The Pursuit of Knowledge
in the Early American Republic

WITHDRAWN

THE PURSUIT
OF KNOWLEDGE IN
THE EARLY AMERICAN
REPUBLIC.

American Scientific
and Learned Societies
from Colonial Times
to the Civil War

EDITED BY ALEXANDRA OLESON
AND SANBORN C. BROWN

The Johns Hopkins University Press
Baltimore and London

Manufactured in the United States of America

The Johns Hopkins University Press, Baltimore, Maryland 21218
The Johns Hopkins Press Ltd., London

Originally published, 1976
Second printing, 1977

Library of Congress Catalog Card Number 75–36941
ISBN 0-8018-1679-3

Library of Congress Cataloging in Publication data will be found on the last printed page of this book.

These essays are the result of an interdisciplinary study program organized by the American Academy of Arts and Sciences and supported by a grant from the National Science Foundation.

Contents

Foreword:
The Learned Society
in American Intellectual
Life

JOHN VOSS

As a promoter and disseminator of knowledge, the learned society has been one of the major institutions of American intellectual life since colonial times. Scientific and humanistic societies have sponsored and organized research, provided opportunities for the exchange and diffusion of knowledge through publications and meetings, and advanced the professional interests of their members. In a larger sense, they have reflected, and often shaped, American life and thought from the challenges of establishing the first new nation[1] to the confrontations stemming from the divisive social and intellectual issues of the present day.

To say that the American learned society has had a long history, however, is not to say that its nature and functions have remained unchanged for the past two hundred years. The learned society of today is markedly different from that established throughout Europe in the seventeenth century or in America in the eighteenth century. In the era of the Scientific Revolution, men of "genius and learning" sought new patterns of social organization that would further the desire to regenerate European society and, at the same time, reflect their sense of cultural superiority. As Roger Hahn observes in his study of the Paris Academy of Sciences, "the intellectual felt both above and responsible for the rest of society. In spirit, [he] was neither an artisan nor a professional, neither a teacher nor a preacher, neither a political leader nor a mere servant of society, even though he shared many of their occupational concerns and ambitions. He prized judgment by peers, the diffusion of knowledge, and the improvement of mankind."[2] It was these three objectives that guided the formation of the great European academies and scientific societies that were subsequently to serve as models for the first learned societies established in the New World.

One of the principal forces behind the creation of societies for the promotion of knowledge was the belief that all aspects of learning lay within the province of the educated man. The membership of the American Philosophical Society and the American Academy of Arts and Sciences included scientists, writers, historians, artisans, physicians, merchants, and gentleman farmers—the formally educated as well as the self-taught. Moreover, the intellectual of the pre-Civil War

[1] Notes to the Foreword begin on page x.

period could, and often did, become a member of several different types of learned societies. In addition to general academies and philosophical societies whose membership encompassed all fields of learning, a host of more specialized organizations—natural history societies, mechanics institutes, library companies, agricultural and medical societies, and organizations for the promotion of industrial arts, manufactures, and the like—were formed in response to the rapid growth of knowledge in the early decades of the nineteenth century. In urban centers stretching from Boston, New York, and Philadelphia in the East to Charleston in the South and Cincinnati in the West, learned societies from the most prestigious to the most provincial became part of what A. Hunter Dupree herein terms an "information network" for the "gathering, processing, and dissemination of knowledge." Before the rise of the American university and at a time when the government had yet to learn the importance of sponsoring research, it was these societies that fostered the development of science and scholarship and provided invaluable communication links between the far-flung members of the young Republic's intellectual community.

Yet the influence that the regional learned society exerted in the first half of the nineteenth century was to give way in the period following the Civil War. Its decline can be traced to the development of more effective organizations for the promotion of specialized knowledge and the impact of the "second scientific revolution." The period after 1860 saw the rise of the great universities, which, in their capacity to advance research, diffuse learning, and promote the exchange of ideas, far surpassed the regional academy. At the same time, there emerged a new publicly supported mechanism for conducting research in the national interest—the government bureau. The "social usefulness" of the privately funded learned and provincial society was dwarfed by the educational and regulatory activities of a whole range of government agencies, including the Coast and Geodetic Survey, the National Bureau of Standards, the various bureaus of the Department of Agriculture, and the Smithsonian Institution. The establishment of the first research institutes, foundations, and industrial laboratories in the early years of the twentieth century was to further diminish the role of the generalized learned society.

Contributing to the strength of these new institutions was the specialization of knowledge and its corollaries: the multiplicity of fields, each distinguished by a highly technical vocabulary; the separation of the humanities and the social sciences into disciplines distinct from the natural and physical sciences; the development of professional standards within disciplines; and a marked growth in the size of the scholarly community, particularly in the scientific fields. In his contribution to this volume, Nathan Reingold estimates that the American scientific community increased sevenfold in the half century from 1850 to 1900. It was these factors, coupled with advances in transportation and communication, that gave rise, in the latter half of the nineteenth century, to new learned and scientific bodies, based on emerging distinctions among fields and disciplines and organized on a national level.

The trend toward national organizations was foreshadowed by the formation of the American Association for the Advancement of Science in 1848 and the National Academy of Sciences in 1863. These were followed by the formation of a number of highly specialized, professional societies, among them the American Philological Association (1869), the American Historical Association (1884), the American Chemical Society (1877), and the American Economic Association (1885). Gradually these organizations, each devoted to a specific field of inquiry, began to issue technical and professional journals of their own. By the early twentieth century, many were serving as clearing houses for information on academic employment. Their annual meetings became a locus for the presentation and discussion of the results of research in a language generally intelligible, or at least of interest, only to other experts in the field. In time they even came to incorporate groups representing subdivisions within fields; the American Historical Association, for example, currently holds its annual meeting in conjunction with some thirty different historical societies representing interests ranging from agricultural, church, and legal history to the history of science, education, and social welfare.

Today the university and the government agency, the professional association, the research institute, and the public and private foundations continue to dominate the American intellectual environment. Yet, in the past several decades, there has been a discernible change in the interests of learned men, as evidenced in the effort to bring together professional specialties and to encourage the collaborative study of problems that belong to no one discipline or institution. Attempts at intellectual integration were long frustrated by the exclusive disciplinary interests of specialists in an increasing number of fields. Not only were the scientists isolated from the nonscientists and, in some cases, from each other, but the humanists and the social scientists were also driven apart. In 1919 ten learned societies concerned with humanistic studies came together to form the American Council of Learned Societies; four years later the political scientists, economists, and sociologists seceded from the ACLS and established the Social Science Research Council. Although the SSRC espoused "interdisciplinary cooperation," its collaborative undertakings were, for many years, confined solely to social scientists.

Yet, apart from artificial institutional arrangements, the boundaries between disciplines were neither clear cut nor impregnable. As Howard Mumford Jones observed, "the relation of fields is not one of pigeonholes but of living, interdependent cells."[3] Certainly the need for interaction among those cells was never greater than in the period following World War II. The critical problems of national and international society in the nuclear age could not be dealt with by experts in any one discipline, or even by the faculty of any one institution. The university, divided by departmental loyalties, sometimes immersed in applied science and research, and often burdened by public responsibilities, found it increasingly difficult to combine the disinterested pursuit of scholarship with the conflicting demands of students, government, industry, and special interest groups. Just as the learned men of the eighteenth century felt a need to meet and exchange ideas, so their twentieth-century counterparts sought a form of organization that would encourage and facilitate communication among scholars, men of affairs, and concerned individuals from various fields and institutions. The result was the gradual revival of the broad-based learned and scientific society, which in recent years has come to be regarded as the most suitable instrument for the analysis and definition of those public and scholarly issues which belong to no one discipline or profession.

Today the federal government looks to the diverse scientific membership of the National Academy of Sciences for advice in such areas as natural resources, technology assessment, and the relationship of science to complex questions of public policy. The ACLS collaborates with the SSRC on a number of foreign area programs involving joint studies and conferences in the social sciences and the humanities. To us, of course, the changing role of the learned society is particularly striking within the American Academy of Arts and Sciences. Through conferences, seminars, and study groups, the Academy—the second oldest learned society in the United States—has provided new insights into such issues as arms control, ethnicity, the role of science and technology in contemporary society, and the future of humanistic studies. When the Academy established its journal *Daedalus* on a quarterly basis in 1958, its editor, Gerald Holton, described the publication as "a medium through which leading scholars in all fields can address one another, . . . an instrument for focusing our attention again on that which does and should make us members of one community." The recent experience of the Academy shows that in a sense the generalized learned society has come full circle: today it is once again a vital center of American intellectual life, a place where men of learning can organize research, engage in discussion, and publish their views on a wide range of issues encompassing the sciences, the humanities, the social sciences, and public affairs.

NOTES

1. Seymour M. Lipset. *The First New Nation* (New York: Basic Books, 1963), pp. 75–85.
2. Roger Hahn, *The Anatomy of a Scientific Institution: The Paris Academy of Sciences, 1666-1803* (Berkeley and Los Angeles: University of California Press, 1971), pp. 41, 42.
3. Howard Mumford Jones, Presidential Address to the American Academy of Arts and Sciences (Boston: American Academy of Arts and Sciences, 1951), p. 4.

Preface

I. BERNARD COHEN

Despite the long tradition and renewed importance of learned societies, their role in the advancement and dissemination of knowledge remains a neglected area of historical scholarship. Most histories of academies and of learned and scientific organizations are no more than institutional records providing specific information but failing to explain the ways in which such institutions are "shaped" by the changing nature of society and by the developing subject matter to which they are dedicated. The want of such studies in general is strikingly evident with respect to America's learned societies, since we have only the barest sketches of their history in any form.

While the most prominent of American learned societies are dealt with in broad historical accounts, there is no major study of the learned society as an institution in American social and cultural life. On the European side, Roger Hahn's recent analysis of the Paris Academy of Sciences set forth the history of a scientific academy in terms of the larger cultural tradition of France.[1] Hahn points to the need for understanding that scientific societies "are the main instrument for the formulation and the transmittal of scientific norms, and that these norms must harmonize with the dominant scientific modes of the time." He stresses that "the scientific institution is the anvil on which the often conflicting values of science and society are shaped into a viable form."[2] There is a need to understand the institutional history of American science and learning in comparable terms, and this was an important factor in the decision of the American Academy of Arts and Sciences to undertake a major examination of the role of societies for the promotion of knowledge in American life. To organize and direct the project, the Academy appointed an advisory committee consisting of Sanborn Brown of the Massachusetts Institute of Technology (chairman), I. Bernard Cohen and Frank Freidel of Harvard University, A. Hunter Dupree of Brown University, John Greene of the University of Connecticut, Brooke Hindle and Nathan Reingold of the Smithsonian Institution, and Walter Muir Whitehill of the Boston Athenaeum (emeritus).

This volume represents the work of the first phase of the study: the history of learned societies from colonial times to the Civil War. A second stage will focus on the period from 1860 to 1920, and a third on the decades since World War I. Our objective is not so much to produce a definitive account of American learned and scientific institutions as to provide a historical framework for understanding their range and variety, a starting point for both the scholar and

[1] Notes to the Preface begin on page xiii.

xi

the general reader concerned with the development of American science and learning.

The papers contained in this volume were commissioned by the American Academy of Arts and Sciences under a grant from the National Science Foundation. In June 1973 the authors met with members of the Academy's advisory committee and commentators representing various aspects of the history of American science, technology, and humanistic learning for a five-day workshop in Cape Newagen, Maine. During this meeting, there were discussions of draft papers and of certain general historical questions associated with them. The final papers published here incorporate suggestions and comments made at these sessions.

It may be noted that our initial goal was far more modest. For some time our fellows have urged that a history of the American Academy be prepared to mark the celebration of our bicentennial in 1980. It was soon apparent that such an undertaking would encounter serious difficulties, first because of the limited nature of the Academy's records, but even more because of the absence of an established body of historical studies dealing with related learned, scientific, professional, and educational organizations.

Preliminary discussions with American intellectual and institutional historians revealed that a sound and maximally useful history of the Academy, one that would transcend local or parochial interests, could not be undertaken apart from a much broader study of the role of learned and scientific organizations in American society. A series of planning meetings emphasized the necessity of viewing the different forms of societies from a variety of perspectives—social, economic, political, intellectual, and ideological. Accordingly, the present volume is not limited to detailed chronological analyses of specific institutions, but deals further with a number of primary historical themes. The latter include the regional and national pattern of development of early American learned societies; the nature and composition of their membership, particularly the beginning of a trend toward professionalization in the first half of the nineteenth century; the influence of public and private support on the formation and growth of learned societies; and the impact of these societies on American science and scholarship in the period up to 1860. To provide a comparative dimension, consideration is also given to some European societies that served as models for the early American learned organizations, notably the Royal Society of London, and to the emergence of learned societies in Canada—a development that stands in contrast to the American experience.

Moreover, since this undeveloped field is sorely lacking in numerical data, the Academy planning committee encouraged authors to contribute what figures they could on the membership of these early societies. In an appendix to his essay on professionalization of science in the nineteenth century, Nathan Reingold estimates the changing numbers of scientific researchers and practitioners throughout the century. Sally Kohlstedt gives a numerical view of early AAAS nationwide membership, reporting in particular on the scientific interests, occupations, age, and geographical distributions of its leadership. James Hobbins's study of the Albany Institute presents significant numerical profiles on ages, occupations, and scholarly output of the members of a provincial society. Other contributors have included preliminary analyses of the membership of their respective institutions. While no facile conclusions may be drawn from the aggregate data in these essays, certain orders of magnitude have emerged that are of considerable importance in understanding the structure of the early American scientific and learned community.

The papers in this volume present much new information, serving both to enlarge and alter the commonly accepted view of organized learning in the early decades of the American Republic. By recapturing some of the themes that were central to our discussions at Newagen, the general introduction underlines the way in which the Academy inquiry has clarified, reinforced, and changed that view. The concluding commentaries deal in a similar manner with the new light these studies cast on the state of American life and thought in the pre-Civil War period.

In sum, this volume presents what is essentially the first broad overview of the activities, influence, and cultural role of learned societies in America's first century. Like all such first essays, it contains personal insights, impressions, and hypotheses that will, hopefully, stimulate questioning, discussion, and further investigation by readers. Above all, it should encourage other scholars to explore certain topics that are either not introduced here or are discussed only briefly. Among these are the relationship between learned societies and educational institutions (both in the quantitative terms of overlapping membership and in relation to shared and unshared projects and activities); the social, political, and intellectual significance of membership or nonmembership in such societies; the public image of American scientific and learned organizations; the comparison and contrast between their stated aims and their actual activities; and the ways in which the societies differed in terms of the various social, intellectual, and geographical communities they were intended to serve. If, as a result of this volume, knowledge of American science and learning is advanced and further scholarship encouraged, we shall have achieved our purpose.

NOTES

1. Roger Hahn, *The Anatomy of a Scientific Institution: The Paris Academy of Sciences, 1666-1803* (Berkeley and Los Angeles: University of California Press, 1971).
2. Ibid., p. x.

Introduction:
To Build a New Intellectual Order

ALEXANDRA OLESON

The desire to enrich the American intellectual environment, to make the new nation a respected part of the international learned community, was a major impetus behind the formation of societies for the promotion of knowledge in the early American Republic. The Revolution inspired what historian Brooke Hindle has termed a spirit of "cultural nationalism";[1] in the midst of the war and in the years immediately following it, statesmen and scientists alike predicted that freedom and liberty would bring forth a scientific and cultural flowering in the New World. In his inaugural address in 1780, the first president of the American Academy, James Bowdoin, hailed the role of the learned society in advancing the progress of European science and expressed the hope that similar organizations of American origin "may aid and invigorate the individual: benefiting by their production not only the communities in which they are respectively instituted, but America and the world in general."[2]

Bowdoin's vision reflected the prevailing belief that learned societies were socially useful instruments created to serve the public through the widespread diffusion of knowledge. Their principal goal was the advancement of knowledge in the expectation that it would benefit the nation, promote the arts, and aid mankind. Most scientists and scholars of the late eighteenth century saw no distinction between theoretical and applied knowledge; indeed, one of the tenets of the Enlightenment was the belief that scientific principles could be applied to, and would ultimately produce, utilitarian results.

This concern with the utility of science not only contributed to the success of the first medical, agricultural, and industrial arts organizations established in the new Republic, but was also reflected in the activities of the two major learned societies of the day—the American Philosophical Society and the American Academy of Arts and Sciences. Both undertook what might be termed "disinterested" scientific investigations: the observations of the transit of Venus and Mercury by the Philosophical Society and the Academy's expedition to Penobscot Bay to study a total eclipse of the sun. Yet each gave special attention, particularly in the early years, to the practical benefits of scientific pursuits. In his 1743 *Proposal for Promoting Useful Knowledge among the British Plantations in America*, Benjamin Franklin defined the purpose of what was to become

---

[1] Notes to the Introduction begin on page xxv.

xv

the American Philosophical Society as the promotion of all subjects that "tend to increase the power of man over matter, and multiply the conveniences or pleasures of life."[3] The incorporators of the American Academy dedicated themselves to "useful experiments and improvements whereby the interest and happiness of the rising empire may be essentially advanced."[4] As they asserted in the first volume of the Academy's *Memoirs* (1785), "societies for promoting useful knowledge may be highly advantageous to the communities in which they are instituted. Men united together, and frequently meeting for the purpose of advancing the sciences, the arts, agriculture, manufactures and commerce, may oftentimes suggest such hints to one another, as may be improved to important ends."[5] By 1815, however, the emphasis on practical improvements began to give way to a growing interest in the advancement of knowledge regardless of its utilitarian implications.

Part of the reason for the change in emphasis was the influence of new institutions for promoting specialized—and practical—areas of knowledge. In Philadelphia, agricultural topics became the province of the Philadelphia Society for Promoting Agriculture (1785). The Academy of Natural Sciences (1812) asserted its leadership in the area of natural history, and the Franklin Institute (1824) took up the question of mechanical improvements. In Boston, the emergence of the Massachusetts Society for Promoting Agriculture (1792), the Linnean Society of New England (1814), and the *New England Journal of Medicine and Surgery* (1812) meant that the American Academy could turn to less utilitarian concerns.

The growth in organizing activity in the opening decades of the nineteenth century can be traced to several factors. Although the country was still beset with serious political and sectional problems, the primary goal of creating a strong federal union had been achieved. The War of 1812 brought cultural nationalism to a new height, and learned societies of every form began to multiply. Difficulties in transportation and communication still hindered the establishment of societies on a national level, but local and regional organizations were formed in large numbers both within and beyond the Phila-delphia-Boston region.

Before considering the growth and development of these organizations, it might be well to set forth a taxonomy of early American learned societies. At the Newagen conference, John Greene proposed a division into three classes: (1) societies for promoting knowledge, (2) societies for the advancement of a profession, and (3) societies for the improvement of the arts.

The societies for promoting knowledge encompassed the literary and philo-sophical groups (whose membership covered the whole field of knowledge), the general scientific societies (in which the literary and historical component was not necessarily present but could sometimes exist as a subordinate category), the specialized natural history societies, the historical societies, and the library companies. Since this is an idealized scheme, specific organizations often repre-sented a blending of categories. For example, during its early years the American

Philosophical Society was both a society for promoting knowledge and a society for improving the practical arts; gradually, however, its program came to be centered largely on basic science rather than practical improvement, and the result was a general scientific society with a relatively insignificant literary and philosophical component.

If there was a common denominator among the various societies for promoting knowledge, it was their concern with natural history or, more properly, the nature and uses of the "various natural productions of the country." The reasons for this widespread interest were, in large part, related to the tenor of American life and thought in this period. Natural history was patriotic in that it called attention to the unique "productions" of the New World; the distinctive plants, animals, fossils, and minerals of the United States were a rich resource for American naturalists and an important drawing card for foreign scientists. In addition, natural history was, for Americans, the most feasible route to international scientific recognition. In the late eighteenth and early nineteenth centuries, the United States lacked the established educational and scientific institutions necessary to promote and carry out advanced theoretical work. Yet, in the area of natural history, scientists such as Louis Agassiz, James Dana, and Asa Gray were able to undertake research that transcended routine taxonomy— research that enabled them to take their place beside Lyell, Hutton, and Darwin as major contributors to the intellectual revolution that was transforming man's understanding of geology and biology. Finally, for the practical-minded, natural history was utilitarian in that it furthered discovery and exploitation of the country's natural resources for the benefit of the people and proved to be of considerable importance in such practical endeavors as agriculture and medicine. Thus, by reinforcing so many strands within American society, it provided a sound base for the formation of viable scientific organizations.

Natural history investigations were encouraged, not only by general scientific societies, but also by numerous specialized natural history groups, among them the Academy of Natural Sciences of Philadelphia (1812), the Lyceum of Natural History of New York (1817), the Boston Society of Natural History (1830), the Western Academy of Natural Sciences (Cincinnati, 1835), the Cleveland Academy of Natural Science (1844), and the Chicago Academy of Natural Science (1856, later to become the Chicago Academy of Science, 1859). What few societies emerged in the South in the pre-Civil War period also included among their objectives "the collection and preservation of specimens in natural history." The patriotic-utilitarian appeal of natural history was in no small part responsible for the substantial increase in the number of societies for promoting knowledge that occurred in the first half of the nineteenth century.[6]

The second group of organizations—the societies for the advancement of a profession—were the forerunners of the specialized professional groups that were to proliferate in the years following the Civil War. In this earlier period, however, their scope was limited primarily to architecture, engineering, and, most important, medicine. Their purpose was clearly defined as the advancement of a specific field and the protection of those who were properly trained to practice it. In 1840 the geologists became the first group of American scientists to form their own professional organization; in 1843 the Association of American Geologists absorbed the naturalists; and in 1848 it broadened its membership to include all aspects of physical and natural science, changing its name to the American Association for the Advancement of Science.

The third category—the societies for improving the arts, namely agricultural societies, mechanics institutes, and societies for promoting the industrial and fine arts—entailed far more complex problems of definition. To differentiate between societies for promoting knowledge and societies for improving the arts, the participants at Newagen drew up a set of criteria based upon three distinguishing characteristics. First, what was the principal aim of the organization: was it the promotion of knowledge in the belief that knowledge would eventually be useful or was it the organized improvement of practice, be it agriculture, technology, or fine arts? Second, what was the nature of the membership? How did the membership of the American Philosophical Society differ from that of another Philadelphia organization, the Franklin Institute? Third, what method did the society use to achieve its objectives? Did it rely largely on discussion and publication or did it employ the variety of methods that in this period came to distinguish the societies for improving the arts not only from the other categories but indeed from each other?

To reward improved practice in agriculture, manufacturing, and even the fine arts, the majority of societies of the arts used premiums and prizes, usually in the form of cash payments. Beyond these economic incentives (but often associated with them and with the government-sanctioned patent system) was the concept of "emulation"—the notion of encouraging talented practitioners to emulate the work of the master. Whether the models to be studied depicted bridge trusses or sculptures from the Louvre, the underlying principle of emulation was the same: improvement was achieved by artists who worked within the traditional pattern of the craft to first equal and then excel the masterpieces of the past. Brooke Hindle's essay explores the efforts of a number of New York societies of art to foster creativity by developing improvement out of deep craft understanding.

To move outside the craft tradition, to seek a new means of solving technological problems through the use of science or scientific methods, was yet another means of achieving the objective of societies for improving the arts. In his paper on the Franklin Institute, Bruce Sinclair points up the distinction between the direct application of science to the mechanical arts and the use of scientific methods, particularly the experimental approach, to advance technology.

In the end, however, the effectiveness of the learned society in stimulating improvement must be measured against that of other forces and agencies in society. Margaret Rossiter's study of agricultural societies within the larger context of agricultural improvement provides this kind of analysis by also taking into account the role of economic and geographical factors, scientific discoveries, popular journals, higher education, and the government in the agricultural reform movement.

The interaction between learned societies on the one hand and related instruments for the advancement of knowledge—educational institutions, proprietary journals, and the government—on the other is considered throughout this volume. So many different patterns emerge that it is difficult to determine the relative influence of one or another element beyond a specific region or time span. What is clear, however, is that in the first half of the nineteenth century the learned society achieved its objective—be it promoting knowledge, improving the arts, or advancing a profession—largely through the efforts of a small group of people who believed in and worked for that goal. Such organizations did not live or die because they were the focus of great enthusiasm or hostility on the part of either the public or the instrumentalities of the nation. What modest support they received from the larger environment was based on a tacit and widespread understanding that they were acting on behalf of society as a whole. Certainly it was within that context that the government took steps to strengthen learned societies through limited financial assistance and other forms of recognition—particularly if utilitarian benefits were likely to result.

In the late eighteenth century, the American Philosophical Society received contributions from the provincial assembly of Philadelphia to support its transit of Venus observations (justified as "an Object, on which the Promotion of Astronomy and Navigation and consequently of Trade and Commerce so much depends")[7] and a project for encouraging silk culture. It was the state of New York, however, that took the lead in providing indirect and direct subsidies for learned societies.[8] As early as 1808, the New York Society for the Promotion of the Useful Arts administered a program of premiums established by the state to stimulate the manufacture of woolen cloth and later to promote "domestic manufacturing." A more direct form of patronage was instituted in 1819, when the state legislature approved an annual appropriation of $10,000 for the formation of county agricultural societies on the condition that these organizations raise by voluntary subscription a sum equal to that awarded by the state. Within five years, fifty-two of New York's fifty-eight counties had established their own societies, complete with annual fairs. In 1816 the city of New York provided support for a nonutilitarian organization by making available rent-free space to several cultural societies, known collectively as the New York Institution for the Promotion of the Arts and Sciences. There is no doubt that New York's repeated efforts to provide monetary and other forms of assistance for learned societies was due, in large measure, to the advocacy of De Witt Clinton, who not only promoted legislative aid but also took an active role as a member and officer of several societies.

On a national level, in 1830 the Franklin Institute for the Promotion of the Mechanic Arts became the first private scientific organization to receive a federal appropriation when the Secretary of the Treasury awarded funds to Alexander

Dallas Bache for the purchase of equipment needed to investigate the cause of steam boiler explosions. Recognition of a different sort was granted by the Commonwealth of Pennsylvania when it selected the Franklin Institute to conduct a state investigation into a uniform system of weights and measures.

Limited amounts of government support continued to be doled out in a piecemeal fashion throughout the period up to 1860. While such assistance was often critical in assuring the continued operation of certain learned societies, it was seldom the motivating force behind their formation.

To understand why learned societies appeared with such persistence in the first half of the nineteenth century, one must again look to less tangible factors, notably the "national pride" and "organizing habit" of the American people. As Richard Storr observed at Newagen, "small groups of people, often in fledgling communities, were seldom content to meet as private clubs; instead they chose to organize formally and to adopt sweeping names—the *American* Philosophical Society, the *United States* Military Philosophical Society, the *Western* Academy of Natural Sciences, the *American* Academy of Arts and Sciences. There appears to have been a kind of formalism combined with a sense of grandeur at work in the minds of these individuals."

Learned men of the 1820s and 1830s no less than those of the Revolution were determined to show that America was not culturally inferior to Europe, that just as this nation was capable of establishing a "new order" of political institutions, so it was capable of establishing a "new order" of intellectual institutions. The learned society brought together the desire to pursue and promote "American" science and learning with the propensity of Americans, then and now, to seek cooperative action through organization. In his essay, James Cassedy provides an interesting perspective on physicians as "the most conspicuous joiners" in early nineteenth-century America. To the physician and to countless other educated men, the learned society represented a way of defining their status in the community, an opportunity "to be or act as learned men."

Ultimately, any analysis of these early societies must take into account the nature and motivations of the people who comprised their membership. As the studies in this volume indicate, learned societies were not "aristocratic" organizations; they attracted the self-made man who had acquired a certain level of education and wanted to associate with persons of similar background. In the late eighteenth and early nineteenth centuries, the composition of the societies (with the exception of those devoted to specific professions) reflected a wide range of interests and competency. As a general scientific organization, the American Philosophical Society embraced political and civic leaders, academicians, physicians, lawyers, clergymen, artisans, merchants, and "gentlemen scientists." In this period there was no attempt to classify the membership in terms of disciplinary interests or professional commitment. The division of a society's membership into distinct occupations is a contemporary methodological device that, while useful, can also be somewhat arbitrary.

As Henry Shapiro pointed out at Newagen, there is a kind of "fallacy of occupational analysis" that stems from the fact that the learned men of the late eighteenth and early nineteenth century were often involved in many different occupations in the course of a lifetime. Cassedy's paper demonstrates that physicians did research in natural history and geology and took part in the temperance and missionary movements. Since physicians and others did pursue such varied interests, Shapiro questioned whether occupational analysis is a meaningful key to defining the character of an early learned society. Walter Whitehill noted that the intellectual community of New England included a number of versatile men who engaged in a variety of occupations. David Cobb, for example, was a physician and one of the incorporators of the American Academy. Yet when the Massachusetts Medical Society was established in 1781, Cobb was occupied elsewhere as an aide-de-camp to General Washington. He subsequently returned to Boston, reestablished himself as a physician, and became a member of the Massachusetts Medical Society in 1786. Still later, however, he appears as one of the principal capitalists in the development of Maine land. Is Cobb a physician first or a general or a land developer?

John Greene indicated that the role of the physician in particular may be better understood in light of the nature of medical education at the time. Chemistry, natural history, mineralogy, and anatomy were all part of the physician's curriculum, and research in any one of those areas would probably not be considered beyond the scope of his professional interest. On the other hand, one can point to Samuel Latham Mitchill, who was not only a physician but also a gentleman farmer and a bit of a poet. In the case of the medical profession, therefore, it is possible to distinguish between those activities which were in some way related to the physician's training and those which were totally removed from it.

Going beyond a specific profession, Nathan Reingold observed that the problems implicit in this kind of analysis arise largely because the occupational distinctions of the present tend to be imposed on the past, on a time when advanced specialization and professionalization had no meaning. To overcome this "fallacy," Hunter Dupree proposed a form of "multiple mapping" based on the concept of a learned society acting as an information system. As the studies in this volume indicate, interlocking intellectual directorates existed in many urban areas during this period; for example, the same men who were the principal lawyers of Boston or officers of government and instruction at Harvard College were among the incorporators of the American Academy of Arts and Sciences and later went on to establish the Massachusetts Historical Society and the Boston Athenaeum. In the course of a year or a lifetime, a given person might be involved in several different information networks, tying in and out of various systems as old interests waned and new interests developed. Therefore, instead of employing a linear occupational table, it would be possible to "map" these individuals into their respective networks and thus obtain a more realistic picture of the ubiquitous learned men who dominated these societies in the late eighteenth and early nineteenth centuries.

Another form of membership classification based not on occupation but on the kind and degree of commitment to the pursuit of *scientific* knowledge was also discussed at the conference. John Greene identified three categories of individuals concerned with the promotion of science in the period 1780-1820. The "wheel horses" or "regulars" included college professors, physicians, surveyors, and the like who manifested a serious interest in science while continuing to pursue their own occupation—which may or may not have been related to science. In the early years of the Republic, it was these people who organized societies, established journals, and otherwise served as the backbone of the scientific enterprise. The second category, the gentlemen scientists, were wealthy individuals such as Colonel George Gibbs of Rhode Island and Benjamin Vaughn of Maine, who provided financial support for the societies and sometimes made minor contributions to science. Finally there were the "mavericks"—the Maclures, the Nuttalls, the Rafinesques. Not tied to a given location or vocation, they were free to undertake a large share of the field research and thus represented the crucial element in terms of research and publication.

By the second quarter of the nineteenth century, however, these distinctions began to lose their meaning in the wake of the increasing professionalization of the scientific endeavor. Of course, learned societies continued to attract those wealthy and cultured individuals with a desire to demonstrate their appreciation of science through financial support and attendance at local meetings. However, if we adopt the terms set forth by Nathan Reingold in his paper, the scientific community of the nineteenth century can be said to consist of three distinct groups: cultivators, practitioners, and researchers. A "cultivator" is best described as a member of the learned culture who participated in a variety of scientific enterprises, always without remuneration. Some cultivators acquired scientific instruments and engaged in meteorological or mineralogical analyses; others built up natural history collections. They were present in every scientific field and regularly attended the meetings of local scientific societies, often taking part in the management of the organization and sometimes delivering a paper. To them, science was a source of pleasure, "a hobby." Although the influence of the cultivators steadily declined in the period up to 1860, they were never wholly supplanted, and indeed were an important element in the membership of the American Association for the Advancement of Science.

Unlike the cultivators, the "practitioners" earned their living in science or science-related occupations; for the most part they were employed by the federal or state governments and by colleges and universities in teaching, administrative, and applied development posts. The practitioners performed some research but in intensity and quality, their work never equaled that of the leaders of the scientific community—the "researchers."

In the pre-professional period, some researchers were actually cultivators who attained great expertise and achievement. With the trend toward professionalization and specialization, the researchers were set apart by their single-minded devotion to research and their major contributions to American science. Their principal goals were to foster significant scientific output, to destroy and subsequently prevent what they termed the "charlatanism" and "quackery" that threatened the "progress of science," and, above all, to elevate the United States to the position of a major scientific power. As a step toward accomplishing these ends, they took the lead in the creation of, first, a broad-based national society for the exchange of scientific knowledge—the American Association for the Advancement of Science—and, second, an elite national society designed to uphold the highest standards of scientific research—the National Academy of Sciences.

By the 1840s modern transportation and communication facilities had made the establishment of learned societies on a national scale a possibility; what made such organizations a reality was the growth of the scientific endeavor, both as an avocation and as a career, coupled with the feeling on the part of a growing body of professional scientists that local groups were no longer satisfactory avenues of publication and vehicles for the exchange of information. As Sally Kohlstedt points out in her study of the AAAS, the local societies effectively promoted scientific activities within a given region, but "none provided a national podium for prominent researchers or a membership broad based enough to encourage conference-quality debate or resolve specific scientific questions." The American Association for the Advancement of Science was established to meet this need. Its objectives, as set forth in a constitution adopted in 1848, were "by periodical and migratory meetings, to promote intercourse between those who are cultivating science in different parts of the United States, to give a stronger and more general impulse, and a more systematic direction to scientific research in our country; and to procure for the labours of scientific men, increased facilities and wider usefulness."[9]

To translate these abstract principles into an effective organization for the promotion of American science at home and abroad was a difficult task, particularly for a democratic body whose membership ranged from distinguished researcher to local observer. The leaders of the AAAS recognized the conflict between professionalism and the public demands on science, but they were reluctant to exclude the cultivators and nonscientific supporters from the Association. While they openly decried popularization and socialization, they found the public response gratifying and, to the dismay of the younger scientists, did little to advance more specialized areas of research that could not be shared with a wider constituency. Yet, despite internal divisions, by 1860 the AAAS had succeeded in displacing local and regional societies as the primary organization of America's practicing scientists. Its role in providing a national forum for science, through meetings and publications, was acknowledged by no less a figure than Alexander Dallas Bache, "chief" of the Lazzaroni—that select circle of prominent scientists whose goal was the establishment of the highest standards of excellence for American scientific research.[10] At the same time, however, Bache and other members of the scientific elite recognized that quackery could not be defeated nor professional standards maintained through peripatetic meetings and an eclectic membership. What they sought—and achieved in 1863—was an organization linked to the federal government and composed of the most prestigious scientists in the country: the National Academy of Sciences.

The formation of two national scientific organizations by the mid-nineteenth century is often regarded by historians as the culmination of a linear progression in institution building that began with the organization of small regional societies in the late 1700s. To stress this progressive development, however, is to overlook the fact that many of the academies and regional societies founded in the early years of the Republic still flourished in the 1850s and later; just beginning to appear were the specialized professional societies, government bureaus, and major universities that were to assume many of the functions of the learned society in the post-Civil War period.

In the first half of the nineteenth century, learned societies in all their variety were the dominant elements in the organized pursuit of knowledge in America. In an age pervaded by Baconian utilitarianism, they were highly useful organizations. For the learned community, they organized and promoted research, fostered the advancement of general science and scholarship, offered opportunities for publication, and provided a means of establishing one's identity as a man of knowledge. For the larger society, they encouraged the improvement of the practical arts and promoted the public diffusion of useful knowledge. For the nation, they symbolized the cultural and scientific independence of the United States.

In the period between the American Revolution and the Civil War, national pride and self-definition were implicit in the organizing activity that surrounded American science and learning. As Richard Storr concluded at Newagen, "A kind of upward suction was at work in the minds of Americans as they contemplated the void between what the country was culturally and what they believed it should be. . . . Talk about the American Dream has become hackneyed; but the early history of the academies suggests that a revolution of rising expectations (admittedly another cliché) did begin shortly after the War of Independence ended. Remember how emphatically Benjamin Rush declared that the Revolution was not over!"

In the years that followed independence, the learned society became one of the focal points in America's attempt to realize those expectations and assert its cultural independence. In 1780, immediately after the American Academy was established, John Adams quickly dispatched a copy of the Academy's charter, together with several publications of the American Philosophical Society, to French publisher Jean Luzac, proclaiming that "at a time when the English Emissaries are filling all Europe with their confident assertions of the distress of the Americans, the inclosed Papers show that both at Philadelphia and Boston, the People are so much at their Ease, as to be busily employed in the pursuits of the Arts of Peace."[11] That spirit was echoed nearly a century later when in 1863 Louis Agassiz declared that the establishment of the National Academy of Sciences would "tell strongly in our favor, where learning is duly appreciated";

indeed, it would be "evidence to go before the civilized world at large of the intellectual activity displayed even in these days of our public troubles. . . . "[12] As the principal instrument for the discovery, preservation, and dissemination of knowledge, the learned society of the early American Republic provided an essential institutional structure for the pursuit of science and scholarship in the New World, and thereby helped lay America's claim to a respected place within the intellectual community of Western man.

NOTES

1. For an analysis of early American "cultural nationalism," see Brooke Hindle, *The Pursuit of Science in Revolutionary America, 1735-1789* (Chapel Hill: University of North Carolina Press, 1956), pp. 248-277, 382-385.

2. James Bowdoin, "A Philosophical Discourse, Addressed to the American Academy of Arts and Sciences," *Memoirs of the American Academy of Arts and Sciences* 1 (1785): 3.

3. Benjamin Franklin, *The Writings of Benjamin Franklin*, ed. Albert H. Smyth, 10 vols. (New York, 1905-1907), 2:230.

4. "Preface," *Memoirs of the American Academy*, p. xi.

5. Ibid., p. iii.

6. The table in Ralph S. Bates, *Scientific Societies in the United States*, 2d ed. (Cambridge, Mass.: M.I.T. Press, 1958), p. 51, indicates that societies for the general promotion of science increased from two in 1795 to thirty-five in 1855. These figures, however, do not take into account either historical societies or library companies.

7. *Votes and Proceedings of the House of Representatives of the Province of Pennsylvania*, Pennsylvania Archives, 8th series, 7 (1935):6289; quoted in Brooke Hindle, *Science in Revolutionary America, 1735-1789* (Chapel Hill: University of North Carolina Press, 1956), p. 135.

8. On New York support of agricultural and other forms of learned societies, see the essays by Brooke Hindle, James Hobbins, and Margaret Rossiter in this volume.

9. *Proceedings of the American Association for the Advancement of Science* 1 (1849):8.

10. The Lazzaroni were a small group of scientists united by their friendship with Bache and their determination to institute and uphold standards of excellence for American science. They included Louis Agassiz, James D. Dana, Charles H. Davis, Cornelius C. Felton, John F. Frazer, Oliver W. Gibbs, Benjamin A. Gould, Joseph Henry, and Benjamin Peirce; with the exception of Agassiz, they were all physical scientists.

11. John Adams to Jean Luzac, 22 August 1780, letterbook copy, The Adams Papers, Massachusetts Historical Society, Boston, Mass.

12. Edward Lurie, *Louis Agassiz: A Life in Science* (Chicago: University of Chicago Press, 1960), p. 331.

The Pursuit of Knowledge
in the Early American Republic

Science, Learning, and Utility: Patterns of Organization in the Early American Republic

JOHN C. GREENE

Nothing is more characteristic of modern Western civilization than the organized pursuit of secular knowledge. If the Greeks valued knowledge for its own sake and the Middle Ages knowledge of a different kind for the sake of salvation, the modern world, taking its cue from Bacon and Descartes, values knowledge as power. On the continent of Europe the emerging nation states took charge of the organized pursuit of knowledge, including it as part of a system of centralized, governmentally sponsored academies and schools for cultivating science, literature, and the fine and practical arts. This system reached its apogee in Napoleonic France, where science and technology, learning and literature became at once the glory and the servants of the state.

In England, free enterprise rather than state patronage guided the search for knowledge, drawing on the private resources of lords and gentlemen rather than the largesse of the state. Societies for the promotion of useful knowledge sprang up everywhere, but the preeminence of London as the political, cultural, and economic center of the kingdom, combined with the limited geographical area of the country, provided an element of centralization without which the organized pursuit of knowledge by private enterprise might have remained dispersed and ineffective. Thanks to these circumstances the Royal Society of London, the Geological Society of London, the Linnean Society of London, the Zoological Society of London, and the Royal Astronomical Society were national as well as London societies. True, there were numerous provincial societies, but these acknowledged the hegemony of the London groups. At the same time, the dominant utilitarianism of the Baconian tradition was qualified and softened by an older tradition of patronage of science, learning, and art for their own sake.

In Britain's daughter nation across the Atlantic a different situation prevailed. Here, too, private enterprise took full responsibility for organizing the pursuit of knowledge, but private resources were less substantial than those in England; the gentleman scientist was a relative rarity; political, economic, and cultural power were diffused over a vast area; and the national capital after 1800 was a raw, new "city" inhabited chiefly by diplomats and government officials. With the defeat of the Federalists and the removal of the capital to Washington, D.C., in 1800, it became clear that institutions for the promotion of knowledge would develop on

1

a regional or local scale for many years to come. Philadelphia, New York, Albany, Boston, New Haven, Charleston, Cincinnati, Nashville, St. Louis, New Orleans—these would provide organizations for seeking knowledge until such time as the development and professionalization of American science required organization on a national scale.

Of these urban centers, Philadelphia was the most active and fecund in generating institutions for the pursuit of knowledge. The largest city, leading commercial port, and political center of the nascent nation until 1800, Philadelphia had established its preeminence as a medical center through the Pennsylvania Hospital and the School of Medicine of the University of Pennsylvania, and had led the way in organizing for the pursuit of knowledge with the formation of the American Philosophical Society, distinguished by the names and researches of Franklin, Rittenhouse, Jefferson, the medical professors at the University, and such notable foreign scientists and savants as Joseph Correa da Serra, William Maclure, Joseph Priestley, and André Michaux and his son, François André. The Chemical Society of Philadelphia, the Philadelphia Society for Promoting Agriculture, Peale's Museum, and the botanical garden created by John Bartram, followed in later years by the Academy of Natural Sciences and the Franklin Institute, gave further evidence of the city's capacity to create institutions for improving knowledge.

These institutions were mutually reinforcing, and were mutually sustained by a community of college professors, medical men, scientifically inclined gentlemen and artisans, and visiting foreign scientists that composed their overlapping memberships. Members of the Chemical Society of Philadelphia—James Woodhouse, Adam Seybert, and Robert Hare, for example—were active in the American Philosophical Society, some of whose members, such as John Vaughan, Benjamin Rush, Benjamin S. Barton, Zacchaeus Collins, Caspar Wistar, and James Mease, were involved in the Philadelphia Society for Promoting Agriculture or contributed articles to its *Memoirs*. The overlap in membership between the American Philosophical Society and the Academy of Natural Sciences was substantial. Most of the leading members of the Academy—Maclure, Troost, Say, Harlan, Morton, Wetherill, Ord, Lesueur, Bonaparte, Nuttall—were also members of the Society. In the physical sciences there was an important overlap between the members of the American Philosophical Society and those of the Franklin Institute. Isaiah Lukens, William Keating, Robert M. Patterson, John P. Wetherill, and William Strickland—all members of the American Philosophical Society—were among the officers of the Franklin Institute when it was founded in 1825, and other leading members of the Society were active in the Institute and contributed to its *Journal*. In the field of the earth sciences there was considerable overlap between the membership of the Institute and that of the Academy of Natural Sciences.

Partly because of their overlapping memberships, these various institutions for promoting knowledge were mutually sustaining rather than competitive. The oldest and most prestigious of them, the American Philosophical Society, had begun as a society for promoting useful knowledge, with a heavy emphasis on practical utility. Franklin and his associates had set the tone in dedicating the Society to the cultivation of "all philosophical experiments that let light into the nature of things, tend to increase the power of man over matter, and multiply the conveniences and pleasures of life."[1] When the first volume of the Society's *Transactions* appeared nearly thirty years later, Baconian utilitarianism was still the dominant theme. "Knowledge," the preface to this volume declared, "is of little use, when confined to mere speculation. But when speculative truths are reduced to practice, when theories, grounded upon experiments, are applied to the common purposes of life; and when, by these, agriculture is improved, trade enlarged, the arts of living made more easy and comfortable, and, of course, the increase and happiness of mankind promoted; knowledge then becomes really useful."[2] To this end the members of the Society proposed to devote their energies chiefly to "such subjects as tend to the improvement of their country, and advancement of its interest and prosperity." Among these were listed improvements in agriculture; the preservation of timber for shipbuilding and other purposes; the improvement of materia medica; the discovery and introduction of "new vegetable juices"; improvements in the manufacture of wine, cider, and vinegar; and methods of constructing highways, causeways, and bridges and of linking rivers and improving inland navigation. Physics, mechanics, astronomy, and mathematics were also mentioned as forms of useful knowledge.

For the implementation of these ambitious plans for human improvement through the pursuit of knowledge, the Society looked primarily to "gentlemen . . . whom Providence hath blessed with affluence, and whose understanding is improved by a liberal education" but also to practical farmers and to "ingenious mechanics," whose knowledge might be communicated to the Society if stimulated by the award of premiums for important discoveries and inventions. Mention was also made of the desirability of forming a cabinet of "fossil," vegetable, and animal substances "that may enlarge the bounds of natural history in general, and of this part of the world in particular." There was, however, no reference to the fine arts or to history, philosophy in the modern sense, or literature. Of the six committees established by the Society to referee communications, the first was responsible for geography, mathematics, natural philosophy, and astronomy; the second, for medicine and anatomy; the third, for natural history and chemistry; the fourth, for trade and commerce; the fifth, for mechanics and architecture; and the sixth, for husbandry and American improvements.

But although practical utility was the central theme in the founding of the American Philosophical Society, it failed to dominate the activities and publications of the Society thereafter. Interest in agricultural improvement lapsed quickly after the publication of the first volume of the *Transactions,* to be taken up by the Philadelphia Society for Promoting Agriculture. Articles devoted to

[1] Notes to this chapter begin on page 19.

mechanical improvements—a "self-moving or sentinel register," an improved ship pump, a horizontal windmill, an improved method of quilling harpsichords, improvements in water mills and gristmills, Jefferson's moldboard, suggestions for improving steam engines, and the like—continued to appear until the 1820s, after which they were few and far between, probably because of the founding of the Franklin Institute and its *Journal.*

Meanwhile, the launching of the Academy of Natural Sciences of Philadelphia (1812) and its *Journal* (1817) had challenged the Society's leadership in the field of natural history. Fortunately for the Society, the naturalists of Philadelphia continued to contribute to the Society's *Transactions,* even though the Academy and its museum now became the focus of research and publication in natural history. In the 1850s the Society recognized the Academy's leadership in this field by transferring its collections of fossils, accumulated since the days of Franklin, Jefferson, and Wistar, to the custody of the Academy.[3]

In 1815 the American Philosophical Society had taken an important step toward expanding its conception of the realm of "useful knowledge" by establishing a Committee of History, Moral Science, and General Literature under the chairmanship of the Philadelphia lawyer and linguist Peter S. Duponceau.[4] To the disappointment of those members who viewed this innovation as a move in the direction of transforming the Society into a "literary and philosophical" society (some of these members went on to organize the Historical Society of Pennsylvania), Duponceau's interests were confined almost exclusively to comparative linguistics, especially the study of Indian languages. The chief result of the committee's work, aside from its occasional publications, seems to have been the addition of comparative linguistics to the list of topics represented in the *Transactions* of the Society. In his annual address to the Society in December 1854, President Franklin Bache reported that the 261 members of the Society resident in Philadelphia included 158 scientific men and "artists," 83 literary men, and 20 naturalists, adding that the literary members, "comprising, for the most part, gentlemen of the legal and clerical professions," had made very few communications to the Society, "as if they considered the object of the Society to be exclusively the cultivation of science."[5]

The literary members' view of the Society was not without foundation. Judging from the contents of its *Transactions* and *Proceedings,* the American Philosophical Society had become a general scientific society, dividing its attention more or less equally among the physical sciences, the earth sciences, and the natural history of plants and animals. In the physical sciences, observational science was represented by astronomy, geodesy, meteorology, and terrestrial magnetism. On the experimental side, chemistry and electricity and magnetism were ably represented by Robert Hare and Joseph Henry respectively, with subsidiary contributions by R. A. Tilghman, James C. Booth, and others in the chemical field. Because of its central location and its early lead in astronomy and related geophysical sciences such as geodesy, meteorology, and terrestrial magnetism, the Society was able to attract contributions on a national scale—from

Lt. James Gillis, William Lambert, and Ferdinand Hassler in Washington, D.C., Elias Loomis at the Hudson College Observatory in Ohio, Dr. John Locke in Cincinnati, C. G. Forshey in Natchez, William H. C. Bartlett at West Point, Robert Treat Paine and Benjamin Peirce in Boston, William C. Redfield and Robert Adrain in New York, and J. N. Nicollet and other explorers. The presence in or near Philadelphia of James Espy, Robert Hare, William C. Redfield, and Joseph Henry—all interested in meteorology—made Philadelphia a center for research of this kind in the period 1830-1850. The interest of Alexander Dallas Bache and Loomis in terrestrial magnetism and Bache's magnetic researches at the Girard College Observatory had a similar effect in this field of inquiry. At the same time the research of Joseph Henry, Robert Hare, and various workers at the Franklin Institute such as Walter R. Johnson, designer of a machine for testing the strength of metals, made Philadelphia the leading center of experimental science in the United States.

But the preeminence of Philadelphia and of the American Philosophical Society in these branches of science in the 1830s and early 1840s was not destined to last. During the 1840s, Hare resigned his chair at the School of Medicine of the University of Pennsylvania, and Henry, Bache, Espy, and Sears Walker moved to Washington, D.C., to become employees of the federal government. Meanwhile other avenues of publication for the research of these and other physical scientists were opening up: Silliman's *American Journal of Science,* the *Proceedings* of the American Association for the Advancement of Science, Gould's *Astronomical Journal,* and the publications of the Smithsonian Institution, the United States Naval Observatory, and the Coast Survey, for example. The federal government was beginning to emerge as a significant patron, organizer, and publisher of science, and Philadelphia was no longer the seat of that government.

For its part, the American Philosophical Society was in no position to make a bid for national leadership in science at this juncture. The "Account of the American Philosophical Society," written in 1841 by the aged treasurer and librarian, John Vaughan, in response to inquiries from the Prussian Minister in Washington, did not give the impression of a flourishing society spurred on by vigorous leadership. Vaughan himself was eighty-six and would die before the end of the year. The president of the Society since 1828, Peter S. Duponceau, was also in his eighties and in very poor health. The financial condition of the Society was not encouraging.

Our annual income is about 1800 dollars [Vaughan wrote], arising from the rents of some property & the contributions of the resident members of 5 Dollars a year. . . . It may appear a matter of surprise that our Society has published so little, but it must be observed that having no assistance from Government, our pecuniary means were small & our exertions paralised for want of funds. . . . It has only been by a rigid economy that we have attained our present situation, which enables us to be more regular in our publications, which will appear from the dates of our more recent ones.[6]

The Society's situation seems to have deteriorated rather than improved during the remaining years before the Civil War. In the mid-1840s an unfortunate financial reverse suffered in connection with the Society's efforts to buy the Philadelphia Museum imperiled the existence of the Society and forced it to appeal to the Philadelphia community for assistance. The interval between successive issues of its *Transactions,* which had been narrowed to two or three years in the late 1830s and early 1840s, expanded to seven years between 1846 and 1860. With the retirement of Hare and the departure of Henry, Bache, Espy, and Walker for Washington, the physical science component of the resident membership was enfeebled, and more reliance had to be placed on the natural historians—especially Joseph Leidy, Isaac Lea, and John P. Wetherill—for contributions to the *Transactions.* In 1859, aware that its position was deteriorating, the Society appointed a special committee to study "the present condition of the Society and the means of increasing its usefulness." In its report, submitted May 6, 1859, the committee described the circumstances that had made the Society "the centre to which more appropriately than towards any other should come the problems which control special investigations." But the Society's preeminence could no longer be taken for granted, the committee warned:

. . . it is well known to the Society that during some years past neither its Transactions nor its Proceedings have equalled the expectations which might justly be entertained of its fruitfulness. In number and in variety of subjects the contributions of its members and others have not corresponded with its claims and means. The attendance of its members has been greatly below the standard consistent with its proper effectiveness, and a constant diminution of general interest in the meetings has been the natural consequence.[7]

The Society's library was in a condition that precluded satisfactory use of it by the members, but the librarian had made progress in analyzing and rearranging the collection, and the expected removal of the Society to new quarters would provide the space needed for proper arrangement of the books, the committee reported. The chief matter of concern was the dearth of scientific and literary communications to the Society by its members. To correct this situation the committee recommended the establishment of a standing Committee on Premiums, charged with advertising and administering the existing premiums of the Society and with recommending new premiums "directly chosen in reference to the actual state of science and the comparative value of particular problems." By these measures and by renewed appeals to the general membership, it was hoped that the Society could be reinvigorated and restored to its original position of leadership in American scientific circles.

Meanwhile the Academy of Natural Sciences and the Franklin Institute had sloughed off their early spirit of Baconian utilitarianism and had emerged as flourishing institutions dedicated to the discovery and dissemination of knowledge through the labors of professional naturalists, physical scientists, and engineers. Organized in 1824 for "the promotion and encouragement of manufactures and the mechanic and useful arts by the establishment of popular lectures on the sciences connected with them, by the formation of a cabinet of models and minerals and a library, by offering premiums on all objects deemed worthy of encouragement, by examining all new inventions submitted to them, and by such other measures as they may judge expedient," the Franklin Institute of the State of Pennsylvania for the Promotion of the Mechanic Arts symbolized its dedication to useful knowledge by adopting the name of Franklin. Indeed, Franklin would have been pleased to belong to an institution of "manufacturers, mechanics, artizans and persons friendly to the mechanic arts" whose membership list included a variety of merchants, manufacturers, engravers, jewellers, carpenters, hatters, dentists, metalworkers, druggists, lawyers, coachmakers, tailors, accountants, and instrument makers, as well as some of Philadelphia's leading physical scientists.[8]

In no other institution in Philadelphia or elsewhere in the nation was there as strong a working interaction between scientists, technologists, educators, and men of business and industry. Within a few years the Institute had erected a building; sponsored a series of public lectures; created professorships of natural philosophy, mineralogy and chemistry, architecture, and mechanics; established a high school with instruction in geography, history, Latin, Greek, French, Spanish, and German as well as theoretical and practical sciences; begun a collection of minerals and mechanical models; built up a library; launched a journal; and inaugurated a series of industrial exhibits that were to continue annually or biennially throughout the period to 1860. On its own initiative, or at the request of the federal, state, or city government, it undertook investigations of water as a source of power, of the causes and prevention of steam boiler explosions, of weights and measures, and of methods of paving highways. The Institute also published monthly weather reports based on the research of its Committee on Meteorology. It was in the lecture hall of the Franklin Institute, not at Philosophical Hall, that the Association of American Geologists was organized in 1840, seven of the eighteen founders being members of the Institute. During the 1850s the Institute experienced difficulty in raising funds for its activities, but in the following decade more than $30,000 was raised by the sale of stock in the Institute to industrial concerns in the Philadelphia area.[9]

In the *Journal* of the Institute the growing interaction of technology with science was reflected throughout the period up to 1860. In its early years the *Journal* eschewed abstract science, devoting its pages almost entirely to technological articles that showed little influence of science, with occasional digressions into natural history from the pens of John Godman, Alexander Wilson, and John James Audubon. In the field of metallurgy, the contributions of the early period concerned such processes as gilding and silvering, methods of producing alloys, and the manufacture of wire. By midcentury, however, the study of metals had become important in relation to railroad and locomotive construction, steam boilers, ship hulls, pumps, canals, and the like; a long series of articles in the *Journal* discussed the virtues of Jacob Perkins's high-pressure steam engine. By this time the main contributors to the *Journal* were no longer artisans, amateur inventors, clergymen and physicians interested in technology, and anonymous contributors, but college professors of science, engineers, and other professionals, most of whom were careful to display their credentials, academic or otherwise, in connection with their reports. These contributions—on steam engines, bridges, the strength of materials, ships, railroads, metallurgy, engraving, and photography—were increasingly of a kind that could properly be described as applied science rather than practical technology, as indicated by the use of mathematical, mechanical, chemical, and geological principles in the discussion of practical problems.

In like manner, the Academy of Natural Sciences grew in membership, resources, and the spirit of professionalism as the century progressed. Founded, like most other Philadelphia institutions for promoting knowledge, in a spirit of Baconian collection and dissemination of useful information, the Academy was preserved in that spirit for many years by its president and benefactor, William Maclure, a devout Baconian empiricist in science and an ardent champion of scientific and technical education for the common man. After Maclure's death in 1840, however, the Academy became increasingly a place for scientific research and publication under the leadership of Samuel G. Morton, John Cassin, Joseph Leidy, William S. Vaux, Timothy Conrad, Samuel S. Haldeman, and others.

Although the Academy never regained the leadership in botany it had enjoyed earlier in the century through the work of Thomas Nuttall, C. S. Rafinesque, and others, it continued to be an important center of zoological and paleontological research. In 1846 Dr. Thomas B. Wilson loaned the Academy the collection of ten thousand birds he had purchased from the Duc de Rivoli, and paid for a sizeable extension of the Academy's building to house the collection. He also helped subsidize a second series of the Academy's *Journal.* In 1860 his entire collection of birds, comprising twenty-six thousand mounted specimens and two thousand skins, was donated to the Academy.

Meanwhile, the building had been enlarged again, and a Biological Department, headed by Dr. Joseph Leidy, had been added. And just as the publications of the American Philosophical Society had served as an outlet for a broad range of studies in astronomy and related sciences in the 1830s and 1840s, so the *Proceedings* and *Journal* of the Academy of Natural Sciences became an important avenue for publication in natural history during the 1850s and subsequent decades. As Edward Nolan, historian of the Academy, has written:

The Academy entered on its second half century under the brightest prospects and with a most gratifying record of honorable achievements. The year 1862 was made notable by the work of illustrious veterans who were still active, and by what there was reason to expect from their successors. But few of the great collections which have since come into prominence were then in existence. The Smithsonian Institution was then rather a distributing agency than a storehouse of scientific material. The United States Government had not become, through the Agricultural Department, the National Museum, the Fish Commission and the Geological Surveys, one of the largest publishing concerns in the world, and a formidable rival in the publication of scientific matter, so that the work of Gill, Meek, Hayden, Coues, Stimson, Kennicott, Yarrow and others in Washington and elsewhere, was issued promptly and accurately in the pages of the *Proceedings* and *Journal*.[10]

In the same publications appeared the research of Joseph Leidy, John Cassin, Isaac Lea, George W. Tryon, Jr., James Meigs, John L. Leconte, and other members of the Academy. The Academy, like the Franklin Institute, ended the ante-bellum period on a strong note.

Throughout the first half of the nineteenth century, the Philadelphia societies for promoting knowledge, although they failed to attain the national prestige and hegemony enjoyed by their counterparts in London, maintained a steady level of intellectual achievement and mutual cooperation, educated the Philadelphia public, kept up contacts with similar institutions abroad and in the United States, served in some degree the needs of the city, the state, and the national government, and provided avenues of publication for a scientific community extending well beyond the limits of Pennsylvania. If the Philadelphia institutions were not national in scope and prestige, at the very least they established the models on which similar institutions in other regions of the growing Republic were formed.

Among the first cities to emulate the example of Philadelphia in organizing societies for promoting knowledge was Boston. Outstripped by Philadelphia in population, wealth, and trade, and lacking the Quaker City's central location on the Atlantic seaboard, Boston nevertheless had pretensions to intellectual eminence based on its Puritan past and institutionalized in "the University at Cambridge," as Harvard College was often called in the early nineteenth century. Not to be outdone by Philadelphia, Boston organized its literati into the American Academy of Arts and Sciences in 1780, swelling the roster of its members with the names of its most illustrious citizens.

According to John Adams, the American Academy was modeled more on the Académie Royale des Sciences in Paris than on the American Philosophical Society, but the absence of government patronage and the strong overtones of Baconian utilitarianism in the preface to the first volume of its *Memoirs* (1785) belied the claim. The preface began by reciting the rise and contributions of societies for promoting useful knowledge in Europe, pointing in particular to the Royal Society of London, the Académie des Sciences in Paris, and the Society Instituted for the Encouragement of Arts, Manufactures, and Commerce in London. Through the efforts of these and similar societies, the preface declared, "knowledge of various kinds, and greatly useful to mankind, has taken the place of dry and uninteresting speculations of schoolmen; and bold and erroneous hypothesis has been obliged to give way to demonstrative experiment."[11]

The American Academy, then, was to be another society for promoting useful knowledge. Its aim was

to promote and encourage the knowledge of the antiquities of America, and of the natural history of the country, and to determine the uses to which the various natural productions of the country may be applied; to promote and encourage medical discoveries, mathematical disquisitions, philosophical enquiries and experiments; astronomical, meteorological and geographical observations; and improvements in agriculture, arts, manufactures and commerce; and in fine, to cultivate every art and science, which may tend to advance the interest, honor, dignity and happiness of a free, independent and virtuous people.[12]

The astronomical papers in the first volume of *Memoirs,* the preface explained, were "chiefly of the practical kind . . . such observations and deductions, as are subservient to the cause of geography and navigation, the improvement of which is of great importance to this country." The articles on natural history and "antiquities," too, were justified in terms of their value, actual or potential, in practical affairs. The medical papers, though containing little that was new, would serve to disseminate useful discoveries recently made in Europe. Looking to the future, the founders of the Academy recommended attention to improvements in agriculture; researches in natural history, especially those useful to medicine; astronomical observations, "particularly those . . . which will serve to perfect the geography of the country, and improve navigation"; mechanical arts, manufactures, and commerce, which would "enrich and aggrandize these confederated States"; and, in general, "useful experiments and improvements, whereby the interest and happiness of the rising empire may be essentially advanced."

Further light on the character and objectives of the American Academy can be derived from the "Philosophical Discourse" delivered before the Academy by its president, James Bowdoin, upon his induction into office on November 8, 1780. After describing the extensive field of investigation opened up to the "sons of literature" by the Academy, Bowdoin devoted himself chiefly to the subjects of civil and natural history, stressing the value of a thorough knowledge of the natural history of one's country for the development of its agriculture, commerce, and manufactures. With a prescient eye, he stressed the central role that Harvard College would play in the activities of the Academy. Most of the Academy's members, he noted, were sons of Harvard. So, too, would most of its future members be Harvard men. Then, somewhat less presciently, he assumed the mantle of the Academy's historian one hundred years hence. Looking backward from that vantage point, he recorded that the Academy's members, true to the philosophy of Bacon and Newton, had

laid it down as a fundamental principle, that as true physics must be founded on experiments, so all their enquiries should, as far as possible, be carried on, and directed by them. . . . This has been the uniform practice of the society: whose members, from time to time, having been chosen from the men of every country, from every class and profession, without any other distinction than was dictated by the dignity of their characters, by their morality, good sense, and professional abilities, we find in the printed transactions of the society, the best compositions on every subject, within the line of their department. We find in those transactions new facts, new observations and discoveries; or old ones placed in a new light, and new deductions made from them.

They have particularly attended to such subjects as respected the growth, population, and improvement of their country: in which they have so happily succeeded, that we now see agriculture, manufactures, navigation and commerce, in a high degree of cultivation; and all of them making swift advances in improvement, as population increases. In short, they have, agreeably to the declared end of their institution, "cultivated every art and science, which might tend to advance the interest and honour of their country, the dignity and happiness of a free, independent, and virtuous people."

This is demonstrably evident from the numerous volumes the society have published of their transactions. These volumes are a noble collection of useful knowledge; and considered together in their miscellaneous state, strike the mind with a splendour, resembling the galaxy in the heavens, derived from the combined light of countless myriads of constellations: and like that too, when the several corresponding parts are viewed in their proper connections, they appear to be parts of a whole; and to constitute the most useful systems: systems distinguished by their beauty, regularity, and proportion.[13]

Alas for prophecy! In the next eighty years the Academy published only eleven volumes of *Memoirs* containing but 206 contributions to knowledge. Of these only two or three were based on experiments. As to practical improvements in agriculture, navigation, commerce, manufactures, and the like, only the first two volumes contained a significant number of articles of this sort. The improvement of agriculture was taken up by the Massachusetts Society for Promoting Agriculture, which was also responsible for the founding of a professorship of natural history and a botanical garden at Harvard College. Medical articles soon disappeared from the Academy's *Memoirs*, probably because of the founding in 1812 of the *New England Journal of Medicine and Surgery*. By 1821, when the fourth volume of the *Memoirs* appeared, articles of immediate practical utility had disappeared from the publication, their place being taken by contributions on linguistics and classical literature.

Thereafter, "useful knowledge" was represented by two contributions from the Rumford Professor and Lecturer on the Application of Science to the Useful Arts (one on cannon construction, the other on a machine for spinning hemp and flax); a description of a new telescope stand by the Reverend John Prince; an account of the inner harbor of Boston "with a Synopsis of the General Principles to be observed in the Improvements of Harbors"; some determinations of latitude and longitude by Robert Treat Paine; and an article "On the Practice of Circummeridian Altitudes at Sea or on Shore" by Captain W. F. W. Owen of the Royal Navy. Technology, manufactures, navigation, and commerce—though not agriculture—were indeed flourishing by midcentury in New England, but not as a result of the research and publications of the American Academy of Arts and Sciences.

The Academy's gradual transformation from a society for promoting "useful knowledge" to a literary and philosophical, or learned, society became apparent in 1851, when the Academy decided to distribute its 280 members (of whom

130 were residents of Massachusetts, 80 lived elsewhere in the United States, and 70 were Foreign Honorary Members) into three classes, each with four subdivisions.[14] The first class, Mathematical and Physical Sciences, included mathematics, practical astronomy and geology, physics and chemistry, and technology and engineering. The second, Natural and Physiological Sciences, embraced geology, mineralogy, and physics of the globe; botany and vegetable physiology; zoology and animal physiology; and medicine and surgery. In the third class, Moral and Political Sciences, were moral and intellectual philosophy; philology and ethnology; politics, political economy, and jurisprudence; and aesthetics. In practice, the publications of the Academy, like those of the American Philosophical Society, were dominated by astronomy (and related geophysical sciences) and natural history, with occasional essays on linguistics. There was less experimental and theoretical science in the Academy's *Memoirs* than in the American Philosophical Society's *Transactions,* but the Academy was more successful in securing contributions from its "literary" members.

Whereas the American Philosophical Society reached its highest eminence in its early period and struggled manfully to maintain that eminence in subsequent years, the American Academy increased gradually in stature as Harvard University developed into an important center of science and learning through increasing financial support from the burgeoning Boston community. Whatever the claims of Boston-Cambridge to intellectual distinction in 1800, they were not based primarily on scientific achievement. Science was at a low ebb at Harvard in the first four decades of the nineteenth century. There was no worthy successor to John Winthrop IV in astronomy until Benjamin Peirce and William C. Bond were brought to the College—Peirce in 1831 and Bond in 1839. However, President Joseph Willard did maintain the Winthropian tradition in the Academy to the end of the eighteenth century, by which time Nathaniel Bowditch had begun to emerge as New England's leading astronomer and the Academy's main ornament for more than thirty years. In natural history nothing much was accomplished until the founding of the Boston Society of Natural History in 1830 and the coming of Asa Gray, Louis Agassiz, and Jeffries Wyman to Harvard in the 1840s.

In vain did Benjamin Vaughan seek to persuade the Academy to expand its horizons, enlarge its membership, and become a regional, if not a national, institution. Writing to Nathaniel Bowditch in 1817, Vaughan lamented that Massachusetts, which, in terms of the number of well educated persons residing there, ought to be the "headquarters of science" in the United States, had done little to establish intellectual leadership apart from Harvard College.

Its American Academy is asleep perhaps in the sleep of death; and while it sleeps, other petty rivals take (as it were) from between its teeth, the materials which ought to go to its support. Instead of being the organ of New England's learning, its own journals and its own petty societies carry away what ought to belong to it; and Connecticut has instituted a rival Society. So far from our dividing the force of *Massachusetts,* it ought to combine the whole of *New*

England in favor of knowledge. Massachusetts will not be allowed to be the *representative* of New England; but it may be the chief mover in a *central society*; other states sending representatives, with authority to select pieces for publication belonging to the whole, and philosophical and literary societies of the other states, and (in default of these) their colleges may provide the representatives . . . remembering that no separate *society* and no separate publication in the joint state [of Massachusetts and Maine] can singly have magnitude or interest enough to attract general notice in the U. S. and much less in Europe. The *whole* of our philosophers and literary men *united* can only do it by making exertions in unison with each other. The American Academy by the suspension or slow rate of its publications, and by its want of zeal in soliciting pieces, must receive the chief share of censure for what has occurred on this occasion. An annual publication would satisfy the impatience of authors and the public; and thus prevent many contributions from being diverted from this channel, and seeking the public notice through other publications. But where would be the difficulty of the Linnean Societies [Society's] having a department in this publication allotted to it? The Agricultural Society also, when it has a piece which conveys to the world natural knowledge, and the Connecticut Society may be provided with similar opportunities. The printing might be so contrived, that each Society might have copies to bind up separately, and make volumes of its own, when its papers admitted of it. . . . For myself I perceive no real objection to collecting the published pieces of New England on the subjects in question, yearly; and annexing them (when consent is obtained) to the Massachusetts Volume: but if that be thought degrading let pieces which can not otherwise be obtained, be first presented to the Academy, then published elsewhere with the *leave* of the Academy (affixed to the head of it), and be resumed by the Academy at the end of the year, with the corrections of the author and the remarks of others. The Academy would maintain an easy ascendancy on this occasion; for, if its own contributions did not exceed *all* of the others, they would at least exceed those of *any* of the others; and it would besides have the merit of giving to the whole a currency which others could not expect by their separate efforts. As matters stand arranged, little can be expected from the dislocated action of each state, in consequence of the favors of each branch of knowledge acting separately.[15]

Yet such cooperation was not to be, despite the fact that the Massachusetts Society for Promoting Agriculture, the Linnean Society of New England, and the American Academy of Arts and Sciences had overlapping memberships and shared an interest in natural history. Perhaps because it enjoyed state support, the Massachusetts Society for Promoting Agriculture felt obliged to apologize for the inclusion of a considerable number of scientific articles in their *Massachusetts Agricultural Repository and Journal* (1801-1832).

. . . We are reproached for introducing articles which are above the capacity of common farmers [the editors wrote]. If it be intended as an intimation that we devote too large a proportion of this work to philosophical agriculture, we deny the fact. We have always given the preference to the home bred practical essays and experiments. But we are not ready to admit the fact that the introduction of rational and scientific speculations, such as those of Kirwan and Davy is inexpedient. Massachusetts has scarcely a town which does not furnish educated men. Knowledge must be first communicated to them and from them it will inevitably reach their less informed neighbors.[16]

The Linnaean Society of New England, organized in 1814, showed no disposition to collaborate with either the agricultural society or the American Academy, and soon went under from inability to pay for the housing and care of its rapidly growing collections. Meanwhile, the Connecticut Academy of Arts and Sciences lost much of its reason for existence when the success of Benjamin Silliman's *American Journal of Science* provided an outlet for publishing scientific contributions of the kind that had formerly been published in the Academy's *Memoirs*.[17] New Haven, not Boston, was to become the site of the most important American scientific journal in ante-bellum America, but this journal was to be a family enterprise, not the organ of a society for promoting knowledge. The Connecticut Academy of Arts and Sciences lingered on—indeed, it is still in existence— but it failed to become the instrument for promoting the arts and sciences envisioned by Ezra Stiles, Timothy Dwight, and Noah Webster.

In Boston events took a different turn. Although the American Academy continued to rely heavily on Harvard professors and graduates for membership and for scientific and scholarly contributions, the rapid growth of Boston as a commercial, industrial, and financial center, combined with a longstanding tradition of philanthropic donations in support of the "University at Cambridge," created conditions favorable to the development of scientific and cultural institutions. Between 1830 and 1860 a series of bequests to Harvard College provided for the establishment of professorships in astronomy, botany and natural history, anatomy, and mathematics and natural philosophy, as well as the Lawrence Scientific School, the Museum of Comparative Zoology, and a first-rate observatory with a powerful telescope. In the same decades in which Philadelphia was losing some of its leading physical scientists to the federal government, Harvard acquired the services of Benjamin Peirce and William and George Bond. Moreover, the operations of the United States Coast Survey and the United States *Nautical Almanac* in the Boston area began providing employment for other astronomers and natural philosophers, such as Lt. Charles W. Davis, Simon Newcomb, John D. Runkle, William and Maria Mitchell, William Ferrel, and Joseph Winlock. In 1849 Benjamin Apthorp Gould began publishing his *Astronomical Journal* in Cambridge. Runkle's short-lived *Mathematical Monthly* began publication in 1858.

In the field of natural history, Harvard acquired Asa Gray, Jeffries Wyman, and Louis Agassiz. Meanwhile the Boston Society of Natural History, aided by benefactions from Jonathan Phillips, provided a meeting place for the devotees of natural history. About the same time the talented and energetic Rogers brothers, William and Henry, moved to Boston, there to promote the founding of an institute of technology and to contribute substantially to the scientific discussions at the American Academy and the Boston Society of Natural

History. In Boston, as in Philadelphia, the natural historians divided their contributions between the publications of the younger natural history society and those of the older and more general scientific society. Naturalists like Asa Gray, William Sullivant, and David Humphrey Storer contributed to the *Memoirs* of the American Academy some of the botanical and zoological studies that might more naturally have found publication in the *Boston Journal of Natural History.* These contributions, added to occasional ones from outside the Boston area—from S. S. Haldeman and Joseph Leidy in Philadelphia, John L. LeConte in New York and later Philadelphia, Edward Hitchcock in Amherst, and James Hall and Fielding B. Meek in Albany—gave the Academy a respectable showing in natural history. Indeed, its *Proceedings* for the 1850s, in contrast to the volumes of the 1840s, showed more activity in natural history than in natural philosophy, perhaps because the Boston-Cambridge astronomers had found a new outlet for their contributions in Gould's *Astronomical Journal,* Runkle's *Mathematical Monthly,* and the *Proceedings* of the American Association for the Advancement of Science.

Besides astronomy and natural history, the chief topics that recurred in the *Memoirs* of the Academy from time to time were Indian languages, the calculation of life expectancy, Indian mounds, and thermometric, barometric, magnetic, and other geophysical records. Humanistic research was represented by "A Glossary of Later and Byzantine Greek," a long article entitled "The Age of Petronius Arbiter," Jacob Bigelow's essay "On the Death of Pliny the Elder," and John Pickering's linguistic research.

In Boston, as in Philadelphia, the natural historians, drawn chiefly though not exclusively from the ranks of medical men, formed a major component of the scientific community. Like the Academy of Natural Sciences of Philadelphia, the Boston Society of Natural History led a precarious financial existence for many years, struggling to house and care for its rapidly augmenting collections until private benefactions enabled it to function more efficiently. A turning point came in 1860, when Jonathan Phillips, a member who had donated $2,000 to pay the debts of the Society a decade earlier, bequeathed an additional $10,000 to the Society. In the following year came the first of a series of large donations to the Society by Dr. William J. Walker. About the same time the state legislature granted a square of land for the use of the Society and the projected Massachusetts Institute of Technology. By the spring of 1864 the Society was established in a handsome new building, the Museum of the Boston Society of Natural History, dedicated and opened to the public on May 27, 1864.[18]

Like its sister institution in Philadelphia, the Boston Society of Natural History attracted contributions from far outside the Boston area—from John Bachman and Lewis R. Gibbes in South Carolina; from Moses Ashley Curtis in Wilmington, North Carolina; from N. M. Hentz in Alabama; from Samuel G. Morton, Joseph Leidy, and S. S. Haldeman in Philadelphia; from Jacob W. Bailey at West Point, James Hall in Albany, and John LeConte in New York; and from Josiah D. Whitney in the Lake Superior region. However, it never became an outlet for publishing the collections of government expeditions. Locally it drew heavily on the Boston medical community, made up of Harvard medical professors and their students, but as Harvard College emerged as a major center of research in natural history through the labors of Gray, Agassiz, Jeffries Wyman, and others, the College began to overshadow the medical school as a center for research in natural history.

In the short run these developments in the College greatly strengthened the American Academy and the Boston Society of Natural History. In the long run, however, Harvard University was to dwarf both of these institutions, rendering them peripheral to its ever-expanding intellectual empire. With the Museum of Comparative Zoology, the Geological Museum, the Gray Herbarium, the Arnold Arboretum, and the Peabody Museum of American Archaeology and Ethnology all flourishing at Harvard University in the twentieth century, what need was there for the Museum of the Boston Society of Natural History? James Bowdoin had spoken truly when he described the American Academy as the offspring of Harvard College. So, too, was the Boston Society of Natural History. But the parent institution was to prove too vigorous and powerful for its offspring. The universities, not the various academies and societies, were to be the chief agencies for promoting knowledge in the United States after the Civil War.

In New York, where population, commerce, industry, wealth, and geographic location might have led one to expect the development of an array of institutions for promoting knowledge rivaling or surpassing the achievements of Philadelphia, nothing of the kind occurred. Reflecting on this anomaly, De Witt Clinton offered in explanation the practical motives of the original settlers in New York; the debilitating effects of a royal colonial government that tended to alienate the governing classes from the governed; the cultural and linguistic diversity of the population, leading to political and religious factionalism; the absence of provisions for elementary education; the low condition of the professions of law, medicine, and divinity; the disastrous effects of the Revolution; the schisms within the medical community; and the dominance of the commercial spirit.[19] Doubtless some, if not all, of these factors were influential, but an even more important circumstance seems to have been the removal of the state capital to Albany, thus dividing the scientific resources of the area between two poles. Since the meetings of the Society for the Promotion of Agriculture, Arts, and Manufactures (later the Society for the Promotion of Useful Arts) were tied to the meetings of the legislature, the removal of the capital to Albany shifted the center of gravity of the Society's operations to that city, although many of the most active members lived in New York. When the Natural History Survey of New York was inaugurated in 1836, Albany, not New York City, became the center of its operations and the repository of its collections, and the Albany Institute mobilized energies that might otherwise have been devoted to building scientific and technical institutions in New York. Just as the removal of the national capital to Washington, D.C., prevented Philadelphia from becoming a national scientific center, so the transfer of the New York State capital to Albany reduced New York City's chances of becoming a strong regional center.

Certainly there was no dearth of scientific talent and enterprise in New York City in the opening decades of the nineteenth century. Samuel Latham Mitchill's *Medical Repository* served as a national scientific journal, drawing contributions from far and wide, and Mitchill himself was a tireless organizer and promoter of useful knowledge. New York's medical community was badly rent by factional strife, but it managed to produce and sustain a high level of scientific activity at the College of Physicians and Surgeons and rival institutions and to generate a surprising number of enterprises for promoting useful knowledge. Dr. David Hosack's Elgin Botanic Garden, established and developed at his own expense, became an important adjunct of the College of Physicians and Surgeons by gift of the State of New York, which purchased it when Hosack could no longer afford to maintain it. Dr. Archibald Bruce's *American Mineralogical Journal* (1810-1814) provided a national outlet and rallying point for Americans interested in geology, mineralogy, and paleontology. Mitchill, Bruce, Hosack, and, later, John Torrey and William MacNeven trained a large number of students in chemistry, the earth sciences, and natural history and played a prominent role in organizing the pursuit of knowledge. John Griscom's popular lectures on chemistry and natural philosophy were well attended for many years, and John Scudder's American Museum, although not the equal of Peale's Museum, stimulated public interest in natural history. At the same time, important public figures—notably Robert R. Livingston, Robert Fulton, and De Witt Clinton—were ardent promoters of useful knowledge. Not far up the Hudson River, the United States Military Academy provided a cadre of professors well trained in mathematics, natural philosophy, and engineering, and Columbia College supplied the talents of Robert Adrain, James Renwick, and others. In 1814 Colonel George Gibbs, a wealthy gentleman scientist from Newport, Rhode Island, established a residence on Long Island and became active in New York scientific and cultural affairs. Soon afterward young John Torrey began building an herbarium and a competence in botany that were to make New York a clearing house for the botany of the Western expeditions in the 1840s and 1850s.

The efforts of the New York scientists, literati, and promoters of useful knowledge to organize in pursuit of their objectives reached maximum intensity in the period during and just after the War of 1812. In these years the Society for the Promotion of Useful Arts was invigorated by the activities of such avid devotees of science—especially chemistry, mineralogy, geology, and general natural history—as Samuel L. Mitchill, Archibald Bruce, Theodric Romeyn Beck, Colonel George Gibbs, Thomas C. Brownell, and Josiah Noyes. Many of these same individuals took the lead in promoting similar studies in the New York Historical Society. A cabinet of natural history was organized in the Society in 1816, and in March of the following year the Society established lectureships in the various branches of science and appointed lecturers who also chaired committees charged with collecting information and specimens in their respective departments. Mitchill was appointed chairman for zoology and geology, David Hosack for botany and vegetable physiology, John Griscom for chemistry and natural philosophy, and Colonel Gibbs for mineralogy.

Soon afterwards Gibbs reported in Biglow's *American Monthly Magazine and Critical Review* that the Society was planning to display specimens of minerals from every state in the Union in specially designed cases, "one case being devoted to each state, after the manner adopted in the national collection at the École des Mines at Paris."[20] Meanwhile, two entirely new institutions for promoting knowledge—the Literary and Philosophical Society of New York and the Lyceum of Natural History of New York—were being organized, and the city was providing meeting space for these and other institutions—the Academy of Fine Arts, the New York Historical Society, Scudder's American Museum, Griscom's chemical laboratory, and the United States Military Philosophical Society—in the Old Almshouse, now designated The New York Institution for the Promotion of the Arts and Sciences.

In examining the membership lists, public pronouncements, and activities of the various societies housed in the Old Almshouse, one is impressed with the strength of the interest in natural history, ranging from mineralogy and geology to paleontology, botany, and zoology. This interest had been present from the beginning in the Society for the Promotion of Useful Arts. It was equally apparent in De Witt Clinton's inaugural discourse before the Literary and Philosophical Society of New York and in the first and only volume of the Society's *Transactions.* It even manifested itself in the New York Historical Society, whose zealous natural historians threatened to transform the Society into an institution for promoting natural history. Finally, the passion for natural history produced in 1817 the Lyceum of Natural History of New York, the one scientific society that was to endure in New York despite many financial vicissitudes and the eventual destruction of its collections by fire.

The Lyceum was to be a worthy though impecunious counterpart of the Academy of Natural Sciences of Philadelphia and the Boston Society of Natural History, but the absence of a counterpart of the American Philosophical Society and the American Academy of Arts and Sciences meant that the mathematicians and physical scientists in the New York vicinity, including West Point, Rutgers University, Princeton, and New York itself, had to look elsewhere—to Philadelphia or Boston or Albany—for stimulation and publication. In vain did William C. Redfield assure Elias Loomis that his contributions to meteorology would be welcome at the Lyceum of Natural History. Philadelphia was a more natural outlet. Joseph Henry, too, looked to Philadelphia for scientific company after he left Albany for Princeton. As for John W. Draper, New York's leading physical scientist before the Civil War, his papers appeared in the *Journal of the Franklin Institute,* the *American Journal of Science,* the *American Journal of the Medical Sciences,* and the *Philosophical Magazine.* The founding of the American Ethnological Society and the New York Academy of Medicine in New

York in the 1840s indicated that the impetus toward organizing for the promotion of science and related arts was not extinct, but the rapid decline of the Literary and Philosophical Society of New York after 1830 brought an end to all efforts to emulate the example of the American Philosophical Society and the American Academy of Arts and Sciences.

And so it went in the various urban centers scattered from Boston to Charleston, from Cincinnati to New Orleans. The number and character of the local institutions for promoting knowledge varied with the resources—economic, cultural, and scientific—of the region, the enterprise of its citizens, and the peculiar circumstances of history, culture, geography, and individual genius. In Cincinnati Dr. Daniel Drake attempted with limited success to replicate the pattern of institutions for promoting knowledge he had admired while a student in Philadelphia. Charleston had its Literary and Philosophical Society for a time, New Orleans and St. Louis their academies of science at a later period. Each began with a broad statement of purposes and aspirations and a framework of classes or committees embracing the whole range of science and literature. In practice, however, natural history proved to be the only area of investigation capable of enlisting a sufficient number of professionals—usually medical men— and amateur cultivators to maintain the society in existence, if indeed it could survive.

It appears, then, that the record of societies for promoting knowledge in the period before 1860 was an honorable, though not a brilliant, one. Deprived for the most part of government support, they could not hope to emulate the model of the academies on the continent of Europe. Scattered in urban centers, none of which could claim national preeminence, dependent for support on members for the most part of limited means, hampered by public attitudes that placed no high value on intellectual achievement per se, they were equally incapable of attaining the eminence and influence of the leading British societies. Yet, despite these limitations, their role was a highly useful one. Without them the scientific communities scattered over the face of the country would have languished for lack of communication among themselves and with each other, and the general public, already too prone to neglect the cultivation of science and letters, would have been denied the stimulus, both practical and intellectual, provided by the publications, the collections, and the example of these societies for the improvement of knowledge and the human condition.

NOTES

1. Benjamin Franklin, *Writings,* ed. A. H. Smyth, 10 vols. (New York, 1907), 2:230.

2. "Preface," *Transactions of the American Philosophical Society* 1 (1771): xvii. The patriotic and utilitarian context of the early activities of the American Philosophical Society is discussed at length in Brooke Hindle, *The Pursuit of Science in Revolutionary America 1735-1789* (Chapel Hill: University of North Carolina Press, 1956), chaps. 6-7. See also *American Philosophical Society; an Historical Account of the Origin and Formation of the American Philosophical Society . . . and the Report of the Committee on the Date of the Foundation of the Society Accepted May 1, 1914* (Philadelphia: American Philosophical Society, 1914).

3. *Proceedings of the American Philosophical Society* 5 (1848-1853): 111-12. See also Whitfield J. Bell, Jr., "The American Philosophical Society and Medicine," *Bulletin of the History of Medicine* 40 (1966): 112-23.

4. "Old Minutes of the Society, from 1743 to 1838," *Proceedings of the American Philosophical Society* 22 (1885), pt. 3:453. A footnote comments concerning the establishment of this committee: "This was in fact the birth of the Historical Society of Pennsylvania."

5. *Proceedings of the American Philosophical Society* 6 (1854-1855): 67. A good account of the Society in the years 1835-1850 is Walter E. Gross, "The American Philosophical Society and the Growth of Science in the United States 1835-1850" (Ph.D. diss., University of Pennsylvania, 1970).

6. John Vaughan, *An Account of the American Philosophical Society* (Philadelphia: The American Philosophical Society, 1972).

7. "Report of the Special Committee on the Present Condition of the Society and the Means of Increasing Its Usefulness," Minutes of the American Philosophical Society, January 7, 1853, to April 21, 1865, Library of the American Philosophical Society, 291(May 1859):6.

8. *First Annual Report of the Proceedings of the Franklin Institute of the State of Pennsylvania, for the Promotion of the Mechanic Arts . . .* (Philadelphia: J. Harding, Printer, 1825), pp. 4-63.

9. Sydney L. Wright, *The Story of the Franklin Institute* (Philadelphia: Franklin Institute, 1938), chap. 1. I am indebted for information concerning the Institute's changing financial fortunes to Bruce Sinclair, whose study of the Franklin Institute is an important contribution to knowledge of scientific and technological activity in Philadelphia.

10 Edward J. Nolan, *A Short History of the Academy of Natural Sciences of Philadelphia* (Philadelphia: Academy of Natural Sciences, 1909), p. 16.

11. "Preface," *Memoirs of the American Academy of Arts and Sciences* 1 (1785): iv-vii.

12. "Charter of Incorporation, May 4, 1780," *Memoirs of the American Academy of Arts and Sciences* 11(1888): 78.

13. James Bowdoin, "A Philosophical Discourse, Publickly Addressed to the American Academy of Arts and Sciences, in Boston, on the Eighth of November, 1780: When the President Was Inducted into Office," *Memoirs of the American Academy of Arts and Sciences* 1:18-19.

14. *Proceedings of the American Academy of Arts and Sciences* 2 (1848-1852): 285-88.

15. Benjamin Vaughan to Nathaniel Bowditch, 13 August 1817, quoted in Nathan Reingold, ed., *Science in Nineteenth-Century America: A Documentary History* (New York: Hill and Wang, 1964), pp. 17-19.

16. *Massachusetts Agricultural Repository and Journal* 7 (1823): 320.

17. Simeon E. Baldwin, *The First Century of the Connecticut Academy of Arts and Sciences, 1799-1899 . . .* (New Haven: Tuttle, Morehouse and Taylor Co. Press, 1901), p. xxii.

18. Thomas T. Bouvé, *Historical Sketch of the Boston Society of Natural History: With a Notice of the Linnaean Society, Which Preceded It* (Boston: Boston Society of Natural History, 1880), pp. 80-88.

19. De Witt Clinton, "An Introductory Discourse Delivered on the 4th of May, 1814," *Transactions of the Literary and Philosophical Society of New York . . .* 1 (1815):21 ff.

20. *American Monthly Magazine and Critical Review* 1 (1817): 48, 124.

The National Pattern
of American Learned Societies,
1769-1863

A. HUNTER DUPREE

A learned society is an information system. This statement does not signify that a learned society in the period of incipient nationalism for both the United States and western Europe, 1769-1863, was something like an information system. The statement is not limited to the assertion of an analogy. It says, rather, (1) that the business of a learned society was in the late eighteenth century, and has remained, the gathering, processing, and dissemination of information; and (2) that purely informal and unstructured means of information exchange had long before the mid-eighteenth century proved inadequate. A pattern had emerged that was well understood by those living at the time. The founders of a learned society knew that they had to form an organization with certain characteristics if information was to flow, and they had a definite pattern, or template, proven by experience to guide their choices. Hence the historian can identify the pattern, ascertain its boundaries, and distinguish it from other patterns. In short, he is justified in calling it a system.

Both words—"information" and "system"—have general meanings deeply imbedded in the language and technical meanings assigned to them as the result of developments since the Second World War. Information in its more general, older sense implied items of knowledge that possess enough structure to be intelligible discreetly. In a strict sense, modern information theory, after the usage of Claude Shannon, is concerned only with the quantity of information flowing in a channel and not with its content. However, before and after Shannon, usage of the word "information" has implied a mixture of quantity and content. The United States Navy in World War II put Combat *Information* Centers on its ships. The National Science Foundation, soon after its founding in 1950, established an Office of Science *Information* Services, which dealt with the same kinds of mixtures of channel and content that are recognizable in the scientific exchanges of the eighteenth century. Information is still a part of the general language as used here, but its meaning has been enriched by the more rigorous usage of the present age.[1]

The word "communication" has some claims to serve in place of "information" in this discussion. It has a meaning in the general language, and has also become the focus for a set of more rigorous theories that only partly overlap

---

[1] Notes to this chapter begin on page 31.

information theories. "Communication," however, emphasizes the channels among interacting individuals or groups at their terminals, whereas "information" implies the inclusion of the terminals as well as the channels. Learned societies are analogous to the terminals, not merely the channels. Therefore, although one would not go completely wrong by substituting "communication" for "information," the system implied by the latter includes the senders and receivers of messages, not just the messages in the channels of communication.

"System" likewise has a long-standing array of general meanings, figuring prominently in the literature of science at least from the time of the comparisons of the Ptolemaic and Copernican systems. With somewhat less success than engineers with respect to information, the enthusiasts for general systems theory have attempted to achieve mathematical rigor in their analyses.[2] Even if a general theory is not achieved, however, the word "system" has been enriched by modern usages, especially those under the rubric of cybernetics, which emphasizes negative feedback circuits as controls and a resulting tendency toward equilibrium. Talcott Parsons, who applied cybernetic concepts to sociology in his book *The Social System* (1951), has also used "system" in a sufficiently loose form—a sense that can easily be assimilated into the vocabulary of historians.[3]

In *The Anatomy of a Scientific Institution: The Paris Academy of Sciences, 1666-1803*, Roger Hahn refers briefly to Parsons's theories and points out the possible advantage of considering a scientific institution as a social unit.[4] Hahn also sees in the scientific societies established in the 1660s three characteristics that "became the trade-mark of all groups seriously concerned with the promotion of science. Each organization, by its very nature, had a communal instinct to share information within its membership, and secondly to make its collective findings generally available to other interested circles. . . . Yet if in our eyes communality and publicity seem crucial, the members themselves placed an even higher value upon a third activity: experimentation."[5] Whether the relative values remained unchanged into the late eighteenth century is less important than that the characteristics Hahn emphasizes are precisely the ones that give meaning to the statement that a learned society is an information system.

In any era a face-to-face meeting has an advantage over other forms of communication, and the slower the alternative form of interaction, the more prized the local meeting. Hence in the eighteenth century all scientific societies give local meetings a central importance. The generalization is as true of the Royal Society of London—the name itself is evidence—and what Hahn calls in his title "The Paris Academy of Sciences" as it is of the "American Philosophical Society, Held at Philadelphia." The ability to travel to meetings periodically to hear communications, to see demonstrations, and to take part in discussions made residency a requirement for full-fledged membership. The local transportation network was a defining limit on the functioning of any society, and on the shared culture of the individuals who made up the membership. The sharing of information on learned subjects, which was the first objective of all the societies, took place, then, within an internal network of relationships that lapped over into other social units, in which the individual members, as residents of the same place, participated.

The overlapping membership in the eighteenth century made possible the combining of cultivators, practitioners, and researchers into one society. At the same time each of these members was also connected with other groups, a profession, a church, a political club, a social class, a family. This multiple mapping of an individual into many templates has often misled observers, because the concept of a single relationship as the one that defines identity to the exclusion of all others is a fallacy. During the period under review the relative weights of the various relationships changed, but the fact of multiple mapping remained. Benjamin Franklin or Thomas Jefferson do not relate easily to a single scientific discipline. Perhaps for that reason they found the American Philosophical Society congenial. Joseph Henry, Asa Gray, and Louis Agassiz are much more clearly related to a single discipline, yet their multiple connections cannot be ignored.

Even before the first appearance of learned societies as formal entities, an informal network of correspondence was in existence, transcending the locality of the isolated individual. A global network of communication was present in the technology-intensive maritime society emanating from western Europe that since the fifteenth century had made possible the exploration, settlement, and commercial survival of the New World. From the time Thomas Hariot rode Raleigh's ships to Roanoke to the continuous trade of the Quaker merchants of eighteenth-century Philadelphia, the sailing fleet formed a network carrying not only heavy goods but mail, which, though of little physical weight, could have a high information content. Furthermore, the network served to connect those with complementary business interests and similar tastes in all the ports open to European trade. Linnaeus's network of collectors extended from North America to South Africa to Japan. The correspondence necessary to keep merchandise flowing could easily be adapted to messages of intellectual import; hence, the role of a Peter Collinson joined in one network the mercantile and scientific information flow. Brooke Hindle's natural history circle, which centered on Collinson, can be understood as a correspondence network that was not dependent on any local society for its structure.[6]

As Collinson's American correspondents discovered, they could not participate in the highly developed global information network centering on western Europe without systematic efforts to get their local findings in a form that would be acceptable generally; that is, they had to publish, not merely write letters. From their start, the learned societies reflected this need to join in formal and generalized correspondence by making an essential part of their functions the publication of transactions, proceedings, and memoirs. The terms "transactions" and "proceedings" imply the collective action of the society. Its imprimatur suggested the act of judgment by which the editor and specially knowledgeable members trusted by him monitored the quality and originality of the contributions emanating from the society. The function of referees evolved from the early days of the Royal Society.[7]

The fact that in the beginning local societies in America had difficulty getting enough original contributions from the presentations before their meetings to mount volumes at regular intervals is a measure of their limited ability to function, rather than a reflection on their nature. A glance through the list in Max Meisel's *Bibliography of American Natural History* shows many abortive efforts at transactions and proceedings, and highlights the performance of the American Philosophical Society and the American Academy of Arts and Sciences.[8]

The use of the memoir for contributions a shade more substantial and more irregular than transactions and proceedings gives an added dimension to the publications of a learned society. In terms of modern computer science, the publications were a memory storage containing information in a form that allowed easy and accurate retrieval. The word "memoir" offers a clue that the founders of learned societies recognized this function and some of the rules that had to be followed if science was not to sink under a load of miscellany. Descriptions must be in good form and good Latin. Figures must be accurately drawn. Slovenliness was to be avoided. Moreover, to repeat a contribution already made by another was both to waste scarce resources in publication and to render the retrieval of the prior report more difficult. The rules of priority and the prohibition on synonymy had their base in the inner workings of a global information system that was already well developed in the age of Linnaeus. The extent to which American societies enforced the rule showed to what extent they matched the global system. This matching, rather than a vague concept of maturity, is the adequate way to conceive of American accomplishments in comparison with those of Europe.

As soon as a society published its transactions, it was in a position to gather in the transactions of other societies by trade. Even if a society had no resources for book purchase, it found itself in the library business at an early stage. The impulse for libraries in the cities of the New World antedated the learned societies, as Carl Bridenbaugh has felicitously shown for Philadelphia.[9] In the mid-nineteenth century the battle over the Smithsonian Institution's library policy was evidence that the tradition of the general library never completely merged with that of the learned society library. A memory bank in the form of stored transactions was, however, necessary for both the local and the global networks to which a society contributed and from which it received information.

A full accounting of information flow into and out of a learned society must include nonverbal communication. In its pure form such data might enter a meeting of the society directly in the form of experimentation. In both the Royal Society and the Paris Academy experimentation had a prominent place. None of the early savants wished the societies to be mere clubs. However, by the late eighteenth century experiments had all but disappeared from the meetings of the Royal Society.[10] A research enterprise as complicated as the observations of the transits of Venus required special sites all over the world, yet, although they were intimately tied to the founding of the American Philosophical Society, the transit observations reached the society in writing.

One reason for the prominence of natural history in early American science is the fact that minerals and biological specimens, especially dried plants, could serve as nonverbal transmitters of information, and could, collectively, form a memory bank of the exploring expeditions that gathered them. The curatorial role was not a passive one. The specimens entered the museum or herbarium in batches identified by their expedition and, hopefully, the locality of their collection. After Linnaeus the act of naming had the effect of tying the local biological assemblages (that is, the specimens) to a global system of nomenclature. This complicated operation, involving both analytical and bibliographical skill, could not take place at the meeting; it required a stable, well-protected location for regular work.

Like the Royal Society, the American Philosophical Society and the American Academy of Arts and Sciences failed to develop the specialized facilities required for natural history. However, in the first round of learned societies established after independence, one often found societies of natural history. The Academy of Natural Sciences of Philadelphia came into being in 1812 not long after Peale's Museum had moved out of the Hall of the American Philosophical Society and begun its wandering toward the clutches of P. T. Barnum. According to an early history of the Academy, "a few gentlemen resolved to meet once in every week, for the purpose of receiving and imparting information."[11] My use of the word "information," and indeed my basic proposition, is thus not an anachronistic analogy but the direct statement of a nearly contemporary observer. A museum, a library, a chemical laboratory, and experimental apparatus were all included in the plan, and a series of papers under the title of *Journal* began in 1817 and became a *Proceedings* in 1841. The list of officers is a standard one, reflecting both the local and the global circulation of information: president, vice-president, corresponding secretary, recording secretary, treasurer, librarian, conservator for various departments. This roster matches closely the older societies, which provided templates for would-be organizers. The California Academy of Sciences (1853) shows the same organization, though it was strong on curators and weak on the corresponding secretary—a sure sign of future chauvinism.[12]

That the California Academy of Sciences in its early isolation published its proceedings in a newspaper, *The Pacific*, shows a connection between the learned societies and a wider information flow through general journalism. Throughout our period the general newspapers provided an alternate channel of scientific news that was under the control of editors not bound by the standards of a society. Quackery and pseudoscience found a place alongside "good" science in the press of the early Republic. Yet, out of the proprietary press arose an important type of scientific publication that most often bore the title "journal." *The American Journal of Science and the Arts*, founded in 1818, had evolved a long way from newspapers and general periodicals. But its editors stood outside the framework of any society and were financially as well as editorially liable. Indeed, one of the important changes brought about by the *American Journal* was its invitation to would-be organizers of societies to submit their proceedings for publication. In this way, the proprietary journal helped to carry the societies and made possible a much greater volume of society publication.

We must pause here to consider again the definition of information. In the beginning we admitted a loose interpretation that would embrace messages as both quantity and content. Even while using this definition, however, the description as it has developed tends to delineate a social structure rather than a body of knowledge. Instead of deploring the distinction that has emerged, we should emphasize it. The template of the learned society, which the devotees of science found already a well-developed tradition in the late eighteenth century, provides channels for the flow of information. As a social unit, its population is bound to a place or a set of places, and communication with the global store of knowledge, while ardently sought, can never achieve a complete exchange of information. One can glimpse in the local-global exchanges a flow of information that passes through the individual societies, but that originates with individuals or groups of investigators and collects in symbolic pattern in a memory store. By our period the memory store can be called "global" in terms of the comprehensiveness of the localities from which the symbols come, and a global network of local stations can be seen emerging.

To follow this second information flow passing *through* the learned societies is to trace the history of science conceived of as a set of bodies of knowledge. Moreover, to adopt an active view of a body of knowledge that has a clearly discernible structure is to admit that it has been *disciplined* by constraints of various sorts. The history of scholarly disciplines and their subject matter is quite distinct from the history of the templates of scholarly institutions. Information theory may provide a way of looking at both the templates that govern the institutions and the disciplinary boundaries that shape the symbols of knowledge itself.

To return to the learned society of 1769-1863, which we described earlier, we can get a clearer idea of its characteristics if we watch it function. Since the societies are social units, they can, like other social units, be observed to function from four distinct points of view:

1. They can be considered as aggregates of people, as communities.

2. Since they mobilize power and even invoke sanctions, the societies can be considered as polities. Certainly when they partake of the power of the sovereign they are a polity, and even when they are purely voluntary associations they have the character of a polity, at least internally.

3. They can be regarded from an economic viewpoint as a mobilizer of resources to support the creation and ongoing flow of an information system.

4. Finally, they can be seen as having a value system which is exhibited both locally and globally by symbolic acts. Both the universal science of the Enlightenment and the nation states of the era of democratic revolution challenge the learned societies to characteristic symbolic responses. These values themselves become as much a part of the information environment of the societies as the substantive scientific symbol-sets that appear within the apparatus of the societies.[13]

The concept of organizing a society, identifying a community of interest, and selecting a group of people as members was deeply engrained in the experience and the heritage of British Americans. By the 1760s they had a vast repertoire of social techniques available to them. Yet potential members of American learned societies had long been organized in networks whose centers were in the Old World. Both the Royal Society of London and the informal networks of correspondence had provided only an indirect access to the global community of science. To achieve face-to-face communication and become an interacting community, the devotees of science had to identify a local population and mobilize it. Such a population could gradually change from a group in which all interested were welcome to one in which members were rigidly selected. Even in extreme cases, however, enough selection existed, through either volunteering or invitation, to make the learned society a body clearly distinguished from other organizations, however many members might overlap into churches, lodges, and professional associations. The mix of members between those who were merely interested and those "under the discipline" could change over time; indeed, it did tend to shift as professionalization proceeded in the nineteenth century. It is the task of analysis to examine the mix in any given case, not to make an all-or-none decision between amateur and professional.

A learned society could begin as an informal global network or as an "invisible college" in a single locality, but its functions would be severely restricted if it did not soon develop a polity. The English template of a voluntary association was dominant in America—hence the reiterated pattern of charters, bylaws, and officers—but the point at which a polity began to operate as more than adornment came with the enforcement of standards. These sanctions could be applied directly in the selection of members. By 1850 the battle against quackery and self-appointed experts who teemed in Jacksonian America had made the nature of membership a serious issue—one that was certainly evident in the founding of the National Academy of Sciences. A more subtle sanction, operating much earlier, was the standard-setting role of editors and referees. The extent to which they functioned, and to which their publications were received into the global systems, is a measure of American stature in science more concrete than individual reputations.

No association could succeed without economic support, and even the relatively slight costs of having groups of amateurs meet occasionally and issue sporadic publications were greater than many societies could bear. Since the scientific societies and even the more practice-oriented societies of arts did not pay their own way, some mechanism for transferring resources from the society at large to the learned society was a necessity. To transfer directly from the state was within the experience of American societies but their more customary means of support was dependence on their own members. It is probably impossible in such instances to draw a clear line between the gentleman-amateur as financial supporter and the professional as financial recipient. Indeed, a case could be made that from very early in our period it was those under the discipline who made the greater contribution economically to the societies because they often donated their collections and services directly. They also wrote the bulk of the papers and held the bulk of the offices in the societies.

As an exemplar of value systems, the learned society faced two ways. In the locality, it symbolized the global network of science with its attendant belief in the tenets of the Enlightenment—a secular but universal truth. In the global network, it was a local station, injecting information from that locality but also saying symbolically that this place—Philadelphia, Boston, or Albany—is civilized and capable of contributing to the good of humanity. As the American nation took shape, it did so in a world in which the local value system, not the global value system, was becoming nationalized. Representing the Royal Society of London, Sir Joseph Banks negotiated hot-war and cold-war issues with his counterpart at the first class of the Institut de France during the period 1794-1815.[14] An American national symbol in science therefore was a part of the information transmitted by the American Philosophical Society and the American Academy of Arts and Sciences even in an age when the transportation network of the country effectively limited these organizations to the localities of Philadelphia and Boston.

The learned societies, as they functioned, had to define for themselves the characteristics that would separate them from other, related information systems also operating in the general society. For example, we have already alluded to the fact that these societies needed libraries but left the function of providing general libraries in America to other groups, public and private. Given their limited resources, they had to avoid assuming a function not defined by the learned society template.

The most obvious boundary established by the learned societies lay at the point of junction with educational institutions. Schools, colleges, and academies (sharing a name) were in the information transmission business. Because they had to initiate young people who were by virtue of age and lack of experience as yet unqualified as members of the society of scholars, the schools and colleges generally required an extended period not only of residence in the general locality but residence inside the walls. Only in this way could advanced instruction go on several hours a day, not just in one meeting a month. The American colleges were well established long before the learned societies. The decentralized pattern of location, the shape of a polity, the economic resources, and the major value systems were all laid down long before 1769. The general line of differentiation between the educational institution and the learned societies was clear from the beginning of our period.

Along the boundary itself, however, grew up a set of learned societies connected with the colleges. As long as the collegiate tradition deemphasized research, and as long as the tools of scholarship needed by colleges bore some resemblance to those in the learned societies, a hybrid society was possible. A glance at Max Meisel's list quickly reveals, as examples:

1793   Harvard College Mineralogical Cabinet, Cambridge
1802   Yale College Mineralogical Cabinet, New Haven
1805   Cambridge (Mass.) Botanic Garden
         College of New Jersey (Princeton) Cabinet of Natural History
1822   Amherst College Natural History Society and Cabinets, Amherst, Mass.
1824   Transylvania University Botanical Garden, Lexington, Ky.
1834   Yale Natural History Society
1835   Williams College Lyceum of Natural History
1836   Cuvierian or Natural History Society of Wesleyan University, Middletown, Conn.
1837   Harvard Natural History Society, Cambridge
         University of Michigan Natural History Museum, Ann Arbor
1839   Agricultural, Horticultural, & Botanical Society, Jefferson College, Miss.
1840   Natural History Society of Geneva College, Geneva, N.Y.
1844   Linnaean Association of Pennsylvania College, Gettysburg, Pa.[15]

The presence of these intermediate institutions and their disappearance from the scene suggests that, as the colleges developed a research capability, the society form of support gradually withdrew, to be taken over directly by the college. The history of the Harvard Botanic Garden bears out this evolution.

Another major boundary existed between the learned societies and the information system that transmitted technological knowledge. Unlike the knowledge in the college system, neatly defined in curriculum and narrowly restricted to a small fraction of the general population, technological information flowed broadly through all classes in many craft traditions. The absence of guilds in America should not mislead us into thinking that craft traditions, with apprenticeship—formal or informal—as the transmitting institution for channeling information from one generation to another, were also absent.[16] Throughout our period most technological information flowed from father and mother to son and daughter or from master to apprentice in a way that perpetuated longstanding ways of doing things. Technologically, America in our period was more medieval than western Europe.[17] This information system, stable in time, was transmittable in space only by moving people around. Even innovations were most easily made by moving a person with a design in his head—Samuel Slater, for example—from one place to another.

Like the colleges, the technological traditions were clearly distinct from the learned societies. But, unlike pure learning, technology had by its very definition a payoff.[18] Traditions did not survive unless they yielded their adherents some value in return for following the discipline of the craft. Therefore, the societies of arts and the American Academy of Arts and Sciences found themselves having to compete with practices of proven value if they wished to improve technology.

In our period the patent system was developing, with the sanction of the government, to provide a substitute reward for deviations from craft practice. The main device open to the societies was the offering of prizes as an alternate reward for innovation. The book that proves that prizes were deleterious to the progress of knowledge has not yet been written, but neither has the case been made that they yield a net gain of information when one takes into account all the losers and secondary effects. As symbols, prizes have not been unsuccessful enough to die out, but other forms of reward for priority, such as reputation, seem to have gained ground in comparison.

Two kinds of societies of arts must be considered within a special category. Agricultural societies and medical societies were more vigorous in our period in America than those societies that aimed to improve on craft tradition. Stephen Toulmin and June Goodfield make a distinction that provides guidance in this area:

> Our practical skills and activities fall into two general classes, which may be called the *natural arts* and the *artificial crafts*. In every age, the farmer and the doctor are concerned with natural processes to the best of their ability—to steer them in a favourable direction, and to remedy the worst disasters that afflict our agriculture or health: in these natural arts, all we can hope to do is to take advantage of certain natural powers stronger than ourselves. But the men who run factories and produce artifacts have more direct control over the timing and end-products of their activities.[19]

Whether or not their distinction has fundamental merit, Toulmin and Goodfield have done us a service by even mentioning the arts and crafts in a work on the history of science. Helpful references are few. It might be more useful to point out that medicine and agriculture are not single crafts organized around a single product, but rather a whole nexus of different crafts that must be selected and organized by the cultivator. Among the information needs of the farmer and the physician were bodies of knowledge that bore some resemblance to the memory stores developed by the natural history societies. Physicians in particular could populate the learned societies while still seeking the goals of the physician's art. In both cases there was no one-to-one comparison of new and old practice, a comparison that would have enabled a price tag to be put on the change. The information requirements of these two arts resembled a scientific endeavor more than an artisan's craft. In them were to be found the first beginnings of that mirror image of science which Edwin Layton sees developing for technology by the end of the nineteenth century.[20]

As the period 1769-1863 went on, the societies showed, not a progressive development from local to global, but rather a series of networks that, once established, tended to remain and to become enveloped in other networks. The American Philosophical Society and the American Academy of Arts and Sciences were symbolically national, and were in touch with the global network. They fell short of providing a national network because of the lack of a single

American metropolis. It was London and Paris with their whole matrix of institutions that made the local societies established in these cities also national organizations.

In the early Republic, American institutions generally fell short of their counterparts in Europe because their local stations were spread too thinly and provided no single focus. The national university and the national learned society underwent the same pressures. As much as could be asked of the period from 1790 to 1830 was the establishment of local stations and the gradual emergence of a few urban centers that would form the bases for a plural-centered national network.

After 1830 two great reorganizations came together to change the environment of the learned society in America. A. D. Bache clearly envisaged both of these tendencies in his speech before the American Association for the Advancement of Science in 1851.[21] He saw that when "modern facilities of communication" were present, and when the cultivators of science became numerous and zealous, a new pattern was needed. His criticism of the early period of the Republic reflects the drive toward specialization in the sciences. "The absence of a minute subdivision in the pursuit of science, the prevalence of general lecturing on various branches, the cultivation of the literature of science rather than of science itself, has produced many of the evils under which American science has labored, and which are now passing away."[22] Bache recognized the AAAS as responding to these needs, and called in addition for an academy that would be both of limited membership and tied to the government. Thus the National Academy of Sciences was a product of the rearrangement of information networks already apparent by 1850.

In another way, however, the reorganization of networks followed specialization not to overall national societies but to a new kind of pluralism. As the specialized scientific traditions gained clarity of standards that could be enforced, the internal sanction of the disciplines formed the boundaries within which information flowed. For Asa Gray, being a botanist was a more fundamental commitment than being a professor or an officer of the American Academy of Arts and Sciences. Yet the 1850s were not quite ready to yield to the specialization that marked the period after the Civil War. As Richard Storr has shown us, the graduate schools, the home of professionalism, were also not quite ready to flower. The sense that information was not flowing efficiently in all these spheres makes the National Academy of Sciences appear as the culmination of a set of institutions that were looking for new ways to adjust the flow. After 1860 the flow of science became a many-channeled flood.

NOTES

1. A brief introduction to modern information theory, selected from a large literature, is Gordon Raisbeck, *Information Theory: An Introduction for Scientists and Engineers* (Cambridge, Mass.: MIT Press, 1963).
2. For a recent roundup of this literature, see George J. Klir, ed., *Trends in General*

Systems Theory (New York: Wiley-Interscience, 1972), especially the introduction and the chapters by Ludwig von Bertalanffy, Anatol Rapoport, and W. Ross Ashby.

3. Talcott Parsons, *The Social System* (New York: Free Press of Glencoe, 1951).

4. Roger Hahn, *The Anatomy of a Scientific Institution: The Paris Academy of Sciences, 1666-1803* (Berkeley and Los Angeles: University of California Press, 1971), pp. 316-17.

5. Ibid., p. 3.

6. Brooke Hindle, *The Pursuit of Science in Revolutionary America, 1735-1789* (Chapel Hill: University of North Carolina Press, 1956), pp. 18-21.

7. Harriet Zuckerman and Robert Merton, "Patterns of Evaluation in Science: Institutionalisation, Structure and Functions of the Referee System," *Minerva* 9 (January 1971): 66-100.

8. Max Meisel, *Bibliography of American Natural History*, 3 vols. (New York, 1924-1929; reprint ed., New York: Hafner, 1967), vols. 2 and 3.

9. Carl and Jessica Bridenbaugh, *Rebels and Gentlemen: Philadelphia in the Age of Franklin* (New York: Reynal and Hitchcock, 1942), pp. 86-95.

10. Raymond P. Stearns, *Science in the British Colonies of North America* (Urbana: University of Illinois Press, 1970), pp. 96-97.

11. S. G. Morton, quoted in Meisel, *American Natural History*, 2:131.

12. Meisel, *American Natural History*, 3:148-49.

13. While using no particular vocabulary or method beyond the usual prose of the historian, I am in a general way trying to follow Talcott Parsons's four-function paradigm. For a brief and relatively recent version of his social system, see Talcott Parsons, *Societies: Evolutionary and Comparative Perspectives* (Englewood Cliffs, N.J.: Prentice-Hall, 1966), pp. 5-29.

14. A. Hunter Dupree, "Nationalism and Science—Sir Joseph Banks and the Wars with France," in *A Festschrift for Frederick B. Artz*, ed. D. H. Pinkney and T. Ropp (Durham, N.C.: Duke University Press, 1964), pp. 37-51.

15. Meisel, *American Natural History,* 2:ix-xiii. Vol. 3:ix-xi lists the comparable foundations for 1845-1865 but lists not a single one with the combination of college and society title, which was the criterion for the cited list.

16. Michael Burrage, "Democracy and the Mystery of Crafts: Observations on Work Relationships in America and Britian," *Daedalus*, Fall 1972, pp. 141-62, states an interpretation the opposite of mine. One of the main historical sources he cites, Carl Bridenbaugh, *The Colonial Craftsman* (New York: New York University Press, 1950) can be interpreted to back my version instead of his, although Professor Bridenbaugh himself might not agree.

17. Lynn White, Jr., "The Legacy of the Middle Ages in the American Wild West," *Speculum* 40 (1965): 191-201, states this thesis succinctly and provocatively, with some unusual examples.

18. A. Hunter Dupree, "Comment: The Role of Technology in Society and the Need for Historical Perspective," *Technology and Culture* 10 (October 1969): 528-34.

19. Stephen Toulmin and June Goodfield, *The Architecture of Matter* (New York: Harper & Row, Harper Torchbook, 1966), p. 28.

20. Edwin Layton, "Mirror-Image Twins: The Communities of Science and Technology," in *Nineteenth-Century American Science: A Reappraisal*, ed. George Daniels (Evanston: Northwestern University Press, 1972), pp. 210-30.

21. A. D. Bache, "Address," *Proceedings of the American Association for the Advancement of Science* 6 (1851): xli-lx.

22. Ibid., p. xlv.

Definitions and Speculations: The Professionalization of Science in America in the Nineteenth Century

NATHAN REINGOLD

By now an appreciable body of literature exists on the development of the American scientific community from its roots in colonial times into the early twentieth century. Not surprisingly, professionalization of science is a major theme in many of these writings, perhaps more so than in the comparable writings on science in other nations. It is a story of how full-time professionals necessarily and inevitably supplanted amateurs, however talented and devoted. From the increasing complexity of scientific knowledge arose the necessity and the inevitability of higher standards of training and recruitment coupled with full-time employment. Accompanying professionalization was an insistance on the self-government of the scientific enterprise under standards arising from within the scientific community. The leading scientists of ante-bellum America advocated this view of professionalization in their public discourse, and even more openly in their private communications.

Others, then and now, saw the matter differently: as an elite establishing a monopoly of competence, and therefore of jobs, by squeezing out sincere, perhaps promising, participants in the scientific endeavor. Because American historians turning to the study of science in their country were acutely conscious of the importance of the problem of an elite in a democracy, there has developed a unique and extensive body of literature on the American scientific community. Few countries have anything comparable. For France, it is true, there are writings on the role of the artisans in the execution of Lavoisier and the dissolution of the Academy during the Revolution. A rather skimpy historical literature exists on the professionalization of science in Britain,[1] but the replacement of gentlemen amateurs by a gentlemanly professoriate is remote from the problem of an elite in a democracy.

Why is there such a difference between the American historical literature and the writings on European science? The first and perhaps inevitable observation is that historians of European science were overwhelmingly concerned with internal history, while Americans were avidly interested in placing science and scientists in a larger national context. Even the Marxists writing on these matters could not tip the scales. Influencing the Europeans, Marxists and non-Marxists alike,

---

[1] Notes to this chapter begin on page 64.

was a second factor: the existence of a hierarchial social structure was usually assumed, with the scientists occupying a specific high place in the structure. Shedding tears over amateurs was then quite inappropriate. In contrast, American scientists and other intellectuals could not assume a fixed exalted position in a social hierarchy. It is one of the glories of the American nation that the learned have achieved great power and prestige without the comforting certainty of a secure position in the national scheme of things.

When historians wrote about the crucial decades, about 1830-1870, in which the American scientific community came into being, we naturally stressed the scientists' expression of a professional ideology with elitist, antidemocratic overtones. Even better, we sought out those incidents in which emerging scientific pride clashed with the misguided sincerity of the amateur, often animated by a Baconian faith. There was the struggle over the Smithson bequest involving that preprofessional body, the National Institute. The Institute itself was involved in maneuvers for primacy with the Association of Geologists and Naturalists, the latter then transmuting itself from a professional to a quasi-professional body—the American Association for the Advancement of Science. This organization, in turn, became the focus of two related incidents in which the leading scientists enforced their standards: the rather pathetic case of John Warner and the confusion over the publication of the proceedings of the Cleveland meeting of 1853. To these we can add the lawsuit involving the criticism of Emmons's geological views, which smacks of a heresy trial, and the very tangled relations of Matthew Fontaine Maury with the Lazzaroni.[2]

The use of the first person plural in the comments above is deliberate; this is a tradition in which I grew up and to which I have contributed. Yet there is a need to stand back and rethink this matter of professionalization. What I propose writing is an essay of definitions and speculations. In order to produce a coherent analysis of the professionalization of American science, I have chosen not to end my discussion at 1860 but rather to consider developments up to the close of the nineteenth century.

Defining professionalization is a thankless task.[3] Many writers start out by warning that fashioning a definition is very difficult because there exists no ideal profession; one would be better advised to talk about the position of any particular profession on a kind of spectrum leading to an ideal. What definitions do emerge are based upon the three traditional professions of law, medicine, and the ministry, to which are added a number of newer professions, notably the sciences, engineering, and several other occupations requiring some particular body of knowledge. A number of near professional or quasi-professional fields are then brought in for comparison.

Further complicating any attempt at precise definition is the pervasiveness of certain common usages of the word that influence individual reactions. There is the connotation that a professional is someone in full-time employment, as in "the world's oldest profession." There is also the connotation of competence, that a professional is necessarily better than an amateur, as in sports. Finally, there is the notion of a professional being very decidedly white collar, as distinct from manual occupations, however skilled.[4] In America the tendency is to merge all these usages and call any occupation a profession if skill is required. While this usage of "profession" does not coincide with the definitions of academics, it reflects something very important in the American scene. In the United States there is a great tendency for all occupations to strive for professional status, to regard themselves so after the attainment of certain stigmata, and to obtain a measure of recognition from the general public, even from the state and local governments in the form of licensure laws—much to the dismay of the more established professions.

Conventionally, professions are defined as occupations that require special training in a particular body of knowledge or a particular technique or technology. Professionals usually form associations to advance the body of knowledge they serve and to enforce high professional standards. These are particularly important because the common definitions of a profession assume an applied component requiring a service ideal. Quite typically, writers on professionalization talk about clients—either individuals, as in the case of law or medicine, or possibly corporate organizations employing professionals. Increasingly, it is recognized that professions are not exclusively practiced individually but in bureaucratic structures, giving rise to concern over whether the profession can function autonomously. Can a professional act according to the best dictates of a body of knowledge and the ethical standards of the profession when subject to the control of a bureaucracy? Pessimists say no; optimists find hope in the professionalization of bureaucracy. As part of the high service ideal, professionals are presumably not primarily concerned with pecuniary gain but with the symbolic recognition that comes from high performance within their fields.[5]

The lack of clients or the lack of a specific application provides problems to some writers on the role of the sciences as professions. Several writers flatly deny that the sciences are professions in any meaningful sense of the word unless there is a very strong applied component. Lewis and Beer, in one of the few articles by historians on the professionalization of science in the twentieth century, categorize the nineteenth century as a nonprofessional era, when scientists were simply gentlemen interested in advancing knowledge. Professionalization comes to American science when scientists become significantly employed in industrial research laboratories and in government policy formation.[6]

In two articles notable for their parallelism, Shils and Ben-David,[7] who are most anxious to show that basic research is the apex of scientific professionalization, begin with general considerations on how a particular body of men go about finding knowledge but conclude by considering the role of the scientist in society, how and when scientists have the autonomy to practice their professions, and what their relationships with government and industry should be. Research achievements, in their view, arise from the high internal standards of the disciplines. What is assumed is that these standards are both applicable and carried over to dealings with outsiders where all the classic problems of client relations exist but on a national and international level. Specifically, Shils and Ben-David are concerned with showing that research—especially the most abstract and basic research—is *the* highest product generated by the professional scientist. Another aim is to illustrate that, despite the absence of any specific individual or corporate body as the client, the scientist maintains the very highest standards in the performance of his task. Talcott Parsons handles this dilemma by making the university and the academic disciplines rather than the traditional learned professions the paradigm of professionalism.[8]

In this interpretation, ethical problems requiring licensure and regulations are avoided in the sciences through informal monitoring by individual scientists or scientific organizations, seen primarily in the refereeing process of the scientific journals. To quote Shils:

The ethical problems which arise in the other professions where an expert deals with laymen have no equivalent at the heart of science, where many experts confront and scrutinize the results of each other's work as embodied in publications. Professional associations and science do not need committees on ethical practices because there are no defenseless laymen. The disinterestedness of scientists is a disciplined concern for truth which is imposed by the watchfulness of many others equally well disciplined.[9]

What Shils is talking about, of course, is not the scientists' relations with the public but only their relations among themselves. What is noticeable here is the high value placed upon science as a body of knowledge and upon scientific research as an endeavor made high-minded by an involved process of self-policing and moral inculcation carried out during years of training. Self-policing is seen as preferable to interference in science by the state in any way, shape, or form. As science becomes increasingly involved in applied areas and scientists become increasingly involved in public issues, the general populace, at least in America, is no longer inclined to accept the self-policing expertise of scientists without question. One writer even reports the development in the state of California of licensure for geology, an old established field of science.[10]

One of the effects of the last two decades of science policy disputes in the United States has been to convince many lay people that, whatever their intellectual expertise, scientists are simply another pressure group. It is widely understood that they have their own viewpoints and interests, and that these do not necessarily correspond to any other group interests in the population or indeed to that of the population at large. That this growing recognition occurred at the time when American historians were beginning to investigate seriously the antecedents of their scientific community is no accident. It helped shape our research. Perhaps this was unfortunate, because, in fact, the ante-bellum scientific community had relatively little power to exercise.

In this essay, I would like to offer two definitions of a profession—one sociological and the other operational. The first is taken from the writings of the Englishman Geoffrey Millerson: "It is a type of higher-grade, non-manual occupation, with both subjectively and objectively recognized occupational status, possessing a well-defined area of study or concern and providing a definite service, after advanced training and education."[11]

Note the complete absence of any rhetoric about ideals. I am willing to accept research and teaching as well as many other activities as being professional activities of scientists, even though this may not fully accord with Millerson's definition. What I propose to use is another rather simplified operating definition. Today, in the twentieth century, we define a scientist as anyone who meets at least two and usually three of the following characteristics: (1) he or she possesses a suitable educational degree (e.g., a Ph.D. or M.S.); (2) he or she is in an occupation or has an occupational title that requires the possession of that degree or at least of the knowledge supposedly entailed by obtaining that degree (e.g., professor of chemistry); (3) he or she belongs to a professional association of people who supposedly have the knowledge for which the degree was acquired and who, as a group, are presumably interested in advancing it (let us say, the American Chemical Society). While these three characteristics can be used quite successfully now and even as far back as 1900, they are not usable in the period prior to 1860. The situation prevailing then was so different that one simply cannot use the definitions of professionalism that appear in most of the current sociological literature. There were very few degrees one can compare to those awarded today. Professional societies were very rare. And only by stretching terms can many positions be categorized as "scientific" by today's standards.

It will be necessary for us to think of another kind of situation that will define the total scientific scene. I shall do this by trying to offer a model of what existed prior to the development of professionalism as we now know it and to suggest in very general terms what happened from then until approximately 1900 when professionalization was clearly rampant. In developing this model, a principal theme is the presence of a real confusion between certification and accomplishment. Most of the sociological writings stress the attainment of intellectual mastery over a body of knowledge, sometimes described as theoretical knowledge. If we look into the historical literature, it is usually assumed that the real professionals have a greater degree of mastery than their opponents, the amateurs. It is further assumed that this mastery is associated with genuine intellectual accomplishments, as it is, indeed, in many cases. Yet reflection on Darwin should cause some second thoughts; accomplishment in his case did not require formal certification. And to paraphrase Walter Cannon, if Darwin was not a professional in terms of accomplishment, who was?[12] What we assume today about degrees and the like was not true in the past.

What is most frequently involved in professionalization, past and present, is certification, that is, some way of determining that a particular person is indeed qualified to practice a given profession. Certification, a process beyond getting a degree or passing a qualifying examination, reoccurs at successive stages of a career. Certification is the nonintellectual aspect of professionalization, the seeking and attaining of place, income, and influence; it is part of the entire social context influencing scientists. The literature, both historical and current, implies that the object of professionalization is the accomplishment of high goals and ideals, whether it be the advancement of knowledge or staving off death and pain. In the case of science, Ben-David rightly points out that the leading scientists were originally charismatic figures, and the attainment, for example, of a professorship in Germany was to some degree an assessment of charismatic quality and thus a guarantee of accomplishment. Something like this happened in other countries of the Western world, even the United States. By now Ben-David notes, "A professorship in the United States becomes little more than the best-remunerated stage of a normal career" rather than necessarily a mark of exceptional gifts.[13]

There are great virtues in this position; most people are not leaders or geniuses. Most scientists do not publish, because most do not do research.[14] Of those who do publish, most publish very little.[15] And authorship may occur within a brief span of professional life. Judging by the recent literature, of those articles published, most are either not cited at all or are cited with extraordinary infrequency.[16] (The mere fact of noncitation, however, does not necessarily mean that an article was not seen and used.) To paraphrase the sociologist E. C. Hughes, training for and the doing of research is often for the purpose of getting a post not requiring research.[17] In sum, research results of a few cast a noble glow over the community.

If most never publish or publish little, the relationship of the leading scientists to the bulk of their fellow professionals becomes a very interesting problem. In the pre-1860 period these assertions about nonpublication and noncitation were more or less true, insofar as we can judge by rather useful but imperfect statistics.[18] What was different was the occupational structure, and indeed the rationale of the whole system. We may define our past scientific community as consisting of three groups:

1. *Researchers* are individuals characterized by a single-minded devotion to research, resulting in an expertise yielding an appreciable accomplishment by past standards certainly and in retrospect in some instances. Most, but not all, are in scientific occupations.

2. *Practitioners* are individuals wholly or largely employed in scientific or science-related occupations. Those who publish are less prolific and less significant in terms of accomplishment than researchers.

3. *Cultivators* are best described at this point rather than defined. In what follows, professionalization is viewed from their standpoint, not from the perspective of the leading scientists, the researchers.

The Cultivators

Unfortunately, the pejorative connotations associated with the word amateur prevent my using it. I say "unfortunately" because I would like to preserve the etymological implication of the word, that is, "lover of," because it says something important. "Cultivator" was chosen deliberately because of the relation of the word to the terms "cultural" and "cultivation." More specifically, it was actually used by Sir David Brewster to describe the mass of people in attendance at early meetings of the British Association for the Advancement of Science.[19] This crowd was not of the "professional" eminence of scientists like Brewster and the other principal leaders of the Association. Using "amateur" is also undesirable, because over the years it has become associated with another term to form the expression "gentlemen amateur." With this goes another connotation—that in the past there was an appreciable body of men in the United States and elsewhere who were not professional scientists but who had a sincere interest in and knowledge of science, and who somehow or other participated meaningfully in the scientific endeavor. What has occurred are some very loose extrapolations from very special cases, like Thomas Jefferson—a very distinguished cultivator indeed.

People who extrapolate from the exceptional case do so because of confusion of terms more than anything else. What they are reacting to is a specific culture (if I may use that murky term) in the United States that one can describe as the culture of polite learning. This could be acquired by attendance at one of the colleges or by self-study. Polite learning included some knowledge of mathematics and various scientific subjects. Possessing polite learning in no way implied being a significant amateur or cultivator of science any more than entering today's American educational system—high school or college—and acquiring a certain standard core of information involving scientific subjects makes one a scientist. Early in the last century there existed in the United States, as well as in the countries of western Europe, what we can call "vernacular" cultures. Most of the people did not possess polite learning. Beyond the illiterates there were, of course, a substantial body of people who had acquired the basics of reading, writing, and ciphering—part of the vernacular culture.

The cultivator was a particular kind of person who possessed learned culture. For various reasons the cultivator had a more specific knowledge in the sciences. Unlike others in the learned culture, the cultivator actually applied his knowledge in some kind of activity. A man who was simply part of the learned culture might very well become a nominal member of one of the local societies with an interest in science. By the Civil War, if not earlier, a certain amount of social prestige was attached to membership in learned societies. When, prior to the Civil War, the American Association for the Advancement of Science came to his city to hold its meetings, such a man might give money to the support of the meetings, serve on the local arrangements committee, and in many other ways throughout his life show himself appreciative of science. In doing this he was simply reflecting, perhaps, the pervasive belief in progress, a progress that arose from science. Science was a good thing, and he was well aware of that, but he was not using science in any way.

A cultivator, on the other hand, would not only join one of the local societies, but, indeed, come to meetings with some degree of regularity. He would help the more advanced devotees of particular disciplines. He might very well participate actively in the meetings. A cultivator might take an active role in the management of the society. He might be moved by the infectious enthusiasms of his friends and his own eagerness to deliver a paper—maybe two. Perhaps stimulated by praise or by his own feelings of satisfaction, this might result in publication by the local society. Perhaps a text might even be sent on to Benjamin Silliman, Sr., in New Haven if the author's friends, whose opinions he respected, so urged him.

In discussing this learned culture, I am carefully avoiding the trap of assuming that there was once one culture. I think that there were always at least two—the learned culture and the vernacular culture. In the learned culture there were ways in which the scientific and the nonscientific interests tended to blend and perhaps even interact at times, just as today. The use of terminology shows how cultivators and noncultivators sometimes viewed the relationship. Early in the nineteenth century, for example, Benjamin Vaughan referred to people in the learned culture, scientists and others, as literary gentlemen,[20] and as late as the very brief heyday of the National Institute, Joel Poinsett referred to literature as the "vehicle of science."[21] In the early years of the Albany Institute, however, the differentiation of science and literature was quite clear.[22] When John C. Spencer asked Francis Wayland to contribute to the 1844 National Institute meeting, he described the Institute as engaged in "the effort . . . to establish a Confederacy of Science and Literature for our whole country,[23] implying an awareness of a disjunction to be bridged. Periodicals and societies sometimes had the words "Literary and Philosophical" in their titles early in the century. Interestingly, as late as 1900 the Census Bureau had an occupational category for "Literary and Scientific Persons,"[24] so even at that date a relationship was presumed. The presence, for example, of an extensive nonmathematical review by Nathaniel Bowditch of technical astronomical works in the *North American Review* in 1825[25] might indicate a fusion of science and literature within a single learned culture before the rise of professionalism, but such instances are misleading.

By examining a number of journals in Joseph Henry's library and other titles found by association, the position of science in the learned culture is somewhat clarified. These journals are mostly from the Mid-Atlantic states before 1840, and, judging from the sample, science had an honored but minor position in the learned culture. At most, 30 percent of a volume might be scientific, as in volume 4 of the *New York Review* (1839); more common are volumes containing 5 percent or 10 percent scientific matter. A Philadelphia periodical, the *American Quarterly Review,* ranges from 10 percent to 20 percent in the years 1827 through 1830, but the percentage drops to zero or a nominal 2.5 percent when Carey and Hart cease being the publishers. The *Belles-Lettres Repository and Monthly Magazine* of New York has sections on mathematical problems and meteorological reports in 1821 but little else of a scientific nature.[26]

This unscientific sample says much about the place of science, even beyond the sparseness of content. To use modern terms, the articles were often reviews or secondary accounts, rather than original science. Natural history, surveys and explorations, and reviews of textbooks are common here. By this period the article rather than the monograph was the common vehicle for dissemination of new research, usually in a scientific periodical. A smattering of secondhand reports or literary reviews did not really convey much of scientific developments to the so-called gentlemen amateurs. If any trend is discernible, it was a diminution of scientific content in these periodicals. A cultivator would have to turn to the scientific literature to maintain any serious interests in research.

Cultivators might go on to become practitioners of science—that is, work at science full time—and, indeed, become fairly eminent research scientists. There are a few cases, one of which I will discuss later. The cultivators were quite often concerned with their own self-education, rather than the increase or dissemination of new knowledge.[27] Not being interested in publishing, the cultivators tended to regard what they did as a source of pleasure—a form of relaxation, a hobby.[28] It was even a sport.

The groups they formed were neither organizations devoted to specialized subjects nor professional associations that were implicitly and explicitly certifying bodies. What was often encountered were social groupings, even though a few members were scientifically proficient. Geoffrey Millerson refers to these groups in Britain as study associations, noting that in the course of time some evolved into truly professional subject groups.[29] Even today a few of the British organizations still retain a mixture of competent specialists and amateur devotees. Study associations, according to Millerson, were the vehicle by which men in the middle class raised their social status. I see few signs of that in America, although in time many of the old general learned societies became prestige groups in their localities. Even the more specialized local societies that were interested in natural history tended in time to have a degree of social prestige attached to them.

I do not use the term "social grouping" in any pejorative sense. I think the societies enabled certain people to do research and stimulated others to aid science. Indeed, a recent British article argues in a very ingenious and forceful manner that the Royal Society's origins are not to be found in any Baconian drive for utility, nor in any particular attribute of a Puritan, Presbyterian, or Anglican bloc, but in the desire of a congenial group of men with similar tastes to meet and to share these interests.[30]

What could a cultivator do? What did cultivators do? W. J. Reader in his book on the rise of professions in England cites a work early in the last century that advised gentlemen going to the country to make and use scientific instruments.[31] This advice was taken, as it were, by a few Americans, who also made and used instruments of various kinds. We have no idea how many cultivators had telescopes to watch the heavens, but we know some actually published their observations. There were also individuals who delighted in solving mathematical problems.[32] Abiel Holmes, the father of the poet-physician Oliver Wendell

Holmes, kept meteorological journals, as did countless other individuals in Britain, the United States, and on the Continent. When Joseph Henry set up his telegraph-linked meteorological service, these men manned the various stations in the network and later in the century also provided readings of barometers and thermometers to the Signal Corps's weather service and its successor, the Weather Bureau of the Department of Agriculture.

Then there were the ladies and gentlemen who filled the lecture halls to hear talks on chemistry by Benjamin Silliman, Sr., and countless itinerant lecturers like E. L. Youmans. One wonders what they actually received from all those varied talents, but some certainly were moved to buy chemical equipment and to delight in getting reactions, spectacular and otherwise. People interested in chemistry sometimes applied this knowledge to mineralogical analysis. Collecting minerals was a widespread scientific activity, and the identification of minerals was of interest both to serious scientists and to casual cultivators of the field. As one leafs through manuscript collections in natural history, there is a seemingly endless procession of collectors of flora and fauna, as well as of geological specimens. Judging by the subject distribution of the articles published by Americans and listed in the *Royal Society Catalogue,* it is safe to say that almost every branch of science practiced in the first six decades of the last century encompassed matters of concern to cultivators of science.

To be more specific, let us consider some events in the life of Joseph Henry. On November 25, 1828, in a meeting of the Albany Institute at which Henry spoke, Major General Erastus Root delivered a talk on two different topics— problems of the design and use of thermometers and an interpretation of the solar spots of 1816.[33] General Root (1773-1846)[34] had gained his military title by virtue of his high rank in the state militia. In the year he spoke, as well as in 1827 and 1830, he was the Speaker of the New York Assembly. Presumably he attended the meeting of the Institute while the legislature was in session in his capacity as a corresponding member. Root never published these papers, nor any other paper I can find. In 1795 he did produce an introduction to arithmetic for common schools that went through additional editions early in the nineteenth century.

In 1837 Henry had another encounter with a politician who had scientific interests or pretensions. While visiting Britain, he was perturbed to discover that the American Minister, Andrew Stevenson (1784-1857), was planning to make a few remarks on the subject of light to the physical section of the British Association. As he later wrote, "I feared he would have made himself ridiculous . . . at this he appeared somewhat offended." Stevenson however made amends, as Henry put it, by a very nice address at one of the dinners.[35]

Andrew Stevenson was a former Governor of Virginia. He served as rector of the university in that state upon his return from Britain, but, as far as I have been able to tell from the usual sources and a fairly good biography,[36] he did not have any noticeable interest in science. His biographer mentions that while at William and Mary at the end of the eighteenth century he received a good standard education, which included mathematics and natural philosophy. Root may very well be a cultivator, but Stevenson hardly seems to have made the grade. One might characterize him as one of the literary gentlemen possessing polite learning who did not realize that professionalism was emerging. He might very well have been one of the men Henry and Bache complained of when they talked about ignorant politicians interfering in scientific matters.

Yet Henry's position on this is not at all unequivocal. If we look carefully at other instances in his life, we find him hobnobbing with rank cultivators. For example, as is well known, Henry had no desire to yield certain points to the National Institute, and even toward the close of his life he was making acid comments about it.[37] Nevertheless, in 1849, 1850, and 1851 he was successively elected as one of the three vice-presidents of the organization, declining reelection the following year. In 1855, when the Institute was nearing extinction, he was elected vice-president again but declined reelection.[38] I do not interpret this as a subtle move on the part of Henry to keep an eye on the National Institute to prevent it from gaining an advantage in any matter of interest to him as secretary of the Smithsonian Institution and as a strong proponent of the development of a proper scientific community in the United States. I think—and here I speculate—that he regarded the National Institute as one of these social societies that could and did serve a real purpose in providing education and stimulation in science. He objected, however, to the Institute pretending to be a proper scientific body, responsible for genuine research tasks. In a later address Henry very clearly indicated the distinction.[39] His position was neither ambivalent nor anachronistic.

In the post-Civil War years Henry actually wrote a clear and revealing statement of advice to people desiring to form local societies with scientific interests.[40] To me this indicates that he did not conceive of a situation in which cultivators would be wholly supplanted. He recognized that the Smithsonian Institution used these individuals not only in the weather service but also as aids in acquiring specimens and in the exchange of publications and information. In the 1850s—the exact date is not too clear to me as yet—Henry joined with other researchers, practitioners, and cultivators in the city of Washington to form a club that met weekly even during much of the Civil War and persisted for years after that conflict. Its members were not young men starting out on their careers but included some very eminent individuals. In the post-Civil War years, a member who participated with delight, according to his recollections, was the Secretary of the Treasury, Hugh McCulloch; his interests seemed largely social, perhaps partly educational.[41]

Consider, also, Charles Nicoll Bancker (1778 [?]-1869). Originally a New Yorker, Bancker moved to Philadelphia and made a considerable amount of money first in importing and then later in insurance and mortgage underwriting. He became a member of the American Philosophical Society, even serving on a few committees to evaluate submitted publications. His eulogist in 1869 referred to him as "a man of general scientific tastes and attainments" who made his instruments available to public lecturers on chemistry and natural philosophy. [42] From the surviving Bancker correspondence in the library of the American Philosophical Society we know that Henry at Princeton did borrow instruments from Bancker. His heir put these up for sale in 1871; there were 787 catalogued items, although the number of individual pieces must have been much larger. It is an extraordinary collection, and a letter of Henry's, partially quoted in the catalogue, states that with the addition of a few of the most recent pieces it would be a complete set of apparatus for the physical sciences.[43] Indeed it would be. I have no idea why a Charles Nicoll Bancker acquired such an enormous body of philosophical apparatus. The catalogue of his private library published two years previously contains a wide range of books from all fields, but only a modest number of scientific works.[44] For some reason Charles Nicoll Bancker simply collected all of these instruments. As in the case of Thomas Jefferson, one should not infer from this evidence that nineteenth-century insurance executives had significant interests in the sciences.

Another man who was part of the wide circle of Henry's acquaintances was Joseph G. Cogswell (1786-1871).[45] A Harvard graduate, Cogswell is perhaps best known as the first head of the Astor Library. His adult career seems devoted to nonscientific pursuits. At Harvard he was close to the natural philosopher John Farrar and apparently had considerable interests in mineralogy and botany. In 1819 he did the conventional grand tour of Europe, visiting not only Goethe but Gauss, and in many other ways displayed interest in the sciences. As he puts it, he was "foolish enough" to pick up an unearned Ph.D. at Göttingen. His memorialist plays down Cogswell's later scientific interests, but Cogswell was not only Librarian of Harvard but served as Professor of Mineralogy and Geology at the College (1821-1823).

Shortly after his return from Europe, Cogswell joined George Bancroft and taught in an experimental school at Round Hill, where, incidentally, one of the instructors was Benjamin Peirce. The 1826 prospectus for Round Hill stated: "A very considerable proportion of time is assigned to the Mathematics. We consider the study of them in connection with the languages as essential to the best discipline of the mind. The natural sciences are pursued rather as a relaxation, and to quicken the powers of observation. . . ."[46]

One student at Round Hill was a precocious but difficult youth from a wealthy New York banking family, Sam Ward. At first Sam Ward did not seem particularly promising in mathematics. But with a little study he became extraordinarily proficient—so much so that, instead of joining the family banking firm, he went to study with Nathaniel Bowditch, which meant, of course, working with Benjamin Peirce, who was then helping Bowditch with his translation of Laplace.[47]

In 1832 Ward became a member of the Examining Board at West Point, and so impressed the faculty that two friends of Joseph Henry, Charles E. Davies and Captain Edward Ross, acting on the authority of Superintendant Thayer, offered him an assistant professorship in mathematics. By this time Ward had already published a little periodical containing mathematical problems that he proceeded to solve, an American edition of an algebra text, and two review articles in the *American Quarterly Review*, one on probability and the other on Locke. Faced with a concrete offer of a teaching job, the eminent status of a practitioner of mathematics, and the certainty of parental disapproval, Sam Ward convinced his father that he needed time to think, perhaps to get further training, and would therefore require a trip to Paris, which he described at the time he arrived as "the City of Sin and Science." While in that city he proceeded to buy the library of Legendre. On his return, Sam Ward abandoned any idea of teaching or full-time practice of mathematics and joined the family firm.[48]

This was the start of a very spectacular career as a bon vivant and lobbyist. Sam Ward is best known in American history as the "King of the Lobby," and for the possible role that he may have played in the "Mystery of the Public Man." And yet, one wonders about his mathematics. Ward's biographer asserts that he only used the knowledge of probability to further his favorite interest, determining what card would come up next. However I note that his papers in the New York Public Library contain collected autographs of eminent scientists. Would a careful examination indicate that he maintained his youthful concern for mathematics so we can consider him a cultivator and not merely the sinner brother of Julia Ward Howe? When Sylvester resided in New York City after leaving the University of Virginia during his first stay in America, Sam Ward was a good friend.[49]

Quite a different case is presented by Lewis Morris Rutherfurd.[50] He was clearly an amateur in the sense of pursuing an activity for the love of it and not being paid in any way for his work. Rutherfurd was a Williams graduate who came from a fairly well-known American family and married a relative of the Stuyvesants. Interestingly, he followed the suggestion of the English author cited previously about building devices in his country estate—the country estate being the traditional Stuyvesant acres in what is now the Lower East Side of Manhattan. There he became a pioneer of spectroscopy and astrophysics. In the period up to 1860 Rutherfurd published very little, and even if we add to it the publications occurring from 1860 until his death, the total is not very large. Nevertheless, his life is clearly one of single-minded devotion to research and the achievement of considerable expertise and accomplishment, so I am inclined to classify Rutherfurd as a researcher. Strictly speaking, he does not belong in a section on cultivators.

Rutherfurd had a number of interesting attributes. His friend and memorialist, Benjamin Apthorp Gould, reports that Rutherfurd was on the *America* when it won the cup now bearing its name.[51] I suspect that the spirit of sports and competition animated Rutherfurd but not simply in the sense of winning. In yachting, for example, attention must be paid to all sorts of details of the construction, design, and outfitting of the boat, as well as the details of the actual handling of the yacht. It is this attention to technical matters, to details, that characterized much of the work of Rutherfurd on diffraction gratings and on the application of photography to astronomy.

Rutherfurd had another characteristic quite often found among cultivators, the reluctance to publish. It was not important for him to publish. He did not need to publish in order to earn a living, to get a job, or advance his position in some bureaucracy. Being independently wealthy, he sought only the satisfaction of good workmanship and of knowing his own achievements. Again a point is the analogy with yachting on the scale of the America's Cup races. There are few of these events. One performs rarely and has to win rarely. If one does well, win or lose, it is very creditable.

Rutherfurds were, however, all too rare to provide the foundation for a scientific community in the mid-nineteenth century. Men of a different stripe—the practitioners—would dominate the scientific scene. But even in 1888 G. Brown Goode could report the existence of about three thousand cultivators.[52] And as late as 1940 the American Philosophical Society issued a publication for the benefit of "laymen scientists."[53] Long before that time, however, the cultivator had nearly vanished from both the research scene and the institutional fabric of science.

The Practitioners

In choosing the term "practitioner" I deliberately want to establish a parallel with the established professions of law, medicine, and the clergy. Practitioners have employment in which they, some way or other, use their scientific training, or at least achieve their positions and salaries by virtue of presumed scientific competence. There is no trouble in differentiating practitioners from cultivators. The latter are simply not usually remunerated for whatever scientific work they do. Some of the practitioners do indeed publish, while others do not, giving rise to an important problem in differentiating researchers from practitioners. The distinction on one level between a practitioner and researcher is that the latter performs more research and of a higher quality than the researching practitioners.

The Elliott statistics enable us to confirm what some people understood from less precise sources of information.[54] There were in the United States in the period up to 1860 a fair number of men who earned their living in the practice of science, and there were two leading sources of employment, the most obvious being the government, primarily the federal government and to a lesser extent the states; the other being the colleges and universities. Indeed, the central point of Daniels's book on Jacksonian science, the Beaver dissertation,[55] the Elliott dissertation, and numerous other works is to stress the role of the professoriate in the development of science. A large percentage of American scientists went to college or obtained some degree or training beyond the secondary school level, and a surprising percentage of these ended up teaching. In 1835 Henry made a distribution list for a reprint of an article of which he was particularly proud;[56] aside from a few old friends from Albany and three Princeton trustees, the list consists largely of men from the American professoriate: Farrar at Harvard, Renwick at Columbia, the elder Silliman at Yale, and Bache at Pennsylvania.

The problem with the professoriate, as well as the government practitioners, from the standpoint of the development of research as a professional activity lies in determining how much research was done within the institutional framework. It is not enough to cite, as Daniels did,[57] that there were twenty-one scientific jobs in 1802, by which he clearly means academic posts; most of these men spent the greatest part of their time teaching rather than conducting research. Somehow or other we must convert figures on practitioners from counts of articles to something like a full-time equivalent measurement. Even today, less than 40 percent of holders of Ph.D.s are engaged in research and development, and no more than 30 percent of all scientists employed in educational institutions are involved in such activities.[58]

The great trend in science in America from 1820 to 1920 is not the growth in accomplishment, considerable as that was, but the near extinction of cultivators and the tremendous expansion of the number of practitioners. By 1900, perhaps, the real problem that animated many of the scientists agitating for increased research output was how to differentiate themselves from practitioners and technicians, as well as from physicians and engineers. The young Linus Pauling and Warren Weaver both took engineering degrees as undergraduates because they were initially unaware of science as a career.[59] Scientists were often animated, I suspect, as much by the desire to avoid a lower place on the occupational totem pole as by any intellectual stimuli.

During the nineteenth century the United States generated a large number of posts for practitioners ranging from the marginal to the first rate. In France someone like Gay-Lussac could occupy multiple posts, a practice known as the *cumul*. This practice was quite common, and young French scientists in the pre-1860 period and afterward often found themselves waiting in the hope that an opening would come. In Britain there were very few academic or other posts for practitioners. One particular possibility that comes to mind was the Military Academy at Woolwich, which employed Sylvester and others. One had to be a gentlemen amateur to practice science in Great Britain; it was often an enforced necessity. Even some of the chairs at the universities paid little to their holders.

In Germany the situation was far more complicated, because there were many more university posts than in either Britain or France, and good ones. In the United States there were many chairs at the college-university level, but they were not good posts in comparison to professorships in the leading German universities of the mid-nineteenth century. I think the German situation was probably far better than we realize because there were quite a number of other institutions employing scientists. We know something of Freiburg, the mining academy, but all too little about agricultural research stations, medical research institutes, and various kinds of other organizations. The German situation, at least in the first three-quarters of the nineteenth century, must have been far better than that in any other major country in the West.

The posts in the United States, however, made it possible for people of modest income to find employment and a lifetime occupation as scientists. They encouraged the development of a large body of trained, competent, middling level scientists. I say this not in any pejorative sense; many of these scientists were far above the average and had quite creditable records. I use the term in contrast to words like "genius" and "charismatic." In a country like France, Germany, or Britain, it was assumed (and may still be) that major posts were awarded after a very intensive sifting out, and that the award of the post was a recognition of eminence, an acknowledgment that a man had become, as Ben-David put it, a charismatic leader of science. The American assumption is quite different, namely, that genius is somehow taken care of but that society must concern itself with providing for myriad needs by widening the number of professional posts. Distinctions between professions are minimized, and gradations of rank within professions are blurred. Not that these differences are not known and felt, but public policy and the ways of the society often combine to overlook them.

This trend goes back quite far in American history. In 1827 the Board of Regents of the University of the State of New York, under the prodding of the state legislature, quietly adopted a policy that placed scientific and technical occupations on the same level with the older learned professions insofar as state support was concerned.[60] I have characterized this trend as "occupational egalitarianism," meaning that it was assumed that all vocations were to be treated equally in the eyes of the government, provided they were based on a suitable level of education and training. In the United States occupations would be encouraged by public policy and by social pressures to become professions, to acquire some kind of a learned component, and to be considered the equal of even some of the older prestige professions. This did not mean that in actual practice each profession received equal shares of power and money. On the contrary, American society has been, from its very beginning, one in which there were great differences in these shares and in the deference accorded to groups.[61]

Lest anyone still harbor a confusion with law, medicine, and clergy, let me state that, in the course of a considerable amount of reading of manuscripts and printed material in this period, I have no recollection whatsoever of seeing any scientist cite the three established learned professions as models to be followed— or to be avoided, for that matter—in the development of science on a specialized professional level.[62] This is by no means surprising. The medical profession in the United States in the period immediately preceding the Civil War was not in the highest repute. Some very eminent scientists did have medical degrees, such as Asa Gray and F. V. Hayden. One can speculate that men interested in science acquired medical degrees because that was a good way to earn a living prior to the full development of scientific occupations. Perhaps an even stronger reason was the fact that acquiring the M.D. was one of the better ways of receiving scientific training in the period before the development of science teaching in the liberal arts colleges, in the specialized scientific engineering schools, and in graduate schools. After about 1840 the number of men who became scientists by way of the medical school dropped markedly.[63] William Harkness, a post-

Civil War astronomer of repute at the Naval Observatory, had a medical degree, but he is an exceptional case.

Most medical men, now and in the past century, are conscious of belonging to a very distinct tradition. They might refer to themselves or be referred to as scientists, but very few of them did any research, medical or otherwise. In the latter decades of the last century a relatively small number of medical men with scientific tastes would turn their talents and interests to clinical subjects and to related areas of basic science. Some of these men can certainly be called scientists and counted in whatever enumeration one makes of the scientific community, but the medical community in the United States has always been a quite distinct body of men with a strong sense of belonging to a specific tradition. Relatively few were part of the emerging scientific community in the mid-nineteenth century.[64]

As to law, my overall impression is that scientists tend to find the law quite alien to their way of thinking. It was thought "unscientific" to take one side or the other for money without considering on which side truth may lie. Law simply did not appeal to many people in the scientific community as a model for their disciplines.[65]

The clergy were certainly held in fairly high repute by many scientists during the early decades of the nineteenth century. Henry was for many years a trustee of the Princeton Theological Seminary, and had clerical friends. Nevertheless, I find in the record no particular awareness by scientists that the clergy constituted a learned group whose practices should be emulated or shunned. There was a growing feeling on the part of some clergy and some scientists that their interests were antithetical, but this feeling did not become serious until much after Darwin. By that time the scientists were on their way to establishing a professional existence, and the clergy was involved in a complicated series of adjustments to a post-Darwin industrialized America.[66]

During the ante-bellum period, engineering did not constitute an organized profession. It was emerging, just as the sciences were. If anything, it was the scientists to whom the engineers pointed, rather than the other way around. The more advanced and well trained were inclined to describe themselves as representing a scientific and learned tradition. Even the more practical men in the group would stress the role of knowledge, although their definition of science in an empirical sense was not at all in accordance with the tastes of a Bache or a Henry. The engineers were not a group scientists would emulate in setting up their own organizations.

What the scientists did in establishing their institutions was to rely upon a knowledge and an understanding, almost mythological, of the history of science, of the development of particular institutions, and of the role of various great men. They would point to Europe, citing the Royal Society, Sir Isaac Newton, Lavoisier, Laplace, the Paris Academy, and the École Polytechnique. Later in the century the German university was singled out.

Being based on a mythology, all the published and unpublished discussions on professionalization—all the literature, the essays, the letters exchanged—assume that the entire goal in developing science in the United States was to yield American research on a scale comparable to that of the leading European countries. There was a real desire to make a contribution commensurate with what many felt was America's greatness; to play a larger role in Western civilization; and, on the part of some, to repay America's debt to the culture of the Old World. The proponents of professionalization quite sincerely confused accomplishment with certification. If scientific posts went to proper scientists, accomplishment would follow. But most of the people involved and most of the posts were not of the kind that would necessarily provide much opportunity or incentive for notable research. There would be a few scientists of considerable talent, a few we can even describe as great. Usually, most would be practitioners, just like today. Advanced degrees and professional societies made no difference whatsoever. Most of the practitioners were necessarily concerned with teaching, administration, applied developments, and other essential, grubby tasks.

Looked at from the standpoint of the practitioners—aided and abetted by the researchers, who were their friends and teachers—the plethora of posts was a consequence, not of specialization and the expansion of knowledge, but of increased social participation. The growth of specialized and graduate schools was as much a means of certification as a means of increasing research accomplishment. Diminishing the general liberal arts classical course was exchanging the old learned culture for a practitioners' culture justified by a research ideology. The number of publications increased by 1920 because of pressures from both the ideology and careerism.

The Researchers

Despite differences with the cultivators and the practitioners, the researchers—the leaders of the emerging scientific community—maintained their hegemony. They managed to overcome the strains of the differing goals of accomplishment and certification, as well as the problems occupational egalitarianism presents to an emerging status-conscious group. Most important, although failing in their specific aims, the researchers were largely successful in their grand goal of making the United States a great scientific power. Complaints were also blunted by the real openness of the community. Despite the few incidents, what strikes me in the pre-1860 period is the surprising ease of entry. The researchers were most conscious of being a very small group, of being surrounded by other groups, who were perceived as indifferent and perhaps hostile. They were anxious to expand research. If anyone seemed genuinely interested and had some ability, they were usually eager to promote entry into their community. The letters of Henry, Bache, Dana, Gray, and Hall, as well as others, show how often young men came to these scientists for aid in entering the field. In many cases the researchers did their best with all too little resources.

In these instances the leading scientists were trying to further the achievement of more significant scientific output.

Further blunting possible hostilities was the fact that the elite researchers were not at all unified on every issue. Henry had reservations about aspects of the Lazzaroni activities; others were indifferent or hostile to the group around Bache. Although an elite intellectually produces a disproportionate share of research in both qualitative and quantitative terms,[67] one can doubt their influence in every sphere and not assume endless occasions for clashes of interests. Elites are, after all, largely self-anointed. Accounts of their power usually stem from themselves and from bitter opponents, hardly objective sources. An elite is best described as a group forever surprised by the course of events; we need add, perhaps unkindly, that as the course shifts some rush frantically to the new front line.

The continued dominance of the researchers is simply explained. All three groups—cultivators, practitioners, and researchers—had a high degree of agreement on essentials. This agreement was rooted in both the sciences performed and in the ideas of a scientific life style. The content of science was received from scientific fathers, the leading scientists of the previous generation who had brought the state of the art to the point perceived by all three groups. But the life styles of the scientists came from their scientific grandfathers. I do not mean this in a literal sense, but there was at least a generation jump in perceptions of scientific roles. Not the fathers but rather the semi-mythological accounts of the great tradition in science dictated how they should act. Henry's peers took their science from, perhaps, Sir Humphrey Davy, but views of the ideal life of science came from, let us say, Sir Isaac Newton. The people in the learned culture who were not cultivators might know the grandfathers, but had only an imperfect knowledge of the fathers; this is really what differentiated them from cultivators. A common core of beliefs from fathers and grandfathers explains why the great disparity between certification and accomplishment did not give rise to any major conflicts. The principal researchers were viewed, not only as being on the leading edge of knowledge, but also as illustrating the ideal behavior for creative scientists.

This relationship of the major scientists to practitioners and to cultivators is greatly obscured by some of the catch words that are used to describe the scientific situation in the past and the present. Some assume the existence of so-called Baconian science in the United States in the past, a kind of routine data-gathering operation. It is also assumed that there was, in the past, something called "little science," as opposed to something called "big science," which we have today. Big science is that of teams—of faceless investigators operating under plans and producing copious quantities of articles. Yet I find it hard to believe in this picture of big science that is so readily drawn by many. Twentieth-century science is not dominated by faceless robot investigators operating under more or less rigid plans; rather, it is marked by animating intellectual or administrative leaders, just as there were in the nineteenth century. There is a real distinction between bigness and changes in kind.

Scientific investigations in the past were routinized and even done by teams. Consider the *Manual of Scientific Inquiry*[68] issued by the British Admiralty for the benefit of scientific travelers overseas—and not the only example of literature of that kind. During the Civil War, Charles Henry Davis, who was one of the Lazzaroni, planned a similar document for Americans. The assumption behind issuing some kind of a manual is that one could describe basic scientific operations in various fields in simple terms and that anyone with reasonable intelligence and education could then perform these operations. What we have here is neither Baconian science nor big science nor little science, but simply the problem of whether a scientific operation can be described and routinized so that it need not be done by people of exceptional ability and training or under unusual circumstances. The idea of having large numbers of cultivators conduct surveys under carefully prepared instructions was one of the early notions of the British Association for the Advancement of Science.[69]

Manualizing was not confined to natural history. Larger portions of meteorology and astronomy were so routinized that men, very skilled it is true, could grind out data in a relatively routine, undeviating manner. In other words, they could be practitioners of science. This leads to one of the real definitions of a practitioner that transcends the occupational category. A mere practitioner is a man who receives from his scientific fathers or his scientific peers a body of scientific method and doctrine, which he repeats more or less in an undeviating manner as part of his work. In this sense most of the cultivators were also practitioners, that is, they took a certain kind of scientific activity and performed it, usually in an undeviating manner. Some of the cultivators and some of the practitioners deviated from the set procedures with enough success to become creative researchers.

Two further explanatory points need to be made. First of all, I am not speaking about normal science in the Kuhnian sense, although some normal science does fall into this category. If a particular kind of problem solving can be done by a standard routine method, even if it requires a person of considerable ability, I would describe this person as a practitioner. Kuhn, of course, thinks of normal science problem solving as being a very high-skilled scientific activity that, when done properly, is the most certain kind of knowledge obtainable from the sciences. What I am concerned about here is whether or not scientific operations have been so described in the literature and are so followed in practice that they could be applied in a straightforward manner, given a reasonable amount of intelligence and training. This is simply a stage in the natural history of scientific concepts. Yesterday's brilliant novelties become today's routine practices; tomorrow they become operations turned over to machines.

The second point is that quite a number of very eminent scientists in various stages of their career carry out routine tasks, either as training or as incidental to their investigations. That is, they are practitioners for at least that moment in their careers. Of course, this does not affect their overall life style as research scientists. Nor does this deny that in the course of routine investigations a perceptive mind can notice a deviation and perceive its meaning. Think of Roentgen's work with photographic plates that other scientists threw away or returned to the dealer. Nor does this imply that a perceptive mind cannot see the routine in a novel manner. Practitioners exist because some scientific activities were susceptible to routinization. Successful routinization is the basis for occupations.

But occupational egalitarianism posed a great problem for the leading researchers in their efforts to develop an American scientific community over the century 1820-1920. What they did not see was the absence of a literal egalitarianism. Lacking in America was the sense of a hierarchy, a social structure, and a system of deference associated in the researchers' minds with the societies of western Europe. The scientists had a problem with a feeling that pervaded American society, as demonstrated by the way the Census Bureau classified occupations in 1860.[70] Actors and showmen were also professionals, as were dancing masters and riding masters. How could the researchers differentiate themselves from the practitioners and the cultivators if they were classed with dancing masters? By 1900 there was even a problem of distinguishing the heirs of Newton and Darwin from technicians.

The researchers' reaction was threefold. Most obvious was to establish honorific organizations or awards to distinguish the best scientists from mere practitioners; the National Academy of Sciences is an obvious example. A second reaction, continuing to this day, was to set up research enclaves, clearly what Joseph Henry had in mind with the Smithsonian Institution, what Alexander Dallas Bache wanted with the Coast Survey, and what Louis Aggasiz thought he was doing with his museum.

The third reaction is more difficult to define: the researchers in the mid-nineteenth century did not want to change the organizational system as it existed. I do not believe that most of them wanted to negate the network of organizations that existed in the form of local societies, academies, and institutes of all sorts. I do not think they really conceived of the people in them as being vulnerable, a dying breed; there were far too many of them. I think the astute leaders of the scientific community saw such people as a potential resource. Some might become scientists, others might become friends of science to be counted on when lobbying was needed in Congress and in state legislatures. Because of that, most of the leading scientists of that day usually did not think in terms of the graduate degree. Somehow people would get specialized training beyond what could be had in the liberal arts schools. The researchers certainly did not conceive of what has happened since; the universities, by awarding a degree, actually provide an essential element in the certification of scientists.

At the same time, they did not envision the post-1860 growth of the many specialized scientific societies. The National Academy deliberately brought together various disciplines, just as most of the local societies did. Even the most specialized of these local societies were broad natural history groupings. What strikes my eye when comparing the American case with the British is the fact that the Americans failed to develop the kind of study associations that began appearing in Britain well before midcentury. The Geological Society of London and the Royal Astronomical Society are good examples; there were very few equivalents in the United States. In Britain some of these societies would remain purely study societies, with a mixture of cultivators and professionals, while others would become specialized societies. In the United States, when these societies appeared after the Civil War, they were almost invariably professional societies formed to facilitate and accomplish development of a specialized field by sponsoring annual meetings and publishing a journal. A few of these societies became concerned with aspects of the certification process, that is, with improving the supply of people. They were involved with the standards of education, and in some cases, particularly through the refereeing process, with proper professional conduct.

The result was that while the mid-nineteenth-century researchers would invariably opt for an older institutional pattern implying accomplishment, reality called for certification, for providing a way of securing a large number of proper practitioners. These leaders of the scientific community preferred national or local groups, rather than disciplinary groups. Bodies like the original kernel from which the AAAS came tended to disappear as many scientists succumbed to pressures to operate on a national level, despite all of the risks, in order to awaken the nation to the need for research. Inevitably this took precedence over strong feelings for the mere development of narrow subject specialities. Since the researchers perceived the sciences as functioning best in nonspecialized groupings, it was an understandable position. But, as the century progressed, disciplinary groups became more common.

By the time George Ellery Hale began revitalizing the National Academy of Sciences, such groups were ascendant. Hale recognized that in order to advance astrophysics there had to be cooperation on an international basis and by various disciplines. His scientific father was Sir William Huggins. Institutionally, he noted that the work of the National Academy of Sciences, a multidisciplinary body, was in decay while the specialized societies were rising. It was a violation of the way of the grandfathers—Sir John Herschel, let us say. In other words, Hale's particular research problems required cooperation across disciplinary lines, and he wanted to restore the unity of the scientific community that he perceived in the generation of his scientific grandfathers. Being an elitist, he did not quite succeed in this attempt because the trends of the time were quite different. The Academy acquired real power only after World War II, under circumstances far different from those Hale envisioned.

But Sir John was only one of the grandfathers. A surprising number of twentieth-century scientists confused him with the whole class of cultivators, now transformed by historical mythology into gentlemen amateurs. In 1892 the

British physicist Arthur Schuster, extolling the dying tradition of amateurism, pointed to Faraday.[71] Faraday was gainfully employed as a scientist—that would make him a mere practitioner—but Faraday was an amateur by lack of formal training. Schuster thought this a virtue, being unconstrained by received doctrines in the university, even though he admitted many untrained amateurs did have strange ideas. What Schuster was extolling was a mythical grandfather, the scientist as romantic discoverer, certainly a more appealing candidate for grandfatherhood than the plodding practitioner and the casual hobbyist.

Eager to differentiate themselves from mere practitioners of science, not to mention the myriads of engineers and physicians, many researchers after 1900 implicitly contrasted the purity of research by romantic discoverers with being in trade. It was the purity of social climbing. For the high-minded seeking of the plan of Divine Providence, for the high-minded certainty of science ameliorating man's lot, some researchers substituted the purity of the play element. Did not Rutherfurd, after all, stand on the deck of the *America*?

APPENDIX: A NUMERICAL EXCURSION

It is quite difficult to give statistical garb to the proposed classification of the ante-bellum scientific community. An element of subjectivity enters into the designation of "researcher." Most cultivators, by definition, leave no traces in the bibliography of science. A majority of practitioners, at least, are also nonpublishers. But, while exact figures are lacking, it is possible to estimate the rough orders of magnitude involved.

As the development of scientific occupations seems a key element in professionalization, let us first consider the practitioners. An obvious source of information is the decennial censuses, which since 1850 have given data on occupations. These present problems perhaps best illustrated by a recent attempt to use this source for twentieth-century data. In *Science: Growth and Change,* Henry W. Menard uses *Historical Statistics of the United States* and later Census Bureau figures to show the expansion of the scientific and technological community from 1900 to 1960, comparing the results to National Science Foundation figures that cover the years 1940 to date.[72] The latter are based on the National Register of Scientific and Technical Personnel, primarily derived from the membership of professional societies. The census data of Menard is given under three rubrics: "scientists," chemists, and engineers. The last matches the NSF results, but the other two are invariably higher. Menard concludes that the census tallies take into account an appreciable number of technicians, "some of whom presumably regarded themselves as scientists when they filled out the census forms."

As 1900, Menard's starting point, is my terminal date, let us examine the numbers involved. *Historical Statistics of the United States* gives 38,000 engineers and 9,000 chemists [all numbers hereafter are rounded]. The former need not concern us; the latter will be treated later. Contrary to Menard, *Historical*

Statistics does *not* give a figure of 12,000 for scientists. That total is given for occupational series 176-181 as follows:

176   Dieticians and nutritionists
177   Foresters and conservationists
178   Natural scientists (not elsewhere classified)
179   Personnel and labor relations workers
180   Social scientists
181   Professional, technical, and kindred workers (n.e.c.)[73]

While the 12,000 in 1900 grows impressively to 302,000 in 1950, this category cannot be used as Menard does. He clearly implies that subtraction of the "technicians" should yield the proper professional total. By this, Menard means those certified by membership in the proper societies. The Census Bureau, for its own purposes, has constructed a systematic classification of occupations; the one in *Historical Statistics* is based on the classification used in the 1950 enumeration. By a complex process of samplings and weightings the classification was applied retrospectively to yield a set of comparable numbers, obviously differing from the original returns.

In 1900, for example, the census reported 43,500 engineers, 8,800 "chemists, assayers, and metallurgists," and 5,800 "authors and scientists."[74] Since the table in *Historical Statistics* reports 3,000 authors for 1900, we can roughly assume 2,800 "scientists." This total, however, does *not* include scientists at institutions of higher learning, or in the employ of federal and state governments; the 1970 census will be the first to give the fields of the professoriate. In recent decades the Census Bureau has made an effort to separate supervisory scientists in public employment from nonsupervisors. From the published figures, I doubt seriously if this was done for 1900.

Instead of 12,000 for 1900 we are left with 2,800 "scientists," plus an unknown number of college faculty and governmental scientists. Who are the approximately 2,800 "scientists" who are not chemists, not at institutions of higher learning, and not in government service? Chatauqua lecturers? Sunday supplement writers? Private consultants?

While I cannot resolve the mystery of the 2,800, using the original published data of the censuses through 1900, it is possible to construct usable estimates of the numbers of scientific practitioners. The point of the Menard example is that these numbers are not readily comparable over time, and normalization of the data may introduce a dangerous degree of anachronism. The censuses of 1850 and 1860 were taken under the same direction, but with unsatisfactory precision of definitions by later standards. After the Civil War a new census establishment was formed, eventually becoming a permanent bureau.[75] By 1900 the census had attained a fairly high degree of methodological sophistication. From discrepancies in the reported data and the previously cited absence of breakdowns for governmental and university scientists, the Census Bureau clearly did not consider the professionalization of science as very important, certainly not in the same class as the changing ratios of agricultural and manufacturing employment.

Of the two missing classes of occupations, the higher education employment figure is the easier one to rectify. From a recent study of leading liberal arts colleges in ante-bellum New England and the Middle Atlantic states, we know that about half of these faculties were scientists by 1860.[76] Assuming this is an unrepresentative sample, I will arbitrarily take one-fourth of the professoriate as scientists for the period 1850 through 1900. Difficulties in determining the total for some census years are discussed below. Of course, more precise figures may be obtainable by taking samplings from college catalogs, old Office of Education figures, and other sources. For our purpose—estimating orders of magnitude for a proposed model—this procedure appears adequate.

Determining the number of scientists in governmental bodies is far more difficult. With some reluctance, I am not attempting any estimates of state employees. They are numerically outbulked by the federal establishment; some are included under the counts for faculty at institutions of higher learning, and I will round upwards to cover others, such as members of state geological surveys. Nevertheless, the figures given below for official scientists are probably slightly on the low side.

For federal employment I will use the published *Official Registers,* sometimes referred to as the "Blue Book."[77] As the listings were made on odd-numbered years, I have used the *Registers* for the years after each decennial census. In the *Registers* are the names of every civil and military employee of the federal government from the top of the hierarchy down to unskilled laborers. Entries give the titles of positions and salaries. I have scanned each volume, tallying the number of scientific posts. In making the count I have had no trouble with posts bearing clear titles like "geologist," "entomologist," or "chemist." In other cases I have relied upon my knowledge of the activities of particular offices and of the official careers of named individuals.[78] The resulting totals, like those for the professoriate, are given in brackets in the tables that follow. For comparison, figures of some related occupations are given in the second column. All numbers are rounded to the nearest hundred (if over 100), except for the official scientists' data, which are rounded upwards (see tables on pp. 58-59).

Practitioners

1850	900
1860	1,500
1870	2,100
1880	3,300+
1890	7,300
1900	14,200

A few observations on these rough tables are in order. Although the Civil War apparently had a retarding effect, the record nonetheless shows a steady growth in the number of practitioners, with the period after 1870 producing a particularly notable expansion. Chemical occupations loom very large in these statistics, but the professoriate and officialdom grow substantially, although at a lesser

Occupation	Scientific	Related
1850[a]		
Astronomical, mathematical, and nautical instrument makers		400
Chemists[b]	500	
Civil engineers		500
Engineers		11,600
Philosophical instrument makers		700
Professors	[250]	
Surveyors		1,600
Officials	[150]	
	900	
1860		
Assayers	50	
Astronomers	2	
Astronomical instrument makers		80
Chemists	600	
Civil and mechanical engineers		27,400
Electricians		200
Explorers	2	
Geologists	3	
Mathematical instrument makers		150
Naturalists	7	
Philosophical instrument makers		60
Physicians		54,500
Professors	[625]	
Officials	[200]	
	1,487 (rounding to *1,500*)	
1870		
Chemists	600	
Engineers, civil		4,700
Inventors		350
Land surveyors		2,600
Metallurgists	200	
Naturalists	300	
Physicians and surgeons		62,400
Officials	[200]	
Professors[c]	[800]	
	2,100	
1880		
Chemists, assayers, metallurgists	2,000	
Engineers, civil		8,300
Physicians and surgeons		85,700
Officials	[200]	
Professors[d]	[1,100]	
	3,300+	

Scientific and Related Occupations from U.S. Censuses
1850–1900 (continued)

Occupation	Scientific	Related
1890		
"Authors and literary and scientific persons"[e]	[1,000]	6,700[total]
Chemists, assayers, and metallurgists	4,500	
Engineers and surveyors		21,800
Physicians and surgeons		104,800
Officials	[300]	
Professors	[1,500]	
	7,300	
1900		
Electricians		50,800
Engineers and surveyors		43,500
Scientists[f]	[2,800]	5,800[total]
Chemists, assayers, and metallurgists[g]	8,900	
Physicians and surgeons		132,225
Officials	[700]	
Professors	[1,800]	
	14,200	

SOURCES: For 1850, U.S., Bureau of the Census, *The Seventh Census of the United States:* (Washington, D.C., 1853), pp. lxvii-lxxxi; for 1860, idem, *Population of the United States in 1860...* (Washington, D.C., 1864), pp. 656-79; for 1870, idem, *The Statistics of the Wealth and Industry of the United States...* (Washington, D.C., 1872), pp. 812-15; for 1880, idem, *Statistics of the Population of the United States at the Tenth Census...* (Washington, D.C., 1883), p. 744; for 1890, idem, *Special Census Report in the Occupations of the Population of the United States at the Eleventh Census: 1890* (Washington, D.C., 1896), p. 11; for 1900, *Occupations at the Twelfth Census.*

[a]This census lists males only; the later ones give figures for both sexes.
[b]Here and subsequently, pharmacists are not included.
[c]In 1870 and 1880 no separate figures were given for teachers at institutions of higher learning. Using the figures for the censuses before and after, I have estimated the series from 1850 to 1900 as follows: 943, 2500, [3100], [4200], 5392, 7272.
[d]The teachers category for 1880 not only lumps together teachers at all levels but also "scientific persons" not further defined; this undifferentiated body of scientists is here noted by a +.
[e]I have not found any way of estimating the scientific persons in this category other than an arbitrary assumption of 1,000.
[f]See previous discussion.
[g]In this census this category was subsumed under the rubric of scientific and literary persons. The 5,800 figure of related scientists is obtained after the subtraction of chemists and librarians.

rate. Given the large number of "chemists" reported by the census, we know very little about their education (in colleges or on the job), their places of employment, and what their activities entailed.[79] Finally, note the other large numbers in the 1900 table. Not only chemical practitioners, but also a veritable horde of engineers and physicians overshadowed the heirs of Newton and Darwin.

For researchers and cultivators, we can crudely estimate the numbers involved for the two ends of the time scale. For one end of the scale, we do have a useful bibliographical tool. I am well aware of the limitations of using counts of articles or citations; used properly, however, these numbers are useful.

A subtle problem arises from the self-selecting nature of the literature counts. Almost invariably, one counts literature to find the most prolific scientists or the most prolific institutions, on the assumption of a correlation between being prolific and being accomplished. By counting the nineteenth-century literature, one is selecting authors and defining their characteristics as being "scientific." It is no surprise to me to look through the literature or some bibliographical reference work and find people who have published twenty, thirty, forty, or fifty articles. And it is no surprise that most of them are specialized in one field, and that they are interested in publishing. If one looks a little further, the authors are fairly well educated. The prosopographical literature for the United States seems to indicate that in the period to 1860 the American scientific community was far better educated than has been thought, was likely to be engaged in full-time occupations involving some degree of scientific competence, and was fairly active in publication.

This interpretation is based largely upon the leaders in terms of publication. It excludes the possibility of a somewhat different picture if one goes below whatever the cutoff point is for the "leading" scientists to the people who publish far less or even to the nonpublishers. In my terminology, this source does not tell anything about individuals at the low end of the publishing scale, not to mention those off the scale—the nonpublishing practitioners and cultivators.

I propose to use information taken from an unpublished dissertation as a basic body of useful data. C. A. Elliott's 1970 dissertation, "The American Scientist, 1800-1863: His Origins, Career, and Interests," is based upon a count of the first series of the *Royal Society Catalogue,* which goes up to 1863.[80] It is not the most sophisticated statistically; Beaver's dissertation probably has that honor.[81] However, Elliott's is by far the most thorough and the most useful source.

I am convinced from Elliott's work that the use of the *Royal Society Catalogue* is a perfectly good way of obtaining a first approximation of data on the nature of the scientific community in the past. If anything, his figures are slightly on the low side, since they minimize the count. An appreciable number of scientists published monographs, not articles, and an unknown small number of articles are not in the indexed journals but in other journals—medical, technological, general, or agricultural.[82] Yet the coverage of the *Royal Society Catalogue,* as Elliott demonstrates, is extremely thorough, and the data is quite reliable.

Author Distribution of Articles in American Serials,
1800-1863

Number of articles	Number of authors
1	1,652
2	354
3	170
4-5	155
6-10	153
11-15	58
16-25	47
26-50	41
51-100	23
100+	6
	2,659 Total authors

SOURCE: C.A. Elliott, "The American Scientist, 1800-1863: His Origins, Career, and Interests" (Ph.D. diss., Case-Western Reserve University, 1970), p. 38.

The problem with using Elliott's total count is that he finds that a number of the authors who are identified as publishing in American journals are foreigners whose papers are being reprinted or abstracted. For his core group—those with three or more articles—Elliott states that approximately one-fifth are inadmissible for this reason, but does not indicate whether the distribution of this one-fifth occurred at the level of three papers, or from the five to ten level, or what. If we assume that one-fifth of the listed names in the lower part of the scale are similarly inadmissible, we could then simply deduct a fifth from the total and arrive, by a process of rounding, at approximately 2,200 names.

A check on this is provided by Beaver. He estimates that the maximum number of scientists in America in the first six decades—from 1800 to 1860—is about 2,600, and it is not by accident that this number is so close to the total maximum figure arrived at by Elliott. However, Beaver's method of determining these numbers is by approximation from particular samples, supplemented by various kinds of statistical tests. And he estimates, very conservatively, that there were about 1,600 active scientists in America in that time span.[83] The figure of 2,200 that we have arrived at by deducting from Elliott's total is approximately half way between the maximum and the very low conservative estimate that Beaver fixes on.[84]

Using Elliott's original table, I will define the researchers as those publishing more than ten times—that is, 175—which I will expand to 200.[85] From various indicators, they will probably divide in a 3 to 2 ratio between natural history and other scientific fields.

Elliott estimates that 16 percent of his core group—those with three or more publications—never worked in scientific or science-related professions. Since his 84 percent—that is, practitioners—includes both individuals who worked only partly in scientific occupations and practicing physicians, determining the number of publishing practitioners and cultivators in terms of my definition is very awkward. Let us assume arbitrarily that three-quarters of Elliott's authors are practitioners and let us assume—a very risky move—that his figures apply also to authors of one and two articles.[86] That yields 1,650 practitioners who published during the years 1800-1860, of whom 150 are in the researcher category.

Scientific Authors, 1800-1860

Researchers   200 [50 being nonpractitioners]
Practitioners 1,500
Cultivators   500

To determine the number of nonauthors, I would do the following: double the number of practitioners on the assumption that at least one nonpublisher exists for every publishing practitioner. This is roughly confirmed by the earlier tables. From a scanning of membership lists and from browsings in correspondence files, I suspect there were between five and ten nonpublishing cultivators for every author. Let us use the lower figure. The resulting cumulative totals are:

American Scientific Community, 1800-1860

Researchers   200
Practitioners 3,000
Cultivators   11,000

In 1906 James McKeen Cattell published the first edition of *American Men of Science.* Cattell had started his work shortly after the turn of the century with the aid of a grant from the Carnegie Institution of Washington. The approximately 4,000 names, he announced, were "a fairly complete survey of the scientific activity of a country at a given period."[87] In what sense did Cattell consider this edition complete?

Originally, Cattell had expected to produce fairly quickly a complete biographical directory of about 1,000 names, an expectation based upon an extrapolation of an earlier estimate of G. Brown Goode, to which we will return. Instead, the first edition was delayed because his efforts initially yielded 8,000 names. Cattell tells us he sent questionnaires to the membership of twenty-two societies, reviewed membership lists of societies in applied fields, consulted catalogs of "institutions of learning" and biographical reference works, scanned the names of contributors to journals, printed requests for names in *Science, Popular Science Monthly,* and *The Nation,* and received "much assistance from individuals."

In a contemporary article Cattell stated he eliminated about 4,000 "who had not done research work in the natural and exact sciences."[88] The first edition preface is a bit more enlightening; it notes that the "men of science" carried on research in North America (therefore, probably including a number of Canadians). But, in addition, the first edition contains the names of those who are supposedly to have advanced science by teaching, by administrative work, or by the preparation of textbooks and compilations. There are also some whose work has been chiefly in engineering, medicine or other applied sciences, and a few whose work is in education, economics, or other subjects not commonly included under the exact and natural sciences. The names are included because they are supposed to represent work that has contributed to the advancement of pure science—the term being used in the narrower sense—or because they are found in the membership lists of certain societies. Indeed, all members who returned questionnaires are included with two exceptions.[89] Cattell's criteria were quite like Menard's, that is, like the National Register.

Cattell's source for his original estimate of 1,000 was Goode's 1888 address before the Biological Society of Washington, "The Beginnings of American Science."[90] Citing the *Naturalists' Directory* for 1886 with its approximately 4,600 names, Goode estimated the "investigators" as not over 500 and the advanced teachers as "perhaps 1,000 strong"—which compares nicely with my figure of 1,100 and 1,500 for 1880 and 1890.[91] But Goode was a man of a different mold than Cattell. In calculating the ratio of scientists to the general population, he included not only his investigators (i.e., my researchers), the advanced teachers (my practitioner professoriate), but also the remaining cultivators, "all who are sufficiently interested in science to have special lines of study."[92] If he had not thought of research accomplishment, Cattell would have used 1,500 rather than 500 to arrive at the 1900 figure of 3,000, which was closer to his actual findings.

Cattell's 4,000 corresponds in my classification to the researchers, the publishing practitioners, some nonpublishing practitioners in universities and government, and the relatively few nonpractitioners who still survived in the scientific scene. We can also guess that the omitted 4,000 are largely nonresearching practitioners and the surviving remnant of nonpublishing cultivators. Assuming Goode's 3,000 in 1886 was down to 2,000 in 1900,[93] Cattell's 8,000 might divide as follows:

American Scientific Community, 1900

Researchers   400 [1/10 the total in first edition] *
Practitioners 5,600
. . . .
Cultivators   2,000

*A rough estimate, in accord with the findings of the importance, qualitatively and quantitatively, of the minority of leading scientists.

Goode would include the cultivators; Cattell excludes them from the community—therefore, I have inserted the dotted line in the table. Comparing the figures above the line with the census returns for 1850, the American scientific community had roughly a sevenfold increase in half a century. If we assume that about two-thirds of the cultivators in the cumulative total of 11,000 were active in 1850, their total had dropped by more than two-thirds in the same period. Yet, even if the estimate of 2,000 proves valid, the numbers do not indicate the extent of the change. Being a cultivator in 1900 was a most unlikely route to a scientific career; the graduate school was the certification mechanism. Even more important, being a cultivator in 1900 was a most unlikely route to research achievement; the graduate school was the accomplishment mechanism.

The practitioners' figure above the dotted line corresponds very well with the previous figures for 1900 if we exclude chemists (scientists + officials + professors). If we add 300 chemists (publishing and leading nonpublishing practitioners), Cattell and Reingold match exactly. Not having claimed statistical validity, I can only express pleasure at this unexpected, if dubious, confirmation.

NOTES

1. A recent example is W. G. Holt, "Social Aspects in the Emergence of Chemistry as an Exact Science: The British Chemical Profession," *The British Journal of Sociology* 31 (1970): 181-98.

2. On these various incidents, see A. Hunter Dupree, *Science in the Federal Government* (Cambridge: Harvard University Press, Belknap Press, 1957), chap. 4; Sally Kohlstedt, "A Step Toward Scientific Self-Identity in the United States: The Failure of the National Institute, 1844," *Isis* 62 (Fall 1971): 339-62; idem, "The Formation of the American Scientific Community: The American Association for the Advancement of Science, 1848-1860" (Ph.D. diss., University of Illinois, 1972); Warner papers, Library of the American Philosophical Society, Philadelphia, Pa.; John D. Holmfeld, "From Amateurs to Professionals in American Science: The Controversy over the Proceedings of an 1853 Scientific Meeting," *Proceedings of the American Philosophical Society* 114 (1970): 23-36; Edward Lurie, *Louis Agassiz: A Life in Science* (Chicago: University of Chicago Press, 1960), p. 180; Nathan Reingold, "Two Views of Maury . . . and a Third," *Isis* 55 (1964): 370-72.

3. The social science literature on professionalization is vast enough without even considering the many writings of members of particular professions. The following selected list is a starting point for historians unfamiliar with this literature, sticking very close to pieces specifically on professions and professionalization, not obviously related topics like role theory:

Ben-David, Joseph. "The Profession of Science and its Powers." *Minerva* 10 (1972): 362-83.

Carr-Saunder, A. M. and Wilson, P. A. *The Professions.* Oxford: Oxford University Press, 1933. The classic work, highly influential and still usable.

Cogan, Morris L. "Toward a Definition of Profession." *Harvard Educational Review* 23 (1953): 33-50. Has useful bibliography of older works.

Holt, B. W. G. "Social Aspects in the Emergence of Chemistry as an Exact Science: The British Chemical Profession." *The British Journal of Sociology* 21 (1970): 181-98. Interesting, but not wholly convincing.

Jackson, John Archer, ed. *Professions and Professionalization.* Sociological Studies, vol. 3. London: Cambridge University Press, 1970. T. Legatt on teaching has interesting comments.

Lynn, K. S., et al., eds. *The Professions in America.* Boston: Houghton Mifflin, 1965. Barber, Beer and Lewis are most relevant.

Millerson, Geoffrey. *The Qualifying Associations: A Study in Professionalization.* London: Routledge & Kegan Paul; New York: Humanities Press, 1964. The best single work by far. Very British, but with a few pointed comments on the United States situation.

Moore, W. E., and Rosenblum, G. W. *The Professions: Roles and Rules.* New York: Russell Sage Foundation, 1970. A fine monograph, but not particularly useful to a historian.

Parsons, Talcott. "Professions." *International Encyclopedia of the Social Sciences.* An unsuccessful attempt at redefinition.

Reader, W. J. *Professional Men: The Rise of the Professional Classes in Nineteenth-Century England.* London: Weidenfeld & Nicolson, 1966. Splendid blend of history and sociology, far superior to Calhoun's *Professional Lives in America.*

Shils, Edward. "The Profession of Science." *The Advancement of Science* 24 (1968): 469-80. A good example of a conventional view.

Strauss, George. "Professionalism and Occupational Associations." *Industrial Relations* 2 (May 1967): 7-13. Good for comparison with engineers.

Vollmer, H. M., and Mills, Donald L., eds. *Professionalization.* Englewood Cliffs, N. J.: Prentice-Hall, 1966. A well-done anthology.

Weber, Max. "Science as a Vocation." *From Max Weber: Essays in Sociology.* Edited by H. H. Gerth and C. Wright Mills. New York: Oxford University Press, 1946.

Wilensky, H. L. "The Professionalization of Everyone?" *American Journal of Sociology* 70 (September 1964): 137-58. An important article in the American context.

4. Millerson, *Qualifying Associations,* pp. 1-2.

5. Bernard Barber, "Some Problems in the Sociology of the Professions," in Lynn, *Professions in America,* p. 18.

6. John J. Beer and W. David Lewis, "Aspects of the Professionalization of Science," in ibid., pp. 110-30.

7. Shils, "Profession of Science," and Ben-David, "Profession of Science and Its Powers."

8. Parsons, "Professions." This presentation is more a reflection of hopes than a description of reality.

9. Shils, "Profession of Science," p. 473.

10. Henry W. Menard, *Science: Growth and Change* (Cambridge, Mass.: Harvard University Press, 1971), pp. 202-204.

11. Millerson, *Qualifying Associations,* pp. 10-11.

12. I am greatly indebted to Dr. Cannon for many stimulating insights on this matter of professionalization. He does not merit any blame, however, for what follows.

13. Ben-David, "Profession of Science and Its Powers," pp. 371-73, passim.

14. Only 37 percent of holders of the doctorate are in research and development. U.S., National Science Foundation, *American Science Manpower 1970* (Washington, D.C., 1971), p. 14.

15. Counts of this are very hard to come by in the contemporary literature, since attention is understandably on the prolific producers and the authors of great impact. But see J. R. Cole, "Patterns of Intellectual Influence in Scientific Research," *Sociology of Education* 43 (1970): 377-403.

16. Menard, *Science: Growth and Change,* p. 99 estimates that 78 percent of all geologists are never cited.

17. E. C. Hughes, *Men and Their Work* (New York: Free Press of Glencoe, 1958), pp. 137-38.

18. For example, C. A. Elliott, "The American Scientist, 1800-1863: His Origins, Career, and Interests" (Ph.D. diss., Case-Western Reserve University, 1970). By adjusting his figures, I estimate about 2,200 American authors of scientific articles. More than two-thirds published only one piece.

19. A. D. Orange, "The British Association for the Advancement of Science: The Provincial Background," *Science Studies* 1 (1971): 315-29, called my attention to Brewster's usage. Since writing this, several have called my attention to this usage in ante-bellum America, including sources familiar to me.

20. Nathan Reingold, ed., *Science in Nineteenth Century America: A Documentary History* (New York: Hill & Wang, 1964), pp. 17-20.

21. Joel R. Poinsett, *Discourse on the Objects and Importance of the National Institution for the Promotion of Science* (Washington, D.C., 1841). Mr. John Kazar of the University of Massachusetts at Amherst called this to my attention.

22. Nathan Reingold et al., eds. *The Papers of Joseph Henry* (Washington, D.C.: Smithsonian Institution Press, 1972), 1: 66, 75, passim.

23. John C. Spencer to Francis Wayland, 2 February 1844, Wayland Collection, Brown University Library, Providence, R.I.

24. U.S., Bureau of the Census, *Occupations at the Twelfth Census* (Washington, D.C.: Government Printing Office, 1904), p. xxiii.

25. *North American Review* 20 (1825): 309-66.

26. The periodicals examined were: *American Quarterly, New York Review, New York Review and Atheneum Magazine, Belles Lettres Repository and Monthly Magazine, American Monthly Magazine and Critical Review, The Literary and Scientific Repository and Critical Review, Boston Quarterly Review.* Further browsings have not altered the picture.

27. Linda Kerber, "Science in the Early Republic: the Society for the Study of Natural Philosophy," *William and Mary Quarterly* 39 (1972): 261-80, is a fine account of this tradition.

28. "For practically the whole century science and many specialized subjects could serve as hobbies, which did not entail very deep, intricate pre-instruction." Millerson, *Qualifying Associations*, p. 22.

29. Millerson, *Qualifying Associations.*

30. Quentin Skinner, "Thomas Hobbes and the Nature of the Early Royal Society," *Historical Journal* 12 (1969): 217-39.

31. Reader, *Professional Men,* pp. 6-7.

32. A fine example of this activity is provided by the Charles Gill Papers, Department of Manuscripts and University Archives, Olin Library, Cornell University, Ithaca, N. Y., with its letters from problem solvers. These include college teachers of mathematics (i.e., practitioners) like Theodore Strong, but also others devoted to this kind of mathematics.

33. Reingold, *Papers of Joseph Henry,* 1: 212.

34. *Dictionary of American Biography,* s.v. "Root, Erastus."

35. Reingold, *Science in Nineteenth Century America,* p. 88.

36. Francis Fry Wayland, *Andrew Stevenson: Democrat and Diplomat* (Philadelphia: University of Pennsylvania Press, 1949).

37. For example, the draft of Henry's address of November 18, 1871, to the Philosophical Society of Washington has strong passages excised from the printed version in *Scientific Writings of Joseph Henry* (Washington, D.C. 1886), 2:468-75. The draft is in box 26 of the Henry Papers, Smithsonian Archives, Washington, D.C.

38. National Institution Journal of Proceedings, entries of 1 January 1849, 6 January and 7 January 1851, 5 January 1852, 15 January 1855, 14 January 1856, National Institute Papers, Smithsonian Archives, Washington, D.C.

39. See note 37 above.

40. Joseph Henry, "On the Organization of Local Scientific Societies," *Scientific Writings,* pp. 511-13.

41. Hugh McCulloch, *Men and Measures of Half a Century* (New York, 1888), pp. 261-69, passim.

42. *Proceedings of the American Philosophical Society* 11:85-91. Delivered March 19, 1869.

43. *Administrators Sale. Extensive Rare and Beautiful Cabinet of Science . . . Catalogue of Valuable Philosophical Apparatus being a collection made by the late Charles N. Bancker* (Philadelphia, 1869).

44. *A Collection of Rare and Valuable Books . . . Catalogue of the entire Private Library of the late Charles N. Bancker* (Philadelphia, 1869).

45. Anna Eliot Ticknor, ed., *Life of Joseph G. Cogswell as Sketched in his Letters* (Cambridge, Mass., 1874), pp. 43-107, passim.

46. Ibid., p. 352.

47. All this is very distressing to me, since I implied in the Bowditch article in the *Dictionary of Scientific Biography* that Peirce is the only one qualifying as a student of Bowditch. Sam Ward was below my level of perception.

48. Robert V. Steele [Lately Thomas], *Sam Ward: King of the Lobby* (Boston: Houghton Mifflin Co., Riverside Press, 1965), pp. 20-21, 30-32; Louise Hall Tharp, *Three*

Saints and a Sinner (Boston: Little, Brown, 1956), pp. 38-39, 45-46, 49-53; Maud Howe Elliott, *Uncle Sam Ward and His Circle* (New York: Macmillan Co., 1938), p. 47.

49. R. C. Archbald, "Unpublished Letters of James Joseph Sylvester and other new Information concerning his Life and Work," *Osiris* 1 (1936): 118.

50. See my Rutherfurd article in the *Dictionary of Scientific Biography*, in press.

51. Benjamin Apthorp Gould, "Memoir of Lewis Morris Rutherfurd," *Biographical Memoirs of the National Academy of Sciences* 3 (1895): 417-41.

52. G. Brown Goode, "The Beginnings of American Science," *A Memorial of George Brown Goode* (Washington, D.C., 1901), p. 463. Originally delivered in 1888.

53. W. Stephen Thomas, ed., *The Layman Scientists in Philadelphia* (Philadelphia: American Philosophical Society, 1940).

54. Elliott, "American Scientist."

55. George Daniels, *American Science in the Age of Jackson* (New York and London: Columbia University Press, 1968); Donald Beaver, "The American Scientific Community, 1800-1860: A Statistical Historical Study" (Ph.D. diss., Yale University, 1966).

56. Reingold, *Papers of Joseph Henry* (1975) 2: 432-38.

57. Daniels, *American Science*, pp. 10-11.

58. *American Science Manpower 1970*, pp. 14, 19.

59. Pauling: "I decided then to be a chemist, and to study chemical engineering, which was, I thought, the profession that chemists followed." Gerald Holton, ed., *The Twentieth-Century Sciences: Studies in the Biography of Ideas* (New York: Norton Co., 1972), p. 281; Warren Weaver, *Scene of Change: A Lifetime in Science* (New York: Scribner's, 1970), pp. 23-25.

60. Reingold, *Papers of Joseph Henry*, pp. 245-46.

61. This is by no means a position original with me. As an example, I can cite the work of Edward Pessen, which has a strange relationship to the writing of historians studying science in America—it is avowedly anti-de Tocqueville. See his "Did Fortunes Rise and Fall Mercurially in Antebellum America?" *Journal of Social History* 4 (1971): 339-57, especially footnote 3.

62. Of course I haven't read everything, and my memory is far from infallible. I would welcome any contrary instances.

63. Elliott, "American Scientist," pp. 107-10.

64. These few were important in their own right. The 1860 census reported 54,543 physicians, however, so that the number doing science was a very small fraction of that total. *Eighth Census of the United States Population* (Washington, D.C., 1864), 671.

65. See Anton-Hermann Chroust, *Rise of the Legal Profession in America*, 2 vols. (Norman: University of Oklahoma Press, 1965).

66. There is surprisingly little specifically on professionalization and the ministry even in such an extensive source as N. R. Burr, *Critical Bibliography of Religion in America*, 2 vols. (Princeton: Princeton University Press, 1961), vol. 4, *Religion in American Life*, ed. J. W. Smith and A. L. Jamison.

67. Beaver, "American Scientific Community," pp. 15-16 indicates that the leading scientists produced at least 50 percent of the literature in this period.

68. Three editions appeared: 1849, 1851, 1859.

69. Orange, "British Association for the Advancement of Science."

70. See note 64, above.

71. British Association for the Advancement of Science, *Report of the Sixty-Second Meeting* (Edinburgh, 1892), pp. 628-30.

72. Menard, *Science: Growth and Change*, pp. 58-60.

73. U.S., Bureau of the Census, *Historical Statistics of the United States, Colonial Times to 1957* (Washington, D.C.: Government Printing Office, 1960), p. 75.

74. *Occupations at the Twelfth Census*, p. xxxiv.

75. Meyer H. Fishbein, "The Censuses of Manufactures, 1810-1890," *National Archives Accessions* (June 1963), is a good introduction to this story.

76. Information furnished by Dr. Stanley H. Guralnick, Colorado School of Mines.

77. *Register of the Officers and Agents, Civil, Military, and Naval, in the Service of the United States . . .* , to give one title of the last century. This biennial publication started in

1816; after 1817 it was issued at two-year intervals; through 1911 it listed *all* employees of the federal government. The last number appeared in 1959.

78. Army and Navy officers present a particular problem. Officers detailed to West Point as assistant professors of mathematics are clearly in scope. How does one count ordnance and engineer officers, especially if some are, in fact, doing science?

79. C. A. Browne and M. E. Weeks, *A History of the American Chemical Society . . .* (Washington, D.C.: American Chemical Society, 1952), pp. 51-58, cite a paper by H. C. Bolton in 1902 giving 2,575 as the number of members in American chemical societies.

80. Elliott, "American Scientist."

81. Beaver, "American Scientific Community."

82. Ibid., p. 16, estimates ten thousand papers, about a thousand books, and several hundred reports. The *Royal Society Catalogue* does give a considerable number of "reports," but if Beaver is correct on the book estimate, this immediately introduces a possible 10 percent margin of error (assuming that 1 book = 1 paper for counting purposes). This, plus the possibility of missing articles, justifies the assumption that Beaver and Elliott are to some extent on the low side in their reported results. See Elliott's article, *"The Royal Society Catalogue* as an Index to Nineteenth Century American Science," *Journal of the American Society for Information Science* 21 (1970): 396-401.

83. Beaver, "American Scientific Community," p. 115.

84. Although I indicated my belief in note 82, above, that these quantitative results of Beaver and Elliott are on the low side in terms of the number of contributions, I am reluctant to follow this by assuming that a higher count of contributions justifies a leap to the highest count of contributors possible (i.e., 2,600). If we assume that the foreign authors are balanced by the authors of books and reports, this completely discounts the problem of name duplication. Many of the thousand books were written by authors who also penned articles. In general, in doing these estimates, I tend to take the lower possibility.

85. This is to allow for additional names from books and reports, as well as a quality factor not part of the Beaver and Elliott figures.

86. Elliott, "American Scientist," pp. 136-40. Using his core group, he excludes physicians and comes up with a two-thirds figure, but cannot deal with men who worked in both science and nonscience occupations. My figure is a rough compromise. In a letter commenting on a draft of this paper, Dr. Elliott took polite exception to my statement that he "cannot deal" with careers of mixed occupations. He recalculated his data to arrive at a 70 percent figure for men solely employed in science occupations and those with a mixed occupational history. Since he excludes physicians and teachers of medicine, I think our results are pretty close, given our initial data and assumptions. My next assumption, about the applicability of this split to authors of one and two articles, he regards as unlikely, given the greater productivity of men in scientific occupations. I remain skeptical and await further evidence on this point.

87. J. McKeen Cattell, ed., *American Men of Science* (New York: Science Press, 1906). This quote and later references are from the Preface.

88. J. McKeen Cattell, "Homo Scientificus Americanus," *Science* 17 (1903): 561-70. Reprinted in A. T. Poffenberger, ed., *James McKeen Cattell: Man of Science,* 2 vols. (Lancaster, Pa.: Science Press, 1947), 2: 185-96.

89. Only fellows of the American Association for the Advancement of Science and the American Ornithologists' Union were included, perhaps an implicit judgment by Cattell of the nature of the regular members.

90. Goode, "Beginnings of American Science."

91. Samuel E. Cassino, ed., *The Naturalists' Directory, 1886* (Boston, 1886).Thirty-one editions were issued by him from 1877 to 1938 and were not limited to persons in natural history by any means. The 1886 title page specifically lists chemists, physicists, and astronomers as well as naturalists within its scope. I have spot checked a number of these volumes for names of physical scientists and of institutions employing physical scientists. Much to my surprise, the coverage is very good. Cassino (1856-1937) (who merits some investigation) has Canadians; later volumes bear the word "international" and "universal" in their titles as he attempted global coverage. In 1886 Cassino announced that the next edition would contain some device for distinguishing amateurs and professionals. No edition

examined by me does this. As Cassino was an entomologist, perhaps the directory originated to facilitate exchange of specimens.

92. Goode estimates the scientists as being 1 per 10,000 of the population. Since he uses 42 million for the U.S. population, he apparently rounded the total in Cassino to 4,200, perhaps an implicit judgment on 400 cultivators.

93. Nonprofessionals have not vanished even today. My colleague, Erle Kauffman of the National Museum of Natural History, a paleobiologist, reports their existence in Great Britain, France, Germany, and Scandinavia, but near absence in the United States. According to a study by Forman, Heilbron, and Weart to appear in volume 5 of *Historical Studies in the Physical Sciences,* as late as 1900 cultivators were still active in *physics* in Britain, France, and Germany, although in small numbers.

The Royal Society
in America

GEORGE F. FRICK

For more than the first century of its existence, the Royal Society of London was the learned society of the British colonies in North America. This is true even if American efforts to form philosophical societies are taken into account. Increase Mather's Boston organization of 1683 succumbed too easily to the political disasters that befell the Bay Colony soon after the philosophers began to meet, even though its collections provided some of the "Curiosa Americana" that Cotton Mather transmitted to the Royal Society long afterward.[1] Similarly, the efforts of Franklin and his Philadelphia colleagues to establish the American Philosophical Society in 1743 proved premature. In the decade of Franklin's electrical experiments, Philadelphia's nearest approach to a scientific institution was its Library Company, to which Peter Collinson, the Royal Society's principal correspondent with America in the middle years of the eighteenth century, transmitted "the earliest accounts of every new European Improvement in Agriculture and the Arts, and every Philosophical Discovery. . . ."[2]

A learned society three thousand miles removed from a part of its constituency had some disadvantages, although philosophical colonists probably did not suffer appreciably more than did provincial Englishmen. The Royal Society *of London* was in many ways just that. London and Middlesex were always heavily represented on the list of fellows as against the more remote parts of the kingdom, and, while it is difficult to tell why many fellows were chosen in this period, it would seem that Londoners frequently were elected with less scrutiny than was the case with those who lived at a distance.[3]

The list of North American and West Indian fellows of the Society compiled by Raymond P. Stearns is clearly indicative of the Englishness or, as there were a number of Scots among them, the Britishness of American science in the seventeenth and eighteenth centuries.[4] In their persons and interests, the colonial fellows resembled very strongly those at home. In some ways the list is as interesting for names omitted—which would prove the point even better—as for those included. Mark Catesby, for example, spent some seven years in Virginia and another three in South Carolina and the Bahamas, but is treated quite rightly as a transient visitor.[5]

Place of death rather than place of birth gives a rough index of primary affiliation. Of fifty-three colonial fellows elected before the end of the American

---

[1] Notes to this chapter begin on page 81.

War for Independence, twenty-seven died in the New World and twenty-four in the Old or in the course of their return there. The slight American majority may have been created by colonial governors who died in office.

Even the "Americans" selected by this arbitrary process constituted an Anglo-American elite whose cultural aspirations were focused on the imperial metropolis. This might well have been expected in the early period, but it remained true down to the time of the American Revolution. Governor John Winthrop, Jr., an adult when he first went to America, was clearly of a kind with the Restoration philosophers who founded the Society. His contributions to the Society while he remained in England and the items that he sent to the secretary, Henry Oldenburg, after he returned to Connecticut indicated the interest of the first generation of fellows in American materials.[6] William Byrd, whose long association with the Society extended from his election in 1696 to his death in 1744, was, despite his Virginia birth, English both in education and in terms of the long periods he spent in the mother country. He was something more than a Chesapeake planter simulating the ways of an English gentleman.[7] Finally, it might well be argued that the Benjamin Franklin who received the Copley Medal in 1753 for his electrical experiments, and who was elected a fellow three years later, was an exceptionally sophisticated Philadelphian, but that the Franklin who served four times on the Society's Council had become a part of the life of London. The colonial agent was a cosmopolitan.

In some ways, this gravitation toward London can be illustrated by a colonial fellow here accounted British, Dr. Alexander Garden of Charles Town. Unlike Franklin, who was "discovered" and nurtured by Peter Collinson, Garden actively sought recognition from leading fellows. Garden's letters to Dr. John Huxham and to Stephen Hales in 1754, shortly after he arrived in the South Carolina capital, were obviously designed to court the attention of influential fellows. This motivation was probably less true of Garden's long and advantageous relationship with the London Society of Arts which began at nearly the same time. Garden may well have been acquainted with William Shipley, the founder of the younger and more practical organization.[8] Whatever the case, Charles Town did not offer this ambitious Scot sufficient ego gratification or philosophical conversation. From the beginning of his life in America, Garden displayed an attitude that would eventually take him as an embittered loyalist to London and active participation in the affairs of the Royal Society.

Both Byrd and Garden were more typical of the natural history emphasis of the American fellows than was Franklin. While it is difficult to discern the scientific interests of many of the fellows, a rough estimate would place the preponderance of those inclined toward natural history and medicine over natural philosophy at slightly more than two to one. Articles by Americans or on American topics published in the *Philosophical Transactions* before the War for Independence give an even greater weight to natural history, although the ratio of about three to one was aided by the fact that transient English scientific visitors in the New World tended to be naturalists. All of this was due to the interests of those who managed much of the Society's correspondence with the colonies, many of whom were members of the English natural history circle, but it was not wholly that, nor was it peculiar to British America. Professor Stearns's figures for letters and papers submitted to the Royal Society during its first hundred years indicate a preponderance of 65 percent in natural history to 35 percent in natural philosophy.[9] And while natural history may not have dominated English science in Newton's century, naturalists were in the majority.

There is a final significant element in the colonial membership of the Royal Society—the proprietors and governors. The list contains thirteen in all, making governors the largest single occupational group. The obvious reason would seem to be that the Society sought to provide a quasi-public, quasi-private patronage of science in their respective governments. The answer is not quite that simple: many would seem to have been elected on merit or at least for other reasons. John Winthrop, Jr., for example, was unquestionably chosen for his talents, although the fact that he held a government position may also have played a part. William Burnet, son of the great bishop, was elected a fellow some fifteen years before he took his first post in New York. James Edward Oglethorpe achieved membership after he returned from Georgia. Henry Ellis was elected before he went to Georgia, and Francis Fauquier before he received his appointment in Virginia, both apparently on the basis of their qualifications. Ellis's certificate cited his Arctic exploration, and Fauquier's a minor reputation for "Philosophical and Mathematical inquiries. . . . " Again, Thomas Pownall was elected after his return to England from his post in Massachusetts, although, unlike Oglethorpe, he retained considerable influence.[10]

The remainder were probably chosen in expectation of benevolence to science, which was, occasionally, provided. Francis Nicholson, who came as near as any to being a professional colonial governor, was probably the most generous of the gubernatorial fellows in support of scientific inquiry. He joined with the great planting Bishop of London, Henry Compton, in underwriting the botanical collections of the Reverend Hugh Jones during his governorship of Maryland in the 1690s and also contributed to the work there of William Vernon and probably to that of Dr. David Krieg.[11] All of this was before he was elected F.R.S. in 1706. Still later, on the eve of his departure to become the first royal governor of South Carolina, he pledged £20 yearly to Mark Catesby, ". . . recommended to him as a very proper person to Observe the Rarities of that Country for the uses and purposes of the Society. . . . "[12] That promise is one of the few mentions of the patronage of colonial science in the Society's Council Minutes during the entire colonial period.

The matter of patronage was significant, as it helped to determine the relationship of the Royal Society to scientific activity in America and, indeed, to scientific activity generally. If, as Roger Hahn has amply demonstrated, the Académie des Sciences reflected Ancien Régime society, so too did the Royal Society mirror the social arrangements of seventeenth- and eighteenth-century England. Of course, if the events of 1688 and 1689 had not intervened, the nation might have moved in a more "French" direction and the Royal Society might also have resembled the Académie. Certainly the Royal Society was aware of the nature of its French counterpart. Shortly after the promulgation of the new statutes of the Académie in 1699, the Council appointed a committee including William Byrd and Hans Sloane to "make an Extract of what they think necessary to be Established for the Society."[13] There is no indication that they found anything of use.

Nonetheless, some of the same elements existed in embryo in the English institution as in the French. The Society early sought to pass on mechanical inventions, and Queen Anne ordered in 1713 that patents be referred to the Society for its approbation.[14] Similarly, the Society possessed the charter right to appoint a printer and to license books. The privilege was exercised throughout the period, although it never constituted a monopoly of scientific writings and had much less meaning after the end of licensing generally in 1694.[15] Imprimatur implied only a cautious approval of books by the Council, which acted on all of them, and did not normally involve a subsidy. Apparently, until the Society took over publication of the *Philosophical Transactions* in 1752, only Francis Willughby's *De Historia Piscium* (London, 1686) was printed at its charge. The failure of the "book of fishes" to pay its costs probably discouraged subsequent sponsorship by the Society which could ill afford the loss.[16]

Certainly the Royal Society was a far less restrictive organization than the Académie, embodying the relative openness of the English social order even during the eighteenth-century domination by the great Whig magnates. Although their entrance was easier than other mortals, peers were not segregated as *honoraires*, and frequently served the Society effectively as ordinary members or as officers. While the same might not be said of all titled presidents of the Society, the tenure in that office of the Earl of Macclesfield (1752-1764) was an effective and reforming one by a man who had real scientific interests and a deep concern for the reputation of the organization he headed.[17] The only segregated members of the seventeenth- and eighteenth-century Royal Society were foreigners, who usually did not make paid contributions but were treated otherwise as ordinary members until the 1770s.[18]

Most significantly, the Royal Society lacked a recognized, professional elite. Distinctions between scientists and amateurs have been imposed upon it anachronistically by modern authors. Without significant support from the Crown, it could not offer pensions or other substantial rewards to those who were dependent upon philosophy for a livelihood. This was dealt with in some measure by appointing scientists to salaried posts. The office of curator, charged with performing experiments, was frequently held by fellows who could be considered full-time scientists. Robert Hooke held that post almost from the beginning of the Society until his death. Denis Papin served with him for a time, as did Nehemiah Grew and Edmond Halley.[19] Still later, Jean Theophile Desaguliers, whose experiments inside and outside of the Society did so much to popularize experimental Newtonianism, held the post for many years. He received as much as thirty pounds for his labors at the beginning of his career and as little as ten guineas in his old age.[20]

Some of the same men also acted with pay as secretaries to the Society, as was the case with Hooke and Grew and Halley.[21] Even so, payment was not always easy, particularly during the difficult late years of the seventeenth century. Edmond Halley was offered fifty pounds or fifty "books of fishes" to measure the "degree of the Earth." He did not accept the offer, but did take as many copies of Willughby in payment of salary and twenty more for other money owed him.[22]

More often, the Royal Society rewarded those who contributed to knowledge or furthered its own ends by excusing them from the payment of fees. On 21 November 1698 these included the treasurer; the secretaries; the professors of Gresham College, where the Society then met; Theophilus Grew, whose work on plant anatomy had already received the Society's support; James Petiver, notable for his promotion of botanical collection in America and elsewhere; John Ray, the premier English naturalist of the age; and a number of others.[23] The practice was apparently intended to be a regular one, as the Council voted shortly afterwards that "any person who Should inform the Society of any matters or observations whereby Natural knowledge may be improved, leaving Such observations in writing with the Secretary, Shall be repaid his charges. . . ."[24]

This would have been a rather expensive policy if it had been carried out in its entirety, but the practice continued. J. T. Desaguiliers was excused his payments from the beginning of his service to the Society.[25] Stephen Hales was excused his arrears and future payments in recognition of his statical experiments.[26] Mark Catesby was returned his bond for payments, not for his *Natural History of Carolina*, but for drawing cuts for the Register Book.[27] And so the practice continued, even though the Council grew more cautious as it appeared that this practice might weaken the Society's resources.

Given the nature of this patronage, there was a certain irony in the reaction of Peter Collinson, who was so deeply involved in the work of the Royal Society, to the first proposal by John Bartram in 1739 to establish a philosophical society in Philadelphia. He cautioned his American friend:

As to the Society that thee Hints att, Had you Sett of Lerned, Well Qualified Members to Sett out with, it might Draw your Neighbors to Correspond with you. Your Library Company I take to be an essay towards such a Society. But to Draw Learned Strangers to you, to teach Sciences, requires Salaries and good Encouragement; and this will require the Publick as well as proprietary assistance, which can't be at present complied with, Considering the Infancy of your colony.[28]

In fact, Collinson seems to have had a firmer grasp of Philadelphia realities than did his correspondents there. The American Philosophical Society, organized four years later, was patterned on the Royal Society and was active for less than a year in that first incarnation.[29] The model that Collinson chose for the

Philadelphians, however, was not the Royal Society but a continental academy. Perhaps he had in mind that of St. Petersburg, to which his friend Johann Amman, the Swiss-born physician who had helped Sir Hans Sloane order his collections, had gone as professor of botany.[30] It may have been that peripheral outposts of European culture required paid professorships to draw "learned strangers" to them.

Actually, the Royal Society of London through most of its seventeenth- and eighteenth-century history either could not or would not have supported such an extensive foundation.[31] The reasons were grounded first in necessity and second in precedent. The Crown provided little for monetary support for the Society or for science in general. Charles II, from whom support might have been expected, lacked resources to accomplish this end. The result for the Society was a great deal of freedom from royal control but also a condition of genteel poverty during most of this part of its existence. Genuinely in need for much of the late seventeenth century, it was then, as the situation eased, required to make considerable expenditure for its new home in Crane Court in 1710. In the period of its founding, the only result of appeals by the Society to Charles II for land for itself or offices for its fellows was the grant of Chelsea College. Similarly, in the case of the Royal Observatory at Greenwich, the benefactions of the Crown covered only the structure, and the Society had to lend its own instruments for the use of John Flamsteed, the Astronomer Royal.[32]

In the years that followed, the situation remained much the same. Royal patrons confined their grants to privileges rather than money. The exception was the frequent and generous use of naval vessels in the service of exploration and scientific discovery, Halley's voyage to the South Seas in the *Paramour* from 1698 to 1700 being the principal early example. In the same way, great trading companies, particularly the Hudson's Bay and East India Companies, lent their ships and the use of their posts for overseas scientific activities, including those sponsored by the Royal Society.

Not until the transits of Venus in the 1760s, however, was there significant royal support. In 1760 the Council successfully memorialized the Board of Trade to support the Society's observations of the next year.[33] More ambitious proposals to view the transit of 1769 required much greater subvention. The Council's memorial to George III was based both on patriotism and also on need, asserting "that the Royal Society are in no Condition to defray this Expence, their annual Income being scarcely sufficient to carry on the necessary business of the Society."[34] Preparation for this great venture coincided with a major financial crisis. Emanuel Mendez da Costa, who had been engaged by the Society because of his work with fossils and ores, his linguistic ability, and his close connections with the natural history circle, had embezzled nearly £1,500 in dues and other fees. Benjamin Franklin, who sat on the Council through these events, alleged that the Society's need was due to the theft by "a wicked Jew, entrusted as our Clerk and Collector, . . . " but, given the past record of the Society, there is no reason to suppose that it would have expended large sums of its own on the project.[35] The grant, a munificent £4,000, was not spent entirely on the transit expedition, and a part of the remainder ultimately was used to pay Charles Mason for his measurement of the attraction of mountains in Perthshire.[36]

The relationship of the Royal Society to science in the American colonies was determined by its own habits and expectations and by the attitudes of the better and middling parts of the English social order who constituted its fellowship. Although it was in a poor position to provide direct patronage, it could give other forms of encouragement. The Society was interested in the New World from the very beginning, as was evidenced in part by Winthrop's election as a charter member, and that interest persisted throughout the period. The second volume of the *Philosophical Transactions* contained "Inquiries for Virginia and the Bermudas," relating principally to natural history, as might be expected of lands still in the process of discovery.[37] The Society was also liberal in distributing instruments overseas, even in its difficult early years. When, in 1673, Nehemiah Grew reported to the Council that a Mr. Mannering was going to the Indies, it "undertook to have Barrometers sent to the Indies and the Barbados with full Directions for the use of them and to procure an Account from thence of what Observations should be made."[38]

Direct subsidy of overseas activities in America or elsewhere by the Royal Society acting corporately was rare before the middle of the eighteenth century, at least as indicated in the Council Minutes. In January 1698/99 the Society, in an unusual action, authorized Hans Sloane to subscribe £20 to encourage a voyage by William Vernon to the Canary Islands.[39] Vernon had already served many of the fellows, who had subscribed privately, as a collector in Maryland. A little more than six months later, however, the members of the Society gave only verbal support to one of their former servants, Jezreel Jones, "as a fit person to make discoveries in Africa." They lacked sufficient money or stock to subscribe financially.[40]

The major instance of direct financing by the Society of a scientific project in America occurred in 1765, when the Council authorized the expenditure of £200 for the measurement of a degree of latitude in Pennsylvania by Charles Mason and Jeremiah Dixon, with an additional £40 for passage to England if it were needed. It is unlikely that this support would have been forthcoming had Mason and Dixon not been on the site to survey the division between the Penn and Calvert proprietaries.[41]

A quarter century before, James Alexander of New York had presented an ingenious proposal to the Society to utilize the frozen surface of the Hudson River, with its nearly northerly course to Albany, for such a measurement. Alexander, who was a lawyer, merchant, land speculator, surveyor, and sometimes amateur astronomer, was, after Cadwallader Colden and perhaps before him, the most capable natural philosopher in New York during the first half of the eighteenth century. The Society requested Peter Collinson, who had communicated the letter, to inform Alexander that a measurement in a middle latitude would be of no use in determining the shape of the earth.[42] They did not say that it would also be expensive unless surveyors were already there. Alexander, however, was like many other colonials in wanting assistance from the Society. As the most active member of and surveyor general for the proprietors of East Jersey, who had long been in conflict with New York over their common boundary, Alexander knew that an observation bearing the Society's approval would have fixed the boundary's eastern terminus.[43]

One alternative to the direct patronage of science at home or in the colonies might have been the creation of some sort of premium fund, such as was ultimately established by the London Society of Arts. That organization, dedicated to more immediate and practical ends than was the case with the Royal Society in the eighteenth century, aroused tremendous interest in the American colonies in the rather brief time between its founding and the American Revolution. The explanation may lie in part in its concern for agricultural and mechanical improvements, but its premiums also attracted American correspondents. Certainly the Society of Arts provided another ideal for American organizations promoting the arts and sciences in addition to and sometimes in conjunction with that provided by the older London institution.[44]

The idea of establishing a premium fund was considered by the Royal Society but was rejected, probably because the Society's aims and devices were already too well established. In 1738 Sir Hans Sloane read a proposal from the president's chair submitted by a Dr. Peck that concerned raising a stock of £1,000 "for the Encouragement of Arts and Sciences." The Council agreed that they "cannot as a Society Assist in the Establishment of Such a Foundation: nor will they give any interruption to the design of any other Society which the Proposer now seems to be in hope may be formed thereon."[45] Certainly the Royal Society did not hinder the organization of the Society of Arts in 1753, and, in fact, many of its leading members, including Stephen Hales, Henry Baker, and John Ellis, were active in the affairs of both organizations. Other fellows of the Royal Society, such as Peter Collinson, actively promoted its objectives.[46] In spite of assertions to the contrary, neither the Society's Minute Book nor its *Philosophical Transactions* give any indication of hostility between "pure" and "applied science." The practical concerns of many of its fellows continued even after the founding of the younger organization.

The Royal Society fostered colonial science in less tangible ways, or at least in ways that were less direct than monetary rewards. It is difficult to measure the influence of the *Philosophical Transactions*, its abridgments, or, after the 1730s, the excerpts from it which were published in the *Gentleman's Magazine*. Nonetheless, it is apparent that the *Transactions* themselves circulated far beyond the libraries of American fellows and the few other philosophical gentlemen who subscribed to them.[47] The *Gentleman's Magazine* reached a larger audience, particularly because colonial newspapers borrowed from it so freely. In a very real sense, the *Transactions* provided the source for English and European science in America.

The journal varied in quality, depending upon the degree of activity of the Society and upon the competency of the editors. The first publication in 1665 was a private venture by the secretary, Henry Oldenburg, although it was licensed by the Society and required review by some additional fellows.[48] The *Transactions* remained in the hands of successive secretaries until 1752, when, following the death of Cromwell Mortimer, the last proprietary editor, and a scandalous libel by "Sir" John Hill, a talented hack and unsuccessful candidate for fellowship, the Society assumed responsibility for its publication.[49] The *Philosophical Transactions* provided, at best, an uneven tutelage of American science and may have been responsible for some of its weaknesses. Even so, as the original learned journal of the English-speaking world, it was the obvious model for early *Transactions* and *Memoirs* published in America.

While the *Philosophical Transactions* provided an example for American activity, the correspondence and patronage of officers and fellows of the Royal Society had a far more direct impact. Certainly the secretaries were expected to maintain a wide philosophical correspondence, and sometimes they did. Henry Oldenburg, who served in that capacity from the time of the second charter in 1663 to his death in 1677, established a vast network of intelligence that reached America peripherally, at least.[50] Few of his successors could match the range of his correspondence, although some were active in seeking or maintaining contacts in North America and the West Indies. Richard Waller, who held the office (except for one year) from 1687 to 1714, renewed the Society's correspondence with the Reverend John Clayton in Virginia, sought returns from Jamaica, and was the recipient of a part of Cotton Mather's "Curiosa Americana."[51] Dr. James Jurin, during his tenure in the 1720s, maintained contacts with a number of New Englanders. Mather, Thomas Robie, Zabdiel Boylston, Benjamin Colman, Isaac Greenwood, and Paul Dudley transmitted their communications to the Society through his hands. Similarly, the efforts of Dr. John Lining of South Carolina to relate climatic conditions with epidemic diseases were sent to Jurin.[52]

A part of Jurin's Massachusetts correspondence was continued after 1730 by Cromwell Mortimer, who also added some minor contacts in Maryland. Zabdiel Boylston together with Isaac Greenwood, the first Hollis Professor of Mathematics and Natural Philosophy at Harvard College, and his successor in that chair, the third John Winthrop to become F.R.S., wrote to him.[53] Paul Dudley continued to send "such Curiosities as I meet with and think worthy of [the Society's] notice," although he could not comply with a suggestion by Mortimer that might have altered greatly the relationship of science in Old and New England. He wrote: "I dare not encourage the Society with any prospect, at least on my part, of setting up a company here subservient to the Royal Society. My poor State of health, with other necessary avocations, will render it impracticable for me to undertake a thing of that consequence."[54] Despite the fact that the suggestion was Mortimer's, it would seem that much of the correspondence of the secretaries with America was initiated in America, or, at least, that New Englanders chose to deal with the Royal Society through formal channels.

Most of the letters and papers that reached the Society from America, and much English patronage of science on that continent, resulted from the private efforts of fellows who sought to enlarge their collections or who simply acted out of generosity and friendship. Admittedly, it is sometimes difficult to ascertain the division between private concerns and those of the Society. The correspondence of Sir Hans Sloane was due in part to his service as secretary, vice-president, and, from 1727 to 1741, president of the Royal Society and to his similar importance in the College of Physicians; but it was also the result of his endless concern for the collection of all kinds of rarities.[55] In the main, private concerns predominated, although for some fellows, if not for Sloane, reputations could be built and even the fellowship itself acquired by a philosophical correspondence with America or other remote parts.

Through the late seventeenth century and the early years of the eighteenth, a number of energetic patrons assisted collection in America. Henry Compton, Bishop of London, played an important, if somewhat obscure, role. His promotion of collectors in Maryland has already been noted, and as the diocesan for North America he was in a strong position to assist "botanizing parsons," the first effective naturalists in Virginia; the clerical collectors, John Clayton and John Banister, were prime examples.[56]

The Temple Coffee House Botany Club, a loose association of naturalists, most of them members of the Royal Society, met from 1689 to about 1720. Its members frequently associated with Compton in American ventures and included a number of men who sometimes shared their returns with the Society, particularly Sir Hans Sloane, Martin Lister, and James Petiver.[57] Petiver was particularly active in American correspondence and occasionally in patronage. In the three decades before his death in 1718, the London apothecary received scientific intelligence from at least eighty residents and itinerants.[58]

The last great effort of those associated with this group was the promotion of Mark Catesby's collection in Carolina and the Bahamas between 1722 and 1725. The principal promoter was William Sherard, a talented botanist who had spent long years in the Levant. He was joined by Sloane, Charles Dubois, F.R.S., and others who had previously been active in the club.[59] In a sense, those travels which produced the *Natural History of Carolina* marked an end to the period in which American collection was dominated by English itinerants rather than by those with more permanent colonial ties.

Certainly there were other fellows, earlier and later, who provided links between the Royal Society and the colonies. John Woodward was the recipient of many of Cotton Mather's communications, and, much later, John Ellis was responsible for Alexander Garden's tie with the Society and also his profitable introduction to Linnaeus.[60]

During the middle years of the eighteenth century, however, when the colonies had achieved a degree of maturity, their traffic with the Society passed largely through the hands of one man. To a considerable degree Peter Collinson can serve as a symbolic focus of the Anglo-American scientific relationship.

At first glance, Collinson seems an unlikely candidate for a philosophical broker. "Citizen and Mercer," he was a Cockney Quaker with little education and only moderate wealth.[61] He minded his counting house between October and March or May, and at the same time maintained a correspondence that reached from Philadelphia to Peking. At heart, though, Collinson was a gardener who sought to domesticate exotic plants in England. He complained in 1729, "It is needless to tell thee with what Industry I have cultivated Friendships and Acquaintance with the principal Men of North America att some pains and expence to Engage them to Comply with what I may call Triffles, because of no Value to them. And yett So many Excuses is on their Side that it is but Seldome that I can obtain the favour of a little parcell of their Country Seeds."[62]

Up to this time, his best source of American materials had been Mark Catesby, whose travels he had assisted. Possibly through his aid to Catesby, and because of his growing reputation as a collector, Collinson moved into the circle of Sir Hans Sloane, who helped secure his election as F.R.S. in 1728. He was an active participant in the affairs of the Society until his death forty years later, serving fourteen years on its Council. Most of Collinson's own contributions to the Society were trivial, even at a time when many minor curiosities found their way into the pages of the *Philosophical Transactions*, but his real service to the Society lay in forwarding its aim and activities.

In this, as in his horticultural activities, Collinson's fortunes improved when, in 1732, the directors of the Library Company of Philadelphia sent their first book order to London along with a bill of exchange drawn on him. This accident began a long career as unpaid buyer and unsolicited adviser to the Company. His most important gift to them was the glass tube that he sent, probably in 1745, along with an "Account of the new German Experiments in Electricity . . . and some directions for using it, so as to repeat those Experiments."[63] Collinson's own interests were best served by still another outgrowth of his relation with the Library Company—his long association with John Bartram's collections of plants and seeds. Yet he served science best by acting as gadfly and middleman in the events that secured the publication of Benjamin Franklin's *Experiments and Observations on Electricity*.[64] He acted in similar ways for other Americans, assisting in the partnership between John Clayton and J. F. Gronovius, which produced the *Flora Virginica* (Leiden, 1739-1743), and aiding in the publication of writings by John Mitchell, Cadwallader Colden, and James Logan.

On January 23, 1734/35, Collinson transmitted the first of James Logan's considerations of sexual generation in plants to the Royal Society. Captain Edward Wright, a shipmaster who carried many of Logan's transmissions to London, described the scene:

. . . I had the pleasure of hearing your discourse on Generation read before those Gentlemen, but it was very much abridged by Mr. [John] Machin, which in their language is call'd extracting the Quintescence of it. But how well they perform that operation I dare not take on me to say. But this I can, that dureing the time of its reading, there was two thirds of them imployed at disscusing a Germain cabbage and looking for the Small fibers in the root of an turnop. . . .[65]

The Journal Book gives no account of the vegetable experiments that so absorbed the attention of the fellows, but it does include a confused version of Logan's speculations, which questioned whether farina floated freely in the air on the grounds that such would be contrary to the economy of nature.[66] In a sense it was like much of the communication between the American colonies and the Royal Society in the eighteenth century. Though garbled and nearly unheard, it represented a shared concern in plant hybridization of British scientists on both sides of the Atlantic, and it passed through the hands of Peter Collinson. Logan's later and fuller account of plant reproduction was not even transmitted to the Society but was sent by Collinson to the Netherlands, where it was published by J. F. Gronovius.[67]

As was the case with Logan's work, much eighteenth-century American scientific writing of high quality reached an English and European public by means other than those available to the Society. Collinson directed most of Franklin's electrical letters to the printer rather than reading them to fellows. Similarly, he sent the most important products of Dr. John Mitchell's Virginia naturalizing to the Nuremberg academy rather than securing their publication in the *Philosophical Transactions*.[68]

As tutor, exemplar, and encourager to American science in the colonial period, the Royal Society undoubtedly had serious weaknesses. It could not have been otherwise, given the localized nature of almost all early academies and philosophical societies. Even so, it can hardly be argued that colonial science would have proceeded along the same lines if the Royal Society had not existed or if it had taken no interest in the New World. English science, and its provincial reflection in America, was shaped to a considerable degree by the principles and actions of that great Restoration institution. Certainly even those private fellows, who provided the link with North America more often than did the Society in its official capacity, learned much of what they transmitted across the Atlantic at the weekly meetings of the Royal Society in Crane Court.

NOTES

1. Otho T. Beall, Jr., "Cotton Mather's Early 'Curiosa Americana' and the Boston Philosophical Society of 1683," *William and Mary Quarterly* 18, ser. 3(1961): 370-72.

2. Benjamin Franklin to Michael Collinson, 8 February 1770, in *The Papers of Benjamin Franklin*, ed. William B. Willcox et al. (New Haven: Yale University Press, 1959-), 17 (1973): 65-66.

3. See the list in *The Record of the Royal Society of London* (London, 1940), pp. 375-428; Raymond P. Stearns, *Science in the British Colonies of North America* (Urbana: University of Illinois Press, 1970), p. 107.

4. Raymond P. Stearns, "Colonial Fellows of the Royal Society of London, 1661-1788," *Notes and Records of the Royal Society* 8 (1951): 178-246.

5. See George F. Frick and Raymond P. Stearns, *Mark Catesby* (Urbana: University of Illinois Press, 1961).

6. For Winthrop, see Robert C. Black III, *The Younger John Winthrop* (New York: Columbia University Press, 1966), and Richard S. Dunn, *Puritans and Yankees* (Princeton: Princeton University Press, 1962). Stearns, *Science in the British Colonies*, pp. 117-39, has the fullest treatment of his science.

7. See Pierre Marambaud, *William Byrd of Westover, 1674-1744* (Charlottesville: University of Virginia Press, 1971), pp. 77-91 passim; Stearns, *Science in the British Colonies*, pp. 280-86, 288-93.

8. Edmund Berkeley and Dorothy Smith Berkeley, *Dr. Alexander Garden of Charles Town* (Chapel Hill: University of North Carolina Press, 1969), pp. 36-39.

9. Stearns, *Science in the British Colonies*, p. 99. The first figure combines natural history, medicine, and meteorology. I have examined all of the pertinent volumes of the *Philosophical Transactions*.

10. Stearns, "Colonial Fellows"; *Dictionary of National Biography* and *Dictionary of American Biography*.

11. Raymond P. Stearns, "James Petiver, Promoter of Natural Science," *Proceedings of the American Antiquarian Society*, n.s., 63 (1953): 303-309.

12. Council Minutes 2:324, 20 October 1720 (copy), MS in Library of Royal Society, London, England.

13. Ibid., p. 151, 22 March 1698/99.

14. See Stearns, *Science in the British Colonies*, p. 93.

15. *Record of the Royal Society*, pp. 36-38.

16. R. K. Bluhm, "Remarks on the Royal Society's Finances, 1660-1768," *Notes and Records of the Royal Society* 13 (1958), pp. 99, 100, 102.

17. Sir Henry Lyons, *The Royal Society, 1660-1940* (Cambridge: At the University Press, 1944), p. 181.

18. *Record of the Royal Society*, pp. 95-96.

19. Ibid., pp. 29-30.

20. Council Minutes 2:293, 10 November 1714; ibid., 3:343-44, 30 November 1743.

21. *Record of the Royal Society*, p. 342.

22. See Council Minutes 2:86, 30 June 1686 and earlier; ibid., p. 94, 6 July 1687.

23. Ibid., p. 135, 21 November 1698.

24. Ibid., p. 144, 8 February 1698/99.

25. Ibid., p. 280, 15 July 1714.

26. Council Minutes 3:2, 4 January 1727/28; ibid., p. 49, 16 April 1730.

27. Ibid., pp. 137-38, November 1732; ibid., pp. 163-64, 30 April 1734.

28. Collinson to Bartram, 12 April 1739, in *Memorials of John Bartram and Humphrey Marshall*, ed. William Darlington (Philadelphia, 1849), pp. 128-33.

29. Brooke Hindle, *The Pursuit of Science in Revolutionary America* (Chapel Hill: University of North Carolina Press, 1956), pp. 67-74.

30. See Frick and Stearns, *Mark Catesby*, pp. 88-89.

31. See Bluhm, "Remarks on the Royal Society's Finances," pp. 82-103.

32. *Record of the Royal Society*, pp. 23-24, 33.

33. Council Minutes 4:228, 26 June 1760, and entries for the remainder of the year.

34. Ibid., p. 295, 15 February 1768.

35. Ibid., entries following p. 211, 3 December 1767; Franklin to Jean-Baptiste Le Roy, 14 March 1768, in Willcox, *Papers of Benjamin Franklin* 15 (1972): 82-83.

36. Council Minutes 6:207, 20 January 1774.

37. *Philosophical Transactions of the Royal Society* 2 (1667): 420-21.

38. Council Minutes 1:342, 10 December 1673.

39. Ibid., 2:140, 11 January 1698/99.

40. Ibid., p. 157, 19 July 1699.

41. Ibid., 5:33, 28 June 1764; ibid., p. 44, 25 October 1764; ibid., pp. 119-23, 17 October 1765; ibid., pp. 124-26, 24 October 1765; Thomas D. Cope, "Charles Mason, Jeremiah Dixon and the Royal Society," *Notes and Records of the Royal Society* 9 (1952): 55-78.

42. Journal-Book 17:192-93, 29 January 1740/41 (copy), MS in Library of Royal Society.

43. Henry N. MacCracken, *Prologue to Independence* (New York: J. H. Heineman, 1964) is an unsatisfactory biography of Alexander.

44. "The American Correspondence, 1755-1840," microfilm, Royal Society of Arts, London.

45. Council Minutes 3:217, 20 October 1738.

46. Lyons, *The Royal Society*, p. 182. For Collinson, see Royal Society of Arts Guard Book 2:70, MS in Royal Society of Arts; ibid., 3:80; ibid., 4:9, 93; ibid., 7:17; Royal Society of Arts Minute Book 3:138.

47. See Stearns, *Science in the British Colonies*, p. 151, for its early circulation in New England, and also *A Catalogue of Books Belonging to the Library Company of Philadelphia* (Philadelphia, 1741), p. 16.

48. Council Minutes 1:99, 1 March 1664/65.

49. John Hill, *A Review of the Works of the Royal Society of London* (London, 1751); Dorothy Stimson, *Scientists and Amateurs: A History of the Royal Society* (New York: H. Schuman, 1948), pp. 140-46.

50. See A. Rupert Hall and Marie Boas Hall, *Correspondence of Henry Oldenburg* (Madison: University of Wisconsin Press, 1965-).

51. Edmund Berkeley and Dorothy Smith Berkeley, *The Reverend John Clayton* (Charlottesville: University of Virginia Press, 1965), pp. 91-92, 122-29; Stearns, *Science in the British Colonies*, pp. 185, 367, 405-407.

52. Stearns, *Science in the British Colonies*, pp. 410-12, 420, 434, 437-38, 445-49, 463-68, 595-96.

53. Ibid., pp. 275-77, 439-40, 451, 646.

54. Dudley to Mortimer, 25 January 1736/37, Letter Book 23:286-87, Library of Royal Society.

55. See G. R. de Beer, *Sir Hans Sloane and the British Museum* (London; New York: Oxford University Press, 1953).

56. See Berkeley and Berkeley, *The Reverend John Clayton*, p. xxiii. Joseph Ewan and Nesta Ewan, *John Banister and His Natural History of Virginia* (Urbana: University of Illinois Press, 1970), pp. 63-71, are less certain of the degree of Compton's support.

57. See George Pasti, Jr., "Consul Sherard: Amateur Botanist and Patron of Learning, 1659-1728" (Ph.D. diss., University of Illinois, 1950), who discovered the group; Stearns, *Science in the British Colonies*, pp. 260-61.

58. Stearns, "James Petiver," pp. 291, 359-62.

59. Frick and Stearns, *Mark Catesby*, pp. 16-19.

60. Berkeley and Berkeley, *Dr. Alexander Garden*.

61. Norman G. Brett-James, *The Life of Peter Collinson* (London: E. G. Dunstan and Co., 1926) must be supplemented with Earl G. Swem, "Brothers of the Spade ... ," *Proceedings of the American Antiquarian Society* 68 (1948): 17-190, and by my sketch in *The Dictionary of Scientific Biography* (New York, 1971), 3:349-51.

62. Collinson to Thomas Story, 18 October 1729, MS in Thomas Story, *A Journal of the Life of . . .* (Newcastle upon Tyne, 1747), Library of Friend's House, London.

63. I follow J. A. Leo Lemay, *Ebenezer Kinnersley* (Philadelphia: University of Pennsylvania Press, 1964), pp. 49-51, in dating Collinson's gift.

64. Benjamin Franklin to Michael Collinson, 8 February 1770, in Willcox, *Papers of Benjamin Franklin*, 17 (1973): 65-66.

65. Wright to Logan, 12 March 1734/35, Yi 2, 741, fol. 9, Library Company of Philadelphia, Philadelphia, Pa.

66. Journal-Book, 15:70-74.

67. *Experimenta et meletemata de plantarum generatione . . . ,* (Leyden, 1739); *Experiments and Considerations on the Generation of Plants* (London, 1747).

68. *Acta Physico Medica Academiae . . . Leopoldina . . . Ephemerides* 8 (1748): Appendix, pp. 178-202.

The Underside
of the Learned Society
in New York,
1754-1854

BROOKE HINDLE

Even in the colonial period, New York was charged with lagging in its intellectual and cultural development, especially by comparison with Boston to the north and Philadelphia to the south. Evidences of this failing became more difficult to explain as the nineteenth century advanced and New York outstripped its rivals in all the material foundations for cultural achievement. It passed both cities in population, in commerce, and in wealth. As a matter of fact, it attained levels of creativity in several fields that destroyed the universality of the charge of cultural inferiority. (It came to excel, for example, in literature, drama, painting, music, aspects of natural history, several fields of technological innovation, and specialized periodical publication.) Despite these achievements, however, it failed notably to establish one of the primary eighteenth-century indices of intellectual maturity—a philosophical or general scientific society.

Philadelphia established the American Philosophical Society in 1769, the first permanent learned society in this country to publish a journal and gain a reputation among the learned societies of Europe. Boston saw the organization of the second society in 1780, the American Academy of Arts and Sciences. Elsewhere societies proliferated with many valuable results, but none acquired the luster of the first two and none of the others similarly regained in the twentieth century the large role that all of them lost somewhere in the nineteenth.

New York tried. It founded what was intended to be a general learned or philosophical society in two conspicuous failures. In 1784 the New York Society for Promoting Useful Knowledge was launched as a general scientific society, but never even began an effective life. The Literary and Philosophical Society of 1814 produced more of value and lasted longer, but it also died. Then, in 1817, the Lyceum of Natural History of New York immediately became an effective but specialized scientific society. But, by the time it was broadened in 1876 and renamed the New York Academy of Sciences, the learned society as a form had lost its vocation.

Why did New York fail to establish a learned society? It is no longer satisfactory to note that the differences between New York and the other cities were those of degree, that the similarities from city to city were enormous.

Inescapably, the differences noted by sensitive observers were significant. It is not enough merely to assert that New York was dominated by commercialism or that it lacked the force of cultural aspirations felt elsewhere. Persuasive as some of the explanations are, they beg the question; in fact, they pose answers constructed from the ingredients of the question itself. More fruitful are such issues as the ends to which New York devoted itself with effort and effect and the ends to which it adapted the form of the learned society. New Yorkers marched to a somewhat different rhythm and in somewhat different directions. To what purpose? With what results?

One analysis of the New York experience can be made in terms of models. New Yorkers did respond to the Royal Society and the Académie des Sciences models, but with less notable success than some of them had hoped. On the other hand, they poured energy into a great variety of organizations, in some of which they pioneered and reached realms of conspicuous success. Not infrequently, New York's leadership was found in enterprises that followed the methods, forms, and mood of the London Society of Arts rather than the Royal Society. Occasionally this response was conspicuously imitative; more often it represented a subconscious harmony of attitude. In both cases the Society of Arts is an appropriate model against which to view the New York effort.

The Society of Arts

"The Society Established at London for the Encouragement of Arts, Manufactures, and Commerce" was sometimes called the Premium Society but more often the Society of Arts. At its beginning in 1754, it was not properly a learned society at all, although in time it assumed most of the forms of the learned society, including hearing papers, publishing a journal, and seeking to advance knowledge. It was not the first organization of its kind, having been preceded by both French and Irish societies. The Société des Arts met regularly in Paris prior to 1723 and continued at least until 1733; the Dublin Society for Improving Husbandry, Manufactures and other Useful Arts began in 1731 and in 1749 became the Royal Society of Dublin.[1] However, the London Society of Arts became the model for men in Britain and her colonies who joined in groups to promote agriculture, arts, and manufactures. It also influenced societies that followed its success from France to Russia, where the Free Economical Society of St. Petersburg was founded, in imitation, by Catherine the Great in 1766.[2]

The primary purpose of the Society of Arts was to improve the practice of the arts, both the fine arts and the useful arts as they applied to agriculture and manufacturing, and to extend such improvements as would be economically beneficial. Its focus was on practice rather than on theory or principle, and in its early years it did not encourage papers even of the most practical sort. It was not, however, in any sense opposed to science, and, while its initial membership

---

[1] Notes to this chapter begin on page 113.

included prosperous craftsmen, several of its members also belonged to the Royal Society. The well-to-do membership supported the Society, anticipating that it would promote the application of science as well as the development of the best practice in ways that might be economically beneficial. The Society's emphasis upon production of economic advantage led it to seek to raise the quantitative output—sometimes with minimal concern for technique.[3]

The Society of Arts owed its origin to William Shipley, a Northampton drawing master who not only provided a broad vision, but gave the Society a twist reflecting his own background.[4] Arts, in the common understanding of the time, embraced not only the useful, mechanical, or practical arts but also the fine arts or "polite arts." Most of the societies that patterned themselves after the London Society of Arts did not follow that society in encouraging the fine arts, especially painting and drawing. Because of Shipley, however, the proto-type society gave much attention to these areas. It adopted rewards in the form of premiums as the most efficacious means of encouraging better practice in agriculture and manufacturing, and applied the same mode of encouragement to the fine arts, awarding premiums for the best paintings, drawings, and even sculptures in various announced categories. The philosophy behind the use of premiums for the improvement of both the fine and the useful arts—or technology—was indicative of a sense that both advanced in the same manner. The assumption was that creative improvement grew out of conscious efforts by talented practitioners to better their own previous work and the models of the best craftsmen in their field. Science and all other accesses to understanding were to be used, but the emphasis was not upon science.

Most of the meetings of the Society of Arts and its committees were occupied with the establishment of premiums to be offered and with their award. Premiums took the form of cash payments usually awarded for a specified quantity of each product—saltpeter, logwood, potash, for example—being encouraged. In this sense they paralleled the system of parliamentary bounties, which offered specified increments over the market price, sometimes for the same products. Premiums of the Society were offered both to English and colonial producers, usually on different products. At the same time some premiums were awarded on the basis of qualitative attainment—often in three-stepped levels of excellence. Another device used by the Society was the gold medal, voted for specific individual achievements or new methods. In addition to such terminal awards, the Society also intervened directly: by exchanging seeds, by sending a sawmill to America, and by dispatching agents to study technological problems.[5]

The Society of Arts in America

Because of its concern with commercial products and its specific interest in the empire's trade, the Society of Arts had a special interest in America. Each year certain of its premiums were earmarked for the colonies and sometimes separate lists of these offers were published. Both William Shipley and Peter Templeman, who succeeded Shipley as secretary of the Society, conducted extensive correspondence with such Americans as Alexander Garden. Shipley had a special relationship with Benjamin Franklin, and he saw fit to record in the Society's first Book of Minutes a copy of Franklin's 1743 American Philosophical Society proposal. This stood in the interesting company of three 1721 letters calling for a "Chamber of Arts, for the preserving and improvement of operative knowledge, the mechanical arts, inventions and manufactures."[6]

Through its premiums, the Society became well known to Americans, dispensing large sums of money for potash in Massachusetts, silk in Georgia, and viniculture in New Jersey. It was widely copied as a model, but each copy differed sharply in accord with perceived needs.

The Society of Arts reached out to the colonies in many ways. While it had no continuing journal until its *Transactions* began in 1783, it used several other periodicals prior to that time. The *Gentleman's Magazine* served as an early vehicle of news, the *Museum Rusticum* ran from 1764 to 1766, and in 1767 Robert Dossie's *Memoirs of Agriculture and other Oeconomical Arts* appeared. These were almost unofficial journals, yet they had some currency in the colonies. Special successes were recognized by the award of medals; Jared Eliot, for example, was given a gold medal in 1763 for his method of producing malleable iron from black sea sand.[7] The Society sent James Stewart to New England in 1763 and to Maryland in 1771 to promote the production of potash and other alkalis. Specific efforts to use science were made in two pamphlets analyzing American potash, one by Robert Dossie and the other by W. N. B. Lewis, both produced in 1767. Lewis was a kind of consulting chemist to the Society, a man more akin to a modern engineer and less concerned with theory for its own sake than with the uses of science for production.[8]

The first great enthusiast was Alexander Garden of Charleston. Before he knew of his March 1755 election to the Society of Arts, Garden wrote Shipley a long letter on the productions that might best be encouraged in South Carolina. He must have had an earlier letter from Shipley outlining the latter's plans for the Society. In any case, Garden's letter and accompanying seeds were received with great enthusiasm, and for several years he served the Society well. He had urged the encouragement of vines, cotton, cochineal, hemp, flax, and potash—all well matched to the Society's objectives. The Society urged him to experiment with the cochineal insect and to test its food; it sent him vine cuttings and established a premium on cochineal. Garden was asked to set up a botanical garden where products not native to Britain or the colonies might be grown and tested. He responded by sending back more seeds, geological specimens, buffalo licks, and several ideas. He suggested the establishment of separate cooperating societies in Georgia, South Carolina, Philadelphia, and New York. He went further by beginning to correspond with American acquaintances in other provinces; he also experimented with various dyes, and placed notices in the Charleston newspaper soliciting help. No organization resulted from these efforts, but he tried. As a naturalist, Garden demonstrated special responsiveness to the Society's efforts to promote products that might be grown in the southern colonies.[9]

Elsewhere, various organizational attempts were in some degree associated with the Society of Arts. The Virginia legislature in 1759 appointed a committee to encourage economic diversification, and some time later Governor Francis Fauquier opened a correspondence with the Society in a specific attempt to encourage products such as saltpeter, hemp, flax, and potash, which were favored by Virginia. In Boston a Society for Encouraging Trade and Commerce was founded in 1763, and the Manufactory House was reopened for a time. In 1771 a Society for Encouraging Manufactures sought to stimulate new productions in Charleston, and the Virginia Society for the Promotion of Useful Knowledge of 1774 is remembered almost solely for the medal it awarded for a new threshing machine.[10]

The Philadelphia response to the Society of Arts was one of the largest, but it did not proceed in a manner that might have been expected. Despite Franklin's early election to the Society and his friendship with Shipley, his activities were restricted to the time he spent in England. He made a fine gesture at the outset by contributing twenty pounds to be allocated for premiums awarded to Englishmen, rather than Americans, and he attended committee meetings of the Society when he could. It was not, however, on his initiative that Philadelphia acted upon the English model.

This occurred in 1766, when the "American Society, Held at Philadelphia, for Promoting and Propagating Useful Knowledge" was established. It developed out of the young Junto of 1750, which had patterned itself upon Franklin's 1727 Junto. Its 1766 plan is best viewed as an effort to fulfill the Society of Arts design in encouraging invention and the introduction of new agricultural products.[11]

The American Society was keyed to the same objectives that dominated the Society of Arts: "the Advancement of useful Knowledge and improvement of our Country."[12] Attention was directed to the improvement of agriculture, manufactures, and commerce—especially agriculture, which was to be studied to introduce the best products and to develop the best methods. The objective was to reduce "speculative Truths" to "practice."[13] It did not eschew astronomy and higher mathematics, but such pursuits were relegated to a secondary position.

The premium approach of the Society of Arts was followed in the granting of a £10 premium for the production of wine. Essays on a ship's pump, a file cutting machine, and a steam valve were received, in addition to others on medical and natural history topics. With the 1769 union that formed the American Philosophical Society, such practical efforts were subordinated—and gradually spun out of the Society into separate groups: the Silk Society in 1770 and the United Company of Philadelphia for Promoting Manufactures in 1775. After the Revolutionary War the process was extended in the formation of an agricultural society, a manufacturing society, a society for developing the steam-boat, and a medical society. Thus, the image of the Society of Arts gradually faded away and the American Philosophical Society became a proper learned society, in which knowledge was expected to prove useful but the ways of the artisan were not much noticed.

The First New York Society of Arts

New York achieved the closest copy of the London Society of Arts late in 1764 in the "Society for the Promotion of Arts, Agriculture, and OEconomy, in the Province of New York, in North America." As in Philadelphia the response was keyed to political and economic distress and did not make use of the personal intellectual channels that had provided the initial connections between New York and the Society of Arts.

Cadwallader Colden was the New Yorker first introduced to the Society of Arts. Alexander Garden wrote him about it in October 1755 and then forwarded an invitation from Shipley to join. No response from Colden survives, but occasional comments suggest that he favored the effort, and years later he did offer friendly advice.[14] Other New Yorkers learned of the Society through premium announcements carried in their own newspapers and in separate pamphlets. Some ran across occasional news of it in the *Gentleman's Magazine*, and a number competed for its premiums.

On November 29, 1764, the new organization was announced as a response to "the present deplorable State of our Trade." Its goal would be to "advance husbandry, promote manufactures, and suppress luxury."[15] A correspondence would be opened with the London Society of Arts to facilitate the collection of premiums offered New Yorkers; at the same time the New York Society would establish premiums of its own for desired products. It intended to encourage linen manufacture more directly, reprint pamphlets on producing various products, and stimulate experiments to discover what modifications might have to be applied to European techniques introduced into New York.

The gentlemen members, most of them merchants and professional people, divided themselves into committees on the arts, agriculture, schemes of economy, and correspondence. The committee of correspondence wrote the London Society as well as individuals on both sides of the Atlantic. It announced as the great purpose of the New York Society, "to encourage such Manufactures as will not interfere with those of England, and to promote such Growths and Productions as may best Answer for Returns to Great Britain."[16]

Although papers were not solicited, a few essays appeared under the auspices of the Society. The *New York Mercury* published two letters to the Society from Henry Guest, who urged the use of sole leather as a roofing material, asserting that it was lighter than slate, cheaper than shingles, not a lightning conductor, and ostensibly would last a century. It was to be applied in sheets, like copper, and in his second letter Guest decided to recommend painting the roof to ensure that it would last a thousand years. The Society received another paper on sheep raising and voted to publish extracts from it.[17]

The Society went no further; it made no effort to encourage the writing of even the most practical papers. In this respect, it was even less responsive to the techniques of the learned society than was the American Society in Philadelphia. It did seek practical improvements, but any experiments it stimulated were evaluated in terms of quality and quantity of produce.

It also established premiums for twelve categories of agricultural products and for twelve manufactured products, following the patterns of the Society of Arts and the even more widely familiar parliamentary bounty system. Most premiums were to be awarded for the greatest quantity produced, and in some cases second, third, fourth, and fifth awards were offered. They ranged from £5 to £30 on most items but went up to £150 for whale oil. The committee on the arts established premiums on potash, stockings, and cloth, all of which carried London Society of Arts premiums, too—with the difference that the New York Society encouraged linens instead of woolens. Also, tiles, slate, and various sorts of leather and shoes were listed. However, quality rather than simple quantity was the basis of the awards on shoes and dressed deerskins. The committee on agriculture posted premiums on hemp and flax, "two of our most natural Objects." Nevertheless, only an honorary medal was offered on hemp because it already enjoyed an £8 per ton parliamentary bounty, £20 from the New York legislature, and up to £100 from the London Society of Arts. Apple trees, cheese, mules, barley, and thorn hedges were also placed on the list. In total, £205 was offered for agricultural products and £464 for manufactures or processed items.[18]

Despite the acknowledged importance of iron, no premium was offered for its production because of preexisting encouragement by both Parliament and the Society of Arts and because the New York Society asserted that shortage of cash was the barrier to expanded output. New Yorkers were offered assistance in recovering premiums offered by the London Society. Those to which attention was called were on wine, sturgeon, hemp, and saltpeter.[19]

Recognizing that premiums alone could not establish the manufacture of linens, the Society made different and greater efforts. In harmony with its general approach, it offered a gold medal for each of the first three flax mills to be erected. Also, it instructed its committee on linen manufacture to procure fifty flax spinning wheels, two reels, two looms, and a reeler. The committee immediately advertised for the needed machines, and very shortly set in operation its own linen manufactory, under the direction of Obadiah Wells. With £600 at his disposal, Wells employed spinners and weavers until he had three hundred at work. The enterprise was countered by a letter from London asserting that the New Yorkers were too "infatuated with foreign trade" to make a success of manufacturing in competition with Silesia, Austria, Bohemia, and Russia. In the end it failed, but the factory did operate for at least eighteen months.[20]

Two spinning schools were associated with the factory, each pupil being furnished with a spinning wheel, a chair, and a reel. At one point thirty additional spinning wheels and ten reels were ordered, to be lent out to the poor. To facilitate sales, a market was opened and homespun much touted in the press. Even the governor wore homespun in public to encourage its production.

A somewhat similar approach was applied to potash production. A potash works was erected with the anticipated output of twenty-five tons a year, the first four hogsheads being sent to London in May 1765. The techniques of potash production were more of a mystery than those required for linen manufacture, and Americans in all the colonies were uncertain how to evaluate their product and how to improve it. The Society's committee of correspondence reported to London that it was uncertain whether its product was potash or pearl ash (a purer product) and that the London Society might offer more help by obtaining the proper valuation than by awarding premiums. Thus, the treatises on potash produced by Robert Dossie and W. M. B. Lewis answered a real need;[21] both described methods of production and suggested chemical tests to determine alkalinity, and both concentrated on the American production of potash.

Another pamphlet deemed of great value was Edmund Quincy's *Treatise of Hemp Husbandry*, published by order of the Massachusetts legislature. The New York Society did not enter hemp manufacturing directly, but it did import one hundred copies of the pamphlet and offered them for sale.[22]

The Society's market brought forth a number of manufactures not specifically solicited but well within its basic objectives. These included scythes, spades and shovels, liquors and cordials, and paper hangings. The market, in fact, was so successful that it was held every two weeks rather than monthly as originally projected.[23]

In March 1766 the Society reviewed New York's accomplishments and plotted a slightly different course. The varieties of encouragement of potash had produced promising results, sturgeon had been cured at Albany for the first time, trials in viniculture were anticipated, and the export of ship timber was anticipated. Its own premiums offered for the ensuing year, however, would encourage only linen, stockings, and women's shoes. Linen would not interfere with English manufactures, stockings needed bolstering to compete with Philadelphia, and women's shoes had to be improved in quality.[24]

The Society was aware that several of the premiums offered by the London Society would not provoke any response because of inadequate knowledge of techniques or inadequate financing. Its committee of correspondence, therefore, advised the London Society of Arts that it might best send over seeds and roots of desired products and publish annual reports of the "Experiments" conducted with them by Americans. This would be "the surest method of Introducing new Productions among us." At the same time and in the same spirit, the committee published in the newspaper a recipe for making potash as practiced in Hungary, Poland, and Germany.[25]

After the repeal of the Stamp Act, the Society declined. A large meeting in the city in 1767 appointed a committee that recommended the encouragement of woolens, worsted, cotton, linen, linsey-woolsey, paper, and glass—with the immediate reopening of the linen manufactory. A subscription to that effect was launched on December 29, 1767, and the newspapers applauded past efforts, but the new attempts did not gather momentum. Neither the town meeting's plan for encouragement of open competition with British manufactures nor the Society's milder approach was resumed. The last reported meeting of the Society was held in February 1768, at which time it referred various pieces of unfinished business to committee and awarded a gold medal to Philip Schuyler for a flax mill erected at Saratoga during the preceding year. Premiums for the year 1767 were the last awarded.[26]

The New York Society of Arts was dominated by efforts to develop profitable products as a means of benefiting New York trade. It was not motivated by the basic quest for knowledge. On the other hand, there was nothing antiscientific nor anti-intellectual about its work. Where science could be used, as in analyzing potashes, the Society was anxious to use it. More directly, it expressed a deep faith in the experimental method for developing new knowledge and it encouraged the experimental approach. It sought to make available the best knowledge through publication—the knowledge being practical, applicable understanding of technique and technology.

The General Learned Society vs. the Utilitarian

In New York as in the other cities, some men aspired to establish a society that would encourage useful knowledge and the experimental method but, more centrally, would seek to advance knowledge and understanding. The image of the Royal Society was strong in New York, and it was heightened by the success of the American Philosophical Society and the American Academy of Arts and Sciences. An effort to establish a parallel learned society could count on some of the same areas of support that sustained societies in the other American cities—notably the medical community, the college faculty, and the commercial and professional patrons who had sustained the Society of Arts.

The launching of such a society, however, was almost an accidental event. The precipitant was the visit of Dr. Henry Moyes to New York in 1784. Moyes, a Briton educated at Edinburgh, was giving scientific lectures to enthusiastic audiences in major American cities. Often referred to as "the blind philosopher," he penetrated the scientific circles in each of the major cities and left an institution behind him in the most responsive centers. In Boston he was largely responsible for the establishment of the Humane Society and in Philadelphia for the Dispensary. In New York he was appointed professor of natural history in the medical faculty of Columbia College, although he never occupied the chair.[27]

More important, it was Moyes who convinced many of his auditors to contribute a guinea each to a fund for founding a "society for the promotion of useful knowledge." This became the New York Society for Promoting Useful Knowledge, which began a hopeful career with monthly meetings held in 1785 and into 1786. Samuel Bard was responsible for lending Moyes's enthusiasm to this accomplishment, as he had been for much of the welcome extended to Moyes.[28]

Dr. Samuel Bard was exactly the man to lead a New York drive toward a philosophical society. In many ways the leader of the New York medical community, he had brought back from his student experience at Edinburgh the enthusiasm that produced the medical school by action of the trustees of King's College in 1767. It was Bard who inspired the campaign that culminated in the establishment of the New York Hospital, a movement that also led to a medical society with attributes of a learned society: the "Society for promoting the Knowledge, and extending the Usefulness of their Profession.[29]

Thomas Paine may have played a role too, for before Moyes's visit he wrote Lewis Morris advocating a philosophical society in New York. He voiced a not uncommon resentment of Philadelphia's success, asserting that "Pennsylvania, with scarcely anyone in it who knows anything of the Matter, except Mr. Rittenhouse and one or two more, is drawing to herself laurels and honors she does not deserve."[30] He did not, however, emerge as a leader of the Society, and no membership rolls survive to indicate his possible involvement.

One of the few things that can be said of the short-lived New York Society is that its officers were more prominent in public affairs than in science. George Clinton, Governor of New York, was elected president for 1785, while James Duane, Mayor of the city, and John Jay, Secretary of Foreign Affairs, served as vice-presidents. Samuel Bard, as secretary, was the active member of the group. He opened communications with other philosophical societies, wrote Benjamin Franklin informing him of his election to honorary membership, and tried to carry the enterprise forward. In 1789 he was elevated to a vice-presidency, while the other posts were given to governmental officials somewhat less prominent than the initial officers.[31]

The only recorded venture of the Society was in a distinctly utilitarian cause: a search for means of controlling the Hessian fly then ravaging wheat crops in the middle states. The Philadelphia Society for Promoting Agriculture, not the American Philosophical Society, attended to this matter in Philadelphia and solicited the aid of the New York Society. In response, Samuel Bard, "By Order of the Society," inserted notices in the newspapers requesting communications on the subject. One possible result was an article published in the New York *American Magazine* by Bard's former student, Samuel Latham Mitchill, recently returned from study at Edinburgh. With only this single sign of life, the Society expired; De Witt Clinton later said it "perished in embryo."[32]

Significantly, such interest as it did arouse was entirely in "practical" affairs or "useful knowledge," narrowly defined; at the same time, other societies were pursuing such objectives more effectively. Of these, three were of some importance: the New York Manufacturing Society, the Society for Establishing Useful

Manufactures, and the General Society of Mechanics and Tradesmen. None was significantly motivated toward the advancement of science, but each clearly reflected aspirations of the Society of Arts for "practical" and profitable improvement.

The New York Manufacturing Society was founded in 1789 in conscious imitation of the Pennsylvania Society for the Encouragement of Manufactures and the Useful Arts. Its two declared objectives were to aid the industrious poor and to reduce dependence upon European manufactures. As in the case of the first Society of Arts, scientists were nowhere to be found among its promoters, but merchants, securities speculators, bankers, brokers, lawyers, and gentlemen were in strong evidence. The initial chairman was Alexander Robertson, who soon became the largest stockholder of the Bank of New York. Other prominent members were Nicholas Low, Josiah O. Hoffman, Judge John Sloss Hobart (who was then president of the New York Society for Promoting Useful Knowledge), and that patron of all New York societies, John Pintard. The Society established a fund through subscriptions of £10, with which it introduced some linen manufacturing and also established a cotton textile factory. It is perhaps best known as Samuel Slater's first stop in this country, but his judgment proved correct: it was not properly developed to succeed. Sometime in 1792 the Society faded away. [33]

Although possessing patriotic and benevolent motives, the New York Manufacturing Society was fundamentally a business corporation and organized as such; the same may be said of Alexander Hamilton's Society for Establishing Useful Manufactures. The latter was founded in 1791 as a joint stock company with various forms of government support, designed as an instrument for fulfilling objectives stated in Hamilton's Report on Manufactures. The SUM attracted a similar group of businessmen and moved to establish a manufacturing center at the Great Falls of the Passaic. It too was deeply concerned with the transfer of technology—again in the quest of profits rather than learning. Although it succeeded only in part, much technological development was associated with it: first cotton textiles and then silk, but ultimately guns and locomotives were produced by its lessees.[34]

The General Society of Mechanics and Tradesmen was an altogether different sort of organization. It began in 1785 as a beneficial federation of master craftsmen in all the trades. Its initial efforts to obtain a charter were denied, and one was not granted until 1792, when the purposes stated were: (1) promoting trade and manufactures and (2) raising a fund to aid distressed members. In fact, the attention of the Society did turn heavily toward the promotion of manufactures, and, while purportedly nonpolitical, it sought to influence the legislature in favor of duties on the importation of manufactured goods. The organization had more in common with the Manufacturing Society and with groups of tradesmen and manufacturers in other cities than with the rank and file of workers. Yet in time it moved to establish an apprentices' school and library and to make some halting efforts toward assembling models and encouraging technological improvement by emulation; it continues to the present.[35]

The Second New York Society of Arts

The New York Society for the Promotion of Agriculture, Arts, and Manufactures, established in 1791, had enough of the attributes of the London Society of Arts that it may be regarded as another essay in that direction. In fact, in 1804 its major stem was renamed the New York Society for the Promotion of Useful Arts and was called the Society of Arts. In its earliest years, however, it was generally known as the Agricultural Society, because agriculture was its first and major focus of attention.

Organized in February 1791 and incorporated in March 1792, the Society enjoyed the most distinguished leadership and support. Robert R. Livingston, chancellor of the state, was the primary founder, the first president, and the apparent source of its vigor and success. When he left for Paris in 1800, the Society declined until his return, and he remained president until his death in 1813. His initial vice-president was Judge Hobart, who transferred his prestige from the presidency of the then deceased Society for Promoting Useful Knowledge, while Samuel Bard, the mainstay of the defunct organization, also became active in the new one. The rules and regulations of the Society were formulated by Livingston, Samuel Latham Mitchill, and Simeon De Witt, Surveyor-General of New York, and its initial membership of seventy-two was made up of gentlemen, among them large landholders and many active in New York government.[36]

The cultivated and well-to-do leadership of the second New York Society gave it a style and responsiveness to the forms of the learned society that had been less marked in earlier New York organizations. This was clearly demonstrated in its collection of papers and in its rapid issuance of a volume of *Transactions*, the first part of the initial volume appearing in 1792 and the final part in 1799. Overwhelmingly, the papers related to the improvement of agriculture in the patterns of the best English and American agricultural groups. Livingston was prominent in the first volume where he wrote on the use of lucerne and gypsum, the Society later claiming credit for introducing both of these items. On the use of gypsum as a fertilizer, Livingston disputed his claim to priority with Richard Peters of the Philadelphia Society for Promoting Agriculture. Mitchill, De Witt, Noah Webster, Ezra l'Hommedieu, later a president of the Society, and Pierre Delabigarre, Livingston's close neighbor, were among many other contributors.[37]

The plan of the Society required that it meet when the state legislature was in session at the site of that meeting. This intentionally coupled the Society to the government with many resultant benefits; for example, the legislature paid for the publication of its *Transactions*. As a result, it was transferred from New York City to Albany when the capital was moved in 1797. Since many of the leaders had business in the state capital as well as in New York City, the immediate impact was limited, but in time the Society contracted and took on an Albany cast. The initial plan established a secretary for each of the senatorial districts charged with convening local members for inquiries into agriculture and manufactures and with forwarding resulting papers for presentation to the Society. Samuel Bard, for example, from his Dutchess County seat, was able to assume the post of secretary for the middle district, while David Hosack served for the southern district. In essence, this was a private state agricultural body with access to state funds and erected upon a federation of local units.

The organizational plan impressed members so much that in 1802 an effort was made to extend it to the national scene by creating a federation of American societies seeking to promote "Arts and Sciences." The objective was to collect and put to use all "experiments and improvements" issuing from general learned and scientific societies, such as the American Philosophical Society, with which the New York Society sought to associate itself. Each member group was asked to appoint delegates to meet together in Washington when Congress was in session. Enough did so to produce the American Board of Agriculture in 1803, an effort that soon failed.[38]

The society of arts mechanism, the premium, was applied effectively. In 1807 a premium in the form of silver plate was awarded for specimens of cloth woven from domestic wool, and in 1808 the legislature gave the New York Society responsibility for awarding premiums established by the state. Woolen cloth was the first product to be encouraged, but others were later added. Papers came before the Society on such subjects as bridges, a hydraulic ram, steel, and an analysis of a bell. The Society also sought to promote a geological survey for the purpose of finding coal, and it authorized the collection of a cabinet of minerals.[39]

At heart, however, it remained an agricultural society and hewed to an image designed by gentlemen farmers. Its papers and publications reported primarily the results of experimental farming by this group. Some findings were influential, but the usual commentary, that the Society lacked means for reaching out to the dirt farmer, is valid.

One of the strongest threads woven into New York's organized efforts to improve the practice of the arts was contributed by Elkanah Watson and his Berkshire Agricultural Society. In 1810 Watson introduced the first Berkshire Fair, an approach he heralded as a critical innovation responsible for solving the outreach problem. Through the mechanism of the local fair, better methods in farming practice could be directly communicated to the dirt farmer; moreover, through the associated mechanism of emulation, stimulated by premiums or prizes, the farmer could be cajoled into using better methods and even into discovering them.

The fair was an ancient rite, the market fair having long served fundamental needs. Its importance as an opportunity for the sale or exchange of goods had declined in modern times, but upon these roots were engrafted the art exhibition, the industrial exhibition, and the agricultural fair. In the development of the first two, the London Society of Arts played a central part. In England it has asserted claim to introducing the first art exhibition, in 1760, and an even stronger claim to the inauguration of exhibitions of manufactures the following year.[40] However, in the rise of the modern industrial exhibition, the agricultural fair is much more important than historians have recognized. This was especially true in the United States, where the effective story begins, as Elkanah Watson insisted, with him.

Watson, a native of Massachusetts and a businessman in places as diverse as Rhode Island, North Carolina, and France, settled in 1789 in Albany where he succeeded very well. In 1807 he retired to Pittsfield, Massachusetts, to engage in farming, seeking to introduce the best practices in developing sheep farming and wool manufacturing. His first effort at organization was a cattle fair including a parade of the local farmers with their cattle; it was followed by the incorporation of the Berkshire Agricultural Society. At the fair of the following year, Watson introduced manufacturing as well. He paraded two floats, one with looms and a spinning jenny manned by English artisans, and the other carrying American machines. Thus contemporary expectations of the harmony of farming and manufacturing were demonstrated.[41]

This conjunction of farming and manufacturing was a customary attribute of early agricultural societies and fairs. Societies not infrequently combined the two objectives in their names, as did, for example, the New York Society for the Promotion of Agriculture, Arts, and Manufactures; even the Society of Arts form preserved the combination within the envelope of arts. One widely publicized event held the same year as Watson's initial fair was Chancellor Livingston's sheepshearing at Clermont. Watson himself attended, as did Samuel Latham Mitchill, Colonel David Humphreys (a leading Merino sheep advocate), and other notables. The wool sheared there from 196 ewes was immediately sold to manufacturers, and the double objective was stated in two signs: "Success to Agriculture" at one end of a long table, and, at the other end, "Success to Manufactures."[42]

The influence of the Berkshire system upon New York was promoted by Watson's return to the state in 1816. Thus began the county agricultural society and fair movement in New York, Watson aiding in the organization of an Otsega County Fair at Cooperstown that very year. Almost immediately he was called upon to lend a hand in fairs introduced in Jefferson, Oneida, Schoharie, Montgomery, Rensselaer, and New York counties.

Enthusiasm rose rapidly, capturing the immensely important advocacy of De Witt Clinton, then governor of the state. Clinton carried the county agricultural society movement another step in 1819 when he proposed aid to the county societies and the establishment and support of a state agricultural society, plus a model farm, to be located near Albany under a professor of agriculture who would supervise continuing experimentation. The legislature declined to underwrite the farm, but did provide remarkable support for the organization of agricultural societies in New York; the structure built upon and fulfilled the 1791 plan of the New York Society for the Promotion of Agriculture, Arts, and Manufactures by federating county societies under a state society. In fact, in 1815 the Society had urged such a program and it now supported it vigorously.[43]

The new legislation provided an annual fund of $10,000 to be made available to county agricultural societies on a matching grant basis, for the purpose of sustaining a vigorous premium program at the county fairs. A specific portion was earmarked for each county, New York receiving the largest amount—$650. In place of a state agricultural society, a Board of Agriculture was to be constituted, made up of representatives of the county societies. Each premium recipient was required to write a description of his device or methods, and the county society president was to forward such papers to the Board of Agriculture, which would meet annually and publish those regarded favorably in an annual volume distributed to the people of the state. This the state would finance as it had the *Transactions* of the Society for the Promotion of Agriculture, Arts, and Manufactures.[44]

Because it took a while to organize the board, Elkanah Watson stepped into the breech. He wrote and published in 1820 his *History of the Berkshire Agricultural Society*, which was distributed as a kind of handbook for organizing the county societies. While still in Pittsfield, Watson kept up a correspondence with the county societies and sent them seeds he had begun to collect from abroad. He had in mind distributing animals and farm implements also, but support for this never materialized.[45]

County societies with their annual fairs multiplied until they existed in fifty-two of New York's fifty-eight counties. In addition, the Board of Agriculture began to publish its *Memoirs*: since hardly any papers were yet in hand, the first volume in 1821 consisted largely of a synthetic treatise put together by G. W. Featherstonhaugh, secretary of what had then become known as the Society for Promoting Useful Arts. A second volume of papers was issued in 1823, but after that the legislative requirement of an annual volume was rescinded and the third and last volume was printed in 1826. Legislative support of the entire program also came to an end in 1826, and the county societies declined in vigor like deflating balloons.[46]

A curious thing then happened to the Society for Promoting Useful Arts, the primary thrust of which had been the promotion of agriculture. The great state program of county societies under the Board of Agriculture took over the agricultural role previously filled by the Society. Stephen van Rensselaer, formerly vice-president of the Society for Promoting Useful Arts, became president of the Board of Agriculture, and other active members also gave strength to the new system. In 1824 the Society for Promoting Useful Arts merged with the recently established Albany Lyceum of Natural History to form the Albany Institute. The Society became one of the three departments of the Institute, namely the Department of Physical Sciences and the Arts. In this step, it emphasized a minor science component in its background, and eventually came to resemble more distinctly a learned society. It also abandoned its role as a state society with strong New York City roots and became a local Albany enterprise.[47]

Thus, the Society for the Promotion of Agriculture, Arts, and Manufactures (later called the Society for the Promotion of the Useful Arts) was extraordinarily successful. Initially effective because of the wealth and political power of its promoters and patrons, it developed forms that were capable of translating its aspirations into positive action. The fusion of the society of arts concept, especially of premiums designed to provoke emulation, with the Berkshire fairs and the support of the state treasury produced the spectacularly successful New York county agricultural societies, county fairs, and the state Board of Agriculture with its own annual fairs, and ultimately a set of transactions. The system broke down when state support, extended in 1819, was permitted to come to an end in 1826. However, this was a renewable process. The mere establishment of a state agricultural society in 1832 was not of any importance, but the restoration of state financial support in 1841 made all the difference. Then, not only agriculture but manufactures and the arts benefited and were encouraged in the same way—the way of the societies of arts.

The importance of government support can scarcely be overemphasized, and the direction in which that support pointed was almost equally important. A truism usually accepted is that government support encouraged the manifestly useful and balked at supporting basic science not directed toward utilitarian goals. Such was the nature of New York's support for agricultural premiums, and well after the restoration of funds, the state agricultural society met rebuff in seeking support for a college directed toward improving agriculture and the arts. Much earlier, the support for college professorships, conspicuously provided by New York State in 1791, had resulted in an unusually utilitarian twist exemplified by Samuel Latham Mitchill's title: "Professor of Natural History, Chemistry, Agriculture and Other Arts Depending Thereon."[48]

The New York Institution for the Promotion of the Arts and Sciences

New York State support for nonutilitarian institutions, especially for learned societies that sought the general advancement of knowledge, must be weighed at this point. The generalization that governments of this era extended little support for anything but utilitarian enterprises requires some amendment. Clearly, the rise of county agricultural societies resulted from remarkable state support, as did the inauguration of a vigorous state agricultural society; the vitality of the American Institute also rested in part upon state funding. New York State support of this sort was unusual, and it was critical. It will not do, however, to assume that in New York useful societies flourished because of government support while basic learned societies languished for lack of it.

The New York Institution for the Promotion of the Arts and Sciences is virtually unique as an instance of government support for institutions not dominated by utility. Established in 1816, the Institution was fundamentally a building in which rent-free space was made available by the city to several societies dedicated to the advancement of one or more of the arts and sciences. It reflected a belief in the interrelationships of the arts and sciences, especially of the fine arts with the basic sciences.

In common with other cities, New York had earlier provided space for cultural institutions, and, indeed, it was the demolition of Government House in 1815 that deprived three societies of such support. Housed there at the time were the New-York Historical Society, the American Academy of the Fine Arts, and the recently formed Literary and Philosophical Society of New York. John Pintard produced little immediate effect when he urged upon the mayor the opportunity for fostering "the Arts, Science & Literature" by housing a number of cultural institutions in the soon-to-be-evacuated almshouse or in Bridewell. De Witt Clinton first branded the idea "too impudent to be submitted to the corporation," but, as he thought about it, he became an advocate, and carried it through to resounding success.[49]

The Common Council of the city voted the requested support on the plea that "The Citizens of New York have too long been stigmatized as phlegmatic, money making & plodding—our Sister Cities deny we possess any taste for the sciences." It caught the vision of an "Institute of the elegant fine & liberal arts," which would include an athenaeum or general reading room; a professorship of mineralogy and natural history; a school for painting, sculpture, and architecture; an astronomical observatory with associated lectures; a chemical laboratory with an enlightened professor; and a hall for discourses and debates.[50]

Specifically, the Common Council sought to encourage and disseminate learning and taste—not to cultivate the useful and mechanic arts. It denied the essence of one petition asking support for a society for the encouragement of arts, manufactures, and commerce and for lectures in chemistry, mechanical philosophy, agriculture, and botany. Agriculture, manufactures, and technology were not to be encouraged here—although, uninvited, some of them nevertheless gained entrance.[51]

First and last, a wide range of societies and institutionalized individuals was accommodated in the New York Institution. Initially admitted were the Historical Society, the Academy of Fine Arts, the Literary and Philosophical Society, and the Society Library—although the Library declined to move in when it was unable to sell its own building advantageously. John Scudder's American Museum was granted the largest amount of space, and John Griscom's chemical laboratory was accommodated. The United States Military Philosophical Society was a ghost in the halls of the Institution, for it never occupied the space provided. On the other hand, the Lyceum of Natural History of New York moved in shortly after its founding in 1817 and flourished. Years later, organizations with little claim to learning were also admitted: the Institution for the Instruction of the Deaf and Dumb, the Savings Bank, and the Society of

Shipwrights and Caulkers—the last institution required to preserve and exhibit models of naval architecture. John Vanderlyn was not given rooms but was permitted to build a rotunda on nearby city land for the display of his paintings.

The New York Institution embodied a strong sense of the interrelationships of cultural and learned societies, and it promoted them. In New York as in other cities, there was a remarkable overlap in membership, and especially in leadership of the societies. New York led, however, in associating the fine arts with science and with the practical arts. This too can be seen in the New York Institution.

Of course, all of the older institutions had diffuse and general objectives, which tended to sharpen as institutions with more limited purposes arose. The Historical Society was concerned with natural history as well as with civil, ecclesiastical, and literary history, and although it divested itself of its natural history cabinet in 1829, it balanced this loss with an increased concern for the fine arts. The Literary and Philosophical Society embraced the practical arts as well as the natural sciences, literature, and history. Science was its central objective, however, and in this it could not compete effectively with the more specialized Lyceum of Natural History. Still, when the *American Monthly Magazine* ran notices of "Transactions of Learned Societies" in 1817, natural history emerged as the dominant activity of each of these three societies. In addition, Scudder's American Museum was primarily a natural history museum.[52]

Despite its emphasis on science and its nonutilitarian intention, the New York Institution's sensitivity to technology was remarkable. Some of this may have followed from the accident of personal involvement, as evidenced in the important roles played by the painter-inventors, Robert Fulton and Samuel F. B. Morse. Strikingly, also, Robert R. Livingston was the man primarily responsible for the founding of the American Academy of Fine Arts, over which he presided at the same time that he served as president of the New York Society for the Promotion of Agriculture, Arts, and Manufactures. A little later, De Witt Clinton, best known for his encouragement of technological development in the form of the Erie Canal, served concurrently as president of both the Historical Society and the Literary and Philosophical Society.

Indeed, one of Clinton's most curious performances was the address he gave to the Academy of Fine Arts when it moved into the New York Institution in 1816. Clinton had been almost solely responsible for reviving the Academy, but, instead of setting before it reasonable objectives in the realm of art, he made a few passing references to art and then devoted the evening to the introduction of the steamboat by Livingston and Fulton. Even more significant was the only joint meeting of the Academy, the Historical Society, and the Literary and Philosophical Society—held in 1817 to hear a eulogium on Fulton by one of the leading defenders of his steamboat contributions, Cadwallader David Colden.[53]

The New York Institution unquestionably supplied critical government support to several cultural organizations, but it did not serve to overcome New

York's deeper concern with practical technology and the improvement of the economy. The Institution succeeded in reviving the American Academy of Fine Arts, but it failed to revive the United States Military Philosophical Society, which was beyond such efforts at resuscitation. It certainly extended the life of the Literary and Philosophical Society and kept it going until the demise of the New York Institution itself in 1830. It made the Historical Society more effective, although the $5,000 legislative grant to aid the Historical Society, obtained by Clinton, proved an even more essential support. Finally, the Lyceum of Natural History grew more remarkably than any other society in the Institution—and it was the only one wholly removed from interest in mechanical technology.[54]

The Practitioners' Societies

In the second and third decades of the nineteenth century, there arose a need to reach out with useful knowledge to groups not deeply involved in earlier efforts led by the more favored elements of society. The need was first felt in farming, where it was a conspicuous part of the Berkshire movement. Farmers were more individualistic and more isolated than artisans or mechanics; the learned societies of gentlemen farmers were understandably ineffective in influencing farming. By contrast, manufacturing societies of the same character could more reasonably hope to influence manufacturing without a great outreach effort. In the 1820s, however, the effort to reach out escaped the farming communities, and new sorts of societies were invented with the diffusion of knowledge more central to their effort than it had been even in the old societies of arts. All still professed the desire to develop new knowledge, stimulate invention, and even discover principles.

The new people's societies are generally understood in terms of the concept of the rise of the common man, and they are intimately associated with familiar educational reforms. The lyceums, mechanics institutes, athenaeums, and apprentices' libraries of the 1820s were primarily concerned with education, and they fed the public school movement. The atmosphere surrounding these efforts not only produced new institutions but created tension and change within the old ones.

The first response by New York mechanics came within the old General Society of Mechanics and Tradesmen, which established an apprentices' library and a school in 1820. The following year it received legislative authority to operate the two, and in November 1821 it formally inaugurated what it called "the Mechanics Institution." The school was intended to serve children of members and continued until 1858, when the establishment of public schools eliminated the need. The apprentices' library began with a small collection of four hundred books but grew into a general library and continues to the present. Even though correctly regarded by historians as an elitist society of entrepreneurs and master mechanics, this group did reach out in the spirit of the felt needs of the time.[55]

The first new institution to emerge within this context was the New York Mechanic and Scientific Institution. It was a people's society cast in the form of a society of arts, that is, in the form of a utilitarian learned society. The organization was chartered in 1822 "for the purpose of instructing and maintaining scientific and practical lectures applicable to the arts, and for collecting and forming a repository of machinery, tools, and generally for enlarging the knowledge and improving the conditions of mechanics, artisans, and manufacturers." John Griscom served as first chairman of the lecture committee, and successful lecture series were instituted. In 1824 the Institution sponsored a Mechanics Fair, held in the old arsenal in New York City and intended as the first such annual event. American products including textiles, iron, paper, and glass were exhibited, and $540 was awarded in premiums. However, internal dissension began to rack the Institution, and a second fair was never held.[56]

De Witt Clinton tried to lend support of the sort he had already pioneered. As Governor, he signed the act of incorporation, and in 1825 he urged the legislature and the city to support the Institution as "the first organized school of its kind in the world." He asked that land belonging to the state and the city be granted to the Institution, but his request failed. The Mechanic and Scientific Institution continued to function for a few years; however, when its charter expired in 1842, its remaining funds were turned over to the General Society of Mechanics and Tradesmen.[57]

The New York City Mechanics Institute was established relatively late, after the New York Athenaeum, the Naval Lyceum of Brooklyn, the Mercantile Library, the Apprentices Library of Brooklyn, and various mechanics institutes in several other cities. It was founded in the winter of 1830-1831, inaugurated by a series of lectures on natural philosophy and chemistry presented by John Steele. Its act of incorporation defined its purpose as the promotion of the general diffusion of useful and practical knowledge among the mechanic class— but it also included the promotion of excellence in the useful arts. Its first annual report mentioned the Académie des Sciences and the Royal Society among models but seemed to give primary attention to the experience of the Franklin Institute. It rapidly built a library, a museum of models and machines, and a membership that by 1836 reached three thousand. It did not issue a journal, but for several years the *Mechanics Magazine* served as its organ.[58]

In 1831 the Common Council gave the Institute the use of rooms in the basement of City Hall, where it tried a small exhibition in July 1835. This was so successful that Castle Garden was rented for September of the same year and an attendance of forty thousand recorded. Premiums were awarded for a great variety of machines, philosophical instruments, and craft products. Following this success, the *Mechanics Magazine* took the subtitle, "Journal of the Mechanics Institute" and began to publish more and more respectable material, much of it reprinted. For example, nearly the whole of Pambour on locomotives and Nicholson's architecture were included, as well as a lecture on the application of chemistry to the useful arts, especially prepared by James Renwick.[59]

Its fairs made the New York Mechanics Institute one of the best known organizations of its kind in the country. Various innovations, including regular conversational meetings, were introduced; models of recent inventions were often displayed in the Institute rooms. At midcentury it continued to serve a useful function, but a ceiling had appeared above its aspirations. When the *Mechanics Magazine* failed, no other outlet was found, and the Institute settled into the routine of an educational body dedicated to the diffusion of knowledge and skill but little concerned with their advancement.

The lyceum movement has, with some straining, been characterized as an aspect of the mechanics institute movement. However its relationship is perceived, it did reach its culmination in New York City. The lyceum movement was established in 1826 by Josiah Holbrook; his Millbury Lyceum became the first branch of a national body, the American Lyceum. Those branches which followed were organized on a federal basis, with state lyceums formed as conventions of local lyceums. At the 1831 meeting of the New York State Lyceum, held in Utica, it was decided that the American Lyceum would establish a national convention to meet in New York City later that year. For the next six years the convention of the American Lyceum met annually in New York and was dominated by New Yorkers. At the convention of 1833, delegates were sent by the New-York Historical Society, the New York Athenaeum, the General Society of Mechanics and Tradesmen, the New York Mercantile Library Association, and several other New York institutions. The next year the Lyceum of Natural History of New York and the Naval Lyceum of Brooklyn were also represented. Thus, while the name "lyceum" in the title of an organization did not denote anything specific about a given body, many of New York's learned and "sublearned" societies considered themselves related to the movement.

Primarily a lecture sponsoring effort, the lyceum was concerned with education generally and with various means of diffusing knowledge. Some lyceums were, or became, respectable learned societies, but this was probably not a result of impulses received from the American Lyceum. In the end, the lyceum system reflected a popular cultural movement, expressive of the times and only peripherally related either to the advancement of learning or to the societies of arts.[60]

Artists were, in one case, directly involved in a successful attempt to replace an old-style learned society of patrons with an organization of practitioners. The American Academy of Fine Arts (later called the American Academy of the Arts) had failed to serve the art community either by diffusing knowledge and skill or by stimulating creativity. A new organization, the National Academy of Design, was founded in 1826. Led by Samuel F. B. Morse, who became its first president, this Academy was composed of working artists, with only a few honorary members, such as David Hosack, Philip Hone, and some literary men. Lectures were established, not only in drawing and painting but in fields conceived to be related, such as chemistry and anatomy. Regular exhibitions were held, but the plan to establish regular premiums was less successful, and they were awarded only occasionally in this era. The National Academy succeeded, while, in 1841, the American Academy of Fine Arts passed out of existence. No journal was published by the National Academy but its methods of schooling, practice, emulation, and premium reward were those of the societies of arts.[61]

In their nature, the popular societies were so structured that they could not easily adopt the forms of the learned societies. They were made up of practitioners of the arts (agricultural, mechanical, and fine). They sought better information, usually by instruction from scientists or experienced practitioners. They strived to encourage better practice through discussion, submission of products to prize competition, and the publicizing of methods and results. Most of them aspired to hearing papers and publishing learned journals—but without success. They represent a fascinating movement away from the pattern of the societies of arts, continuing the direction taken by the societies of arts when they moved away from the classical learned societies. The popular societies emphasized the diffusion of knowledge and technique at the expense of creative improvement. They sought to be consumers of principle. They had absolutely no quarrel with science; they venerated it, but they wanted to use it as a tool, rather than add to it.

The American Institute—Third New York Society of Arts

The American Institute was a significant organization, cast in the form of a society of arts and employing its methods. In its origin, it was curiously similar to the first New York Society of Arts; in both cases the founders were political and economic leaders, not scientists or mechanics. It has been pictured by some as a mechanics institute because of the time of its appearance; by others it has been viewed as an agricultural society. It was neither; it was the most successful of the American societies of arts that sought to stimulate the improvement of the technology of production by the award of premiums.

The American Institute was the product of a high-tariff group in New York, committed to the position that the government should protect manufactures and intervene in other ways to encourage a balanced and prosperous economy. It seems to have derived from the American Society of New York for Promoting Domestic Manufactures, a group active between the tariffs of 1816 and 1824. The founders of the American Institute were admirers of Henry Clay and his American System. They felt that the tariff of 1824 finally set the seal "to the American System" and represented the beginning of correct policy. They asserted that after 1824 "the sound of the loom, the trip hammer, and the spinning jenny were heard again" and looked back on the Harrisburg convention of 1827 with enthusiasm. It was no accident that the American Institute was formed in 1828, the year of the "Tariff of Abominations." Its purpose, to some of its members, was "to sustain the American system."[62]

On February 10, 1828, a small group met in Tammany Hall and voted to establish the American Institute of the City of New York. The following year it was incorporated, its charter spelling out purposes in less political tones than did earlier speeches and in less emotional tones than the toasts drunk at its early meetings. The official purpose was "encouraging and promoting domestic industry in this State and the United States, in Agriculture, Commerce, Manufactures and the Arts, and any improvements made therein, by bestowing rewards and other benefits on those who shall make any such improvements, or excel in any of the said branches."[63] Its initial plan was to hold annual exhibitions of agriculture, commerce, manufactures, and the arts and to establish a board of agriculture, which would hold cattle fairs; a board of science and the arts, which would encourage inventions; and a library.

Among the founders, Thaddeus B. Wakeman was perhaps the most devoted. Until his death in 1848 he served as secretary and gave continuity and direction to the efforts of the Institute; he was generally regarded as the father of the organization. However, General James B. Tallmadge was propelled to the presidency in 1832, and, except for one brief interval, held the reins until his death—which occurred just after he had attended a session of the 1853 Fair of the American Institute.[64] A politician and protectionist, he was ably backed by Mahlon Dickerson, one-time Governor of New Jersey, who maintained an experimental farm and was even more identified with protectionism.

The American Institute retained its American System orientation, and, no doubt, some of its success was owing to its political position. However, much of the authority it gained in the encouragement of invention and inventors came from the association of an important group of entrepreneurs and inventors. Among them were Peter Cooper, Richard M. and Robert Hoe, F. W. Geissenhainer, William and James Bogardus, Erastus Fairbanks, James Francis, Zadock Pratt, and Samuel Colt. Also involved were men with some scientific and intellectual competence, such as James Renwick, James J. Mapes, Henry Meigs, and Felix Pascalis.[65]

The Institute met monthly, but its annual fair became its major effort. In the early years the fair was held in Masonic Hall, but in 1834 Niblo's Garden was used; after that very popular site burned in 1848, Castle Garden (or Castle Clinton, the old Battery) served effectively, permitting transportation by water and the presentation of "aquatic galas" at the fair. (These were not shows by swimmers, but demonstrations of lifeboats, underwater explosions, diving bells, and pontoons.)[66]

The first fair attracted an attendance of fewer than twenty-five thousand, receipts of $1,600, and six hundred or so exhibits, but the fair of 1852 boosted attendance to five hundred thousand, and receipts to $25,000, while premiums offered amounted to $5,000. Initially, premiums were given in the form of diplomas alone, but by 1852 gold, silver, and bronze medals, silver cups, cash, and books were also awarded. The Institute took a degree of pride in pointing to a distinction between its premiums and those of the Franklin Institute, which specified articles to be put in competition. In contrast, the American Institute accepted almost all products within very broad classes; all were submitted to a panel of judges for evaluation. Most of the exhibits came from New York City or the surrounding Connecticut-New Jersey-New York region, but Philadelphia, upstate New York, and New England were always represented. By 1852 twenty-four states were among the exhibitors.[67]

Many of the most famous inventions were exhibited at one time or another in the Institute's fairs. McCormick's reaper, Singer's sewing machine, Morse's telegraph, Borden's meat biscuit, and Colt's guns all appeared. Some noted inventions of the day, which have since been largely forgotten, such as Francis's unsinkable lifeboat, also received credit and attention. From an early point, steam power was supplied for the machines on display, many of the exhibits being mechanical in character. Some had already received patents, and, previously or subsequently, many were exhibited at other fairs. What was the function of the fair for these exhibitors? Whether it played the role forecast by those who saw it as a means of encouraging inventiveness by emulation is hard to demonstrate. Certainly fairs encouraged exhibitors by giving a sense of achievement; they were also of obvious use in promotion and advertisement of products. For visitors, fairs were shows to which they went for entertainment, and, for all, they fed the faith in technology as the means for improving man's condition on earth.[68]

The American Institute carried farther than any other New York society one of the strongest principles in the society of arts philosophy—the breeching of craft secrecy. Traditional technology had been perpetuated under the cover of craft secrecy, and at many levels trade secrets and mysteries continued to be protected. The exhibition of technological products, the award of premiums, and the publication of details combined to make known the best, discoverable techniques. The Farmers Club and the Mechanics Club of the Institute also sought to replace secrecy by the effective communication of information about techniques. Many other institutions of society were at the same time contending against craft secrecy: the mechanics institutes, lyceums, schools, and even the patent system were deeply committed to the elimination of secrecy. This objective of the American Institute was always implicit in its efforts and occasionally voiced; its contribution to the elimination of secrecy was significant.

The example of Samuel Colt's relationship to American Institute fairs is illustrative. Colt was always a great drawing card, and he apparently used the fair, usually following the receipt of patents, to publicize his products and improve their sale. Colt won ten medals at Institute fairs and was elected a member of the Institute. At the same time, competing gunmakers tended to exhibit at competing fairs; Mighail Nutting, for example, showed his repeating firearms at several of the Mechanics Institute fairs in New York. Colt not only exhibited his revolving chamber pistol, but repeating rifles and carbines and waterproof cartridges. A great showman, Colt not infrequently demonstrated his own firearms personally. When objections were raised to so much stress upon weapons of death, the faith of the time easily provided the answer: "All the great inventions of the world have tended to humanize and civilize." Gunpowder was cited as an example of this. There was no need to worry: the internal beneficence of technology could be trusted totally—even against contradictory appearances.[69]

The Institute disavowed any intention or need to look behind inventions; that was the job of the Patent Office and of the courts sitting on patent cases. Institute judges seem to have performed rather superficial jobs and left none of the fine records of the Franklin Institute's committee on arts and sciences. Occasionally committees were appointed to report upon specific questions, to visit a manufacturing plant or a vineyard.

The response to the great concern about steamboat boiler explosions, especially following the *Aetna* explosion, provides another striking contrast. Instead of establishing a competent committee to conduct a scientific investigation, the American Institute used its primary approach. It offered a hundred-dollar gold medal for the best essay on the subject. Then, when James Frost submitted his pamphlet, *Descriptions of the Causes of the Explosion of Steam Boilers,* it appointed a committee, consisting of James Renwick, Henry Meigs, and Henry R. Dunheim, to visit Frost's laboratory to examine his assertions. Their competent report rejected Frost's wild ideas—but nothing more constructive resulted.[70]

The genuine conviction of American Institute leaders that science was a support of technology that should be cultivated was given embodiment in several ways. They established a faculty, consisting of James Renwick as professor of mechanical philosophy, James R. Chilton as professor of analytical philosophy, and James J. Mapes as professor of natural philosophy and chemistry applicable to the useful arts. They also made use of Thomas Antisell, an immigrant chemist who in 1848 established a private laboratory in New York. Antisell was several times called upon as a consultant and then moved on to become a Patent Office examiner and, for a time, chemist to the Department of Agriculture. This faculty presented an occasional lecture series, but, more centrally, was expected to respond to inquiries from members, providing such needs as chemical analyses of soil.

Still, established scientists looked askance at the Institute's basic emphasis upon individual emulation and improvement out of the state of the art. Charles T. Jackson urged more attention to science, and Alexander Dallas Bache put down the Institute's efforts in his insufferable manner with the classic comment that empiricism was "the lowest form of knowledge."[71]

Three separate efforts were made to establish a journal, following the practice of learned societies but perhaps more directly in imitation of the influential *Journal of the Franklin Institute.* The first *American Institute Journal* was launched in 1835 and ran to 1839. Its initial number announced the intention of filling a void in New York City, which, despite its great commitment to domestic industry, had no periodical devoted to the combined interests of agriculture, manufactures, commerce, and the arts.[72] It concerned itself primarily with the news and activities of the American Institute but also ran essays and papers. The second *American Institute Journal* was not dissimilar but lasted only about a year; launched in 1851, it had still less chance of success, for the institute by then already had a periodical organ of sorts—the *Annual Report of the American Institute.*

First issued in 1842, the *Annual Report* followed the 1841 act of legislature that provided a sum of $10,000 to be distributed annually on a matching basis to county agricultural societies to support the premium programs of their fairs. The act not only called for annual reports from recipients, among whom the American Institute functioned as the society for the City and County of New York and received by far the largest allotment—$950—but it also provided money to pay for the publication of such reports. For this reason the *Annual Report* seems to reflect an organization overwhelmingly concerned with agriculture, which was not the Institute's major interest. For a time the reports were ambiguously issued as *Annual Reports* or *Transactions,* but after 1849 they became simply the *Transactions.* This series carried the Institute's financial report, the statement on its fairs, addresses given at the fairs, and committee reports. The fair reports, addresses, and fair catalogs had previously been separately published—and often continued to be; other separate publications included occasional committee reports and membership lists.[73]

The *Transactions* did not include many scholarly or scientific papers but did introduce one interesting category of reports, namely, the commissioned paper on a technological process by a successful entrepreneur or practitioner. A good example is Zadock Pratt's 1848 "Description of the Prattsville Tannery."[74] Pratt had previously been awarded a gold medal for sole leather he had submitted, and he agreed to write up an account of his processes, including the improvements he had introduced as a "result of experience." Neither Pratt nor his report was in any sense antiscientific. Nevertheless, this sort of report emphasized the empirical route to technological improvement sought in the award of premiums and exhibitions at fairs: the artisan's improvement of his art through conscious effort based upon insights developed in his own practical experience.

This approach was probably more effective in the diffusion of technology than in its advancement; it did help to breech craft secrecy. Other techniques of the Institute also had this characteristic. The Farmers Club was designed to offer farmers, on the day they came to market, the opportunity to talk about techniques and improvement. The Mechanics Club, later called the Polytechnic, sought a parallel goal for mechanics and those involved in mechanical efforts. The library of the Institute, numbering about six thousand volumes by 1850, was strongest in practical manuals. The Repository, established on a permanent basis when the Institute bought its own building in 1848, was a collection of machines and models, preserved for the purpose of instruction and stimulation by the same processes envisioned in the American Academy of Fine Arts when it imported casts of busts and sculptures.[75]

The American Institute was, indeed, a fine monument to the concept of technology embodied in the London Society of Arts and all its American copies.

It reflected the same views that contemporaneously led the state legislature to its sweeping support of agricultural improvement. Critics first saw the organization as a tariff lobby or a "humbug" and a little later as possessing "zeal wanting in knowledge."[76] In a measure they were right, for neither the Institute nor the society of arts movement as a whole included a study of science sufficiently serious to aid in developing a science-based technology. The science community did not praise the American Institute, except for such castoffs as James Renwick—who, perhaps, had simply reached the point where he could not keep up with current science.

Many, however, did applaud the Institute. Regardless of whether Levi Woodbury really felt the Institute was responsible for New York's substantial record in patenting new devices, he clearly announced that its efforts had worked in this direction. In 1849 he reported that one-third of all patents annually awarded went to New York State inventors, while New York City alone was responsible for 15 percent of the national total. The press aimed at farmers and mechanics continued to display a high level of emotion. The *Cultivator,* for example, asserted that the American Institute's fairs were "to the manufacturing and mechanic arts, what cattle shows are to agriculture—schools of instruction, and stimulants to industry, enterprise and laudable competition." *Farmer and Mechanic* reported that, if the Institute did nothing more than hold its fairs, "it will exert a vast practical influence for good and secure the lasting gratitude of the country." Emulation to invent and improve was viewed as the critical factor. Thaddeus Wakeman continued to describe "vast emulation" provoked by "even a single gold medal." In the end the Institute recognized technology for the art it was and in a measure must always remain. It sought to encourage the creativity of the craftsman in his craft.[77]

The New York Crystal Palace

For New York, the capstone to the society of arts philosophy was set in the Exhibition of the Industry of All Nations which opened in 1853—the United States' first World's Fair. The Crystal Palace Exhibition, as it was generally known, was a direct and almost immediate copy of the London Crystal Palace Exhibition of 1851. The New York fair was presented by an association organized as a stock company, a business enterprise; it bore no relationship to the learned society. It represented, however, much more than a moneymaking effort.

The London Crystal Palace had grown out of the London Society of Arts, by then the Royal Society of Arts. The concept emerged in England at a Society of Arts meeting (although it had been suggested in France earlier) and was carried forward to resounding success under the leadership of Prince Albert, president of the Royal Society of Arts. The United States sent exhibitions that, though small in number, had a large impact. Britishers, who were first disinterested in American technology, were impressed and a bit shocked at the effectiveness of some of the American advances and methods. They suggested to members of the American delegation that such an exhibition should be held in the United States. They wanted to learn what America was about, and, indeed, Britain sent a notable commission to visit the New York Crystal Palace.[78]

The message was carried back and developed by Edward Riddle, an American delegate to London and former Massachusetts auctioneer, who foresaw numerous profit-making possibilities. He sold the idea to a group of New York bankers and businessmen, including August Belmont, Watts Sherman, and Francis W. Edmonds. The election of Theodore Sedgwick as president of the Crystal Palace Association revealed a curious difference in orientation from the American Institute. Sedgwick was a free-trade Democrat with objectives in direct opposition to the protectionism of the American Institute. Supporters of the American Institute were among those who criticized the proposed show of foreign manufactures as "hostile to American industry." Even so, the Crystal Palace built upon the still-rising successes of the industrial fairs of the American Institute. So many regular exhibitors at American Institute fairs moved to the Crystal Palace when it opened that the attendance at the 1853 Institute Fair plummeted and its first deficit was recorded. By a similar measure, the Crystal Palace was strengthened and enriched.[79]

Despite the shortness of time (the association was not formed until 1852) a remarkable building was constructed, foreign and American displays were put together, and the spectacle opened only two months late. Although the delay was deprecated by critics, it is a feat that could not be duplicated today.

The restriction laid down by the Common Council of New York in making the reservoir site available was that the building be of iron and glass in imitation of the London structure. That ruled out the more imaginative, suspended-roof design of James Bogardus, but the successful design of a domed Greek cross upon an octagon by Georg Johan Carstensen and Charles Gildemeister was nevertheless something of a jewel. The glass of the dome was enameled in translucent blue, and at night the entire structure sparkled with its gas lights. Inside the exhibit floors were small compared with London, but good foreign representations were present. Fine arts, of course, were displayed in true society of arts tradition, along with useful arts. Here, however, the American showing was poor, only 40 of 654 paintings being American. On the other hand, of the remaining thirty classes of craft and industrial exhibits, the Americans accounted for three times as many as Britain and Ireland, the largest foreign exhibitors.[80]

It was a good show, but it failed. It failed financially and somehow it failed psychologically—the bright hopes of a permanent exhibition following the pattern of the Conservatoire des Arts et Métiers expired. Premiums were awarded in traditional pattern by panels of judges. There was not sufficient foreign participation to provide a valid comparison of American and European technology, and, as the visiting British Commission discovered, the most important aspects of American technology were poorly depicted inside the Crystal Palace.

Still, Americans who visited it never quite lost the vision. As financial deficits mounted, P. T. Barnum was called upon to revive the effort, and his not inconsiderable talents did give it a "kick" of life for a time. It expired, nevertheless, and in 1855, 1856, 1857, and 1858 the American Institute rented the Crystal Palace for its annual fairs. This was in a way symbolic, and so was the brief and devastating conflagration that totally destroyed the edifice on October 5, 1858.[81] Horace Greeley correctly predicted, "As we grow in wealth and strength, we may build a much greater Crystal Palace and accumulate therein more imperial treasure than we could now afford to purchase; but a second Fair cannot bring the exhilaration and glory of the first."[82]

That was not the end of fairs. America's most successful World's Fair lay a quarter of a century ahead, and fairs, however much deprecated, play a significant role to the present. It was not the end of the American Institute, which had a long and lingering death to endure—finally expiring in the 1930s, by which time it had become a children's science show.

The End of the Society of Arts Era

What did end, however, was the era of societies of arts. New York, like the rest of the nation, turned to other means of encouraging technology and the arts. As professionalization and the emphasis upon basic science became more and more demanding, the society of arts approach became less and less respectable. The contrasting fortunes of the National Association of Inventors and the American Society of Civil Engineers illustrate the changed atmosphere. The professionalization of science, evident in such institutions as the Lyceum of Natural History, was followed, after a delay, by the professionalization of engineering and the erection of professional societies dedicated to practical arts based upon science.

In October 1845 the National Association of Inventors was organized, with James Renwick as president and James J. Mapes as secretary, both of them prominent in the American Institute. This was an organization that sought to promote useful knowledge by the processes of the societies of arts, that is, by encouraging invention by practitioners of the art. It did not long endure because that was not the route into the future. The American Society of Civil Engineers, established in New York in October 1852, experienced one hiatus, but then began a life that reaches to the present. This was a grouping of civil, mechanical, and mining engineers, as well as architects, led by specialized, professional engineers. James Laurie, a railroad engineer, became the first president, and Charles W. Copeland, a naval engineer, one of the vice-presidents.[83]

The fate of James Renwick is significant. He was the primary science professor at Columbia and a practical engineer who had consulted on a variety of engineering projects and sought strenuously to apply science to practice. However, he had lost credence in both science and engineering communities by midcentury. The disaffection was great enough, indeed, to oust him from his Columbia chair in 1853. He had contributed nothing to science and nothing in the way of principles to engineering, but he had carried forward the faith of those who promoted creativity by emulation in the pattern of the societies of arts. With the societies of arts, he belonged to the past.[84]

The future of technology and of practical improvement lay in professionalization and in the cultivation of the science base. The new professional engineering societies bore relationships to the learned societies as well as to the societies of arts, and they benefited from the experiences of both. The societies of arts had played important roles but now moved off the stage, superseded by new attitudes and new forms. The most central element of their philosophy, the concept of creativity by the effort to develop improvements out of deep craft understanding, was not lost. It was too much an inescapable part of things. It was, however, submerged—at a cost only now beginning to be perceived.

NOTES

1. Roger Hahn, *The Anatomy of a Scientific Institution: The Paris Academy of Sciences, 1666-1803* (Berkeley and Los Angeles: University of California Press, 1971), pp. 108-109; H. F. Berry, *A History of the Royal Society of Dublin* (London, New York: Longmans, Green & Co., 1915).

2. Sir Henry T. Wood, *A History of the Royal Society of Arts* (London: John Murray, 1913).

3. Derek Hudson and Kenneth W. Luckhurst, *The Royal Society of Arts, 1754-1954* (London: John Murray, 1954); A. E. Musson and Eric Robinson, *Science and Technology in the Industrial Revolution* (Manchester: Manchester University Press, 1969).

4. See D. G. C. Allan, *William Shipley, Founder of the Royal Society of Arts* (London: Hutchinson, 1968).

5. *Premiums Offered by the Society Instituted at London for the Encouragement of Arts, Manufactures and Commerce* (London, 1769); Wood, *History of the Royal Society of Arts*, p. 92.

6. Minute Book of the Society of Arts 1, n.p., extracted in *Journal of the Society of Arts* 2 (1852-53): 1.

7. Jared Eliot, *An Essay on the Invention, or Art of Making Good, if not the Best Iron, from Black Sea Sand* (New York, 1762).

8. Brooke Hindle, *The Pursuit of Science in Revolutionary America* (Chapel Hill: University of North Carolina Press, 1956), p. 208; Robert Dossie, *Observations on the Pot-Ash Brought from America* (London, 1767); W. M. B. Lewis, *Experiments and Observations on American Potashes* (London, 1767); Musson and Robinson, *Science and Technology*, pp. 53-55; Theodore Wertime, *The Coming of the Age of Steel* (Chicago: University of Chicago Press, 1962), p. 220.

9. Edmund Berkeley and Dorothy Smith Berkeley, *Dr. Alexander Garden of Charles Town* (Chapel Hill: University of North Carolina Press, 1969), pp. 93-103, 155-57.

10. Robert L. Hilldrup, "A Campaign to Promote the Prosperity of Colonial Virginia," *Journal of the Royal Society of Arts* 108 (1958-1959): 940; *Virginia Gazette* (Purdie and Dixon), 19 November 1772, 5 August 1773, 16 June 1774; Hindle, *Pursuit of Science*, p. 106; Carl Bridenbaugh, *Cities in Revolt* (New York: Alfred A. Knopf, 1955), p. 268; Richard P. McCormick, "The Society, the Grape, and New Jersey," *Journal of the Royal Society of Arts* 110 (1962-1963): 119, 266.

11. Hindle, *Pursuit of Science*, pp. 122-38.

12. *Pennsylvania Chronicle*, 7 March 1768.

13. Ibid.

14. *The Letters and Papers of Cadwallader Colden*, 5, New-York Historical Society, New York, N.Y., *Collections for 1921* 54 (1923): 53, 70; Colden to Peter Templeman, 6 February 1761, the American Correspondence of the Royal Society of Arts, Microfilm 6:9.

15. *New York Gazette; or the Weekly Post-Boy*, 29 November 1764.

16. James Duane, William Smith Jr., Walter Rutherfurd, and John Morin Scott to Peter Templeman, 30 March 1765, Society of Arts, Microfilm 9:127.

17. *New York Mercury,* 12 October 1767, 17 March 1766.

18. *New York Gazette; or the Weekly Post-Boy,* 20 December 1764, 27 December 1764.

19. Duane, et al. to Templeman, 30 March 1767, Society of Arts, Microfilm 9:127; *New York Gazette; or the Weekly Post-Boy,* 10 January 1765.

20. *New York Gazette; or the Weekly Post-Boy,* 22 July 1767, 15 October 1767, 31 December 1767; William Smith, Jr., and Walter Rutherfurd to Templeman, 10 November 1766, Society of Arts, Microfilm 11:98.

21. Philip Livingston and Peter Remsen to Templeman, 3 May 1765, Society of Arts, Microfilm 9:139.

22. *New York Mercury*, 10 June 1765.

23. *New York Gazette; or the Weekly Post-Boy,* 5 December 1765, 24 October 1765.

24. Rutherfurd to Templeman, 29 March 1766, Society of Arts, Microfilm 10:132.

25. Ibid.; *New York Mercury*, 31 March 1766.

26. *Report of Committee,* Broadside dated January 1767; *New York Journal,* 4 February 1768, 28 January 1768.

27. Hindle, *Pursuit of Science,* pp. 284-85, 287, 315.

28. Samuel Latham Mitchill, *A Discourse on the Life and Character of Samuel Bard* (New York, 1821), p. 28.

29. Hindle, *Pursuit of Science,* pp. 117-18; Samuel Bard, *A Discourse upon the Duties of Physicians* (New York, 1769), p. i.

30. Thomas Paine to Lewis Morris, 16 February 1784, Duane MSS, New-York Historical Society.

31. *New York Directory and Register for the Year 1789,* p. 121; Samuel Bard to Benjamin Franklin, 13 May 1785, American Philosophical Society Archives, Philadelphia, Pa.; *New York Packet,* 7 March 1785.

32. Minutes of the Philadelphia Society for Promoting Agriculture, 4 September 1787, 18 April 1787, pp. 60, 63; *New York Journal,* 1 February 1787, 18 April 1787; *Worcester Magazine* 2 (1787): 575; *American Magazine* 1 (1787): 73ff.; De Witt Clinton, *An Introductory Discourse* (New York, 1815), p. 13.

33. Minutes of the New York Manufacturing Society 1, 8, 20, 46, New-York Historical Society; *New York Journal,* 2 April 1789.

34. Minutes . . . Directors of the Society for Establishing Useful Manufactures 1 (1791-1928), 20 August 1792; Joseph S. Davis, *Essays in the Earlier History of American Corporations,* 2 vols. (Cambridge: Harvard University Press, 1917), 1:340ff; *Universal Asylum* 7 (1791): 169-74, 435-37.

35. Minutes of the General Society of Mechanics and Tradesmen, typescript copy (1785-1832), pp. 2-63; *Charter and Bye-Laws of the General Society of Mechanics and Tradesmen* (New York, 1798); Thomas Earle and Charles T. Congdon, eds., *Annals of the General Society of Mechanics and Tradesmen* (New York, 1882), pp. 9, 12, 42.

36. *New York Directory for 1792* (New York, 1792), pp. 198-99; *Transactions of the New York Society for Promoting Agriculture, Arts, and Manufactures* 1 (1792-1799): iv, xiii.

37. *Transactions of the New York Society for Promoting Agriculture, Arts, and Manufactures,* pt. 2, p. 63; *Memoirs of the Philadelphia Agricultural Society* 1 (1808): 158; David M. Ellis, *Landlords and Farmers in the Hudson-Mohawk Region, 1790-1850* (Ithaca, N. Y.: Cornell University Press, 1946), pp. 94-96.

38. Ezra L'Hommedieu to Thomas Jefferson, 3 April 1802, American Philosophical Society Archives, *Resolutions,* Broadside dated 24 March 1802.

39. *Transactions of the New York Society for Promoting Useful Arts* 1 (1792-1794): 232; ibid., 4 (1819): 7, 340-42.

40. Kenneth W. Luckhurst, *The Story of Exhibitions* (London, New York: Studio Publications, 1951).

41. Elkanah Watson, *History of the Berkshire Agricultural Society* (Albany, 1820), pp. 118-20.

42. Ellis, *Landlords and Farmers,* p. 144.

43. Ibid., pp. 139-40; *Memoirs of the New York Board of Agriculture* 1 (1821): vi-viii.

44. *Memoirs of the New York Board of Agriculture*, p. v; Ulysses P. Hedrick, *A History of Agriculture in the State of New York* (Albany: State of New York, 1933).

45. Watson, *History*, pp. 153, 174.

46. *Memoirs of the New York Board of Agriculture* 1 (1821): v; ibid., 2 (1823): 1; L. H. Bailey, *New York State Rural Problems* (Albany: State of New York, 1913).

47. *Transactions of the Albany Institute* 1 (1833): 25-32.

48. Hindle, *Pursuit of Science*, p. 315.

49. Kenneth R. Nodyne, "The Role of De Witt Clinton and the Municipal Government in the Development of Cultural Organizations in New York City, 1803-1817" (Ph.D. diss., New York University, 1969), pp. 14-15, 99; Austin B. Keep, *History of the New York Society Library* (New York: DeVinne Press, 1908).

50. Minutes of the Common Council of the City of New York (New York, 1917), 8: 233, 235.

51. Ibid., 7: 269-70.

52. *American Monthly Magazine* 1 (1817-1818): 122, 193, 236.

53. De Witt Clinton, "Discourse," pp. 22-29; Nodyne, "Role of Clinton," p. 94; Minutes of the Common Council 9:18-19.

54. See Jonathan Harris, "New York's First Scientific Body: The Literary and Philosophical Society, 1814-1834," *Annals of the New York Academy of Sciences* 196 (1972): 329-37; *Records of the Literary and Philosophical Society of New York* (1814-1834), p. 72, New-York Historical Society; Kenneth R. Nodyne, "The Founding of the Lyceum of Natural History," *Annals of the New York Academy of Sciences* 172 (1970): 141-45.

55. Minutes of the General Society of Mechanics and Tradesmen 2: 222; Earle and Congdon, eds., *Annals*, pp. 60, 65; Stephen M. Wright, "Historical Sketch," General Society of Mechanics and Tradesmen *Centennial Celebration* (New York, 1885), pp. 42-43.

56. Edward A. Fitzpatrick, *The Educational Views and Influences of De Witt Clinton* (New York: Teachers College, Columbia University, 1911); Charles P. Daly, *Origin and History of Institutions for the Promotion of the Useful Arts* (Albany, 1864), p. 26.

57. Fitzpatrick, *Educational Views*, p. 132; Wright, *Centennial History*, p. 44.

58. *American Repertory of Arts, Sciences, and Manufactures* 1 (1840): 34-35; *First Report of the Board of Directors of the Mechanic's Institute of the City of New York* (New York, 1833), pp. 9-11.

59. Minutes of the Common Council 19: 295; *Circular of the Mechanics Institute* (New York, 1835); *Mechanics Magazine* 7 (1836): title page.

60. Carl Bode, *The American Lyceum* (New York: Oxford University Press, 1956), pp. 13-14, 60; Josiah Holbrook, *American Lyceum, or Society for the Improvement of Schools and Diffusion of Useful Knowledge* (Boston, 1829), pp. 3, 19.

61. Eliot Clark, *History of the National Academy of Design, 1825-1953* (New York: Columbia University Press, 1954), p. 10; William Dunlap, *Address to the Students of the National Academy of Design* (New York, 1831), p. 4; Thomas Cummings, *Historic Annals of the National Academy of Design (1825-1863)* (Philadelphia, 1865), p. 37.

62. *An Address of the American Society for the Encouragement of Domestic Manufactures* (New York, 1817); Frederick W. Wile, ed., *A Century of Industrial Progress* (New York: Doubleday, Doran & Co., 1928), p. v; Ralph Lockwood, *Address Delivered Before the American Institute* (New York, 1829), p. 10; Henry M. Western, *Address on Domestic Manufactures* (New York, 1828), p. 7.

63. *Charter of the American Institute* (New York, 1862), p. 1.

64. George B. Andrews, *Sermon Occasioned by the Death of the Hon. James Tallmadge* (Poughkeepsie, 1833), p. 17; L. E. Chittenden, *The Value of Instruction in the Mechanic Arts* (New York, 1889), pp. 6-8.

65. *Transactions of the American Institute* (1846-1856), passim; Wile, *Century of Industrial Progress*, p. xiii.

66. *Scientific American* 2 (1846-1847): 27, 45; *Annual Report of the American Institute* (1842), pp. 103-104.

67. *Transactions of the American Institute* (1852), pp. 17-23; Daly, *Origin and History*, p. 30.

68. *Transactions of the American Institute* (1851), p. 247; John Abbott, "Some

Account of Francis's Life-boats and Life-cars," *Harpers New Monthly Magazine* 3 (1851): 162-71; Wile, *Century of Industrial Progress,* p. xiii.

69. *Journal of the American Institute* (November 1837); John E. Parsons, "Samuel Colt's Medals from the American Institute," *New-York Historical Society Quarterly* 33 (1949): 189-98.

70. *Transactions of the American Institute* (1850), pp. 188-90; *Journal of the American Institute* 1 (1850): no. 3; "Minutes of the American Institute Committee on Manufactures," 14 January 1841, New-York Historical Society.

71. *Transactions of the New York State Agriculture Society* 5 (1846): 508-10, 463; *Transactions of the American Institute* (1850), pp. 190-99; *Transactions...* (1851), p. 228; *Transactions...* (1856), pp. 73-108; Thomas Antisell, *Address... On the Philosophy of Manufactures* (New York, 1849), pp. 15-16; Windham D. Miles, "CSW's First President, Thomas Antisell," *The Capital Chemist* 18 (1968): 7-9.

72. *Journal of the American Institute* 1 (1835): 1.

73. Daly, *Origin and History,* p. 31; *Transactions of the American Institute* (1855), p. 9.

74. *Transactions of the American Institute* (1848), pp. 182-98.

75. *Alphabetical and Analytical Catalogue of the American Institute Library* (New York, 1852), p. 3; Description of Models, Machines, etc., etc., at the Repository, 1839, New-York Historical Society.

76. *Journal of the American Institute* 1 (1835): 47; *Mechanics Magazine* 5 (1835): 68-80.

77. Levi Woodbury, *Twenty-second Anniversary Address* (New York, 1849), p. 23; *The Cultivator* 3 (1836): 173; *Farmer and Mechanic* 1 (1847): 282, 47.

78. Kenneth W. Luckhurst, *The Great Exhibition of 1851* (London: Royal Society of Arts, 1951), pp. 3-4; *Transactions of the New York State Agriculture Society* 6 (1846): 15, 16; Richard D. Cummings, "The Growth of Technical Cooperation with Governments Abroad, 1849-1853," *Pacific Historical Review* 18 (1949): 202-203.

79. Cummings, "Growth of Technical Cooperation," p. 205; C. B. Norton, *World's Fairs from London 1851 to Chicago 1893* (Chicago, 1893), p. 17; Ivan D. Steen, "America's First World's Fair," *New-York Historical Society Quarterly* 47 (1963): 258; *Transactions of the New York State Agriculture Society* 11 (1851): 163.

80. *Transactions of the New York State Agriculture Society* 11 (1851): 259; William Chambers, *Things as They Are in America,* 2d ed. (London, 1857), p. 201; clippings, Crystal Palace Papers, New-York Historical Society.

81. P. T. Barnum, *Struggles and Triumphs* (Buffalo, 1871), p. 363; George Templeton Strong, *Diary* (New York: Macmillan Co., 1952), 2: 416.

82. Quoted by Charles Hirschfeld, "America on Exhibition: The New York Crystal Palace," *American Quarterly* 9 (1957): 101.

83. *Eureka* 1 (1846-1847): 15; ibid., 3 (1849): 223; Charles W. Hunt, *Historical Sketch of the American Society of Civil Engineers* (New York, 1897), pp. 16, 24, 28.

84. Strong, *Diary,* pp. 103, 120.

Shaping
a Provincial Learned
Society: The Early History
of the Albany Institute

JAMES M. HOBBINS

Like the history of most other early American learned and scientific societies, the history of the Albany Institute has typically been studied by well-intentioned officers of the society but has never served as the subject of modern historical scrutiny from an outsider's view.[1] The historiographic legacy assumes that the virtues of the great founders in 1791, the cultural wealth of Albany's great families, and the industry of a few outstanding gentlemen insured the steady progress of the Institute to the present, making it one of America's oldest learned societies. This essay departs from those facile assumptions and asks instead who really were the participants, what did they intend to do, and what were the internal and external factors that determined their course, their accomplishments, and failures? To what part of American culture did they intend to relate, and how did they do it?

Such questions, never before asked of the historical records of the Albany Institute, will be the central consideration here in the course of describing more than sixty years of activity of the Institute and the societies that preceded it. The earliest organization, the Society for the Promotion of Agriculture, Arts and Manufactures, founded in 1791, was reshaped as the Society for the Promotion of Useful Arts in 1804. The Albany Lyceum of Natural History, founded in 1823, was linked with the latter society in 1824 to become the Albany Institute. Formed by the association of two largely scientific societies, the Institute gradually developed into a general learned society, so that by the 1850s it had a character quite different from any of its forerunners or constituent societies.

The changes exhibited in the history of the Institute were not simply isolated, local phenomena. Albany was indeed an idiosyncratic provincial setting, but it also participated in many broader, more sweeping cultural trends. Likewise, the early history of the Albany Institute reflects simultaneous developments both within Albany and far beyond.

---

[1] Notes to this chapter begin on page 143.

The Society for the Promotion of Agriculture, Arts and Manufactures

The Society for the Promotion of Agriculture, Arts and Manufactures (SPAAM) was the 1791 product of a few well-established private citizens of New York City and a far greater number of politicians and other members of officialdom.[2] Of the seventy-two incorporating gentlemen, twenty-five had been active in the state legislature in the years 1791-1793. Twenty-seven others were members of officialdom by virtue of their involvement, earlier or later, with national political positions, state positions, judgeships, or mayoralty. And sixteen members (some already representative of the officialdom) were state regents, Columbia trustees, or Columbia professors. An analysis of the occupations[3] of forty-one identifiable SPAAM members produces this profile:

	Attorneys	*Physicians*	*Educators*	*Scientists*	*Businessmen*	*Clergymen*	*Miscellaneous*	*Occupations Identified*	*Average Age*	*Ages Identified*
SPAAM in 1793	16^2	5^2	2	6^3	10	1	1*	41 of 72	43.7	40 of 72

*Playwright-artist-historian William Dunlap

Note that in this profile table, and in others to follow,
N^n n = number of members within N who published at least one scholarly
    contribution in a field of interest to the Society
     N = total number of members in occupational category

Of the thirty-one whose primary occupations have not been determined, twenty-three were active, at one time or another, in state or local politics. In short, the membership incorporating the SPAAM was characteristically a well-established, educated group, no fewer than seven of whom had published in the fields of agriculture, useful arts, or manufactures. While not necessarily typified by them, the SPAAM was led in spirit by such scientist-politician-learned archetypes as Samuel Bard, Matthew Clarkson, George Clinton, Simeon DeWitt, James Duane, John Sloss Hobart, John Jay, Ezra L'Hommedieu, Robert R. Livingston, and Samuel Latham Mitchill.

Not in any sense a learned society with a wide range of scholarly interests, the SPAAM was primarily concerned with improvements in agriculture and its implements, and only secondarily with the other useful arts and manufactures. At the outset it barred "works of mere ingenuity, [and] essays upon speculative and abstract subjects." Its "humbler" pursuit was to "supply the wants and relieve the necessities of mankind and thereby to *render human life more comfortable*; to multiply the productions of the land, to shorten or facilitate the toils of the labourer, and to excite a spirit of honest industry, whereby *riches may become more abundant . . . ."*[4] Ten of its eleven concerns were agricultural; the eleventh was "manufactures."

By design, the Society was closely associated with the state government not only in membership but also in schedule. Its biweekly meetings were held at the time and place of the legislative sessions, during the first four months of the year. All members of the legislature were *ex officio* honorary members of the Society. The object was to bring together the most recent agricultural advances from regions throughout the state, through the meeting of learned representatives from each county; each section of the state could then learn from the other, and the increase of regional prosperity was thus assured.

Publication of the *Transactions* was provided for in the 1791 bylaws, and between 1792 and 1799 four numbers appeared, the first single volume being published in 1801. The articles were predominantly agricultural, although after 1798 other useful arts were increasingly represented.[5] Twenty-two different authors contributed the sixty-nine articles in the *Transactions I,* but, of those, four authors were especially active contributors: Robert R. Livingston (the Society's president), sixteen articles; Ezra L'Hommedieu, fourteen; Simeon DeWitt, seven; Samuel Latham Mitchill, five. These four were also among the most active in the founding of the SPAAM in 1791.[6]

In the early years of the nineteenth century the example of the SPAAM served as a model for a national organization with similar purposes.[7] But the charter that had incorporated the SPAAM in 1793 was allowed to expire in May of 1804. Several factors had affected the Society's effective pursuit of its stated objectives. With the movement of the state capital to Albany at the close of the century, SPAAM had moved too, thus abandoning a good number of New York City area residents who had been active a decade earlier. In addition, it was difficult to conduct most of the operations of the Society at the stated meetings of the general membership which were held only during legislative sessions. Similarly, such arrangements prevented the accumulation of permanent collections, a potential drawing card for new members and a continuing source of intellectual stimulation for all members. It was only through reorganizing the Society that more practicable procedures could be implemented.

The Society for the Promotion of Useful Arts

In April 1804 the New York State Legislature incorporated a new society to replace the expiring SPAAM. Retitled the Society for the Promotion of Useful Arts (SPUA), in membership and purpose it was merely a continuation of the former society; the new name intended no real change from the focus of the SPAAM. "Although the title of the Society points at THE USEFUL ARTS generally, it is intended to consider agriculture the chief, and improvement in it always a principal aim." The same close relationship with the state government, especially the legislature, was explicitly maintained. The legislature provided a room for the SPUA's use in the Capitol. But the SPUA needed even more encouragement: "The future usefulness of the Society will ... depend on an extension as well as a continuance of the patronage of the state."[8] That patronage would come.

The membership profile of the reconstituted Society is essentially a scaled-down version of the SPAAM 1793 profile.[9] The total number of members of the SPUA in 1806 was only one-third that of the SPAAM, but then too Albany's population in 1800 was less than one-sixth of New York City's in 1790, or about one-twelfth of New York City's in 1800.[10]

	Attorneys	Physicians	Educators	Scientists	Businessmen	Clergymen	Miscellaneous	Occupations Identified	Average Age	Ages Identified
SPAAM in 1793	16^2	5^2	2	6^3	10	1	1*	41 of 72[a]	43.7	40 of 72
SPUA in 1806	6^2	2^1	1	2^2	5^1	0	1**	17 of 25[b]	47.8	17 of 25

*Playwright-artist-historian William Dunlap
**Stephen Van Rensselaer
[a]23 of 31 unknowns are active politicians but have no other identifiable primary occupation
[b]5 of 8 unknowns are active politicians but have no other identifiable primary occupation

Though fewer in number, the members of the SPUA were generally established members of the community, similar in learning, age, and occupation to their SPAAM predecessors. Eight of the original incorporators of the SPAAM were among the twenty-five SPUA founders, and of that twenty-five no fewer than fifteen had been active in the SPAAM in its later days.

Although the act to incorporate the SPUA was passed in 1804, no meetings were held until the legislative session of 1806. The new structural feature was the "council," comprised of nine elected "counsellors" who would act as the main administrative body of the Society. Their responsibilities would include, by means of meetings throughout the year (not simply during the legislative session), proposing members, plans, and regulations as well as editing and publishing the *Transactions*. Although restricted from executing business without the consent of the general membership, the council could, nonetheless, keep the house in order so that meetings could be more orderly and interesting than they had been during the years of the SPAAM.[11]

The SPUA enjoyed increasingly good health from 1806 through 1815 or so. Enthusiastic leadership, exemplified by the SPUA president, Robert R. Livingston, had its encouraging effects. The second volume of the *Transactions*, a continuation of the *Transactions* of the preceding society, appeared as a single publication in 1807, containing some thirty-five notes and articles, many of which had originated during the SPAAM period. Twenty-six of the thirty-five articles focused on agricultural matters, and nine related to other useful arts. But the leadership was clearly in evidence: Livingston authored no fewer than eleven articles, while Ezra L'Hommedieu had six and Simeon DeWitt had four.

With few exceptions the meetings increased in number from year to year, reaching a high of fourteen in 1815. Internally, too, changes were taking place. The Society had overwhelmingly emphasized the study of agriculture, with only a smattering of other useful arts appearing in either their published *Transactions* or in their recorded meetings. But in 1810 a fresh topic of consideration not only broadened the interests of the Society but also set the precedent for a new mechanism within the SPUA organization. The Society resolved to collect and preserve mineralogical specimens from within state borders. Members were encouraged to forward to the Society any interesting specimens "of earths, earthly fossils and metalic [sic] ores" which they can find, and likewise to encourage "lovers of the science in every part of the State." Within two years a mineralogical committee was elected which, like the council, held regular meetings during the "recess."[12]

Much of the prosperity of the SPUA was affected by the Society's increasing role in the state's prewar and wartime political economy, a natural role by virtue of the Society's quasi-official status. In 1808, at the request of the Society, the legislature passed an "Act for the Encouragement of the Manufacture of Woolen Cloth."[13] For more than ten years the SPUA administered the state government's competition for the best quality of wool cloth manufactured in New York. Premiums up to $80 per prize were awarded for the best cloths in county and statewide contests. By 1815 $20,965 had been awarded.[14] In 1811 the Society proposed to the legislature an act to encourage "domestic manufacturing" by means of a similar bounty system; by 1812 such a system was enacted and the SPUA was entrusted with its administration.[15] Only a month later the Society proposed an act to encourage annual agricultural fairs in the state. Frequent and casual communications with the legislature exemplified the increasingly secure relationship between the SPUA and its legislative patronage.

Needing more room in the Capitol, the rapidly expanding Society inserted its request in a clause of another proposal to encourage manufacturing in the state. Additional space was needed for the SPUA's rapidly expanding membership. An 1807 revision of the rules eliminated the two-week waiting period for the admission of new members.[16] From 1808 through 1815 an average of over 20 new members were elected each year; the recording secretary claimed 169 living members in 1815.[17] Additional space was also required for the Society's library.

First mention of a substantial library came in 1811, when the SPUA considered installing shelving in the room in the Capitol. By 1813 the Society had procured a separate library room.[18] An exchange program, formally initiated in 1814, accelerated substantially the growth of the library, bringing in the publications of such societies as the New-York Historical Society, the American Philosophical Society, the Connecticut Academy of Arts and Sciences, the Literary and Philosophical Society of New York, and several agricultural societies.[19] Private donations from a dozen members accounted for nearly forty titles in the library. Samuel Latham Mitchill, Robert R. Livingston, and Simeon DeWitt headed the list in generosity. The Society purchased eleven more titles, including complete sets of the *Repertory of Arts, Manufactures, and Agriculture* and the *Transactions* of the London Society of Arts. In all, by 1816 the library boasted of over two hundred volumes. Subject emphasis was equally distributed among works on agriculture, inventions, and mineralogy-geology.[20] After 1816 the SPUA annually allocated $100 for library purchases, establishing the library's growth as a permanent priority.[21]

Several administrative changes illustrate the burgeoning activity of the SPUA. In 1812 the two corresponding secretaries (based in Albany and New York) were replaced by four, one from each state senatorial district.[22] The New York area membership continued to be so substantial, at least on paper, that the SPUA appointed a committee in 1814 to consider the expediency of establishing a branch of the Society in that city; a year later, however, the committee rejected the idea without comment.[23] The most important change came as a result of an 1813 resolution to consider dividing the SPUA into "several committees or classes," an idea based on the apparent effectiveness of the then year-old mineralogical committee. Within a year three members were appointed to each of the four committees in the following areas:

Agriculture—to include Domestic economy, Husbandry, Horticulture, Botany, Implements & Machinery, Grasing, Dairy, Diseases, & Management of domestic animals, soils & manures.

Chemistry—to include mineralogy, metallurgy, Arts of Dyeing, Brewing, Baking, Malting, Glass making, Potter's arts, and all the arts connected with Chemistry.

Mechanical Arts—to include every specie of handicraft for necessaries, conveniences, or elegancies of life. . . . [Also,] all those Arts & Sciences which depend for their illustration on the Science of Mathematiks, as Mechanicks, Opticks, Astronomy, Pneumaticks, &c.

Fine Arts—Painting, sculpture, engraving, music, Architecture. . . . [24]

Each committee was responsible for all communications within its area and for periodic reports on its branches. While there is little evidence that the committee system greatly enhanced the level of operations of the Society, the efficiency of the system may have helped to avert an earlier, more rapid, or more total decline than that which the SPUA eventually suffered.

More importantly, the committees signified a broadening range of interests which were at least officially recognized as legitimate areas of scholarly concern for the SPUA. Botany, never before explicitly included in the Society's subject areas, was assigned to the agricultural committee. Although it had received earlier attention as a special project, mineralogy along with metallurgy was now included as a stated inquiry of the chemistry section. And in the mechanical arts the Society expressed for the first time its concern for a range of the physical sciences that would later become a mainstay of the Society's interests. The inclusion of the fine arts, an unrelated activity, was little more than a dream; the committee's only recorded contribution over the next few years was to procure a portrait of Robert R. Livingston for the Society's chambers. While agriculture was still a primary area of activity, the focus of its committee's responsibilities was considerably broader than that of the ten specific agricultural concerns of the SPAAM in the 1790s. These changes, included in revised bylaws passed by the Society in 1815, signified at least the formal beginning of the SPUA as a scientific society.

Not only a broader, but also a more dynamic society was evolving. One of the most energetic and tireless contributors to this evolution, T. Romeyn Beck, enthusiastically wrote to his former teacher in 1812, "The Society has never had so many communications as it had the last winter. Every week there was one, and in general they were very good." A few years later Beck bragged, "The society intend publishing every spring, if they have sufficient materials."[25] The first number of the fourth volume of the *Transactions* appeared in 1816. Two hundred and eighteen pages, this one number could have constituted a whole volume, or certainly one additional year's communications would have filled a complete volume well. But the council was explicitly anxious to demonstrate the Society's new range of interests: four papers on agriculture, three on strictly natural history topics (of no immediate applicability to agriculture), and five on a wide variety of the useful arts, broadly conceived. As the editors emphasized, "although Agriculture is a paramount, yet it is not an exclusive subject of enquiry, and accordingly, papers on any subject connected with the Useful Arts, in their most extensive sense, have been thought worthy of a place."[26]

By 1816 and 1817 there was evidence of a leveling off and later a gradual decline in SPUA activity. The number of meetings per year fell below the number for 1815, but, even more important, attendance at meetings was off as well. Recruitment of new members dipped below the previous average between 1816 and 1818, suffering a sharp decline in 1819 and 1820, with no new members from 1821 through 1823.[27] In 1819 the second part of the fourth volume of *Transactions* appeared, containing slightly more emphasis on agricultural matters but also a continued high representation of the other useful arts. These original notes and articles comprise the first 152 pages of the second part; an additional 182 pages are devoted to "selected" (i.e., reprinted from other journals) pieces, with a heavy emphasis on agricultural matters. While this second part of the fourth volume was by no means unworthy of a scientific society, especially in a provincial setting, its contents did not measure up to those of the first part in terms of the originality of its contributions.

After the zenith year 1815, the wartime bubble burst. Since 1808 the SPUA had enjoyed the warm patronage of the legislature—the prewar and wartime political economy had provided for the SPUA an important role in state affairs and the Society had flourished. But after the war the legislature was less convinced that such a program needed continuation. The program of premiums for the best woolens generally declined after 1815. In 1818 the SPUA committee complained of the "small number of specimens that have been offered and also generally . . . their inferior quality." The last year of the SPUA's involvement with the program was 1819. The State Board of Agriculture, established that year, inherited these responsibilities, thus changing the whole bearing of the SPUA to a "city institution."[28] Might the heavier emphasis on agriculture in the *Transactions* in 1819 have been aimed at convincing legislators of the SPUA's devotion to that study, to convince them that no Board of Agriculture would be needed? To take away the agricultural functions of the SPUA was to excise its very heart and original purpose. The Society was left with only its concerns for the development of the useful arts and its nascent interests in the sciences.

In general, the SPUA's ability to deal effectively with legislators had slipped but not from lack of patriotism and regional chauvinism. A number of the SPUA's petitions, urging further government programs to insure, at last, comparability to and independence from Europe, fell on deaf ears. In 1816 the Albany Academy trustees, well represented in the SPUA membership, petitioned jointly with the SPUA for a state-endowed professorship of chemistry and mineralogy, but the plea was repeatedly unsuccessful.[29] A year later the SPUA urged the legislature and even the U.S. Congress "that it is expedient to encourage domestic manufactures." The U.S. Congress, they pleaded, should take measures "conducive to the promotion of the manufactures of this country & which in their full exercise will render us independent of foreign relations." Two weeks later the SPUA resolved to petition the state legislature for an act to encourage agriculture, arts, and manufactures, noting explicitly that the SPUA would consider it a "mark of confidence."[30] But there were again too few in sympathy. Repeated frustrations made the Society acutely sensitive to their declining stature. "While other bodies . . . possess the patronage and favourable eye of the State, it cannot be expected that the exertions of the Society will be either very extensive or conspicuous. Like most literary and scientific institutions in this country, it has now to depend on the talents and industry of its Members alone, and like them also, it must be liable to seasons of occasional depression."[31]

By 1817 the Society was beset with "depression." Treasurer Isaac Hutton had bankrupted the Society, leaving it seriously indebted after years of enjoying reported treasury balances in excess of $1,000. As T. R. Beck wrote to John Wakefield Francis:

. . . our Treasurer is a Bankrupt, has $1200 of our money in his hands, of which we cannot get any thing. The expectation of this event, & the very provoking conduct of the members in not exerting themselves to prevent the loss, have indisposed me in such a manner towards the Society, that I shall decline hereafter taking any active part in its affairs. Apart from the little Library we were forming, the Society never was very useful—always excepting its encouragement of *Domestic* Manufactures.[32]

Now, instead of contemplating opening an SPUA branch in New York City, Beck was asking Francis to urge the members there to pay up past dues. And, in soliciting such past dues, the Society burst still another bubble. In 1818 an investigative committee found that many members had been elected without their consent or even knowledge, and the recording secretary had often been slow in notifying them. "In numerous instances individuals have been members for several years before they became acquainted with [the SPUA]." Naturally, these members were reluctant to pay up the arrears. "Again, several members have joined when called to Albany by public duties, and probably have not again visited it for several years."[33]

Corrective measures did not begin until the reshaping of membership procedures in 1818.[34] Several years of tight financial management alleviated the worst symptoms by 1820 and accompanied other well-intentioned innovations. Amos Eaton offered to give a course of lectures on agriculture. On its own, the SPUA began a program of premiums to be awarded for the best original memoirs in a range of topics from the most advantageous agricultural exports to the diminution of imports, and from mineralogy and botany to animal husbandry.[35]

Nonetheless, other problems persisted. By 1820 a drop in attendance was apparently serious enough to T. R. Beck to initiate a study of how to make meetings "more useful and interesting."[36] An SPUA committee was even appointed to confer with the Board of Agriculture on the subject of a union of the two groups, but no report was ever recorded.[37]

Following Beck's suggestions, an investigating committee proposed several stopgap reforms. The order of business at meetings was reshuffled. Papers could be read even when no quorum was present. Volunteers for papers would be asked to announce their topics in advance. If no volunteer were scheduled for the next meeting, the president could appoint a member to prepare an original contribution. Soon enough, such a circumstance arose. President Simeon DeWitt called upon Dr. Joel Wing to present a communication. Illustrating the futility of such a procedure, Wing complied one week later with a paper on "Cooking of Food."[38]

Financial troubles continued to plague the SPUA, even though it had avoided collapse in 1817 and had recovered significantly. In the years 1821 through 1823 attendance dropped more than before, despite stopgap reforms. Desperate attempts were made to rectify the organization. The initiation fee was raised to $25 for revenue, but had to be dropped when no new members joined. Extra levies were laid on members residing in Albany, but only a small portion was collected. Finally, attendance at a minimum of two meetings per legislative session was required to maintain membership.

By 1823 the demise of the Society was almost inevitable. "When the Members of this Society shall have been reduced within the number of officers mentioned in the charter, ie. shall be less than sixteen, then the provisions of the charter cannot be fulfilled . . ." and the properties must be divided up.[39] Only two meetings had attracted a quorum in 1823. No additional *Transactions* had been or would be forthcoming.

The skeletal Society met in early 1824 almost exclusively for the business of joining with the upstart Albany Lyceum of Natural History. In profile the SPUA membership in 1824 looks somewhat different from the profiles of members in 1793 and 1806.[40]

	Attorneys	Physicians	Educators	Scientists	Businessmen	Clergymen	Miscellaneous	Occupations Identified	Average Age	Ages Identified
SPAAM in 1793	16^2	5^2	2	6^3	10	1	1*	41 of 72^a	43.7	40 of 72
SPUA in 1806	6^2	2^1	1	2^2	5^1	0	1**	17 of 25^b	47.8	17 of 25
SPUA in 1824	3	4	2	4^3	6	1	4^1***	24 of 31	49.0	23 of 31

*Playwright-artist-historian William Dunlap
**Stephen Van Rensselaer
***Stephen Van Rensselaer, E. C. Genet, 2 engravers
[a]Twenty-three of 31 unknowns are active politicians but have no other identifiable primary occupation
[b]Five of 8 unknowns are active politicians but have no other identifiable primary occupation

There had been a decrease in the number of attorneys, especially those who had published scholarly contributions. None of the members with unidentifiable primary occupations is known to have been politically active, in contrast to significant numbers in that category in 1806 and 1793. The archetype scientist-politician-learned gentleman, so characteristic of the SPAAM and the early SPUA, was no longer strongly in evidence. Rather, the SPUA in the 1820s was spearheaded by active scientists and known scientific enthusiasts; Simeon De-Witt, T. Romeyn Beck, Edmund C. Genet, John Randel, Jr., and even Stephen Van Rensselaer were the spiritual core. Whereas agricultural concerns had been paramount in the SPUA in its early life, by the 1820s the members of the Society had been channeled into the sciences and other useful arts. Of the 1806 incorporators, only the eighty-two-year-old John Tayler and sixty-eight-year-old Simeon DeWitt were still active.

The Albany Lyceum of Natural History

The Albany Lyceum of Natural History was the 1823 product of a plan originated by a small group of Albany residents. Young and enthusiastic, these men consciously began a lyceum in the image of the New York Lyceum of Natural History,[41] making no pretensions about the scope of their interests and being remarkably pragmatic in planning their organization. Their objective was the study of natural history exclusively, and they felt confident of the best approach.

Who were these few founders? Unlike the founders of the SPAAM and the

SPUA, they were young men, similarly well educated, but having practically no political experience; instead they possessed eagerness, enthusiasm, and energy. Half of the fourteen founders had been contemporaries at Union College and/or the Albany Academy.[42] Only two of the founders were over thirty years old. The average age of twelve of them, twenty-four years, suggests that they were, in general, only a few years out of school.[43] Their occupations were as follows:[44]

	Attorneys	*Physicians*	*Educators*	*Scientists*	*Businessmen*	*Clergymen*	*Miscellaneous*	*Occupations Identified*	*Average Age*	*Ages Identified*
ALNH Founders	5[1]	1	1	4[3]	3[1]	0	0	14 of 14	27.5	13 of 14

The group included four scientific practitioners or researchers. In addition, five of the fourteen had published, or would eventually publish, in natural history or closely related areas.

These founders set up the constitution and bylaws of the Lyceum with an eye toward the practical success of the society. Their canvass had shown that there were several individuals in Albany who were willing to deposit their minerals and botanical collections: some five hundred minerals and one thousand plants were promised if the proper cases could be built. The founders knew that the collections and library would be crucial to the growth of the Lyceum, and they accordingly planned to construct a greater number of cases than were immediately needed to attract further donations. They confidently expected that Stephen Van Rensselaer, who sponsored several county agricultural and geological surveys locally, would deposit the collected specimens in the Lyceum. Such a spectacular collection would draw the assistance of the state's most wealthy citizens, but membership was to be open to those of far less fortunate circumstances. Estimating their total costs at $100 and confident of getting fifty members at $2 each, the founders emphasized the importance of inexpensive dues in the society's infancy. "For if it were otherwise, many persons who would be very useful to us would on this account be deterred from joining the institution." And the Lyceum seemed particularly certain to attract the interest of the "intelligent and scientific" state legislators who would proudly bring and deposit specimens from their home territories.[45]

In all, the Lyceum was conceived by a few young men as a place for serious natural history work in an environment that could provide the energy and support. On the eve of the opening of the Erie Canal, such optimism in this particular provincial setting was not unwarranted.

The group that was proposed and elected as original members of the Lyceum was similar in profile to those fourteen founders.[46]

	Attorneys	Physicians	Educators	Scientists	Businessmen	Clergymen	Miscellaneous	Occupations Identified	Average Age	Ages Identified
ALNH Founders	5[1]	1	1	4[3]	3[1]	0	0	14 of 14	27.5	13 of 14
ALNH Original Members	11	6[1]	1	3[1]	1	0	5*	27 of 30	29.2	25 of 30
ALNH Total in 1823	16[1]	7[1]	2	7[4]	4[1]	0	5	41 of 44	28.6	38 of 44

*Stephen Van Rensselaer, Stephen Van Rensselaer, Jr., 1 engraver, 2 druggists

All but eight of the forty-one identified members were clustered within the twenty- to thirty-year-old bracket.

Was there any relationship with the SPUA at the founding? Only one member of the SPUA, T. R. Beck, was among the active founders of the Lyceum. Four more were included in the thirty new members. As the ages might indicate, if there were any relationship between the SPUA and the Lyceum, it could nearly be symbolized by that of fathers and sons. In fact, six original members of the Lyceum were sons of active SPUA members. Stephen Van Rensselaer, who was included along with his son in the list of thirty new members, remarked that he was pleased to see "the rising generation taking a higher stand in the literary & scientific world than their fathers."[47]

In its aggressive first year the Lyceum was quite a contrast to the SPUA. Not confined to the legislative schedule, the Lyceum held thirty-one meetings throughout 1823, adjourning only two for want of a quorum. The Lyceum met temporarily in the Chamber of Commerce building until they received permission to use the Board of Agriculture's room in the Albany Academy building; the Academy trustees soon complied with an additional room for the Lyceum's use, provided that the Lyceum equip the room. The Lyceum publicly solicited funds for the work, a procedure they would resort to many times in the future. Their receipts totaled an unexpectedly high $223, all from nonmembers who were characteristically older, established Albany lawyers, politicians, and businessmen.[48]

Other business was quickly attended to. The Lyceum was incorporated in April of 1823. Committeemen were elected for their four standing committees: geology, botany, mineralogy, and zoology. Officers were elected: Stephen Van Rensselaer, president, and T. R. Beck, first vice-president; three curators were named too, along with the corresponding secretary, the recording secretary, the treasurer, and a draftsman. Unlike the situation at the SPUA, the presidency of the Lyceum was proffered to a great science patron, not because he had been or promised to be a tireless worker in the society but because of the potential prestige and wealth he would bestow upon the Lyceum. As president, Van Rensselaer was certainly not a worker; in fact, he only reluctantly accepted the presidency and he attended only one of the thirty-one meetings in 1823. But his worth as a patron would be felt many times. It was proven for the first time in November 1823 when he donated a goniometer (an instrument for measuring angles) and a collection of minerals so valuable that a special meeting was held to acknowledge the event.[49]

The Lyceum's collections had grown in the first year far beyond the wildest dreams of the organizers; even the extra cases had been filled, and more were needed. Then, too, membership had increased by 75 percent. Between February of 1823 and May of 1824, some thirty-three new members had joined.[50] In profile they changed the Lyceum little:

	Attorneys	Physicians	Educators	Scientists	Businessmen	Clergymen	Miscellaneous	Occupations Identified	Average Age	Ages Identified
ALNH in 1823	16[1]	7[1]	2	7[4]	4[1]	0	5*	41 of 44	29.6	38 of 44
New Members, 1823-1824	8	6	2	2[2]	3	1	3**	25 of 33	25.2	24 of 33
ALNH Total in 1824	24[1]	13[1]	4	9[6]	7[1]	1	8	66 of 77	28.0	62 of 77

*Stephen Van Rensselaer, Stephen Van Rensselaer, Jr., 1 engraver, 2 druggists
**One engraver, 2 military

The low average age of new members continued; the Lyceum, which was created by young, well-educated and energetic men, was continuing to attract such types.

With the spectacular growth in membership and collections and the problems of establishing rules, committees, cabinets, and meeting places, the Lyceum was slow in gathering speed in other areas. Scientific publications had not been discussed in the course of organizing the Lyceum. Once organized, the Lyceum paid only lip service to republishing a guide for naturalists which was never forthcoming. The library was recognized as essential from the beginning, but purchases were made cautiously and growth was modest.[51] Many meetings were held without any scientific papers, donations, or learned discussions. Fewer than a dozen presentations had been read in the first year, most of which were done by only a few men. L. C. Beck addressed the Lyceum six times on a variety of natural history topics, and Matthew Henry Webster and Simeon DeWitt Bloodgood each gave two talks. The lack of a full schedule of papers and wide distribution of authors may have been simply the mark of a society still in the throes of organizing. But the Lyceum was hardly topheavy with a vast number of established naturalists. Given the groundwork of the first year, the Lyceum's potential was surely greater than its scholarly achievements. By 1824 it was enthusiastically led by a respectable group of scientific practitioners and researchers, but its well-educated, youthful cultivators had not yet exhibited much learning in natural history.

The Albany Institute

By early 1824 Albany had two established scientific societies, as distinct in their subject areas as they were in membership. Judging from the profiles above, both had only a handful of scientists who accounted for the bulk of scholarly publications and leadership.[52] While both societies were composed of generally learned members (neither society had significant numbers of the uneducated or laborers), the Lyceum membership was more than twice the size and barely half the age of the SPUA's. There was no appreciable overlap in membership; only T. R. Beck had been active in both.[53] The most significant contrast was between the momentum of the youthful, burgeoning, but almost clumsy Lyceum and the disappointing decline of the small but sophisticated SPUA.

The impetus for a union came from the SPUA. That Society was, in essence, barely alive; something had to be done to prevent its properties from being divided up. Adding breadth to the scholarly scope of the Society was considered; as T. R. Beck recalled a decade later:

> On the establishment of the Board of Agriculture by the legislature, the society for the promotion of useful arts became a city institution. It possessed a small but valuable library, and many of its members were unwilling that this should be dispersed and the society abandoned. It was thought that a union with the Lyceum of Natural History, and the extension of the objects of the society, so as to comprehend general literature, might be useful to all engaged, and, if properly sustained, honorable to the city. Of this plan, Mr. [Simeon] DeWitt was a warm and zealous supporter.[54]

The SPUA proposal of February 18, 1824, contained an outline of the projected society. It would consist of a confederation of three departments, with the SPUA being the First Department (of physical sciences and arts), the Lyceum being the Second Department (of natural sciences), and a Third Department to be formed for the study of history and general literature.

The notion of a section devoted to history and general literature was, in the long run, significant. Why would these societies have entertained such an idea at this time? Apart from the justification offered by T. R. Beck, the SPUA had earlier accorded at least token acceptance to the fine arts. Moreover, the Third Department may have attracted many members of the Lyceum who joined, not because they were ardent naturalist cultivators but simply because the Lyceum was Albany's only young, viable learned society in the early 1820s. For some within the societies, and hopefully for many others in Albany, the section of history and general literature might thus elevate both societies into a grand-scale learned institute.

According to the proposed rules for union, the properties of the existing societies were to be combined but not legally alienated, such that the SPUA's specimens would be "deposited" in the Lyceum and the Lyceum's books would be "deposited" in the SPUA. The effect would be a single library in the care of the First Department's librarian, and a single collection in the custody of the Second Department's curators. The integrity of each society would be maintained in other ways: each would elect its own officers and members; each would handle its own finances; each would continue to hold its own meetings. Biweekly joint meetings would be held for the annual election of a president and treasurer, the presentation of papers, donations, departmental reports, and other Institute business.

Perhaps surprised and not wholly enthusiastic, the Lyceum's response was hesitant. The proposal was nearly rejected at first. But Henry J. Linn, a twenty-three-year-old attorney, recommended that the SPUA proposal be accepted with modifications insuring, among other things, continued inexpensive dues and election of Institute officers by a plurality of all members. Linn's resolutions carried, and by early April two committees of five men, each working jointly, drew up formal articles of union. The societies were allied and officers elected at their first joint meeting of May 5, 1824.[55] As they saw it, the union was a credit to both constituent societies. Through careful manipulations, neither had anything to lose. The major gains would be a larger audience for papers, a larger but consolidated base for communications with corresponding members, and a broader spectrum of subjects of inquiry.[56] The chance to form a more "learned" society could be taken with practically no risk, as the union would be effective even in the event that the Third Department failed to form.

Stephen Van Rensselaer was elected the first president of the Institute and was unanimously reelected until his death in 1839. His presidency was similar to his presidency of the Lyceum. While he attended only three meetings in fifteen years, he was a serviceable titular head and an almost inexhaustible patron of science and the Institute.

Any member of the SPUA was a member of the First Department, and Lyceum members were members of the Second. In 1824, then, the composite profile of Institute membership looked like this:

	Attorneys	Physicians	Educators	Scientists	Businessmen	Clergymen	Miscellaneous	Occupations Identified	Average Age	Ages Identified
SPUA in 1824	3	4	2	4[3]	6	1	4*[1]	24 of 31	49.0	23 of 31
ALNH in 1824	24[1]	13[1]	4	9[6]	7[1]	1	8**	66 of 77	28.0	62 of 77
Total Albany Institute	27[1]	17[1]	6	13[9]	13	2	12[1]	90 of 108	34.1	85 of 108

*Stephen Van Rensselaer, E. C. Genet, 2 engravers
**Stephen Van Rensselaer, Stephen Van Rensselaer, Jr., 2 engravers, 2 druggists, 2 military

Possibly indicating that the formation of the Institute was not to the liking of a significant number of the thirty-one SPUA and seventy-seven Lyceum members, the first meeting was attended by only five from the SPUA and fifteen from the Lyceum.[57] But if enthusiasm was limited to only a few members at the time of the formative meeting, it was not easily exhausted that year. The Institute held nine meetings throughout the remaining half of 1824 (taking no "recess" in this first year). In these meetings, four major original papers were delivered in addition to two exhibitions of a secondary nature. Seemingly endless donations of books and specimens from members and outsiders alike were presented. Albany newspapers published notices of meetings, lists of donations and donors, and occasional abstracts of proceedings.

From the outset publications were viewed as essential for two reasons: "The utility of periodical publication under the auspices of an active & intelligent Society is unquestionable, both as it respects the Members & the Public. It incites and awakens investigation among the former, & it attracts the favorable notice of the latter." The only hesitation stemmed from the society's lack of confidence respecting its competency to furnish original articles of merit in a balanced journal reflecting the Institute's range of interests from the physical and natural sciences to literature.[58] The Institute boldly decided affirmatively, appointing a permanent publications committee charged to issue numbers, then volumes, of the new journal.

The development of the Third Department (of history and general literature) came slowly, in a less formal and determined way. By February 1825 the Third Department announced it had formed and elected its officers. The initial membership was almost wholly an assembly of new members from outside the Institute, not transfers from the First or Second Departments. Until 1829, however, the Third Department was never formally organized and was of little consequence in Institute activities.

The First Annual Report of the Albany Institute, published in July 1825 primarily for public relations purposes, gave the picture of an organization considerably smaller than the constituent societies had been in pre-formative days. The nominal, inactive membership of both societies apparently dropped out; no evidence has survived to indicate any widespread rejection of the union. According to the *Annual Report,* twenty remained in the First Department, thirty-eight in the Second, and the Third was "just organizing." Some financial troubles had persisted. The First Department had leftover debts,[59] and the Second Department had incurred debts in installing new cases needed to receive the overwhelming flow of donations. The promise and problems of the Institute were continuations of those from earlier days.

In the period 1824 through 1829 the Institute became, rather methodically, a steadily growing more confident society. During these years it held an average of eight meetings per year, in which an average of twelve papers were given, eight of them being significant original contributions of which half would be published. Using T. R. Beck's impression of the SPUA in 1812 as a yardstick (he was pleased with one paper per meeting), the Institute could point to one and one-half papers per meeting, at least one per meeting being original.

Interestingly, the members of the small First Department led in presenting 55 percent of the significant scholarly, or original, contributions, while only 43 percent came from the Second Department. On the other hand, the Second Department originated 64 percent of the lesser contributions (translations of foreign works, exhibitions of specimens, readings from journals, etc.), while only 36 percent of these presentations came from the First. The older, more accomplished membership of the First Department was responsible for the bulk of key scholarly papers, but the energy and interest of the neophyte Second Department were contributing significantly to the building of a more solid, science-educated society. Only one paper was contributed by a Third Department member, and only one paper in the history-literature realm was given by a member of another department.[60] At least eight of the scholarly papers addressed topics outside the subject areas of the departments to which the authors belonged; significantly, the bulk of this subject crossover was represented by members of the Second Department giving papers related to the physical sciences, the realm of the First Department. The broadened spectrum of subject areas, made possible by the 1824 union, was having positive effects.[61]

Growth was also evident in an unending stream of donations. By 1829 the library had more than doubled in size, from 329 volumes to 682, and the museum had more than doubled its original count of 1,867 specimens. This period's most significant single donation of both natural history books and specimens came from the heirs of De Witt Clinton in 1828.[62] Increased space was provided by the Albany Academy trustees, and cash donations solicited from the public provided more cases and furnishings.[63]

During this period the publication commitments also came to fruition. A pamphlet containing four papers was released as the first number in 1828. By October 1829, the second number was issued, containing six papers. The published papers, all of which had been delivered by and before the Institute members, represented a range of contributions from terrestrial magnetism to botany, electromagnetism to geology and climatology, and from T. R. Beck's efforts on "Americanism" to his "Statistics on Insane Asylums." The first number was sent to seventeen different societies in the United States and Europe and was well enough received to be abstracted in a number of important journals.[64]

Minutes of meetings were occasionally abstracted in Albany newspapers, and special meetings, such as the one for the annual address open to the public, often received editorial comments. Institute contacts beyond the Albany environs were expanded by means of an ever-increasing body of corresponding members—highly respected scientists from both sides of the Atlantic elected to free membership in the hope they would contribute papers, make donations, or simply spread the reputation of the Institute.[65] Some complied.

Reflecting the Institute's success in the first five years of operations, an act of incorporation was passed by the state legislature in late February 1829. A committee of the Institute had drafted the incorporating act in the fall of 1828, but in the process of review the Senate Committee on Libraries added amendments. The Institute was surprised to learn that the Third Department for History and General Literature, which had languished since its informal organization in early 1825, must be formally constituted. The Institute scrambled to write the constitution and bylaws and to elect officers. T. R. Beck even suggested that a literary journal be added to the list of four scientific journals received by the Institute.[66]

A profile of the eighteen incorporating members of the Third Department shows a group somewhat different than in preceding profiles:

	Attorneys	*Physicians*	*Educators*	*Scientists*	*Businessmen*	*Clergymen*	*Miscellaneous*	*Occupations Identified*	*Average Age*	*Ages Identified*
Third Department in 1829	7[3]	0	2[2]	1	3	3	2*	18 of 18	34.9	18 of 18

*One politician, 1 journalist-politician

The average age was nearly thirty-five years, but the ages were more evenly distributed than in other departments: five in their teens or twenties, eight in their thirties, and five in their forties or fifties. Six of the members had transferred from the Second Department, while none had switched from the First.[67] The Third Department was established to bring a new learned dimension to the Institute, and in time that dimension would radically change the Institute's course.

Following the 1824-1829 period of solid growth, the Institute spent the next four years at its highest level of activity. An average of eleven meetings were held per year between 1830 and 1833, and this increased number meant an overall increase in Institute productivity. Of an average of one and one-half papers presented at each meeting, slightly more than one per meeting was an original contribution of apparent publishable quality. One-third of those papers were, in fact, published by the Institute.

Membership had grown gradually since the 1825 dip, and continued to grow during the apex period.[68]

	Attorneys	Physicians	Educators	Scientists	Businessmen	Clergymen	Miscellaneous	Occupations Identified	Average Age	Ages Identified
1830										
I	3	3	1	4[3]	6	0	2*	19 of 22	50.5	17 of 22
II	7	6[2]	2	7[4]	16[1]	1	4**	43 of 46	34.2	36 of 46
III	7[4]	0	1[1]	0	3	4[3]	1***	16 of 16	37.4	16 of 16
Total Albany Institute	17[4]	9[2]	4[1]	11[7]	25[1]	5[3]	7	78 of 84	39.3	69 of 84

*Stephen Van Rensselaer, 1 engraver
**Stephen Van Rensselaer, Stephen Van Rensselaer, Jr., 2 druggists
***One journalist-politician

	Attorneys	Physicians	Educators	Scientists	Businessmen	Clergymen	Miscellaneous	Occupations Identified	Average Age	Ages Identified
1833										
I	2	3	1	4[3]	4	0	1*	15 of 21	54.7	16 of 21
II	18	6[2]	1	5[3]	15[1]	2	1**	48 of 65	33.0	46 of 65
III	12[7]	0	3[1]	1	3	2	1***	22 of 24	36.0	22 of 24
Total Albany Institute	32[7]	9[2]	5[1]	10[6]	22[1]	4	3	85 of 110	37.9	84 of 110

*Stephen Van Rensselaer
**Stephen Van Rensselaer, Jr.
***One journalist-politician

Growth from 1830 to 1833 was not evenly distributed among the departments. The First Department actually sustained one net loss, and the increase in average age indicates that younger members were not being attracted to that Department. Successful recruitment in the Second and Third Departments is indicated by healthy increases in membership, coupled with slight decreases in the average ages. Young people were still being attracted to the Institute.

During this period the Institute enjoyed an unprecedented warm relationship with the Albany public. As before, local newspapers continued to note meetings, donations, and some proceedings. Editorial remarks were even more enthusiastic than before. As the *Argus* commented in 1830:

> While noticing this society, it will be proper to add that new cases have been recently erected, and that the whole collection is now arranged in order. As it is in every respect a public collection, so admittance can be gained at all times, and we know that it affords high gratification to the members to exhibit it. As an institution emanating from the citizens and mainly supported by their liberality,

it is one in which all may feel a proper degree of pride from its present highly flourishing state.[69]

The "flourishing state" was evident in the increases in the collections. In April 1830 William Caldwell, a prominent local businessman, had belonged to the Institute just two weeks when he gave $200 for the "completion" of the mineralogical collection and the purchase of books on mineralogy.[70] John Delafield, Jr., a local citizen and not a member, donated roughly four hundred mineralogical and geological specimens two months later.[71] These donations, combined with a constant flow of smaller gifts, exhausted the cabinet space, forcing the Institute to make another public appeal. By late 1833 over $400 had been donated and an appeal to the Academy trustees had succeeded in acquiring more room for the collections.[72] The Institute's museum, after doubling in size from 1824 to 1829, doubled again in the four years 1830 through 1833.

The library also benefited as a result of donations. It had increased from 329 volumes in 1824 to 682 in 1829, then from 761 in 1830 to 1,592 in 1833. In 1832 Joseph Henry, then the Institute's librarian, was proud to "have access to a valuable collection of scientific works and most of the European periodical publications."[73]

The publications program had progressed so favorably during the 1824-1829 period that the Institute was encouraged to incur the expenses of publishing a complete volume of their *Transactions*. A third number appeared by early spring, 1830; it contained contributions from Henry, T. R. Beck, L. C. Beck, Amos Eaton, and Jacob Green. All contributions had been read before the Institute, and they ranged over such topics as topography, geology, and natural history. With greater emphasis on the physical sciences, the fourth number contained articles from Stephen Alexander, George W. Clint, and Benjamin F. Joslin and a lengthy anniversary address by Benjamin F. Butler. The completed volume was published in late 1830, embellished with an appendix containing the charters and the history of the Institute, a catalog of the library, an abstract of Institute proceedings, and a catalog of members. By October 1833 the first number of the second volume was issued, containing articles on astro-omy, meteorology, natural history, and geology, as well as Amos Dean's annual address. Again, these contributions—by T. R. Beck, Stephen Alexander, James Eights, and Simeon DeWitt—had all been delivered before the Institute.

The subject areas of the published articles and the authors themselves reflected the relative contributions of the departments within the Institute. In a change of role from the 1824-1829 period, the Second Department contributed the largest single share, 39 percent of the original papers read at Institute meetings from 1830 to 1833. The First Department's contribution had dipped to 24 percent of such scholarly contributions, while the Third began to show strength with 13 percent. The remote corresponding members had communicated a significant share, some 24 percent. The Second Department continued to perform most of the secondary presentations, 67 percent, while the First delivered 20 percent and the Third 13 percent.

In the period 1830 through 1833 the Institute enjoyed unparalleled prosperity. Scarcely having been in the black in the earlier period, the treasury could boast of growth to a balance of $50 in 1830 and a balance of $171 in 1833. Much of the strength of the Institute had been due to the maturing of the Second Department. They had more than taken up the slack from the aging and dwindling First Department, while the contributions of the Third Department were beginning to appear in meetings, if not yet in print. With varying degrees of momentum in each department, the Institute by 1833 had achieved its most effective balance and its apex as a learned society.

Even the decline that followed was not without accomplishments. The Institute resolved late in 1833 to petition the legislature to establish a state natural history museum. Though unsuccessful, that particular plea has been viewed as an essential contribution toward legislation for the organization of a State Natural History Survey. Significantly, however, when the American Institute of New York City successfully petitioned for the State Survey two years later, the Albany Institute did not offer its support as a resolute body. Rather, the Survey was pushed into the political arena by a coterie of lobbying science enthusiasts who were nearly all active members of the Albany Institute. There was no official representation from a lively and effective Institute as late as 1835.[74]

During these few years following the apex of Institute activity, the publications program continued but showed symptoms of decline. The second number of volume two of the *Transactions* was completed by June 1836. Mainly tables of meteorological observations, annual addresses, and a historical piece, the contents were a significant departure from earlier tendencies toward the more exact sciences and reflected a diminution of the Institute's creative capabilities.

Despite a good deal of activity, the earlier vivaciousness, enthusiasm, and momentum began to fade. A leveling off of activity characterizes the period 1834 through 1836; while there were an average of eleven meetings per year, the average number of all presentations per year dropped to twelve, barely assuring the attending members of one presentation per meeting. There was an average of a mere 6.3 scholarly papers per year, and only one paper from each year was published. By 1837 a more radical decline had begun. Meetings dropped to an average of 5.3 per year through 1843, maintaining an average of just over one presentation per meeting. Scholarly papers dipped to a lower average, 3 per year, and only 2 papers during that period were every published.

Membership too reflects a decline from the 1833 high point.[75] Drops in membership since 1833 occurred most significantly in the First Department (nearly 50 percent net) and in the Second Department (about 37 percent net) while the Third Department sustained a net loss of only 8 percent. The average age of members in the Second Department increased significantly, indicating that recruitment was

	Attorneys	Physicians	Educators	Scientists	Businessmen	Clergymen	Miscellaneous	Occupations Identified	Average Age	Ages Identified
1836										
I	2	2	0	1^1	3	0	0	8 of 11	53.5	8 of 11
II	14	3^2	0	4^3	11^1	0	0	32 of 41	36.7	31 of 41
III	9^6	2	2^1	1	4	1	1*	20 of 22	36.2	20 of 22
Total Albany Institute	25^6	7^2	2^1	6^4	18^1	1	1	60 of 74	39.2	59 of 74

*One journalist-politician

	Attorneys	Physicians	Educators	Scientists	Businessmen	Clergymen	Miscellaneous	Occupations Identified	Average Age	Ages Identified
1837										
I	2	2	0	1^1	2	0	0	7 of 10	53.6	7 of 10
II	7	2^2	0	3^2	7^1	0	0	19 of 24	37.5	18 of 24
III	8^4	1	2^1	1	4	1	1*	18 of 19	37.2	17 of 19
Total Albany Institute	17^4	5^2	2^1	5^3	13^1	1	1	44 of 53	40.8	42 of 53

*One journalist-politician

failing to bring in younger members. These trends are again prevalent in membership changes between 1836 and 1837. In essence, the membership of the Second Department had peaked around 1833 and was beginning to subside. The First Department, which had never really peaked in membership numbers, continued its slow but steady decline. The Third Department was at best holding its own amidst the general recession.

The Library and museum further evidenced the leveling off and decline. Whereas the library had consistently received more than 200 volumes per year in the apex years, from 1834 through 1836 additions never reached 200 and averaged only 144 volumes per year. In the years 1837 through 1843 additions were normally below 100 volumes per year, dipping to a low 30 volumes in 1839. The yearly rate of museum acquisitions, which had averaged 1,497 specimens per year in 1830-1833, dipped to an average of 840 specimens in 1834-1836, and to 377 per year in 1837-1843.

Further shifts could be seen in the relative scholarly (original) contributions of the three departments. In the period 1834-1836 the First Department roughly maintained its previous share of scholarly contributions, 25 percent; the Second Department again claimed the largest share, 62 percent; and the Third contributed at about the same rate as before, roughly 13 percent. Significantly, however, no scholarly papers came before the Institute from the corresponding members during these years. In the period of more serious decline (1837-1843), the First Department's share declined to 17 percent and the Second's declined to 28 percent, while the Third Department contributed by far the greatest share, 44 percent, and 11 percent (two papers on meteorology) were contributed by corresponding members. But if the Second had slipped in its scholarly contributions, it continued to dominate the lectern with 80 percent of the secondary presentations in 1834-1836 and 90 percent in 1837-1843.

More specifically, in the period of greatest decline Institute activity was dominated by meteorological interests. Largely the work of a colorful character, Matthew Henry Webster, the Institute became informally a coordinating agency for the State Board of Regents' meteorological observations system.[76] Moreover, Webster went beyond state and national boundaries in his role as the Institute's chief meteorological enthusiast. As corresponding secretary of the Second Department, he worked to coordinate stateside horary observations, keying in with Sir J. F. W. Herschel's worldwide network of meteorologists. At meeting after meeting Webster would instruct the Institute members in meteorology, including translations from Pouillet's *Meteorology,* presentations of meteorological tables, and readings from Herschel's letters. It was not unusual in the years from 1836 through 1840 to hear M. H. Webster giving two or even three presentations in one evening!

The overemphasis on meteorology, combined with Webster's own overbearing performances, may have contributed notably to the decline in Institute activities in the period 1837 through 1843. By 1837 the weaknesses of the Institute were clearly in evidence. If we are to believe Webster's diagnosis, poor attendance at meetings was discouraging those who might otherwise be interested in giving papers. Coupled with poor attendance were diminishing membership rolls and financial difficulties which, appearing as early as 1834, forced a cessation of publishing activities.[77] The debts of the Institute continued to be pestilential throughout the period 1837-1843. Not only were members not attending, but many were not paying. The treasurer listed nineteen members unpaid in 1837, and no fewer than thirty-two members unpaid in 1838![78] The lack of direct evidence notwithstanding, some of these difficulties could have been reflections of the national financial crises of 1837 and 1839.

The declining state of the Institute did not pass without notice. Aware that something was wrong, Elias Loomis asked W. C. Redfield the pointed question in October 1838: "What has become of the Albany Institute? I cannot learn that they have published any thing new for a long time. Are they defunct or quiescent? I have understood that Mr. Webster, their former Secretary, had been unfortunate in business and was obliged to abandon entirely his scientific pursuits. Is it so?"[79] What had become of the Institute? M. H. Webster blamed the state legislature for forcing the Institute to become too broad in its concerns.[80] But, in retrospect, diversity within the Institute was not the primary reason for its decline.

Changes had taken place in the 1830s not only in the Institute, but also in the learned Albany community and, indeed, beyond. It was not that Albany had become devoid of learned individuals who could continue to support the Institute—quite the contrary. Albany had established several other learned institutions which added to its cultural milieu. Beginning with the State Natural History Survey in the mid-1830s, the Albany scientific community took on more substantial proportions. By 1838 the Albany Medical College was incorporated with a full complement of professors possessing considerable scientific interests and attainments.[81] Nearby, in Troy, Rensselaer Polytechnic flourished, and in Schenectady Union College proudly ranked among the best colleges in the nation, especially for science.

Institutionally, Albany in the 1830s was stronger in learning than ever before. Another institution was born in 1833 that, although at a different level, vied with the Institute for public attention. The Young Men's Association for Mutual Improvement, established for the cultivation of good, learned citizenry among young people, developed rapidly in size and attractiveness and soon far outweighed any other Albany society. Whereas in the early 1830s the Albany newspapers had brought the Institute before the public's eye, from 1835 on the papers did a far more thorough job from day to day for the Young Men's Association. The Young Men's Association held lectures twice a week and consistently drew large audiences; topics ranged from the physical sciences to art, history, philosophy, and law. Essentially a self-help organization receiving no government funds, the Association depended upon public support and succeeded handily. It attracted gifted lecturers from great distances, built a large library, acquired philosophical apparatus, and boasted of a membership exceeding one thousand. Not a direct competitor of the Institute, the Young Men's Association did, however, compete successfully for the public's attention.[82]

In 1842 the Institute attempted a change of character to reestablish itself in the heart of Albany culture. Two free public lectures were scheduled, beginning with the Reverend Horatio Potter on "Imagination." If not immediately and totally successful, the initial results seemed promising. The *Albany Evening Journal* praised the Institute's public-mindedness in initiating the series and urged the public to show greater enthusiasm.[83] Yet, when the Reverend William D. Snodgrass lectured on "The Course of Civilization" one month later, no such enthusiasm was evident in the newspapers, either before or after, or in the attendance. No additional public lectures were forthcoming. The Institute's attempts at sponsoring popular lectures as a means of reestablishing the relationship of the society with the public failed.

By the year 1843 the Institute was weakened beyond hope. In the four meetings held that year, not one scholarly paper was read, not one presentation was made. Symbolic of the changes that had been taking place outside of Albany, as well as within, at the last meeting in 1843 an invitation from the

American Association of Geologists was read, inviting interested members to attend their meetings in Albany that spring. Eight Institute members did in fact attend, but afterwards there was no further Institute meeting at which they might have presented a report.[84]

The demise of the Institute in 1843 was somewhat ironic. Albany at that time was far from a depressed community, especially intellectually. The Natural History Survey, the Medical College, and other growing institutions had attracted more learned and scientific men than ever before gathered in the Albany area. The Institute failed not because of a lack of scientific or learned people to support it. It failed because it could not maintain the broad base of public enthusiasm that was so explicitly integral to its rise in the earlier years. This inability was due, at least in part, to a growing dichotomy between the level of science and learning that the productive members espoused and the level of interest and understanding at which the supportive public was comfortable. For their part, the Institute's scientists began to look beyond the Institute for intellectual camaraderie, to such ventures as the Natural History Survey and the Association of Geologists. Many of these same scientists gave popular lectures to the young audiences at the Young Men's Association. In the meantime, by 1842 only the Third Department literateurs cared enough to make their own attempt, in vain, to reestablish the Institute as a viable society in the Albany learned community.

But the irony of the demise goes back to the interest and enthusiasm of the scientific cultivators who had provided the foundation, if not the leadership, for the early Institute. In Albany by the 1840s the growth of a more professional scientific community was accompanied by a decline in the enthusiasm among the cultivators of science. These cultivators were no longer a continuing source for provincial institution building. As the *Albany Evening Journal* wrote in 1843, "... in this city, where Silliman's Journal formerly had some fifty subscribers, there are now scarcely twenty." That drop is symbolic of the fading of cultivator interest in good general science.[85] Ironically, it was just that kind of interest which fostered the Institute in the first place and which the Institute should have continued to foster, at least for its own sake.

EPILOGUE

Albany reached a peak in cultural excitement in 1851. With the likelihood of the establishment of a national university there, the city became the focus of attention of the nation's most influential educators and scientists; such notables as Louis Agassiz, Benjamin Peirce, John P. Norton, and James Dwight Dana promised to lend their support. The American Association for the Advancement of Science showed its interest by meeting in Albany that summer. The University of Albany, as it was called, announced its courses for 1852 in the medical school, the law school, and the science department.[86]

In the midst of the excitement the Albany Institute was awakened from its eight-year slumber. In the spring of 1851 T. R. Beck called the meetings through newspaper notices. Twenty-two former members responded. By the end of the year seventy-one new members, a noticeably younger and more accomplished group, had changed the profile of Institute membership:

	Attorneys	Physicians	Educators	Scientists	Businessmen	Clergymen	Miscellaneous	Occupations Identified	Former Members'* Average Ages	New Members' Average Ages	Total Members	Ages Identified
1851												
I	3	2	0	5⁴	2	0	0	12 of 13	66.8	34.8	47.0	12 of 13
II	3¹	7³	3¹	5⁴	4	0	3**	25 of 28	47.8	33.8	37.9	21 of 28
III	8¹	3¹	11⁶	2	15	3¹	0	43 of 52	40.3	37.0	37.6	39 of 52
Total Albany Institute	14²	12⁴	14⁷	12⁸	21	3¹	3	80 of 93			40.0	72 of 93

*I, 5 former members; II, 11 former members; III, 6 former members
**1 artist, 1 military, 1 gentleman farmer

The Institute's strongest single department in total members was now the Third, but its membership continued to be dominated by scientists and members of the two science departments with records of scholarly publications. For the first time, however, the Institute had a near balance between science and history-literature members.

The newly reorganized Institute hosted the AAAS convention in August of 1851, and many Institute members attended. No fewer than sixteen meetings of the Institute were held that year, with an average of nearly two presentations per meeting. Contributions of papers at both levels (original and secondary) were evenly divided between the science and history-literature departments. In subsequent years the level of activity dropped to an average closer to one paper per meeting, and the average number of meetings leveled off to about ten per year. In 1852 the second volume of the *Transactions* was finally released, comprised entirely of works presented to the Institute before 1843. In 1855 the third volume was published, being a catalog of the Institute library. Reflecting the near-completion of a process so long in the making, the Institute first considered abolishing the departments in 1856 to consolidate the entire membership into a single learned body, but the traditional departments survived into the 1870s.[87]

What made it possible for the Institute to regain that momentum lost in the 1830s and 1840s was perhaps a conscious rededication to its original implied purpose. At the very least, the problem of the 1840s had been made explicit in some of the remarks presented at the 1851 AAAS meetings. The Reverend Horatio Potter, an Institute member, attended those meetings and listened especially intently to Alexander Dallas Bache's famous presidential address.

During the concluding ceremonies many of the visiting notables heaped praise on the Albany community for its gracious hospitality and support. But Potter, in some apparently unrehearsed, unscheduled comments, pointed out to the meeting that the obligation was Albany's, not the AAAS's. Thanking the AAAS for coming to Albany, he pointed out the cleavage that had contributed to the Institute's demise a decade earlier:

Mr. Chairman, I rejoice in this meeting and feel myself grateful for it, as it has been the means of bringing the People into contact with men of Science—of leading persons engaged in the ordinary pursuits of life to see and feel how much there is that is beautiful and exalted and useful in the labors of the Cultivators of Science. There is too apt to be a feeling in certain quarters that the two classes have nothing in common. Why, gentlemen, what do we sometimes hear? We are told, and what I say is in part suggested by a remark communicated to me by my friend in the chair, (Prof. BACHE) a day or two since, that it is not necessary or desirable to give support to scientific inquiries; that the people have little concern in them, but that they are and ought to be chiefly interested in promoting popular instruction! Why, gentlemen, what a stupendous mistake and absurdity![88]

The question of the Institute's relevancy as a scientific society in a provincial setting, first felt and most strongly evident in the late 1830s and 1840s, would remain a problem throughout the remainder of the century. The Albany community continued to attract a number of respected scientists, primarily because of the dynamic James Hall and the State Natural History Survey. Whereas in the 1820s and 1830s such scientists had enthusiastically supported the Institute as a good, general scientific society, by the 1840s and the 1850s these scientists were devoting a significant share of their energies to the newly established professional organizations and research institutions. The Institute revived at mid-century, not simply as a scientific society but rather as a society of general learning, with an increasing emphasis on history and literature. The humanities, and later the arts, not yet professionalized, attracted the bulk of the young cultivators of learning, as science had done earlier in the century. The Albany Institute of History and Art survived into the twentieth century on the strength of those cultivators.

NOTES

1. The most scholarly attempt in this genre is that of John Davis Hatch, Jr., "The Albany Institute of History and Art: A Sketch of Its Early Forerunners," *New York History* 25 (1946): 311-25. But Hatch drew heavily on Orlando Meads's "Annual Address" of 1871, *Transactions of the Albany Institute* 7 (1872): 1-34. Other examples of such sympathetic orations are sprinkled through the *Transactions.*

2. The membership list used here for study was compiled from the seventy-two names appearing in "The Act of Incorporation," *Transactions of the Society for the Promotion of Agriculture, Arts and Manufactures,* 2d ed. rev. 1 (1801): v-x (hereafter cited as SPAAM *Transactions*). Names from this list, as well as names from other membership lists to be discussed below, were systematically checked in standard biographical sources, state and local histories, and specialized biographical directories too numerous for listing here. Each name was also checked for publications in the *Royal Society Catalogue, Poole's Index to the*

Periodical Literature, and the Library of Congress printed card catalog. The information most sought after consisted of dates of birth and death and occupations, offices held, and, where possible, education. Of the 438 names in the file, 308 (70.3 percent) were satisfactorily identified, 58 (13.2 percent) lacked only their dates, 20 (4.6 percent) lacked only clues to their occupations, and 52 (11.9 percent) eluded the search for significant information. The author gratefully acknowledges the assistance of Kathleen Waldenfels in these biographical searches.

3. Since careers in early American life were often undifferentiated and entailed more than one occupation, generalizations about occupations are hazardous. In this profile, and others to follow, "occupation" is taken to mean "primary occupation," that which was central to the individual's career at the time of the profile or, lacking record of that contemporary occupation, that occupation for which historians have generally remembered him. But placing individuals in occupational categories which are historically accurate and still meaningful to today's scholars raises additional problems. Where occupations have not fallen readily into general categories that are meaningful today, the careers have been listed in the "miscellaneous" category. Engravers, for instance, varied in their devotions to artistry, science, and business; druggists similarly ran the gamut from near-physicians to chemists to businessmen. And a number of other careers are simply best described by the individual's name, such as Stephen Van Rensselaer or William Dunlap.

Primary occupational categories are used in the profiles according to the following general criteria. "Attorneys," "physicians," and "clergymen" are those individuals who were accredited and practicing in those professions. "Educators" are those whose energies were primarily devoted to teaching at any level, as well as those who served as educational administrators. "Scientists" are those who were "practitioners" or who distinguished themselves as "researchers" according to the criteria in Nathan Reingold's "Definitions and Speculations: The Professionalization of Science in America in the Nineteenth Century" (pp. 33-69 of this volume)."Businessmen" includes a wide range of primarily commercial occupations, from retailers to merchants to manufacturers.

4. "Letter of the Agricultural Society to the Friends and Promoters of Rural Economy," ca. 1791, SPAAM *Transactions,* pp. ix-xiv.

5. The first three numbers of the first volume, all published by 1798, contained thirty-six articles on strictly agricultural topics, six articles on related topics (meteorological observations and a geological smattering), four general orations, and one paper on salt springs and salt manufacture. But in the final number (1799), there were thirteen agricultural papers, one general oration, and there were no fewer than eight papers relating to the useful arts—ranging from steam engines, to profits on whale oil, to paper manufacture, to the heating of rooms.

The schedule of publication is not clear from the 1801 volume, but is clarified in the Minutes of the Society for the Promotion of Useful Arts, vol. 1, 7 March 1815, Library, Albany Institute of History and Art, Albany, N.Y. That is, no. 1, 1792; no. 2, 1794; no. 3, 1798; no. 4, 1799.

6. L'Hommedieu was chairman of the formative meeting. Livingston, DeWitt, and Mitchill drew up the bylaws. Livingston served as president of the SPAAM and its successor institution without interruption from 1791 to his death in 1813. For the early meetings, see SPAAM *Transactions,* pp. i-iii.

7. Established in 1803 with national pretensions, the American Board of Agriculture was a short-lived product of the efforts of Isaac Briggs (1763-1825, Maryland agriculturalist and engineer), L'Hommedieu, and Mitchill. James Madison was its president. Briggs Papers, Library of Congress, Washington, D.C.; Mitchill Papers, Library, Albany Institute of History and Art; Courtney R. Hall, *A Scientist in the Early Republic: Samuel Latham Mitchill* (New York: Columbia University Press, 1934), p. 103; Irving Brant, *James Madison, Secretary of State: 1800-1809* (New York: Bobbs Merrill, 1953), pp. 45-46.

8. *Transactions of the Society for the Promotion of Useful Arts* 2 (1807): iv (hereafter cited as SPUA *Transactions*).

9. The twenty-five members of the newly reconstituted society were listed in the minutes of their first meeting. See the Minutes of the Society for the Promotion of Useful Arts 1: 19 February 1806 (hereafter cited as SPUA Minutes).

10. *American Almanac and Repository of Useful Knowledge for 1848* (Boston: James Monroe and Co., 1847), p. 213.

11. See SPUA *Transactions* 2 (1807): 233-36 for the April 2, 1804, act of incorporation. The establishment of the council was authorized in that act, but its responsibilities were specifically defined in the SPUA's first few meetings. SPUA Minutes 1: 5 March and 10 March 1806.

12. SPUA Minutes 1: 14 March 1810, 10 February 1812.

13. SPUA *Transactions* 3 (1814): Appendix, pp. 225-50. This was an attempt to establish real American independence, in the economic as well as cultural sense, in an era of challenge to the new nation and increasing tensions between the United States and Great Britain. The arguments for establishing such a bounty system for American wool manufacture are especially appetizing for the student of political economy. See, for instance, SPUA Minutes 1: 7 March 1810.

14. SPUA *Transactions* 4 (1816): pt. 1, app., p. 6.

15. Ibid., 4 (1819): pt. 2, p. [2]; SPUA Minutes 1: 27 February 1811.

16. SPUA Minutes 1: 13 March, 21 March and 28 March 1811, 4 March 1812, 7 April 1807.

17. Ibid., 13 June 1815. In 1815 alone thirty-four new members were elected. Note, however, that certainly not every member was active in attendance, nor in contributions to SPUA activities. In the period up to 1816, normally one or two meetings per year were adjourned for want of a quorum of nine members. The problem of attendance will be discussed below in reference to the later years of the SPUA.

18. Ibid., 2 February and 21 March 1811, 3 March 1813.

19. Ibid., 16 March 1814. The societies are named in the library report cited in the next note. Several of these societies had contributed their Transactions before the exchange program had been formalized.

20. Ibid., 7 March 1815 and 19 March 1816; "Donations to the Library," SPUA *Transactions* 4 (1816): pt. 1, app., pp. 42-45.

21. Ibid., 2: 10 February 1817.

22. Ibid., 1: 5 April 1812.

23. Ibid., 2 March 1814 and 21 February 1815.

24. The original resolution was passed and recorded in ibid., 17 February 1813. The committees' subjects and responsibilities were approved a year later, February 16, 1814, and incorporated in new bylaws passed February 21, 1815.

25. T. R. Beck to John Wakefield Francis, n.d., J. W. Francis Papers, New York State Library, Albany, N.Y. Internal evidence indicates that the first letter dates from the spring of 1812, while the second is from 1814 to 1817.

26. SPUA *Transactions* 4 (1816): pt. 1, "Advertisement."

27. From 1816 through 1819 an average of ten meetings were held successfully each year, but in three of those four years three meetings per year were adjourned without a quorum. After 1819 the number of meetings successfully held drops: 1820, seven; 1821, seven; 1822, four; 1823, two. In addition, the number of meetings at which no quorum appeared had increased: nine, six, eleven, six respectively. The SPUA added only three new members in 1819 and five in 1820.

28. SPUA Minutes 2: 11 March 1818 and 10 March 1819. The Board of Agriculture was a government agency, established primarily for coordinating county agricultural societies and allocating public funds thereto. See Nathan Reingold et al., eds., *The Papers of Joseph Henry* (Washington, D.C.: Smithsonian Institution Press, 1972), 1:52-53 (hereafter cited as *Henry Papers*).

29. SPUA Minutes 2: 5 March 1816. For the story of successive attempts by the Academy and their motivations, see the *Henry Papers*, pp. 25, 43-44.

30. SPUA Minutes 2: 4 February and 25 February 1817. The petition to the legislature is printed in SPUA *Transactions* 4 (1819): pt. 2, 343-47.

31. This quote followed a statement on the glorious role that the SPUA had played under the legislature's patronage and the tragedy of its end. SPUA *Transactions* 4 (1819): pt. 2, [2].

32. Beck to Francis, 24 September 1817, J. W. Francis Papers. Beck's disappointments did not prevent him from continuing to act as a counselor and future leader of the Society.

33. SPUA Minutes 2: 24 March 1818. This practice of carrying inactive members on the membership lists has an unfortunate effect for today's historians. No reliable statistical

membership profile was possible, as there was no list or even clues to who were the real participants between 1806 and 1823.

34. Essentially, nonpaying members were to be dropped from the rolls and admission procedures would be tightened. New memberships had to be maintained for at least three years before dismissal, which would be granted only if dues were paid up. Life memberships were offered for $25. Two dollars was the annual rate. SPUA Minutes 2: 31 March and 7 April 1818.

35. Ibid., 19 January 1819 and 31 January 1820. There is no evidence that a premiums program of any consequence was ever brought to fruition.

36. Ibid., 17 April 1820.

37. Ibid., 6 March and 3 April 1820.

38. The reforms are noted in ibid., 20 February and 27 February 1821. The appointment and compliance of Wing are noted in ibid., 7 March and 13 March 1821.

39. "Council Report on the By-Laws," ibid., 2 April 1823.

40. No membership list was ever recorded after 1819, but names of members attending meetings were recorded (roll was called in accordance with the reforms noted in the text and in note 38, above.). In addition, dues-paying members were listed in ibid., 21 January 1824. The membership profile is based on a list comprised of dues-paying and/or attending members.

41. Their constitution was drafted "upon the plan of that of the New York Lyceum with such alterations as our situation requires." Minutes of the Albany Lyceum of Natural History, 15 January 1823, Library, Albany Institute of History and Art (hereafter cited as ALNH Minutes). The original constitution is also preserved in the Institute library.

42. There were six Union graduates and two Albany Academy graduates, and one young man who had studied at both schools.

43. One man's age is unknown; the age of the other, then-Chancellor James Kent, was sixty, so uncharacteristic (the twelve other ages are between twenty and thirty-two) that his age was eliminated from the average of these twelve. In the profiles, however, Kent's age has been included.

44. There is no original list of the "meeting of the several gentlemen of the City of Albany" and of the individuals who participated in formative activities. The fourteen members represented here are those whose names appear in the minutes of the meetings prior to the acceptance of the first wave of membership. ALNH Minutes, 7 January through 18 January 1823.

45. Report of the "Committee appointed to consider the practicability of forming a Lyceum of Natural History," ibid., 15 January 1823.

46. The list of the thirty new members is contained in ibid., 18 January 1823.

47. Stephen Van Rensselaer to the Albany Lyceum, 7 February 1823, Albany Institute Correspondence 1795-1840, Library, Albany Institute of History and Art; also quoted in the *Henry Papers*, p. 70.

48. ALNH Minutes, 17 February 1823; "Licence for Begging for the Lyceum," 24 February 1823, Albany Institute Correspondence 1795-1840 (and printed in the *Henry Papers*, pp. 61-62). The thirty-five donors are listed, with the amounts of their donations, on an inside flyleaf of the ALNH Minutes.

49. The honorary election of Stephen Van Rensselaer had been calculated as one of the factors assuring the success of the Lyceum (see the discussion above on where the collections would come from and note 45). An anonymous tipster warned the president-elect, then serving in Washington as a congressman, of the "sinister motives of the Albany Lyceum in electing you President" (see "Amicus" to Stephen Van Rensselaer, postmarked 15 February [1823], Albany Institute Correspondence 1795-1840). Van Rensselaer at first declined (see the "Committee Report of the Albany Lyceum," 29 January 1823, Albany Institute Correspondence 1795-1840), but the patroon mysteriously reversed that decision. His "honorary" presidency was a contrast to the history of the SPUA's presidency. Such SPUA leaders as Robert R. Livingston, Simeon DeWitt, and Edmund C. Genet had distinguished themselves as founders, tireless workers, and repeated contributors of original works both before and during their presidencies. But Van Rensselaer was widely respected as a patron of science, and the Lyceum founders were pragmatic enough to seek his attention. At the meeting held in November to commemorate his donation, it was resolved

to publish a note of appreciation in the newspapers for his services as a science patron. See ALNH Minutes, 6 November 1823; "Albany Lyceum," *Albany Argus,* 10 November 1823.

50. The names of new members were gathered from the minutes of meetings at which they were elected, from 3 February 1823 through 19 April 1824.

51. Specific purchases were *Silliman's Journal,* the *Journal* of the Academy of Natural Sciences of Philadelphia, Torrey's *Flora of the Northern and Middle Sections of the United States,* the *Annals of the Lyceum of Natural History of New York,* and the Royal Institution's *Journal of Science and the Arts.* See ALNH Minutes for 16 May and 13 October 1823 and 9 February 1824.

52. Scientific practitioners or researchers represent only 16.6 percent of the SPUA identified occupations and only 13.6 percent of the ALNH identified occupations. But note that in the SPUA in 1824, of the four members who published, three were scientific practitioners or researchers and the fourth, E. C. Genet, was a well-accomplished cultivator. And three of these four—T. R. Beck, Simeon DeWitt, and Genet—were active leaders of the SPUA. Examining the Lyceum in 1824, note that two-thirds of those who published in natural history were science practitioners or researchers, namely: T. R. Beck, L. C. Beck, Jesse Buel, James Eights, Joseph Henry, and Winslow C. Watson. All but Watson were officials of the Lyceum, 1823-1824.

53. Three other Lyceum men, Stephen Van Rensselaer, John S. Walsh, and Peter Van O'Linda had paid dues to the SPUA in 1823 but had not attended meetings there. Even as members of the Lyceum they were not among the most active.

54. T. Romeyn Beck, "Eulogium on the Life and Services of Simeon DeWitt..." (delivered before the Albany Institute, 23 April 1835), *Transactions of the Albany Institute* 2 (1852): 325.

55. The minutes of the first joint meeting provide a euphemistic summary of the spring's proceedings. They are recorded in the Albany Institute Minutes 1: 5 May 1824, Library, Albany Institute of History and Art, and they are reproduced in the *Henry Papers,* pp. 65-72. Additional details on the proceedings within the SPUA and the Lyceum appear in their minutes of meetings.

56. One major advantage of union for both societies would be that members could now deliver papers in realms well outside their own constituents' major interests. For instance, a naturalist of the Lyceum may feel an urge to give a paper on steam engines, or a surveyor from the SPUA might wish to discuss some flora or fauna he discovered. This kind of subject crossover does occur in the early period of the Institute and will be mentioned in the text as well as in note 61.

The fact that the bulk of subject crossover was by members of the Second Department giving papers in areas of physical science and the useful arts gives rise to speculation about the Lyceum's interest in union with the SPUA. A number of Lyceum members may have joined the Lyceum because they could best relate with that age group and because they had at least a latent interest in science or other learning. They may not have been ardent naturalists and they may not have sincerely preferred the natural sciences over the SPUA's physical sciences and useful arts. But the SPUA in the early 1820s may not have been attractive to a young, aspiring cultivator of science or learning. The fact that very few members of either society switched membership after the union suggests that age-group cohesion may have continued for many years. But in 1829 six members of the Lyceum crossed to the Third Department, indicating that the Lyceum members may have had more of a need for the expanded breadth than the SPUA members, none of whom made the transfer. See below in the text and note 67.

57. Sizeable general attendance at meetings was, of course, then a problem for the SPUA, and may have been appearing as a difficulty for the Lyceum. But the formative meeting was obviously for many not as auspicious an occasion as in retrospect it might have been. Even T. R. Beck, whose enthusiasm could not be questioned, was absent.

58. Report of the Publications Committee, Albany Institute Minutes 1: 13 October 1824, reproduced in the *Henry Papers,* pp. 72-77.

59. Manuscript Report of the Treasurer of the Society for the Promotion of Useful Arts, 30 June 1825, Library, Albany Institute of History and Art.

60. T. R. Beck's "Notes on Mr. Pickering's 'Vocabulary of Words and Phrases... Peculiar to the United States' with Preliminary Observations," *Transactions of the Albany*

Institute 1 (1830): 25-31. Beck's address was read at the March 18, 1829, meeting, at which time the Third Department was formally being incorporated (see below in the text). It may have served more as a warm, welcoming hand to the newly organized group than as a demonstration of the Institute's interests in nonscientific matters in the period 1824-1829.

61. For instance, such members of the Second Department were L. C. Beck, who gave a talk "On Magnetism," 14 February 1827; George W. Clinton, "Repulsion as a Distinct Property of Matter," 21 March 1827, and "Essay on Light," 10 October 1827; Richard V. DeWitt, "Steam Engines," 25 April 1827; and Philip Ten Eyck, "On Steam Engines, Models and Designs," 4 March 1829. Before he joined the First Department and maintained dual membership, Joseph Henry gave several papers on the physical sciences, including his lecture, "On the Chemical and Mechanical Effects of Steam," 30 October 1824, printed in the *Henry Papers,* pp. 78-92. Henry joined the First Department to serve as the Institute's librarian. Only a few other members, notably T. R. Beck and Stephen Van Rensselaer, maintained dual memberships. Despite the overlap in interests, peer groups functioned most strongly as cohesive factors. See notes 56 and 67.

62. Albany Institute Minutes 1: 27 February and 12 June 1828.

63. Ibid., 25 April 1827 and 4 March 1829. Contributors, all nonmembers, were given free, nonvoting memberships.

64. The societies to which the *Transactions* were sent are listed in the Albany Institute Minutes 1: 10 July 1828 (reproduced in part in the *Henry Papers,* pp. 208-10) and 22 August 1828. The encouraging reception for the number is reported in the Institute Minutes 1: 15 April 1829 (also reproduced in part in the *Henry Papers,* pp. 217-21).

65. There were, for instance, such Americans as Asa Gray, John Torrey, Benjamin Silliman, William C. Redfield, and Henry R. Schoolcraft. Included among the foreigners were Adolphe Quetelet and Sir J. F. W. Herschel. A list of 420 corresponding members of the Institute, including all nonresident members of the constituent societies, as well as all corresponding members elected up to 1870, is printed in the *Transactions of the Albany Institute* 6 (1870): 323-31.

66. The act of incorporation is printed in *Laws of the State of New York Passed at the Fifty-first Session, Second Meeting, 1828; and Fifty-second Session, 1829* (Albany: Edwin Croswell, 1829), pp. 106-108. The legislative history can be traced through the *New York Assembly Journal, 52nd Session, 1829,* pp. 39, 110, 162, 517; *New York Senate Journal, 52nd Session, 1829,* pp. 128, 167, 205, 217-18. Preparations by the Institute are reported in Albany Institute Minutes 1: 22 August and 25 November 1828. T. R. Beck's remarks are recorded in the Institute Minutes 1: 15 April 1829 (reprinted in the *Henry Papers,* pp. 217-21).

67. This is further evidence of the Lyceum's interest in broader subject coverage. Note that changing membership affiliation to a new group with a wide distribution of ages was more acceptable to Lyceum members than was crossing over to the SPUA or First Department, where the members were considerably older. See note 56, above.

68. The 1830 membership list was gleaned from the list printed in the *Transactions of the Albany Institute* 1(1830): pt. 2, app., pp. 65-74. The 1833 membership list was taken from the Annual Report for 1833 in the Institute Minutes 1: 6 February 1834.

69. "Albany Institute," *Albany Argus,* 9 April 1830.

70. Albany Institute Minutes 1: 8 April 1830, printed in part in the *Henry Papers,* pp. 269-70. By 1833 the Caldwell fund had been expended. The Institute had purchased fifty-five volumes representing thirty-one titles in mineralogy, as well as forty-nine specimens of considerable rarity. Albany Institute Minutes 1: 10 July 1833.

71. Ibid., 29 June 1830.

72. Ibid., 3 October 1831; 7 March, 10 October, and 11 December 1833.

73. Joseph Henry to John Maclean, 28 June 1832, Princeton University Archives, Princeton, New Jersey. Reproduced in the *Henry Papers,* pp. 435-37.

74. The New York State Survey represented a model that was followed by many other state natural history and geology surveys. As a result of the visible activities of the lobbying coterie (such Institute members as T. R. Beck, L. C. Beck, John A. Dix, Governor William L. Marcy, and James Hall), the Institute soon became popularly associated with the beginnings of the survey. For the origins and early years of the survey, see Michele L. Aldrich, "New

York State Natural History Survey, 1836-1845" (Ph.D diss., University of Texas, 1974). By the 1840s the kind of state museum that the Institute had proposed in 1833 inevitably resulted from much of the survey's collecting activities.

75. The lists for these profiles were recorded in the Annual Reports for 1836 and 1837 in the Albany Institute Minutes 1: 13 April 1837 and 14 February 1839. These are the only reliable lists of members available for the period 1834 through 1843.

76. Webster's role, and indeed the Institute's role, in the New York State meteorological network was never by official designation. The state's meteorological observations system was initiated by Simeon DeWitt early in the century. Under DeWitt's plan, the regents required each state-supported academy to keep meteorological data and to submit it annually. Conceivably the arrangement with the Institute was informal; in the late 1830s as many as fourteen of the twenty regents were members of the Institute. Nevertheless, the identity between the Institute and the meteorological system was clear enough to Joseph Henry in 1851, according to his remarks in "Proceedings of the Association for the Advancement of Science," *Albany Evening Journal,* 26 August 1851. The origins of the regents' system and Henry's role in it are portrayed through the documentation in the *Henry Papers,* passim.

77. See Matthew Henry Webster, "Annual Address for 1837," *Transactions of the Albany Institute* 2 (1852): 234-36.

78. The treasurer's accounts are recorded in a manuscript volume entitled "Treasurer of the Albany Institute," Library, Albany Institute of History and Art. The accounts were not kept in a consistent manner, but it is evident that unpaid memberships were continuing through 1843.

79. Elias Loomis to William C. Redfield, 22 October 1838, Loomis Papers, Yale University, New Haven, Connecticut, as reproduced in Nathan Reingold, ed., *Science in Nineteenth-Century America* (New York: Hill and Wang, 1964), p. 100.

80. Matthew Henry Webster to A. W. Smith, 17 June 1836, A. W. Smith Papers, Brown University Library, Providence, Rhode Island.

81. Samuel Rezneck, "The Emergence of a Scientific Community in New York State a Century Ago," *New York History* 43 (1962): 211-38; Franklin B. Hough, comp., *Historical and Statistical Record of the University of the State of New York* (Albany: Weed, Parsons and Company, 1885), pp. 169-72.

82. Some of the local lecturers were Amos Dean, T. R. Beck, Amos Eaton, James Hall, and Jesse Buel, to name just a few. Outsiders included Benjamin Silliman, Sr., and, later, Louis Agassiz. Wallace K. Schoenberg, "The Young Men's Association, 1833-1876: The History of a Social Cultural Organization" (Ph.D. diss., New York University, 1962).

83. "The Albany Institute," *Albany Evening Journal,* 23 January 1842.

84. As of the spring of 1843 the Institute Minutes stop, and no meetings or other activities are reported until the spring of 1851. Similar gaps are apparent in the minutes of each department, which were kept in separate volumes and have been preserved in the Library of the Albany Institute of History and Art.

85. "Silliman's Journal," *Albany Evening Journal,* 2 May 1843. *Silliman's Journal* may have begun as America's best scientific journal, but with the passage of time and the increased specialization and sophistication in the sciences it became less relevant to the practitioners' and researchers' work. The Connecticut Academy of Arts and Sciences, which had relied on *Silliman's* as its publishing arm, learned to regret "the disadvantage of excluding abstract and technical memoirs, which are unsuited to the pages of a periodical [such as *Silliman's Journal*] which depends upon popular patronage, although containing discoveries of the highest importance to pure science." See Elias Loomis, "Connecticut Academy of Arts and Sciences," in William L. Kingsley, ed., *Yale College: A Sketch of its History,* 2 vols. (New York: Henry Holt & Co., 1879), 1:329-37; quote is from p. 334. A drop in the Albany subscriptions reflects a decline in the popular science patronage there.

86. The cultural outlook was characterized by a comment in the *New York Times:* "While New York has become the London of the Western hemisphere, Albany will soon be its Gottingen and Leipsic." As quoted in Howard S. Miller, *Dollars for Research* (Seattle: University of Washington Press, 1970), p. 40; *University of Albany Circular of the Scientific Department . . . for 1852* (Albany: Charles Van Benthuysen, 1851). The hopes for the

university had died by the mid-1850s, not because of any lack of local enthusiasm; see Robert Silverman and Mark Beach, "A National University for Upstate New York," *American Quarterly* 22 (1970): 701-13.

87. Albany Institute Minutes 1: 17 January and 14 February 1856.

88. "Proceedings of the Association for the Advancement of Science," *Albany Evening Journal,* 26 August 1851.

Early Learned Societies in Boston and Vicinity*

WALTER MUIR WHITEHILL

The American Academy of Arts and Sciences

The American Academy of Arts and Sciences, the second oldest learned society in the United States, regards John Adams, the second President of the United States, not only as its second president but also as its founder. Admittedly, John Adams was inspired by the American Philosophical Society which he came to know while in Philadelphia as a delegate to the Continental Congress. On a hot Sunday morning in August 1776, he attended a Baptist meeting in Philadelphia and was disgusted by the furious, vociferous boisterousness of the preacher. In writing home to his wife, he compared "scholars educated at the southward" and "southern preachers" unfavorably with products of Harvard College:

Particular Gentlemen here, who have improved upon their Education by Travel, shine; but in general, old Massachusetts outshines her younger sisters, still. In several Particulars they have more Wit than We. They have Societies, the Philosophical Society particularly, which excites a scientific Emulation, and propagates their Fame. If ever I get through this Scene of Politics and War, I will spend the Remainder of my days, in endeavoring to instruct my Countrymen in the Art of making the most of their Abilities and Virtues; an Art, which they have hitherto, too much neglected. A philosophical society shall be established at Boston, if I have Wit and Address enough to accomplish it, sometime or other.[1]

In traveling from Boston to Philadelphia, John Adams had several times amused himself at Norwalk, Connecticut, with Mr. Arnold's "very curious collection of birds and insects of American production"; they made so deep an impression upon him that he could not but consider it a reproach to his country "that so little was known, even to herself of her natural history."[2] In the Continental Congress he had introduced a resolution that each colony establish "a society for the encouragement of agriculture, arts, manufactures, and commerce," and "maintain a correspondence between such societies, that the rich and natural advantages of this country, for supporting its inhabitants, may not be neglected."[3]

---

*This paper deals only with early societies that have survived to the present day with purposes akin to those for which they were established.
[1] Notes to this chapter begin on page 172.

Such thoughts were constantly in John Adams's mind. Recalling the events leading to the foundation of this Academy in 1780, he wrote in 1809:

When I was in Europe, in the years 1778 and 1779, in the commission to the King of France, with Dr. Franklin and Mr. Arthur Lee, I had opportunities to see the king's collection and many others, which increased my wishes that nature might be examined and studied in my own country, as it was in others.

In France, among the academicians and other men of science and letters I was frequently entertained with inquiries concerning the Philosophical Society of Philadelphia, and with eulogiums on the wisdom of that institution, and encomiums on some publications in their transactions. These conversations suggested to me the idea of such an establishment at Boston, where I knew there was as much love of science, and as many gentlemen who were capable of pursuing it, as in any other city of its size.

In 1779, I returned to Boston in the French frigate *La Sensible,* with the Chevalier de la Luzerne and M. Marbois. The corporation of Harvard College gave a public dinner in honor of the French ambassador and his suite, and did me the honor of an invitation to dine with them. At table, in the Philosophy Chamber, I chanced to sit next to Dr. Cooper [Rev. Samuel Cooper, Fellow of Harvard College, 1767-1783]. I entertained him during the whole of the time we were together, with an account of Arnold's collections, the collections I had seen in Europe, the compliments I had heard in France upon the Philosophical Society at Philadelphia, and concluded with proposing that the future legislature of Massachusetts should institute an academy of arts and sciences.

The doctor at first hesitated, thought it would be difficult to find members who would attend to it; but his principal objection was that it would injure Harvard College, by setting up a rival to it that might draw the attention and affections of the public in some degree from it. To this I answered,—first, that there were certainly men of learning enough that might compose a society sufficiently numerous; and secondly, that instead of being a rival to the university, it would be an honor and advantage to it. That the president and principal professors would no doubt be always members of it; and the meetings might be ordered, wholly or in part, at the college and in that room. The doctor at length appeared better satisfied; and I entreated him to propagate the idea and the plan, as far and as soon as his discretion would justify. The doctor accordingly did diffuse the project so judiciously and effectually, that the first legislature under the new constitution adopted and established it by law.

Afterwards, when attending the convention for framing the constitution [of Massachusetts], I mentioned the subject to several of the members, and when I was appointed by the sub-committee to make a draught of a project of a constitution, to be laid before the convention, my mind and heart were so full of this subject, that I inserted the chapter fifth, section second.[4]

This section, concerning the encouragement of learning, was a characteristic and unique contribution of John Adams to the Constitution of Massachusetts. As his grandson, Charles Francis Adams, observed some seventy years later: "The recognition of the obligation of a state to promote a higher and more extended policy than is embraced in the protection of the temporal interests and political rights of the individual, however understood among enlightened minds, had not at that time been formally made a part of the organic law."[5] After indicating that "it shall be the duty of legislators and magistrates, in all future periods, to cherish the interests of literature and the sciences, and all seminaries of them" and enumerating Harvard University and public and grammar schools, John Adams outlined these additional duties, "to encourage private societies and public institutions, rewards and immunities for the promotion of agriculture, arts, sciences, commerce, trades, manufactures, and a natural history of the country; to countenance and inculcate the principles of humanity and general benevolence, public and private charity, industry and frugality, honesty and punctuality in their dealings, sincerity, good humor, and all social affections and generous sentiments among the people."[6]

In his 1809 memorandum John Adams confessed that he was "somewhat apprehensive that criticism and objections would be made to the section, and particularly that the 'natural history', and the 'good humor' would be stricken out; but the whole was received very kindly, and passed the convention unanimously, without amendment."[7]

Four months after his return from France, John Adams was off to Europe once more on a diplomatic mission. He sailed on November 13, 1779, again in *La Sensible,* and was abroad in France, the Netherlands, and England until the spring of 1788. In his absence the Reverend Samuel Cooper indeed acted "judiciously and effectually" upon the subject that John Adams broached at the Harvard Corporation dinner on August 24, 1779. "An act to incorporate a Society for the cultivation and promotion of Arts and Sciences" was read for the first time in the Massachusetts House of Representatives on December 15, 1779, and was passed on May 4, 1780. In accordance with this act a charter was granted, incorporating Adams, Cooper, and sixty other citizens of Massachusetts into "a Body Politic and Corporate, by the name of The American Academy of Arts and Sciences." The charter thus defined the "end and design" of the Academy:

to promote and encourage the knowledge of the antiquities of *America,* and of the natural history of the country, and to determine the uses to which the various natural productions of the country may be applied; to promote and encourage medical discoveries, mathematical disquisitions, philosophical inquiries and experiments; astronomical, meteorological, and geographical observations, and improvement in agriculture, arts, manufactures, and commerce; and, in fine, to cultivate every art and science which may tend to advance the interest, honor, dignity, and happiness of a free, independent, and virtuous people.[8]

The aspirations and scope of the new Academy were graphically represented in an allegorical corporate seal, which was described in the following manner in the first volume of the Academy's *Memoirs*:

The principal figure in it is Minerva. At her right-hand is a field of Indian Corn, the native grain of *America.* The prospect on that side is bounded by a hill, crowned with Oaks. On the declivity of the hill, towards the sea, appears the out-skirt of a town, the body of which is concealed by the hill. About the feet of Minerva are scattered several instruments of husbandry. On her left-hand are a quadrant and a telescope, a prospect of the sea, with a ship steering towards the town; and the sun rising, and appearing completely above the cloud, in which it rose. Over the whole, the motto SUB LIBERTATE FLORENT.

The device represents the situation of a new country, depending principally on agriculture; but attending at the same time to arms, commerce, and the sciences. The sun above the cloud represents, not only our political state in 1780, when the Academy was first incorporated, but also the rising state of *America,* in regard to empire, and the arts and sciences. The motto conveys the general idea that arts and sciences flourish best in free States.[9]

The engraving of this device was not very skillfully carried out. On the title page of Volume I of the *Memoirs,* its details are far from clear, and, as new cuts were made from ink-clogged impressions, it became worse, decade after decade. Finally in 1954, when it had degenerated into a black gob that disfigured any page it was intended to adorn, Rudolph Ruzicka, a fellow of the Academy more highly skilled in the graphic arts than the original engraver, redrew the seal in a handsome manner that clarifies the iconography.

Hardly had the first meeting of the Academy taken place before John Adams was spreading the word in Europe of the Academy's foundation. On August 22, 1780, he sent Jean Luzac, publisher of *Nouvelles extraordinaires de divers endroits,* popularly known as the *Gazette de Leyde,* copies of the Academy's charter and recent publications of the American Philosophical Society, explaining in his covering letter that "at a time when the English Emissaries are filling all Europe with their confident assertions, of the distress of the Americans, the inclosed Papers show that both at Philadelphia and Boston, the People are so much at their Ease, as to be busily employed in the pursuits of the Arts of Peace."[10] Luzac achieved something of an eighteenth-century record for up-to-the-minute reporting by publishing a French translation of the Academy's charter, with a paraphrase of John Adams's letter, in the August 29, 1780, issue of his *Gazette,* one day previous to the third meeting of the Academy, at which statutes were adopted and Governor James Bowdoin was elected president and Samuel Cooper vice-president.

For the next sixty years the Academy convened quarterly, with a reasonable pattern of summer and autumn meetings at Harvard College and winter and spring meetings at a variety of places in Boston. When Bowdoin was formally inducted at the fourth meeting on November 8, 1780, he gave a "philosophical discourse" that was soon printed in pamphlet form and subsequently included as the leading article in the first volume of the Academy's *Memoirs.*[11]

A fortnight before Bowdoin's affirmation of faith in the experimental principle, the Academy and Harvard College had sent a scientific expedition to Penobscot Bay to observe a total eclipse of the sun.[12] It was led by Samuel

Williams, Hollis Professor of Mathematics and Natural Philosophy and a member of the council of the Academy. The party included Stephen Sewall, Hancock Professor of Hebrew and vice-treasurer of the Academy; James Winthrop, librarian of the University and cabinet keeper of the Academy; Fortesque Vernon, who had taken his A.B. degree at the last Harvard commencement; and six undergraduates.

The Commonwealth "though involved in all the calamities and distresses of a severe war . . . discovered all the attention and readiness to promote the cause of science" by providing transportation in the state galley, *Lincoln.* The party embarked on October 9, 1780. The officer in command of the British garrison permitted the expedition to enter the enemy-held Penobscot Bay while Captain Henry Mowatt of H.M.S. *Albany* made himself most helpful. Landing at Islesboro on the nineteenth, the party set up their instruments. When the eclipse took place on the twenty-seventh, following two days of thick fog, the observers found to their sorrow that they were just outside the path of totality. In view of the limited time allowed for this excursion into enemy-held territory, they had not had sufficient opportunity to check their latitude.

By the curious workings of what Horace Walpole called "serendipity"—"the faculty of making happy and unexpected discoveries by accident"—their location made them the first to see and record what are now known as "Baily's Beads." Fifty years later the English astronomer Francis Baily gave his name to the beads of light that appear along the edge of the sun a few seconds before or after totality; this effect is created when the almost completely obscured sun shines through the mountain-lined valleys of the moon. However, it was the new academicians from Cambridge, looking through their telescopes at Islesboro, who first discovered this phenomenon—a remarkable event that was the result of the respect for learning shown by neighbor and enemy alike during the American Revolution.

The results of this and numerous other experiments and observations were published in 1785 in a handsome 622-page illustrated quarto volume of *Memoirs.* John Adams, then Minister to the Court of St. James's, lent his copy to John Singleton Copley, with a request for his opinion of the unsigned copper engraved plates. Copley replied candidly: "I think them well engraved, much better than I should have expected, as there was no person that knew much of that Art, in the State of Massachusetts when I left it; but there is a total want of the knowledge of Perspective in every part of them."[13] This, incidentally, is amusing evidence of Copley's opinion of Paul Revere, who had been turning out not very inspired engravings for more than a decade before 1774, the year Copley left Boston, never to return.

James Bowdoin held the presidency of the Academy until his death on November 6, 1790. The following spring John Adams, then Vice-President of the United States, was elected to succeed him. While two generations of Adamses have been Presidents of the United States, three have presided over the American Academy of Arts and Sciences. John Adams was president of the Academy from

1791 to 1814; his son, John Quincy Adams, and his grandson, Charles Francis Adams, held the same office, while his great-great-grandson, Thomas Boylston Adams, has been the Academy's treasurer since 1955.

The sixty-two men who were named in the Charter of Incorporation as fellows of the Academy were all citizens of Massachusetts.[14] Moreover fifty-six of them were graduates of Harvard College. The senior was clearly the Reverend Charles Chauncy of the class of 1721, long minister of the First Church of Boston; not far behind him stood the Reverend Samuel Mather (A.B. 1723), son of Cotton and grandson of Increase Mather. Oddly enough, the next to the youngest incorporator, Theodore Parsons of Newburyport of the class of 1773, was already dead when the charter was issued. In the list of incorporators in the Academy's Centennial Volume,[15] this young physician is enigmatically described as "lost at sea, 1779, aged 28." This entry perplexed me until my late classmate Clifford Kenyon Shipton (1902-1973) who, through having prepared fourteen volumes of *Sibley's Harvard Graduates,* knew more about eighteenth-century New Englanders than any man who has ever lived, furnished the clue. Young Parsons had gone to sea as surgeon in a revolutionary privateer that was reported missing. As there was apparently still hope that he might turn up when the application for the charter was submitted in the spring of 1780, his name was included among the sixty-two incorporators. Since he never did, his older brother Theophilus (A.B. 1769) later Chief Justice of Massachusetts, was included in the first group of fellows elected on January 31, 1781.

Of the six incorporators who had not taken a Harvard bachelor's degree in course, four were recipients of honorary degrees. The Reverend Daniel Little (1724-1801), who had reached the pulpit of the First Congregational Church of Kennebunk without benefit of a college education, received an honorary A.M. from Harvard in 1766. This, as Clifford Shipton well said "was not an honorary degree in the modern sense, but an invitation to join the tight circle of educated men."[16] Parson Little was a rustic scientist, who contributed a paper on "Observations upon the Art of Making Steel" to the first volume of the Academy's *Memoirs.* Shipton remarks that "his efforts at the furnace which he set up by his house at the Landing were unsuccessful. No doubt he was inclined to be too sanguine, for he once announced that he had discovered a way to cure cancer by clay poultices."[17] James Sullivan, a justice of the Massachusetts Superior Court in 1780, had never seen the inside of the college either, for he was a self-taught Maine lawyer. At the 1780 commencement, however, Harvard made him an honorary Master of Arts. John Bacon, a 1765 graduate of the College of New Jersey, received an honorary A.M. from Harvard in 1771 when he was pastor of the Old South Church in Boston. When sacked by his congregation in 1775, he moved to Stockbridge, where he combined law with farming, serving on the Court of Common Pleas of Berkshire County from 1779 to 1811. At various times Bacon was a member of both houses of the Massachusetts legislature; as a Jeffersonian Republican, he served in the national House of Representatives from 1801 to 1803. Theodore Sedgwick of Sheffield was graduated from Yale in 1765. In 1780 he was a member of the Massachusetts House of Representatives. After a career that included both houses of Congress and a seat on the Supreme Judicial Court of Massachusetts, Harvard College gave him an LL.D. in 1810.

Thus sixty of the sixty-two incorporators of the Academy were holders of some Harvard degree. The Northampton lawyer Joseph Hawley, who was influential in the dismissal of his cousin Jonathan Edwards from his church in 1749-1750 and was the leading spirit of the Revolution in the Connecticut valley, was a Yale man of the class of 1742 without Harvard connections. The sixty-fourth, described as "Elijah Lothrop, Boston. Died in 1797?" was never a student at Harvard. Thus far, I have been unable to discover who he was or what he did that brought him into this distinguished company.

In local terms the incorporators were an eminent lot for they included John Adams (A.B. 1755), elected by Congress in September 1779 to negotiate treaties of peace and commerce with Great Britain; his cousin Samuel Adams, (A.B. 1740), delegate to the Continental Congress and the chief magistrate of Massachusetts; John Hancock (A.B. 1754), Governor; Thomas Cushing (A.B. 1744), Lieutenant Governor; Henry Gardner (A.B. 1750), Treasurer; Robert Treat Paine (A.B. 1749), Attorney General and, with Hancock, a signer of the Declaration of Independence; William Cushing (A.B. 1751), Chief Justice, and Nathaniel Peaslee Sargeant (A.B. 1750) and James Sullivan, justices of the Massachusetts Superior Court.

Nearly all the principal officers of government and instruction of Harvard College were in the list. President Samuel Langdon (A.B. 1740) and Fellows Samuel Cooper (A.B. 1743), Caleb Gannett (A.B. 1763), James Bowdoin (A.B. 1745), and Edward Wigglesworth (A.B. 1749), with Treasurer Ebenezer Storer (A.B. 1747) represented six-sevenths of the Harvard Corporation. For some reason not clear at this distance John Lathrop (A.B. College of New Jersey 1763, hon. A.M. Harvard 1768), although a member of the Harvard Corporation from 1778 to 1815, was only elected to the Academy on August 25, 1790. The holders of the only three endowed chairs that then existed were incorporators: Edward Wigglesworth, Hollis Professor of Divinity; Samuel Williams (A.B. 1761), Hollis Professor of Mathematics and Natural Philosophy; and Stephen Sewall (A.B. 1761), Hancock Professor of Hebrew and Other Oriental Languages. So were James Winthrop (A.B. 1769), the librarian, and Benjamin Guild (A.B. 1769), a tutor. Joseph Willard (A.B. 1765), although at the time minister of the First Church in Beverly must be mentioned with this group, for he had earlier been a tutor and a fellow and was to return to Cambridge the following year as president of Harvard College.

Learning in an earlier stage was represented by two schoolmasters. Samuel Moody (A.B. 1746) was the first master of Dummer Academy in Newbury when it opened in 1763. The Duxbury schoolmaster George Partridge (A.B. 1762) was also Sheriff of Plymouth County, a member of the Continental Congress and, later, of the House of Representatives.

Lawyers and judges formed the largest group among the incorporators: in addition to John Bacon, Theodore Sedgwick, Robert Treat Paine, William Cushing, Nathaniel Peaslee Sargeant, and James Sullivan, who have previously been mentioned, there were William Sever (A.B. 1745) of Kingston; Andrew Oliver (A.B. 1749) of Salem; David Sewall (A.B. 1755) of York, an enthusiastic amateur astronomer; John Pickering (A.B. 1759) of Salem, Register of Deeds for Essex County; John Lowell (A.B. 1760), a future fellow of Harvard College; Francis Dana (A.B. 1762), future Minister to Russia and Chief Justice of Massachusetts; Nathan Cushing (A.B. 1763) of Scituate; Caleb Strong (A.B. 1764) of Northampton, a future United States Senator and Governor of Massachusetts; John Sprague (A.B. 1765) of Lancaster, who farmed as well; and Levi Lincoln (A.B. 1770) of Worcester, later Attorney General of the United States under Jefferson and Governor of Massachusetts.

There were eleven clergymen beyond those who were represented in Harvard College. The venerable Charles Chauncy and Samuel Mather, who have previously been mentioned, were almost indispensible ornaments to any group organized in Boston; at the other end of the scale came the Reverend John Clarke (A.B. 1774), one year junior to the unfortunate Theodore Parsons. Clarke was Chauncy's colleague in the First Church of Boston and later his successor. The Reverend Phillips Payson (A.B. 1754) of Chelsea, who was greatly interested in astronomy, was the only one close to Boston. Otherwise the clergy, like the previously mentioned Parson Little of Kennebunk, were scattered throughout Massachusetts; also like him, most of them had scientific predilections. In order of age they were the Reverend Abraham Williams (A.B. 1744) of Sandwich, the Reverend Samuel West (A.B. 1754) of New Bedford, the Reverend Samuel Deane (A.B. 1760) of Portland, the Reverend Perez Fobes (A.B. 1762) of Raynham, the Reverend Nehemiah Williams (A.B. 1769) of Brimfield, and the Reverend Zedekiah Sanger (A.B. 1771) of Duxbury. Parson West, although notably credulous, had a reputation for omnivorous learning that extended far beyond his isolated New Bedford. He was elected to the American Philosophical Society in 1768; to the American Academy he contributed hints on the making of porcelain and a study of the supposedly volcanic origin of Gay Head. Samuel Deane, far away on Casco Bay, was fascinated by science and reputed to be more successful with agriculture than with sinners. He made the long journey to Boston to attend early meetings of the Academy; encouraged by the Academy's committee on agriculture, he published in 1790 his *The New England Farmer, or, Georgical Dictionary* that went through three editions. Later, believing that the District of Maine should have a college of its own, he had a hand in the creation of Bowdoin. Perez Fobes in Raynham was fascinated by botanical classification; later in life he commuted to Providence to lecture as professor of natural history at Rhode Island College, the forerunner of Brown University.

The ten medical men who were among the sixty-two incorporators were Edward Augustus Holyoke (A.B. 1746) of Salem, Cotton Tufts (A.B. 1749) of Weymouth, Oliver Prescott (A.B. 1750) of Groton, Micajah Sawyer (A.B. 1756) of Newburyport, Ebenezer Hunt (A.B. 1764) of Northampton, Joseph Orne

(A.B. 1765) of Salem, Charles Jarvis (A.B. 1766) of Boston, David Cobb (A.B. 1766) of Taunton, John Barnard Swett (A.B. 1771) of Marblehead, and the missing privateer's surgeon, Theodore Parsons (A.B. 1773) of Newburyport.

Finally, as in all traditional Boston enterprises, there was a leavening of prosperous merchants and gentlemen of inherited property. The eldest of these was James Bowdoin's classmate, James Warren (A.B. 1745) of Plymouth, who began life in an inherited shipping business. Having married James Otis's sister, Mercy, Warren was early in the forefront of the resistance movement. He was at various times President of the Provincial Congress, a major-general, Speaker of the Massachusetts House of Representatives, and a member of the Navy Board, Eastern District. There were three Newburyport merchants: Tristram Dalton (A.B. 1755), long a warden of St. Paul's Church there, who became United States Senator from Massachusetts in 1789; Jonathan Jackson (A.B. 1761), who in the last years of his life was Treasurer of Harvard College; and Nathaniel Tracy (A.B. 1769), who suffered heavy losses by the operation of revolutionary privateers. Samuel Phillips (A.B. 1771) of Andover, although less than a decade out of Harvard, had with financial aid from his father and uncle already established Phillips Academy in his native town. He long served in the Massachusetts Senate, and in 1785 succeeded Samuel Adams as its president.

Save for Elijah Lothrop, *un illustre inconnu* who has thus far defied identification, these sixty-one were a varied and distinguished company that well represented the intellectual community of Boston of 1780 as well as its government. Their occupations may thus be summarized:

High public officials	9
Officers of Harvard College	11
Schoolmasters	2
Lawyers and judges	13
Clergymen	11
Physicians	10
Merchants and gentlemen of property	5
Unidentified	1
Total	62

In many cases these divisions are arbitrary, for some of the incorporators were versatile men who engaged in a variety of occupations. For example, David Cobb who is reckoned with the physicians was at the time of the incorporation of the Academy on active duty as a lieutenant colonel. Later he was aide-de-camp to General Washington who in 1798 recommended him for the command of the United States Army. Although he did not achieve that post, he was at various times a major-general of militia, a judge of the Court of Common Pleas, Speaker of the Massachusetts House of Representatives, and a conspicuous figure in the development of Maine land. James Bowdoin, although counted with the officers of Harvard College because he was a member of the Corporation in 1780, was always very much a gentleman of property.

A number of the incorporators occupied significant places in the years ahead:

John Adams became second President of the United States; Tristram Dalton, Caleb Strong, and Theodore Sedgwick were United States Senators; while for the next thirty-six years Governors of Massachusetts were without exceptions fellows of the Academy. John Hancock, James Bowdoin, Samuel Adams, Caleb Strong, and James Sullivan were incorporators; Increase Sumner and Christopher Gore were elected fellows in 1791 and 1796 respectively.

Among the incorporators we have noted that the men of position and property stood side by side with certain representatives of the rural philosophers of the type so admirably depicted by Professor Harry J. Carman and Rexford G. Tugwell in the preface to their 1934 edition of the Reverend Jared Eliot's *Essay upon field husbandry in New England:*

There used to be a kind of man found rather often in earlier generations, who stood to a whole countryside as the representative there of learning. He might be a doctor or a lawyer; sometimes he was a craftsman; at any rate his ubiquitous interest in things of the mind made him notable. Men of this sort have a tendency now to flock together and, having done that, they specialize and develop a fantastic exclusiveness. This spoils the unique quality of the village philosopher. For this kind of man had an interest in all the branches of knowledge: archaeology, geology, astronomy—none of the sciences excluded him. Likely enough he had a chemical laboratory in the woodshed; and it was far from strange if his wife should catch him, on cold winter nights, gazing at the stars through a long brass telescope, he being meanwhile all too thinly protected from the weather. Perhaps his hobby was to discover the burial places of earlier inhabitants and to lay Indians' bones bare to the weather on some local hillside. He may have been the local atheist, his bent for learning taking a theological cast and he being by temperment contentious; or he may have been the schoolmaster interested to test for himself the conclusions which seemed too easily reached in books; then again he may have been the minister with interests other than those which were strictly legitimate to his profession, so that the things of this world came rather distinctly into Sunday's discourse. It did not seem effrontery in earlier years to combine one's interests in this way; it has come to seem so now. But what has been gained in precision of scholarship and in depth of knowledge is certainly partly offset by a loss in breadth of interest and in speculative temper.[18]

The first crop of fellows elected in January 1781 included Benjamin Franklin of Philadelphia; George Washington of Mount Vernon, Virginia; Ezra Stiles; Benjamin West; Elbridge Gerry; and Benjamin Lincoln.[19] Thomas Jefferson was elected in 1787; Charles Bulfinch, John Trumbull, and Alexander Hamilton in 1791; James Madison in 1794; Benjamin Waterhouse in 1795; John Quincy Adams in 1797; John Thorton Kirkland and Nathaniel Bowditch in 1799. All the early elections included not only such national figures but men from Brimfield and Stockbridge, Massachusetts; Killingworth, Connecticut; Hampton, New Hampshire; and similar places, who clearly stood "to a whole countryside as the representative there of learning."

In the nineteenth century, as specialization increased, the number of rural philosophers within the Academy declined markedly. In the first half of the century, one finds public figures such as Daniel Webster, Edward Everett, and Lemuel Shaw; the historians William Hickling Prescott and George Ticknor; the poet Longfellow; such artists as Washington Allston, J. J. Audubon, and Horatio Greenough; and scientists of the magnitude of Louis Agassiz, Asa Gray, James Hall, Joseph Henry, and Jeffries Wyman. In the second half of the century, Francis Parkman and Henry Adams succeeded Prescott; Emerson, Bryant, and Whittier came to keep Longfellow company; and the earlier scientists were followed by such figures as James D. Dana, H. A. Newton, Simon Newcomb, George W. Hill, Edward C. Pickering, Josiah Willard Gibbs, T. W. Richards, Seth C. Chandler, Samuel P. Langley, Alexander Graham Bell, O. C. Marsh, Joseph Leidy, A. S. Packard, H. P. Bowditch, and Charles W. Eliot. Similarly, in the early decades of the twentieth century appear the names of A. A. Michelson, Thomas C. Chamberlain, Elihu Thomson, Percival Lowell, Alexander Agassiz, William T. Sedgwick, Maxime Bôcher, and Charles P. Steinmetz.

In the earliest lists of the Academy, fellows were divided into three groups—home members, American members, and foreign members—thus indicating the representation of the local, the national, and the international scenes. The first foreign honorary members, elected in 1781, were John Adams's traveling companions of 1779, the Chevalier de la Luzerne and the Marquis de Barbé-Marbois. The Marquis de Chatellux, the Comte de Buffon, Joseph Priestley, Thomas Brand Hollis, the Marquis de Lafayette, Sir Joseph Banks, "Benjamin Thompson, Graf von Rumford," John Singleton Copley, Sir William Hamilton, and the Marquis de Condorcet were among those elected in the first twenty years. Fabre, Sir Humphry Davy, Humboldt, Arago, Gay-Lussac, John Stuart Mill, Theodore Mommsen, Benjamin Jowett, Gladstone, Tennyson, Viollet-le-Duc, Carlyle, and Ruskin lent distinction to the Academy's roster of foreign honorary members during the nineteenth century as did Niels Bohr, Sir Winston Churchill, Jawaharlal Nehru, and Albert Schweitzer in more recent times.

The nomenclature of the original three groups has often varied. Early in the nineteenth century there were but two classes: resident members and honorary members. After 1833, they were, for a time, described as members resident in Massachusetts, American honorary members, and foreign honorary members, but in 1854 the constitution was amended to provide for the election of fellows (resident in Massachusetts), of associate fellows (resident in other states of the Union), and of foreign honorary members. Today the membership consists simply of fellows, with nearly two-thirds of the membership residing outside the Boston area, and of foreign honorary members.

The Academy began its publications in normal eighteenth-century manner with a quarto series of *Memoirs*, four volumes of which were published between 1785 and 1821. In 1833, for no apparent reason other than the confusion of librarians, a new series was begun, of which nineteen volumes were issued during the next 113 years. Then in 1848 was added a series of octavo *Proceedings* appearing at more frequent intervals; over the next century these volumes constituted the chief means of periodical communication between the Academy and its Fellows.

In the half century after the 1780 foundation of the American Academy of Arts and Sciences, substantial fortunes were made by Bostonians, first through the expansion of maritime commerce into distant seas, and then through the development of textile manufacturing. The town began to grow. To make room for the expanding population, hills were cut down to fill in the coves on what was originally a hilly peninsula, almost completely surrounded by water. The ambiance of the town changed greatly through the activities of the remarkable amateur gentleman-architect Charles Bulfinch (elected to the Academy on August 24, 1791), who was not only personally responsible for the design of most of the new private and public buildings but, as the perennial chairman of the Board of Selectmen, was the competent head of local government. In these years of prosperity and increased leisure a number of new institutions, both philanthropic and learned, were created. In many cases fellows of the Academy were intimately involved.

The Massachusetts Medical Society

On November 1, 1781, the Massachusetts Legislature passed and Governor Hancock signed "An Act To Incorporate certain Physicians, by the Name of The Massachusetts Medical Society," which began, "As Health is essentially necessary to the Happiness of Society; and as its Preservation or Recovery is closely connected with the Knowledge of the Animal Oeconomy, and of the Properties and Effects of Medicines; and as the Benefit of Medical Institutions, formed on liberal Principles, and encouraged by the Patronage of Law, is universally acknowledged. . . ."[20]

By this act thirty-one Massachusetts physicians were constituted as a body with power "to examine all Candidates for the Practice of Physic and Surgery." Among these were eight of the ten physicians who had been incorporators of the American Academy the previous year—Holyoke, Hunt, Jarvis, Orne, Prescott, Sawyer, Swett, and Tufts; Theodore Parsons was by then known to be lost at sea. The tenth, David Cobb, although then absent from Boston as aide-de-camp to General Washington, became a fellow of the Massachusetts Medical Society in 1786. Another of the thirty-one incorporators was John Warren (A.B. 1771), who had been elected to the Academy on August 22, 1781. In 1782 he was to become the holder of the first Harvard chair in medicine: the Hersey Professorship of Anatomy and Surgery.

It is worth remembering that Harvard College only began to give medical degrees in course in 1788. Until 1811 the M.B. was conferred on graduation from the Medical School and the M.D. upon examination at least seven years later. In 1811 the doctor's degree was granted to graduates of that year and to earlier graduates who had not received it; since that date it has been conferred upon all graduates. Once Harvard became formally involved in medical education with the creation of the Hersey Professorship, the College from time to time recognized older physicians by the awarding of honorary degrees in medicine. The first honorary M.D. was given in 1783 to Edward Augustus Holyoke (A.B. 1746). Subsequently, a similar honor was given to four other physicians who had been incorporators both of the Academy and the Massachusetts Medical Society: Cotton Tufts in 1785, Oliver Prescott in 1791, Micajah Sawyer in 1793, and Ebenezer Hunt in 1811. Seven of the thirty-one founders of the Massachusetts Medical Society were subsequently elected to the Academy.

The Massachusetts Historical Society

Just as the Massachusetts Medical Society is the oldest organization of its kind in the country, with a record of uninterrupted meetings from its incorporation in 1791 to the present, so the Massachusetts Historical Society is the oldest historical association in the United States.[21] Its founder, the Reverend Jeremy Belknap, minister of the Federal Street Church in Boston, had been elected to the Academy on January 26, 1785. On August 26, 1790, Dr. Belknap met with four friends—the Reverend John Eliot, minister of the New North Church; the Reverend Peter Thacher, minister of the Brattle Street Church; the lawyer William Tudor; and James Winthrop, formerly librarian of Harvard College—to found what was called initially "An Antiquarian Society." They agreed to invite the assistance of five friends, of whom each would choose one, to achieve a membership of ten. Consequently the physician William Baylies; the Reverend James Freeman, minister of King's Chapel; George Richards Minot, Historian of Massachusetts; Judge James Sullivan, future Historian of the District of Maine and Governor of Massachusetts; and Thomas Wallcut, an impassioned book collector, joined the enterprise. It should be noted that Winthrop and Sullivan were incorporators of the American Academy; that Baylies, Belknap, and Minot were fellows at the time; and that Eliot, Thacher, and Freeman were elected later. Only two of the ten founders of the Massachusetts Historical Society— Tudor and Wallcut—had no connection with the Academy. Eight of the ten were graduates of Harvard College; and Sullivan, as we have seen earlier, held a Harvard honorary degree. Only Wallcut was without academic ties.

The purposes of the society, which was formally organized on January 24, 1791, were broad:

The preservation of books, pamphlets, manuscripts, and records, containing historical facts, biographical anecdotes, temporary projects, and beneficial speculations, conduces to mark the genius, delineate the manners, and trace the progress of society in the United States, and must always have a useful tendency to rescue the true history of this country from the ravages of time and the effects of ignorance and neglect.

A collection of observations and descriptions in natural history and topography, together with specimens of natural and artificial curiosities, and a selection of everything which can improve and promote the historical knowledge of our country, either in a physical or political view, has long been considered as a desideratum; and, as such a plan can be best executed by a society whose sole and special care shall be confined to the above objects, we, the subscribers, do agree to form such an institution, and to associate for the above purposes.[22]

The original limit of 30 on resident membership was raised to 60 in 1794 and to 100 in 1857; today it is only 150, with allowance for not more than 125 corresponding and 10 honorary members. The society has thus retained the semihonorary character of an eighteenth-century learned society. Although the corresponding membership consists almost entirely of distinguished professional historians in other parts of the country, resident members are chosen from a broader group. Normally about half will be members of university faculties or persons professionally concerned with history; the other half includes lawyers, doctors, clergymen, and a considerable number engaged in public life, business, or banking.

The preamble to the act of February 19, 1794 that incorporated the Massachusetts Historical Society defined "the collection and preservation of materials for a political and natural history of the United States" as a desirable object. [23] Although some "natural curiosities" found their way into its cabinet in early years, their preservation always presented a problem. Twenty-two portfolios of herbarium sheets of European plants, given to the Society in 1795 by the China trade merchant Thomas Handasyd Perkins (who was never a member) soon excited the concern of the entomologist William Dandridge Peck (elected to the society on October 8, 1792, and to the Academy on January 30, 1793), who then lived on a farm in Kittery, Maine. Pointing out the danger of destruction by insects, Peck asked to borrow the collection for a year so that he might put it in order and place the sheets in tight boxes impregnated with camphor. His application continued:

He will make out a correct catalogue, containing every plant, and forward it to the Corresponding Secretary, to be placed in the Historical Chamber; and if, before the plants are returned, any inquirer shall wish for information, or to acquire the knowledge of any individual in the catalogue, he will on application by letter, forward such a drawing of the plant as shall enable the inquirer to recognize it wherever he shall find it in the field, and will be at the expense of the postage. He would observe that the professed object of the donor is public utility, and that this object may be in some measure attained by assisting Mr. Peck in investigating the plants of our own country. He confesses he is young in botanic science. An accurate attention to these plants may give him some experience; and it is in the power of the Society, of which he has the honor to be a member, to lend him a helping hand in detecting the vegetable riches of New England.[24]

Peck's request was granted, and the loan subsequently extended for two years. On October 31, 1797, Peck was appointed, with Dr. Redford Webster and Dr. William Spooner, as a member of a committee of the Massachusetts Historical Society "to consider the necessary measures to preserve the Library and the preparations for the Museum from destruction by insects and the intermeddling of strangers."[25] From the beginning, books, manuscripts, and maps of historical interest predominated in the accessions of the Massachusetts Historical Society. Some indication of relative values is provided by a vote of October 25, 1796, in which Samuel Turell, who was then cabinet keeper, was authorized "to exchange some of the shells belonging to the Society for Governor Hutchinson's picture."[26]

Many Boston institutions started with very broad purposes that have been narrowed over the years as newer institutions have been founded for more specialized interests. The creation of the Boston Society of Natural History in 1830 permitted the Massachusetts Historical Society to relinquish any obligations that it originally felt in the field of natural history. On April 25, 1833, the librarian and cabinet keeper were authorized to deposit with the new institution "such articles in the Museum, relating to that subject, as they may think proper."[27] Since that date the Massachusetts Historical Society has made no claim to an interest in science. When the late Edward P. Hamilton succeeded me as cabinet keeper of the Massachusetts Historical Society in 1957, he found in early memoranda the mention of a 417-pound giant clam, given in 1803, which was once in the cabinet. As the object could no longer be located, he publicly accused me of having eaten it!

The Massachusetts Historical Society has long confined its activities to the collection, preservation, and publication of manuscripts and printed source material relating to the political and social life of the United States, with special reference to Massachusetts. Its manuscript collection is second only to that of the Library of Congress; its publications in letter-press, photostat, and microfilm make its resources available to scholars throughout the world.

The initial plan for the organization of the Massachusetts Historical Society included the proposal that "its quarterly meetings shall be held on the days next following those appointed for the meetings of the American Academy of Arts and Sciences."[28] The pattern persists today, although both organizations now meet monthly from fall through spring. The Academy meets on second Wednesday evenings; the Massachusetts Historical Society on second Thursday afternoons. For the past sixteen years Thomas Boylston Adams has served simultaneously as treasurer of the Academy and president of the Society, while I have been for almost as long librarian of the Academy and recording secretary of the Society. Indeed, from 1791 until 1925 all presidents of the Society were fellows of the Academy. The list follows, with dates of the presidency on the left and of election to the Academy in parentheses.

1791-1806   James Sullivan (incorporator)
1806-1818   Christopher Gore (November 9, 1796)
1818-1835   John Davis (May 29, 1792)
1835-1841   Thomas Lindall Winthrop (November 10, 1813)
1841-1855   James Savage (February 18, 1824)
1855-1885   Robert Charles Winthrop (August 8, 1849)

    1885-1894   George Edward Ellis (May 27, 1856)
    1895-1915   Charles Francis Adams (February 14, 1871)
    1915-1924   Henry Cabot Lodge (November 13, 1878)

Of the ten presidents of the Academy in the century between 1780 and 1880, five were members of the Massachusetts Historical Society. With the dates of their election to the Society in parentheses, these were:

    1791-1814   John Adams (June 30, 1800)
    1820-1829   John Quincy Adams (April 27, 1802)
    1839-1846   John Pickering (January 29, 1818)
    1846-1863   Jacob Bigelow (February 12, 1838)
    1873-1880   Charles Francis Adams (March 25, 1841)

A sixth, Asa Gray, president of the Academy, 1863-1873, was invited to join the Massachusetts Historical Society but declined.

The Massachusetts Society for Promoting Agriculture

The Massachusetts Society for Promoting Agriculture was incorporated on March 7, 1792.[29] Of the twenty-eight initial trustees, eleven were fellows of the American Academy of Arts and Sciences then or later. Five were incorporators of the Academy: Samuel Adams, John Lowell, Samuel Phillips, James Sullivan, and Cotton Tufts. Aaron Dexter had been elected to the Academy in 1784, Thomas Russell in 1788, and the architect Charles Bulfinch in 1791. Three others were subsequently elected on the dates indicated in parentheses: Charles Vaughan (May 27, 1794), Christopher Gore (November 9, 1796), and Thomas Lindall Winthrop (November 10, 1813). Of the first nine presidents of the Massachusetts Society for Promoting Agriculture, all save John Welles, the eighth, were fellows of the Academy.

    1792-1796   Thomas Russell (April 30, 1788)
    1796-1802   John Lowell (incorporator)
    1802-1805   Caleb Strong (incorporator)
    1805-1813   John Adams (incorporator)
    1813-1823   Aaron Dexter (August 25, 1784)
    1823-1828   John Lowell (January 24, 1804)
    1828-1841   Thomas Lindall Winthrop (November 10, 1813)
    1841-1846   John Welles
    1846-1847   John Chipman Gray (November 14, 1855)

The Society concerned itself with practical improvements in agricultural methods; its seal, showing a plough, oxen, fences, sheep and cattle, bore the motto "Source of Wealth." It offered prizes for improved breeds of animals, began in 1813 to publish the *Massachusetts Agricultural Journal,* and in 1818 built a hall in Brighton for the exhibition of farm implements and mammoth vegetables, with cattle pens nearby. Although agriculture no longer figures as a source of wealth in Massachusetts, the Society has survived as a pleasant rallying point for gentlemen farmers.

The Boston Athenaeum

The Boston Athenaeum, incorporated on February 13, 1807, was a proprietary institution whose library was "designed to contain *the works of learning and science in all languages;* particularly such rare and expensive publications, as are not generally to be obtained in this country; the most valuable of the encyclopedias of the arts and sciences in the English and French languages; standard dictionaries of the learned and principal modern languages; books of general reference, useful to the merchant and the scholar; and finally the works of the best authors, ancient and modern."[30]

Also included in the plan were a reading room of newspapers, periodicals, and gazettes; a museum or cabinet "which shall contain specimens from the three kingdoms of nature, scientifically arranged, natural and artificial curiosities, antiques, coins, medals, vases, gems and intaglios"; a "Repository of Arts, in which shall be placed for inspection models of new and useful machines; likewise drawings, designs, paintings, engravings, statues, and other objects of the fine arts, and especially the productions of our native artists"; and lastly "A Laboratory, and an Apparatus for experiments in chemistry and natural philosophy, for astronomical observations, and geographical improvements."[31] The scientific laboratory never materialized, nor did the cabinet with a display from the "three kingdoms of nature," but most of the rest of this ambitious plan was carried out. From 1827 the Athenaeum maintained the principal art gallery in Boston. It patronized the work of Gilbert Stuart, Washington Allston, and many other "native artists," and acquired for its permanent collections the works of earlier European artists. By 1870 the artistic activities of the Athenaeum led to the incorporation of the Museum of Fine Arts as a separate institution, to which the Athenaeum has ever since lent the greater part of its works of art for public exhibition.

In 1807 completeness in a library was a more attainable aspiration than it is today. Within its first quarter of a century, the Boston Athenaeum had assembled a higher percentage of "the works of learning and science in all languages" and "the works of all the best authors, ancient and modern" than one is likely to find today in a library of several million volumes. Forty-four years later, when Charles C. Jewett, librarian of the Smithsonian Institution, published the first census of libraries in the United States, the Athenaeum (with 50,000 volumes) was one of the five largest in the country.[32] The others were the Harvard and Yale College libraries, the Library Company of Philadelphia, and the Library of Congress. In the past 120 years, as the Boston Public Library and many specialized ones have been created in the area, the Athenaeum has deliberately and consistently narrowed its field. It has divested itself of law, medicine, and the sciences, and restricted its holdings to the humanities and the fine arts. In this narrower area it has today in excess of 460,000 volumes.

Relations between the Boston Athenaeum and the American Academy have always been intimate. Of the ten founders of the Athenaeum who were mentioned in the 1807 act of incorporation, all but two were fellows then or later. Five were then fellows: Chief Justice Theophilus Parsons (January 31, 1781); John Davis (May 29, 1792), United States District Judge; the Reverend William Emerson (May 24, 1803), minister of the First Church of Boston and father of Ralph Waldo Emerson; John Lowell (January 24, 1804), lawyer and political writer; the Reverend John Thornton Kirkland (May 28, 1799), minister of the New South Church in Boston, later president of Harvard College. William Smith Shaw, Clerk of the United States District Court, was elected to the Academy on November 14, 1810; the Reverend Joseph Stevens Buckminster, minister of the Brattle Street Church, was elected on August 9, 1809. Peter Oxenbridge Thacher, judge of the Municipal Court in Boston, and the Cape Codder Obadiah Rich, later a United States Consul in Spain and an antiquarian bookseller in London, were never elected to the Academy.

With the single exception of the great China trade merchant Thomas Handasyd Perkins, all of the first eleven presidents of the Boston Athenaeum were fellows of the Academy; nine of these ten had already been elected when they took office in the Athenaeum. They were:

1807-1813	Theophilus Parsons (January 31, 1781)
1814-1815	John Davis (May 29, 1792)
1816-1819	John Lowell (January 24, 1804)
1820-1829	Josiah Quincy (May 24, 1803)
1830-1832	Thomas Handasyd Perkins
1833-1836	Francis Calley Gray (May 25, 1819)
1837-1845	George Hayward (May 26, 1818)
1846-1859	Thomas Greaves Cary (May 27, 1856)
1860-1876	John Amory Lowell (November 10, 1841)
1877-1879	Charles Francis Adams (January 28, 1857)
1880-1898	Samuel Eliot (November 5, 1865)

The American Academy of Arts and Sciences in 1817 settled in with the Boston Athenaeum, then in a house on Tremont Street overlooking the King's Chapel Burying Ground. Five years later, when the Athenaeum moved to a large house on Pearl Street, given to it by James Perkins, the Academy went along. In 1825, when the Athenaeum was contemplating the construction of an art gallery and lecture hall on land behind the Perkins house, it was suggested to the Academy, the Massachusetts Medical Society, and the Massachusetts Historical Society that if each contributed $3,000 to a fund, the building might be so constructed as to afford each society a convenient room for its library and private meetings, while all public meetings could be held in the lecture room.[33]

This cooperative plan did not materialize. The Massachusetts Historical Society remained until 1833 in the upper room of the central pavilion of Charles

Bulfinch's elegant Tontine Crescent on Franklin Street (over the arch that gave its name to Arch Street), where it had settled in 1794 when the Crescent was new. Although the Athenaeum put up its building without outside help, the Massachusetts Medical Society rented a room in the basement of the new structure in 1827. In 1829 the new Athenaeum building was becoming overcrowded; a coup d'état, based on matters unconnected with learning, was simultaneously taking place within the Academy. In the election of 1828 John Quincy Adams, who had been president of the Academy since 1820, was defeated in his bid for a second term as President of the United States by Andrew Jackson. Adams returned home in June 1829, with the expectation of passing his remaining years in learned rather than political matters, but he met with a chilly reception. His Federalist neighbors, who could nurse a grudge as long and lovingly as anyone outside Ireland, had never forgiven him for supporting Thomas Jefferson's Embargo twenty-one years earlier. They had, among other evidences of their displeasure, dumped him out of the presidency of the Academy on May 26, 1829, electing the upright, tight-lipped, and vinegary navigator Nathaniel Bowditch in his place.

Bowditch, who was actuary of the Massachusetts Hospital Life Insurance Company, moved the Academy to the 50 State Street premises of that firm. Such an association seemed entirely reasonable to Bostonians of the period. For example, from 1833 to 1856 the Massachusetts Historical Society and the Provident Institution for Savings shared a building at 30 Tremont Street, overlooking King's Chapel Burying Ground, in which James Savage, an officer of both organizations, would run happily up and down stairs as he turned from receiving deposits to editing historical documents. After a dozen years on State Street, the Academy moved to 7½ Tremont Row, in that part of Scollay Square consecrated to tattooing parlors until the recent construction of Government Center.

The Boston Athenaeum had, in the meantime, so far outgrown its quarters on Pearl Street that Edward C. Cabot's plans for the present building at 10½ Beacon Street were approved in April 1846. The cornerstone was laid a year later, and the building occupied in July 1849, although the interior was not then completely finished. The Athenaeum's dignified new premises attracted the Academy in several ways, for in 1851 a committee was considering "the expediency of electing as Associate Members of the Academy gentlemen not known as scientific men, strictly so called, but interested in literary and scientific subjects."[34] In urging the inexpediency of electing such members, Samuel Atkins Eliot reported the committee's opinion "that this class of persons would be found among the proprietors of the Athenaeum, and also that by removing from the rooms now occupied by the Academy to the very eligible apartment in the Athenaeum which the Proprietors are desirous of leasing, and granting to such of these gentlemen as might desire it, the privilege of attending the meetings of the Academy, much good would be effected to both parties."[35] The first floor front room to the left of the Athenaeum entrance proved so attractive that the

Academy leased it and remained there for forty-seven years—the longest that this peripatetic society has remained quietly in one building.

The Salem East India Marine Society

Although the "cabinets" of the Massachusetts Historical Society and the Boston Athenaeum, which were organized as learned institutions, soon fell by the wayside, that of the Salem East India Marine Society, formed in 1799 for charitable and sociable purposes, has become an ethnological and historical museum of high importance.[36] On August 31, 1799, twenty-two seafaring men met in Salem and signed an agreement "to form an association to consist of such Ship Masters only as have had a Register from Salem and who have navigated those Seas at or beyond the Cape of Good Hope, to continue our friendly association by dining in Company together each month or quarterly, forming a Society by the name of the East India Marine Society." Only thirteen years before, Elias Hasket Derby's ship *Grand Turk* had been the first Salem vessel to reach China, and so the company that could qualify for the new society was both small and select. The closest hypothetical parallel today would be a club restricted to astronauts.

The objects of the founders were broader than mere sociability, for members of the East India Marine Society bound themselves:

First, To assist the widows and children of deceased members, who may need it, from the income of the funds of the Society . . . obtained from the fees of admission and the annual assessments.
Second, To collect such facts and observations as may tend to the improvement and security of navigation.
Third, To form a Museum of natural and artificial curiosities, particularly such as are to be found beyond the Cape of Good Hope and Cape Horn.[37]

While some of the objects brought back to the museum were mere curiosities of the idlest sort, those from the Pacific islands and other uncivilized regions, where natives were living by their own primitive hunting, fishing, and agriculture, are today of high historical and scientific importance. As Ernest S. Dodge, Director of the Peabody Museum of Salem, has well said, "It mattered not what the captain received in exchange for his hatchets and glass beads. Anything that he got at that early period, judged in the light of present day ethnology, was certain to be good. Weapons, household utensils, fans, ornaments, canoe paddles, tattooing instruments, in short, anything of native manufacture which could be found, was brought back to Salem.[38]

As the native cultures of the Pacific were changing with remarkable rapidity under the impact of traders and missionaries, the early nineteenth century was an extraordinarily favorable period for collecting evidences of material culture that cannot today be studied in the field. The fact that the objects brought to Salem and given to the East India Marine Society were cataloged with record of the name of the donor, who usually was also the collector, and the date of accession, adds enormously to their significance. A catalog of the museum, listing 2,269 objects and compiled by Dr. Seth Bass, who was librarian of the Boston Athenaeum from 1825 to 1846, was published in 1821. Although Dr. Bass recorded good, bad, and indifferent objects with disarming impartiality, his catalog bears witness to the scientific conscience of these adventurous mariners.

The members of the East India Marine Society were men who had gone to sea at an early age and risen rapidly through their own efforts, without benefit of extended formal schooling. Only one of them, Nathaniel Bowditch (1773-1838) figured in the other institutions described in this paper. He had left school at the age of ten, and, after working in a cooper's shop and ship chandlery, had gone to sea in 1795. By determined private study he acquired languages and a knowledge of mathematics. Between 1795 and 1803 he made five voyages, one as ship's clerk, three as supercargo, and a final one as master and supercargo. At the suggestion of a Newburyport publisher, he checked the accuracy of the tables in J. H. Moore's popular *The Practical Navigator,* first published in London in 1772. From the thirteenth edition of Moore, Bowditch prepared a revised first American edition, which appeared in 1799. This led to his election as a fellow of the American Academy of Arts and Sciences on May 28, 1799. Further revision led to the publication under Bowditch's name of *The New American Practical Navigator* in 1802, and Harvard College awarded him an honorary A.M. that same year. Having left the sea for good after a voyage that ended on Christmas day, 1803, Bowditch became president of the Essex Fire and Marine Insurance Company in Salem. He joined the East India Marine Society in 1800 and was its president from 1820 to 1823, in which year he moved to Boston to become actuary of the Massachusetts Hospital Life Insurance Company. He became an overseer of Harvard College in 1810, serving until 1826 when he became a member of the Harvard Corporation, where he served until his death in 1838. Bowditch received an honorary LL.D. in 1816 from the hands of President Kirkland, whom he nevertheless hounded out of office in 1828. Bowditch was a trustee of the Boston Athenaeum from 1826 to 1833, and president of the American Academy from 1829 until his death. On taking over the latter office, he promptly moved the Academy from the Athenaeum to his own premises at the Massachusetts Hospital Life Insurance Company! During his residence in Salem, Bowditch published twenty-three papers in the *Memoirs* of the Academy and completed his translation of the four volumes of Laplace's *Mécanique céleste,* which was his most notable piece of scientific work.

Even before Bowditch's death, Salem shipping was in decline; with each year there were fewer shipmasters who could qualify for membership in the East India Marine Society. Consequently, in 1867 a group of trustees established and endowed by George Peabody of London, the international banker and philanthropist, bought the building and collections of the East India Marine Society, thus perpetuating them as the basis for today's Peabody Museum of Salem. Through having been in continuous existence since 1799, this is the oldest museum in the United States. Today it specializes in maritime history, the ethnology of the Pacific Islands and Japan, and the natural history of Essex

County. Indeed, it is the only one of the early Massachusetts institutions whose "cabinet" has served a serious scientific purpose.

The personal intertwinings between these institutions are numerous. I spent a decade as assistant director of the Peabody Museum of Salem, and for the past twenty-four years have been one of its trustees. William Smith Shaw, the first librarian of the Boston Athenaeum (1807-1822) was also librarian of the American Academy of Arts and Sciences from 1818 to 1823. I, who was the ninth librarian of the Athenaeum (1946-1973), continue to serve as librarian of the Academy. I have earlier noted the way in which a few gentlemen still follow each other from the second Wednesday evenings of the Academy to the second Thursday afternoons of the Massachusetts Historical Society. Such coincidences are neither wholly accidental nor consciously arrived at. In the first place, the Boston temperment more readily accepts change in large matters than in small ones and accepts change in ideas rather than in the details of daily life. If people do not tinker endlessly with dates and times and meetings, one knows without recourse to notices or engagement books when certain things occur, thus avoiding conflicts and minor hassles. Secondly, Boston institutions are usually on good terms with each other with remarkably little evidence of duplication, empire building, or internecine warfare. It is recognized that, as there is only so much time and money, it is undesirable to waste either. Finally, a respect for learning, reaching back to Puritan beginnings, has led to the development of a tradition of nonacademic scholarship in which professionals and amateurs happily foregather both in the older learned societies and in a multiplicity of clubs. Thus Bostonians of many sorts are constantly doing business with each other and sometimes with themselves, in different capacities in a great variety of places including the American Academy, which, after 194 years, still (in John Adams's words) "countenances and inculcates sincerity, good humor, and all social affections and generous sentiments among the people."

NOTES

1. John Adams to Abigail Adams, 3 August 1776, in *Adams Family Correspondence,* ed. Lyman H. Butterfield (Cambridge, Mass.: Harvard University Press, Belknap Press, 1963), 2:75.

2. John Adams, *Works of John Adams,* ed. Charles Francis Adams (Boston, 1851), 4:259, footnote.

3. *Journals of the Continental Congress,* ed. Worthington C. Ford, 34 vols. (Washington, 1904-1937), 4:224.

4. J. Adams, *The Works of John Adams,* 4:259-60, footnote.

5. Ibid., p. 259, footnote.

6. Ibid., p. 259.

7. Ibid., p. 261, footnote.

8. The charter of the American Academy is printed in *Memoirs of the American Academy of Arts and Sciences,* 11, pt. 1 (1882): 77-79.

9. Ibid., 1 (1785): xix.

10. John Adams to Jean Luzac, 22 August 1780, letterbook copy, The Adams Papers, Massachusetts Historical Society, Boston, Mass.

11. *Memoirs of the American Academy,* 1:1-20.

12. Ibid., pp. 86-102.

13. John Adams to John Singleton Copley, ante 15 October 1786, *Daedalus* 86 (September, 1956): 167; original in American Academy of Arts and Sciences, *Letters,* 1:57-58, Boston Athenaeum, Boston, Mass.

14. Details on the founders and fellows are derived from *Harvard University Quinquennial Catalogue of the Officers and Graduates, 1636-1930* (Cambridge, Mass.: Harvard University, 1930); Clifford Kenyon Shipton, *Sibley's Harvard Graduates, Biographical Sketches of Those Who Attended Harvard College,* vols. 6-16 (classes of 1713-1767) (Boston: Massachusetts Historical Society, 1942-1972); *Dictionary of American Biography,* 1st ed.; and *Biographical Directory of the American Congress, 1774-1961* (Washington, D.C.: Government Printing Office, 1961).

15. *Memoirs of the American Academy,* 11, pt. 1 (1882): 33-34.

16. Shipton, *Sibley's Harvard Graduates,* 12:43.

17. Ibid., p. 44.

18. Jared Eliot, *Essays upon Field Husbandry in New England and Other Papers, 1748-1762,* ed. Harry J. Carman and Rexford G. Tugwell (New York: Columbia University Press, 1934), preface.

19. The list of fellows, 1780 to 1881, is printed in *Memoirs of the American Academy,* 11, pt. 1 (1882): 35-75.

20. Walter L. Burrage, *A History of the Massachusetts Medical Society with Brief Biographies of the Founders and Chief Officers, 1781-1922* (Boston: privately printed, 1923), p. 63. The charter of the Massachusetts Medical Society and a detailed description of its founding appear in Burrage, pp. 37-67.

21. Sources used for material on the Massachusetts Historical Society are *Handbook of the Massachusetts Historical Society, 1791-1948* (Boston: Massachusetts Historical Society, 1949) and Walter Muir Whitehill, *Independent Historical Societies* (Boston: Boston Athenaeum, 1962).

22. *Handbook of the Massachusetts Historical Society,* pp. 1-2.

23. Ibid., p. 170.

24. *Proceedings of the Massachusetts Historical Society* 1 (1791-1835): 93.

25. Ibid., p. 107.

26. Ibid., p. 101.

27. Ibid., p. 467.

28. Jeremy Belknap, "Plan of an Antiquarian Society," reproduced in facsimile in M.H.S. *Collections,* 5th ser., 3, opp. p. 231, Massachusetts Historical Society.

29. *An Outline of the History of the Massachusetts Society for Promoting Agriculture* (Boston: Massachusetts Society for Promoting Agriculture, 1942).

30. Josiah Quincy, *The History of the Boston Athenaeum* (Cambridge, Mass., 1851), pp. 27-28.

31. Ibid., p. 28.

32. Charles C. Jewett, *Notice of Public Libraries in the United States of America,* Appendix to the Fourth Annual Report of the Board of Regents of the Smithsonian Institution (Washington, D.C., 1851).

33. *Proceedings of the Massachusetts Historical Society* 1 (1791-1835), 384.

34. Report of the 354th Meeting of the American Academy of Arts and Sciences, 3 December 1851, Manuscript Records of the American Academy, 2:334, Boston Athenaeum.

35. Ibid.

36. Walter Muir Whitehill, *The East India Marine Society and the Peabody Museum of Salem: A Sesquicentennial History* (Salem, Mass.: Peabody Museum, 1949), p. 3.

37. Ibid., p. 6; also printed in *The East India Marine Society of Salem* (Salem, Mass., 1821).

38. Ernest S. Dodge, "Captain Collectors, the Influence of New England Shipping on the Study of Polynesian Material Culture," quoted in Whitehill, *The East India Marine Society,* p. 38.

The Academy
of Natural Sciences
# of Philadelphia
1812-1850

PATSY A. GERSTNER

The Academy of Natural Sciences of Philadelphia was established in 1812. Two possible divisions of the Academy's history up to 1850 suggest themselves. The history can be viewed as a two-phase development, with the first phase lasting from 1812 to 1825 and representing an amateur scientific period, and the second lasting from 1825 to 1850 or beyond, and representing a transitional phase from the amateur toward a more professional outlook. The other possible division, and the one I have chosen to use, is a three-part approach, in which the years 1817-1840 are treated as a distinct phase that embodies both the amateur and transitional elements; these years are held together as a unit by the personality and strength of William Maclure, who served as president of the Academy and dominated its activities during the period.[1]

The First Period: 1812-1817

In the early 1800s interest in natural history was growing rapidly throughout the United States. In Philadelphia the public flocked to Charles Willson Peale's Museum to view the curiosities of nature, and an early version of the roadside zoo, exhibiting everything from elephant to jaguar, was popular.[2] On a more sophisticated level, the work of William Bartram and Benjamin Smith Barton in botany and Alexander Wilson in ornithology excited interest in the flora and fauna of the United States. Yet those who found the works of Wilson and others more exciting than the public exhibits had few opportunities to meet. The American Philosophical Society and the Linnaean Society of Philadelphia were in existence, but the first was a multipurpose society and the second was restricted to botany. For those taken with the new interest in natural history, neither was satisfactory.

To meet the need, seven young men who had frequently discussed their various interests in natural history gathered in 1812 to create a society based on those interests. The seven were John Speakman, an apothecary; Jacob Gilliams, a dentist; Gerard Troost, a physician and chemist, later a geologist; John Shinn, Jr., a chemist; Nicholas S. Parmentier, a distiller; Camillus Macmahon Mann, a

---

[1] Notes to this chapter begin on page 189.

physician; and Thomas Say, a naturalist.[3] Their goals and purposes in forming an academy devoted to natural history were stated at the first meeting, held on Saturday evening, January 25, 1812:

At a meeting of gentlemen friends of Science and of rational disposal of leisure moments held by mutual concurrence and desire at the house of John Speakman Esquire, and from deference to the usage of politeness and hospitality and in compliance with the unanimous request of the other gentlemen . . . agree to form, constitute and become a Society for the purpose of occupying their leisure occasionally, in each other's company, on subjects of Natural Sciences interesting and useful to the country and the world and in modes conducive to the general and individual satisfaction of the members, as well as to the primary object [which is] the advancement and diffusion of useful, liberal, human knowledge.[4]

The founders emphasized that all those elected to the Academy should be absolutely devoted to science, and that all members should be free from religious and political prejudice and animosity at least within the confines of the Academy. These provisos and goals were incorporated in a Constitutional Act signed by all members on March 17. The Act stated, that "for the common benefit of all the individuals who may be admitted" the Academy would contain a museum of natural history, a library of scientific works, a chemical experimental laboratory, experimental philosophic apparatus, "and every other desirable appendage or convenience."[5]

Several historians have singled out various elements characteristic of science in an amateur stage. These include an emphasis, first, on collecting and description (fact gathering) that made science democratic, since everyone could participate equally and, second, on the diffusion of knowledge, particularly useful knowledge, rather than its advancement. In addition the amateur expected his relations with others of similar interests to be a friendly and pleasant pastime. These elements are embodied in the goals of the Academy and the method chosen for their implementation,[6] and they are reflected in the activities of the Academy from 1812 to 1817—activities that also demonstrate a useful involvement with the larger community of learned men.

The locations of the early meetings prohibited any collection of those materials thought by the Academy's founders to be so necessary to the pursuit of science. In April of 1812, however, the members rented a small room for their meetings, which were to be held weekly, and at this time

the formation of a Library was . . . commenced by some of the members depositing in the rooms of the Academy books from their private librarys [sic]. The formation of a museum was commenced about the same time by a donation from C. M. Mann of a few specimens of very common insects & shells, to these were soon added, some specimens of small birds stuffed, some foreign shells, a fine herbarium collected in the vicinity of Paris, and some artificial christals [sic]. The birds were presented by Mr. T. Say, the shells by Dr. Barnes, the herbarium by N. S. Parmentier and the christals were presented by Dr. Troost.[7]

The collection of specimens was the principal activity of the Academy in its initial period. Early in May 1812 the members visited the coal mines on the Schuylkill near Perkiomen Creek to collect minerals, and returned to the Academy with both mineral specimens and a variety of other things.[8] In the summer an attempt was made to buy, at public auction, a collection of minerals, but the Academy was outbid. Knowing the Academy's interest in acquiring such material, Dr. Adam Seybert offered to sell his collection of nearly two thousand minerals to the Academy for $750. Since the Academy had no funds to meet this price some of the members agreed to buy shares of stock in the collection at $20 per share, to be redeemed by the Academy whenever possible.

In an obvious effort to reach out of their own confines so that their knowledge could be communicated to other naturalists, the Academy almost immediately initiated a program of electing corresponding members. During the first three years, at least fifty-one correspondents were elected, eleven of them foreign correspondents, and by 1817 there were about one hundred correspondents.[9] Through these correspondents, the regular members hoped to foster an exchange of information and specimens to further their goals. How much response came from elected corresponding members is difficult to determine, but several people who might not have heard of the Academy from any other source were made aware of its existence in this manner.

Sporadic attempts were made before 1817 to gather useful information that involved, or could have involved, the Academy with the community at large rather than the community of naturalists. At the end of 1812, the Academy prepared a circular addressed to "farmers, planters and owners of land throughout the United States." It was a plea for information and samples of rocks, minerals, ores, soil, and other materials. Such samples were to be forwarded to members of the Academy for analysis so that the Academy could locate and identify those things "as would be beneficial to the country at large [and] to bring forth the resources that God has given us within ourselves to enable us to withstand the deprivation of foreign trade and render ourselves as independent as possible of other countries and governments."[10] While this was an idea in keeping with the goals of the Academy, it was surely fostered by the War of 1812 as well. In spite of good intentions, however, the circular was not sent to anyone.

In 1816 the Academy received a circular from the Boston Linnaean Society addressed to the captains of vessels on the methods to be used in collecting and preserving quadrupeds, birds, fishes, insects, shells, plants, and minerals. This notice attracted the attention of Academy members, and they decided to issue a similar document.[11] Unlike the earlier one, this was prepared and printed; how widely it was distributed and the results it achieved are unknown.

Although the Academy preserved and perpetuated its goals, it met with many failures. For one thing, membership remained small throughout these early years. In 1812 there were only seven additions to the membership of seven founders. In 1813 there were six and in 1814, twelve. Meetings were seldom attended by more than half a dozen members. It has been suggested that the Academy was generally unpopular during this period, primarily because of its stand against discussion of religion in the Academy. The members did make a strong point of this issue, and it is possible that such a restriction lent an aura of uncertainty to the Academy insofar as the general public was concerned. People feared that the Academy was an atheistic body, and association with such an organization would have been considered hazardous by many who might otherwise have joined.[12]

A ray of hope for increased membership came, however, at the end of 1815, and it directed some interest toward the potential of the Academy as an institution available to the public.[13] In 1812 and 1813 Gerard Troost gave a series of lectures on mineralogy and crystallography based on the Seybert Collection which the Academy had purchased. These lectures, open to members and others, were so well received that the following year a number of lectures on botany, given by Drs. John Barnes and John T. Waterhouse, were arranged by the Academy for the ladies; these were held in the hall of the Agricultural Society since the Academy had no room in which to hold lectures. Although open by invitation of a member only, they were so successful that in 1815 they were offered to anyone upon payment of a $10 fee. Also in 1815 a course of lectures in chemistry was given by Dr. John Shinn, Jr.,[14] and Troost's lectures were repeated. By this time the Academy was in another building, with sufficient room to accommodate these public meetings.

The advantage of community exposure through lectures was of immediate benefit to the Academy in terms of new members. In 1815 the number of new members almost equaled that for the three previous years combined. At the end of 1815 Richard Randolph, treasurer of the Academy, reported that the public lectures had caused the Academy to rise "into public notice, has attracted the attention of strangers and has established for [the Academy] a character and reputation far exceeding our most sanguine expectations."[15] This success set the stage for the acceptance of even greater involvement with the general public in the following years.

Unfortunately, the library collection did not grow during these early years, and its failure was a great concern to members; by 1817 there were less than 150 volumes available. However, the most significant of the problems encountered was financial. Dues and public lectures were the only source of income for the Academy. Rental of rooms and the occasional purchase of books and specimens had put the Academy $1000 in debt by the end of 1815. Various efforts were made to alleviate the situation. Members who did not pay dues, and there were apparently several, were dropped. In 1816 the Academy adopted a formal constitution, and proceedings for incorporation were started in the hope that a legally constituted body might be able to handle money in a more effective manner. The society was incorporated in April of 1817, but the financial difficulties were still very much in evidence at the beginning of 1817.

The Second Period: 1817-1840

The second era of the Academy's history was dominated by the paternalistic leadership of William Maclure as president. Maclure was responsible, in many ways, for a stabilizing of the financial situation of the Academy. This was done primarily through the donation of personal funds to help the Academy through difficult times and to allow for its expansion. During this period the Academy grew in terms of total membership and the size of the collections, but its activities, while more intense, were not very different from those of the earlier period and were directed largely toward collecting and diffusing knowledge. The way in which these activities were carried out was often related to the activities of Maclure.

The first major act in the Academy's second era was the creation of a journal. Early in 1817 a committee of four was appointed to study the possibility of issuing a publication; by May it was agreed that the Academy should publish a journal devoted to the diffusion of knowledge through the sharing of interesting facts and observations with the community of naturalists at large. To insure that this would be its purpose, papers of a theoretical nature were considered undesirable,[16] and those dealing with subjects in natural philosophy were excluded.[17]

The members believed that the *Journal of the Academy of Natural Sciences of Philadelphia* would serve the American community of naturalists as well as "those enlightened foreigners who make our country the object of their attention" by offering a place of frequent and expeditious publication.[18] The *Journal* was a principal source of publication for regular Academy members and some corresponding members, but the hope that foreigners would use it was never fulfilled. Of 233 papers published in the *Journal* between 1817 and 1842, only 3 were by foreigners. The most active members in the Academy were those who used the *Journal* most frequently, and they included Thomas Say, Richard Harlan, Thomas Nuttall, Charles Lesueur, Isaac Lea, Samuel George Morton, and Timothy Conrad. The financial problem in publishing a journal was recognized by the members, who vowed to make the publication as "cheap and as unostentatious as the nature of the subjects will admit."[19] Despite this vow, however, the Academy found itself unable to maintain the *Journal,* and after 1817 publication was halted until 1821. The *Journal* was published sporadically from that time until 1842.

In spite of its financial difficulties, the *Journal* was generously distributed to learned societies in the United States, and whenever possible to European societies as well. Through this distribution the Academy achieved a recognizable position among the learned societies. Membership in the Academy grew steadily to almost two hundred in 1840, and some of this growth must be attributed, at least indirectly, to the *Journal.*

The collections of the Academy, both specimens and books, multiplied rapidly. The library grew from 150 volumes in 1817 to 7,000 volumes by 1840, and the collection of specimens increased from a few hundred items to a collection containing 2,500 mineral specimens, 3,000 fossils, 10,000 insects, 2,400 shells, 1,000 fish and reptiles, 1,300 birds, and 35,000 herbarium specimens.[20] Without funds for the purchase of books and specimens, this growth was dependent on the generosity of members. Maclure was largely responsible for the expansion of the library, adding over 3,000 volumes to its collection. Thomas Say, who died in 1834, bequeathed his entomological library to the Academy. The collection of specimens was aided by private collecting trips of members who then made gifts to the Academy. For instance, Maclure, with a few members of the Academy, made trips to the West Indies in the winter of 1816-1817 and to Florida in 1817-1818 and subsequently presented some specimens from these trips to the Academy.[21] In 1834 Say's collection of insects was given along with his books, and that same year the Academy received from the estate of its member, the Reverend Lewis David von Schweinits a herbarium containing several thousand specimens, including those collected by Thomas Nuttall.[22]

Specimens were also added to the collection through the exchange of objects with Europeans, and in 1832 the Academy passed a resolution making it routine for all unusual specimens to be cast, and the cast made available to all institutions with which the Academy was in the habit of exchanging specimens. Although the Academy was involved to some degree in the gathering of specimens through exchange, it was more often the individual member who exchanged specimens with European acquaintances and then deposited the specimens in the Academy.

Since there were no funds available, exchanges and gifts remained the principal mode of adding to the collection. Occasionally, however, money was given to purchase a collection. In 1829 Joseph Dorfeuille of Cincinnati offered for sale his large collection of fossils.[23] The Academy's paleontological collection had begun with donations as early as 1815, and by the late 1820s the membership included many whose principal interests were in fossils, among them Samuel George Morton and Richard Harlan, both of whom were eager that the collection of Dorfeuille come to Philadelphia. Both men were members of the American Philosophical Society as well as the Academy, and at each of these institutions interest was stirred in the Dorfeuille collection.

The precise details of the effort to secure the collection are lost, but may in some manner be reconstructed from a letter written to Dorfeuille by Morton on July 25, 1829.[24] Morton reported that he had been assured by John Vaughan of the American Philosophical Society that the Society was going to purchase the collection, but, in the event that this should not happen, Morton had written to an unidentified influential member by the Lyceum of Natural History of New York suggesting a joint purchase by the Academy and the Lyceum. Finding that the Lyceum, like the Academy, was too heavily burdened with debt to consider this, Morton tried to raise purchase money at the Academy by subscription. This too failed, and Morton next sought to arrange a joint purchase by the Academy and the American Philosophical Society, even though Vaughan still assured him that the American Philosophical Society would make the entire purchase. Whether the Society eventually declined to do so or not, the collection did come to the Academy through the gift of an individual member, John Price Wetherill, who was persuaded to make the purchase by another member, Richard Harlan. Harlan reported in 1831 that "my estimable friend John Price Wetherill, Esq. with that distinguished liberality which he has so repeatedly displayed toward the sciences and those who cultivate them, authorized me, when on a visit to Cincinnati in the autumn of the same year [1829], to purchase these invaluable relics, which together with other admirable contributions in this department, he has caused to be arranged in the cabinet of the Academy of Natural Sciences of Philadelphia."[25]

Through the gifts of Maclure, Say, Wetherill, and the others, and through the efforts of individual members who arranged for exchanges or for purchases, the collection grew. This increase in specimens, plus the increase in the library and the size of the membership, made new quarters a necessity for the Academy. In 1826 the Academy moved to a building purchased from the Swedenborgian Church, but, even before the building was completely converted to Academy use, it was found that a still larger building was needed. In 1839 the cornerstone was laid for a new, fire-proof structure with room for some expansion and for meetings and lectures.

The collection of specimens in the Academy was kept in good order and carefully displayed in cases purchased by the Academy or through members' subscriptions. Members had access to the collections at the discretion of the Academy, and this was freely given. They were expected to see that the items were properly arranged in some scheme, basically a Linnaean taxonomic one. In essence, then, the collections formed a museum for the use of members.

In August of 1828 it was decided that the museum should be opened "two half days in every week for citizens" as long as they held a ticket signed by a member of the Academy; the afternoons selected were Tuesday and Saturday. This move in 1828 can be understood as a logical extension of the Academy's experience with public lectures in an earlier year, but was also the probable outcome of Maclure's influence (as will be discussed later). With the opening of the museum the Academy assumed the role of public institution in the community—a role it continues to play. Other, less important efforts to involve the Academy in the life of the community occurred from time to time; for example, on February 28, 1832, it was decided that particularly interesting proceedings of the Academy should be published in local newspapers.

It was in the period from 1817 to 1840 that the Academy, through its growing number of members, came into contact with many other organizations. Memberships were commonly held in the American Philosophical Society and the Franklin Institute as well as in the Academy. For a time there was a strong relation between the Academy and the Philadelphia Museum as well. Titian Peale had been an active member of the Academy since 1817 and was largely responsible for the operation of the Philadelphia Museum. Part of the Museum's program was a series of semipopular lectures on such subjects as anatomy, mineralogy, zoology, and physiology. John Godman, Thomas Say, Gerard Troost, and Richard Harlan, all Academy members, were lecturers in the series in the early 1820s.[26] This kind of multiple membership or activity in several organizations allowed a free and easy "information network" to operate among the organizations of Philadelphia; through corresponding memberships in other natural history organizations, especially the Lyceum of Natural History in New York, the exchange of information was carried out on an even greater scale.[27] Ties with English scientists, especially geologists, were also quite strong within the Academy. Samuel George Morton maintained a very extensive correspondence with Gideon Mantell; Henry Darwin Rogers of the Academy was the first American elected a fellow of the Geological Society of London and kept in contact with his English friends; Rogers and Richard Harlan visited England and attended the 1833 meeting of the British Association for the Advancement of Science. Through these men the Academy received a continuous flow of information from England.

Within the Academy itself, however, the dominant force in the period 1817-1840 was William Maclure. Maclure was a successful businessman who had earned a reputation as a philanthropist among the scientific societies of the early nineteenth century. His survey of the eastern United States established his claim to a position of importance as a geologist.[28] In 1817 the Academy honored Maclure's achievement by electing him president to succeed Gerard Troost, the Academy's first and only president to that time. Maclure was rarely present in Philadelphia, especially after 1825 when he joined Robert Owen's New Harmony experiment in the hope of bringing to fruition a number of his ideas on education. However, in spite of his absence, he was always reelected, and only his death in 1840 brought his presidency to an end.

Not only the financial condition of the Academy but also its general development were aided by Maclure's philanthropy. As noted earlier, the collections of both specimens and books increased through his generosity. Many of the books he gave were carefully selected for the Academy during his travels in Europe. For his work at New Harmony he amassed a sizable library. When the New Harmony venture faltered in 1827, Maclure left for Mexico, where he spent most of his remaining years. In 1835 he gave the Academy over 2000 volumes from his New Harmony library. Since there were no funds for purchases of books, it is clear that the library would not have fared well without Maclure.

Maclure was also influential in sustaining publication of the Academy's *Journal.* Despite the members' determination to keep the cost of publication low, financing the *Journal* would have been impossible without Maclure's help. He purchased a used printing press, on which the first issues were printed by members themselves, and occasionally improved the general financial state of the *Journal* with personal contributions of money. Although there is no official notation in the Academy's records that Maclure was the moving force behind the decision to publish the *Journal,* his efforts in making the venture possible, his well-known zeal for the diffusion of knowledge, and his position as president of the Academy leave little room for doubt that he was in large measure responsible for the publication.

In moving to new buildings, Maclure was also helpful. The Academy was still deeply in debt from the first move in 1826, but between 1837 and 1839 Maclure gave the Academy several thousands of dollars, with which it was able to liquidate the old debt and carry on plans for the new building. Although the opening of the public museum in 1828 was without doubt encouraged by earlier successes with the public, it was probably helped along by Maclure; at least it was an activity that would clearly appeal to him.

Maclure's interest in New Harmony stemmed from his progressive ideas on education in the Pestalozzian tradition. Emphasis on the education of the young in a manner that allowed self-exploration and openness to new ideas was the stock and trade of the Pestalozzians. What better way to open up the world of nature and science to the young mind than by exposure to a museum where the child's interests might be developed and encouraged through his own exploration? In 1839, to insure the continuation of the Academy's role for the public benefit, Maclure addressed a letter to the Academy from Mexico in which he strongly suggested "the necessity of some legal instrument specifying the liberality of the Academy in gratuitously giving access to all classes," not only to the museum but to the library as well. He specifically cited the following as desirable:

That the library, museum etc. shall be open to the public gratis,
That the library shall be furnished with tables, chairs, etc. heated and lighted,
That the library shall be accessible 4 or 5 days in the week,
That the library shall be open to the public the whole of Sunday or Sunday night,
That there shall be a librarian who shall attend at least 6 hours on the days of admission and the nights until 9 o'clock,
That the lecture room shall be open for the use of any one who wishes to lecture, particularly on Sundays on any species of science, etc. etc. admission for males 5 cents and females gratis.[29]

On August 27 it was reported that the bylaws of the Academy had been amended in partial accordance with Maclure's suggestions. The library was to be open to the gratuitous admission of the public on as many days as a librarian could be present, but all persons using the library were required to have the permission of the librarian, except the members. No specific action was taken in regard to the lecture room; however, it was indicated in a letter to Maclure dated November 21, 1839, that the new building would allow more room for public lectures.

The tradition of amateurism as defined earlier, that is, the friendly gathering and diffusion of information, remained apparent in the activities of the Academy during this second era of its history, and this tradition was further manifested in the Academy's steadfast refusal to involve itself in any way as an official body with other institutions, with the government, or, for that matter, even with the city of Philadelphia. In March of 1819 the Academy had its first opportunity to participate in an expedition of major significance. On March 11 a letter from the Secretary of War, requesting that the Academy furnish a set of suggestions for the western expedition of Major Stephen Long, was introduced to the members. The letter indicated that it was the government's desire to make the trip useful to the sciences and that it sought the Academy's recommendations in this regard. Long had been a member of the Academy since 1817 and was well known to the members. The expedition promised to yield quantities of useful information and specimens, but rather than consider any involvement with it, the Academy decided that the expedition was to leave too soon for it to prepare any suggestions.[30]

Late in 1821 a committee was appointed to study the possibility of "conferring with other institutions on the propriety of presenting a joint memorial to Congress on the Subject of the existing duties on foreign books imported into the United States and petitioning for a repeal of the same." On January 15, 1822, the committee voted against the proposal. In 1825 (May 10) a proposal was presented to the Academy that it join with the Pennsylvania Society for Promoting Public Improvement to undertake a geological survey of the state. No action was taken. At a meeting on July 14, 1829, a letter was read asking the Academy to join with the Franklin Institute in petitioning the Secretary of State for the reinstatement of Dr. Thomas P. Jones as superintendent of the U.S. Patent Office, from which position he had been removed. There was strong feeling among members of the Academy that this should be done, since Jones was one of the oldest members of the Academy (1812); an initial resolution was passed in favor of the move but was rescinded at the next business meeting of the Academy on July 28. In 1820 and again in 1832 the Philadelphia Athenaeum, a library founded in 1814, suggested that the learned societies of Philadelphia come together to construct a hall for their mutual use, but both times the Academy resolved not to join such an effort. In 1831 a member proposed that the Academy assume the responsibility for preparing a list of American equivalents for a British geological chart; the membership did not act.[31]

In 1839 the Academy was contacted by Joel Poinsett, the Secretary of War, concerning the bequest of James Smithson to establish a national scientific institution. Poinsett wanted to use the bequest to found a national museum, and sought the approval of scientific men for his plan. Some support existed in the Academy and at the American Philosophical Society, and the two organizations were in touch on the matter.[32] But the American Philosophical Society declined because the request for assistance was made unofficially to them,[33] and on September 24, 1839, the Academy committee appointed to consider the request reported "that they considered it inexpedient at the present time to take any action on the subject."

The Academy's decision not to involve itself in joint ventures can be explained in part by its financial condition, but there is also ample evidence that the Academy did not see itself as a representative of the scientific community. A willingness to take a stand on subjects of mutual concern is a mark of a modern professional society; conversely, an unwillingness to become involved, to the degree manifested by the Academy, would seem to be a legitimate mark of a group still in its amateur stage. One cannot help but think that this tradition was perpetuated by William Maclure, who, although not often in residence in Philadelphia, stayed in constant contact with the organization. Maclure was an industrious, far-sighted man, but he was not a professional scientist. In fact, his activities took him farther and farther away from the area of science. Elected to membership in the Academy in 1812, he was of the same tradition as those who founded the Academy; indeed, Samuel George Morton, writing in 1841, intimated that it was only because Maclure was away from Philadelphia that he was not present at the founding meeting.[34] Had it not been for Maclure and the perpetuation of this tradition through his leadership, the Academy's view of itself and its role in the scientific community might have changed noticeably in the 1830s, for there is evidence that some members, between about 1825 and 1835, were thinking of science in new terms. A conflict of traditions is apparent in bitter confrontations within the membership and in the reaction of the old guard to new ways.

The first and most important confrontation occurred in 1825, when Richard Harlan, a member since 1815, published a general account of natural history entitled *Fauna Americana, being a description of the mammiferous animals inhabiting North America.*[35] Devoted to the living and fossil species of America, it is basically a work of nomenclature and classification (the classification is Linnaean). Although such systems were followed by other Americans of the period, few if any of Harlan's predecessors were so consistent or complete with regard both to nomenclature and classification. The first criticism of the work appeared in the *North American Review* which termed the classification confused and unwarranted; in addition it found the book not useful for beginners.[36]

John Godman, a member of the Academy since 1821, was essentially in agreement with the review.[37] From Godman's remarks it is evident that his argument with Harlan was in great measure over the role of classification and nomenclature in zoology. Godman had little respect for systems of nomenclature and classification because they were, in his view, arbitrary and, therefore, of secondary importance. He failed to realize that a universally adopted system of classification and nomenclature could benefit science. Harlan, on the other hand, recognized this as well as the arbitrary nature of classification.[38]

It has been suggested that the first stage of the professionalization of science is preemption, that is, science passes through a stage that makes it comprehensible to a few rather than to many, and that one sign of preemption is the attempt to standardize nomenclature.[39] If this is true, Harlan's recognition of the importance of classification and nomenclature as "the foundation of all natural science," and his use of it as the basis of his *Fauna Americana,* puts him in the role of at least a semiprofessional scientist when opposed to Godman.[40] Further, Harlan viewed his book as a foundation for the growth of zoology, and in this sense his work is of a distinctly different tradition than that of many other Academy members, who were still concerned with the diffusion of knowledge rather than its advancement.[41] Between 1826 and 1828 Godman published a three volume work called *American Natural History,* which was, like Harlan's, intended to be a general study of American mammals. Unlike Harlan, however, Godman intended "to render this study pleasing and intelligible, more than to discuss minutiae of classification; to give *Natural History* instead of the nomenclature of American animals; to impart information to those seeking for knowledge, rather than to prepare a book for such as consider themselves the founders of systems."[42] Here the difference in approach between Harlan and Godman is apparent. The difference is equally striking in their descriptions of animals as illustrated by their respective accounts of the American black bear. Harlan's description of the black bear begins with a listing of the various names, scientific and common, assigned to the bear and the authors of those names, followed by a list of the essential characteristics of the species that distinguish it from other species, the dimensions of the animal, a description of how it differs from the brown bear, a comment that in New York two varieties of the species are distinguished, and a summary of its range. Harlan's description occupies about half a page compared with Godman's sixteen-page treatment.[43] Like Harlan, Godman also lists the various names assigned to the black bear, but from that point on his essay deals with the ecology, disposition, habits, and use of the bear, with no further information on its taxonomic characteristics. In sum, Harlan's *Fauna Americana* is a book on classification and nomenclature; Godman's, although using a classificatory approach as a kind of outline, is an essay on the natural history of the American quadruped. Godman's closest friends in the Academy were Thomas Say and Titian Peale. Together with Gerard Troost and George Ord, they appeared to share Godman's reaction to Harlan, as would be expected, since they all represented the earlier tradition.

An interesting aspect of this clash stems from questions raised by Godman about the creation of new species in the *Fauna.* These were not invalid questions, and the matter of "species-making," its potential problems and hazards, was a concern to American naturalists in general at the time. But the important point is that Say, Godman, and the others were species-making all the time without condemnation.[44] Isaac Hays, a member of the Godman-Ord-Peale group, created many different mastodon species but was much admired.[45] It would seem that it was acceptable to engage in species-making as long as it was done in the confines of a long-standing tradition, but not when it was seen as part of the creation of a new foundation for the advancement of science.

A confrontation of a different sort is also indicative of the threat to old ways. In 1824 John James Audubon visited Philadelphia and became acquainted with the Academy and its members. Audubon cannot be designated as even a semiprofessional scientist; nonetheless he was greeted with a bitter reception. This was undoubtedly because Ord had an interest in another ornithologist, Alexander Wilson, the same Wilson who had inspired much of the serious interest in natural history that had led to the founding of the Academy. Ord was devoted to Wilson, who had died in 1813, and was in the process of preparing an edition of Wilson's *American Ornithology*. Since Ord feared that Audubon would eclipse Wilson's stature as an ornithologist,[46] he fostered a campaign against Audubon with Thomas Say as one of the co-conspirators. Ord was successful in keeping Audubon from membership in the Academy and in the American Philosophical Society by a variety of means. He failed to give credit to Audubon for any achievement. There are no doubt many valid points on which one can find fault with Audubon in relation to Wilson, particularly the charges that have been made so many times that Audubon plagiarized some of Wilson's work. However, the whole bitter attack initiated by Ord, and carried out with the help of Ord's friends in the Academy as well as William Cooper in New York and Charles Waterton in England, is difficult to characterize as one of sound merit.[47] Everything Audubon said or did was considered suspect, and Audubon's friends, including Richard Harlan at the Academy, John Bachman in Charleston, and J. J. Abert, future chief of the Topographical Engineers, were criticized for their friendship with him.

The point to be made in evaluating this reaction is that Audubon was a threat to a tradition and to one of the leaders of the tradition; if Wilson were overshadowed by Audubon, the early American naturalist tradition from which the Academy sprang might be overshadowed as well.

That the old order indeed felt threatened may have been a factor in the creation of the Maclurian Lyceum of the Arts and Sciences in Philadelphia in 1826. Founded as a natural history society on almost the same basis as the Academy, it was named in honor of Maclure, and its first president was Thomas Say.[48] Neither Say nor Maclure were in Philadelphia at the time, and they never attended a meeting. Both supported the organization, however—Maclure by gifts of specimens and Say by the contribution of papers to be published by the Lyceum. Its initial membership is revealing in that it included Gerard Troost and Jacob Gilliams as well as Say and Maclure, all early or original members of the Academy. Godman was probably a member. The papers published in the short-lived *Contributions of the Maclurian Lyceum to the Arts and Sciences* are also revealing, in that of three papers by Say one is an attack on Harlan and another is a paper rejected by the Academy.[49]

Whether Harlan represented a professional scientist is open to much question, and he is characterized above as a semiprofessional. This second period of the Academy's history was certainly more amateur in outlook than professional or semiprofessional, but both elements were to be found. Many events in the Academy in the 1830s show in small ways that a subtle trend toward professionalism was present. There was, for example, a reaction against the museum as a department of the Academy open to the public.[50] Questions about the museum were voiced throughout the decade, although the museum continued to be open.

In 1832 the Geological Society of Pennsylvania was organized by a group interested in geology in Philadelphia and particularly in the formation of a state survey. One member of the Academy, Richard Harlan, was a founding member of the Society, and it is probable that Harlan viewed this new society as offering a better opportunity for the expression of his own semiprofessionalism. More interesting than Harlan's membership in the organization is the reaction to the Geological Society expressed by Samuel Morton. By 1832 Morton was recognized as one of this nation's leading geologists and had been the first to use fossils as geological indices to any extent in America. George Daniels has suggested that professional scientists were often recognizable by their "marked caution regarding the formation of associations. They generally recognized that there were as many dangers, if not handled carefully, as there were advantages. There was the ever present fear of charlatanism gaining control with the result that 'true science' would be subordinated to extra-scientific considerations and perhaps misdirected."[51] Such a reaction to the Geological Society was demonstrated by Morton. Shortly after the Society was formed, Morton wrote to his friend Benjamin Silliman: "I see by one of our yesterdays newspapers that we have in this city a Geolog. Society of Penn—but among the dignitaries of the Institution I could not recognize a single geologist! Excepting Mr. Peter A. Browne who is a very reputable learner. Something else than science is at the bottom of it. Not one of the well informed geologists of Philad. has been consulted in this matter."[52]

During the 1830s the Academy showed a little more interest as an official body in participating in exploring and collecting trips than before. As early as 1834 the Academy provided $100 to John Townsend for his exploring venture to the mouth of the Columbia River,[53] but the first more than superficial association came with the Wilkes Expedition. If, as Hunter Dupree has said, the Wilkes South Sea exploring expedition of 1838-1842 was to the United States "a mark of her growing scientific stature,"[54] the Academy recognized it as such and recognized its own ability to act on behalf of the scientific community.

On September 6, 1836, a letter from the Secretary of the Navy, Mahlon Dickerson, was read to the Academy. It requested suggestions and nominations for the proposed national exploring expedition to the South Seas. The Academy declined officially to nominate anyone for the scientific corps of the expedition but made recommendations that amounted to nominations. Most of the members of the Academy supported Charles Pickering as naturalist for the voyage, and a letter with twenty-five signatures of Academy members was sent to Dickerson in Pickering's behalf.[55] Pickering was eventually chosen to be one of the naturalists on the voyage along with his fellow Academy member, Titian Peale.[56] Richard Harlan wanted the post of surgeon and naturalist on the voyage and wrote to Daniel Parker in Washington to the effect that the Academy was "addressing a memorial to the President . . . containing the most flattering recommendations in my favour."[57]

The Academy drew up recommendations for the expedition, which included ideas on the general organization of the scientific corps and on procedures for collecting. A committee of eight, appointed on September 13, 1836, prepared the reports that embodied the thoughts of the Academy. The preparation of the reports proceeded smoothly, with the only question being whether the physical sciences should be included. Since the Academy had for some years carefully excluded articles on the physical sciences from its *Journal* this was a legitimate issue. It was ultimately decided to include the physical sciences for this purpose. On September 27 the reports of the committee, each on a special area of natural science, together with a report on the general organization of the scientific corps of the expedition, were submitted to Dickerson.[58] However, as has been well documented, plans for the expedition were not to proceed smoothly, and the attention actually paid to the Academy reports is questionable.

The Third Period: 1840-1850

William Maclure died in 1840, and an era in the Academy's history came to an end. In the following years the trend toward professionalism that first emerged in the 1830s continued and became stronger. Yet this period should not be characterized as a professional one in the Academy's history. It was, rather, a transitional phase, as might be expected to occur on the road from amateurism to professionalism. Were it not that William Maclure and his role in the Academy distinguish the years 1817-1840 as a unit, the whole period from 1825 to 1850 might best be considered as a transitional period for the Academy.

The years from 1840 to 1850 were essentially quiet ones within the Academy. Financial problems were still a concern, but fortunately the Academy had friends who were able and willing to help with personal funds.[59] Membership at meetings declined, perhaps a reaction to the end of the tradition brought about by Maclure's death. In spite of these problems, the Academy began the publication of its *Proceedings* in 1841, and, although the *Journal* ceased publication in 1842, a second series was started in 1847.

A different attitude regarding the purpose of the collections of the Academy is seen in the 1840s. Almost as soon as Maclure was gone, the Academy ruled that on the days the museum was open to the public the library was to be inaccessible to all but members, and in 1841 entrance to the museum was restricted to those over sixteen. The collections were viewed as matters of scientific concern, and the unhappiness with public access to them, evident in these actions, continued in discussions reported in the Minutes throughout the decade. Not only had it become desirable to keep the public away from the collections, it was now considered advisable to give the scientific community greater access to the material. Instead of making casts of specimens available for exchange, for example, the Academy freely allowed qualified persons who were not members to borrow the actual specimens.[60]

Moreover, during these years, the Academy never failed to take a stand on issues of interest to the community of scientists if it felt it had any right to do so. For instance, it expressed great concern over the fate of the information collected by the Wilkes Expedition. When Congress decided to limit the publication of the scientific reports of the expedition to one hundred copies, the ire of many naturalists was aroused. On February 6, 1846, the American Academy of Arts and Sciences wrote to the Academy of Natural Sciences asking for its cooperation in securing a larger printing. In response, the Philadelphia Academy prepared a series of resolutions, sending one copy to Boston and another to the Library of Congress. The resolutions stated that by virtue of the fact that the Academy had provided counsel concerning the formation of the expedition at the request of the Navy Department, it "deems itself justified in complaining of the treatment, which in common with all the other scientific bodies thus consulted, it received by the existing arrangement," permitting only one hundred copies to be printed. Such a number was "utterly inadequate to supply the demand for the work, especially as about one half of that number is understood to be distributed in donations to Foreign Governments, while none are allowed to scientific societies at home."[61]

The varied interests and activities of the members of the Academy in the 1840s are indicative of its transitional state. Some of its members, like Henry Darwin Rogers, may be called theoretical scientists; others, like Joseph Leidy, carried the descriptive sciences to a high level of development.[62] Some members were involved in the creation of new, highly specialized professional bodies. Among the founders and first officers of the American Medical Association, organized in Philadelphia in 1847, were George B. Wood, a member of the Academy since 1824, and Isaac Hays, a member since 1818. The Association of American Geologists grew out of the need for communication channels among state geological surveys, and Henry Darwin Rogers as Director of the Pennsylvania Survey was active in its organization in 1840. In the years after 1850 the move toward professionalism continued, but the Academy as a professional society was to an extent eclipsed by the efforts of its own members to create more specialized organizations and by its renewed interest in pursuing a public role in the Philadelphia community through its museum.[63]

NOTES

1. The following is a list of histories of the Academy of Natural Sciences of Philadelphia before 1850. Most of these histories tend to be repetitive, and none include much information on the relation of the Academy of American society. For general information on the Academy's early years they are, however, very useful. They are listed in order of publication or preparation date.

John Barnes, "Rise and Progress of the Academy," inserted in Minute Book of 1816, Academy of Natural Sciences Archives.

"Notice of the Academy of Natural Sciences of Philadelphia," *American Journal of Science* 19 (1830): 88-96. Also published separately in 1830, 1831, 1836, and 1837.

Walter R. Johnson, *Address Delivered on Laying the Corner Stone of the Academy of Natural Sciences of Philadelphia May 25, 1839* (Philadelphia: T. K. and P. G. Collins, printers, 1839).

Samuel George Morton, "History of the Academy of Natural Sciences of Philadelphia," *American Quarterly Register* 13 (1840-1841): 433-38.

W. S. W. Ruschenberger, *Notice of the Origin, Progress and Present Condition of the Academy of Natural Sciences of Philadelphia* (Philadelphia: T. K. and P. G. Collins, printers, 1852).

W. P. Foulke, *Discourse in Commemoration of the Founding* (Philadelphia, 1854).

W. S. W. Ruschenberger et al., *Addresses Delivered on Laying the Corner-Stone of an Edifice for the Academy of Natural Sciences of Philadelphia, October 30, 1872* (Philadelphia: T. K. and P. G. Collins, printers, 1873).

W. S. W. Ruschenberger, *Report of the Condition of the Academy of Natural Sciences of Philadelphia, on Its Moving Into Its New Edifice, S. W. Cor. of Race and Nineteenth Sts. April 28, 1876* (Philadelphia: T. K. and P. G. Collins, printers, 1876).

Edward J. Nolan, *A Short History of the Academy of Natural Sciences of Philadelphia* (Philadelphia: Academy of Natural Sciences, 1909).

Edward J. Nolan, "History of the Academy of Natural Sciences," 1912, Academy of Natural Sciences Archives.

Max Meisel, "Academy of Natural Sciences of Philadelphia," *A Bibliography of American Natural History. The Pioneer Century: 1769-1865,* 3 vols. (New York: Premier Publishing Co., 1924-1929), 2 (1926): 139-218.

Morris Albert Linton, *The Academy of Natural Sciences of Philadelphia. 150 Years of Distinguished Service* (New York: Newcomen Society of North America, 1962).

2. Entertaining advertisements for such exhibits frequently appeared in Philadelphia newspapers of the day.

3. Say was not present at the first several meetings of the Academy, but his name was included by the other six as a founding member, and we may assume that he was in perfect accord with the others regarding the formation of the Academy. It was, no doubt, an accident of chance that he was not present at the first meetings.

4. Minutes of the Preliminary Meeting, Academy of Natural Sciences Archives, Philadelphia, Pa.

5. The chemical experimental laboratory never became a reality, and there is no evidence that the experimental philosophic apparatus ever existed.

6. Although the members stated their goals as the "advancement and diffusion" of knowledge, diffusion and advancement were essentially the same to them.

7. John Barnes, "Rise and Progress of the Academy," 1816, inserted in Minute Book of 1816, Academy of Natural Sciences Archives. Barnes was the first person elected to membership by the founders.

8. Ibid.

9. The number of correspondents elected has been determined from a list kept by the corresponding secretary of the Academy, Reuben Haines. Although Haines was elected to this position in 1814, he made an effort to record all outgoing correspondence from 1812. Data for 1813, however, is not in the notebook, and so the figures given are not accurate. They do, nevertheless, give some indication of the extent of the corresponding membership. The one hundred correspondents elected between 1812 and 1817 were from the following areas:

Other areas of Pennsylvania	17
New York	15
Massachusetts	8
Maryland	6
France	5
Kentucky	4
Connecticut, Delaware, New Jersey, and South Carolina	2 each
England	2
Maine, North Carolina, Ohio, U.S. Navy, Virginia, and Washington Brazil, East Indies, Guadaloupe, India, Ireland, Nova Scotia, Portugal, Spain, Switzerland, and the West Indies	1 each

There are fifteen entries in Haines' notebook that do not give clear addresses for the correspondents. These are not included in the above list.

10 Following Minutes of 1812, Academy of Natural Sciences Archives.

11. Minutes of the Academy, 23 July 1816. Detailed minutes of the Academy meetings have been carefully kept and preserved since the first meeting of the founders. Much of the information contained in this paper has come from those minutes. If no other source is given in a footnote, it can be assumed that the minutes are the source. A few years ago the Academy microfilmed all the minutes, and much of its official correspondence and documents. References like that given in note 10, above, refer to the location of an item on the microfilm.

12. Ruschenberger, *Notice of the Origin, Progress and Present Condition of the Academy of Natural Sciences of Philadelphia,* p. 48.

13. A willingness to be available to the general public is probably a nonprofessional attitude. This is suggested in comments by George H. Daniels in his "The Process of Professionalization in American Science: The Emergent Period, 1820-1860," *Isis* 58 (1967): 151-66.

14. Minutes, 15 November 1815.

15. Treasurer's Report following Minutes of 1815.

16. *Journal of the Academy of Natural Sciences of Philadelphia* 1 (1817): preface.

17. There are miscellaneous comments recorded throughout the Minutes of the Academy after the *Journal* was begun that rule out the inclusion of any papers that did not deal specifically with a subject in natural history. Such papers were, however, welcomed as papers to be read before the Academy.

18. Minutes, 26 February 1817. Expeditious publication was very often essential to the nineteenth-century naturalist who, in his role as taxonomist was concerned with giving the first description of some new animal or plant.

19. *Journal of the Academy of Natural Sciences of Philadelphia* 1:2.

20. From a note following Samuel George Morton, *A Memoir of William Maclure, Esq.* (Philadelphia: T. K. and P. G. Collins, printers, 1841).

21. Ibid. The trip to the West Indies included Lesueur, and the Florida trip included Thomas Say, George Ord, and Titian Peale.

22. "Notice of the Academy of Natural Sciences of Philadelphia," *American Journal of Science* 19 (1831): 94.

23. Exactly what was included in this collection is not known, as no record of its contents now exists, but according to Harlan the purchase included Dorfeuille's collection of fossils from the Mississippi Basin and a collection from Mr. Clifford of Kentucky, which was in the possession of the Western Museum. A Western Museum record of 1826 indicates that there were one hundred mammoth and Arctic elephant bones, fifty megalonyx bones, and a thousand miscellaneous fossils in the museum's possession at that time. These may have been included in the collection purchased from Dorfeuille, since he virtually owned the Western Museum. Elizabeth R. Kellogg, "Joseph Dorfeuille and the Western Museum," *Journal of the Cincinnati Society of Natural History* 22 (1945): 4, 23.

24. Dreer Collection-Physicians, vol. 3, Pennsylvania Historical Society, Philadelphia, Pa.

25. "Description of the Fossil Bones of the Megalonyx, Discovered in 'White Cave,' Kentucky," *Journal of the Academy of Natural Sciences of Philadelphia* 6 (1831): 269.

26. See list of professors in *The Philadelphia Museum or Register of Natural History and the Arts,* 1 (1824).

27. Although physicians accounted for about 30 percent of the Academy's members between 1812 and 1840, and although a great many of the papers read before the membership were on medical or very closely related subjects, there was no apparent interchange between the Academy and the University of Pennsylvania medical faculty. There is nothing, in fact, to suggest any particular bond between the Academy and the university in any department. A few Academy members were faculty members, but they seem not to have brought the two organizations into any form of alliance.

28. "Observations on the Geology of the United States Explanatory of a Geological Map," *Transactions of the American Philosophical Society* 6 (1809): 411-28. An expanded version was published in Philadelphia in 1817.

29. 23 June 1839, incorporated in the Minutes of 13 August 1839, Academy of Natural

Sciences Archives. Also see Maclure to S. G. Morton, 15 June 1839, American Philosophical Society Collection, Philadelphia, Pa.

30. Minutes, 27 April 1819.

31. Minutes, 16 August and 30 August 1831.

32. Sally Kohlstedt, "A Step Toward Self-Identity in the United States: The Failure of the National Institute 1844," *Isis* 62 (1971): 343.

33. Minutes, 20 August 1839.

34. Morton, *Memoir of William Maclure,* p. 15.

35. Philadelphia: Anthony Finley; J. Harding, printer, 1825.

36. "Review of Harlan's *Fauna Americana,*" *North American Review* 22 (1826): 120-36.

37. "Remarks on an Article in the North American Review," *Journal of the Franklin Institute* 1 (1826): 19-20. One of Godman's principal reasons for becoming involved in a discussion of the *Fauna* was his belief that it represented a case of plagiarism. Harlan's reason for writing the book was, in part, a conviction that errors and confusion about American animals in the minds and works of Europeans had arisen because there was not such a book available, that is, a general compendium of American living and fossil mammals. Citing as a particular example A. G. Desmarest, *Mammalogie ou description des espèces de mammifères* (Paris: Agasse, 1820), Harlan showed that there was misunderstanding and lack of knowledge concerning the animals of North America (*Fauna,* p. v). It was his expressed intent to correct and add to the information as given by Desmarest. However, Godman accused Harlan of virtually copying Desmarest's work without acknowledgment and passing it off as his own. Harlan responded almost immediately to this, and to the criticisms in the *North American Review,* in a small booklet entitled *Refutation of Certain Misrepresentations Issued Against the Author of the Fauna Americana, in the Philadelphia Franklin Journal, No. 1, and in the North American Review, No. 50* (Philadelphia: Wm. Stavely, printer, 1826). What Godman said in general of Harlan, Harlan now said of Godman. He asserted that Godman spoke of things he knew little about, pointing out that Godman's ideas of the subject scarcely "soared above 'Goldsmith's Animated Nature,'" and that Godman himself was guilty of plagiarism in using the ideas of Bell and Bichat as his own in a work entitled *Anatomical Investigation, Comprising Descriptions of Various Fasciae of the Human Body* (Philadelphia: H. C. Carey & I. Lea, 1824). This charge had been made against Godman by others as well. Godman's reply to Harlan was that he had given full credit to Bichat in the preface of the work in question (see Godman's *A Letter to Dr. Thomas P. Jones, Editor of the Franklin Journal* [Philadelphia: Printed for the author, 1826], p. 20). This, of course, was exactly what Harlan had done in regard to Desmarest.

38. Harlan once wrote to John James Audubon that "God made the *Species*—man has attempted to make classes, orders, genera—" thus expressing his recognition of the artificiality of classification. 27 January 1832, Houghton Library, Harvard University, Cambridge, Mass.

39. Daniels, "The Process of Professionalization," p. 155.

40. Harlan, *Refutation of Certain Misrepresentations,* p. 14.

41. Harlan, *Fauna Americana,* intro.

42. John Godman, *American Natural History,* 3 vols. (Philadelphia: H. C. Carey and I. Lea, 1826-1828), 3:247.

43. Harlan, *Fauna Americana,* p. 51; Godman, *American Natural History,* pp. 114-30.

44. On the relationship of species making to the rise of professional science see Daniels, "The Process of Professionalization," p. 156.

45. "Description of the Inferior Maxillary Bones of Mastodons in the Cabinet of the American Philosophical Society, with Remarks on the Genus Tetracaulodon (Godman) etc.," *Transactions of the American Philosophical Society* 4 (1834): 317-39.

46. On this point see Alice Ford, *John James Audubon* (Norman: University of Oklahoma Press, 1964), p. 143.

47. The extent of Ord's bitterness appears most clearly in letters like the following: Ord to Titian Peale, 8 January 1830 and 19 July 1835, Peale Manuscripts, Pennsylvania Historical Society; William Cooper to Charles Lucien Bonaparte, 20 March 1826, Microfilm no. 542, American Philosophical Society; Ord-Waterton correspondence at the American Philosophical Society, especially the letter dated 23 April 1832.

48. A brief history of the Maclurian Lyceum is that of John T. Sharpless, *Report of the Transactions of the Maclurian Lyceum of the Arts and Sciences* (Philadelphia: J. Richards, printer, 1830), pp. 1-6.

49. See the unpublished history of the Academy by A. J. Nolan, p. 150, in the Academy's Archives and *Contributions of the Maclurian Lyceum to the Arts and Sciences* 1 (1827): 37-39.

50. Minutes, 15 March 1831. Reaction against public access to scientific collections has been recognized as a mark of a more advanced science. See, for example, Nathan Reingold, *Science in Nineteenth Century America: A Documentary History* (New York: Hill & Wang, 1964), p. 30.

51. Daniels, "The Process of Professionalization," pp. 9-10.

52. 29 February 1832, Morton-Silliman Correspondence, Yale University, New Haven, Conn. By 1834 the Geological Society's membership included many well-known geologists, including Morton's protégé, T. A. Conrad, who was also a member of the Academy.

53. Although the money was raised by special subscription of individual members, the transaction was an official one, and made in exchange for specimens to be collected. When it was time to claim the specimens, the Academy reacted in its original tradition by saying that only members and not the Academy had contributed to the venture and therefore the Academy could not, apparently, participate in the spoils. It was, however, pointed out that this had not really been the case and the specimens were claimed by the Academy. Minutes, 19 December 1837. The Academy received about one hundred birds and one hundred shells. In 1838 (March 27) the Academy approved the expenditure of $100 to purchase more of Townsend's collection.

54. A. Hunter Dupree, *Science in the Federal Government: A History of Policies and Activities to 1940* (Cambridge, Mass.: Harvard University Press, Belknap Press, 1957), p. 57.

55. R. Harlan and twenty-four others, October 1836, U.S. Exploring Expedition Collection, Academy of Natural Sciences.

56. There was probably strong support for Peale in the Academy, as evidenced by a letter in his favor sent by Isaac Lea, 2 October 1836, U.S. Exploring Expedition Collection.

57. 28 December 1828, Daniel Parker Papers, Pennsylvania Historical Society.

58. The reports were prepared by R. E. Griffith on botany, S. G. Morton and R. C. Taylor on mineralogy and geology, R. Bridges on chemistry, B. Coates on the medical sciences, R. Harlan on vertebrate zoology, R. Coates on invertebrate marine animals, and Morton and R. Coates on the general organization of the corps.

59. Thomas B. Wilson, for example, supported the Academy and secured specimens, among others the collection of birds of the Duc de Rivoli numbering about twenty-five thousand specimens. His money allowed significant extension of the Academy's building in 1846-1847.

60. Requests from W. C. Redfield (26 October 1847) and from Charles Lyell (8 January 1846) for the loan of fossils met a willing response, and articles of the bylaws restricting such loans were put aside in both instances without discussion.

61. Minutes, 17 February 1846.

62. Rogers published a paper on mountain elevation that was in part a theoretical treatment of geological dynamics. "On the Physical Structure of the Appalachian Chain, as Exemplifying the Laws which Have Regulated the Elevation of Great Mountain Chains, Generally," *Reports of the First, Second, and Third Meetings of the Association of American Geologists and Naturalists at Philadelphia in 1840 and 1841, and at Boston in 1842* (Boston: Gould, Kendall, and Lincoln, 1843), pp. 474-531. Leidy's work was mainly in paleontology and is the basis for many papers.

63. The relatively early trend toward public involvement in the Academy through its museum may have been a factor in the survival of the Academy through the first half of the nineteenth century, when other societies rose and then disappeared with some frequency. Whether the presence of a public museum had any effect on the survival of other societies or not would require, of course, a special study. The tendency after 1850 to emphasize the museum at the Academy suggests that the museum may have been looked upon as the road to long-term survival and security.

Science, Technology, and the Franklin Institute

BRUCE SINCLAIR

Historians are familiar with the proposition that nineteenth-century scientists often proclaimed the practical value of their research as an argument for financial support of science and its institutions. Almost implicitly, this assertion seems to connote a hollow argument. Yet there were, in fact, significant examples of a fruitful science-technology relationship that scientists could draw upon—suggestive models for research programs that served as precedents for public support. It should be noted, however, that two of the best examples—the Franklin Institute's water power experiments and its investigation into steamboat boiler explosions—originated not in science but in technology, and grew out of the efforts of a technical society that itself was committed to a relationship between science and technology.

The idea that there should be a positive connection between science and technology was widely popular in nineteenth-century America. It was a stock item in the rhetoric of the mechanics' institute movement and involved visions of democratic educational reform. The founders of the Franklin Institute believed that the union of theory and practice, the combination of scientific principles and craft skill, would lead to a new era in human history. It would be an era, moreover, in sharp contrast to past ages, when a profound gulf separated science and practice. The same sentiments were echoed by speakers before lyceums and apprentices' libraries, at college commencements and industrial exhibitions, and on similar ceremonial occasions. Audiences were reminded that, until Lord Bacon and his new experimental philosophy, mankind had labored in fear, ignorance, and superstition.[1] Monopolistic guilds had limited production and suppressed technical advance. Contempt for manual work had reduced the productive classes of society to a degraded and servile status. And the artisan himself had been forced to guard his craft secrets jealously in order to gain a slender livelihood from his skills.

Science, in this interpretation, was locked away in remote towers. At the universities, only an anemic remnant of Greek thought remained in the idle speculations of closet philosophers. The libraries and cabinets of wealthy aristocrats contained the truths of nature, but they were just as closed to the artisan as was the university. Science was denied the corrective of experience; the mech-

[1] Notes to this chapter begin on page 205.

anic arts were deprived of knowledge. Bacon ended the despotism. By directing science to practical ends, by redefining its goals in terms of bettering the human condition, he opened the long-closed door separating theory and the arts. Reason gradually prevailed, and men discovered that education and freedom led to prosperity and happiness.

By setting their aims in a broad chronological panorama, the founders of mechanics' institutes claimed an essential role in the historical process. Bacon had made the philosopher aware of the lessons to be learned in the workshop. Educational reformers meant to make philosopher and workingman the same person. In an explicit effort to identify this new individual, they called him the "intelligent mechanic," or the "scientific mechanic."[2] He had several distinguishing characteristics. In the first place, he was a skilled craftsman, so knowledgeable about the properties of materials and so practiced in the use of tools that he had an intuitive understanding of both. He was an able draftsman, an ability that allowed him to communicate his ideas clearly and effectively. The intelligent mechanic was inventive. He had a flexibility of mind that transcended the boundaries of craft lines and that was uncharacteristic of what Americans assumed Old World guildhall thinking to be.

Nor were his intellect and interests limited to the workshop. He took part in community affairs, was able to turn a phrase, perhaps even to write a piece of poetry. Indeed, as Americans described the scientific mechanic, his talents, and his role, it becomes clear that he was Jefferson's idealized yeoman farmer, moved to the workshop. Just like that sturdy son of the soil, the intelligent mechanic was a repository of wit, wisdom, and virtue. He needed only education to allow him to rise to his proper station in a republican society. In turn, his contributions to the country's material advancement would ultimately demonstrate the superiority of its political system.

But what most distinguished the intelligent mechanic was his knowledge of science. More particularly, it was his understanding of the scientific principles that lay behind his art. A thorough background in those basic and unchanging natural laws, when joined with his practical skills, would allow him to correct old mistakes and devise new procedures, to see different combinations of materials and new uses for them. If the mechanic understood fundamental principles, he would also be able to recognize incorrect principles or faulty design. Science would save him from wasting his time and money on things that would not work. While there was an obvious practical point to the approach, it also included a mission. The scientific mechanic would escape that cycle which had limited craftsmen for centuries, that old need to rediscover the same truths every generation. Besides its ideological implications, then, the union of theory and practice described a set of mechanisms to stimulate technological advancement.

Philadelphia's Franklin Institute provides a good example of the kind of program devised to advance the artisan and the state of his art.[3] The board of managers first organized evening lectures on various topics, mainly to capitalize on the popular interest surrounding the society's formal incorporation early in 1824. But then, in very rapid succession, the managers appointed an academic faculty to conduct lecture courses in natural philosophy, mechanics, and chemistry; opened one evening school to teach architectural and mechanical drawing, and started another to teach mathematics; formed a committee to examine and report on new inventions; sponsored an exhibition of domestic manufactures; and built a handsome new hall to house the organization. There were also notions of publishing a mechanics' magazine and perhaps of creating an experimental laboratory to join classroom instruction and practical application. In fact, even those hopes were shortly realized, although not in their original dress.

Indeed, within little more than two years the Franklin Institute had put together the most ambitious program in the country to stimulate and coordinate technical advance. Its lecture courses, evening schools, and the *Franklin Journal,* which Dr. Thomas P. Jones began in 1826, were all mobilized to diffuse knowledge of science and its applications. Identification of those technical problems most in need of solutions came from the work of the committee on inventions, from Dr. Jones's pages, and from the committee on exhibitions, which distributed an advance schedule of awards, with the value of prizes keyed to selected areas of industrial activity.[4] In their efforts to organize American technical development, the Institute's managers employed a number of devices that had long been familiar, both at home and abroad. It was the combination of these instruments, wielded in such a self-conscious fashion, that was novel.

But in a period of time almost as brief as the two years it took to assemble the program, it became apparent at the Institute that the formula didn't work. To begin with, the lectures were a failure, or rather, they failed to teach workingmen the scientific principles upon which craft skill supposedly rested.[5] Part of the problem was that the mission was an ideological posture as much as anything else and difficult to implement. Whether the mechanic arts did depend on the principles of science was an assumption no one bothered to examine. If so, precisely how an artisan might utilize Newtonian physics, and how he might translate the link into pedagogical forms were issues without answers. The committee on instruction grappled with these problems and with alternate proposals for their solution, because out of their experience they had arrived at at least one firm piece of evidence: workingmen could understand only science lectures so elementary that they had no real application.[6]

Dr. Jones discovered the same problem with respect to his magazine. He saw the editor's task in a simple and straightforward way. The *Journal's* major objective was to diffuse knowledge, and Jones made no attempt at originality. He selected articles from foreign periodicals in terms of their practical value and plain language, the same basis on which he accepted communications from the mechanic community.[7] Even with those predilections, to simplify technical language and still convey precise meaning was a difficult business. For a brief time, Jones tried to include a vocabulary in each number of the *Journal* to explain unfamiliar words. But that quickly proved a tedious and unsatisfactory solution. He then experimented with a series of special features designed to convey a simple stock of scientific ideas and terms.[8] Compared to the drama of real events, however, the series seemed pale and remote. Steam transportation, large-scale internal improvements, and industrial development were more exciting issues, and they posed more interesting problems.

In the Institute's experience, the connection between educational reform and technical advance was difficult to establish. At that level, uniting theory and practice proved a conception with little more than rhetorical value. And yet it seemed obvious that the nation's material progress was somehow crucially tied up with science. The answer to that particular puzzle came out of a set of efforts at the Institute that, relatively speaking, carried little ideological thrust.

The one element in the society's early activities that distinguished it from other mechanics' institutes was its attempt to organize and coordinate industrial development. Prize awards at exhibitions served that purpose and identified specific technical problems, as well as types of industrial production to be encouraged. At the second exhibition in 1825, for instance, silver medals were offered for the best treatises on the efficient use of water power and on the best methods for preventing boiler explosions in steamboats. Both were significant problems. Industrial development depended on prime movers, and for most Americans during the first half of the nineteenth century that meant water power. During the same period steam power was most successfully applied to transportation, but often without any detailed understanding of the technology. In both instances, mechanics used rule-of-thumb methods more than they did engineering principles, and the results were frequently either inefficient or disastrous. Furthermore, in neither case were the problems likely to be solved by random efforts.

By 1829 the Institute's managers recognized that some issues called for a more systematic approach than prize awards, and they hit upon an idea. The organization would itself conduct an investigation into water power and the most effective means of using it, if industry would support the costs of experimentation. Samuel V. Merrick, a founder of the Institute who later became one of Philadelphia's most prominent industrialists, explained the reason behind the proposal. The technology of water power, he argued, "has never been fix'd by actual experiment on a scale of sufficient magnitude to settle principles upon which it is to be calculated."[9] He proposed, therefore, that the Institute circularize American manufacturers to raise the money for a course of experiments, devise suitable apparatus for the purpose, and publish the results.

Nothing better illustrates the widespread appreciation of the problem and of the need for rational technology than the response to the Institute's appeal. Letters came from New England, the mid-Atlantic states, and from across the Appalachians.[10] They provided both the encouragement and financial support the managers wanted, and by the spring of 1830 the committee in charge of the experiments had constructed its testing facility.

The primary purpose of research could be stated with simplicity. It was to determine "the mode of applying any given head of water, so as to produce the greatest ratio of effect to power expended."[11] In practice, however, that was a complicated analysis, involving variations in the head of water, wheel size, and type; in the size of the aperture that let water to the wheel and the form of gate used in the chute; in the number of buckets on a wheel, their shape and position; and finally in the velocity of the wheel. The effect of friction and inertia for each wheel combination had to be determined, and, in the interest of further accuracy, each experiment for each variation of each variable was run twice to double-check the results, or additionally if necessary to secure reliable figures.[12] In all, the experimenters recorded 1,381 trials in their reports—which meant, of course, that they went through the procedures twice as many times.

When the results of the water power investigation were made available, the first report was published in the *Journal* of the Franklin Institute in March, 1831; it provided precisely the information the committee had intended to discover. By recourse to the tabular data of the reports, millwrights could determine the limits of efficiency in whatever combination of elements they had at their command. Or perhaps a better way of putting it is that they could discover how to combine the elements of water power to achieve maximum efficiency. The research did not produce radically new ideas, nor had anyone expected that it would. Instead, it was designed to extend existing knowledge by a careful consideration of all known parameters in tests with full-scale apparatus. The conclusions, as George Rennie noted in 1832 before the British Association for the Advancement of Science, "eclipse everything that has yet been effected on this subject."[13]

The water power research was remarkably important for the Franklin Institute and for the development of American technology. It defined a transition from emotionally powerful but vague ideas about theory and practice to a technology that advanced by using scientific methods. When Merrick talked about principles, he did not mean fundamental natural laws. He meant engineering principles cast in the form of tables. Just like scientists, engineers needed rigorously validated information but to describe different phenomena and for different purposes. Technology, Edwin Layton has pointed out, progressed by using the methods, not the principles of science.[14]

Foreign comment illuminated another significant result of the work. The editor of the London *Mechanics Magazine* reprinted the committee's first report as an example of the power of "organized and co-operative" research.[15] Individual discoveries might be made along the technological frontier, but the most dramatic advances came through combined efforts. Major problems were solved by an enterprise larger than the talents and funds of a single individual. And when the editor compared the water power research with the work expected of the newly formed British Association, it was implicitly suggested that organization also meant standards of intellectual activity. Technology, like science, required institutions, norms of professional conduct, the cooperative effort of its practitioners, and outside financial support for research.

There is an important connection between the formulation of an experimental style for technical investigations and the development of scientific institutions in America. Indeed, at the Franklin Institute the style grew out of efforts to define science and the role of scientific organizations. The central figure was Alexander Dallas Bache. Most of the general details of Bache's life are familiar to historians of American science, except for his activities at the Institute. When he returned to Philadelphia at the age of twenty-two, his West Point record already indicated a brilliant future. Bache joined the Institute in 1829 and almost immediately came to dominate all of the society's programs that related to instruction, publication, and research.[16] Shortly after his election to membership, he was added to the committee conducting the water power experiments and was responsible, along with James P. Espy and Benjamin Reeves, for publishing its reports. But, most crucial, Bache led the Institute's research into steamboat boiler explosions.

The hazard of exploding steam boilers had always been an easily identifiable problem. The difficulty was in doing something about it. There was a fog of confusion surrounding the causes of these disasters: eyewitness accounts were notoriously unreliable; the industry was unable and unwilling to police itself; and government had yet to draw the line between private interest and public welfare. There had been previous investigations, but they were limited in scope and without the authority to compel action.[17] In that vacuum of uncertainty the Institute's managers, fresh from the success of their water power research, decided in 1830 to undertake an investigation of their own. Coincidentally, the Secretary of the Treasury, Samuel D. Ingham, received an appropriation for a governmental inquiry, and he provided the funds for a series of experiments Bache had drafted.[18]

Those experiments and their relation to federal regulatory measures have been described elsewhere.[19] But their significance to attitudes about science and scientific institutions is worth notice. To begin with, the experiments marked the first use of federal funds to support research outside the governmental establishment. It was also the first such experimental investigation in America. The research was directed at the level of a national problem; at stake was the country's scientific reputation, and Bache's reputation as well. Bache became chairman of the committee in charge of the experiments and wrote two of the three reports that issued from the project. They constituted the bulk of the scientific credentials he carried with him to Europe in 1836.[20]

Probably more important, however, the investigation provided an ideal sample of mission-oriented research and the justification of public support for science. Both were epitomized in Bache's *General Report on the Explosions of Steam Boilers,* published in 1836.[21] In his view, it was his responsibility as chairman to describe the nature of the inquiry, summarize the experimental data, and make the recommendations necessary for legislative action. He meant to survey the problem and to provide definitive answers. The report outlined in crisp methodical fashion the major causes of boiler explosions. Equally important, in Bache's mind, was to show "what are certainly not causes," and one of his main objectives was to settle conclusively the variety of popular notions that confused the subject.[22] Catastrophic theories fitted the instantaneous nature of explosions and seemed appropriate to their disastrous consequences. But explosions were not beyond science, Bache argued. And once facts had been applied to prevent the danger, there would be ample time to look for "occult" causes. The report included an analysis of various safety devices; contained advice on the design, materials, and construction of steam boilers; and provided information for proper maintenance and safety-checking procedures. It was a model presentation of the current state of a problem that had engaged scientific men throughout the world.

From the beginning of the investigation, the committee had entertained no doubt of the necessity for regulation in the interest of public safety, or of the power of Congress to legislate accordingly. If anything, that view was strengthened during the course of the investigation. Bache's *General Report* was cast in near perfect form to secure legislative action. Experimental results were translated into three proposed categories of regulation: the establishment of an inspection and certification system for steam boilers; minimum standards for safety devices, operating procedures, and personnel qualification; and penalties for improper operation or noncompliance. And all of these features were incorporated in a bill that Bache had drafted at the end of his report. In order to be effective, the Institute's labors had to be cast in a form that Congress could most easily digest. Bache understood the role of a science administrator long before he went to Washington.

The boiler explosion investigation focused the Institute's attention on research and gave Bache the opportunity to transform the organization with a program that in microcosm mirrored his later efforts at the national level. In concert with a scientific circle composed of James P. Espy, Walter R. Johnson, Sears C. Walker, James C. Booth, John F. Frazer, and on occasion Henry D. Rogers and his friend Joseph Henry, Bache redirected the Institute toward original research, publication, and public funding.[23] With state money from Rogers's geological survey (which also furnished occupation for Booth and Frazer), the society carried out meteorological observations for a number of years, providing a job for Espy and a corps of observers, which Henry later amalgamated into his Smithsonian network. The Institute devised and carried into effect a plan for a uniform system of weights and measures for the Commonwealth, an interest Bache pursued later in his career.[24] Walter R. Johnson headed a boiler explosion subcommittee that investigated the strength of boiler materials in a remarkably sophisticated set of experiments. His subsequent research, particularly a study of the burning properties of American coals conducted under Navy auspices, reflected the same approach. And the testing apparatus he devised at the Institute was afterwards used by the committee that Joseph Henry chaired to investigate the U.S.S. *Princeton* disaster in 1844.[25]

To Bache and his colleagues, research always implied publication. Publishing was infused with the same values and the same ambitions as original investigations. It was the way to reputation for men with career aspirations but also the yardstick of a man's talents. Publication revealed the ability to frame important questions and to provide significant results. Reforming the Franklin Institute's *Journal* was therefore an important part of Bache's program.

Dr. Jones had conducted his magazine firmly in the belief that workingmen needed their information in "a style as familiar, and as little technical, as the subject will admit."[26] In his opinion, most of the books designed to give artisans an understanding of science failed in their purpose because their authors recognized neither the needs nor the comprehension of the audience. "To pretend that artisans will, or can, become men of general science" was a "ridiculous" notion. Jones had no doubts of the value of science to workingmen, but he was convinced that the form of its presentation determined its utility. The *Journal*'s task was therefore to diffuse the principles of science in such a clear and straightforward fashion that they had a direct bearing on the improvement of mechanics and manufacturers, "a class of our fellow citizens," Jones claimed, "whose importance we are only beginning to appreciate correctly."[27]

Nothing could have been further from the ambitions Bache had for the *Journal*. Ultimately geography gave him the advantage he needed. In 1828 Jones moved to Washington to superintend the Patent Office, and the difficulties of organizing content and overseeing the printing shifted control over the periodical back to Philadelphia. The emergence of a strong committee on publications dominated by Bache made conflict with Dr. Jones inevitable. For instance, Jones criticized a report from the water power investigation for its lack of editorial revision.[28] In the same fashion, when the committee printed a long article on meteorology by Espy, Jones claimed that anything over eight pages was "destructive" to the magazine, and would not be read by a third of those who would have looked at it if the piece had been divided into parts.[29]

None of the editor's complaints altered the circumstances, and when a long piece from the steam boiler investigation was printed, it was Jones who exploded. The article was too long by half, he wrote, and some of the unrevised parts were "disgraceful to the Journal." If the committee on publications insisted on printing material without the editor's prior consideration, the articles should be so identified. "The present number," Jones concluded, "shows that the body will let that pass which no individual would be willing to father."[30] His outburst brought an angry retort from the committee. The formal letter was written by William Hamilton, the Institute's actuary, but the draft is in Bache's hand. The editor was crisply notified that he was incorrect in his charges and improper in his conduct. "Dr. Jones is informed," Bache concluded, "that as the committee of the Institute are responsible to that body and to the public for their acts, they cannot receive such communications from the Editor of the Journal of the Institute as are referred to above."[31] With that exchange, the issue was clearly joined.

Over the course of the next year, Jones and the committee contended for authority over the *Journal.* "I have never relinquished, and I never design to relinquish, the entire control," Jones wrote Hamilton. Once proofs left his hand, he argued, it was improper for any changes to be made without his approval. "I cannot believe," the editor further claimed, "that the committee of Publications, or any individual concerned, intend to contest my rights on points of this kind." Jones clearly stated what he believed to be the editor's responsibility and area of authority. None of his remarks were intended personally, he assured Hamilton, but "I am not inclined to make a stand capriciously, nor am I disposed to be driven from ground which I have a right to occupy."[32]

The committee outlined its position in a long letter that settled the dispute. Once Jones moved to Washington, they stated, it was clear that some sort of co-editorship arrangement was necessary for the *Journal's* survival. To that end, the members of the committee sought original contributions from their friends and wrote articles themselves; they instituted regular meetings of the group and devised a plan for the arrangement of the magazine's contents. As a result of their efforts, the committee claimed, "the character of the Journal has been greatly elevated" and it was nearer than ever before to paying the printing costs. The editor's distance from the place of publication had necessitated such efforts, the committee continued. Were circumstances otherwise, they would "cheerfully abandon all superintendance of the Journal," and they assured Jones of their regard for his labor.[33]

But behind the assurances, there was a hard note. The committee pointed out that their authority came from the Institute's board of managers. The committee had no intention of yielding to the editor's "absolute control" and hinted none too subtly that the *Journal's* continuance depended upon the present arrangement. With the effective power in their own hands, the committee easily carried the dispute. In the future, Jones would be responsible for his articles and selections, and the committee for theirs, as well as for the "general arrangement" and financial concerns of the publication.[34] What that really meant was that Jones was limited to his comments on patents (a feature he had inaugurated when he went to Washington), to reading proof, and to whatever minor editorial aid he provided in preparing indexes and tables of contents.

Unchastened, Jones continued to grumble about the new style. For instance, he objected to a "heavy" article on capillary attraction by John W. Draper on the grounds that "none but a master in science will understand a page of it." Had he control of the *Journal,* Jones wrote Hamilton, he would have referred the article to Silliman's *American Journal of Science.*[35] In a like spirit he wrote that an article by Walter R. Johnson was already overlong in proof, "and will be a blank to the general reader."[36]

Bache and his group used their control to make the *Journal* a serious scientific and technical publication. Basically, there were three elements involved in the changes they brought about. First, the Institute's scientific circle used the magazine to express their own professional interests and standards. Second, a conscious attempt was made to link the *Journal's* content with current scientific problems, as defined both in this country and abroad. Finally, the talents of a rising generation of scientists and engineers were encouraged by opening the periodical to their articles. In addition to these changes, all of which had as their objective the elevation of the subject matter, the magazine's format was altered in 1836.

The committee organized subject matter along disciplinary lines, with subcategories in each case to distinguish between original and reprinted material. Original articles were grouped into three specialized fields: physical science; practical and theoretical mechanics and chemistry; and civil engineering. Abstracts and translations of current foreign and domestic work in those fields were published in corresponding sections under the headings "Progress in Physical Science," "Progress in Practical and Theoretical Mechanics and Chemistry," and "Progress in Civil Engineering." Foreign and domestic patent specifications, the editor's comments on American patents, and any other miscellaneous material of interest to artisans and manufacturers were gathered under a separate section entitled "Mechanics' Register." General science, a phrase incorporated in the *Journal*'s earlier title, reflected amateurism, and, while the magazine had begun in that vein, Bache and his committee completely reordered its format and policies to meet their own professional ideals.

Concepts of professionalism, of mission-oriented research projects that linked science, its applications, and the public purse, provided occupations for the Institute's scientific circle and models for other organizations. When Joseph Henry wanted to identify the kind of research activity the Smithsonian Institution should pursue, the steam boiler investigation served as his example.[37] Later in his career Bache also used the Franklin Institute's water power and boiler explosion experiments to illustrate the value of science and the need for its support.[38] Indeed, even at a less formal level a series of social groups established by the Institute's men of science led them to think about research in the context of its applications.[39]

Paradoxically, while their Institute experience gave Bache, Johnson, and Epsy a basis for their ideas about science and the locus of its support, the experimental style they stimulated in the organization found more immediate utility in solving the technical problems of the private sector. Samuel V. Merrick's study of European methods for producing lighting gas reveals some aspects of the new approach. Merrick had been sent abroad in 1834, at public expense, to discover the best plan for Philadelphia to employ in its projected gas works. When he arrived in England, however, Merrick discovered considerable variation in processing techniques since, as he put it, manufacturers there often conducted their business "without any definite idea of the principle to be aimed at."[40] In that situation, a descriptive account of English technical practices would have served little point. Instead, Merrick carried out a series of experiments in several establishments, using the specific gravity of the gas produced as a standard against which to measure the efficiency of different methods of production. His report, published in Philadelphia in 1834, described those experiments and their results, giving the city a clear plan for its own works and gas producers throughout the country an analytical basis for judging their own performance.

Merrick's firm built the gas works and for a time he served as its engineer. When the pressures of his foundry and machine business forced his retirement from the gas company, Merrick and Bache successfully advanced the candidacy of John C. Cresson—who also later replaced Merrick as president of the Institute—for the position. And there were other connections. Merrick, Bache, and John Wiegand, cashier of the gas company, were among the members of a group known as the "Franklin Institute Clique," which combined business and scientific interests with sociability.[41] The gas works benefited from these associations. By the 1850s, according to a British technical observer, the enterprise was "celebrated for the perfection to which the manufacture of gas is carried, and the scientific principles upon which every detail of the establishment is carried out."[42]

Ellwood Morris's efforts to promote the use of the reaction water turbine in the United States was a similar example of the technical style stimulated at the Institute. The turbine was an advancement of considerable importance, but there were several problems that inhibited its usage in America. To begin with, until 1839 most of the significant literature was published in French.[43] Its design and construction also called for greater knowledge of hydraulics and ironworking than most country millwrights would have possessed. Finally, because it was difficult to make a turbine, unsuccessful early trials had prejudiced many mill operators against the new device. Convincing Americans to use turbines called for data solidly based on experimental evidence. First, Morris translated for the Institute's *Journal* French tests of Fourneyron's turbines and, using the Institute's water power results as a baseline, argued for the superiority of the new technique. He then drew up working plans for a turbine of the French design, which Merrick manufactured at his Southwark Foundry, and subsequently installed several of them in nearby manufacturing establishments. Experiments were made with those wheels, and the results also published in the *Journal.*[44]

Morris worked within a well-developed community. He had access to the Institute's collection of foreign periodicals, to its conversational meetings, to Merrick's foundry, and, as one of its collaborators in Bache's reorganization of the magazine, to the Institute's *Journal.* In that respect, the introduction of the Fourneyron turbine to America was essentially a Philadelphia story. But industrial power and its efficient transmission within a factory were issues of wider geographic importance, which linked the efforts of engineers in various localities. Zebulon Parker of Ohio submitted his turbine to the Institute for examination and published articles about it in the *Journal.*[45] Ithamar Beard, who was the *Journal*'s agent in Lowell, conducted experiments on the use of belting and shafting for power transmission, using the dynamometer his neighbor Warren Colburn had earlier offered for the Institute's water power investigation. The use of belts and shafts was an important advance over gear systems of power transmission and was a technique more widely developed in the United States than abroad. Beard published his results in the *Journal*, as James B. Francis did when he carried out later experiments on power transmission for the Locks and Canal Company at Lowell.[46] By 1855, when Francis published the conclusions to a notable series of turbine trials at Lowell, the American industrial community had at its disposal a sophisticated corpus of knowledge for the generation and transmission of water power.[47]

One could multiply examples—industrial chemistry and materials testing, for instance—that also suggest the ever-widening influence of a scientifically inspired technology. From the beginning, the Franklin Institute's leaders had expected that joining science with practice would lead to impressive industrial accomplishments. Their initial conception of the union was as naïve as their picture of science. But in the water power and steam boiler experiments they discovered the potential of a scientific method for technology. The research that provided Bache and his like-minded colleagues with a mechanism for their ambitions for American science also illuminated the most fruitful program for technical advance. It led, moreover, to a professionalism and specialization analogous to that which Bache called for on science's behalf in his presidential address to the American Association for the Advancement of Science in 1851. By that date, Philadelphia industrialists like Samuel V. Merrick commanded large and complex industrial enterprises and employed engineers who thought in terms of research and publication. In a sense, these technical specialists were a new breed of the "scientific mechanic." But, to them, theory defined a body of engineering knowledge and the ability to use it, while practice meant the rational manipulation of power and materials in an industrial context.

NOTES

1. For a general treatment of these themes see Arthur A. Ekirch, *The Idea of Progress in America, 1815-1860* (New York: Columbia University Press, 1944), and Perry Miller, *The Life of the Mind in America* (New York: Harcourt, Brace, 1965). There is no history of the mechanics' institute movement in America. Some information is available in Charles A. Bennett, *History of Manual and Industrial Education up to 1870* (Peoria, Ill.: Manual Arts Press, 1926). The English story is told in Thomas Kelly, *Adult Education in Great Britain from the Middle Ages to the Twentieth Century* (Liverpool: At the University Press, 1962). Two very good samples of the aspirations of mechanics' institutes in their early phase are *Charter, Constitution, and By-Laws of the New-York Mechanic and Scientific Institution* (New York, 1822) and *First Annual Report of the Proceedings of the Franklin Institute of the State of Pennsylvania, for the Promotion of the Mechanic Arts* (Philadelphia, 1825).

2. According to some, one of "the most scientific and intelligent mechanics in the city of Boston" was Timothy Claxton, whose *Memoir of a Mechanic. Being the Sketch of Life of Timothy Claxton, written by himself, Together with Miscellaneous Papers* (Boston: George W. Light, 1839) is a classic account of the training, interests, and attitudes of the type.

3. For the Institute's history, see Bruce Sinclair, *Philadelphia's Philosopher Mechanics: A History of the Franklin Institute, 1824-1865* (Baltimore: Johns Hopkins University Press, 1974). Major portions of this paper have been adapted from my study of the Franklin Institute, and I am grateful to The Johns Hopkins University Press for permission to use the information here in a slightly revised form.

4. At first, greatest emphasis was laid on encouraging the use of anthracite coal, particularly in the iron industry. For examples, see the *Report of the Second Annual Exhibition of the Franklin Institute of the State of Pennsylvania, for the Promotion of the Mechanic Arts* (Philadelphia, 1825).

5. While the lectures failed to achieve their original purpose, they were a great popular success, attracting both sexes and members of all classes of society. *The Franklin Journal*

and American Mechanics' Magazine 1 (March 1826): 131; *The National Gazette* (Philadelphia), 31 October 1833.

6. After the second year of evening lectures, the committee on instruction reported, "It has been the opinion of many that the Institution has not fulfilled all the objects for which it is intended and not produced all the effect which was expected." Minutes of the Board of Managers, 2 February 1826, Franklin Institute Archives, Philadelphia, Pa.

7. "Address," *The Franklin Journal and American Mechanics' Magazine* 1 (January 1826).

8. *The Franklin Journal* 2 (November 1826): 353.

9. Minutes of the Board of Managers, 12 March 1829.

10. The records of the committee on water wheels in the Franklin Institute Archives contain the correspondence. The most interesting pieces are those from Lowell textile interests, the Society for Useful Manfactures at Patterson, New Jersey, and Brandywine millers. The Franklin Institute library and archives are rich resources for the study of American technology. Efforts are currently under way to make the archival materials more accessible to scholars.

11. *Journal of the Franklin Institute* 12 (August 1831): 80.

12 The best description of apparatus and test procedures is in the committee's first report in ibid., 11 (March 1831): 145-54.

13. Bache quoted Rennie's remark in his *Anniversary Address Before the American Institute of the City of New York* (New York, 1857), p. 28. Part of Rennie's paper was published in the *Journal of the Franklin Institute* 29 (January 1835): 57-64; ibid. (February 1835): 125-35.

14. Edwin Layton, "Mirror Image Twins: The Communities of Science and Technology in Nineteenth-Century America," *Technology and Culture* 12 (October 1971): 562-80.

15. As quoted in the *National Gazette*, 7 July 1832.

16. Merle M. Odgers, *Alexander Dallas Bache: Scientist and Educator 1806-1867* (Philadelphia: University of Pennsylvania Press, 1947), is the most available biographical study, but Nathan Reingold, ed., *Science in Nineteenth-Century America: A Documentary History* (New York: Hill & Wang, 1964), adds valuable interpretive insights into Bache's career.

17. The report of an 1817 Philadelphia investigation into boiler explosions is republished in *Journal of the Franklin Institute* 12 (October 1831): 234.

18. S. D. Ingham to William Hamilton, 15 August 1830, Steam Boiler Committee, Franklin Institute Archives.

19 Bruce Sinclair, *Early Research at the Franklin Institute: The Investigation into the Causes of Steam Boiler Explosions, 1830-1837* (Philadelphia: Franklin Institute, 1966); John G. Burke, "Bursting Boilers and the Federal Power," *Technology and Culture* 7 (Winter 1966): 1-23.

20. Joseph Henry to Prof. James Forbes, 19 September 1836, Joseph Henry Private Papers, Smithsonian Institution Archives, Washington, D.C.

21. *General Report on the Explosions of Steam-Boilers, by a Committee of the Franklin Institute of the State of Pennsylvania for the Promotion of the Mechanic Arts* (Philadelphia, 1836).

22. Ibid., pp. 4-5.

23. *The Dictionary of American Biography* contains sketches of most of these men. See also George E. Pettingill, "Walter Rogers Johnson," *Journal of the Franklin Institute* 250 (August 1950): 93-113.

24. The report of Bache's committee on weights and measures can be found in *Journal of the Franklin Institute* 16 (November 1833): 304-309; ibid., 18 (July 1834): 13.

25. Johnson's report on the strength of materials investigation was published serially in the *Journal of the Franklin Institute* from February to August 1837; *A Report to the Navy Department of the United States, on American Coals applicable to steam navigation and to other purposes* (Washington, 1844); Lee M. Pearson, "The 'Princeton' and the 'Peacemaker': A Study in Nineteenth-Century Naval Research and Development," *Technology and Culture* 7 (Spring 1966): 173.

26. *The Franklin Journal and American Mechanics' Magazine* 1 (January 1826): 2.

27. Ibid., 3 (January 1827): 42; ibid., 5 (January 1828): iii.

28. Thomas P. Jones to William Hamilton, 6 November 1831, Thomas P. Jones Letters, Franklin Institute Archives, Philadelphia, Pa.

29. Ibid., 1831.

30. Ibid., received 1 March 1832.

31. Hamilton to Jones, 10 March 1832, Jones Letters.

32. Jones to Hamilton, 14 April 1833, 11 May 1833, Jones Letters.

33. Committee on Publication to Jones, 16 May 1833 (draft), Jones Letters.

34. Ibid.

35. Jones to Hamilton, 4 August 1834, Jones Letters.

36. Ibid., 8 October 1834.

37. A. Hunter Dupree, *Science in the Federal Government* (Cambridge, Mass.: Harvard University Press, Belknap Press, 1957), p. 82.

38. See, for example, Bache's presidential address in *Proceedings of the American Association for the Advancement of Science* (Washington, D.C., 1852), p. xlix; and A. D. Bache, *Anniversary Address Before the American Institute* (New York, 1857), p. 28.

39. There were several informal associations. The earliest was one simply called "the Club," which Bache mentioned in his eulogy of James P. Espy in the *Annual Report of the Board of Regents of the Smithsonian Institution . . . for the Year 1859* (Washington, D.C., 1860), p. 109. Another was the United Bowmen's Company of Philadelphia, a group which combined interests in archery and science. Information on it is available in Jessie Poesch, *Titian Ramsay Peale, 1799-1885, and His Journals of the Wilkes Expedition* (Philadelphia: American Philosophical Society, 1961). A third group, the Franklin Institute Clique, is described in Mary Williams Brinton, *Their Lives and Mine* (Philadelphia: privately published, 1973), p. 23.

40. S. V. Merrick, *Report, Upon an Examination of Some of the Gas Manufactories in Great Britain, France, and Belgium* (Philadelphia, 1834), p. 8.

41. Brinton, *Their Lives and Mine*, p. 23.

42. Nathan Rosenberg, ed., *The American System of Manufactures* (Edinburgh: Edinburgh University Press, 1969), p. 276.

43. Louis C. Hunter, "Origines des Turbines Francis et Pelton," *Revue d'Histoire des Sciences et de leurs Applications* 17 (July-September 1964): 209-42, describes early French and American turbine efforts.

44. *Journal of the Franklin Institute* 34 (October 1842): 217-27; ibid. (November 1842): 289-304.

45. *Journal of the Franklin Institute* 45 (January 1848): 49; Records of the Committee on Science and the Arts, Franklin Institute Archives.

46. *Journal of the Franklin Institute* 15 (January 1833): 6-15; ibid., 83 (1867): 379.

47. James B. Francis, *Lowell Hydraulic Experiments* (New York, 1855).

The Growth
of Learned and Scientific
Societies in the Southeastern
United States
to 1860

JOSEPH EWAN

A letter from a naval surgeon in St. Mary's, on the Georgia-Florida border, dated May 27, 1817, reads in part:

When I left the University of Pennsylvania, I calculated that I had formed a league of friendship with a group of young men, which would be lasting as life. But how uncertain and unstable are all things in this little busy dirty world of ours! I have not heard from one of them since I have resided in Georgia. I suppose they think I have become a negro or something worse. Now although I have since formed a pretty extensive correspondence among strangers, in the South, &c, the opening of a correspondence with you, has been among the most pleasing little events I have experienced for a long time.[1]

This response by William Baldwin to Henry Muhlenberg of Lancaster, Pennsylvania, presents a view of the early scientific society as "a league of friendship" to open correspondence, a means of encouraging communication "which would be lasting as life." What became of such scientific societies as were organized in the South before 1850 is the subject of this introduction to what is a thinly scattered aspect of the history of American science.

All ten of the scientific organizations founded in the United States before 1800 were located in port cities. However, the only southeastern port city to establish such an organization was Charleston. Whether in the North or South, scientific societies took shape in cities because a certain concentration of inhabitants with strong scientific interests was essential. Virginia in the eighteenth century lacked a scientific society because the population was scattered on large plantations along the rivers: the density of scientifically inclined persons was insufficient for forming local societies, and only a few isolated persons "curious" about science allied themselves with national organizations such as the American Philosophical Society. John Brickell wrote in 1737 that "chiefly owing to the want of Encouragement to a select number of travelling Gentlemen," we are without observations "that might tend to the Improvement of Natural Knowledge." This lack was due, he says, to the fact that "young

[1] Notes to this chapter begin on page 215.

travelling English gentlemen are not encouraged, as are the French and Spaniards, by a 'handsome pension' to become well acquainted with the country, to keep a strict Journal of all their Passages. Such laudable Encouragements as these," Brickell continues, "would undoubtedly breed an honourable Emulation amongst the Gentlemen of our own Nation, to out do one another . . . to be serviceable to their King and Country."[2]

The Charleston Museum was begun in 1773 as a child of the Charleston Library Society; its purpose was to provide a full and accurate "natural history of the province embracing the three kingdoms."[3] "Though the English began to plant [Carolina] since the Year 1663," says Edmund Bohun in his *Geographical Dictionary* of 1688, "yet being extremely fruitful, and temperate, the inhabitants are already very numerous, and have built two considerable towns, Charles Town and Albemarle. . . . The Colonies are endeavouring to improve this Country to Wine and Oil, which the English chiefly want."[4]

As it turned out, Charleston did not excel in wine and oil, as Bohun reported, but became a shipping point for the loblolly pine as timber or naval stores and thus complemented the role of the New England ports where the "Weymouth pine," which is the native white pine, was esteemed by the Crown for masts of sailing ships.

Why any city should launch a scientific organization, as Charleston alone of southern cities did before 1800, will be considered from four perspectives: politics, economy, climate, and religion. In the eighteenth century, Charleston was a Crown colony that enjoyed an organic connection with the mother country, politically as well as scientifically. Just as there was traffic in goods to and from the British Isles, there was also an exchange of "curious" persons. Alexander Garden[5] came from Scotland to Charleston; Charles Cotesworth Pinckney,[6] born in that city, went to England, and so on. In a like association, especially after the Revolution, southerners corresponded and visited with northerners. Stephen Elliott[7] studied at Yale; John and William Bartram traveled south from Pennsylvania.[8]

As Everett Mendelsohn observed, after 1730 "Charleston was one of the liveliest intellectual centers in colonial America"—a fact that was "in no small measure due to the physicians who gathered there during the eighteenth century."[9] Of forty American medical students studying in Edinburgh between 1755 and 1766, five were from Carolina, and they returned.[10] The southern complexion of American students in Edinburgh was underlined when fourteen Virginians were added to these five Carolinians, making about one-half of the total students from the American colonies.

From another viewpoint, the early decades of the eighteenth century in South Carolina were economically bountiful. There were increased shipments of timber and foodstuffs to the West Indies and naval stores to England, while fur traders numbered between two and three hundred. Rice had become the most important agricultural export, thereby fixing the plantation system—with the planters as the dominant social class.[11] Rice, then, was an economic tie with

British culture and Protestant curiosity. In a minor way, indigo added to the agricultural pattern of the colony.[12] The *South Carolina Gazette* for October 19, 1744, announced that "the true wild indigo plant" may be seen "with seed on the branches" and that seed would be offered to all persons desirous of sowing seed in spite of the advanced season. The search for new crop plants resulting in some successes was as important a reason for the founding of scientific societies in the colonies as it had been in England. An occasional planter with leisure ventured into scientific subjects and became one of the "amateur" members of the societies.

At the same time, scientific as well as other forms of endeavor were hampered by the climate. The southern climate was an obstacle to optimum effort, whether it be in the classroom, laboratory, or museum or in the observation and collection of fauna and flora in the field. Sometimes even in January heat deterred the scientific visitor: on the second of January, Dr. William Bromfield wrote from Charleston to W. J. Hooker at Kew, "warm and indeed hot as the weather is."[13] Abraham Vickers, having returned from a trip into the southern states, wrote to Humphry Marshall in 1790: "Had the climate been agreeable to me I should have delighted to have stayed there some time longer and made what discoveries I could in the vegetable Productions of those Southern States which appears to contain many valuable simpils which might be a great and valuable Addition to the Materia Medica."[14]

Finally, the Protestant ethic of the British colonies seems to have favored scientific activities more than the Roman Catholic environment that prevailed in southern Louisiana. In a study on the education of American scientists, Knapp and Goodrich remark that "Catholicism has permitted comparatively little secularization of outlook among its constituents and has maintained a firm authoritarian structure. And Catholicism has been a consistent opponent of physical monism, that philosophic tradition under which science has for the most part advanced."[15] Another contributing factor is suggested by the fate of scientific reports in Catholic versus Protestant cultures. For example, possibly the earliest account of natural history observations in Louisiana is a manuscript entitled *"Relation de la Louisiana par le Maire,"* of 1714, relating to timber, trees, wine, medicinal plants, snakes, climate, Indians, and so forth. The manuscript was sent to a Catholic monastery, where it was given sanctuary but not publicity. Corresponding reports from the British colonies were sent to individuals who kept private cabinets of curiosities or to public museums. Those manuscripts sent to Bishop Henry Compton in England, for example, were circulated among devotees of the natural sciences, physicians, and apothecaries, who in various ways published their contents and thus stimulated the growth of the natural sciences.[16]

Frederick Bowes comments that the "multiplying artistic, social and political interests of Charlestonians pushed religion into the background."[17] If this was true in the Anglican city of Charleston, it was surely in contrast to the dominant allegiance of New Orleans under Catholicism. Yet there was in Carolina no absence of piety; what Bowes mentioned as a "rationalist faith of the age" dominated the community. T. C. Johnson's verdict is valid: "At the outbreak of the Civil War [Charleston] was still the most intellectually urbane of the urban communities of the South."[18]

Scientists, especially those visiting from abroad, saw slow progress in the sciences in the southern states. When the Oxford professor Charles Daubeny visited the United States in 1837, he observed: "It is too true, that Americans in general interest themselves but little in anything but politics. What science there is seems broken up into little knots and cabals. [There] are men who have risen to eminence without favour or aid from the state, which has no idea of encouraging any kind of knowledge not possessing some immediate practical bearing. . . . Science and literature seem almost unknown, schools are very rare, and it is said, extremely bad."[19]

In 1837 New Orleans had fourteen banks with a paid-in capital of $40 million; the Louisiana Sugar Refinery built in 1832 produced thirty-five thousand pounds of refined sugar and two thousand gallons of rum a day, yet the city made no provision for public schools. The successful founding of a scientific society in New Orleans was not to come until 1853.[20] Caleb Cope wrote from Philadelphia, April 21, 1851, to William Jackson Hooker at Kew: " 'How magnificently they do everything in England' is the common observation of every intelligent American. . . . We must judge by comparison of our means, however, as well as by that of your refinement and enterprise. We have no large fortunes among us to encourage the production or growth of non-essentials."[21] New Orleans, with an annual export of over $37 million and imports of over $15 million in 1837, certainly created fortunes.[22]

Knapp and Goodrich have offered their explanation of the "almost singularly low scientific production of the South":

One might invoke here simply an economic explanation—that the South has been the poorest section of the nation and therefore unable to afford the education of scientists. But this explanation seems to us hasty. . . . Certain cultural hypotheses immediately present themselves. Until the Civil War, the South was, at least in many respects, a feudal order, with a large mass of imported slaves, a segment of impoverished whites, and, as the dominant social group, a gentry of reactionary attitudes and genteel conventions. From this society there sprang indeed certain individuals of scientific learnings whose contributions were largely rendered under the aegis of natural philosophy. It was, until the Civil War, a social order that looked for its intellectual heritage largely to the eighteenth century. There never developed in the South, for economic, sociological, and ideological reasons, anything paralleling the Yankee inventor. Popular education was not acclaimed as in the puritan North, while caste, family, chivalry, and gentility were the dominant forces in the social order.[23]

The role of the *individual* as a nucleus about which other persons are oriented has always been decisive in the emergence of social organizations. The birth of a

scientific society in the South, as elsewhere, turned on the happenstance of a
few like-minded persons having common residence. The social attitude of individuals has always played an important part. John Bachman said of Audubon
that "he taught me how much can be accomplished by a single individual who
will unite enthusiasm with industry."[24] Audubon could never have served as the
core of an organization; John Bachman easily could have. Individuals were the
"encouragers" of such enterprises as Mark Catesby's *Natural History,* sold by
subscription.[25] The encouragers sometimes became the promoters of museums,
as in the case of the Charleston Museum for which a prospectus was printed in
1773. Friendships also played a part: two Charleston physicians, Peter Fayssoux[26] of that city and Alexander Baron,[27] a Scot, were medical students in
Edinburgh at the same time. Baron decided to come to Charleston in 1769 when
Fayssoux returned, and in 1773 the two joined Charles Cotesworth Pinckney[28]
and Thomas Heyward[29] as curators of the newly founded museum. (Contrary to
the oft-repeated statement, the Charleston Museum was *not* the first museum in
the United States, having been preceded by about a decade by DuSimitiere's in
Philadelphia.)[30]

"Organization men" typically multiply their enterprises. Drs. Fayssoux,
Baron, and David Ramsey organized the Medical Society of South Carolina in
1789. Heyward was president of the South Carolina Society for Promoting and
Improving Agriculture and other Rural Concerns, founded in 1785.

The Charleston Botanic Garden was founded in 1805, four years after Hosack
established the Elgin Botanic Garden in New York and two years before the
Harvard Botanic Garden was founded at Cambridge. Mitchill's *Medical Repository* reported in 1806 that the "first concern" of the Charleston garden "will be
the examination and arrangement of our indigenous plants, among which are
doubtless many non-descripts. To extend the knowledge of our favorite pursuit,
we beg leave to propose . . . an exchange of our indigenous plants. . . ."[31] The
garden was opened under the most favorable auspices, enriched by valuable
acquisitions, and flourished for a few years. Yet Dr. Ramsey's pupil, John
Shecut, reported that, despite the efforts of the Medical Society, it had fallen
into a mere farm plot by 1819 for want of sufficient subscriptions.[32]

On more than one occasion, scientific enterprises in Charleston were inspired
by a visitor from the West Indian colonies which were economically bound to
the Atlantic colonies, especially the South. In 1814, for example, there occurred
the "opportune arrival of that distinguished naturalist and practical chemist, Dr.
Felix L'Herminier, from Guadeloupe, with an extensive collection of specimens,
the fruit of twenty years application, expense and industry, which he offered to
[the Literary and Philosophical Society of South Carolina] as an advantage not
to be lost sight of."[33] Thomas Say wrote to George Ord in 1818 of having seen
the "handsome collection" of the Guadeloupe naturalist purchased by the
Charleston Society.[34] In many instances, products of the Caribbean were
compared with their Carolinian counterparts—for example, the vermifuge worm-
grass or pinkroot, *Spigelia anthelmia,* prized from the early eighteenth century.

About 1755 Thomas Knowlton wrote to Peter Collinson, "there is another larger species [of *Spigelia*] that grows in Virginia and Carolina, where it is much extolled likewise for an anthelmintick, or destroyer of worms."[35] Alexander Garden of Charleston was keenly interested in this native plant related to the West Indian medicinal staple.

On the other hand, the scientific activities of individuals living in isolated communities, such as small town and country doctors, often remained local and out of contact with existing organizations. Dr. Clarendon Peck lived at Sicily Island in Catahoula Parish, Louisiana and was evidently in correspondence with Dr. Charles Wilkins Short of Kentucky, although out of touch with any New Orleans associates.[36] It was only *after* Dr. Josiah Hale of Alexandria, Louisiana, moved to New Orleans that he joined with Dr. Riddell and others in founding the New Orleans Academy of Sciences in 1853. Dr. James Hamilton Couper of Darien, Georgia, was an isolated scientist.[37] Beginning in 1836 he collected mollusks for Isaac Lea of Philadelphia on St. Simons Island and contributed the account of recent shells to George White's *Statistics of the State of Georgia* (1849). Couper discovered and Richard Harlan later described what was thought to be the bones of a hippopotamus at Brunswick Canal, Georgia.[38] Lyell corresponded with G. S. Morton of Philadelphia about the bones, and in turn Morton corresponded with Richard Owen in London. James Couper, then, was part of a Philadelphia-London circle rather than of a nonexistent Savannah scientific society.

Benjamin L. C. Wailes, owner of two cotton plantations and about 150 slaves, had been educated at Jefferson College at Washington, near Natchez, Mississippi.[39] Caleb Forshey, later a member of the New Orleans Academy of Sciences, taught there. Wailes was a correspondent of Henry, Leidy, Agassiz, and Silliman. The Agricultural, Horticultural and Botanical Society of Jefferson College was organized by Wailes in April 1839.[40] The Society centered its attentions on animal husbandry and farm fruits, with incidental notice of topics apart from use. The Society had a brief flowering, but 1842 was evidently its last year. Wailes tried to organize another society, the Mississippi State Historical Society, in 1858, but it survived only one year. Wailes was a tragic figure: in his publication of the state report of 1854 on the "agriculture and geology" of Mississippi, a 388-page digest of the three kingdoms,[41] he showed that he had organizing abilities, was ready to make a contribution, and that he was related to the national scene, yet, because of his isolation and later the disruption of the Civil War, his scientific influence was limited.

Another scientist-resident of the South, talented, and known to men of importance, was Thomas Cooper, friend and associate of Priestley and admired by Jefferson.[42] Cooper lived his last nineteen years at South Carolina College (later the University of South Carolina). So far as I can determine, he did not participate in any scientific organization in the South.

A gifted student of Cooper's was Henry William Ravenel, mycologist, whose 14,450 specimens of cryptogams were sold to the British Museum after his death.[43] Although Ravenel's work was not identified, it was referred to in the *Southern Quarterly Review* in 1849: "But it is not to our honor that, while every political squib has its thousands of readers, and every extravagant or licentious fiction runs through a heavy edition, these lucubrations of these laborious men, adding much to our positive knowledge, will see the light only in England, and in connection with the researches of an eminent English botanist."[44] Reference is made here to Reverend M. J. Berkeley, "the finest mycologist in Great Britain," who was interested in Ravenel's collections.[45] "Some consolation, indeed, we may take to ourselves, that our true men of science are appreciated abroad if not at home. Would we could say that our quacks and our popular lecturers, who bepuff themselves in the newspapers, and our flimsy writers, who know scarcely the alphabet of the sciences which they undertake to teach, were also appreciated at their true value. But were science once more generally cultivated, the number of discriminating hearers and readers would be so largely increased that it would not be possible for quackery to succeed."[46]

During Cooper's presidency at South Carolina College, Josiah Clark Nott was a student.[47] A graduate of the University of Pennsylvania (M.D. 1827), Dr. Nott was an effective writer on a wide variety of medical topics. He was a founder of the Mobile-Medical Society in 1841 and presented a paper on animal magnetism before the Society in 1846. He was also evidently a prime mover in the Mobile Franklin Society, about which it has been impossible to learn the barest details.

The first institution of higher learning in New Orleans was the College d'Orleans, founded in 1811. In 1821 French-born Joseph Lakanal became its president.[48] Lakanal was interested in the natural sciences and corresponded with Cuvier and other savants in France. It was not long before the College "sank in a sea of troubles." The Louisiana state legislature passed a law in 1826 prohibiting any but an American citizen from teaching in the schools of the state, and this brought the closing of the College. Lakanal then joined the French communal "Vine and Olive Colony" on the Tombigbee River in Alabama, and, after residence on a plantation he owned on Mobile Bay, returned to France in 1837. Lakanal's talents were lost to the growth of science in New Orleans.

Joel Roberts Poinsett,[49] a native of Charleston whose diplomatic career in Latin America is well known, was a friend and mentor of John C. Fremont and played an important role in the founding of the National Institution for the Promotion of Science. The National Institution was organized in May 1840 and patterned after the broad-based learned societies of the late eighteenth and early nineteenth centuries. As A. Hunter Dupree has observed, Poinsett "was trying to create another American Philosophical Society for Washington" but one that would assume a national character.[50] In 1841, however, Poinsett returned to South Carolina and the Institute eventually faltered.[51]

A nameless writer in the *Southern Quarterly Review* said of Poinsett's *Discourse on the objects and importance of the National Institution for the Promotion of Science* ... (1841) that the reader "seldom enjoyed a richer treat than has been furnished us by the perusal of this excellent discourse. It is a profound and luminous production, is pervaded by a truly patriotic spirit, and is written in a style of great purity and elegance."[52] Poinsett noted in his *Discourse* that it would be the province of the National Institute to "aid the societies already formed." In the end, the National Cabinet of Curiosities, housed on the second floor of the Patent Office and maintained by the Institute, became the repository of the Wilkes Expedition collections and served as the nucleus of the National Museum. Joseph Henry assumed direction of the Museum in 1846 after he was assured of the organic orderly structure of the national collections. Thus, in a sense, Poinsett may be seen as a transitional figure in the growth of national scientific organizations above and beyond local societies.

The period under review closed with the auspicious annual meeting of the American Association for the Advancement of Science in Charleston in 1850, its third since the founding of the Association in 1848. About one hundred persons attended that meeting. Forty-eight papers were read by twenty-seven members, about half of those from southern cities. The president of the Association, Alexander Dallas Bache, felt "unalloyed pain" that in the course of the meeting science was regarded with suspicion by the religious. "Science is emphatically progressive. Who would be so indiscreet as to hinge his religious faith upon changeable, progressive science."[53] This accolade, generously supported by the Corporation of Charleston, which assumed all expenses for the convention, brought some lasting benefits beyond the temporary rousing of popular interest.

Under the stimulus of Louis Agassiz, the cabinet of curiosities in the old Charleston museum, lodged in the Medical College, was importantly enlarged by additions in paleontology, ichthyology, mineralogy, and conchology; these were to be put in a new museum at Charleston College. Three years later the Elliott Society of Natural History was founded in the city with John Bachman elected the first president.[54] This Society soon numbered forty members.

It was Thoreau who said "one generation abandons the enterprises of another like stranded vessels." What became of the scientific societies founded before 1850 in the South? The lineal descendent of the Charleston Library Society's museum, founded in 1773, is the only survivor. The rest have disappeared from the scene, leaving behind only the spirit of a "league of friendship that would be lasting as life."

NOTES

1. William Darlington, *Reliquiae Baldwinianae* (Philadelphia, 1843; reprint ed., with introduction by Joseph Ewan, New York: Hafner, 1969), p. 229.

2. John Brickell, *Natural History of North-Carolina* (Dublin, 1737; reprint ed., Raleigh, N.C., 1910), p. 213.

3. See Max Meisel, *Bibliography of American Natural History, Pioneer Century, 1789-1865,* 3 vols. (New York, 1924-1929; reprint ed., New York: Hafner, 1967), 2:35-38.

4. Edmund Bohun (d. 1699), Chief Justice of South Carolina, whose son collected naturalia in Carolina for James Petiver. Edmund Bohun, *Geographical Dictionary* (London,

1688), p. 213. See J. E. Dandy, *Sloane Herbarium* (London: British Museum, 1958), p. 93; Raymond Phineas Stearns, *Science in the British Colonies of America* (Urbana: University of Illinois Press, 1970), pp. 295-97.

5. Cf. Edmund Berkeley and Dorothy Smith Berkeley, *Dr. Alexander Garden of Charles Town* (Chapel Hill: University of North Carolina Press, 1969); Stearns, *Science in the British Colonies,* pp. 599-619.

6. See *Dictionary of American Biography,* 1st ed., and note 26, below.

7. See Joseph Ewan, introduction to Stephen Elliott, *Sketch of Botany of South Carolina and Georgia* (reprint ed., New York: Hafner, 1971), l:ix-xxxvii.

8. John Bartram, "Diary of a Journey Through the Carolinas, Georgia, and Florida from July 1, 1765 to April 10, 1766," with annotations by Francis Harper, *Transactions of the American Philosophical Society,* n.s., 33 (1942): 1-124; William Bartram, "Travels in Georgia and Florida, 1773-74, a report to Dr. John Fothergill," with annotations by Francis Harper, ibid. (1943): 125-242; William Bartram, *Travels through North and South Carolina, Georgia, East and West Florida* (Philadelphia, 1791; "Naturalist's edition," ed. Francis Harper, New Haven: Yale University Press, 1958; facsimile of 1792 London edition, with introduction by Gordon DeWolf, Savannah, Ga.: Beehive Press, 1973); Joseph Ewan, ed., *William Bartram: Botanical and Zoological Drawings, 1756-1788* (Philadelphia: American Philosophical Society, 1968), pp. 1-180; Stearns, *Science in the British Colonies,* pp. 575-93.

9. Everett Mendelsohn, "John Lining and His Contribution to Early American Science," *Isis* 51 (1960): 278.

10. See Whitfield J. Bell, Jr., "Some American Students of 'that shining oracle of physic,' Dr. William Cullen of Edinburgh, 1755-1766," *Proceedings of the American Philosophical Society* 94 (1950): 275-81.

11. Frederick P. Bowes, *Culture of Early Charleston* (Chapel Hill: University of North Carolina Press, 1942), pp. 5-6.

12. See Lewis Cecil Gray, *History of Agriculture in Southern United States to 1860,* Carnegie Institution of Washington Publication no. 430 (Washington, 1933), 1:290-97.

13. Journal of William A. Bromfield, M.D., Library, Royal Botanic Gardens, Kew.

14. Vickers to Marshall, 5 March 1790, H. Marshall Correspondence, Dreer Collection, Lot 175, 2:7, Historical Society of Pennsylvania, Philadelphia, Pa.

15. Robert H. Knapp and H. B. Goodrich, *Origins of American Scientists* (Chicago: University of Chicago Press, 1952), p. 288.

16. See Dandy, *Sloane Herbarium,* pp. 114-15; Joseph Ewan and Nesta Ewan, *John Banister and His Natural History of Virginia, 1678-1692* (Urbana: University of Illinois Press, 1970), pp. 31-32; Stearns, *Science in the British Colonies,* pp. 166-67.

17. Bowes, *Culture of Early Charleston,* p. 31.

18. Thomas Cary Johnson, Jr., *Scientific Interests in the Old South* (New York: Appleton, 1936), p. 126.

19. Charles Daubeny, *Journal of a Tour Through the United States, and in Canada, made during the years, 1837-38* (Oxford, 1843), p. 148.

20. Meisel, *Bibliography of American Natural History,* 3:188-89; Ralph S. Bates, *Scientific Societies in the United States,* 3rd ed. (Cambridge, Mass.: MIT Press, 1965), p. 50.

21. W. J. Hooker Letters, vol. 64, fol. 79, Royal Botanic Gardens, Kew.

22. George B. Goode, "Beginnings of Natural History in America," *Report of the United States National Museum for 1897,* pt. 2 (Washington, 1901), pp. 463-64. Goode collected figures on the memberships of scientific societies in the United States for the year 1880. In that year, the proportion of scientific men in New Orleans to the population was 1:8,800. Incidentally, Washington, D.C. had the highest proportion in 1880: 1 scientific man to every 500 persons. The average proportion for the country was 1 for every 10,000 persons.

23. Knapp and Goodrich, *Origins of American Scientists,* p. 284.

24. Francis H. Herrick, *Audubon the Naturalist: A History of His Life and Times,* 2 vols. (New York: Appleton, 1917), 2:6.

25. George F. Frick and R. P. Stearns, *Mark Catesby, the Colonial Audubon* (Urbana: University of Illinois Press, 1961), p. 19, n. 59. See Mark Catesby, *Natural History of Carolina, Florida and the Bahama Islands* (London, 1729-1748; facsimile reprint in part

with introduction by George F. Frick and annotations by Joseph Ewan, Savannah, Ga.: Beehive Press, 1974), pp. ix-xvi, 89-107.

26. Dr. Peter Dott Fayssoux (1745-1795), graduate of Edinburgh (1769), had been apprenticed to Alexander Garden. He joined David Ramsey and Alexander Baron in founding the Medical Society of South Carolina in 1789. See Joseph Ioor Waring, *History of Medicine in South Carolina,* 2 vols. (Columbia: South Carolina Medical Association, 1964-1967), vol. 1, *1670-1825* (1964), p. 214; vol. 2, *1825-1900* (1967).

27. Dr. Alexander Baron (1745-1819), a Scot who came to Charleston in 1769, after graduating at Edinburgh in 1768. See Waring, *Medicine in South Carolina,* 1:177-80.

28. Charles Cotesworth Pinckney (1746-1825), born in Charleston, the son of Eliza Pinckney. The botanical enthusiasm of the Pinckneys is supported by Michaux's dedication of the genus *Pinckneya* (Georgia bark or fever tree) to them. See *Dictionary of American Biography* and Elise Pinckney, *The Letterbook of Eliza Lucas Pinckney, 1739-1762* (Chapel Hill: University of North Carolina Press, 1972).

29. Thomas Heyward, Jr. (1746-1809), was one of the four curators of the Charles Town Museum in 1773 and president of the South Carolina Society for Promoting and Improving Agriculture and other Rural Concerns, founded in 1785 and modeled on its Philadelphia counterpart. See *Dictionary of National Biography* and Brooke Hindle, *The Pursuit of Science in Revolutionary America, 1735-1789* (Chapel Hill: University of North Carolina Press, 1956), p. 362.

30. See Robert B. Gordon, *Science* 115 (1952): 217-18. Pierre Eugene DuSimitiere's museum was dispersed by sale of his collections in 1772, and the founder died in 1784 at the age of forty-eight. Some of DuSimitiere's exhibits came from Charleston. His letter of May 8, 1765, to Mr. Frey of Basle, includes a list of various natural specimens. George P. Goode does not mention DuSimitiere in his comprehensive history of museums in the United States.

31. Samuel Latham Mitchill, *Medical Repository,* 23 vols. (New York, 1797-1824), 9:434-36.

32. Meisel, *Bibliography of American Natural History,* 2:115; cf. Darlington, *Reliquiae Baldwinianae,* pp. 54-55, where equivocal comments suggest the disparaging opinion of John Linnaeus Edward Whitridge Shecut (1770-1836) held by Charleston physicians, including Stephen Elliott. Johnson, *Scientific Interests in the Old South,* p. 127, Waring, *Medicine in South Carolina* 1:303-309, and A. R. Childs, *Dictionary of American Biography,* scarcely suggest this opinion, Waring concluding with the edict that Shecut was a "colorful and energetic practitioner." It is noteworthy that Elliott, who was careful to accord thanks to his Charleston botanical colleagues, does not mention Shecut in his classic *Sketch* of the Carolina flora. There is wide disagreement in the spelling of his surname, his place of birth, and other details of Shecut's life.

33. Johnson, *Scientific Interests in the Old South,* p. 129.

34. Harry B. Weiss and Grace M. Ziegler, *Thomas Say: Early American Naturalist* (Springfield, Ill.: C. C. Thomas, 1931), p. 57.

35. Peter Collinson Mss., fol. 83, Linnean Society, London.

36. Charles Wilkins Short in *Transylvania Journal of Medicine and Associated Sciences* 9 (1836): 349. We know almost nothing of Dr. Peck but that he is said to have known 285 plant species from his district and that he published, perhaps under Dr. Riddell's encouragement, a list in *De Bow's Review* 12 (1852): 271-73.

37. James Hamilton Couper (1794-1866) had far-flung associations. See *Dictionary of American Biography;* Johnson, *Scientific Interests in the Old South,* passim; Una Pope-Hennessey, *Aristocratic Journey, being the Outspoken Letters of Mrs. Basil Hall written during a Fourteen-Month's Sojourn in America, 1827-28* (New York: Putnam, 1931), p. 232, passim.

38. *American Journal of Science,* 1st ser., 43 (1842): 141-44. Harlan's contribution to American paleontology is ably fortified by George Gaylord Simpson, "Beginnings of Vertebrate Paleontology in North America," *Proceedings of the American Philosophical Society* 86 (1942): 130-88. Harlan visited London (Richard Owen, etc.) in 1839; for continuing commentary, see *American Journal of Science* 44 (1843): 341-45 and ibid., 45 (1843): 208-11.

39. Johnson, *Scientific Interests in the Old South,* p. 30; Charles S. Sydnor, *A Gentleman of the Old Natchez Region: Benjamin L. C. Wailes* (Durham, N.C.: Duke University

Press, 1938). There was also a Jefferson College in St. James Parish, Louisiana, in the same period.

40. Meisel, *Bibliography of American Natural History,* 2:673.

41. Entitled *Report on the Agriculture and Geology of Mississippi, embracing a Sketch of the Social and Natural History of the State.* Ibid., 3:124.

42. Cf. *Dictionary of American Biography* and Johnson, *Scientific Interests in the Old South,* p. 24. Not to be confused with Thomas Cooper, graduate of Wadham College, Oxford (B.A. 1720), of Charleston, and a close friend of Catesby; cf. Stearns, *Science in the British Colonies*, p. 289, n. 114.

43. For H. W. Ravenel (1814-1887) see Meisel, *Bibliography of American Natural History,* 3:643; Johnson, *Scientific Interests in the Old South,* n. 4, passim; Neil E. Stevens, "Mycological Work of Henry W. Ravenel," *Isis* 18 (1932): 133-49; Ravenel-L. R. Gibbes Letters, Charleston Museum Archives, Charleston, S.C.; Ravenel-John Torrey Letters, Torrey Correspondence, New York Botanical Garden, New York, N.Y.; miscellaneous important documents, W. C. Coker Collection, University of North Carolina, Chapel Hill, N.C.

44. *Southern Quarterly Review* 15 (1849): 48.

45. James Britten and George S. Boulger, *A Biographical Index of Deceased British and Irish Botanists,* 2d ed. rev. and completed by A. B. Rendle (London: Taylor and Francis, 1931), p. 31.

46. *Southern Quarterly Review* 15 (1849): 48.

47. Meisel, *Bibliography of American Natural History,* 3:631; Johnson, *Scientific Interests in the Old South,* p. 86; Clement Eaton, *The Mind of the Old South* (Baton Rouge, La.: Louisiana State University Press, 1964), p. 155.

48. Joseph Ewan, "French Naturalists in the Mississippi Valley," *French in the Mississippi Valley,* ed. J. Francis McDermott (Urbana: University of Illinois Press, 1965), p. 173.

49. Meisel, *Bibliography of American Natural History,* 3:639.

50. A. Hunter Dupree, *Science in the Federal Government: A History of Policies and Activities to 1940* (Cambridge, Mass.: Harvard University Press, 1957), p. 71.

51. In 1842 the name was changed to National Institute "to assert its superiority over the proposed Smithsonian Institution." Ibid., p. 72. See also Sally Kohlstedt, "A Step Toward Scientific Self-Identity in the United States: The Failure of the National Institute, 1844," *Isis* 62 (1971): 339-62.

52. *Southern Quarterly Review* 1 (1842): 277-78.

53. *Proceedings of the American Association for the Advancement of Science* 4 (1851): 164. See Nathan Reingold, ed., *Science in Nineteenth-Century America: A Documentary History* (New York: Hill & Wang, 1964), pp. 200-225 for commentary and quotations from Bache letters.

54. Meisel, *Bibliography of American Natural History,* 3:164-65.

The Western Academy
of Natural Sciences of Cincinnati
and the Structure of Science
in the Ohio Valley
1810-1850

HENRY D. SHAPIRO

Between 1810 and 1850 Cincinnati emerged as America's principal city west of the Alleghenies, and indeed one of the major cities of the still young and rapidly growing nation. If one included the Kentucky cities across the Ohio River, metropolitan Cincinnati in 1850 contained in excess of 150,000 persons, as compared to 67,871 in Pittsburgh, 43,277 in Louisville, or 120,951 in New Orleans itself.[1] In manufactures and trade Cincinnati's prominence was equally apparent. By 1850 her woodworking shops had established a virtual monopoly on the construction of steamboat superstructures and railroad car bodies. Cincinnati shops produced steamboat engines and books, fine furniture for distribution throughout the West, ornamental ironwork for New Orleans, and prefabricated housing parts for settlers on the treeless plains of Illinois and Kansas. Her butchers had already made the city into the first "Porkopolis," and in the process had invented the assembly line—or, more properly, the disassembly line—to speed production and increase profits.[2] Throughout this period, moreover, her city fathers, not being content with dominance over the city's hinterland, sought quite consciously to establish economic and cultural hegemony over the entire "great interior valley of North America." By 1850 her wealthier citizens took their vacations in Michigan's Upper Peninsula and the Mammoth Cave area of Kentucky as frequently as in the surrounding hilltop areas of Mount Healthy and Mount Airy, and they traveled as freely to St. Louis and New Orleans as to Philadelphia or Washington.[3]

If Cincinnatians saw their future in the West, however, they did not for that reason forsake their traditional ties with the East. Indeed, throughout the nineteenth century Cincinnati remained an eastern city set in the West. To the degree that the life of any American city could be planned during this period, Cincinnati was quite consciously designed to replicate the best aspects of eastern civilization in the more fluid, more democratic social and economic environment of the West. Her streets were named after the streets of Philadelphia. Her institutions were patterned after eastern institutions. Her elites maintained close personal, financial, and political ties with eastern elites. To foreign visitors

---

[1] Notes to this chapter begin on page 242.

during the first half of the nineteenth century, Cincinnati both looked and felt familiar, an oasis of Euro-American civilization in the western desert.[4]

In certain respects the attempt to establish hegemony in the West and replicate the culture of the East was eminently successful. In one area in particular, however, it failed. Despite its early promise, Cincinnati in the first half of the nineteenth century did not establish itself as a center for science. The most ambitious effort launched in this direction, the attempt to organize a viable scientific community through the Western Academy of Natural Sciences, failed in and of itself. But even before its demise the Western Academy proved unable to establish either a hegemony comparable to that of Cincinnati business and manufacturing within its immediate hinterland or parity with the societies and academies of New York, New England, or Philadelphia. Yet popular interest in and support for science was widespread. The number of "scientists" in the city was substantial and included several distinguished workers in their respective fields.[5] The institutional network was mature and extensive. The ever-necessary financial base was solid. Why then did Cincinnati not develop a viable and productive scientific community? Why did the Western Academy itself fail?

It is in the answer to questions like these that we may find the most productive insights into the nature of American science in the first half of the nineteenth century, the role of scientific societies in the organization of science and of scientists, and the relationship of science to the American social order during this period. Because we usually concern ourselves with success rather than failure, our questions lead inevitably into a set of generalizations, which end in the thought that "the time was right" or that the abilities and personalities of individuals were responsible for the maintenance of a particular institution or the conduct of productive scientific work. In contrast, the history of science in Cincinnati during the first half of the nineteenth century, and of the Western Academy of Natural Sciences in particular, provide an opportunity to study "pure" phenomena, a set of processes uncomplicated by success and unalloyed by the presence of great men whose distinction and achievements alter both the history and our judgment of the history of the institutions with which they are associated.

Even more important, by asking questions about failure rather than about success we achieve the necessary distance from both the historical phenomena we are seeking to examine and the process of historical inquiry itself. Questions about failure—and, for that matter, questions about success—are circular in the sense that they begin with an assumption about the nature of the process to be explicated, and this assumption then becomes the conclusion drawn at the end of our endeavor. It is only by becoming aware of the circular nature of much historical inquiry that we can begin to free ourselves from this circularity. It is only by recognizing the constraints placed upon us by the relationship between the questions we ask and the answers we find in the sources that we can begin to assess the appropriateness of asking particular questions of particular data. There is no better way of initiating self-consciousness in inquiry than by asking such an overtly artificial and wrongheaded question as the one about failure. In this situation, the kinds of generalizations we normally offer when our questions concern success—that is, that the time was right or that particular individuals had particular abilities—appear totally inadequate. Instead we are necessarily led to ask whether success and failure are in fact the aspects of history we wish to know about, and whether these do not imply judgments about the role of individuals or institutions in the process of history that we perceive clearly by hindsight, but that were entirely foreign to the vision of those whose efforts and activities we seek to explicate and thus to understand.

The Western Academy of Natural Sciences, for example, was not concerned with success as we would define it. It had no real product to produce. It had no explicit goals to achieve. It existed for its own sake. And if contemporary observers, including some of its members, chose to represent its existence as a sign of Cincinnati's cultural, intellectual, and institutional maturity, and hence to grieve at its decline in the 1850s, that matter is ultimately extraneous to the purposes of the society itself. It lived a tenuous life and died a lingering death as the interest of its members alternately waxed and waned, and as the energies of those most able to provide the Academy with leadership were drawn off into other activities. Yet even in that sense it cannot be said to have failed.

Indeed, if we are judging solely in terms of success and failure, the Academy was doomed from the start. All we can in fact say about its demise is that it ceased to be functional—but that is enough. For if Cincinnati failed to develop a viable scientific community, if the Western Academy died its slow death through inactivity, it was not because the times were wrong or because individuals lacked the necessary ability or commitment. It was because the rules by which success and failure are defined were changed, because what was acceptable science by the old standards had ceased to be acceptable science by the new standards, because the purposes for which such an association of scientists as the Western Academy had been organized in 1835 were not consonant with the purposes for which the new professional and paraprofessional societies that emerged in the 1850s and flourished in the 1870s were organized. By 1850 the Western Academy could no longer meet the needs of its members. The Western Academy of Natural Sciences of Cincinnati was appropriate to its time, but not to ours, and that is important because its nonfunctional character, which is evident to us and was evident to contemporaries after 1850, may be seen as a sign of real transformation both in the content and in the structure of science in America during the mid-nineteenth century.

An examination of the early history of science in America cannot in and of itself help us to understand the later history of science in America. But it is an interesting subject for study, and until it is made, and made in terms of its own time and place rather than in terms of ours—that is, until we acknowledge that continuity and identity in history are not the same—we cannot begin to understand the process of transformation that appears as the crucial event in the whole history of American science. The focus of this paper, then, is on the history of the Western Academy of Natural Sciences and its relationship to the scientific community of Cincinnati during the first half of the nineteenth century, but its concern ultimately is with the structure of science itself and with the role of such institutions as the Western Academy in the process of normal science in America during this period.

In the history of science in the Ohio Valley during the first half of the nineteenth century, no name looms as large as that of Dr. Daniel Drake, both in the consciousness of his contemporaries and in the eyes of historians. Yet Drake's own contributions to science were minimal, judged either by our standards or by comparison with the work of his contemporaries, such as John Locke, John Riddell, Joseph Ray, Robert Buchanan, Charles Wilkins Short, or David Dale Owen. Rather, it was Drake's role in the encouragement of science in the Ohio Valley through the establishment of scientific institutions that earned him his reputation as a major figure in the history of American science. Initially, he appears to have viewed such societies as natural extensions of the civilization of the East into the West, and to have regarded their function as serving as centers for the collection of specimens and data relating to the climate and natural resources, including the indigenous flora and fauna and the geological characteristics of a new and largely unexplored region. So in 1812, as secretary of the First District Medical Society in Cincinnati, which he helped organize, Drake sought to establish, as a duty of members, the task of transmitting "as early as possible, specimens of the roots, leaves, flowers and seeds of those vegetables indigenous to this state, which he may know to be reputed useful in Medicine or the Arts, together with such information concerning their qualities and virtues as he can collect . . . [and] to make a quarterly report concerning the Diseases of the district in which he practices accompanied with such topographical and meteorological observations as may be necessary to illustrate their causes."[6]

The knowledge thus to be obtained, interesting in and of itself, had practical value for the residents or potential residents of the West, and its collection was in any case the conventional obligation of physicians of Drake's generation. According to Drake, the observation of nature was not the exclusive province of physician-adepts, nor were philanthropy and social utility the only motives that might lead to the study of philosophy. Indeed, Drake distinguished between the "observer" and the "philosopher" by remarking that "the eye of the one travels over the exterior of creation, and stores the memory with independent facts" while "the mind of the other comprehends its laws," but he argued that all could aspire to become philosphers: "Hitherto, the philosophers have formed a distinct caste from the people; and like kings have been supposed to possess a divine right of superiority. But this delusion should be dispelled, is indeed fast disappearing. Philosophers like kings, are but men; and all men to a certain extent may become philosophers. Our Faculties are the same and if exercised in the same manner we should at length differ only in degree."[7]

It was in the spirit of this commitment that Drake joined with Peyton Short Symmes and Josiah Meigs in organizing, in October 1813, a "School of Literature and the Arts"—a kind of self-improvement society that met on a regular basis during the next year and devoted itself to the discussion of problems in pure and applied science. In an Anniversary Discourse delivered on November 23, 1814, Drake reviewed the year's activities, and after suggesting that the "gentlemen of the town" might like to participate in future meetings of the group, took the occasion to assert the appropriateness of intellectual activity in a society so new as that of Cincinnati and the advantages to individuals of such activity. "Learning, philosophy, and taste, are yet in early infancy, and the standard of excellence in literature and science is proportionably low," Drake pointed out, and as a consequence "acquirements, which in older and more enlightened countries would scarcely raise an individual to mediocrity, will here place him in a commanding station." The opportunities for the establishment of a reputation in new and unexplored countries were hence comparatively greater than in older and better known areas, and, indeed, Drake noted that the Ohio country abounded in opportunities that would "immortalize the names of a greater number of [scientists] than the United States can at present boast." And lest any be concerned about how one chose an area in which to specialize and hence in which to make such a reputation, Drake explained that

the operations of the intellect, in an old country, are like the waters of a deep canal, which, flowing between artificial banks, pursue an equable and uniform course; while in a new country, they resemble the stream which cuts its own channel in the wilderness; rolls successively in every direction; has a current, alternately swift and slow; is frequently shallow; but always free, diversified and natural. The former is extremely useful for a single purpose—the latter can be made subservient to many. . . . In new countries, the empire of prejudice is comparatively insignificant; and the mind, not depressed by the dogmas of licensed authority, nor fettered by the chains of inexorable custom, is left free to expand, according to its original constitution.[8]

It was thus in the context of the realities of life and culture in Cincinnati, generalized to the West and ultimately to the nation at large, that Drake came to see the crucial role that scientific societies could play by guiding and supporting the activities of untutored individuals in the collection of specimens and data for subsequent examination and classification and by making this knowledge available to the society at large. Because they could not be associations of enlightened men, they had to be associations for the enlightenment of mankind. What was needed in every case, Drake argued, was "a point of concentration—a sensorium commune where all intelligence should be received, compared, digested and again radiated . . . like the beams of heat and light which emanate [sic] from the sun to warm the earth and make it prolific."[9] By the time Drake made these remarks in 1823, however, he had already had considerable experience with the establishment of institutions designed to function in such a way. He had seen them succeed, and then he had seen them fail. He must have known that only through a commitment to the pursuit of science as an abstract goal could such institutions develop an esprit that would permit them to stand independent of the shifting patterns of personal relations that constantly threatened their dissolution. That at least should have been the lesson of the last decade's work.

In 1818, as he entered his mid-thirties, Drake stood at the height of his career, with both a local and national reputation firmly established. His account of the geology of the Ohio Valley had been read before the American Philosophical Society during the previous fall, resulting in his election as a corresponding member of that distinguished association. In April 1818 he was elected to membership in the American Antiquarian Society as well. And, following his return from a successful year as a member of the first medical faculty organized west of the Alleghenies at Lexington, Drake initiated five related projects. He organized the Cincinnati Medical Society. He inaugurated the course of medical lectures at the Hall of the Lancasterian Seminary, which led to the organization of the Medical College of Ohio. He delivered the botanical lectures at the Lancasterian Seminary and began the organization of a Western Museum Society to support both the collection of specimens and formal and informal instruction in scientific topics. He initiated a movement to recharter the Lancasterian Seminary as the Cincinnati College. Finally, he inspired the effort to establish a hospital in Cincinnati that would not only serve the health needs of residents of the community and transients, including the riverboat men for whom there was no regular provision for medical care, but would also become a kind of physician's cabinet of disease for the instruction of students and the systematic study of pathology by the profession. The Cincinnati Medical Society was to support the Medical College, which, in turn, was to staff and utilize the hospital. The Medical College, the Cincinnati College, and the Western Museum Society, all to be located in the Hall of the Lancasterian Seminary (now to be renamed College Hall), were to provide parallel courses of instruction in medical, literary, and philosophical subjects respectively. Interlocking boards of trustees or managers institutionalized the agreements concerning purpose and operation which preceded the organization of the several entities. All were to serve the city in one way or another, and the enthusiasm of the people and the press seemed to guarantee success for the total plan.

By the winter of 1819-1820, the first breach in the wall of this complex edifice appeared as disputes over the appointment of physicians to the faculty of the Medical College of Ohio resulted in the resignation of Drake and Elijah Slack from the Cincinnati Medical Society. Drake and Slack subsequently organized the Medico-Chirurgical Society of Cincinnati as a competing professional association. In January Drake and Coleman Rogers, his partner in medical practice since 1817 and his collaborator in the plan to organize the Medical College of Ohio, had a falling out, and Rogers challenged Drake to a duel. Drake refused to meet Rogers on the field of honor; after all, he had the votes. Later that month Drake and Slack voted Rogers out of the chair in anatomy and surgery that he was to hold in the new Medical College. Two years later Slack and his colleagues voted Drake out of *his* chair as professor of the practice of physic on the grounds that he was ambitious, quarrelsome, and "cultivated other branches of science than [his] profession."[10] By 1823 economic depression in Cincinnati, combined with the crisis in leadership precipitated by the personal quarrels in which Drake, Slack, and the others were involved, forced the Cincinnati College, the Medical College of Ohio, and the Western Museum Society to close their doors.[11]

Drake returned to Transylvania University in 1823 and continued to preach his gospel of the need for "accurate observation, judicious arrangement, and logical induction," coupled with the need for institutions or societies to guide the efforts of individuals in their search for an understanding of nature's ways. Perhaps because the failure of his schemes in Cincinnati was fresh in everyone's mind, he appears to have been unable to convince anyone of the appropriateness of his vision. This may have contributed to his decision to return to Cincinnati in 1827 to join Dr. Guy W. Wright in the establishment of the *Western Journal of the Medical and Physical Sciences.* Consciously patterned after Barton's *Philadelphia Medical and Physical Journal,* the *Western Journal* must have appealed to its editors as a kind of scientific institution that would function as just the "sensorium commune" that Drake had earlier advocated, and one moreover that could be controlled by its editors and hence stand independent of faction and personality conflicts. That at least was the character of the journal from the time Drake assumed sole ownership of it in 1828 until he turned both ownership and editorship over to the faculty of the medical department of the Cincinnati College in 1837. The *Western Journal of the Medical and Physical Sciences* was Drake's journal; it was known as such throughout the Midwest and nationally, and his own concerns provided direction to the enterprise.[12]

Between 1828 and 1837 the *Western Journal* published articles on the nature and treatment of disease, reviews of current medical literature, and the normal complement of notes on the state of the profession and editorials urging the establishment of professional standards in medical education and the conduct of physicians. In addition, it contained articles on natural history and geology, including catalogs of western flora and fauna, meteorological tables, and news of scientific societies and their activities, both in the West and in the East. Like a museum or a cabinet of specimens, the *Journal* functioned as a repository for data illuminating problems in both the medical and the "auxiliary" sciences. Like a society or an educational institution, it served as a place in which communication and debate could take place and from which knowledge of nature and nature's ways might be dispersed to the society at large. But it had advantages over the institutional forms with which Drake had previously been associated. Its operations did not require the maintenance of a hall, cabinets, and the payment of regular salaries. It could appear from time to time as the finances of its publishers and the energies of its editor permitted, and, while it depended upon the support of the public through subscriptions, that support was offered at a distance rather than face to face. Most important, its utility was not strictly local. It could serve the needs of physicians and naturalists in the West, as well as those of the profession and the sciences nationally.[13]

If the *Western Journal* was in certain ways continuous with those scientific and educational institutions whose establishment Drake had encouraged during the previous quarter century, it also of necessity lacked the essentially casual and public quality these had displayed and that ultimately had been their undoing. By its very nature as a journal, it distinguished between the producers and the consumers of knowledge. Drake regularly encouraged his subscribers to become "collaborators" by submitting material for publication and providing financial support; he even offered a year's free subscription to any person whose article was accepted for the *Journal*. Nonetheless, the very fact of editorial control over the content of any issue implied the utilization of standards of scientific competence that had not been appropriate to the goals or the organizational structure of the cooperative institutions with which Drake had been associated earlier. While Drake did not take what we would regard as the logical next step and use the journal to encourage the development of specialization and an interest in systematics, choosing instead to retain his conviction that the publication of data systematically obtained was itself sufficient to the discovery of nature's ways, he did make his pages available to those who were moving in the direction of specialization and systematics, including that group of Cincinnati scientists who organized themselves into the Western Academy of Natural Sciences in 1835.

Drake's own role in the organization of the Western Academy is unclear, but it seems safe to say, first, that he was only one among many rather than the driving force behind the enterprise, as had been the case in his previous ventures; and, second, that his contribution consisted primarily in lending his prestige and his presence, as the public representative of the possibility of science in the West, to the movement to create a scientific academy in the city. Drake appears to have been chairman of the meeting on April 25, 1835, at which the academy was organized, but that itself is a sign that his function in its activities would necessarily be different from what it had been twenty years earlier. It was not Drake but James Hall who proposed the resolution the meeting was called to consider: "that in the opinion of this meeting it is expedient to form a society for the promotion of natural history; to be composed of such naturalists and friends of natural science as may be disposed to devote themselves to the preservation and collection of facts and specimens in the various branches of this department of knowledge."[14] Although Drake attended meetings of the Academy on a fairly regular basis as long as he remained in Cincinnati, he never served as an officer and does not seem to have played a major role in the work of the Academy even during its initial years.[15]

Unlike the institutions and societies with which Drake had formerly been associated, the Western Academy did not need, and indeed could not have survived—any more perhaps than those did—the kind of entrepreneurial leadership Drake had sought to provide the Western Museum Society, the Medical College of Ohio, the Cincinnati College, and the various local medical societies with which he was affiliated. Those had been designed to encourage the pursuit of science as an abstract quest for the understanding of nature's ways. To a significant degree they succeeded in this, yet they failed to provide the coordination for the efforts of untutored individuals, which Drake had also seen to be necessary, precisely because they existed as one-man shows. In a real sense, the Western Academy of Natural Sciences stood as their heir, but of a different generation. It was the creation of its scientist members who sought to found an institution that would not only provide them with companionship, mutual support, and encouragement but also sponsor a semipublic museum collection of specimens in natural history for study and analysis. They saw the Academy as an institutional base for the conduct of their own scientific work, a body that would legitimize individual projects and coordinate cooperative efforts in natural history and which could, in its corporate capacity, approve or disapprove the identification of new species, the designation of old species as synonymous with other old species, the articulation of new systems of classification, and the appropriateness of utilizing old systems of classification in new ways. In such a work Drake could be of little assistance himself. But he was welcomed as a participant in the meetings of the Academy, listened to politely, thanked when thanks were appropriate, and otherwise ignored. So far as Drake himself was concerned, that seems to have been fine. He announced the formation of the Academy proudly in an editorial note in the *Western Journal*, published the work of its members from time to time, but otherwise stayed out of the picture.[16]

In its goals as in its form, the Western Academy was not significantly different from the other local and regional scientific societies and academies that were established in the mid-thirties, and indeed the impetus for its formation may have come as one more attempt to replicate the institutions of the East in the West. Its significance in the history of science in the Ohio Valley is not lessened for that reason, however. The very fact of its organization as an association of scientists serving the needs of scientists as well as of science marks the conclusion of the period of simple collecting and abstract generalization out of which it emerged. At the same time, the character of its activities and its apparent commitment to specialization and systematics link it to the more sophisticated and more highly professionalized scientific societies of the period after the Civil War. Indeed, the Western Academy worked to transform the nature of scientific activity in the Ohio Valley in these directions.

Membership in the Western Academy was by election only. Although the usual number of politically helpful individuals were made regular or corresponding members, especially in its initial years, election more often seems to have amounted to a public recognition of scientific accomplishment and to have been based not only upon interest in natural history but upon competence in a particular area as demonstrated through diligence in collecting and classifying specimens. There is no evidence that quotas were established for maintaining a balance in the interests of the members. After 1837, however, members were expected to affiliate themselves with one or more of the sections of the Academy according to their specialty and to participate in the organization and maintenance of the Academy's collections in those areas.

Perhaps the clearest index to the nature and goals of the Western Academy is to be found in the fact that it did not engage in educational work at any time during its more than twenty-year history. To some extent this may be seen as the result of a natural and desirable division of labor. By the mid-thirties science education of a sort was being provided by a variety of specifically educational institutions in Cincinnati, including the Cincinnati College and its medical department (both of which were established or reestablished during this period), and numerous academies, seminaries, and high schools. In addition, the Ohio Mechanics Institute was organized in 1828 in order to make "the sciences, which have heretofore been taught only in our higher seminaries of learning . . . accessible to all who possess talent and taste to cultivate them." After this date, the Ohio Mechanics Institute sponsored not only classes for mechanics and apprentices but also public lectures on a wide range of scientific topics.[17] At the same time, the Academy's failure to adopt an educational function may also have stemmed from a sense of the political realities of "society" life in Cincinnati. Despite these "constraints," it is still significant that the Western Academy sought neither to educate its own members nor, by educating the public to the delights of systematic investigation into nature and nature's ways, to recruit new members. Instead, the members of the Academy accepted as their fellows those already possessed of a degree of expertise in one branch of science or another, and assumed without question—although perhaps for the sake of vanity—a similar degree of expertise among those already enrolled as members.

This is not to say that all members of the Western Academy were of equal competence, or that they did not themselves distinguish between experts and novices in the study of a particular field. Those with greater knowledge, competence, or experience in collecting and classifying specimens in natural history were expected to lead their respective sections and undertake the major part of the Academy's work, but all members were expected to participate in the meetings and to share with their fellows the particular skills they possessed. As we shall see, the system of deference sometimes broke down or was felt to have broken down; but at those times the Academy itself generally broke down and was in each case subsequently reconstituted on a slightly different basis.

Few of the members of the Western Academy can be identified as "professionals" in even the loosest definition of that difficult term, and these few—John Locke, for example, a physician and sometime member of the faculty of the Medical College of Ohio, and at various times an assistant in the geological surveys of Iowa, Wisconsin, Illinois, Michigan, Missouri, and Ohio,[18] or Joseph Ray, a physician by training who served as professor of mathematics, chemistry and natural philosophy at the Woodward College and High School and was the author of a series of school arithmetics that paralleled the McGuffey's readers in their popularity[19] —were among the less active members of the Academy, either because of the divergence of their interests from those of the majority of the members or because of conflicting professional and/or professorial duties.[20] Many of the members of the Academy were physicians by training if not by profession, although it is unclear how many of these were in medical practice at any particular time; then as now, doctors and lawyers sometimes practiced their profession and sometimes did not, and in any case often did a little business on the side. Those "in business," including lawyers, were in any case the great majority. Whatever their occupation, however, the members of the Academy were "amateurs" in the original sense of the term: dedicated students of natural history whose interest led them to engage in private and public activity in support of science and as practitioners of science.[21]

It was precisely because the Academy was an association of scientists designed to serve the needs of scientists as well as the needs of science more abstractly conceived that it was able to survive for more than twenty years despite periodic financial crises, a shifting roster of members, and from time to time what appeared to be an extraordinary lack of interest on the part of the members, demonstrated through low attendance at the fortnightly or later the weekly meetings. When the Academy treasury could not support the rent of meeting rooms, the collections of the Academy were simply stored or returned to the membership, and meetings were held in members' homes. When an individual became too busy to attend meetings or lost interest in the Academy or in natural history more generally, he simply dropped out. Sometimes he turned up again and sometimes he did not, but, because the Academy existed for the sake of its members rather than the reverse, it continued to meet and continued to function as long as it served the needs of any group, however small. And as men with an interest in natural history took up residence in Cincinnati, or as young men reached their majority, they were duly elected to membership in the Academy.

By 1854, when the recorded minutes of meetings end, the membership of the Academy had almost completely changed from that of 1835. Of 117 persons whose names appear in the minutes as regular members of the Academy, 21 were in the group of "founders" by virtue of having attended the organizational meeting in 1835, and 27 were elected to membership during the remaining months of that first year. Of these regular members, only Robert Buchanan, Joseph Clark, and George Graham, of the founders, and John Gould Anthony, elected late in 1835, remained active through the 1840s, however, and leadership in the Academy gradually passed to younger men from among a larger group of 69 elected after 1836. Among these, the most active were John Bartlett (1851), Samuel T. Carley (1836), Thomas G. Carroll, M.D. (1842), Robert C. Carter, M.D. (1849), Robert Clarke (1847), H. C. Grosvenor (1844), John P. Foote (1840?), Uriah P. James (1844), J. W. Jayne (1851), Jacob Resor (1847), John Aston Warder, M.D. (1837), and Levi Hale Warren (1847). Indeed, during the twenty or more years of its existence, the membership of the Academy comprised at least two and perhaps three distinct generations of Cincinnati naturalists.[22]

If the activities of the Academy during its first year of existence are any index to the interests of its members at that time and the goals they envisioned for the association, it is clear that few of the founding generation thought about natural science in terms other than those of the "utility and pleasures" of its study; this was, in fact, the title of an address Drake was requested to deliver at an early meeting of the group in May, 1835. Although one of the original goals of the Academy, according to the resolution of April 25, was the establishment of collections in natural history, for example, little was done to achieve this purpose by the members directly. Instead, curators were appointed (some of whom do not appear to have been members) and charged with filling and organizing the Academy's cabinets. The members themselves sought to demonstrate their literary and oratorical gifts through the presentation of papers on a variety of subjects more or less related to natural science, or by discussion of the merits of appointing committees to memorialize the state legislature concerning the need to establish a geological survey or to investigate the feasibility of "obtaining coal, by boring, in the vicinity of Cincinnati."[23]

Although there is no direct evidence of open conflict between the generation of the founders and their somewhat younger colleagues during the Academy's early years, one can imagine the distress with which John Gould Anthony, for example, or even Robert Buchanan and Joseph Clark listened to Dr. John Riddell's reminiscence of a recent geologizing tour of Ohio or Dr. Drake's paper on the geology of Cincinnati and vicinity, or with which the older members heard Buchanan deliver his paper on the bivalves of the Ohio River.[24] The necessity of repairs to College Hall, where the Academy's rooms were located, required the suspension of meetings from April 1836 to February 1837, and lack of a quorum (which rarely bothered anyone in later years) resulted in the cancellation of most of the scheduled meetings during the remainder of 1837. By the end of 1837, however, a quiet revolution in the nature and purposes of the Academy had taken place. The majority of the founding members of the Academy no longer attended the meetings, and with Buchanan as president, Anthony as secretary, and Clark, Oakley, Graham, and Warder in regular attendance, the Academy got down to business. It was a new kind of business, having little to do with the celebration of the utility and pleasures of the study of natural science, but a great deal to do with study of natural science itself.

On December 9, 1837, Anthony proposed "that members be requested to bring at each meeting of the society one or more specimens which may serve as subjects of discussion at such meetings," and that "the society proceed to divide themselves into committees upon the several branches of science, and that each committee agree to furnish its department, either by personal acquisition or by soliciting donations, with a collection illustrating each department."[25] To both resolutions the members present agreed, and the Academy's cabinets began to fill. At a meeting on March 31, 1838, "it having been suggested that some confusion and inconvenience arises from want of some fixed and certain names by which the different localities of specimens in natural history may be designated," a committee was appointed to draw up a map of the Cincinnati region indicating suitable names for the various collecting spots. This was presented on April 7 and adopted on April 14, 1838, as an authoritative guide for the use of naturalists collecting in the vicinity of the city.[26]

In March 1838 the members of the Academy were informed that Dr. John Riddell, who upon his departure from Cincinnati for New Orleans had inadvertently taken with him the Academy's constitution, was now unable to find this document and that a new one ought to be drawn up. Anthony and Graham were designated a committee to prepare a new constitution and took the occasion to establish standards for the maintenance of the Academy's collections. "The cabinet and collections shall be divided into distinct departments . . . embracing such specimens as may be deposited with the Academy." Each department was to be under the supervision of a curator and a committee chosen by the curator and was to be kept separate from the other departments—the separation reiterated in the constitution not simply for completeness but for emphasis. It was the obligation of the committees and the curators "to preserve in due order the specimens belonging to the several departments, have each numbered or labelled and the corresponding number and name entered in a Book with the locality and name of the donor and date of donation."[27]

The business of collecting thus organized on a more or less orderly basis, the members of the Academy turned to and, in subsequent months, began in earnest the collection of specimens, first for their own cabinets, and then, when duplicates were available, for the cabinet of the Academy. Discussions on nomenclature absorbed much time at meetings during the next several years, as members sought to ascertain by consultation with their colleagues whether or not they had discovered a new species and whether or not a particular species should more properly be located in a different genus than current convention defined. As early as April 1837, Anthony had presented a recommendation that "as members ought to be frequently on the look-out for new specimens in Natural Science, and as it will happen that new discoveries may be made by those thus engaged, I have thought that it would be an encouragement to members if some notice were taken of such discovery," and therefore proposed "that whenever a person shall claim any new thing, it be referred to a committee whose report shall be entered on the Journal [i.e., Minute Books] and such notice be taken of them as the Academy may direct." With this suggestion he submitted a list of fossils he had discovered, but this list does not appear in the minutes, and it was not until January 12, 1839, that a description of a new trilobite, *Calymene bucklandii (Anthony)*, was entered in the minutes of the Academy, apparently the first time that an attempt was made to establish priority in discovery through presentation of a paper to the Academy.[28]

From this time on, problems of nomenclature and classification absorbed increasing amounts of the Academy's time and the members' efforts. Indeed, the activities of the Academy centered largely on attempts to deal with problems of this nature, as well as such auxiliary matters as the maintenance of a hall or rooms in which cabinets might be preserved, and the authorized publication of the innumerable reports prepared under the Academy's aegis during the next dozen years by individuals, committees, or the members present sitting as a committee of the whole. What was to be classified and named, however, was not simply the specimens collected by the members or received through donation, but the actual divisions of science. Indeed, in Cincinnati as elsewhere, the 1840s were noteworthy for the emergence of a new interest in both the taxonomy of natural history and the taxonomy of natural historians.[29]

During the early years of the Academy, no attempt was apparently made to list those branches of science in which the society or its members were interested. The Academy was designed to encourage the study of natural science more generally. Following 1840, however, periodic attempts to "reconstitute" the Academy in an effort to encourage the participation of more persons in its activities, or to make it more responsive to the needs and interests of those members in regular attendance, provided the occasions on which reclassification of the departments of science and their practitioners was attempted. The first of these, in the summer of 1840, originated not in the Academy itself but in the organization of the Educational Society of Hamilton County at a public meeting held in the Hall of the Cincinnati College on March 27 of that year.[30] Designed as an "auxiliary" to the Western Literary Institute and College of Professional Teachers,[31] the Educational Society was established "for the purpose of aiding in the improvement and extension of practical education, and of laying the foundation of a great Western Academy of the Sciences and General Literature."

At subsequent meetings, the name of the society was changed to the Cincinnati Society for the Promotion of Useful Knowledge, a constitution and bylaws were approved, and an agreement reached on June 15, 1840, that the members should divide themselves into sections according to the following scheme: (1) Practical Teaching, (2) Exact and Mixed Science, (3) Natural Science, (4) Practical Arts, (5) Fine Arts, (6) Medicine, (7) Law, (8) Political Economy and Political Science, (9) Moral and Intellectual Philosophy, (10) History, (11) Language, (12) Commerce and Agriculture, (13) Polite Literature, and (14) Statistics. Each section was to meet separately and organize itself as seemed appropriate.[32]

The Section on Natural Science, which had elected John P. Foote president and John G. Anthony secretary, met for the first time on June 18. When "the question respecting what should be our plan for the promotion of the cause we are engaged in" was taken up, the members present agreed upon the policy of "subdividing the section so that each should devote his time and attention to some particular branch of Natural Science and agree to collect specimens in and investigate the difficult or doubtful questions relating to each." The subsections thus constituted and their chairmen were: geology, T. J. Biggs; conchology, J. G. Anthony; botany, S. B. Holley; mineralogy, John P. Foote; chemistry, William F. Hopkins. (Other members of the Section at this time were E. A. Atlee, John

A. Warder, Milo G. Williams, James E. Perkins, and the mysterious T. Maylin.)[33]

The Section met again once in July and once in August before a recess was called because of warm weather. When meetings were resumed on December 16, only Anthony, Buchanan, Foote, David H. Shafer, and Warder were in attendance. All but Shafer were members of the Western Academy, and the conversation must have turned naturally to the advantages of merging the Section on Natural Science with the Western Academy of Natural Sciences, which had apparently continued to meet during the months that the Section was being organized. Not the least of these advantages would have been the existence of a charter from the state of Ohio establishing the Academy as a corporate entity. This document could not only guarantee the Section a degree of independence from its parent organization but could also make possible more businesslike arrangements for the development of collections in natural history. Given the virtually identical membership in the two groups, separate and potentially competitive existence would have been foolish in any case. As a consequence, on December 24 Joseph Clark and Samuel T. Carley sat with the Section as representatives of the Western Academy of Natural Sciences to discuss the possibility of union, which was achieved on December 30. The constitution and bylaws of the Academy were adopted as covering the united society, with the addition of a regulation that provided for the election of "ladies of scientific tastes" as "complimentary" members.[34] Despite the union, the Section on Natural Science continued to exist as a paper organization, reporting from time to time to its parent association, and both "Academy" and "Section" are used interchangeably in the minutes.[35]

The matter of the classification of the branches of science and of scientists was introduced again, in May 1841, at the annual public meeting of the Academy, at which John A. Warder—the featured speaker of the day—proposed that "this society constitute subsections of the leading branches of our extended subject, which may again be divided, as may hereafter be found necessary, and, that we recommend our members unite themselves to one or more of these subdivisions as their tastes may direct." Warder's scheme of classification reflected both his own interest in horticulture and scientific agriculture as a field related to but distinct from botany and the strong interest of other members of the Academy in conchology and meteorology. It thus appears as a truly empirical rather than an abstract system. Warder's divisions were:

I. Botany and Horticulture embracing the physiology and arrangements of plants, the selection, preservation and uses of timbers, grains and roots, their introduction and cultivation.

II. Zoology and Comparative Anatomy, embracing the physiology, natural history and habits of animals, their uses, introduction and improvement.

III. As a subdivision of the above, Conchology or the habits, uses, description and arrangement of the mollusca.

IV. Geology including the examination of rocks, soils, mineralogy, inorganic chemistry, and paleontology.

V. Meteorology and Electrology, or Hygrometric and Thermometric observations, the history of storms, and investigations in electricity and magnetism, especially the variation and dip of the magnetic needle.[36]

Throughout the history of the Western Academy, the availability of rooms in which to hold meetings and in which to maintain a library and cabinets of specimens was regarded as essential for the Academy's viability, in the early years as much for their symbolic utility as a visible manifestation of the Academy's existence as for convenience or practical utilization. From 1835 until sometime in 1837 the Academy rented rooms in the Cincinnati College building, although during most of the latter year no meetings were held. From December 1837, the date of the Academy's first revitalization, until the summer of 1838, rooms were rented in the Ohio Mechanics Institute. In October 1838 a move was made to the Fire House on Fourth Street between Sycamore and Broadway; and in early 1841 another move, back to the Mechanics Institute. The cost of rent, wood for the stove, and candles to light the rooms for late afternoon and evening meetings proved too great a strain on the Academy's treasury, however, and from November 1841 until January 1843 meetings were held "on the social plan," that is, at members' homes in rotation.[37]

Apparently a sociable group, the members of the Academy seem to have enjoyed this visiting around town, which had certain advantages beyond the financial, notably the availability of the members' cabinets for inspection and discussion by the Academy as a whole. As the Academy became increasingly concerned with problems of classification and the preparation of catalogs of such items as local fossils and freshwater mollusks, however, the acquisition of permanent rooms in which collections might be maintained became essential. In this context, meetings held on the social plan seemed pointless, and from January 1843 until November 1844 no meetings at all appear to have been held. Without an endowment, with a small membership paying low annual dues, which were often in arrears, with no income from a regular publication, and with no desire to generate income by establishing a public museum, the Academy remained dependent upon the possibility of obtaining suitable space gratis.

During the autumn of 1844 this possibility was finally realized, when John Talbot offered the Academy the second story of his schoolhouse for a period of five years, renewable, as a place to hold meetings and establish its cabinets. In return, Talbot would have access to the Academy's collections for the use of himself and his family and for the instruction of his pupils.[38] Talbot's offer was accepted, and, following this move into more or less permanent quarters in November 1844, the Academy entered the most productive phase of its history, during which a second library collection was established, extensive collections of specimens in natural history and perhaps also in Indian relics were made and organized, suites of specimens for exchange were prepared, and a variety of reports and catalogs concerning the natural history of the Cincinnati area were authorized for publication under the Academy's name.

At the conclusion of the five-year agreement with Talbot, during the summer of 1849, the Academy accepted a similar offer from J. P. Broadwell, owner of the recently constructed "Apollo Building" on the northwest corner of Walnut and Fifth Streets, who agreed to provide space for meetings and for the preparation of collections in return for the deposit of the Academy's collections in his "museum."[39] Broadwell's plan for a museum apparently did not work out, however, despite the encouragement of the members of the Academy and their donation of $100 toward the cost of a collection of specimens that Broadwell wished to purchase in the East.[40] By March 1851 the Academy had moved again, to a location at the northwest corner of Fourth and Vine Streets.[41]

This also proved to be a temporary move, for in November 1851 the Academy began negotiations with the directors of the Ohio Mechanics Institute for space in their newly constructed building at Sixth and Vine. Although this move is referred to in the Academy's minutes as a "merger," the terms of the lease signed in December 1851 provided that the Academy should retain its identity and maintain exclusive control over its collections and its library, but that these would be located in the second-floor reading room of the Institute and be available for the instruction of students in natural science. The members of the Academy were to have access to the cabinets at all times during the day, and on any evening when a class or lecture was not being held in the room, and the room itself was to be reserved for meetings of the Academy on Monday nights.[42] This relationship was to last for ten years, subject to prior termination by mutual agreement. So far as anyone now knows, the relationship in fact lasted longer than ten years, for although John Foote noted in 1855 that the Academy was but a shadow of its former self, and the minutes end in 1853, the library and cabinets were maintained intact until 1870, when they were turned over to the Cincinnati Natural History Society to form the basis of the public museum planned by that organization.[43] In 1870 not only was there someone authorized to turn the Academy's collections and library over to the new Society, but there was also money in the treasury. How that stayed intact for fifteen years is simply not clear.[44]

From the time of its revitalization in 1840, the Academy directed increasing attention toward the desirability of the preparation of catalogs of the flora and fauna of the Cincinnati area and the proper arrangement of specimens in its cabinets. Although the absence of a permanent location for the Academy's collection before 1844, and the need to engage in simple identification prior to any attempt at analysis of the relationships among species in a genus, for example, prevented this work from developing into anything with more than private utility, it did provide members of the Academy with the experience of cooperative effort and also engendered a familiarity with the characteristics of local species.

In January 1841 John Gould Anthony proposed that the Academy engage in a systematic investigation of the characteristics of the freshwater mollusk, *Unios,* and a year later that "we constitute ourselves a committee of the whole on the priority of authorship &c. &c. of Western *Unios,* to report from time to time."[45] This committee of the whole did report from time to time, as did the earlier committee, composed of Anthony investigating "erosion of the beaks"; John A. Warder, "color of nacre"; John P. Foote, "tubercles and undulations"; and Robert Clarke, "epidermal vestures." Although these reports probably facilitated the revision of Anthony's "Catalogue of Terrestrial and Fluvatile Shells of Ohio,"[46] the reports themselves were not published except in précis in an "Abstract of the Proceedings of the Section of Natural History" prepared by Foote and Warder for the Society for the Promotion of Useful Knowledge in May 1842.[47] During this period also, the members of the Academy sought to "settle" specimens from their cabinets by comparing them with descriptions in Lamarck and Rafinesque, appointed Robert Clarke chairman of the subsection on geology with responsibility to prepare weekly reports "on the fossils of our hills," and authorized Milo G. Williams to organize the Academy's collections in botany.[48]

The visit of Sir Charles Lyell to Cincinnati in May 1842 provided the members of the Academy with the occasion for a series of collecting expeditions as they showed their distinguished guest the geological curiosities of Cincinnati and vicinity; it also resulted in the organization of the great Naturalists' Picnic of July 19, 1842, to the Big Bone Lick in Kentucky for the purpose of answering a series of questions propounded by Lyell during his visit. More important, however, Lyell's presence and his participation in the activities of the Academy introduced its members to a series of problems concerning the role of time in determining the interaction among and the distribution of species, the relationship of environmental characteristics to the persistence or disappearance of species, and the implications of differing patterns of stratification and of the distribution of fossils and current forms in Europe, the eastern United States, and the Ohio Valley.[49] During the next months these problems absorbed the attention of the members. On June 7 they noted in examining specimens of fossils collected during an expedition to the Mill Creek that the eighteen species they found "are precisely similar to those now found living in and around the same stream." On June 21 they discussed the characteristics of the alluvial and diluvial formations of the Little Miami River, and on June 28, "the meaning of the terms Newer Pliocene and Recent, which was settled by reference to Lyell's elements." Lyell's queries, sent to the Academy with a note of thanks for their hospitality, touched on issues of this sort. Among other things, he wished to know "the height of the mineral spring [at Big Bone Lick] above low water mark [on the Ohio River] and the greatest thickness of loamy and gravelly deposits which overlies the quagmire," and posed the following: "Suppose the Ohio to be so high as to deposit the upper terrace at Cincinnati, Big Bone would be under water. Consider this in speculating upon the relative age of the Older Ohio Terrace in which Elephant's teeth are found, and Big

Bone. In collecting the *fossil* shells at Big Bone and those in the adjacent waters, have some regard to the relative abundance of particular species."[50]

The immediate consequence of Lyell's visit to Cincinnati was the emergence of interest in new problems of this kind among members of the Academy, who began to consider the nature of geological drift, the distribution of fossils, the continuity of geological formations between the eastern and western sections of the country, and the disappearance of species of mollusks from the Ohio River and its tributaries. In addition, Lyell's visit and the Academy's success in providing the information he desired concerning the geology and paleontology of the Cincinnati region (for which he rendered personal thanks but no public acknowledgment in his published discussion of these matters)[51] provided the Academy as an entity with its first real contact with the larger world of the emerging international scientific community, and must have given its members a new sense of their own participation in this community and of the real contributions the Academy could make to its work.

The mid-forties thus saw the beginning of a new phase in the history of the Western Academy, a period of maturity marked by the Academy's increasing concern with both the broader issues of classification and the narrower issues of naming the specimens in its collections, a new commitment to the public distribution of its reports and catalogs in printed form, and a willingness to take its place in the emerging network of cooperating scientific societies in America. In this, the establishment of more or less permanent quarters was crucial. Without an extensive collection of type specimens, the work of cataloging and classification could not take place and a publication program would have been simply inappropriate. The existence of the collection and the need to develop a library in natural history to support it, moreover, provided preliminary points of contact between the Academy and the scientific community outside the Ohio Valley, while the existence of a settled location for the weekly meetings facilitated the attendance of corresponding members residing in communities near Cincinnati and of visitors to the city.

During the mid- and late-1840s, accessions to the Academy's library included donations from John Witten Van Cleve of Dayton; David Christy of Oxford, Ohio; James D. Dana of New Haven; James M. Lea of Philadelphia, who transmitted his father's catalog of Ohio Valley plants; James Hall of Albany; Charles Lyell; members of the Geological Society of France; and various governmental entities, including the Ohio Geological Survey and the Smithsonian Institution. Donations were also made by resident members of the Academy, and publications like the *American Journal of Science* and the *Proceedings* of the American Association for the Advancement of Science were obtained through purchase or subscription. During the same period botanical specimens were exchanged with Professors Guthwick and Henslow of Cambridge, England; suites of fossils were sent out to Hall at Albany and to the managers of the New York Exhibition of the Industry of All Nations; a collection of minerals was received from David Dale Owen of New Harmony, Indiana; and a collection of "granitic bowlders" was submitted for identification by a Mr. Robert Way. In July 1845 the only known circular distributed by the Academy was printed and sent out, requesting donations of Indian relics for its collections, but on this subject the minutes are silent.[52] The Academy's guests during these years included E. H. Davis of Chillicothe, the pioneer American ethnologist; James Hall of Albany; B. F. Shumard of Louisville; as well as such visiting corresponding members as D. D. Owen; David and Robert Christy of Oxford, Ohio; Nathaniel B. Shaler of Newport, Kentucky; and J. W. Van Cleve of Dayton.

However, neither the degree of activity that characterized the Academy's work after the mid-1840s nor the directions that activity took can be attributed exclusively to the existence of permanent quarters for the Academy and the sense of self-confidence that accompanied its public recognition as a legitimate and responsible participant in the network of scientific societies in the United States. This was the period of the return of prosperity following the long economic depression that began with the panic of 1837. Cincinnati generally, like the rest of America, was in the midst of a revival of interest in natural science and especially in natural history. Manifested nationally by the establishment of the Smithsonian and the organization of the American Association for the Advancement of Science, in Cincinnati it took the form of a revitalization of the Ohio Mechanics Institute, the establishment of the Cincinnati Astronomical Society on a firm basis of popular support, the effort to organize a new broadly based society of natural history in 1847, the widespread introduction of scientific courses into the secondary schools and academies of Cincinnati, and the desire of educators like Talbot and entrepreneurs like Broadwell to establish cabinets of specimens in natural history for the instruction of students and the delectation of the public.[53]

In the context of this revival of interest in natural science, new members joined the Western Academy. These younger men, who composed a third generation, rapidly assumed positions of leadership within the Academy, and, after its demise, worked for the establishment of the Cincinnati Natural History Society in 1870. While one can only speculate concerning their motives at this time, it does not seem inappropriate to suggest that, unlike Drake and his generation in the late teens and early 1820s, these younger men did not believe the Academy could achieve a national reputation on the basis of minor accomplishments. When the western limits of the United States reached to the Pacific, Cincinnati was no longer the West; with a population approaching 150,000, Cincinnati was no longer "the backwoods." And with scientific standards of competence and relevance established by the new *national* scientific institutions, it must have seemed inappropriate to spend time discussing the peculiarities of the elk or the "correct" names of specimens in the Academy's cabinet.

In any case, it was these men who seem to have led the Academy to its first systematic program for the publication of reports and catalogs prepared by its members and into its first confrontations with the issue of the continuity between the East and the West, principally the question of whether to accept both the natural history of the eastern states—their climate, geology, paleontology, botany, zoology—and the natural historians of the eastern states as standards against which to judge the quality of accomplishment in the Ohio Valley. In this last they finally yielded, and on their ultimate deference to the prestige and power of the Halls, the Agassizes, the Henrys, and the rest may be laid the causes both for the failure of the Western Academy and the failure of Cincinnati itself.

Following the establishment of the Academy's rooms in Talbot's schoolhouse in January 1845, Anthony proposed that the Academy "take measures for determining as far as possible the Fossils which abound in our blue limestone," and urged that "members be requested to furnish specimens for that purpose, as well as books necessary to determine them." To Anthony, all that seemed necessary was comparison of specimens in the cabinets of the Academy with published descriptions, and he led the members in their effort to "name" the *Strophomenae* and the *Atrypa* in January, and the *Pterinea, Avicula,* and *Cypricardata* in February. In this process of naming, there must have been both practical difficulties and personal difficulties between Anthony and the other members of the Academy interested in paleontology, for, when a report was called for on March 3, it had not yet been completed and, in fact, appears never to have been completed.[54] A better index to the difficulties faced by the members on this project, however, is the fact that the same process was initiated again during the summer of 1846, following receipt of a communication from David Dale Owen concerning the need for a uniform system of nomenclature for Western fossils. This time it was not Anthony but two younger naturalists, Samuel T. Carley and Uriah P. James, who began the analysis of the *Strophomenae*.[55] Their report was presented to the Academy on August 31, 1846. They noted that they had

examined and compared a great number of specimens and are satisfied that, by far, too many species have been made;—that a number of those named by the Academy [in 1845, i.e.], as species, are only *varieties* or the young of the same species. Although many individuals vary so much as to appear like different species, yet upon comparing a number of specimens they approach each other so nearly as to make it impossible to decide which they belong to;—in such cases, your committee think it best to make but one species. By this rule have they been governed in making the examination.[56]

Carley and James then began an examination of the genus *Orthis,* and Joseph Clark was asked to begin an examination of the genus *Delthyris.* On November 30 Clark reported to the Academy in almost identical words.

After carefully examining several hundred specimens, young and old, your committee is led to believe that those now known by several names . . . and in fact all the Delthyris of this vicinity, in the blue limestone, ought to constitute one species; for although the extremes, as D. trilobata and D. prolongata, for instance, seem sufficiently different to constitute separate species, yet we find them so united by intermediate gradations, that it is impossible to draw distinct lines of separation; and where this cannot be done your committee would suggest that they ought to be considered one species.[57]

Although the paleontological reports of 1846 were ordered published in the Cincinnati newspapers, no attempt appears to have been made to print a proper catalog of local fossils for distribution either to the members of the Academy or to its correspondents outside the city. While there may have been some uncertainty as to the utility and the relative weight accorded scientific work published in a local newspaper as compared to a journal, it is also likely that the members of the Academy hesitated to offer so radical a challenge to establishment paleontology as the publication of these reports in more definitive form would have implied, for they subsequently authorized the publication of other catalogs in an appropriate journal or in pamphlet form. The receipt of Hall's *Palaeontology of New York State* (1847) in any case brought confusion to the members of the Academy as they sought to compare the specimens in their cabinets, upon which the catalogs of 1846 had been based, with Hall's plates. In the end they abandoned the attempt. "Nothing could be done," Robert Clarke noted in the minutes for July 10, 1848, "the engravings being so indistinct and incomplete that we could not compare specimens with them, with much hope of recognizing each separate species; another difficulty arose from his names which were entirely different from those given by the Academy."[58] John Gould Anthony at least must have regarded the disparity between the Academy's published names and those in Hall's book with some pleasure, since his own lists of 1845 had been rejected by his colleagues. One of the last entries in the extant Minute Books records the fact that he introduced a motion on April 10, 1854, that the Academy authorize the preparation of a catalog of "the fossils in our blue limestone."[59]

When the scientific authority was closer to home than Hall, the members of the Academy were not so deferential as they appear to have been in the case of the paleontological reports. On October 23, 1848, in Anthony's absence, probably because of illness with scarlet fever,[60] the following resolution was introduced and passed by the members present:

Whereas, the members of this Academy consider it important to correct the many errors which are known to exist in the various publications describing the fluvatile shells of the Western waters and they also consider it important to have a correct catalogue of the names of such shells, therefore resolved that a committee of three members be appointed to make such a catalogue of the Unios &c. and their synonyms of the Ohio and its Northern Tributaries, and to furnish such catalogue as soon as practicable for the purpose of publication for the use of members if desirable by the Academy.[61]

Carley, Joseph Clark, and U. P. James were appointed to prepare such a catalog, which was completed by January 14, 1849, and, after some discussion, ordered printed. However, publication came only over Anthony's objections, for he saw this catalog not only as taking precedence over his own revised "Catalogue of

Terrestrial and Fluvatile Shells of Ohio" (1843), which had been widely circulated and stood as the current standard, but as a conscious personal insult. (And so of course it may have been both.) "The Catalogue of Unios you allude to," Anthony wrote to E. R. Mayo, one of his own correspondents in New York City,

was got up here more out of a feeling of jealousy and spite than from any better motive. No *Conchologist* had anything to do with it, unless you call those such who merely pick up shells and use them as a child does broken bits of china and odd pieces of looking glass as an ornament to a babyhouse. Not one of them could identify half the species and not one had all of them in his possession—it was an off-hand, guessing sort of affair—no research, no attempt to understand priority—the great stimulus being to create themselves arbiters in what they were totally ignorant of and especially to put down by the specious appearance of Associated Action my individual catalogue—hence you will note that they have all along copied my catalogue for synonyms, taking good care to reverse my conclusions. . . . The fact is they ignored all books and their "ipse dixit" was to be Supreme Law. . . . You have asked my opinion of the list and I give it fully. I need not say "I do not accept it"—I repudiate it altogether. Not one of the parties concerned would be taken as an authority for a clam shell.[62]

It is impossible at this point to determine the accuracy of Anthony's contentions or even the relative merits of the Academy's work as compared to his own. But this incident, like that of the paleontological reports of 1846, points to a series of difficulties endemic to the pursuit of science in this period and upon which the Academy may ultimately be said to have foundered. There was no uniform system of zoological nomenclature, of firmly established collections of type specimens, and of authoritative catalogs of species and synonyms. In the absence of "quality control," the merits of any "authority" remained permanently subject to personal determination, and the dicta of such an "official" body as the Western Academy could be simultaneously regarded as "supreme law" by some and as of no value at all by others. The inadequacy of contemporary theory concerning the pattern of distribution of species and the relationship of environment to the presence or absence of species created a kind of ambiguity of the sort suffered by the members of the Western Academy when their observations did not agree with the scheme of classification contained in Hall's *Palaeontology* or Anthony's *Fluvatile Shells.* Moreover, there was the unclear relationship between "observation" and "research" as a basis for scientific work; the unwillingness of amateurs to specialize—and indeed the unwillingness of most professionals to specialize—hence the absence of adequate professional role models for the proper conduct of science; and the almost universal tendency to competition among individuals and societies, which represented a principal obstacle to the establishment of a viable scientific "community" and the possibility of achieving cooperative and commonly acceptable solutions to the problems all shared. To this list may be added the problem of money, but unlike the others, it was not a problem solved by the processes of professionalization in the next decades nor did it present the same kind of obstacle to the effective pursuit of science during the first half of the nineteenth century.

From the mid-1840s the members of the Western Academy of Natural Sciences recognized many of these problems and sought in a variety of ways to solve them, but without avail. As other organizations with the ability to deal with such problems made their presence felt during the 1850s, the Western Academy simply faded away. It is no accident, it seems to me, that the members of the Western Academy voted that they should entertain their scientific colleagues visiting Cincinnati for the 1851 AAAS meeting in private, and participate in the meetings as individuals rather than through the Academy.[63] In the end it was only by abandoning such institutions as the Western Academy and presenting themselves as individuals that they could hope to establish their credentials for membership in the emerging national scientific community.

NOTES

1. Charles Cist, *Sketches and Statistics of Cincinnati in 1851* (Cincinnati: William H. Moore & Co., 1851), p. 45 (based on the census of 1850).

2. Ibid., "Statistics of Manufactures" and "The Hog and Its Products."

3. Cincinnati's inevitable dominance of "the great interior valley of North America" was a constant theme in the literature describing the history and prospects of the city from the time of Daniel Drake's *Natural and Statistical View, or Picture of Cincinnati and the Miami Country* (Cincinnati: Looker & Wallace, 1815) to the time of Cist's *Sketches and Statistics of Cincinnati in 1851.* More revealing, perhaps, is the choice of names for things; the history of Cincinnati in this period records the organization of a *Western* Museum Society (1819), a *Western* Journal of the Medical and Physical Sciences (1828), a *Western* Literary Institute and College of Professional Teachers (1830), a *Western* Academy of Natural Science (1835), a *Western* Horticultural Review (1851), and a number of other institutions with similar names, the establishment of all of which clearly transcended simple town-boosting and looked rather to the development of a function in a larger region.

4. E.g., Harriet Martineau, *Retrospect of Western Travel,* 2 vols. (London and New York, 1838); Charles Lyell, *Travels in North America, Canada, and Nova Scotia, with Geological Observations,* 2d ed. in 2 vols. (London, 1855); idem, *A Second Visit to North America,* 2 vols. (London, 1855); Borosovich Lakier, *A Journey Through the North American States, Canada and Cuba (1856-58),* trans. Arnold Schrier, in process. I am indebted to Professor Schrier for making portions of his translation available for my examination.

5. My current count covering the period 1835-1866, including persons residing or working in Cincinnati's suburbs but excluding physicians with no visible interest in the natural sciences, now stands at 190.

6. *Liberty Hall and Cincinnati Mercury,* 9 June 1812. On the organization of the First District Medical Society, see Otto Juettner, *Daniel Drake and His Followers, 1785-1909: Historical and Biographical Sketches* (Cincinnati: Harvey Publishing Co., 1909), pp. 85-86. On Drake generally, see Henry D. Shapiro and Zane L. Miller, eds., *Physician to the West: Selected Writings of Daniel Drake on Science and Society* (Lexington: University Press of Kentucky, 1970).

7. "Address to the Louisville Medical Society, November 27, 1840," reprinted in Shapiro and Miller, *Physician to the West,* p. 171.

8. *Anniversary Address, Delivered to the School of Literature and the Arts at Cincinnati, November 23, 1814* (Cincinnati: Looker & Wallace, 1814; reprinted in Shapiro and Miller, *Physician to the West*), p. 57.

9. "Address to the Lexington Medical Society, November 14, 1823," Cincinnati General Hospital Library, Cincinnati, Ohio. See also Henry D. Shapiro, "Daniel Drake's 'Sensorium Commune' and the Organization of the Second American Enlightenment " *Cincinnati Historical Society Bulletin* 27 (Spring 1969): 43-52.

10. Daniel Drake, *A Narrative of the Rise and Fall of the Medical College of Ohio* (Cincinnati: Looker & Reynolds, 1822), pp. 36-40. On the Cincinnati Medical Society and the Medico-Chirurgical Society, see Juettner, *Daniel Drake and His Followers,* pp. 437-38.

11. In addition to Drake's *Anniversary Discourse on the State and Prospects of the Western Museum Society* (Cincinnati, 1820; reprinted in Shapiro and Miller, *Physician to the West,* p. 131), see Louis Leonard Tucker, " 'Ohio Show Shop': The Western Museum Society of Cincinnati, 1820-1867," in Whitfield Bell et al., *A Cabinet of Curiosities: Five Episodes in the Evolution of American Museums* (Charlottesville: University of Virginia Press, 1967), pp. 73-105; Walter B. Hendrickson, "The Western Museum Society of Cincinnati," *Scientific Monthly* 63 (1946): 66-72; Elizabeth R. Kellog, "Joseph Dorfeuille and the Western Museum," *Cincinnati Society of Natural History Journal* 22 (April 1945).

12. Publication of the *Western Journal* was suspended by vote of the medical department faculty in 1838. Shortly afterwards, the medical department suspended instruction as well. Upon Drake's acceptance of a position at the new Louisville Medical Institute in 1839, ownership of the *Journal* was transferred back to him. In 1839 it was merged with the *Louisville Journal of Medicine and Surgery,* edited by Lunceford P. Yandell. From 1839 to 1849 Drake served as senior editor of the new *Western Journal of Medicine and Surgery,* but except for his own contributions on the climate, demographical characteristics, and social conditions of the "great interior valley," the new *Western Journal* concerned itself primarily with medical topics and discussions of the professional needs and obligations of physicians. It was a "professional" journal, in other words.

13. Locally gathered data could be distributed widely, whereas locally gathered specimens in natural history were each unique and their distribution then diminished the richness of the cabinets from which they were taken.

14. Minute Books of the Western Academy of Natural Sciences, 25 April 1835, Cincinnati Historical Society Library, Cincinnati, Ohio (hereafter cited as Minutes.) This initial meeting was held in the "hall" of the Cincinnati Medical Society (not the same one Drake and Slack had wrecked in 1819, but a new one organized in 1831; like the medical department of the Cincinnati College, which it supported, it also folded in 1838) in the Cincinnati College building. According to Juettner, *Daniel Drake and His Followers,* pp. 439-40, the Society maintained a library, an herbarium of plants useful in medicine, and a cabinet of minerals useful in pharmacy. Papers presented at its meetings were published in Drake's *Western Journal.* Four of the officers of the Society attended the organizational meeting of the Academy: Drs. James M. Mason, John T. Shotwell, Isaac Colby, and John L. Riddell; three others were subsequently elected to membership in the Academy during the spring of 1835: Drs. Landon C. Rives, Charles R. Cooper, and Israel S. Dodge. Of all of these, only Riddell was at all active, and he soon left Cincinnati for New Orleans.

A convenient but not always accurate summary of the history of the Western Academy is Walter B. Hendrickson, "The Western Academy of Natural Sciences of Cincinnati," *Isis* 37 (1947): 138-45.

15. Drake attended eight of sixteen meetings in 1835, six of eight in early 1836, three of seven in 1837, five of thirty-six in 1838, one in 1839, and one in 1842.

16. Daniel Drake, "Western Academy of Natural Sciences," *Western Journal of the Medical and Physical Sciences* 9 (April-June 1835): 155-56; John L. Riddell, "Synopsis of the Flora of the Western States, part III. Prepared for the Western Academy," in ibid. (January-March 1836): 567-92; Joseph Ray, "Abstract of Meteorological Observations for the Calendar Year 1835," in ibid., pp. 547-66.

17. Cist, *Cincinnati in 1851,* p. 128; John P. Foote, "An Address in Behalf of the Mechanics' Institute," *Transactions of the Western Literary Institute 1837* (Cincinnati, 1838), pp. 61-69; idem, "The Present Condition of the Ohio Mechanics' Institute," *Transactions . . .* 1840 (Cincinnati, 1841), pp. 250-54.

18. On Locke, see George P. Merrill, *The 1st Hundred Years of American Geology* (New Haven: Yale University Press, 1924); Juettner, *Daniel Drake and His Followers,* pp. 155-62.

19. I know of no biographical material on Ray and have been unable to locate any correspondence. He is mentioned in Cist, *Cincinnati in 1851,* as a member of the Woodward College faculty, and he prepared a summary of meteorological observations for that volume. He is listed among the Meteorological Correspondents of the Smithsonian in 1851-52, which Institution sent him in August 1851 "1 barometer no. 489, 1 thermometer no. 461 best, 1 psychrometer no. 499, 1 max. and min. thermometer, 1 rainguage" for which he was

charged $56 ("Meteorological Instruments [Sent]," Smithsonian Institution Archives, Washington, D.C.). Ray joined the American Association for the Advancement of Science at the New Haven meeting in August 1850, and hence received one of Spencer Baird's circulars in early 1853, on which he described himself as "Professor of Mathematics, Natural Philosophy, and Astronomy, and Principal, Cincinnati Woodward City High School. Joseph Ray is the author of Ray's Arithmetics Parts 1st, 2nd, and 3d and Ray's Algebra Parts 1 and 2d embracing Elementary and Higher Algebra—These are among the most popular school books in the United States. The Cincinnati Woodward School ranks with the Philadelphia High School and New York Free Academy. The salaries of the Principal and Professors are higher than of any College or University in Ohio" (Circular, Smithsonian Institution Archives, reprinted in Henry D. Shapiro and Hamilton Cravens, eds. *The Smithsonian Circulars: A Guide to the American Scientific Community in the Nineteenth Century* [Westport, Conn.: Greenwood Press, forthcoming]). The popularity of Ray's *Arithmetics* is attested by their availability in secondhand book stores. They are no duller than Professor McGuffey's *Readers*.

20. I have been unable to identify any other "professionals" among the members of the Western Academy at this time, except perhaps John Gould Anthony, who later became a curator of conchology at Harvard's Museum of Comparative Zoology. During this time he supplemented his income by selling shells to collectors, and following a scarlet fever attack that resulted in partial blindness for a while, depended on these sales as the sole source of income. On Anthony, see Ruth D. Tucker, "John Gould Anthony, With a Bibliography and Catalogue of His Species," Museum of Comparative Zoology, *Occasional Papers on Mollusks* 1, no. 8 (July 20, 1946): 81-97; Anthony to E. R. Mayo, 15 January 1850, J. G. Anthony Papers, Harvard University Archives, Cambridge, Mass. Anthony was in almost constant attendance at the meetings of the Academy, but then I do not regard him as a "professional" during this period; neither did he, I suspect, which was a cause of some bitterness on his part.

21. I have not completed my occupational analysis of the membership of the Academy. It does not seem to be a particularly useful matter to pursue, however, since most of them appear to have done a variety of different things at different times.

22. I am indebted to my good friend and former colleague, Hamilton Cravens, of the Iowa State University, for calling my attention to the crucial role generational conflict plays in the emergence of scientific disciplines and in the process of professionalization.

23. Minutes, 1835.

24. Minutes, 1 November 1835; 9 January 1836; 2 and 16 February 1836.

25. Minutes, 9 December 1837.

26. Minutes, 31 March 1838; 7 and 14 April, 1838. So far as I have been able to ascertain, it was never published, however. I discovered what appears to be the original map on the reverse side of John A. Warder to Milo G. Williams, n.d., J. A. Warder Papers, Cincinnati Historical Society Library. Warder had used the back of the map to leave a note for Williams, asking him to come in and look at the specimens and saying he would return soon.

27. Constitution, art. III, in Minutes, following entry for 30 April 1838.

28. Even at a time when the mechanism for the establishment of scientific priority was not well defined, Anthony appears to have been more than casual about establishing priority for his own "discoveries," often sending out specimens to his conchological correspondents before publishing descriptions of them, and sometimes, as in the case of *Calymene bucklandii,* never publishing descriptions at all. After 1840, however, perhaps because of earlier experiences of losing credit for species he had isolated, he did begin publishing the papers he presented before the Academy—e.g., the paper concerning the circumstances under which he first described *Anculotus kirtlandianus Anthony,* and his subsequent conclusion that it was identical with *Melania dilatata* and *Melania rogersii Conrad* and *M. inflata Say,* and hence should be designated *Melania rogersii Conrad* (Minutes, 16 February 1841), is in *Proceedings of the Boston Society of Natural History* 1 (1841). The original description of *Calymene bucklandii Anthony* is in the J. G. Anthony Papers, Harvard University Archives.

29. In this connection, cf. the shifting arrangement of disciplines apparent in the tables of contents of the several volumes of the *Transactions of the American Association for the Advancement of Science* during this period, or Roswell Park, "Address on the Classification

of Human Knowledge," *Transactions of the Western Literary Institute 1840* (Cincinnati, 1841), pp. 151-68.

30. John P. Foote, "Formation, Constitution, etc. of the Cincinnati Society for the Promotion of Useful Knowledge," *Transactions of the Western Literary Institute 1840,* pp. 243-50.

31. The Western Literary Institute and College of Professional Teachers, organized in 1830, met annually in Cincinnati to discuss general topics in education and in the improvement of literary culture in the West. See its *Transactions* and Daniel Drake, *Remarks on the Importance of Promoting Literary and Social Concert in the Valley of the Mississippi* (Louisville, Ky.: Louisville Herald Printing Co., 1833); reprinted in Shapiro and Miller, *Physician to the West,* pp. 223–25.

32. Foote, "Formation, Constitution," p. 245; Minutes, 15 June 1840. Volume 2 of the Minutes begins with a record of the organization and activities of the Section of Natural Science. There are no extant minutes for the Western Academy during this period of overlap prior to the union.

33. Minutes, 15 and 18 June 1840.

34. Minutes, 16, 24, and 30 December 1840; 5 and 12 January 1841. So far as I have been able to ascertain, no "ladies of scientific taste" were ever elected, although the Academy did receive a communication from Margaretta Hale Morris of Germantown, Pennsylvania, and some pamphlets she had written concerning the Hessian fly, *Cecydornia.* Her letter was ordered published (Minutes, 1 and 17 February 1842), but I have not found it. The only other ladies mentioned in the minutes are Mrs. Robert Buchanan, who attended the great Naturalists' Picnic of July 19, 1842, and Mrs. J. G. Anthony, who served pears as refreshments at the meeting of August 16, 1842.

35. The Society for the Promotion of Useful Knowledge existed at least until the spring of 1842. Except for Foote's account of its founding, I have found no other information on its organization, membership, activities, or even the date of its dissolution. It may still exist. Its only publication to my knowledge is J. P. Foote and J. A. Warder, *Abstract of the Proceedings of the Section of Natural History* (Cincinnati, 2 May 1842), Cincinnati Historical Society Library. The terms "natural history" and "natural science" were used interchangeably.

36. Minutes, 3 May 1841.

37. The Section of Natural Science met "on the social plan" throughout its existence as a disparate entity, and apparently at Anthony's house exclusively. Minutes, 1840.

38. Minutes, 2 and 15 November 1844.

39. Minutes, 13, 20, and 27 August 1849; 3 September 1849. The "Apollo Building" is described in Cist, *Cincinnati in 1851,* p. 161, as containing "Wood's Museum" on its second floor. Which Wood is not clear, however.

40. Minutes, 14 January 1850.

41. Minutes, 3 March 1851.

42. Minutes, 17 and 24 November 1851; 8 December 1851.

43. Hendrickson, "The Western Academy of Natural Sciences of Cincinnati," summarizes the extant information about the last days of the Academy and the transfer of its property to the Natural History Society, based on an account in *Cincinnati Society of Natural History Journal* 1 (1878): 5. Hendrickson regards the Academy as a failure from the start, it seems, and apparently because of the foolishness of trying to do real science in a burg like Cincinnati. I think there is more to be said, even about the last days of the Academy.

44. Minutes, vol. 4 contains treasurer's reports for 1860, 1865-1867, and 1871.

45. Minutes, 5 January and 2 March 1841; 4 January, 1 February, October 1842.

46. Ibid., J. G. Anthony, *List of Land and Freshwater Shells Found Chiefly in the Vicinity of Cincinnati,* n.p., n.d. (1839?), and idem, *Catalogue of Terrestrial and Fluvatile Shells of Ohio* (Cincinnati, 1 January 1843), "2nd edition," Cincinnati Historical Society Library. The first list contains 163 species; the second 171 species and synonyms.

47. Foote and Warder, *Abstract of Proceedings.*

48. Minutes, 12 and 19 April 1842. Williams was originally a corresponding member from Dayton.

49. These were, of course, central issues, especially in the absence of any knowledge of

the existence of glacial action in North America, for, upon the identification of the relationship of fossils to strata, Lyell and others sought to develop their history of the earth. By 1851 the unnamed author of the article "Geology" in Cist, *Cincinnati in 1851,* could state as simple fact that "our blue limestone at Cincinnati is . . . very different in its character from the Silurian Formation of England, being infinitely more abundant in fossils, most of which are of a different species." It was not so simple a fact when Lyell first examined the collecting sites in the vicinity of Cincinnati, however. At a meeting of the Academy on May 24, 1842, for example, "Mr. Lyell expressed the regret that we had not commenced the study of the older secondary rocks here instead of the partial formations in Europe" (Minutes, 24 May 1842). On the persistence of such problems, cf. F. B. Meek, "Descriptions of Invertebrate Fossils of the Silurian and Devonian Systems," in J. S. Newberry, *Report of the Geological Survey of Ohio,* vol. 1, *Palaeontology* (Columbus: Nevins and Meyers, State Printers, 1873), which acknowledges the assistance of many former members of the Western Academy, including U. P. James, David H. Shafer, and Samuel T. Carley.

50. Minutes, 7 June 1842; 19 July 1842.

51. Lyell, *Travels in North America,* 2:61.

52. J. A. Warder, who succeeded Anthony as secretary in 1841, did not enter the minutes of meetings after March 3, 1845, however, according to a note by Jacob Resor (a later secretary of the Academy), dated 24 May 1847 (*Minutes,* following 3 March 1845). H. C. Grosvenor took over as secretary in 1846.

53. We scarcely do our duty as historians when we persistently overlook the impact of the business cycle on the process of science during the nineteenth century and insist on talking of "development" as a process of uniform and unidirectional growth. When all but a very few were "amateurs" whose primary activity was outside of science, financial depression meant less money for more work, or less time and less money available for the *private* pursuit of science; and among amateurs this private pursuit of science almost always came first, before their participation in public or semipublic activities. We are aware of the consequences of economic depression on the availability of funds for public institutions like the Museum of Comparative Zoology or the Smithsonian. We must also be aware that the same effects appeared earlier among private persons.

54. Minutes, January-March 1845; see also note 49, above.

55. Minutes, 3 and 10 October 1846.

56. Minutes, 31 August 1846; printed in *Cincinnati Daily Gazette,* 5 September 1846, as a simple list without this commentary.

57. Minutes, 30 November 1846.

58. Minutes, 10 July 1848.

59. Minutes, 10 April 1854.

60. The date of Anthony's illness is not certain, but a correct chronology would help us understand the circumstances surrounding the preparation of the Academy's catalog. A biographical sketch prepared by Anthony's granddaughter, Miss Fanny Garrison, "John Gould Anthony, 1804-1877," typescript, J. G. Anthony Papers, Harvard University Archives, states on the basis of family tradition that he caught scarlet fever from his younger daughter Annie (Miss Garrison's mother) "in 1847 or 1848." Ruth Tucker, "John Gould Anthony," states, based probably upon the same memoir, that the illness was in 1847. Anthony was absent from five consecutive weekly meetings of the Academy in January-February 1847, four consecutive weekly meetings in December-January 1847-1848, six consecutive weekly meetings in March 1848, and seven consecutive weekly meetings in October-December 1848. In May and June 1848, however, Anthony was one of those charged with selecting a suite of fossils from the Academy's cabinets for donation to Mr. Talbot's school (Minutes, 15 May, 26 June 1848), an activity that would probably have not been possible for him during the early stages of his post-illness partial blindness, if this was as severe as seems to have been the case. Moreover Anthony's complaint (see p. 241) to the effect that the conchological catalog was prepared behind his back may be a response to the fact that this work was done during a period when his colleagues knew him to be home with scarlet fever. And if his colleagues did in fact prepare the catalog behind his back, what better time than when they knew him to be secluded at home.

61. Minutes, 23 October 1848.

62. Anthony to E. R. Mayo, 15 January 1850?, J. G. Anthony Papers, Harvard University Archives. The catalog was published as *Catalogue of the Unios, Alasmodantas, and Anodontas of the Ohio River and Its Northern Tributaries. Adopted by the Western Academy of Natural Sciences of Cincinnati* (Cincinnati: J. A. & U. P. James, January 1849), Cincinnati Historical Society Library. Anthony's catalog was not limited to these three genera. For these three, however, Anthony included 64 species and 130 synonyms, the Academy's catalog 64 species and 130 synonyms. The Academy's catalog was to be distributed free to members and correspondents, and sold at $.05 per copy to the public at the Jameses' bookstore. Minutes, 14 and 22 January, 12 February 1849.

63. Minutes, 24 March, 3 May 1851.

The Nature
of Humanistic Societies
in Early America

MARCUS A. McCORISON

What was the nature of early, noncollegiate, humanistic enterprises within the United States? What was their place of beginning—intellectually, chronologically, and circumstantially? Were they concerned with science?

In examining these questions, it may be helpful first to take note of what it meant to be a learned man in eighteenth-century America. In terms of Lockean principles, the educated American was to be virtuous in order to conduct a good life based upon Christian principles, to be wise in the management of his affairs, to be well bred and courteous toward his own person and to others, and to be learned, with an ample store of useful and entertaining knowledge. These four principles, clearly utilitarian in their intent, were a vulgarization of Bacon's concept of a learned man. Bacon's man was to know the "causes, and secret motion of things and [was to enlarge] the bounds of human empire, to the effecting of all things possible."[1] The scholar pursued this knowledge for the benefit of mankind with compassion and humility, honoring God by studying His works. Men of learning, in a Baconian Utopia would rule the new land through their intellectual and ethical capacities, and each would reach this Platonic goal through the merit of his striving, rather than by his birth or the size of his worldly possessions.

Carrying these Baconian goals into practice, the curriculum at Harvard College, for example, was designed thus:

Grammar Rhetoric Logic	to discipline the mind
Mathematics Astronomy	to understand the universe
Philosophy: Moral Mental Natural	to understand man and his world
Theology Belles Lettres	to appreciate man's expression of all of the above

Prepared for a fruitful life of the mind and spirit, students went forth to minister to mankind or to become men of affairs themselves. In addition, some became

[1] Notes to this chapter begin on page 260.

amateurs of literature, of civil history, or of natural history. It was these individuals and their colleagues, not trained at college, who joined together, following the English pattern, in convivial literary and philosophical debating clubs.

It was just such a society that Benjamin Franklin organized in Philadelphia in 1727. Finding his confrères among the craftsmen of the city, Franklin formed the Junto, a "club of mutual improvement," which he termed the "best school of philosophy, morals and politics that existed in the province."[2] The members included Franklin and Hugh Meredith, printers; Joseph Breintnall, a scrivener with a poetical bent; Thomas Godfrey, a glazier and a mathematician who invented a mariner's quadrant; William Parsons, a cobbler who became a map maker and surveyor; William Mangridge, a jointer; and William Coleman, a clerk. The only exception from toil was Robert Grace, in whose house in Pewter Platter Alley the Junto met each Friday evening. There, a paper on matters of morals, politics, literature, or natural philosophy was read and discussed over a glass of wine.

Within a short time, the members of the Junto brought together their books in a common library. As Franklin explains in his autobiography, the reasons for this were eminently practical. First, the members of the Junto often referred to books in their discussions, so "it might be convenient to us to have them all together where we met." In addition, "by thus clubbing our Books to a common Library, we should, while we lik'd to keep them together, have each of us the Advantage of using the books of all the other Members, which would be nearly as beneficial as if each owned the whole."[3] However, this scheme soon collapsed and the books were retrieved by their various owners.

Still, Franklin was not deterred, and in November 1731 he organized the Library Company of Philadelphia. With the aid of his friends in the Junto, he gathered fifty men, "mostly young tradesmen," each man contributing forty shillings at the outset for the purchase of a collection of books. In addition, each member of the library agreed to pay ten shillings a year so that more books might be obtained. Those who subscribed could borrow books from the library, which was open for one hour on Wednesday and six hours on Saturday, "on their promissory notes to pay Double the Value if [the books were] not duly returned."[4] The Company received a charter and land from the proprietors of Pennsylvania in 1742, and thus came into being the earliest, formal, noncollegiate institution in America to encourage humane learning. Franklin's library was also a "public" institution in that it served not only its subscribers, who could borrow volumes, but also the "civil gentlemen" of Philadelphia, who were allowed to read books during those times when the library was open.[5]

There was, in fact, one nonmember, James Logan, who was permitted to borrow books from the Library Company. Logan embodied the learned man of the colonial period, and he assisted the Company in drawing up the first list of books that the Library Company purchased in 1732. Those books provide a clear indication of what informed men believed was important for the training of their intellect. The first catalog listed books by Puffendorf, Rapin, Salmon, Vertot, and Plutarch in history and Palladio and Evelyn in architecture. Tacitus, Homer, Socrates, Cato, and Dryden's edition of Virgil were present in translation; Euclid, books on conic sections, fluxions (calculus), and Oznam in five volumes were in the mathematics section. Keil and Drake were represented on medical matters, Sidney on government, and the gentlemen of Port Royal as well as Crousay on moral and mental philosophy. Gravessand and Boerhaave were the principal figures in natural philosophy and chemistry, with a large assist from the five volume abridgment of the *Philosophical Transactions* of the Royal Society. Addison and Steele, and that old chestnut *The Turkish Spy,* were part of the holdings in literature.[6] This list is repeated in virtually every eighteenth-century American library catalog and represents a settled opinion on useful works for "public" libraries.

In addition to gathering books, the Library Company also came to serve as a museum of sorts.[7] Since some who desired membership had difficulty raising the money to join, they paid for the privilege in kind, presenting such items as stuffed snakes, an old sword that had been dug up on a farm, Indian robes made of skins, and fossils. The Library's historian, Austin Gray, reports that "these payments in kind were displayed in the Library. They were officially known as 'the Curiosities' and it was one of the Librarian's duties to show visiting scholars round 'the Curiosities.' " The Library's collection of artifacts was increased by such items as an air pump donated by John Penn in 1739 and various mechanical devices sent by Peter Collinson of London. When the Library moved to its third home in 1773—two rented rooms in Carpenter's Hall—one of the rooms contained the books, while the other was reserved for the air pump. A telescope and microscope were also acquired soon after, and they, too, were kept in this room, on whose walls were hung "the most impressive of 'the Curiosities.' "[8]

Libraries of various types were established in other states as well. The founding of the Redwood Library Company in Newport, Rhode Island, can be compared with that of the Library Company of Philadelphia. The Redwood Library owes its existence to a debating society—the Literary and Philosophical Society, which came into being in 1730, not long after Bishop George Berkeley arrived in Newport from London. Although the members of Franklin's Junto were of Philadelphia's "leather apron" crowd, the Bishop's colleagues were of much more exalted origins, coming from the leading and most powerful families of the colony. These young men used experiences gained in the Literary and Philosophical Society to develop interests which in 1747 led to the establishment of the Redwood Library Company. Abraham Redwood, a wealthy native of Antiqua, offered the sum of £500 for "purchasing a library of all arts and sciences, whereunto the curious and impatient inquirer, after resolution of doubts, and the bewildered ignorant might freely repair for discovery and demonstration to the one, and true knowledge and satisfaction to the other."[9]

The now matured debaters responded to the opportunity with haste. They raised the money to construct a handsome Doric library building which was designed by Peter Harrison. The Company made up a list of books to be purchased in London, and by March 1750 the volumes were cataloged and shelved in their beautiful building.

The proprietors spent Redwood's entire £500 for 750 titles in 1340 volumes. The correlation between the Philadelphia and Newport lists, allowing for the discrepancy of size (the 1741 catalog of the Philadelphia collection listed but 375 titles), is remarkable. The Redwood library collection included works by every author represented in the Library Company collection and in greater profusion. Not only were the classical authors present in translation as at Philadelphia, but their works, in the original languages, were on the Newport shelves as well. The section of books on civil history was much larger and included a number of histories of modern nations.

The collection relating to science or technology included John Harris's *Lexicon Technicum, or an universal English dictionary of arts and sciences* (London, 1708-1710), 2 volumes, folio; Gerard's *Herbal,* enlarged by Thomas Johnson (London, 1633) folio; *A New Survey of the Globe,* by Templeman and with maps by Herman Moll (London, 1729); Colin MacLaurin's *Account of Sir Isaac Newton's Philosophical Discoveries* (London, 1748); *Physicae Experimentales et Geometricae de Magnete* (Leyden, 1729), the *Philosophical Transactions and Collections of the Royal Society* through 1733, and Sprat's *History of the Royal Society* (London, 1734); Bacon's *Philosophical Works* abridged by Shaw (London, 1733) 3 volumes; *The Philosophical Works* of Robert Boyle, edited by Shaw (London, 1725), 3 volumes; works on optics, hydraulics; Whiston on astronomy; translations of Newton's *Mathematical Principles*—and many more—were also present in the Newport Library, ready to enlighten the "bewildered ignorant."[10]

The line of descent from the debating societies to the subscription libraries to the early learned societies appears to be quite direct and not a particularly difficult intellectual leap. When John Bartram proposed the establishment of a general scientific society to the London merchant, Peter Collinson, in 1739, Collinson replied: "Your Library Company, I take to be an essay towards such a society."[11] The Library Company of Philadelphia was, in fact, the spawning ground for the American Philosophical Society, which in turn formed a historical committee, which, in its turn, in 1824 became the Historical Society of Pennsylvania. In 1791 the Massachusetts Historical Society came forth through an association of members from the American Academy of Arts and Sciences.

The early organizations, such as the American Philosophical Society and the American Academy of Arts and Sciences, were broadly oriented in their intellectual interests. Within a generation of their own life, as the quest for knowledge sharpened or grew more specialized, technical or scientific subgroups were established. Historical societies came next, followed by those devoted to other humanistic disciplines. It is nowhere explicitly stated why learned societies, separate from a collegiate situation, were established. Their intellectual bulwarks were shored against college foundations, yet a substantial portion of memberships were not directly associated with academic institutions. Some members had not obtained even a formal, grammar school education. Thus, we may assume that the laymen and the academics joined forces for similar but not necessarily identical felt needs. The laymen, who were truly interested in intellectual matters and who often were the promulgators of these early learned societies, were eager to engage their talents in matters of the mind and to find the means of associating with other like individuals, in or out of the learned professions. No doubt, that desire operated at more than one level and may well have included social aspirations. At the same time, the academics, including many of the clergymen, looked for means of stimulating their learned interests. Then as now, the training of the young may have been a trial and not always intellectually rewarding for the professor of knowledge. The learned society gave the academic the opportunity to associate with adults having similar interests but varying backgrounds. Further, the society made available a means of publication, either orally or in print. Beyond these amenities, learned societies undertook the collection of specimens, artifacts, and books, and did so in different areas of knowledge and with more vigor than did the colleges. Finally, and perhaps most importantly, the early learned societies were humanistically oriented. They sought unity between natural knowledge, human knowledge, and divine knowledge. Their members were interested in expanding that knowledge rather than in passing on to the next generation that which was already known.

The history of the American Antiquarian Society illustrates the nature and function of the noncollegiate humanistic organization in the nineteenth century. The American Antiquarian Society was the third historical society established in the United States, following the Massachusetts Historical Society (1791) and the New-York Historical Society (1804). The goal of Isaiah Thomas and the other founders was to fulfill a broader national purpose and to obtain a membership drawn from a wider area than their Boston and New York counterparts. Thomas was a self-educated printer and publisher who had energetically collected the manuscripts, books, pamphlets, broadsides, and newspapers which served as the sources for his *History of Printing in America* (1810). By 1812, when the Society was established, his Worcester press had earned him a sizable fortune, and he was regarded as one of the principal printer-publishers in America. Since the Society was in effect "the creature of Thomas' fortune," Worcester was the clear choice for its location. However, other rationalizations for the selection of this site were also put forth at the time of the Society's founding in the midst of the War of 1812:

For the better preservation from the destruction so often experienced in large towns and cities by fire, as well as from the ravages of the enemy, to which seaports in particular are so much exposed in time of war, it is universally agreed that . . . an inland situation is to be preferred; this consideration alone was judged sufficient for placing the Library and Museum of the Society forty miles distant from the nearest branch of the sea, in the town of Worcester, Massachusetts.[12]

Thomas added his own justification for the Worcester location: "Any to whom the Library and Cabinet of this Society may be useful, will not greatly regret the distance which separates them from the objects of their pursuit, if they can but eventually obtain in one place, what, otherwise, they would have to seek in many."[13]

In the petition for the establishment of the American Antiquarian Society presented to the General Court of Massachusetts (the petitioners did not believe that Congress had the authority to grant charters to "publick societies without the District of Columbia"), Thomas wrote that the founders were

influenced by a desire to contribute to the advancement of the Arts and Sciences, and to aid, by their individual and united efforts, in the collecting and preserving of such materials as may be useful in marking their progress, not only in the United States, but in other parts of the globe, and wishing also to assist the researches of the future historians of our country. . . . The rapid progress of science, and of the useful and ornamental arts, in our country, may be ascribed in a great degree to the numerous publick institutions originated by patriotick individuals, but deriving their countenance and support from legislative authority. . . . [Our] immediate and peculiar design is, to discover the antiquities of our own continent; and, by providing a fixed and permanent place of deposit, to preserve such relicks of American antiquity as are portable, as well as to collect and preserve those of other parts of the globe.[14]

They were gratified in their desires by the granting of a charter dated October 24, 1812.

The original petitioners were men from Worcester. Having no evidence to the contrary, we must assume that they joined with Thomas in the belief that a society whose purpose was to document the natural, civil, and literary history of the continent would be a worthwhile undertaking. They were a mixed lot of businessmen, academics, clergymen, politicians, and amateur historians. Nathaniel and William Paine were former loyalists and successful merchants. Levi Lincoln was a lawyer, politician, and Jefferson's first Attorney General. Aaron Bancroft was one of the fathers of American Unitarianism and the father of the historian, George Bancroft. In the act of incorporation they were joined by John T. Kirkland, the president of Harvard College; Josiah Quincy, later another president of Harvard and Mayor of Boston; John Lowell, the Federalist pamphleteer; William Dandridge Peck, professor of natural history at Harvard; William Smith Shaw, librarian of the Boston Athenaeum; Thaddeus Mason Harris, a Unitarian clergyman of Dorchester, an antiquary, and a member of the council of the Massachusetts Historical Society; Elijah Hunt Mills, United States Senator from Northampton, Massachusetts; Edward Dwight of Springfield, Massachusetts, the wealthy manufacturer, merchant, and founder of the Western Rail Road; Thomas Walcutt, an oil merchant of Boston, a portion of whose enormous collection of early American pamphlets and books came to the AAS

in 1834; and Benjamin Russell, the publisher of the Boston *Columbian Centinel.*
This sampling demonstrates the kind of men and interests typical of other,
similar societies.

Thus, the American Antiquarian Society began as a learned, historical society
that proposed to collect and preserve the natural, artificial, and literary antiquities of our country, because the founders believed that "curious and valuable
productions of art and nature have a tendency to enlarge the sphere of human
knowledge, to aid the progress of science, to perpetuate the history of moral and
political events, and to improve and interest posterity."[15] Throughout the
nineteenth century, the work of the AAS was concentrated in three areas
outlined by the Reverend William Jenks at the first anniversary meeting of the
Society in 1813:

The ancient Indian nations of our continent demand our first attention. Here an
extensive field of enquiry opens at once. . . . To collect complete vocabularies of
the Indian tongues, to ascertain the boundaries of their ancient governments,
and the progress they made in the few arts, which were practised among them;
to obtain a knowledge of their numbers and circumstances at the various epochs
of their progress or declension, are objects of laudable curiosity. . . .

A second general subject of enquiry is *the Western Mounds of Earth.* These
may in fact be considered as belonging to the preceding division. But as they are
the only striking evidence we have of ancient population, and the progress of
arts in remote times, they demand a distinct notice. . . .

A third branch of enquiry offers itself in *the early European Settlements.* To
ascertain by whom, at what time, and for what purpose settlements were made,
and how long, if now deserted, they were held; or their subsequent progress, if
retained, belongs, in all its branches of Spanish, French, English, Dutch, Por-
tuguese, Danish and Swedish population, to the history and antiquities of our
Continent; as do also the fossil remains of animated nature, or primitive art.[16]

To carry out its program, the AAS looked to a membership that consisted of
professional scholars, amateur scholars, and nonscholars, with each group reinforcing the work and interests of the other. Before the year 1851 the total
number of persons elected to membership was approximately 490 (excluding
foreign residents—perhaps three dozen from Europe, Canada, and Central or
South America). Of that figure, 242, or 54 percent, were listed in the *Dictionary
of American Biography.* A rough division of that number, classified by professional interests, follows:

Politicians		
Presidents of U.S. or candidates	8	
U.S. Senators and Representatives	30	51
Governors	13	
Academics		
College presidents	20	
Teachers of humanities	8	35
Teachers of medicine or science	7	

Lawyers or Jurists	17	33
Amateurs or authors of history	16	
Clergymen	4	25
Amateurs or authors of history	21	
Signers of the Declaration or		
Revolutionary War patriots		21
Businessmen	12	17
Amateurs or authors of history	5	
Physicians	2	
Amateurs or authors of history		17
or natural sciences	15	
Authors and journalists		11
Naturalists and explorers		11
Historians		9
Ethnologists		5
Mechanical Engineers or inventors		4
Physical scientists		3
		242

From these numbers, it would appear that nearly 30 percent of the group were to some degree intellectually involved with the work of the Society, while the majority were on the rolls as persons useful as leaders in the financial and business affairs of the Society. Yet all had been elected to membership by their colleagues because they had exhibited some serious interest in historical matters. De Witt Clinton, a vice-president of the Society for several years, surely was a member of AAS because of his abiding interest in and knowledge of historical matters, rather than because of his political office. In turn, his involvement in learned societies such as the AAS was due to the fact that in the early nineteenth century these were the chief places where the encouragement and publication of scholarship occurred.

Of those listed in the DAB, 113 were engaged in research and writing—62 of them in humanistic studies and 51 in the natural sciences. We should bear in mind that nearly all of the practicing scholars and lay members were chiefly interested in man's hand upon the land and that this interest centered upon the study of the American Indian. I have classed only 45 of the 113 members as being fully occupied with the increase and dissemination of knowledge; they include Caleb Atwater, Loammi Baldwin, George Bancroft, Benjamin Smith Barton, Neville B. Craig, Daniel Drake, Peter Stephen DuPonceau, John Farmer, John Farrar, Albert Gallatin, George Gibbs, Josiah Willard Gibbs, Sr., Ferdinand Rudolph Hassler, Samuel Foster Haven, Benjamin Hawkins, Samuel P. Hildreth, Abiel Holmes, David Hosack, Washington Irving, Thomas Jefferson, Benjamin Henry Latrobe, William Lincoln, William Maclure, Samuel Latham Mitchill, Jacob Bailey Moore, Jedediah Morse and his son Samuel F. B. Morse, Samuel G. Morton, Eliphalet Nott, Francis Parkman, John Pickering, William H. Prescott, C. S. Rafinesque, David Ramsay, Obadiah Rich, Henry Rowe Schoolcraft,

Nathaniel Shurtleff, Benjamin Silliman, Jared Sparks, William B. Sprague, Francis Adrian van der Kemp, Benjamin Vaughan, Elkanah Watson, Sidney Willard, Hugh Williamson, Andrew Wylie, and Alexander Young. The remaining sixty-eight were, however, closely engaged in intellectual activities.[17]

The members of the Society came from twenty-four of the then thirty-one states of the Union. Not surprisingly, the largest number came from Massachusetts (204), followed by New York (48), Pennsylvania (36), Ohio (29), Rhode Island (27), New Hampshire (25), Maine (16), Connecticut (13), District of Columbia and New Jersey (10), Kentucky, Maryland, and Tennessee (9), Louisiana and Virginia (7), South Carolina (5), Mississippi (4), North Carolina (3), Georgia and Vermont (2), Arkansas, Delaware, Michigan, and Missouri (1).

It seems clear that the management of AAS made a sincere effort to get outside the boundaries of New England in order to facilitate the collecting of historical materials and to obtain a truly national representation among the membership. There was, as there is now, a considerable overlapping of memberships in the American Antiquarian Society, American Academy of Arts and Sciences, American Philosophical Society, Massachusetts Historical Society, and the New-York Historical Society. Beyond that, I am not entirely sure how much intellectual interaction through personal interchange occurred between members drawn from Boston or Worcester and New York or Philadelphia. Probably attendance at meetings was not very large, lively, or even terribly profitable except as proof of one's endurance. Certainly, the papers delivered at AAS tended to be hortative, designed to expose the orator's extensive knowledge of classical literature and history, rather than to be enlightening or instructive for the listener.

The real work of the Society lay in its collections and publications. They tell much of the intention of the institution and have been the determining and vital factors in its work. The collections at the AAS have served as a fundamental source for research into the nation's culture for both staff and readers. Its holdings, by their very existence, have made inquiry possible or in some cases have even formulated the inquiry, while its publications have spread knowledge of these inquiries.

The direction of collecting at AAS has been and remains bibliographical. In 1813 Isaiah Thomas established the tradition by the gift of his library of several thousand volumes valued at $5,000; immediately afterwards, he bought the library of the Mather family and presented it to the Society.

His regime as president, librarian, mower of grass, and financier lasted until his death in 1831. Thomas also set the pattern of financial and intellectual support of the Society. He not only gave his library to the AAS in 1820; he built the Society's first building, and at his death he bequeathed his fortune to the Society.

Thomas was followed as principal administrator of the AAS by Christopher Columbus Baldwin, a single-minded bibliomaniac. Two passages by Baldwin show the cast of his thinking. The first is from a letter concerning a friend who is to be married: after examining the genealogy of the bride's family and finding no fault in it, he writes, "[Mr. Stephen Salisbury] should do nothing that may diminish his affections with venerable books. You know we cannot serve two masters, much less two mistresses; and my mistress is my profession, for which I have the most solid affection."[18] The second quotation is from his description of the library of the New-York Historical Society written in 1833: "There are very few objects of curiosity or antiquity in the collection. This is correct taste. A library should contain nothing but books, coins, statuary, and pictures. I admit now and then that an antiquity should be admitted. But how absurd to pile up old bureaus and chests, and stuff them with old coats and hats and high-heeled shoes! The true history of all these things are handed down by paintings. And besides, if they are once received, there will be attempts making to gull somebody with the 'Shield of Achilles' or 'Mambrino's helmet.' I have discouraged sending them to the Antiquarian Hall for this reason."[19]

Although the AAS did not look for natural curiosities, it did collect artificial and literary antiquities. The most famous artificial example was the mummified Indian maiden found in a remarkable state of preservation in a Kentucky cave. It was forwarded to the Society by member Charles Wilkins, through the good offices of Nahum Ward. Because of public exhibitions by which he made traveling money, Ward spent some time getting to Worcester with his musty charge. This caused no satisfaction to the council of the Society, nor to the maiden, who arrived in 1816 somewhat worse for wear. She ended her career some years later at the Smithsonian Institution. Mr. Wilkins was but one of several receiving agents of the AAS whose self-imposed duties were to seek out and send to the Society notable examples of American antiquities. Another such agent was William Jenks of Bath, Maine, who in 1817 sent a French ax head and an Indian stone sinker for a fish net.

The fate of the Society's collection of natural and artificial antiquities is described by C. K. Shipton in an amusing book, *A Cabinet of Curiosities*.[20] The volume contains articles on the museums of the APS, AAS, William Clark's Indian Museum in St. Louis, the Western Museum in Cincinnati, and others. In all these places, the comingling of functions did little to advance knowledge; to fully exploit the resources of an institution, it was necessary to apply oneself single-mindedly—as C. C. Baldwin correctly observed in 1833—to the function one could do best. Thus, in 1910, when the AAS moved into its third building, almost all of its natural and artificial wonders were distributed to those who would take them. Henceforth, the AAS has devoted itself to the literary antiquities of America.

Fortunately, the collecting of books, and to a lesser extent manuscripts, had not slackened since the gift of the Founder in 1813. In 1820 AAS received the bequest of the late Reverend Mr. William Bentley of Salem, consisting of his American and German books, as well as his pictures, manuscripts, and cabinet. It was a great gift and still a jewel in the Society's crown. Moreover, the bequest so annoyed those proud Salemites that they established their own historical society, the Essex Institute. Silliman and Rafinesque in 1827 also presented gifts of publications, a practice the present administration of AAS encourages among members. During the summer of 1834 C.C. Baldwin broiled himself in the attic of Thomas Walcutt's office gathering up two tons of early American pamphlets and books. Thus, in 1837, when the Society published C.C. Baldwin's catalog of the books in the library, the volume was made up of 284 pages, listing 9,500 titles.

Baldwin died before his catalog was published. In August of 1835 he went to Ohio to investigate the Indian mounds there. Near Zanesville the coach in which he was riding overturned, killing him. Baldwin's death was a calamity for he was an enormously talented book collector, and the Society was deprived of that talent at a time when practically no other institution was active in the field of collecting Americana.

On the other hand, Baldwin's successor made contributions to the Society's work that the collector could not have done. Samuel Foster Haven was appointed librarian in 1838 and served until his death in 1881. He was a man of learning and an excellent editor. He guided the Society into a period of intense archaeological work, which culminated in pioneering efforts in Central America in the 1870s and 1880s. In 1856 Haven concluded the earlier phase of the Society's archaeological interests by publishing his *Archaeology of the United States,* volume 8 in the Smithsonian Institution's series *Contributions to Knowledge.*[21] In the book he summarized all of the work published by AAS since 1820 that dealt with Indian culture in North America. Haven continued the bibliographical interests of the Society and prepared texts on colonial Massachusetts history. He was active in the professionalization of librarianship, taking part in the formation of the American Library Association in 1876.

Following Haven's death and with the increasing specialization of anthropological knowledge, the Society retired from the archaeological field. Here again it should be noted that encouragement of humanistic learning during the nineteenth century was a private matter and that government at any level took little or no interest in it. It was the independent learned society that played the crucial role by providing a focus and, through its publications, a forum for the pursuit of humanistic knowledge.

Throughout the first half of the nineteenth century, the publications of the Society had an undeniable ethnological bent to them, and it was not until 1850 that anything was published by the AAS that concerned the white man's presence in America. The first volume of *Transactions* of the Society was issued in 1820 under the title *Archaeologia Americana.* Its major article was Caleb Atwater's "Description of the Antiquities discovered in the State of Ohio and other Western States." As the council of the AAS noted in a 1850 review of the Society's activities, "this work goes far towards putting to rest the supposition that this region was once inhabited by a race of civilized men. Nothing discovered by the writer, or by subsequent research, sustains this supposition."[22] To the same volume, Samuel Latham Mitchill contributed several short statements on the American Indian, including one on the poetry and songs of the Osage tribe and another on the Asiatic origins of American aborigines. Interestingly, he commented in print that he had not earnestly investigated the history of the native peoples of this continent until after his election to AAS. Other articles included Charles Wilkins's account of his Indian mummy and Moses Fisk's discussion of the Indian history of his district in Tennessee. John Farnham described the Mammoth Cave of Kentucky of which he was co-owner. Finally, William Sheldon, a member resident in Jamaica, inserted a brief account of the Caribs of the Antilles.

The second volume was published in 1838. Its chief contribution was Albert Gallatin's "Synopsis of the Indian Tribes of North America," which was followed by a communication from Don Juan Galindo describing the Mayan ruins at Copán in Honduras. De Witt Clinton's explication of the Celeron Plate also appeared in this volume, as did Daniel Gookin's "Historical Account of . . . the Christian Indians in New England," a document written in the seventeenth century.

The third volume in 1850 was edited by Samuel Haven and consisted of two lengthy and important documents on Massachusetts history: "The Records of the Company of Massachusetts Bay" and the diary of John Hull, mintmaster of the colony for the years 1646-1681. Again the council commented, "To the philosopher, or the antiquarian, it may be less attractive than its predecessors, but to the theologian, the statesman, and the advocate of free inquiry and free institutions, it is of the deepest interest in developing the germs of the great future in which we live."[23]

From the beginning, the purpose of the American Antiquarian Society has been to explore, examine, and explain the life of man in North America—how he was influenced and directed by the land and his fellow inhabitants as well as the impact he made upon his once new world. The intense investigations of the native peoples of America by so many nineteenth-century scholars is an interesting and indicative manifestation of religious and humane concerns. Examination of the antiquities of the continent, until so recently undisturbed, was thought to reveal the works of God, as well as provide new insights into the relationships of man and nature.

Although the other older humanistic learned societies no doubt entertained slightly different means to reach their goals, all worked to encourage learning in order to enable their members and the larger society to arrive at a better understanding of man's place in the world. The writer is hardly a dispassionate viewer of these activities, but it appears that a learned society in the mode of the American Antiquarian Society has provided (and continues to provide) a meeting place as well as services for the public weal which are rarely found in the twentieth century. In a small way, a good work is done to enrich our common experience upon earth.

NOTES

1. Francis Bacon, "New Atlantis," *Great Books of the Western World*, ed. Robert Maynard Hutchins (Chicago: Encyclopaedia Britannica, Inc., 1952), vol. 30, *Francis Bacon*, p. 210.

2. Benjamin Franklin, *The Writings of Benjamin Franklin*, ed. A. H. Smyth, 10 vols. (New York, 1905-1907), 1:298.

3. Leonard Labaree et al., eds., *The Autobiography of Benjamin Franklin* (New Haven: Yale University Press, Paperbound ed., 1964), p. 130.

4. Ibid., pp. 130, 142. See also Austin Gray, *Benjamin Franklin's Library . . . a Short Account of the Library Company of Philadelphia, 1731-1931* (New York: Macmillan Co., 1937), pp. 9-13.

5. Gray, *Benjamin Franklin's Library*, p. 13.

6. Library Company of Philadelphia, *A Catalogue of Books Belonging to the Library Company of Philadelphia, a facsimile of the edition of 1741* (Philadelphia: Library Company of Philadelphia, 1956).

7. A more extensive explanation of the museum function of the Library Company may be found in Gray, *Benjamin Franklin's Library*, pp. 16-21.

8. The microscope and telescope were actually used by members and could even be borrowed. See Ibid., p. 20.

9. Arthur S. Roberts, *Two Centuries of the Redwood Library and Athenaeum, 1747-1947* (Newport, R.I.: Redwood Library, 1948), p. 9.

10. The Redwood Library and Athenaeum, *The 1764 Catalogue of the Redwood Library Company at Newport, Rhode Island*, ed. M. A. McCorison (New Haven: Yale University Press, 1965).

11. Collinson to Bartram, 10 July 1739, in William Darlington, *Memorials of John Darlington and Humphrey Marshall* (Philadelphia, 1811), p. 132.

12. American Antiquarian Society, *A Society's Chief Joys* (Worcester, Mass.: American Antiquarian Society, 1969), p. 8.

13. Ibid.

14. Isaiah Thomas et al., "Petition to the Legislature of Massachusetts, October, 1812," *Proceedings of the American Antiquarian Society*, n.s. 78, pt. 2 (October 1968): 204-05.

15. Ibid., p. 206.

16. Address by Rev. William Jenks, Meeting of the American Antiquarian Society, October 23, 1813, *Proceedings of the AAS, 1812-1849* (Worcester, Mass.: American Antiquarian Society, 1912), pp. 33, 35, 36, 37.

17. Frederick L. Weiss, *A List of Officers and Members of the American Antiquarian Society, 1812-1947* (Worcester, Mass.: American Antiquarian Society, 1947).

18. C. C. Baldwin, "The True Antiquary," *News-Letter of the American Antiquarian Society*, no. 1 (January 1968), pp. 5-6.

19. C. C. Baldwin, *Diary* (Worcester, Mass., 1901), p. 224.

20. C. K. Shipton, "The American Antiquarian Society," in Whitfield Bell et al., *A Cabinet of Curiosities* (Charlottesville: University Press of Virginia, 1967).

21. Samuel F. Haven, *Archaeology of the United States* (Washington, D.C., 1856).

22. Report of the Council, 30 April 1851, *Proceedings of the AAS, 1851-1852* (Worcester, Mass.: Henry J. Howland, 1852), p. 8.

23. Ibid., p. 9.

Medicine
and the Learned Society in the United States, 1660-1850

JAMES H. CASSEDY

Throughout history, medicine has demonstrated, to one degree or another, a certain ambiguity in its relations to society and the world of learning. On the one hand, it has played out its role as a practical art or technique; on the other, it has coexisted as one of the fundamental areas of knowledge and inquiry. Although the physician has been in demand primarily as a practitioner of a necessary profession, he has also often enjoyed something of an image (not always deserved) as a learned man and seeker after new knowledge, medical and other. If medical societies have sprung up primarily as trade associations to organize and regulate the members of the profession, they have, in addition, frequently acted to sponsor the pursuit of knowledge.

This search for fundamental knowledge in the medical societies is a matter well worth greater attention than it has received. This essay can do little more than acknowledge the need for such research, while it moves past that topic to concentrate upon the physician's learned pursuits outside the medical societies, specifically in other types of learned and scientific organizations. The ambiguous role of medicine is well reflected in the profession's relations with the early learned societies—in the devotion of such societies to medical matters, in the participation of physicians in these societies, and in some of the general intellectual and scientific activities that appealed to the physicians in them.[1] The development of these relationships reveals much about the anatomy of eighteenth- and nineteenth-century American intellectual life and institutions.

As far back as the Tudor and Stuart eras, English physicians must sometimes have felt tensions between their professional and trade needs or identities and their scholarly propensities as learned men. This was particularly true of those physicians who were involved in the gradually developing impulse of the time— to question ancient authority and look for new knowledge in nature or experiment. In London, physicians were able, at least for a time, to find an outlet for both needs in a single professional body: the Royal College of Physicians. To advance the economic and professional interests of its fellows, the College carried on a running battle with the Society of Apothecaries, the Barber-Surgeons Company, and assorted quacks or imposters. At the same time, as

[1] Notes to this chapter begin on page 274.

Gillispie, Webster, and others have pointed out, by the 1650s the College had assumed a considerably broader role as a learned society. It had become, in the view of some contemporaries, a veritable Baconian "Solomon's House" of ongoing research. Partly for this reason, fellows of the College (and physicians generally) did not play a very large role in the founding and early activities of the Royal Society, though many became members of the newer body.[2]

Subsequently, however, with the rise of the Royal Society during the 1660s, together with the destruction of the College's library and museum in the great fire of London, the Royal College of Physicians quickly lost much of its importance as a general learned society. Since it did not again systematically build up its general scientific collections nor did it publish transactions of broadly scientific information, the College never served as the sort of clearing-house for colonial scientific (or even medical) communications that the Royal Society soon became. While the College never obtained the monopoly of English medical practice that it sought, it was apparently sufficiently successful in maintaining its privileged medical role in London that few, if any, of its fellows ever migrated to the mainland American colonies. Again, since the College remained essentially a local licensing body for London, only the slightest handful of American physicians ever took steps to become licentiates.[3] In the end, the Royal College of Physicians did serve as a conspicuous model for the many medical societies that sprang up in America during the eighteenth and nineteenth centuries, but it was primarily the model of a professional guild or trade society, not that of a learned society.[4]

The Royal Society, of course, provided colonial Americans with a viable example of the latter kind of society in its broadest form, a group whose members felt free to range over the whole known world of knowledge. This catholicity ensured an ample forum for medically related inquiries. In fact, despite the limited participation of many of its earliest physician fellows, the Society from the outset devoted about as much attention to such topics as to any other area of knowledge.[5] Early communications discussed the circulation of the blood, recipes for fevers and other diseases, anatomical investigations, optics, and the health effects of dampness in mines. A 1667 report of the secretary, Henry Oldenburg, summarized other medical matters that received the Society's attention during its first year or so:

In medicinals we have now and then occasionally inquired after some rarities, medical applications and experiences; what the uses and performances are by Phlebotomy, Frictions, Simples or Compounds not ordinary, by Diet or Chymical Operations in some of the remotest parts of the World, particularly in the famous China. Neither have we altogether omitted to commemorate those obvious reliefs, which the Divine Bounty has offered freely and in common, for distressed Mortals, by Springs, Baths, Bolus's, Medicated Earths, &c.... By Anatomy we have sometimes enter'd into the Chambers and Cabinets of Animal Functions, to find many Meanders and changeable Varieties, and the immediate Organs and Conduits of Life and Sensation.[6]

During the early years, Oldenburg steadily extended the Society's scientific correspondence with travelers, governors of new colonies, officials in trading companies, and other individuals in foreign lands. The scientific inquiries he sent out included special questions to each person about his particular part of the world, many dealing with medical subjects. His thirteen special inquiries in 1666 for persons going to Virginia and Bermuda embodied questions about medicinal baths, uses of tinctures and drugs, the growth of herbs and poisons, the fertility of cattle, and the heights of certain Indian tribes.[7]

Despite the good intentions and occasional replies of a few correspondents, such as John Winthrop, Jr., the early scientific communications about America that flowed to the Society were scanty and provided only fragmentary information.[8] Unfortunately, some of the better observations, particularly the detailed reports of royal governors to the Lords of Trade, were not generally available to most of the Society's members. As a result, fellows who were really curious had to resort to other sources to obtain further scientific information. William Petty, a conspicuous if not entirely typical example, thus tried to establish his own network of informants—returned sea captains, proprietors of colonies, explorers, and the like—to furnish him with raw data of all kinds about America which helped him calculate his political arithmetic.[9] But neither Petty, the Lords of Trade, nor the Royal Society obtained much medical illumination from the New World during the seventeenth century.

The eighteenth century was manifestly better, medically speaking. A few well-trained physicians began to trickle into the colonies in the early decades. Because of them, as well as a growth in the general population, the sources of medical information multiplied rapidly. Moreover, leaders such as clergymen, ship captains, and militia commanders, who had long been called upon for occasional empirical treatment of diseases and wounds, now found more time to read medical and scientific treatises and even to comment upon them. The fact that a score of colonists became fellows of the Royal Society after 1700 reflected both these medical concerns and this increased leisure. Seven out of this number were physicians by training or occupation, while another four had some medical training and/or strong medical interests.[10] Meanwhile, the active leadership roles of prominent British physicians like Hans Sloane, Richard Mead, and James Jurin in the eighteenth-century Society served as a strong stimulus to medical correspondence from the colonies. While the volume of this medical correspondence was never more than a tiny proportion of the *Philosophical Transactions* as a whole, it did form a significant part of the total contribution to the *Transactions* from the mainland colonies.

More importantly, some of the medical communications began to reflect a degree of originality. While William Byrd's "Account of a Spotted Negro" was perhaps little more than another of the curiosities with which the early Society was deluged, a few contributions proved to be much more than that. The 1721-1722 experiment of Cotton Mather and Zabdiel Boylston with smallpox inoculation, that pioneering application of preventive medicine, was fully reported in the *Philosophical Transactions,* where it became an important stimulus to even broader studies of smallpox in England, particularly the one by James Jurin, secretary of the Society.[11] Another American medical experiment reported in the *Transactions* was John Lining's account of the quantitative physiological observations he kept on himself over the course of a year. While Lining acknowledged that he had received inspiration for these experiments from previous iatromechanical studies by the Italian Sanctorius and the Englishman James Keil, his own contribution was significant in its careful correlation of regular meteorological observations with the physiological data.[12] This was, of course, but one of many eighteenth-century attempts to get closer than the ancient Hippocratic hypotheses to the truth about the effects of weather on health. Colonials were understandably concerned about these matters in their New World setting, and several other observers besides Lining sent meteorological readings to the Royal Society, though not all with medical applications in mind.

If the *Philosophical Transactions* provided a significant medium for circulation of the occasional medical contributions from the colonies, they played an even more important role in helping to keep colonial readers abreast of important medical ideas or innovations in Great Britain and on the continent. The dissemination of the *Transactions* was aided by abridgments, as well as by extracts published, after 1730, in the *Gentleman's Magazine,* both of which found their way into collections of colonial library companies. In addition, fellows sometimes loaned their copies of the *Transactions* to friends and neighbors, and colonial newspapers frequently reprinted items from the *Transactions* in their entirety or in abbreviated versions. The emergence of local learned and medical societies in the colonies was to some extent the result of a broadening of these formal and informal processes of sharing knowledge. The earliest local societies were, among other things, devices to help a certain segment of colonial America keep up with scientific developments in Britain and Europe by pooling or sharing the fragments of knowledge that reached certain of the members, sometimes through the *Philosophical Transactions,* sometimes through other printed sources, often in direct correspondence of individuals with given scientists, physicians, or collectors of the Old World. William Douglass's short-lived Boston Medical Society of the late 1730s performed this function to a considerable degree, as did Franklin's Junto and the original American Philosophical Society.[13]

But local organizers did not envisage merely passive roles for their new colonial societies. Rather, like members of the Royal Society, as well as of comparable European societies, they wanted to investigate the secrets of nature themselves. And, like scholars everywhere, colonials recognized the study of medicine as an important part of that quest. Thus, Ezra Stiles, in his proposal of the mid-1760s for an American Academy of Sciences, felt that original medically related inquiries would be among the Academy's necessary areas of concern. He particularly stressed the need for further evaluation of smallpox inoculation, for continuing meteorological and climatological observations, and for the systematic registration of vital statistics and population data in order to permit demographic and genetic studies.[14]

Like Stiles's hoped-for academy, the two learned societies which did emerge during the Revolutionary period and which proved permanent regarded medicine as a natural object of attention for learned men. The reorganized American Philosophical Society distributed its members in 1770 among six standing committees or sections, one of which was devoted to medicine and anatomy, while the American Academy of Arts and Sciences made one of its original stated objectives "to promote and encourage medical discoveries." In 1770, 42 of the Society's 228 American members were M.D.'s or "Dr.'s," and in the first volume of the Society's *Transactions,* 8 of these 42 contributed ten papers, four on medical subjects. The Academy had a similar ratio of medical men among its 61 original members, but its first volume of *Memoirs,* which appeared in 1783, contained a somewhat higher proportion of medical contributions than had the *Transactions.*[15] To some extent this was the result of an effort on the part of the Academy to make up for the paucity of European medical publications reaching the United States during the Revolution. As the editor explained, "The medical papers may, probably, contain many observations not entirely new. However, this ought not to be considered a sufficient objection to their being inserted in this work, because many important [European] discoveries in pathology, as well as in the animal oeconomy, have been in a great measure useless to this part of the world, in consequence of a situation so remote from ancient seats of learning and improvement."[16]

Both societies went on to receive, listen to, and publish substantial numbers of medically related papers for some years after the Revolution. Around the turn of the century, however, a change set in. In 1799 the Philosophical Society published only one paper on a medical topic out of a total of seventy-six; however, there were also several papers on such medically related subjects as chemistry and pharmaceuticals. From then on through 1850 the *Transactions* contained very few strictly medical papers, although a somewhat greater number appeared on programs of the Society's meetings.[17] The Academy's *Memoirs* of 1804 still included two medical papers, along with four on medically related subjects, but in the 1809 volume there was but one medical communication, and medically relevant papers appeared only sporadically in subsequent volumes.

The truth is that, despite their avowed medical objectives and the continuing large numbers of physicians among their members, neither of these general learned societies became very deeply involved in scientific discussion of the important medical advances or questions of the late eighteenth and first half of the nineteenth centuries. In contrast to the Royal Society's considerable interest in inoculation, neither the Philosophical Society nor the Academy played a really substantial role in the American introduction and evaluation of vaccination.[18] And, similarly, no critical assessment was attempted either of such ancient medical therapies as blood-letting or of such revolutionary new measures as anesthesia.

The reasons for this neglect are doubtless many. Prominent among them, however, was the rapid growth that took place in medical institutions during those years. The spread of medical societies and medical schools in the several decades after the Revolution, along with the construction of hospitals and dispensaries, brought into being greatly expanded opportunities for the observation, discussion, and dissemination of medical information. Simultaneously, the emergence of a cluster of specifically medical journals following the launching of the *Medical Repository* in 1797 provided a wealth of new outlets for medical articles. Medicine as a profession and specialty had progressively less need in the nineteenth century for the outlets the learned societies provided.[19]

This is not to say that physicians themselves had a decreasing interest in the learned societies. On the contrary, those with broad scientific interests not only continued as members but often, throughout this entire period, played influential roles as officers. One can point to a number of years in which medicine was the preponderant profession of the officers of both the American Philosophical Society and the American Academy of Arts and Sciences. Two vice-presidents and two curators of the Society in 1771 were physicians, while in 1799 eight out of twenty-three officers (including counselors) were physicians. Comparable ratios continued well into the nineteenth century, with seven out of sixteen officers in 1841 and eight out of twenty-three in 1843 being medically trained men. In the Academy two out of ten council members in 1785 were physicians, while in 1804 three of thirteen officers were medical doctors; in 1845 physicians filled four of six Academy offices, along with six of fourteen committee seats.

From the first, physician-members of these two leading learned societies displayed interest in a wide variety of subjects. If they sometimes presented communications on topics that were fairly closely related to medicine, such as botany or chemistry, at other times they went as far afield as maple sugar culture, astronomy, and geology. As enthusiastically as their fellow members, they built up collections of prehistoric bones, sea shells, bird's nests, and zoological specimens, and listened to papers on anthropology, evaporation, and Indian languages. And, with their colleagues from many professions and fields of interest, they tried, on a recurring basis for half a century after 1780, to obtain scientific illumination of a complex protomedical matter.

In the societies there came together much of the American nation's Revolutionary and post-Revolutionary self-conscious desire to know itself, to proclaim its uniqueness and virtue to the rest of the world, and to defend itself from the aspersions of European critics. As the Revolution ended, Americans wanted to know how strong they were as a nation, how soon they would be numerous enough to rank as a first-class power, what diseases impeded progress toward that goal, what climatic factors peculiar to America were contributing to these diseases. If it was true, as the Europeans had claimed, that animal species, including man, were smaller in the American environment, that they were deficient in sexual vigor, and that their life spans did not measure up to European expectancies, then every effort would have to be exerted to alter that environment.[20] Complete answers to these problems were never worked out in the societies, or in European learned circles either, for that matter. But in the course of the discussions, meteorology, demography, and public health took long strides toward becoming separate scientific specialties.

In the first few decades of the American Philosophical Society, the discussions of these problems of environmental salubrity and population adaptability involved such nonphysicians as Jefferson, Franklin, William Barton, and Nicholas Collin, along with the physicians John Foulke, Benjamin Rush, Thomas Bond, and Anthony Fothergill. Foulke, in his oration to the Society in 1789, described not only the nature of the environmental hygiene ideal but the scientific and emotional consensus of how to go about achieving it, as well as the use of political arithmetic techniques to express it. It was pretty much of a truism with Foulke and others "that paucity of inhabitants, salubrity of climate, and a moderate degree of temperature must insure length of life every where." Unhealthful extremes of climate were to be diminished by such internal improvements as clearing forests, draining swamps, and cultivating fields. Longevity would be further stimulated by preserving America's republican institutions, maintaining a broad distribution of wealth, and shunning the bad habits and luxuries of Europe. Perhaps, as Foulke summed up in a poem, the most important measure of all was to preserve America's rural way of life.

> Ye who amid this feverish world would wear
> A body free of Pain, of cares a Mind;
> Fly the rank City, shun its turbid air
> Breathe not the Chaos of eternal smoke
> And volatile corruption, from the dead
> The dying, sickening, and the living world
> Exhal'd, to sully heaven's transparent dome
> With dim mortality.[21]

For reasons that are not entirely clear but that may have been mainly historical accidents, the early demographic-hygienic-environmental deliberations of the American Academy of Arts and Sciences were somewhat less general than those of the Society, more practical, based on more original data, and more productive of concrete results. At any event, the Academy, soon after its establishment, agreed to act momentarily as an investigative body in seeking illumination about the salubrity of the American community. And while its 1785 survey of physicians and clergymen of Massachusetts and New Hampshire did not accomplish its main objective of launching a permanent system for collecting health information and vital statistics, the original response to the questionnaire made it possible for Edward Wigglesworth to prepare the first American life expectancy table for a general population. The questionnaire also set a useful precedent for local New England communities. With such a model, citizens of dozens of these communities in subsequent decades went on to conduct public health surveys that resulted in comprehensive topographical descriptions of their areas as well as extensive collections of demographic data. It was no accident that, starting in the 1840s and for many years afterwards, Massachusetts had the most advanced vital statistics as well as the best sanitary provisions in the United States.[22]

During the nineteenth century, occasional papers presented before the two older learned societies continued to bear upon the subject of environmental salubrity.[23] Increasingly, however, these were papers by specialists who confined themselves to technical aspects of meteorology, actuarial science, geology, and other sciences. Discussion of the applied medical and public health aspects of the subject was more and more diverted to medical societies and medical journals. There, in the form of medical-topographical surveys and medical climatological inquiries, the subject accounted for a substantial part of the medical energy of the era and filled many of the published medical papers.

It was thus no accident that, when the American Medical Association came into being in the mid-1840s, one of its prominent scientific objectives was to make a coordinated attack upon the ancient weather-disease relationship. This seemed at the time to be a promising enterprise, but in reality the Association could play only a limited role. With little real authority and without an adequate scientific secretariat of its own, it could scarcely do more than form committees to stimulate more medical-topographical surveys. However, it did urge state medical societies to collect statistics on the causes of death from their members in the hope that these could be collated with the meteorological data which were anticipated from the Smithsonian Institution's developing nationwide system.[24]

Actually, only the weather half of the weather-disease inquiry began to benefit materially from nationwide data before the Civil War, for the science of meteorology did flourish under the Smithsonian data-gathering arrangements. The advancement of national vital statistics, however, fared only indifferently under medical society federalism. Rather than rely upon a professional society, achievement of the ideal of reliable and uniform national data had to wait another several decades and the formation of a public agency.[25]

Meanwhile, with the country's growth and the spread of democracy, various other aspects of medicine had become the concern, not only of the older organizations but of all sorts of new societies. The rapid nineteenth-century proliferation of medical institutions did no more than barely keep pace with the growth of other elements of society in America's headlong rush into new geographical areas. The new hospitals, medical schools, medical journals, and medical societies that sprang up were often part of the competitiveness that accompanied this rush.[26] And the fierce localism that sometimes helped them sprout was part of the general challenge to central authority that came to fruition in the democratic urges of the Jacksonian era. In this social environment, orthodox medicine itself lost the last vestiges of whatever absolute authority it once had or pretended to have had. Physicians who became Thomsonians, homeopaths, hydropaths, or eclectics demanded and got from society the same rights to practice as those who retained the orthodox viewpoint.[27] And each group quickly started its own schools, journals, and societies, originally local but eventually national as well. The American Institute of Homeopathy, in fact, appeared in 1844, almost three years before the orthodox American Medical Association. Likewise, a number of medical specialties formed national organizations before the general physicians; among these were the American Society of Dental Surgeons (1840) and the Association of Medical Superintendents of American Institutions for the Insane (1844), which later mercifully shortened its name to the American Psychiatric Association.

In many ways, early nineteenth-century American medicine reflects the paradoxical operation of society's broader tendency to seek unified or cooperative action through organization at the very time when individualism and competitiveness were at their height. On the one hand, contentious medical professors attacked critics of their professional ideas in the most personal and vituperative fashion, while the proprietary medical schools to which they belonged as business ventures noisily fought each other to attract students.[28] On the other hand, changing social conditions were creating problems that could be dealt with only by individuals acting together in a large variety of organizations. Some of these bodies were deeply concerned with medical questions. Although most of them had quite different aims from the general learned societies, many drew upon somewhat the same membership, including the clergy, public officials, and others, but particularly the physicians.

For instance, local and national missionary societies enjoyed the active participation of considerable numbers of physicians. From the 1820s on, some doctors even signed up to serve with missions in frontier communities, in Indian country, or overseas. By 1850 medical missionary societies were being formed to help raise support for a number of overseas missions, particularly those with hospitals.[29]

Probably even more medical doctors were involved in the temperance movement than in the missionary movement. Benjamin Rush's 1784 tract on spirituous liquors was doubtless the principal influence on the turn-of-the-century clergy and others who organized the early local temperance societies. William P. C. Barton was prominent among the physicians who fought to eliminate the liquor ration in the navy, while many medical officers worked for similar ends in the army. Meanwhile, Daniel Drake's Physiological Temperance Society at Louisville was only one of several similar groups organized within the medical profession to try to reduce both the medicinal use of alcohol and the consumption of spirits by physicians.

Another aspect of community improvement from the 1820s on, the lyceum movement, also derived much of its local support from medical men. Physicians not only frequently joined the clergy and other leaders in organizing lyceums, but they were also called upon to present lyceum lectures on physiology, natural history, and any of a wide variety of subjects.[30] Sometimes their topics included mesmerism and phrenology. Then, continuing their discussions of these topics outside of the lyceums, physicians frequently joined other interested persons in phrenological societies. In the Boston phrenological society, Dr. John C. Warren played a leading role in building up a large collection of skulls. The skull collection of Dr. Samuel George Morton of Philadelphia was even more extensive, and was eventually given to the Academy of Natural Sciences in that city.[31]

Of more immediate medical importance than some of the above activities was the gradual buildup of community sanitary awareness and action by a variety of societies and the ad hoc reform committees established in most of the larger cities—efforts that eventually turned into a coherent public health movement. Medical societies naturally were prominent in this. With them, however, was a prolific mix of charitable associations and religious tract societies.[32] Sometimes particular reform groups such as the Prison Discipline Society became involved. At certain times, special circumstances brought about fruitful local collaboration, such as that of the Massachusetts Horticultural Society and other groups, which in 1831 engaged in a joint effort to realize Jacob Bigelow's proposal of a rural cemetery, Mount Auburn, near Cambridge. This work gave an important impetus, not only to the public park movement in America, but to the elimination or improvement of crowded and unsightly urban cemeteries with their frequently nauseous odors and presumedly unhealthful emanations.[33]

A much more extensive enterprise undertaken on a continuing basis was the public health involvement of a new learned society, the American Statistical Association (organized 1839). Like its English model, the London Statistical Society, the Association proclaimed its interest in statistics related to all the "different departments of human knowledge." Nevertheless, in its early years at least, it placed special emphasis on the collection of vital statistics, board of health reports, medical school statistics, and hospital and asylum data. The Association's membership list for 1840 included seventeen physicians out of a total of sixty-nine domestic members (regular and corresponding). But the Association also counted among its members such laymen as Horace Mann and Lemuel Shattuck, whose strong interest in social, sanitary, and medical improvement helped focus much of the organization's early attention upon these matters. Some of the physician members, notably Edward Jarvis and Henry I. Bowditch, played leading parts in compelling the Association first to challenge the accuracy of 1840 federal census statistics relating to insanity among Negroes of the northern states and second to petition Congress for a correction. But it was the nonphysician Shattuck who, more than anyone, successfully persuaded the Association in 1847, a year before the Massachusetts Medical Society took action, to petition the Massachusetts legislature for a sanitary survey of the state.[34]

The involvement of physicians in such a wide variety of community reforms and societies was both typical and necessary in early nineteenth-century America. In the rapidly changing communities of that era, physicians were often not only among the more intellectual elements of the population but also among the more affluent, and those that were able to build up substantial practices were among the more solidly rooted. Hence there was a fundamental rationale for them to share in the organization of the new societies, learned and otherwise. The demand was not just for whatever scientific or other intellectual contributions the physicians could make for sometimes these were minimal. Specifically, the societies needed medical men for their general interest and advice, their financial backing and patronage, and any reflected standing in the community that their participation might bring.[35]

Physicians thus became among the most conspicuous joiners in American society, both because they were interested and because society wanted them. They were among the active founders and leaders of every kind of learned group. Among many familiar examples was Edward A. Holyoke, who was successively one of the founders of the American Academy of Arts and Sciences, the Massachusetts Medical Society, and the Essex Historical Society, and was president of each for several years. Daniel Drake helped found at least sixteen institutions in Ohio and Kentucky between 1807 and 1851 and was active in perhaps twenty-five more.[36] But physicians in other communities could boast almost equally lengthy lists of institutional affiliations.

In New York, Samuel Latham Mitchill may well have exceeded Drake; at any rate, the poet Joseph Rodman Drake reported that Mitchill had a reputation as "Fellow of forty-nine societies."[37] The forty-nine included, of course, a variety of medical, scientific, educational, and civic organizations, including the Society for the Promotion of Agriculture, Manufactures, and Useful Arts; the Rutgers Medical College; and the *Medical Repository*. Particularly prominent in terms of numbers were the natural history societies. Mitchill himself summarized some of these affiliations in an 1826 list:

Honorary President of the Parisian Branch of its Linnaean Society at New York; Lecturer on Botany and Vegetable Physiology to the Horticultural Society; Member of the American Geological Society at New Haven; of the Academy of Natural Sciences at Philadelphia; of the Western Museum Society at Cincinnati; of the Linnaean Society of New England; Honorary Fellow of the Lyceums at Hudson, Delaware, Catskill, and Pittsfield; of the Agricultural Society in the Bahama Islands; of the Literary and Philosophical Society at Montreal; and of the Philo-Phusian Society in Brown University; Correspondent of the Society for Promoting Natural and Physical Sciences at Buenos Aires; etc., etc., etc., etc., etc., etc.[38]

The list should also have included the New York Lyceum of Natural History, of which Mitchill was one of the founders and the first president.

Mitchill's list highlights the ever-growing formal involvement of American physicians in natural history pursuits through the early nineteenth century. The Lyceum of Natural History's original resident membership of thirty-one included nine M.D.'s, one veterinary surgeon, and four medical students. Four of the original officers were M.D.'s, and, as in the older learned societies, physicians frequently held office in subsequent years. The Lyceum's early medical ties were further strengthened by its repeated dependence upon the New York medical community for a place to hold meetings. In 1817 it met for several months at the College of Physicians and Surgeons, while during the 1830s and 1840s it had quarters in buildings of other medical schools.[39]

Despite the considerable proportion of physicians in its membership, the Lyceum made no attempt to publish strictly medical papers. The same was true of the Academy of Natural Sciences of Philadelphia and other natural history societies, in contrast to the early patterns of the general learned societies.[40] In fact, in the natural history societies the ambivalence of those physicians who were interested in science was clearly evident, and certain physicians broke decisively from medicine in favor of careers in science. Some, like Mitchill continued to maintain something of a balance between their medical and scientific interests. But others increasingly used their medical training simply as a livelihood to support their scientific activities or as a jumping stone to non-medical scientific careers.[41] In New York, for example, Dr. John Torrey, who dominated the Lyceum for several decades after Mitchill, gained his principal income from his position as professor in a medical school, the College of Physicians and Surgeons; his principal interests and contributions, however, were in botany. On the other hand, Torrey's protégé, Asa Gray, received his M.D. degree and then arranged to pursue other endeavors; with the exception of a few months early in his career, he never did have to practice medicine or teach in a medical school.

In Philadelphia two prominent physicians, Samuel G. Morton and Joseph Leidy, who played leading roles in the Academy of Natural Sciences, resembled Mitchill in the rough balance they maintained between their medical and scientific work. During the years between 1825 and 1851, Morton served the Academy successively as auditor, long-time secretary, vice-president, and president. In the mid-1840s Agassiz found Morton to be "a man of science in the best sense; admirable both as regards his knowledge and his activity. He is the pillar of the Philadelphia Academy."[42] Still, while making a name in such sciences as geology, zoology, paleontology, and anthropology, Morton was almost equally prominent in scientific medicine. He taught anatomy for many years and produced important works on consumption, pathology, and human anatomy.

Leidy's career before 1850 demonstrated a versatility fully equal to that of Morton. If Leidy had by then already published his classic paper on the fossil horse of America, he had also published noteworthy researches on the structure of the liver, together with his pioneer observations of *Trichina spiralis* larvae in pork. Although he was devoting some time to his duties as a teacher of anatomy, he had also in the mid-forties begun the comprehensive studies that marked him as one of America's first original microbiologists. He reported early phases of these studies at meetings of the Academy in 1849 and 1850, particularly his investigation of the possible relationships between contagious diseases and cryptogamic spores. By this period he was reflecting "upon the possibility of plants of this description existing in healthy animals as a natural condition," and he had already rejected the theory of spontaneous generation. In a few such studies, use of the achromatic microscope by Leidy and other scientists was slowly beginning to open up to Americans new worlds for research in the basic medical sciences. In contrast to clinical medicine, these new worlds were as compatible to the natural history societies as to the medical societies.[43]

For Leidy and Morton the rich physical resources of the Academy materially aided the various facets of their research. By 1847 the Academy had amassed, from the donations of over thirty years, important collections of specimens in many areas of natural history, along with a substantial library.[44] The demand to use these resources had become so considerable that both the librarian and the chairman of curators were required to maintain regular hours at the Academy. Leidy, as chairman of curators for several years during this period, thus had an incomparable opportunity to become acquainted with the collections and to use them for research. Similarly, a few years earlier Asa Gray, from his position as the librarian and superintendent at the Lyceum of Natural History, was able to utilize the various collections more fully than most of the other members, to the immense profit of his scientific career.

The factors that were turning increased numbers of physicians into full-time scientists seemed by the 1840s to have created a pattern for the future, one in which practical and clinical medicine would henceforth be conspicuously missing from the publications, if not from the actual agendas, of the various learned and scientific societies. But the pattern turned out to be reversible, and in that decade it was reversed in at least two instances. At that time the aim of science for status and recognition as a national enterprise seemed to require the cooperation of all segments of science gathered together in a single national scientific society. The National Institution, to be sure, was not really what scientists had in mind; it was much too local, while its program reflected too much of the general educational objectives of the lyceum movement and not enough of the increasingly rigorous scientific outlook.[45] Still, it did defy the scientific separatism of the age to the extent of providing a central forum, not only for agriculture, history, the sciences, literature, and the arts, but also, as something of an afterthought, for medicine.[46]

The American Association for the Advancement of Science overcame both excessive specialization and excessive localism to emerge as a truly national scientific society. And, as it took shape in the late 1840s, the new society from the beginning made a place in its deliberations for medicine. Its members began their own attempt to organize the weather-disease inquiry, particularly through a committee on meteorology and another on vital statistics registration, and they delivered papers on a variety of other medical topics. The Cambridge meeting of 1849, for instance, included papers on vision, cholera, and the assay of quinine. Medically trained men with every degree of involvement in medicine constituted almost a third of the original membership. Some of these became officers of the Association; others simply demonstrated the diversity of mid-nineteenth-century American science. Of the latter, some of the medical men, like Josiah Nott of Mobile, Alabama, reflected older theological preconceptions of medicine and science that had not yet passed away.[47] But others, such as the physician members who dominated the committee to evaluate Charles Spencer's achromatic lenses (chosen at the Albany meeting of 1851) represented commitments to new scientific standards and methodologies that promised much for the future of medicine.[48]

The motivation of the medically trained men who joined the Association at midcentury was tinged with not a little of the continuing ambiguity that has ever marked medicine at its interface with society and the learned world. Some certainly joined in order to further their aspirations in sciences other than medicine. Some doubtless looked to the new organization to bring them a degree of status in society, status that the disorganized medical profession of Jacksonian America had signally failed to ensure. And probably not a few became members because the Association seemed to offer them yet another chance, however illusory, to be or act as learned men.

NOTES

1. My study of these matters is based heavily, though not exclusively, upon an examination of published transactions and/or proceedings of the following six societies for the relevant years: the Royal Society of London, American Philosophical Society, American Academy of Arts and Sciences, Academy of Natural Sciences of Philadelphia, New York Lyceum of Natural History, and American Association for the Advancement of Science.

2. Charles C. Gillispie, "Physick and Philosophy: A Study of the Influence of the College of Physicians of London upon the Foundation of the Royal Society," *Journal of Modern History* 19 (1947): 210-25; Charles Webster, "The College of Physicians and 'Solomon's House' in Commonwealth England," *Bulletin of the History of Medicine* 41 (1967): 393-412.

3. While the reasons for this are too complex to explore here, they do deserve further consideration elsewhere. A preliminary inspection of *Munk's Roll* revealed only two prominent American physicians, John Morgan and Nicholas Romayne, among the eighteenth-century licentiates of the College, and none among the fellows. William Munk, *The Roll of the Royal College of Physicians of London,* 2d. ed. (London: The College, 1878), vol. 2, *1701 to 1800.*

4. A series of short-lived local medical societies were formed in New York City beginning about 1749. Other early city organizations included the Philadelphia Medical Society (1765), the Boston Medical Society (1735, 1780), and the College of Physicians of Philadelphia (1787). In Connecticut county medical societies were established in nearly all counties between 1767 and 1800. Among the earliest state societies were the Medical Society of New Jersey (1766) and the Massachusetts Medical Society (1781), but there were medical societies in five other states by 1800. Large numbers of other societies were organized at all levels after 1800. A convenient listing, by states and dates, of important regular medical societies before 1860 appears in William G. Rothstein, *American Physicians in the Nineteenth Century: From Sects to Science* (Baltimore: Johns Hopkins University Press, 1972), pp. 327-31.

5. Gillispie, "Physick and Philosophy," pp. 216-17. Gillispie identifies 24 physicians among the 115 official founder-members of the Society, but less than half of these seem to have been active.

John Lowthrop's three-volume abridgement and rearrangement of the *Philosophical Transactions of the Royal Society* for 1664-1700 (hereafter cited as *Philosophical Transactions*) provides a convenient rough indication of the quantitative standing of medically related communications in relation to other subjects:

Vol. 1: 620 pages on astronomy, navigation, optics, architecture, physics, and mathematics.

Vol. 2: 915 pages on meteorology, hydrology, mineralogy, botany, agriculture, and zoology.

Vol. 3: 317 pages on language, antiquities, history, and explorations, plus 371 pages on anatomy, physic, chemistry, physiology, diseases, longevity, and pharmacy.

Thus, papers on medicine and the medical sciences took up about one-sixth of the total space of the three volumes, exclusive of indexes. John Lowthrop, *The Philosophical Transactions and Collections to the end of the year MDCC, Abridged and Disposed under General Heads,* 3 vols., 4th ed. (London: J. & J. Knapton et al., 1731).

6. Henry Oldenburg, "Preface," *Philosophical Transactions* 2 (1677): 410.

7. Ibid., pp. 420-21.

8. For examples of Oldenburg's correspondence with Winthrop, see A. Rupert Hall and Marie Boas Hall, eds., *The Correspondence of Henry Oldenburg* (Madison: University of Wisconsin Press, 1965–), 1:105 and 3:525-26.

9. For some discussion of Petty's American sources, see James H. Cassedy, *Demography in Early America* (Cambridge, Mass.: Harvard University Press, 1969), pp. 47-52, 55-56.

10. The seven physicians were Zabdiel Boylston, Thomas Robie, John Mitchell, John Tennent, Arthur Lee, Alexander Garden, and John Morgan. The other four with medical interests were William Byrd, Cotton Mather, Benjamin Franklin, and Benjamin Thompson. The seventeenth-century member, John Winthrop, Jr., should also be added to this latter group.

11. Among the fuller discussions of the Boston experiment, see Otho T. Beall, Jr., and Richard H. Shryock, *Cotton Mather: First Significant Figure in American Medicine* (Baltimore: Johns Hopkins University Press, 1954), pp. 93-122; John B. Blake, *Public Health in the Town of Boston 1630-1822* (Cambridge, Mass.: Harvard University Press, 1959), pp. 52-73. For some of Jurin's work on this problem, see James Jurin, "A Comparison Between the Danger of the Natural Smallpox, and that Given by Inoculation," *Philosophical Transactions* 32 (1722):213ff.

12. "A Letter from Dr. John Lining at Charles-Town in South Carolina to James Jurin, M.D., . . . Statistical Experiments Made on Himself for One Whole Year Accompanied with Meteorological Observations, and Six General Tables," *Philosophical Transactions* 42 (1743): 491-98; together with a supplementary letter in ibid., 43 (1744-1745): 318.

13. For details about the Boston society as well as Douglass's 1729 reaction to a proposal of Cadwallader Colden to organize a scientific society, see *Letters and Papers of Cadwallader Colden,* 9 vols. (New York: New-York Historical Society, 1918-1937), 1:271-73; 2:146-47; 3:190-93. See also *Boston Gazette,* 10 November 1741.

14. The fullest discussion of Stiles's Academy is in Edmund S. Morgan, *The Gentle Puritan: A Life of Ezra Stiles, 1727-1795* (New Haven, Conn.: Yale University Press, 1962).

15. While the list of members in Volume 1 of the Academy's *Memoirs* does not identify M.D.'s as such, five members are given the title "Dr." Several known physicians, notably Edward Holyoke, were given no special titles.

16. *Memoirs of the American Academy of Arts and Sciences* 1 (1783):ix.

17. The Society's 1843 meeting, for instance, seems to have been something of a revival and an exception, so far as medical matters were concerned. Upon that occasion three papers on medical topics were presented, while arrangements were made for all of the members to visit the Pennsylvania Institution for the Instruction of the Blind. *Proceedings of the American Philosophical Society* 3 (1843): 38, 127-74.

Whitfield J. Bell, "The American Philosophical Society and Medicine," *Bulletin of the History of Medicine* 40 (1966): 112-23, gives much more detail about the medical papers and confirms that "medical men ceased almost completely after 1820 to send medical papers" to the Society, chiefly due to the onrush of specialization.

18. While a scattering of communications came to the Society on the subject of vaccination, no special action was taken on them, and none of the communications were published in the *Transactions.*

19. The particular effect upon the *Transactions* of the American Philosophical Society brought about by appearance of the *Philadelphia Medical and Physical Journal* is discussed in some detail in Bell, "American Philosophical Society and Medicine," pp. 120-21.

In a related development, the substantial launching of hospitals began to open up, particularly after 1830, a new resource for medical research that did not exist before in the United States to any appreciable extent, one in which newly available instruments of medical research could be applied—particularly the stethoscope, statistics, chemistry apparatus, and eventually the achromatic microscope. While development of this resource was slow, some curious physicians whose research energies had formerly gone into geological, chemical, and botanical studies began by midcentury to find increasingly attractive outlets in medical research. To some indeterminate extent, such individuals may have offset those others who left medicine in favor of other sciences. I will treat aspects of these matters in a forthcoming book.

20. The classic examination of the roots and early phases of this inquiry is Gilbert Chinard, "Eighteenth Century Theories of America as a Human Habitat," *Proceedings of the American Philosophical Society* 91 (1947): 27-57. See also Cassedy, *Demography,* pp. 243-304.

21. [John Foulke], "Oration pronounced by Doctor Foulke before the American Philosophical Society, Feb. 7 [1789]," MS at New-York Historical Society, New York, N.Y., Microfilm no. 540, American Philosophical Society, Philadelphia, Pa.

22. See AAAS broadside, *Sir, The American Academy of Arts and Sciences. . . ,* (Boston: S. Hall, 10 November 1785); Cassedy, *Demography,* pp. 237-40, 251-55. The Academy's *Memoirs* also provided an outlet for an early paper of Noah Webster, "On the Theory of Vegetation," *Memoirs of the American Academy of Arts and Sciences* 2 (1793), pt. 1:178-85. This paper, which was concerned with the effects of atmospheric conditions on the growth of crops, represents an early aspect of Webster's developing ideas on environment, which culminated in his famous 1799 work on epidemic diseases.

An attempt to emulate the Academy's initiative was the unsuccessful effort of Webster and Timothy Dwight, through the new Connecticut Academy of Arts and Sciences, to collect data about the state of Connecticut. Their questionnaire, however, sought economic, political, and social information, as well as sanitary, demographic, and scientific data. For comment on this venture, see Harry R. Warfel, *Noah Webster, Schoolmaster to America* (New York: Macmillan Co., 1936), pp. 252-58; Timothy Dwight, *Travels in New England and New York*, ed. Barbara Miller Solomon, 4 vols. (Cambridge, Mass.: Harvard University Press, 1969), l:xlv.

23. In addition to such papers, both societies, as well as other American groups, discussed a number of European proposals during the 1840s for collaboration in related scientific projects of worldwide scope. In one, the British Association for the Advancement of Science tried unsuccessfully to get substantial American participation in connection with its system of British and Indian meteorological observations. See Walter E. Gross, "The American Philosophical Society and the Growth of Science in the United States 1835-1850" (Ph.D. diss., University of Pennsylvania, 1970), pp. 60-90. In another, L. A. Quetelet, perpetual secretary of the Académie Royale of Brussels, had an equal lack of success in canvassing several American societies to supply regular data on the "periodical phenomena of man"—i.e., vital statistics, anthropological observations, and medical-meteorological information. For notices of this ambitious project, see "The Periodical Phenomena of Man," *Boston Medical and Surgical Journal* 34 (1846): 18-20; *Proceedings of the American Philosophical Society* 2 (1844): 235, 266. While the two older learned societies expressed interest in both of these proposals, their reluctance and failure to undertake active roles in either reflects, among other things, the societies' diminished national standing by the 1840s, as well as their lack of the necessary full-time scientific secretariats to handle large scientific operations.

24. For a discussion of the Association's aspirations and the practical difficulties in the way of realizing them, see the "Report of the Committee on Hygiene," *Transactions of the American Medical Association* 4 (1851): 536-38. Joseph Henry's comment on the potential role of the Smithsonian appears in Smithsonian Institution, *Fourth Annual Report* (1849), pp. 13-15.

25. James H. Cassedy, "The Registration Area and American Vital Statistics," *Bulletin of the History of Medicine* 39 (1965): 221-31.

26. A concise historical review of medical society formation in the United States is W. B. McDaniel, "A Brief Sketch of the Rise of American Medical Societies," *International Record of Medicine* 171 (1958): 483-91.

27. The resulting rivalries between these various medical sects relates to and forms a phase of the general tensions and increasing differentiation between scientific professionals and amateurs.

28. In some cases, medical societies themselves became the instruments of individualistic ambition and self-glorification, and some were badly torn by dissension arising from such conditions.

29. Among these were groups organized to support the work of the Medical Missionary Society of China in Canton, including the Ophthalmic Hospital begun there by Peter Parker.

30. The wide variety of lectures that were available to listeners in the 1840s, as well as the American thirst for the knowledge imparted in them, were carefully noted by the Boston architect, Charles Bulfinch:

"The prevailing passion of our people seems to be the attendance at Lectures; we have them of every grade: the bare enumeration of them is enough to convince one that if we are not the most intellectual city in the world, it is because we do not keep our ears and eyes open to instruction. I begin with the Lowell lectures, 5 courses, on Geology, by Dr. Lyell; on Christianity, Dr. Palfrey; on Mechanics, Lovering; on Chymistry, Silliman; and on Natural Religion, Dr. Walker.

"Lectures by the Society for Diffusion of Knowledge; others, of the Lyceum, from the Mercantile library association; the Mechanic association; the Historical society;—then we have Professor Bush from New York to explain the Prophecies to us; and Mr. Miller in Chardon Street chapel, proving that the world will come to an end in the next year; Mr. Espy on Storms; Mr. Emerson on the Times; Capt. Partridge on War and preparation for it . . . musical performers on one string of the violin are the rage, and *divine Fanny* has drawn enthusiastic crowds to the theatre, and even old Faneuil hall has vibrated in all its bricks and timbers in honor of a French prince" (Charles Bulfinch to Greenleaf Bulfinch, 30 November 1841, Ellen S. Bulfinch, ed., *The Life and Letters of Charles Bulfinch, Architect* [Boston and New York: Houghton Mifflin, 1896], p. 292).

31. Agassiz, upon visiting the Academy in 1846 and seeing Morton's collection, wrote back to Switzerland about the latter: "Nothing like it exists elsewhere. This collection alone is worth a journey to America" (Louis Agassiz to his mother, December 1846, in *Louis Agassiz, His Life and Correspondence,* ed. Elizabeth Cary Agassiz, 2 vols. [Boston: Houghton Mifflin, 1885], 2:417).

32. For an examination of the influence of such societies upon public health in New York City, see Charles E. Rosenberg and Carroll S. Rosenberg, "Pietism and the Origins of the American Public Health Movement," *Journal of the History of Medicine and Allied Sciences* 23 (1968): 16-35.

33. John W. Reps, *The Making of Urban America* (Princeton: Princeton University Press, 1965), pp. 325-31.

34. For early minutes, officers, and members of the Association, see *Journal of the American Statistical Association* 35, no. 209 (March 1940), pt. 2:298-308. For explicit reference to the role of the Association in these events, see Edward Jarvis, "Insanity among the Colored Population of the Free States," *American Journal of Insanity* 8 (1851-1852): 268-69; idem, Review of "Report of the Sanitary Commission of Massachusetts," *Boston Medical and Surgical Journal* 44 (5 March 1851): 89.

35. Similarly, in many newly established and growing communities, physicians were among the principal backers and sources of capital in the establishment of local banks.

36. Henry D. Shapiro, "Daniel Drake's *Sensorium Commune* and the Organization of the Second American Enlightenment," *Cincinnati Historical Society Bulletin* 27 (1969): 43-52. Shapiro's partial list of Drake's affiliations, national and local, includes thirty-nine institutions. Among these, Drake was one of the founders of seven colleges or other educational institutions and founder of nine societies.

37. Quoted in Herman LeRoy Fairchild, *A History of the New York Academy of Sciences* (New York: Published by the Author, 1887), pp. 60-61. Drake's figure of forty-nine societies apparently was not just a product of poetic license. Mitchill's biographer, in fact, found that Mitchill belonged to considerably more than forty-nine organizations. Courtney Robert Hall, *A Scientist in the Early Republic: Samuel Latham Mitchill 1764-1831* (New York: Columbia University Press, 1934), pp. 129-31.

38. *Catalogue of the Organic Remains . . . presented . . . by . . . Samuel L. Mitchill* (New York: Lyceum of Natural History, 1826), title page.

39. *Annals of the Lyceum of Natural History of New York* 1 (1824); Fairchild, *New York Academy of Sciences,* passim. In Philadelphia, a reversal of this situation occurred

where the College of Physicians occupied space in the American Philosophical Society building for over twenty-five years.

40. Exceptions were the published reports made by some few physicians during the late 1840s on their researches on some of the newer basic medical sciences, notably microbiology, histology, and cellular pathology. Among these scientists were Joseph Leidy and Waldo I. Burnett (see page 272 and note 43, below). It should be made clear that the meetings of natural history societies often included papers and discussions of such medical subjects as anatomy and physiology, although these never appeared in the published transactions; also, the collections of such societies were often useful for medical studies as well as research in other sciences.

41. The total number of such individuals, while undetermined, is substantial. Estimates have been made that "almost half of the American scientists who made significant research contributions during the nineteenth century were physicians." Phyllis Allen Richmond, "The Nineteenth Century American Physician as a Research Scientist," in Felix Marti-Ibañez, ed., *History of American Medicine: A Symposium* (New York: M.D. Publications, 1959), pp. 142-55.

42. Louis Agassiz to Milne Edwards, 31 May 1847, in Agassiz, *Louis Agassiz,* 2:438.

43. *Proceedings of the Academy of Natural Sciences of Philadelphia* 4 (1848-49):225-33; 5(1849-50):7-8. During these same few years, the brilliant young anatomist Waldo I. Burnett was using the Boston Society of Natural History as one of his forums for discussing his researches in histology. Burnett's mentor, Oliver Wendell Holmes, used the Boston Society, among other things, to try out new microscope lenses and equipment.

44. It was particularly proud of its collections in ornithology, geology, zoology, herpetology, entomology, conchology, comparative anatomy, botany, paleontology, and mineralogy. See, for example, *Proceedings of the Academy of Natural Sciences of Philadelphia* 3, no. 12 (December 1847).

45. For a review of the Institute's history, see Madge E. Pickard, "Government and Science in the United States: Historical Backgrounds," *Journal of the History of Medicine and Allied Sciences* 1 (1946): 265-89.

46. The medical department of the Institution (Institute) had only a handful of active members, most or all local Washington physicians. Some of these read papers at meetings, and some had ambitions, through a series of questionnaires, of collecting nationwide statistical information on public health. Two of them, James Wynne and John M. Thomas, played a role in the beginnings of the American Medical Association's committee on hygiene. Medical activities of the Institution received some notice in the *Boston Medical and Surgical Journal* and other medical journals of the period. See also *Bulletin of the Proceedings of the National Institution for the Promotion of Science,* especially vols. 1-4 (1840-1846).

The Columbian Institute, in some ways a predecessor of the National Institution, had, under its first president, the naval surgeon Edward Cutbush, a variety of specific medical aims: the collection of medicinal plants and drugs, the collation and dissemination of information about mineral springs, the study of veterinary medicine, and the gathering of data on medical topography, meteorology, and disease distribution. Pickard, "Government and Science," pp. 254-65.

47. Josiah C. Nott, "An Examination of the Physical History of the Jews, in its Bearings on the Question of the Unity of the Races," *Proceedings of the American Association for the Advancement of Science* 3 (1850):98-106.

48. Those composing the committee were the geologist Jacob W. Bailey, together with four scientists having M.D. degrees, John Torrey, J. Lawrence Smith, Waldo I. Burnett, and Alonzo Clark. The committee concluded that Spencer's objectives "are of unrivalled excellence, ...the best in the world" (*Proceedings of the American Association for the Advancement of Science* 6 [1852]: 397-98). A committee of the New York Lyceum of Natural History had reached substantially the same conclusion in 1847. *American Journal of Science* 2d ser., 5 (1848): 238-39.

The Organization
of Agricultural Improvement
in the United States,
1785-1865

MARGARET W. ROSSITER

In examining the various kinds of learned and scientific societies that developed in the United States before 1865, one of the most important questions to be considered is whether these early "learned societies" were "progressing" toward the later "professional societies" or whether something else was happening. In the case of the agricultural societies, the answer lies in the second alternative.

In brief, the early learned societies, with their numerous purposes, carried out a great many agricultural functions that would later become the task of more specialized organizations, such as the agricultural press, the agricultural colleges, the state agricultural and geological surveys, the bureaus of the U.S. Department of Agriculture, the state experiment stations, and the public schools. In the period before 1820, when agricultural improvement was largely an upper-class activity, the general learned society and the learned society of agriculture were the chief foci of interest, but in succeeding decades, as improvement became an increasingly democratic activity, other institutions arose that were better adapted to the new purposes and methods and, as a result, bypassed the old societies that still remained. Since the new democratic interest in agricultural improvement was partly the result of recent breakthroughs in agricultural chemistry, the public also came to demand a new level of scientific expertise from its journals, societies, and government. This grass-roots demand in turn created a few full- and part-time jobs for professional agricultural scientists. These phenomena contributed to the democratization and "professionalization" of agricultural improvement, transforming the agricultural society from a gentlemen's club interested in agricultural improvement as a form of national betterment into an active self-interested lobbyist group that played an important part in a wider system. But before we draw too many analogies between the role and development of scientific and agricultural societies, there are important differences that should be noted.[1]

The chief difference between science and agriculture in this period was that agriculture had far stronger ties to geography and economics than did science. The period 1785-1865 was one of tremendous economic change in the United States, with whole new areas opened to cultivation, new transportation

[1] Notes to this chapter begin on page 296.

networks established, new urban markets created at home and abroad, and new crops and industries introduced. All these factors had important effects on agriculture. The result was that, by 1865 and frequently before then, American farmers, especially those that remained in the East, had to make drastic readjustments in their farming practice if they were to compete with the fertile and newly accessible lands of the Midwest. Individual farmers who wished either to benefit from this increased commercialization of agriculture or just to hold their own had to make a great many more sophisticated market and technical decisions than had their fathers. What crops should a farmer grow now that the soil would not yield a good crop of wheat? Should he specialize in one crop or grow several? How could he increase his output of hay or tobacco or should he try sorghum? Should he raise livestock or sheep or go into dairy farming? Should he sell the farm and move to the city? Should he go West? All these questions were under discussion in farm circles before the Civil War. They were very unsettling to established routine and made those farmers who wished to remain in New York or New England increasingly eager for new crops and new practices and more receptive to innovation and improvement.

Agricultural specialization was one such means of adjustment, although it implied additional changes as well. According to economic theory, as cities grow the lands near them become more valuable for nonagricultural usage. In their simplest form—that is, without different types of soil, without mineral deposits, without competing cities, mountains and other complicating factors—the land values separate out into the "von Thünen rings" predicated by the nineteenth-century German economist. Thus, in the era before refrigeration, it became most advantageous for a farmer near a city to specialize in dairy farming. He took his milk into the city daily to sell it, bought hay for his livestock and perhaps fruits for his family from another farm farther out, and purchased his wheat, which is relatively nonperishable and cheap to transport, from a distant area. But such specialization also brought problems. As farmers became increasingly dependent on a single crop, one new cattle disease or fruit pest could be a far more serious threat than it would have been in the prespecialized era. In the period after 1865 such specialized agricultural problems would justify the establishment of whole bureaus of entomology and plant and animal diseases in the U.S. Department of Agriculture. Before the Civil War the specialized farmers were only beginning to form their own societies and journals and to lobby for special government attention. In the long run, however, specialization would become an important force in the organization of agricultural improvement, for it broke down geographic lines and required such expertise to solve its problems that federal support would be necessary. The horticulturalists in the 1850s would be among the first to ask for it.

Another important and largely independent area of change for the farmers in the period 1785 to 1865 was the development of whole new sciences of use to farmers: agricultural chemistry, agricultural botany, agricultural entomology, agricultural geology, and even agricultural meteorology. In the pre-Civil War period agricultural chemistry was the most prominent, the result of very rapid developments in organic chemistry between 1800 and 1840. In 1785 there had been no organic chemistry, but by 1813 Humphry Davy could write his *Elements of Agricultural Chemistry* and in 1840 Justus Liebig his important *Organic Chemistry in its Applications to Agriculture and Physiology*. Both were very popular in America, but Liebig's in particular had widespread repercussions. Among farmers who sought helpful hints or panaceas for declining yields, Liebig raised great hopes when he claimed that such problems were capable of "easy solution by well-known facts" and promised to make fertilizing, a practice hitherto not fully understood, completely scientific. Guaranteed fertility seemed only a step away. Many agricultural chemists and "quacks" popularized these ideas, but in their reforming zeal they overrated the efficacy of their soil tests and remedies and created a craze over agricultural chemistry in the 1840s and early 1850s. Unfortunately, when their hopes were not fulfilled, the farmers became angry and bitter and strongly opposed any further advice. The search for an effective and reliable means of agricultural improvement was to be a difficult one.

One reason why the diffusion of agricultural innovations went through a boom-and-bust cycle in the nineteenth century was that there was available no adequate experimentation including statistical controls and cost-benefit analysis to determine what was or was not a useful innovation. There were so many factors—climate, rainfall and other moisture, soil porosity, previous use of soil, etc.—the effects of which were neither measurable nor subject to controls, that it was practically impossible to tell what constituted an improvement or really applicable "useful knowledge" and even harder to tell if it was economic or transferable to other soils and localities. Nevertheless, the agricultural editors and local suppliers urged everyone to try indiscriminately the latest development, be it soil analysis, electroculture, silkworms, or sorghum. Then, when the farmers reported mixed success, the editors were inclined to reject that innovation as not living up to its earlier claims and suggest a newer one. In the 1850s, when such repeated failures began to irritate the farmers, the scientists began to use the need for systematic experimentation as a major argument for state funding of experiment stations. The farmers, they said, needed *more* science, not *less*, in order to improve agriculture, but twenty years would pass before the farmers believed them.

All these pressures, especially strong after 1840, forced the agricultural societies and other organizations of agricultural improvement into a particular mold. The demand for the latest scientific views of agricultural chemistry or entomology was great, but there was little time, patience, or understanding (even among the most eminent scientists, such as Liebig himself) of the complexities of agricultural experimentation and the need to support extended research. Earlier, certain elite farmers had done rough experimentation on their farms and estates, but, from about 1850 until state governments began to support it in the 1870s, there was little sustained agricultural research in the United States. Thus the "demand" side of agricultural improvement, the popularization and diffusion, took precedence over the "supply" side of research and the presentation of papers in the United States before 1875. This orientation may have affected the makeup, as it certainly did the function, of the agricultural societies.

Likewise, agricultural thought "progresses" in ways unlike science, and this process affected the organization of agricultural improvement. Scientists frequently saw farmers as "anti-intellectual," practical men who were intolerant of theories and wanted only facts. The farmers were to a large extent justified in this attitude for very few agricultural theories, even scientific ones like those of Liebig, were reliable in practice—something that was, for the farmers, the only valid test. If, for example, a scientist said mineral manures were more effective than nitrogenous ones yet practice on a particular farm indicated otherwise, the farmer scorned the theory and adopted that which worked best. The scientist, on the other hand, would probably reject the test as invalid, attribute the failure to other factors, and cling to the theory. Since the actual underlying theory made little difference to the farmers, they could be, by the scientists' standards, surprisingly eclectic, that is, willing to believe even contradictory theories at the same time (as in humus and not in humus), if both led to useful practices.[2] As a result, many of the farmers laughed at the scientists, and they in turn shook their heads over the farmers, but these differences were inherent in the different ways that each group looked at agriculture.

The nature of their membership and audience reflect some of these similarities and differences between the agricultural and the general scientific societies. On the whole, the membership of the agricultural societies remained primarily local (countywide or at most statewide) and amateur. They began in the 1780s and 1790s as elite institutions, but after 1830 their leadership and methods of operation changed drastically. Social differences, however, such as a man's class, politics, or economic standing, seem to have provided greater barriers to participation in an agricultural society than in the scientific groups. It would certainly take more than scientific evidence or interest in betterment to make a landlord and his tenant agree on anything!

If social factors affected the agricultural societies' membership, they were even more important in the groups' relations with their audience. In a scientific society the membership and audience it tried to reach were usually like-minded fellow scientists or appreciative and influential laymen who were all presumed to be literate and receptive. But since the chief purpose of an agricultural society was diffusion of new practices to a less enlightened audience, its listeners often did not hold similar views. In fact, as the agricultural improvers began to reach out beyond their own circle, they often encountered criticism, opposition, apathy, and ridicule, which the scientists in their more limited and protected enclaves never experienced. The agricultural reformer thus took on something of the role of a political figure seeking votes or a preacher seeking converts from among the apathetic or reluctant wayward masses. Moreover, too much education, as evidenced, for example, by advanced study in Germany, was a much admired asset in scientific circles; among farmers, however, it was likely to be a liability,[3] and such an individual had to be especially careful when he tried to tell others how to farm. Far more convincing than education would be a prosperous farm nearby.

Ultimately, if publishing the scientific discovery completes the task for the scientist, describing the agricultural remedy is only half the job (and perhaps the easiest half) for the agricultural improver whose task is not complete until he has communicated the idea to the farmers and it is adopted. Extension work would always be a large and difficult part of agricultural improvement.

The organization of agricultural improvement thus had many more inter-actions with society than seems to have been true of the scientific societies before the Civil War. It was highly dependent on changes in economics, geogra-phy, social structure, and attitudes. The history of agricultural improvement in its fullest extent is not only a complex story, but one that is more subject to local variation than the history of scientific societies. In fact, it is a wonder that the agricultural societies were at all analogous to the scientific societies which seem so isolated and homogeneous in comparison. Yet one must remember that both groups were undergoing some of the same transformations in the period 1785 to 1865 in response to similar social, scientific, and economic forces. Therefore, a study of the agriculturalists and their problems may provide a useful perspective from which to look at the scientists and their organizations in this period.

Learned Societies

Organized agricultural improvement first appeared in the United States in the work of two early learned societies, the American Philosophical Society (1768) and the American Academy of Arts and Sciences (1780). Both groups deliber-ately included agriculture among the many subjects to which they wished to contribute and published a sizable number of papers on it in the first volumes of their *Transactions* and *Memoirs.* The topics included such items as worms, fruit trees. Smyrna wheat, and foreign plants. It is hard to assess the value of these papers. Some of the practices they advocated have since been accepted, although it is doubtful such writings had anything to do with their adoption. Most papers just noted curiosities, as was common in the medical and meteorological reports of the time. The only papers of lasting interest in these volumes are those of Jeremy Belknap on the preservation of parsnips in 1786 and Thomas Jefferson on an improved moldboard for a plow in 1799, and they are of value more for what they say of these men's inventive minds and wide-ranging interests than for the impact they had on farmers of the time. On the whole, these papers reveal that the early learned societies had a genuine interest in agriculture from the late 1760s through the 1780s and into the 1790s, but a very naïve impression of how to go about improving it. They thought of agriculture as a branch of science and the useful arts, and they felt that short essays contributed to a philosophical society would have some effect. They were not alone in this belief, for it had a noble English heritage.

For the most part, the members of these two learned societies were prominent, often wealthy, professional men who worked in a major city, but who resided on a relatively large family estate just outside the urban area. Undoubtedly, they were a very small percentage of the population. When they met in the society of Boston or Philadelphia in various social and intellectual settings, it was perhaps natural that they should discuss agriculture, a subject on which, as landowners if not actually farmers, they thought themselves well informed. As educated men they had read the classics and frequently quoted Cato, Virgil, and Varro on the satisfactions of the rural life. Many had also traveled abroad and become aware of the growing interest in the new scientific agriculture in England in the last half of the eighteenth century, which can perhaps be most easily summed up in the work of Arthur Young and the British Board of Agriculture. The English improvers felt that, if useful improvements were described and diffused to other like-minded agriculturalists, then these practices would spread still further to other neighboring farmers anxious to "emulate" them. In this way the British landowning gentry might hope to improve all of British agriculture by its example.[4]

Likewise, the American improvers, many of whom had played an important part in the Revolution and its aftermath, were aware of their country's backwardness in agriculture and were anxious to do all they could to improve it. The need for agricultural improvement appealed to their sense of national duty, and whether still in political life or temporarily in retirement, they worked hard to bring the latest developments to the attention of their countrymen. When writing each other, especially from abroad, they took pains to describe the local agricultural practices, and, when at home on their estates, they experimented with crop rotations, artificial manures, tillage, fencing, and drainage. Lacking a governmental Board of Agriculture, they dutifully reported their experiments to the new philosophical societies to which they already belonged and which they found a convenient forum for discussion and publication. They did not seem to worry that such a means of publication would be seen by only a small part of the nation's farmers, for such "bookfarming" had been very effective in Britain. Caught up in their enthusiasm for the new movement and the solutions it seemed to offer to pressing national problems, the promoters of agricultural improvement began to expand beyond the learned societies into additional separate groups of their own, though often with overlapping membership and clearly in the image of the learned societies.

Learned Agricultural Societies, 1785-1830

Of the several learned societies of agriculture formed before 1800, three stand out as the most important: the Philadelphia Society for the Promotion of Agriculture and Agricultural Reform (1785), the New York Society for Promoting Agriculture, Arts and Manufactures (1791), and the Massachusetts Society for Promoting Agriculture (1792). Although they all aspired to nationwide representation (by electing corresponding members from each others' groups), their membership was, like that of the learned societies themselves, largely local, amateur, and elite. Most of the members were active in business or the professions rather than in farming, with physicians in Philadelphia and merchants and lawyers in Boston particularly well represented. Actual farmers, in fact, constituted only a small percentage of the membership. Of the twenty-six original members of the Massachusetts group, only two were active farmers, although several, but by no means all, owned large farms on the outskirts of the city. The membership was in addition quite restricted, with most of the members being personal friends, business and professional associates, and even relatives. Their overlap with the learned societies was also considerable; in the case of the twenty-three charter members of the Philadelphia society, at least twelve were members of the American Philosophical Society.[5]

Despite their similarities with the learned societies, the new groups had a somewhat different motivation and method of operation. They were, despite their limited membership, more anxious to reach a group outside their own circle. Rather than passively awaiting the "emulation" they might have expected earlier, they now seemed willing to undertake a limited program of agricultural extension by providing premiums for essays on agricultural topics and later through competitions at state fairs. Although their expressed motivation was still national betterment, in order to promote "a greater increase of the products of the land within American states" in the case of the Philadelphia group, a note of urgent social control or, more euphemistically, "philanthropy," began to creep in. This was particularly the case in Massachusetts where the agricultural poverty of the western part of the state and the frequent migrations to the Northwest Territory seriously disturbed the Boston group.[6] Many of the Boston members who rented their farms to tenants stood to lose considerably if western lands proved too attractive and their area declined; a program to improve the state's agriculture was necessary to retain their own prosperity and that of the entire area. One solution that both the Boston and New York group settled upon was to raise money to establish professorships in botany at Harvard and in chemistry and related arts at Columbia, indicating a rather conservative response to the need for social change. Otherwise, the groups had rather uneven histories, dependent on the efforts of a few leading men and lapsing for long periods of inactivity. They continued to rely on learned publications for communications but supplemented them with occasional newspaper accounts. By 1830 most of these groups had ceased to function and, except for a few limited accomplishments, had exerted little impact on their areas. They remain, however, interesting examples of the learned gentleman trying to cope with social change beyond his control.

The first society was formed in Philadelphia, the center of a wheat-growing area before 1800. As in most eastern farm areas at the time, prices were high due to a strong demand, and thus farmers were content with low yields per acre. The reformers, however, were familiar with the more intensive agriculture of the English and urged their countrymen to take up the new practices—crop rotations, new manures (gypsum and lime), improved livestock, deeper tillage, and more varied crops—that would either give greater yields or preserve the soil. Since these practices were known and employed in England, the Pennsylvanians' failure to use them seemed wasteful to the reformers. Unfortunately, the improvers seemed unaware that, with an abundance of cheap land available, such labor-intensive practices were probably not worth the effort.[7]

The Philadelphia Society had two periods of activity, 1785-1793 and 1805-1828. In the earlier period the members used their own limited funds to amass a library of the latest works on agriculture from Europe and attempted to communicate with farmers outside their group through committees of correspondence and local newspapers. In the later period, under the active leadership of Judge Richard Peters, the Society offered premiums for essays and published five volumes of *Memoirs,* of which four had over sixty articles on sheep raising, gypsum, wheat smut, peach trees and various other topics of the day. Peters became such a strong advocate of the use of gypsum, writing over a hundred articles on this topic alone, that he is credited with making Chester County, Pennsylvania, the leading county in its use before 1840. Despite the vigor of the revived Society, however, dissension broke out shortly after Peters's death in 1828, and the Society became inactive. Nicholas Biddle became president in the 1830s, but it is unclear whether he did more than make an address at the annual banquet.[8]

Likewise, in New York City, the Society for the Promotion of Agriculture, Arts and Manufactures was dominated by the large landowners of the region, especially the estate-owners along the Hudson River and on Long Island who were, in the 1790s, also facing the problems of "worn-out soil" and looking for new alternatives to wheat farming. Under the strong leadership of Robert Livingston, the Society's president from 1791 until his death in 1813, the Society published two volumes of *Transactions* which were partially subsidized by the State of New York. Like Judge Peters, Livingston contributed many of the articles. His particular interests were gypsum and livestock, especially Merino sheep, which he studied and imported for himself and his friends. Largely through his efforts, eastern New York became a sheep-raising area for a time. Another active member of the Society was Ezra l'Hommedieu of Long Island, who experimented with alternative manures, such as crushed shells and seaweed. The New York Society also proved hardier than many other agricultural groups, surviving two serious dislocations without a setback. In 1797, when the state capital moved to Albany, the Society followed without losing its vitality, and in 1813 it recovered quite rapidly from the death of its leader, Livingston. Stephen van Rensselaer succeeded Livingston as president, and under his brief leadership the Society published two more volumes of the *Transactions* and increased its membership to an all-time high of 169. But even if the Society had overcome two such crises, it began to decay from within in 1817. Rensselaer resigned, the membership began to decline, and seven years later the Society joined with the Albany Lyceum of Natural History to form the new Albany Institute.[9]

The third learned society of agriculture, established in Boston in 1792, lacked the strong leadership of the other two groups in its early years, but after 1813 it grew more active and wealthy. Although the group had been formed to alleviate the plight of poor Massachusetts farmers, it is doubtful that it had much effect in solving this problem, and over the years it grew increasingly concerned with the gentlemanly agriculture of horticulture and animal breeding. At first the Society had been content to meet at the members' Boston homes, award $50 premiums for essays on agricultural topics, and make contributions to Harvard's botanic garden and its professorship of natural history. In 1813 Aaron Dexter, who had served in the militia suppressing Shays' Rebellion and had been a professor of chemistry and materia medica at Harvard, succeeded the aged John Adams as president. Dexter inaugurated a vigorous new period for the Society by publishing the *Massachusetts Agricultural Journal* from 1813 until 1832, holding an annual cattle fair from 1816 until 1835, and, most importantly, obtaining an annual appropriation of $1000 from the Massachusetts legislature to help defray the costs of the fair and provide the premiums. The annual fair was the most visible activity of the Society, but it aroused resentment among those who had to use their cattle on the farm, because its premiums favored the useless and expensive breeds of the gentlemen farmers.[10] As a result the Society lost its appropriation in 1830, but it continued to exist, devoting its treasury of $13,000 almost exclusively to improving the breeds of the members' cattle. In 1829 the organization was further weakened when several of the members joined the new Massachusetts Horticultural Society, one of the first such groups in the nation. By this time the members of the Massachusetts Society for Promoting Agriculture, the richest, longest-lasting, and initially public-spirited of the learned societies of agriculture, had long since given up their original goal of improving the condition of the state's poor farmers and retired to their own gentlemanly agriculture.

Thus, by about 1830 the learned societies of agriculture had either collapsed or retreated from their earlier purpose of trying to reform the nation's agriculture. Each society had achieved some improvement in its own area, as in gypsum, sheep raising, and cattle breeding, but these were only a small part of the big changes that were taking place in American agriculture between 1790 and 1830. This was the period when New York was settled and Ohio opened by New Englanders, for many of whom westward migration had become a way of life. In fact, it was certainly more advantageous for a New England farmer in this period to give up his poor and rocky farm and move West rather than to try to improve it as the reformers kept urging him to do. The reformers tacitly admitted this by going into the noncompetitive fields of horticulture and cattle breeding. For their own reasons they wanted the poorer farmers to stay, but they were fighting an uphill battle, and the agriculture they were striving to improve was increasingly a rich man's preserve. Despite their good intentions, they were out of touch with the mainstream of American agriculture at the time.

Emergence of a New Pattern: The Rise of Albany, 1825-1841

Most secondary sources on agricultural improvement agree that (1) the early learned agricultural societies (with the possible exceptions of the groups mentioned above) were largely ineffective, (2) it was only after 1840 that the great boom in agricultural improvement took place, and (3) the middle period was relatively quiet and uneventful. This view is somewhat oversimplified, since by 1841 a new pattern of agricultural improvement had already emerged in New York State. By then Albany had become the primary center for agricultural reform in the East, the home of the most active journal, the strongest lobby, the best organized society, and the seat of the most generous legislature. The city of Rochester had also grown into a major center. Boston, Philadelphia, and New York City, however, had all reverted by 1840 to the status of minor centers with less influential journals and less active groups.[11] How this primacy of Albany, which lasted roughly twenty years from 1835 to 1855, came about is one of the major phenomena in agricultural improvement in the United States before 1865.

Part of the answer lies in geographic and economic factors. After the Revolutionary War had cleared western New York of Indian threats, many farmers left New England for better soil along the Mohawk River and in the Genesee Valley. The opening of the Erie Canal in the 1820s brought these fertile areas into easy contact with eastern urban markets and made it possible for the farmers of upstate New York to export their wheat to Albany, New York City, and other areas. This new "commercial agriculture" provided more of an incentive for farmers to increase yields than had been true earlier, when farmers had generally lacked market outlets. But the Erie Canal had opened not only western New York, but Ohio and Michigan as well. As a result, many New York farmers, who were sensitive to the market prices for their crops, began to worry about competition from the West, where fresher and more fertile soils made possible even greater yields and lower prices than in New York. These increased market incentives might be one reason why the New York farmers of the 1830s and 1840s were very responsive, as farmers go, to agricultural change.

In addition, the settling of New York seems, and this is something we can only speculate about, to have created a different social structure for the farming community than had been true earlier in New England. In New York there appears to have been less polarization between the rich and poor farmers and something of a middle class of farmers who were more literate and informed than earlier and more inclined to turn to agricultural improvement rather than to migration to better their lot. Under such conditions many farmers, not just professional men in the cities, began to take a new look at the agricultural improvement they or their fathers had formerly scorned.

Another reason for the rise of Albany in agricultural improvement thus becomes psychological and sociological. Who in society decides to change or innovate, who to follow, and who to resist is a difficult question to answer, but Clarence Danhof has designated certain groups in upstate New York in the period between 1820 and 1870 as "innovators," "imitators," "gradualists," and "traditionalists."[12] Since most farmers, perhaps 90 percent or more, will resist change to some extent even in periods of great innovation, the small minority who are receptive to change and take up leadership is a particularly important body. New York State was fortunate at this time in having so many strong and resourceful men to lead this second movement for agricultural improvement. The names of these leaders constantly recur in the agricultural journals: Luther Tucker, B. P. Johnson, Joseph Delafield, Edward C. Delavan, Jesse Buel, John Johnston, Erastus Corning, Robert Pell, and others. Together, at the state and local level, they could do much to bring change to the rest of the farmers of New York State.

A third reason for the rise of Albany is political and financial, for not only were these New York agriculturalists innovative, but they were also organized and effective in getting support from their state legislature. By 1841, when they succeeded in getting an annual appropriation of $8,000 from the state legislature for agricultural societies and fairs, they were at least ten and maybe twenty years ahead of such other states as Massachusetts, Connecticut, Pennsylvania, and Virginia in their awareness of the need to organize at the county level, to support strong agricultural journals, and to lobby with the state legislature. One had only to examine the case of Virginia in this period to observe the difference.

Between 1790 and 1820 Virginia had been the home of several distinguished agricultural reformers: George Washington, Thomas Jefferson, and James Madison. Most effective had been Edmund Ruffin, who had read Arthur Young and Humphry Davy and started his own agricultural journal, the *Farmer's Register*, in 1819. He popularized the use of marl as a fertilizer for depleted tobacco lands, but despite his efforts Virginia never pulled together a cohesive group that could lobby effectively at the state legislature. Agricultural journals in Richmond complained about the lack of organization and muscle but to little avail, and, when Ruffin's journal collapsed in 1842 due to an unpopular stand on a bank issue, Virginia slipped quietly into the backwater. Baltimore likewise had shown signs of activity in the 1820s, but was unable to sustain it. Albany's success looks all the stronger in comparison.

As early as 1797, when Robert Livingston and the New York Society for the Promotion of Agriculture, Arts and Manufactures had moved up the Hudson, Albany had been the site of a group of men interested in agricultural reform. But it was paradoxically in 1819, when the Society's strength seemed to be waning, that its leaders had their greatest success. At that time Livingston's successor, Stephen van Rensselaer, and Governor DeWitt Clinton convinced the state legislature, first, to establish a state Board of Agriculture similar to that of Arthur Young in England, and, second, to grant $10,000 to county societies for democratic agricultural fairs such as reformer Elkanah Watson had recently been popularizing across the state. The idea of a Board of Agriculture was an old one, having been suggested by George Washington in 1796, but it had never been established on either the state or national level. By contrast, the second provision allocating extensive state funds to county agricultural societies was a strikingly new idea which proved very effective in broadening participation in agricultural reform in New York State. It created more than fifty new agricultural societies and encouraged them to work for the improvement of their own areas.

The New York Board existed for six years, 1819-1825, and published two volumes of *Memoirs*. The first volume contained an extensive essay on agriculture by G. W. Featherstonhaugh and the second, Amos Eaton's geological and agricultural survey of Rensselaer County. At the county level, although the agricultural societies and their fairs were popular for a time, they were not effective enough to override partisan criticism, and the Board and its appropriation became the victims of anti-Clintonian politics in 1825.[13] Later leaders, however, would find it a useful precedent for generous state aid to the agricultural societies.

Of greater importance for agricultural improvement in New York in the 1830s was the rise of a popular agricultural press. In 1831 Luther Tucker started his *Genesee Farmer* in Rochester and in 1832 Jesse Buel began publication in Albany of the *Cultivator,* whose motto was "to improve the soil and the mind." These were not the first such popular agricultural journals in the United States, but they became the most widely read. In 1839, when Tucker took over the *Cultivator* after Buel's death, it had a circulation of over twenty-three thousand in New York and its surrounding states. Although this readership was probably still only a fraction of all farmers, Clarence Danhof has estimated that it was the largest in the world at the time. Americans, when compared to English and other farmers, were the greatest readers of all.[14] The success of these journals indicated once again that by the 1830s upstate New York had a population with the social structure, mental attitude, and income distribution able and willing to support such journals. Interest in agricultural improvement was in the 1830s rapidly spreading beyond the elite, and the men who would replace the Livingstons and van Rensselaers of an earlier generation as the leaders of agricultural reform would be the editors of these new journals.

After Buel started his journal, he and several others petitioned the state legislature to start a state agricultural society. They were successful in 1833 and made the *Cultivator* their mouthpiece a year later. They lobbied for a state appropriation through the rest of the 1830s but were not successful until 1841, when they obtained an annual grant of $8,000 to support the society, its *Transactions,* and the county societies and their fairs. With this funding New York became the leading state for agricultural improvement in the nation. Other states' efforts look weak and disorganized in comparison, and most, twenty or even forty years later, would still not grant this much to agricultural improvement. Somehow New York had succeeded where others had failed.

By 1841 New York had thus established a new tripartite pattern of agricultural improvement: a strong state society situated in the capital to lobby with the state legislature, several county societies to collect statistics and to run local fairs, and a popular journal to advocate new practices and to rouse support for legislative bills. Under this arrangement, agricultural improvements was no longer a philanthropy run by the physicians and lawyers in the city. Such groups persisted, as in the American Institute, or "Fifth Avenue Farmers" as they were called, of New York City, but with greatly diminished importance. The farmers had been roused to help themselves and had strong leaders who were organized to press for action from their state legislatures. In succeeding decades this new pattern would spread, usually in modified or diminished form, to other states. In this new order of things there would appear room—and a role—for the trained agricultural expert and the professional scientist.

Growth and Incipient Professionalism, 1840-1865

After 1840 there was a tremendous growth of interest in agricultural improvement. One calculation reveals that in 1858 there were 912 agricultural societies in the United States, almost all of which had been founded since 1840 on the local or county level.[15] The number of agricultural journals likewise increased rapidly after 1840 and reached an estimated fifty to sixty active journals with a combined circulation of 250,000 in 1860.[16] In fact, there were so many societies and journals they may have undercut each other's support. But even if many existed for only a brief time, others, such as the *Cultivator* and *American Agriculturalist*, had an almost national reputation and circulation. It was becoming increasingly common for the "average farmer" in a given county to read an agricultural journal, belong to an agricultural society, and attend an annual fair. What had occurred first in New York was becoming increasingly widespread.

This great upsurge of interest in agricultural improvement after 1840 can be attributed to several factors. Not only were competitive pressures, as mentioned above, making it increasingly advantageous for farmers to be informed of market conditions and new practices, but also agricultural technology and, for the first time since Arthur Young and Humphry Davy, agricultural science began to offer dramatic new ideas and equipment that promised to lead to improved prosperity, greater security, and less work for farmers. When the farmers began to feel that the improvers might really have something practical to offer, they became curious to hear more about them; gradually, farmers began to think of themselves as an interest group that viewed government as something that might provide benefits rather than merely charge taxes. During the 1840s the farmers also became more tolerant, and even for a while receptive, to the improvers' demands for state agricultural surveys, colleges, chemists, and subsidies. Once the movement was under way, the momentum grew in the mid-1840s as one new innovation begat another and one convert convinced another. Suddenly, not only were farmers ready to subscribe to journals and to read about the latest reapers and threshers and Liebig's ideas from Germany, but legislatures, with

New York leading the way, were increasingly willing to grant subsidies to county and state societies and to create state boards of agriculture to collect data and issue annual reports. Spurred on by the agricultural editors and secretaries of the state boards and societies, the farmers in turn began to demand better and better agricultural information and to expect that every agricultural problem or curiosity would have a scientific explanation. All this grass-roots demand for agricultural information created not only positions but also problems for the new agricultural experts.

The agricultural editors and secretaries, themselves publicists and middlemen with limited scientific training (although more than one might expect), began during the 1840s to turn increasingly to trained scientists for intelligible expertise. Men such as Eben Horsford, a student with Liebig at Giessen; John Pitkin Norton, a chemistry professor at Yale; Ebenezer Emmons, a New York physician and geologist; and Asa Fitch, a New York physician and entomologist began to write regular columns in agricultural journals, address state fairs, give popular lectures, write textbooks, and perform soil analyses. Despite these numerous part-time opportunities for scientists, especially chemists and geologists, there were very few full-time opportunities for agricultural experts before 1865. There were a few positions in the U.S. Patent Office and a few in the societies and at the state boards, but these were subject to political pressures and did not attract the best men. In fact the problem of harnessing the great popular demand for agricultural chemistry in the 1840s and channeling it into jobs for competent men who would do reputable work and thereby "maintain standards" was a severe one for the emerging profession. There was only a limited amount of qualified manpower, and despite the widespread popular interest there were even fewer adequate jobs for such men. The unfortunate result was that many chemists, often self-trained, became self-proclaimed experts in agricultural matters overnight, undersold those chemists who tried to do thorough soil tests, and thereby incurred the hot but ineffectual wrath of the reputable chemists who denounced such men as "quacks." Eventually, in the early 1850s, when farmers became impatient with the inadequacies of soil analysis and agricultural chemistry, they turned on chemists as a whole and indiscriminately labeled them all "quacks." What had once been a very popular and promising area of science came to an abrupt halt, and most chemists immediately retreated from further contact with farmers. The next generation of agricultural chemists would have the difficult task of trying to reconvince the public that their science had some value.

Part of the chemists' problem in the 1850s was that, though they had sought to institutionalize their field in the enthusiastic 1840s, they had not quite succeeded. They had tried to strengthen their position by lobbying for agricultural colleges, agricultural surveys, lectureships, prizes, premiums, state chemists, and an agricultural bureau in the government, and had, in fact, aroused some popular support for these projects; in the end, however, only the least expensive of these proposals had usually been successful. Farmers were willing to subscribe to an agricultural journal for a few dollars as a cheap way to get the latest information about markets, crops, and other matters, especially when it came in the palatable form of a monthly family magazine. In this sense they had come a long way since 1790. But they were not yet willing to be taxed to support a standing army of agricultural research experts or extension officers to tell them what to do. Even New York State, so progressive in so many ways, resisted the idea of an experiment station in the mid-1850s. Later the farmers would become impatient with the weaknesses of existing agricultural knowledge and begin to respond to the scientists' argument that only new research and rigorous experimentation under controlled conditions at an experiment station could hope to solve their problems. But until the 1870s, when the farmers began to listen to such arguments again, the agricultural chemists had a difficult time convincing farmers of anything. The farmers had been burned once by the "experts," and it would take some time before they would be willing to subsidize such men any further.[17] The farmers thus had in the period before 1865 an ambivalent attitude toward the support of agricultural improvement, and agricultural science in particular. They wanted it and admired it, yet they ridiculed its failures. They needed the professional, but they distrusted him. They were interested in his work but were reluctant to provide stable financial support for him. Fortunately for the agricultural chemists, the reformers were a hardy and persistent group who would cause some of this attitude to change during the Civil War, in, of all places, the federal government.

Specialization and the Federal Support of Agriculture

By the mid-1850s the movement for agricultural reform had taken root in most states, but it was encountering increased local opposition from many of its former friends. Perhaps because the reformers were stymied at home, but also because they were becoming increasingly sophisticated politically, some of the agricultural improvers began to seek help from the federal government. Unfortunately, previous attempts to obtain direct or even indirect federal support for agriculture had come to nothing, as in George Washington's plan for a Board of Agriculture, Charles Fleischmann's plan for the use of the Smithson bequest, and repeated plans for a national university.[18] In the 1850s the only agency in the federal government helping farmers was the Patent Office in the Interior Department, which, through a curious history, had come to circulate free seeds to farmers and publish an annual report on agriculture. The reformers began to think the federal government should do more. Agriculture had, however, by its very nature, long been considered primarily a local activity. The reformers' problem in the 1850s was how to convince the federal government to expand its role and support in this area.

During the 1850s two quite separate campaigns developed toward this goal. Both were successful in 1862, and suddenly put the federal government in a central position in the movement for agricultural reform. Although these two successes, the formation of a separate U.S. Department of Agriculture and the passage of the Morrill Land-Grant Act to support agricultural and mechanical colleges, had little immediate impact on American agriculture, they would do much to transform it in the decades ahead.

Those agricultural societies which had in the past petitioned the federal government for support had usually been based in one particular state. Since they had lacked a national constituency, Congress had found it easy to disregard their requests. But by the 1850s various specialized groups, led by the horticulturalists, began to organize on a national level and to petition the federal government. Since the first step in appealing for state funds had usually been to set up a society, which was in fact a lobby or pressure group, several agricultural improvers, led by Marshall P. Wilder of Massachusetts, formed the U.S. Agricultural Society in Washington in 1852. Wilder, the former president of the Massachusetts Horticultural Society and the current president of the newly formed American Pomological Society, was one of the most effective agricultural leaders of the century on the state and national level. In order to create a nationwide constituency, the group established its headquarters in Washington, published a journal, met annually at the Smithsonian Institution, and held an annual fair in various states, including Massachusetts, Ohio, Pennsylvania, Illinois, Kentucky, or Virginia. From the start the group advocated creation of a separate Department of Agriculture in the federal government, but met with little success until 1856 when it began to focus on the Patent Office, attacking it for inadequate treatment of agricultural problems. In 1858 the Department of the Interior responded by creating a separate bureau of agriculture within the Department. Still dissatisfied, the Society demanded a separate Department again in 1860 and obtained it in 1862.[19] Expansion began almost immediately with the hiring of a chemist, a botanist, and an entomologist. The establishment of the Department was a victory for the forces of specialized agriculture which had seen the federal government as the source of greater centralization, paid expertise, and improved communication. In these desires they differed from the other agricultural forces active at the time who favored direct federal support but resisted central direction and control.

During the 1840s and 1850s, the improvers had managed to establish agricultural colleges in several states, most notably Michigan, Pennsylvania, Iowa, and Maryland, but they had not been as effective in other areas. Either way, their efforts usually interacted with those of other groups. They were supported by individuals who had their own ambitions to advance new forms of training such as manual work schools, vocational education, and popular technical education (exemplified by the People's College in New York), but opposed by still other groups: the advocates of sectarian schools, the older colleges, and those farmers who opposed "bookfarming" and the excesses of the agricultural chemistry movement. The improvers saw a way out of this impasse by asking the federal government to support the new agricultural colleges and to do it by selling western public lands. Easterners, especially Senator Justin Morrill of Vermont, were especially fond of this proposal for it gave them new institutions primarily at the West's expense. Others, such as the U.S. Agricultural Society and the backers of the "industrial university" movement in Illinois, also sponsored the bill. Senator Morrill introduced the bill in late 1857; it passed in 1858 but was vetoed by President James Buchanan in 1859. After the South seceded in 1861, Senator Morrill reintroduced the bill which again passed and was signed by Lincoln in 1862. The agricultural schools that were already in existence were glad to receive the extra support, and new institutions sprang up rapidly in other states to claim their share. Such federal support to state institutions seemed the best of all possible arrangements to this branch of agricultural improvers who wished to retain local control. It provided relatively large sums to those in the area who could best attack and solve certain local agricultural problems but demanded few immediate results and asked few hostile questions in return.

In subsequent decades the federal government would move agricultural improvement into a new era whose achievements would far outshine the earlier efforts of the learned societies of agriculture and the state agricultural societies. Likewise, the agricultural societies themselves would be transformed. With the federal government providing funds for research and extension far more effectively and imaginatively than the states had earlier, the societies would become nationwide pressure groups of a new sort, representing either the specialized interests of, for example, dairy husbandrymen or the populist feelings of the members of the National Grange to the state and federal governments. By then the problem of organizing agricultural improvement had largely been solved, and, instead of urging farmers to adopt reforms, the societies would be trying to protect their constituents from the economic repercussions of overproduction and too much technological change.

Conclusion

The period from 1785 to 1865 saw a great many important changes in agriculture in America. These were largely economic, both in terms of the geography of agriculture—transportation and marketing practices and patterns— and in terms of science and technology, which offered new forms of improvement involving gypsum, livestock breeding, sheep raising, and reapers. By 1865 agriculture was a fairly sophisticated industry in which prosperity or failure depended on a farmer's response to changes around him. More and more farmers were realizing that they had to be informed and up to date in order to survive. The increasing number of abandoned farms in New England were living testimony that a modern farmer could not necessarily follow his father's ways and hope to succeed.

During this period, the movement for agricultural improvement finally came into its own. The dire warnings of the reformers before 1800 began to seem real, and by about 1840 more of the middle-rank farmers began to adopt improved practices and to demand more. But the change and final acceptance of agricultural reform was not the result of the efforts of the early learned societies of agriculture, most of which had died out by 1830, but of a change in economic factors and a great advance in agricultural science. In the 1830s a new type of agricultural reformer, the editor of agricultural periodicals, started a second and more popular movement for agricultural improvement, first in New York and subsequently elsewhere. This grass-roots demand for reform created jobs for agricultural experts who would be paid for their labors in an indirect way— through their writings or lectures or posts at agricultural colleges or societies. Starting in the 1850s, some of these men would form groups to lobby for more state and federal support to establish the experiment stations and government laboratories that would employ agricultural scientists full time in investigating soil, crop, and animal problems. By 1865 the organization of agricultural improvement had gone through two eras and was gearing up for the third. Agricultural reform had been accepted as a governmental responsibility, and the foundation had been laid for a greatly expanded federal role in the future.

Likewise, the forces that were doing so much to democratize, professionalize, specialize, and federalize agricultural improvement were affecting scientific organization in the United States before 1865. The early multipurpose learned societies had performed many tasks that were later undertaken by several different types of organizations, such as the lyceums, mechanics institutes, public schools, museums, popular magazines, and systematic geological surveys. The older scientific societies might or might not persist, but they would have to share their audience and functions with these other groups. In fact, as science became increasingly professionalized, the demand for popularization, rather than diminishing, became increasingly widespread, so that a whole group of middlemen and institutions arose to meet and present science to the mass audience, usually through new ways that bypassed the old societies. Before 1865 this task would be largely filled, as in agriculture, by part-time lecturing and governmental advising by scientists already otherwise employed. After the Civil War, men like Edward Youmans and John Fiske could make full-time careers out of popularization, and Charles Wetherill and Thomas Antisell became full-time chemists for the government. In geology the transformation came even earlier, as part-time amateur geologists were largely superseded by full-time, though temporary, employees of the state surveys in the 1830s. These employees would in time form new organizations to represent their interests and to lobby for their projects. Perhaps in ways such as this, the example of agricultural improvement can offer a perspective and point of comparison from which to examine important changes taking place in scientific societies and other institutions in the period before 1865.

NOTES

1. We usually make the following distinctions in talking of scientific societies, but correlations between them are as yet unclear:

Status	Membership	Leadership	Geography	Facilities
Amateur	Democratic (open)	Open Changing	Local (urban)	Rooms
Professional	Elitist (selective)	Selective Entrenched	Statewide	"Cabinet"
Honorary			Regional National Colonial	Other collections Library

Purpose	Audience		Scope	Subject
Social	Polite society		Broad	Technology
Self-education (popularization)	Artisans, farmers		Specialized	Applied science
Professional (communication)	Students			
	Fellow scientists (information, roles, morale)			Pure science
Power (lobbyist)				
Honorary (glory)	Other learned societies Government			Nonscience (literature, history)

2. Margaret W. Rossiter, *The Emergence of Agricultural Science: Justus Liebig and the Americans, 1840-1880* (New Haven: Yale University Press, 1975), pp. 35-36.

3. But farmers were ambivalent in their attitude toward German learning. At one moment they favored Liebig as a genius, but ridiculed him as an incompetent farmer the next.

4. Rodney Loehr, "Arthur Young and American Agriculture," *Agricultural History* 43 (1969): 43-56 is an excellent recent study of the British Board of Agriculture and its influence on America.

5. Olive M. Gambrill, "John Beale Bordley and the Early Years of the Philadelphia Agricultural Society," *Pennsylvania Magazine of History and Biography* 66 (1942): 436.

6. *Centennial Year (1792-1892) of the Massachusetts Society for Promoting Agriculture* (Salem, Mass.: Massachusetts Society for Promoting Agriculture, 1892), pp. 15-16.

7. James T. Lemon, *The Best Poor Man's Country: A Geographical Study of Early Southeastern Pennsylvania* (Baltimore: Johns Hopkins University Press, 1972) is an excellent study of the area and its agriculture. Lemon also points out how the Philadelphia reformers, in their eagerness to point to English examples of agricultural reform, largely overlooked their neighbors, the German Pennsylvania Dutch farmers in Lancaster County, who were thought at the time to have more intensive agricultural practices than their Scotch-Irish neighbors.

8. Lucius Ellsworth, "The Philadelphia Society for the Promotion of Agriculture and Agricultural Reform, 1785-1793," *Agricultural History* 42 (1968): 189-99; Gambrill, "John Beale Bordley," pp. 410-39.

9. James Hobbins, "The Provincial Learned Society: The Early History of the Albany Institute," and Brooke Hindle, "The Underside of the Learned Society in New York, 1754-1854," both in this volume; Donald B. Marti, "Early Agricultural Societies in New York: The Foundations of Improvement," *New York History* 48 (1967): 313-31.

10. Paul W. Gates, *The Farmers' Age: Agriculture, 1815-1860* (New York: Harper Torchbooks, 1960), pp. 313-14. Fairs could, like societies, be either elitist or democratic, depending on the types of exhibits, contests, prizes, sponsorship, publicity, location, and duration.

11. New York City would rise again and eclipse Albany around 1850, when it became publishing center for the national agricultural press with Orange Judd's *American Agriculturalist* and Horace Greeley's *New York Tribune*.

12. Clarence Danhof, *Change in Agriculture: The Northern United States, 1820-1870* (Cambridge, Mass.: Harvard University Press, 1969), chap. 11.

13. Marti, "Early Agricultural Societies," p. 322. The exact relationship of the Society for the Promotion of Agriculture, Arts and Manufactures to the passage of the 1819 act remains unclear, however.

14. Danhof, *Change in Agriculture,* p. 57.

15. Wayne C. Neely, *The Agricultural Fair* (New York: Columbia University Press, 1935), pp. 83-87.

16. Albert L. Demaree, *The American Agricultural Press, 1819-1860* (New York: Columbia University Press, 1941), p. 17.

17. Rossiter, *Emergence of Agricultural Science,* chaps. 8 and 9.

18. Gates, *The Farmers' Age,* pp. 367-70; A. Hunter Dupree, "The Morrill Act and Science," 1962, unpublished manuscript.

19. Lyman Carrier, "The United States Agricultural Society, 1852-1860," *Agricultural History* 11 (1937): 278-88; Paul W. Gates, "The Morrill Act and Early Agricultural Science," *Michigan History* 46 (1962): 289-302.

Savants and Professionals:
The American Association
for the Advancement of Science,
1848-1860

SALLY GREGORY KOHLSTEDT

The emergence of scientists as professionals is a common theme for historians of nineteenth-century American science. The most visible public forum for debating and promoting professional concerns, and the first to create a national organization specifically limited to science yet encompassing regional, specialized interests, was the American Association for the Advancement of Science (AAAS).[1] In several practical ways, the organization predicted future developments. National membership made it a vehicle capable of affecting changes associated with the rise of modern scientific standards. But the Association's early membership was a heterogeneous mix of practicing scientists, interested participants, and onlookers. This fact, together with an understanding that the leaders were firmly grounded in past experiences, makes it imperative for the historian to look backward from 1860 as well as forward. The founders were inspired but also limited by the self-image and aspirations of their age. Although the AAAS was formed as a complement to earlier societies as well as to promote new goals, it confronted the same social, political, and personal imperatives that shaped other pre-Civil War scientific societies. In fact, it is questionable whether the peripetetic national society could have existed without the experience and support of local societies. During the first thirteen years, 1848-1860, the AAAS mirrored the internal tensions perhaps implicit in any new organization and also the difficulties associated with emerging professionalism. This paper will consider first the nature of the new organization, then the characteristics and aspirations of its leadership, and finally the limits of the model it offered to a coming generation of scientists.

Reflecting an organizational tendency pervasive in the 1840s, leading scientists increasingly argued the need for institutions to promote and legitimize science in the young United States. Like many other American groups, and even America itself, the scientists sought self-definition. These spokesmen hoped to improve the status of American science abroad, to gain financial support from the public (sometimes perceived as government and sometimes as private patrons), and to improve education for and communication among scientists. Impetus came in part from a self-conscious and often unrealistic comparison

---

[1] Notes to this chapter begin on page 321.

between American institutions and those with status and financial backing in Europe.[2] Americans were especially aware of German education and of the French and English academies and were envious of the prestige accorded such prominent scientists as Charles Lyell, Michael Faraday, and Georges Cuvier. In America science had not been the exclusive domain of wealthy dilettantes, nor were most political and social leaders particularly interested in science during the colonial and early national period.[3] It appealed most obviously to medical doctors, agriculturalists, and other individuals with leisure to investigate natural history or natural philosophy. Such persons grouped together in local societies in order to share books, journals, and new ideas; the result, though mutually edifying, only rarely advanced science.[4]

In the second quarter of the nineteenth century, science changed markedly. When colleges and government agencies created occupations in science by hiring teachers who did research in specific disciplines, the new opportunities made science more legitimate and publicly recognized. Yet at the same time science assumed the mundane posture of a demanding and often poorly paying job.[5] New societies emerging in major eastern cities described their interests more narrowly than did the American Philosophical Society and the American Academy of Arts and Sciences. Such societies as the Academy of Natural Sciences of Philadelphia, the New York Lyceum, and Boston's Society of Natural History provided the same informal social and intellectual alliances as the older societies, even as they sought a specialized membership and promoted public programs in science. Locally successful in the 1830s, not one of the societies represented science on the national level.

Programming a National Organization

Institutions designed to facilitate communication among scientists and to provide support for research, the information networks suggested by A. Hunter Dupree, were needed. Yet the movement toward a national scientific society was cautious. From 1835 onward, various American scientists corresponded with each other about the possibility of founding a broad-based organization.[6] These individuals carefully scrutinized models at home and abroad that might provide both a general philosophy and the working details of administration for national organizations. For over ten years they evaluated the characteristics of various groups (especially the philosophical and natural history societies) in the United States, each of which reflected local pride and scientific preferences. They also considered the British Association for the Advancement of Science (BAAS) and other European societies, although some Americans expressed skepticism about whether these organizations were models appropriate to the American experience.

Local societies, as several studies in this volume have indicated, had difficulty sustaining themselves but contributed substantially to the quality of effort and the general interest in science for their geographical area. None, however, provided a national podium for prominent researchers or a membership broad based enough to encourage conference quality debate or resolve specific scientific questions. Growing specialization outdated discussion of natural history. A more educated nation with a proliferation of colleges made science accessible to greater numbers, often as an avocation but increasingly as background for individuals dedicated to science. Practically, the transportation revolution made possible a single, centrally located annual convention for scientists.

The earliest efforts to found a society were undermined by established organizations that anticipated competition from a new scientific society and by skeptical scientists who feared the effect of local amateur tradition. As a result, the American Society for the Cultivation of Science, formulated by Boston's John Collins Warren in 1838, was effectively killed by the American Philosophical Society's rejection of the proposal for its establishment.[7] The National Institute in Washington, D.C., was derailed in 1844, after four uncertain years, by the organized roadblock of the geological community and the hostility of other leading scientists who mistrusted the political implications of the organization.[8] During these years, scientists warned each other of the danger of popular science even as they articulated the need for some institution capable of meeting their needs as new professionals. Alexander Dallas Bache, in his address as retiring president of the AAAS in 1891, explained the delay as simple caution and lack of personal familiarity among the practicing scientists:

The opposition came not more from those who were habitually conservative, than from those who, being earnest in regard to the progress of science, are usually in favor of all progressive measures. It proceeded from no under-estimate of the strength which there was among the cultivators of science. Some of us had studied the workings of the British Association, and had been convinced of the absolute necessity for the attendance there from year to year of the men of the universities, to give a tone to the proceedings; . . . So far from having been trained in the name schools, we scarcely knew each other personally. How could we irregulars venture into conflict, when the files to our right and to our left were strangers to us, and when the cause might thus have suffered from the want of discipline of its volunteer support?[9]

Bache went on to explain that, instead of founding a national society in the late 1830s, "it was very prudently left for the geologists to begin the work."

As a result, when established in 1848, the AAAS grounded itself securely on eight years of experience provided by the Association of American Geologists and Naturalists. The older Association, which met annually in various eastern cities from 1840 through 1847, had grown to include nearly all active American geologists. It was successful as a specialized society primarily because geology enjoyed the greatest visibility and financial support of any science in the decade.[10] In general, its members were persistent in attendance and presented their best work at its meetings. Certainly European approval of the group, as expressed by geologist Charles Lyell after he attended the 1842 meeting in Boston and by Swiss naturalist Louis Agassiz in 1847, helped increase the self-confidence and aspirations of the group.[11] The geologists also found the small, informal meetings useful in providing new ideas, encouragement, and personal friendship.[12] However, the Association was not an unqualified success. It never fully incorporated the naturalists into its discussions, the quality of its presentations was not uniformly high despite the excellent work of some members, and it was not able to maintain an ongoing journal. A few dedicated and active members sustained the Association, particularly Henry and William Rogers, Edward Hitchcock, the elder and younger Benjamin Silliman, William Redfield, and James Dwight Dana. Their enthusiasm and seven years of substantive, productive meetings proved adequate to overcome the earlier skepticism. The decision to transform the geological society into the AAAS came as no surprise to most members, because early letters suggest that the founders of the Association of American Geologists and Naturalists had had in mind an organization like the BAAS as their ultimate goal.[13]

The geologists provided practical proof that a national scientific organization was possible, but it was the British Association whose example remained essential to further expansion. The origins of the British Association are debated, and several interpretations suggest reasons for its emergence in 1831. Contemporary debates over the so-called "decline of science" articulated by Charles Babbage and others in the early 1830s raised questions about the older institutions for science in Great Britain and, in particular, fueled dissatisfaction with the rather aristocratic Royal Society.[14] But, in fact, science and interest in science were very lively in the first half of the nineteenth century, and the negativism of Babbage is, in part, explained by impatience with older institutions whose response to the changing goals and needs of science was sluggish.[15] Both these interpretations imply that the BAAS was a reaction to the established institutions. Arguing more positively, Walter Cannon has pointed out that at the Yorkshire meeting the founders repeatedly sought to link active local societies and to allow provincial scientists to communicate among themselves regularly and personally and to meet with the lions of contemporary science through peripetetic annual meetings.[16] The British Association sought to meet the needs of specialization while keeping scientists in communication across still loosely defined disciplinary boundaries and throughout the entire nation.[17] Similar concerns precipitated an American movement. Even more than the British, Americans felt geographically segmented by vast spaces and regional consciousness and turned to central, voluntary groups as a way to surpass distinctions and boundaries. Supplementing older organizations inadequate for new science, overcoming regional tendencies, correlating data gathered by various subgroups of researchers, increasing rural participation, and advancing national priorities in research—each of these goals appealed to certain groups within a still amorphous scientific community. Some American skeptics commented on popularization as handled by the BAAS.[18] Others questioned readiness among scientists.[19] But no one offered a successful alternative to meet the pressing institutional needs of American science. The American Association for the Advancement of Science, when formally proposed in 1847, was burdened with numerous and at times conflicting expectations that had accumulated over nearly two decades.

The AAAS and Its Leadership

In a public statement of purpose, written for the American Association for the Advancement of Science in 1848, Henry Darwin Rogers was quite specific in outlining the new organization's goals.[20] The Association had to meet both the "high wants and controlling practical tendencies of the country and of the age!" Therefore, it had to be willing both to support research and popularize new findings. The dual goals of stimulating broad interest in science and providing guidance and direction for the impulse through support of selected research were not always consistent with one another.

The constitution, similar to that of the Association of American Geologists and Naturalists, and in certain ways more democratic than that of the BAAS, passed easily at the first meeting. Although procedures for eliminating delinquent members, creating a permanent core of officers, and giving specific authority to an enlarged standing committee gradually modified the constitution, it stood as basically outlined in 1848 until more dramatic changes occurred in the 1870s and 1920s.

Beginning with the first session in Philadelphia, the peripetetic meetings produced what members had anticipated. The annual conventions enlivened local interest, at least temporarily, and produced more visible support for science and for the Association. A cumulative analysis of the membership records reveals that over 2,000 persons joined the AAAS from 1848 to 1860 and that at least 132 additional persons participated at one or more meetings without formally joining.[21] The numbers are deceptive, however, in terms of persistent support, as Table 1 reveals. Although large numbers joined when the Association held a meeting near their home, many dropped out or failed to pay dues in following years and were eliminated from the AAAS roster. Thus, by 1860 only 23 percent of the total number of members joining remained in the Association. Still, the temporary enthusiasm led to the contribution of funds necessary to publish annual *Proceedings,* provided visible local support at each meeting, and resulted in a net gain in members from year to year.

Indicative of popular interest was local response. Usually several cities bid for the honor of hosting an annual, week-long meeting, and the AAAS traveled widely from Boston, Massachusetts, to Charleston, South Carolina, to Cincinnati, Ohio (see Appendix I). Several cities, following the example of Charleston in 1851, provided financial assistance toward publication of the *Proceedings.*[22] Local receptions were often gala, and the visiting scientists were feted at parties in the homes of local dignitaries, college presidents, mayors, and philanthropic citizens. Meetings were extensively covered by the local newspapers and in the

Table 1

Year-by-Year Participation Level of Total Membership

This two-dimensional frequency table tabulates the percentage of members, based on the 2,073 total, who having joined in year "Joined" left in year "Left." Percentage totals are not always 100 percent because each entry is rounded to the nearest tenth of a percent. In addition, the table indicates the number joining each year who remained active through 1860, the percentage of individuals joining each year, and the number joining in each year who were dropped by 1860.

| Left | Joined | | | | | | | | | | | | Total |
	1848	1849	1850	1851	1853	1854	1855	1856	1857	1858	1859	1860	
1848	0.4												0.4
1850	5.3	1.0	0.6										7.1
1851	0.4	0.1	0.1	0.2									3.3
1853	5.3	1.0	5.3	5.4	2.6								18.6
1854	0.9	0.2	0.4	0.6	1.5	0.1							5.2
1855	0.2	0.1	0.1	0.2	2.5	0.1	0.5						3.8
1856	0.2	0.3	0.2	0.5	0.5	1.2	0.1	1.4					5.0
1857	0.2	0.1	0.2	0.4	0.7	0.2	1.2	1.7	1.6				3.7
1858	1.0	0.4	0.4	1.0	0.7	0.1	0.2	3.7	8.0	2.5			16.9
1859	0.4	0.2	0.5	0.4	1.3	0.3	0.7	1.4	1.2	0.1	0.1		7.9
1860													
Died*	3.0	0.2	0.2	0.1	0.1	0.1	0.1	0.1	0.1	0.1	0.0	0.0	4.1
Active in 1860	4.3	0.9	1.2	1.4	1.7	0.8	1.3	2.6	2.8	1.5	3.3	1.5	23.4
Total % joining	21.6	4.5	9.2	10.3	12.1	3.3	4.4	11.0	13.8	4.3	3.4	1.5	99.4
Total % dropped	14.3	3.4	7.8	8.8	10.3	2.4	3.0	8.3	10.8	2.7	0.1	0.0	71.9

*A member's death was indicated on the roster, often a year or more after the actual death date. This table indicates the actual year of death when known.

New York Times. Frequently, reporters characterized meetings as the congregation of savants or the congress of science, suggesting that the public viewed
AAAS members as "representatives" of national science.

While local citizens often attended the general evening sessions and social
functions, interested amateurs joined the leading scientists at the specialized
section meetings. The goals of these "cultivators" are difficult to ascertain, but
most seem to have been content to meet leading scientists and perhaps to
communicate their meteorological, zoological, or botanical observations. Primarily interested in meeting and hearing the more prominent scientists, the
amateurs readily promoted these leaders to positions of prominence in the
organization. The overall membership was relatively heterogeneous in educational level, occupation, and scientific interest, but the emerging leadership was
markedly alike.

Outstanding but by no means exclusively important were the group later
self-styled as the scientific Lazzaroni, led by Alexander Dallas Bache and
Benjamin Peirce, and including Joseph Henry, Oliver Wolcott Gibbs, and Benjamin A. Gould.[23] In addition, geologists Henry and William Barton Rogers,
Benjamin Silliman, Jr., and James Hall, as well as Spencer F. Baird, appeared
prominently at the meetings. The total number of members presenting papers
and holding office in the AAAS was relatively large (337), even excluding those
persons who simply held a position on the local committee. Of that group,
fifty-nine men held two or more offices and presented two or more papers; this
subgroup was the most visible and vocal sector of the organization.[24] They were
the primary leadership of the Association (see Appendix II). They had an active
interest in science, as indicated by their formal presentations (no attempt was
made to evaluate the quality of research), and their election or appointment to
office suggests colleague respect.

The new scientific leaders were self-conscious of their role in the national
society. Most of them were members of regional societies, and that status
permitted them quickly to join the effective group within the AAAS. As a result,
the men whose speeches and private discussions shaped the organization in the
1840s and 1850s were locally well known, and the new Association gave them
an opportunity to move to national prominence. Perhaps because they felt
special responsibility for the first national organization or because they realized
its potential, they demonstrated an ongoing commitment. Forty-two of the
fifty-nine leaders were on the original roster in 1848, and the persistence of the
group is documented by the fact that thirty-eight of the entire group remained
members through 1860 (eight others died during their period of membership).
Older leaders who, now in their forties and fifties, worked as much in administration as in research dominated the primary leadership group, but the recently
established or promising younger men in their thirties were encouraged to
participate (see Table 2). The entire group was unusually well educated for its
day. At least forty-six had a bachelor's degree, a medical degree, or both, and
only two had no college education. Moreover, by midcentury most members

Table 2
Membership and Leadership by Decade of Birth

The number and relative percentage of persons born in each
decade are tabulated for the 522 members and 58 leaders
whose birthdate was ascertained.

Birth decade	Members	% of 522	Leaders	% of 58
1760-1769	1	0.2		
1770-1779	16	3.6		
1780-1789	29	5.5	1	1.8
1790-1799	85	16.2	9	16.6
1800-1809	125	23.9	16	27.6
1810-1819	129	24.6	20	34.5
1820-1829	84	16.0	12	21.2
1830-1839	52	10.0		
1840-1849	1	0.2		

were in occupations that utilized their expertise in science. A majority (thirty-one men) retained their academic ties by teaching in a college or medical school.[25] Of the remainder, twelve worked for a state or for the national government and four were in military service.[26] Occupations involving research provided opportunities for personal advancement in science; the AAAS leadership held among the best of such positions in the 1850s.[27]

Regional and disciplinary propensities are evident in an analysis of the primary leadership group, but the extent to which these reflected or reinforced personal, social, and professional ties is not easily determined. Table 3, showing birthplace and residence, pinpoints regions most congenial for science. Massachusetts, New York, and Connecticut, which predominate as birthplaces of AAAS leaders, are also states relatively populous at the turn of the century. More important for understanding the AAAS itself is knowing the place of residence of the scientists while leaders of the organization. As Table 3 shows, they were concentrated near the seaboard, despite the general population movement westward. Although the table suggests that the Mid-Atlantic region gained in relative numbers, Washington, D.C., alone accounts for the increase. Without the addition of persons working with federal agencies, the region would have had a net loss. Urban areas were magnets; while thirty-two of the scientists were born in rural or semirural areas with less than ten thousand inhabitants, only six resided in such areas while members of the AAAS. These scientists apparently appreciated the benefits of frequent communication with each other and the importance of institutions to support research—advantages afforded by major cities. Such scientists achieved eminence and opportunities to do research in part because they were in centers of research activity.

Research areas of interest among the Association's leaders varied considerably. Mathematics and the physical sciences head the list (Table 4). Geology and natural history are closely related, and taken together offset the seeming dominance of the physical sciences. The only significant correlation between resi-

Table 3
Birthplace and Adult Residence of Leadership

The known birthplace and adult residence of the fifty-nine leaders are tabulated by state; the percentages indicate the relative number in each geographical region.

	Birthplace	Percent	Residence	Percent
Northeast		44		34
Maine	2			
Massachusetts	15		15	
Connecticut	8		4	
Rhode Island			1	
Mid-Atlantic		32		41
New York	13		7	
New Jersey			2	
Pennsylvania	5		3	
Maryland			3	
Washington, D.C.			9	
South		14		15
Virginia	1			
North Carolina			1	
South Carolina	3		6	
Georgia	2			
Kentucky	2			
Missouri			1	
Mississippi			1	
Midwest				5
Ohio			3	
Europe	5	9	1	2
Canada	1	2	2	3
Totals	57	101	59	100

dence and scientific interest is that all three leaders from Maryland and four of the nine leaders from neighboring Washington, D.C., were physical scientists. In most cases the fields of interest and residences were random in association.

The above statistical data provide an informative profile of the fifty-nine leading AAAS members: they were born in the most populous eastern states, well educated, resided in urban eastern centers, and worked at occupations related to their scientific interests. This group not only represents all the major areas of science but also the outstanding spokesmen for science in the period. The activities of the individuals comprising this group were scrutinized most closely for the purposes of this study. The common characteristics noted above do not by themselves account for the internal dynamics of the group, for its perceptions of the AAAS, or for the specific activities selected to fulfill both the needs internal to the group and the expectations of the outside world. Sociologist Joseph Ben-David argues that understanding the social, political, and economic context in which a scientist operates and the expectations of that community of interests are essential to the study of scientific institutions.[28] In

Table 4
Major Fields and Subfields of Leadership

The following table presents the major and secondary fields of
the fifty-nine AAAS leaders, based on scientific activity of
individuals during their period of membership.

Area of Activity*	Major Field	Second Field
Mathematics and physics	21	15
Chemistry and mineralogy	10	9
Natural history	11	5
Geology and physical geography	12	7
Mechanical science	3	1
Ethnology	1	2
Statistics	1	

*This list is based on categories found in Spencer F. Baird's
manuscripts, evidently pertaining to his organization of the
AAAS proceedings.

the case of the American Association, the leaders are quite similar in background
and in the goals they articulate.

An analysis of the public conception of science in the pre-Civil War period
would be invaluable to analyzing the interaction between the scientist and his
society, but to date none exists. The older image of "dabblers" and wealthy
philosophes was inappropriate by the 1820s, although some Jacksonians might
have retained this earlier conception.[29] The inclusion of science lectures on the
lyceum circuit suggests that science was not seen as the exclusive domain of
intellectuals, or at least that such knowledge should be accessible to all Americans. In the 1830s Alexis de Tocqueville's *Democracy in America* captured and
commented on another image, the scientist as Yankee inventor. Certainly neither
the model of dilettante nor inventor was acceptable to the emerging professionals whose occupations were based on a scientific specialty. These individuals
looked to Europe for their career models and for institutional patterns that
might be appropriate to the fabric of American experience. Nonetheless, the
image of scientist as intellectual was familiar and comfortable, while the suggestion that science was useful had advantages easily recognized by most scientists.

Savant or Professional?

Some historians have suggested that science was distracted from professionalism by the expectations of an inquisitive, democratic society with its practical
insistence that the key to progress lay in public education and open opportunity
to participate in investigation. Certainly, many contemporary scientists reinforced this conclusion through their continuing complaint that democratic
tendencies strained the research scientists physically and emotionally. In their
frustration they ignored the alternative reality of a still highly structured
community and the existence of elites, betraying a personal predeliction toward

the traditional hierarchy of social and occupational groups found in all American society. Current work in social history has elaborated the importance of elite groups in the nation's cities, even during the period of Jacksonian democracy.[30] The American Academy of Arts and Sciences and the American Philosophical Society, for example, often invited local social and political leaders to full membership. Literature as well as science provided topics of common interest for individuals influenced by the ideals of the Enlightenment. Although science in itself was not a path for upward mobility, it did provide one credential of intellectual attainment. The older societies recruited like-minded members. The self-selection process of such societies reinforced local elite patterns that coincided roughly with social standing and occupation. Thus in the 1830s a nonscientist still could be invited into a "scientific" society. The local tradition that included the "better" community members was in part translated to the national level.[31]

There had been attempts, in general unsuccessful, to form specialized societies for researchers. A group of young men living near Philadelphia (including Joseph Henry, A. D. Bache, and John Torrey) were perhaps most successful in their efforts to test ways to pursue science free from interference by interested local amateurs (including members of the American Philosophical Society). The shared enthusiasm of the young scientists, concentrating on their research careers before assuming administrative responsibilities, resulted in a private and deliberately informal club.[32] The Rogers brothers and other state geologists sought similar opportunities to meet in small groups and to exchange ideas on current research. But their solution was a more formal organization whose membership was explicitly related to scientific interest. Because they soon found common interests and problems, they formulated the Association of Geologists within two years after initial discussions. Invitations were originally limited to working state geologists.

Selection of members concerned both groups. Without ever clearly articulating their goal, the scientists coming of age in the 1830s sought a cadre of professionals, an elite composed of men with particular training for careers in science. Elitism need not be a pejorative term, and the leadership of the AAAS in the 1850s, although self-selecting, was not wholly negative. It had very personal and practical ends. The close relationship that the scientists felt toward each other inspired them to work together. They also recognized the importance of collective action. Benjamin A. Gould observed in a speech defending a national university scheme:

Centralization is a word and an idea now far from popular. But this, like most other principles, has its good as well as evil consequences. And while we, under democratic and republican institutions feel the full force of the objections to that political centralization under which we see so many nations of the old world tottering and sinking, we are too apt to overlook the incalcuable, the unspeakable advantages which flow from the concentrated accumulation of a whole nation's genius and talent.[33]

Whether in the popular East or the unsettled West, scientists were impelled to see the advantages of organization.[34] Even the skeptical A. D. Bache speculated that the large, amorphous National Institute might serve some function when he attended its gala meeting in Washington in 1844.[35] The unresolved dilemma was to find a way to match the experiences in small peer groups with the need for larger, more visible societies. Bache found his personal solution in the parallel meetings of the Lazzaroni and the AAAS, one a private and the other a public gathering. Neither, after a few years experience, proved satisfactory to him, and he led the movement for the National Academy of Sciences.

Charles Peirce, recalling the friends of his father, Benjamin Peirce, wrote, "The word science was often in those men's mouths, and I am quite sure that they did not mean by it 'systematized knowledge,' as former ages defined it . . . but the devoted, well-considered life pursuit of knowledge; devotion to truth. . . ."[36] Idealized though his reflection might be, Peirce was suggesting that the mid-century scientists did not see themselves simply performing research but pursuing a truth whose implications were profound for the human experience. While striving for some new, still vague goal of precise, scientific exchange, they were unwilling to give up attractive opportunities to be spokesmen for larger causes. A sense of responsibility shaped their activities as scientists and citizens.

Once committed to the idea of a national organization for science, such men felt impelled to direct it. Alexander Dallas Bache and Joseph Henry exchanged knowing letters about scientific organization and administration that assumed their personal leadership.[37] Similarly the Rogers brothers (especially Henry and William) self-consciously worked to shape the new AAAS into their image of what was appropriate.[38] Thus, when William Rogers wrote to the president-elect, William Redfield, he commented, "My attendance at the coming meeting will be at great sacrifice but I will do my best to be present. I trust there will be a full gathering of the *experienced* members [of the Association of American Geologists and Naturalists] as the fate of the new organization will greatly depend upon their prudent control."[39] James Dwight Dana, inspired by Bache's retiring address in 1851, expressed the sentiments of many of his peers when he wrote, "There are a few men in the country upon whom its scientific reputation has seemed to me to rest; and of regard are therefore the more valued. Instead however of increasing self-confidence, they produce an oppressive sense of responsibility. . . . I shall certainly not refuse to take my proper place for this end, be that a contributor simply of papers, which I most like, or, if thought best, the office of *Secretary*."[40] Busy with his positions in New Haven, Dana was reluctant to take on more duties but felt compelled to aid the fledgling group.

The 1851 address by Bache inspired a number of young scientists, many just beginning their careers.[41] The speech was a call for action and criticized younger scientists who had failed to take "the laboring oar" for detailed work of organization. In effect, Bache made himself a center for activity while suggesting a program for action. Parts of the address were detailed and practical: the

Association must have a regular publication, continue recommending and supporting specific activities, and assume responsibility for arbitrating priority questions. On the matter of standards for science, he was less clear and direct; instead of outlining guidelines for evaluation he mentioned that Joseph Henry was working on a code of scientific ethics. Consistent with his long-time skepticism about amateurs, he insisted that researchers be distinguished and their work supported. At the same time he did not forget the importance of reaching the public and the AAAS's annual meetings had a healthy component of public presentations. The AAAS provided a platform and an unofficial but dedicated coterie hinted at plans for education, sponsorship of science, and ultimately a more exclusive organization.

Although scientists resentfully discussed "public demands" on science,[42] much of the popularizing and involvement of nonscientists resulted from the initiative of the leadership.[43] Public recognition was personally gratifying to the scientists. At each meeting there were public receptions, speeches of welcome by mayors and others, and an opportunity to mingle with the "best society" of the community. Letters home from Spencer F. Baird and others raved about the unexpectedly good reception of the AAAS in Cincinnati.[44] Such attention was exhilarating to many. To Maria Mitchell it was "really amusing to find one's self lionized in a city where one has visited quietly for years; to see the doors of fashionable mansions open wide to receive you, which never opened before. I suspect that the whole corps of science laughs in its sleeves at the farce."[45]

At the conclusion of each meeting the scientists responded to the enthusiasm of their hosts by a resolution of thanks. This attention was directed toward a select group. In planning for the New Haven meeting, for example, Benjamin Silliman suggested that the public lectures would be for "the better portion of our citizens—to be admitted by tickets but free and distributed at our discretion."[46] The effect on the local scientific groups was mixed; while Charleston and Cincinnati enjoyed an obvious resurgence of enthusiasm for science, the effect was short lived. Many of the scientists were at home in the prominent social circles of their home town. Bache, a member of the American Philosophical Society, was well acquainted with local doctors, lawyers, and professors in Philadelphia. In the 1850s elite groups, formal and informal, existed in most major American cities; and leading scientists by virtue of accomplishment if not birth were frequently guests if not actual members of such groups. In Cambridge the famous Saturday Club of Oliver Wendell Holmes boasted Agassiz and Peirce as members.[47] The Century Club of New York included Oliver Wolcott Gibbs and Lewis M. Rutherford, while nearly all American Philosophical Society members could join the Saturday night Wistar parties in Philadelphia.[48] All such groups were known for their congenial atmosphere and prestigious associates. The leading scientists, as members and guests at such gatherings, accepted without question the community leadership of these men. Such social familiarity could bring a working relationship, which for the energetic, ambitious Bache was the ultimate justification for participation.

A local committee, appointed by the executive or standing committee of the AAAS, arranged for each annual meeting. Typically, this group contained active members of the AAAS but was often nominally headed by and included local dignitaries. Table 5 details the occupations of all persons serving on a local committee from 1848 to 1860 and indicates that nearly half of the individuals serving on such committees were never members, while less than half of the remainder did no more than simply pay dues and attend the meetings. Among the committeemen in "business" and "law" were local politicians and prominent community leaders.[49] The relationship of this group to the AAAS marks a new sophistication among the scientists who sought to make the Association more professional. The invitation to hold an essentially honorary position sustained a tradition of participation, while the responsibilities involved were explicitly social and unrelated to actual governance of the Association. The arrangements for social gatherings proved time consuming and distracting to some of the scientists who attended specifically to present and to hear research findings; by mid-decade, complaints about these activities were increasing.[50] Yet the older corps of scientists were reluctant to exclude old friends and potential supporters or to eliminate their participation, a stance not always understood and appreciated by younger scholars still eager to follow Bache's verbal insistence that they seek scientific truth first.

Nonetheless, all the scientists recognized the importance of fellowship with colleagues. Correspondence among scientists indicates that the opportunity to hear papers and to discuss scientific problems was the primary motivation for most members to attend meetings. AAAS sessions supplemented other chances for eastern scientists to interact, but for a western naturalist like George

Table 5
Local Committee Occupation Compared to AAAS Role

Occupations for 257 local committee members are tabulated by the individual participant's role as nonmember, member, or leader (in this instance broadly defined as a person presenting a paper or holding any office other than local committee member) in the AAAS.

	Nonmember	*Member*	*Leader*	*Total*	*% Total*
Business	19	19	5	43	16.6
Higher education	0	15	24	39	15.1
Law	11	11	2	24	9.5
Government	1	7	14	22	8.6
Military	3	12	7	22	8.6
Medicine	4	12	5	21	8.2
Theology	1	3	6	10	3.9
Editor	4	2	1	7	2.7
Education	2	4	1	7	2.7
Consulting scientist	0	2	4	6	2.3
Other	1	2	1	4	1.6
Unknown	36	16	0	52	20.3
Total	141	98	70	257	99.9

Englemann it was a singular event to meet with colleagues not seen for eleven years and to hear personally the prominent Louis Agassiz.[51]

Each of the men in the close circle of scientists who mutually nominated each other for office in the 1850s was aware that his expertise was known and respected in his specialized area of research. As suggested in the statistical analysis, the principal leaders were already identified locally. However, without a national organization they could not speak as a group for science. Government sponsorship of meteorological observation, explorations, and surveys, as well as agricultural and military investigations, suggested that the scientists sought to persuade politicians of the value of their work rather than rely on general public support.[52] Shortly after assuming his position as secretary of the Smithsonian Institution, Henry wrote Asa Gray: "If the scientific men of the country will only be properly united they can do much for the advance of their pursuits through assistance from Congress. . . . Politicians as a class are timid except when they have an object which they know is worthy and in advocating of which they are sure of being sustained by authority."[53] The scientists wisely followed his direction; Bache submitted annual reports from the Coast Survey and the AAAS commonly appointed committees to investigate and recommend particular projects.[54] In such cases the communication with the public was controlled; the information flow was voluntary and scrutinized.

The scientists were far less pleased with general coverage of the AAAS meetings in the public press. Certain scientists felt that the possibility of newspaper coverage offered a temptation to a "gregarious fraternity" that attached itself to the Association "for the sake of newspaper prominence.[55] When certain dissidents attempted to use the newspapers to put pressure on the AAAS, reaction from the leadership was swift and hostile; they refused even to engage in debate before the general public.[56] Moreover, newspaper reporters were not always accurate in their synthesis of a scientific presentation. Many were more interested in commenting on personalities than in reporting on the rather detailed scientific discussions.[57] The fears about the effects of press coverage on participants and about the adequacy of popularized accounts of proceedings resulted in an insistance that special reporters be hired to record the meetings and supplement the public newspapers. Managing the press proved as difficult as advising politicians.

With the AAAS came a regular journal for publishing American research. Producing a record of the papers presented had been a major, if unsuccessful, goal of the geologists. The AAAS, with a broader membership base, was able to produce annual *Proceedings*. But publication required both control of quality and submission of enough good papers to justify publication. These, too, became felt responsibilities. Before the Cincinnati meeting in 1851, Agassiz reminded Joseph Henry that "the character of the communications received in each section by the Association must be maintained high" in order to sustain the progress then being made in scientific investigation in this country, and went on to say that he would present a paper himself.[58] Many scientists felt that the annual meetings provided the best time to present new research; the leaders in each field were usually present to offer comments and the paper could subsequently be published. Some even planned their research schedule in order to be ready for the annual sessions.[59] Evaluation was originally informal, but the presentation and publication of questionable papers forced that power into the hands of the standing committee and especially the permanent secretary who supervised the final publication.[60]

Perhaps because the officers were uncertain about how and where to draw lines of responsibility and authority, they acted inconsistently and, at times, arbitrarily. The leaders desired to sharpen the quality of American science but had few models from which to derive professional standards. Certainly, the issue of certification was complex. The amateur tradition was long standing and incorporated the democratic belief that any diligent individual might make some contribution to even specialized knowledge. In general the American public supported this view of science as open enterprise—it fitted its vision of self-culture and progressive technology. The new professional aspirants responded with a system that denigrated or eliminated amateur activity in its review of research efforts. Decision-making powers came to reside in a leadership whose standards were still vague or imprecise. As a result, men excluded from participation and observers unable to understand the new procedures became resentful when the new policies were applied.

Not everyone showed the self-restraint and perception that Joseph Henry did when he wrote to Bache, "Let us take our place in the arena as individual competition asking nothing on account of place [social standing, authority] but resting all on personal [individual research] merit."[61] Too often self-confidence and presumption of responsibility had the negative result of giving some scientists an arrogance that antagonized the public and alienated colleagues sympathetic to the principles outlined. Papers submitted by the "mutual admiration society" seemed to be published automatically.

Internal disaffections with such attitudes and procedures appeared gradually and resulted in open antagonism after only three years of initial optimism and harmony.

By 1851 the Association appeared well-established. Public response was positive. A review of the *Proceedings* in 1851 noted:

... every truth connected with the condition or the laws of matter, whether in the organic or the inorganic form, they [the Association] welcome, ... It meets every year and sometimes oftener, not in one fixed place, but by turns in our principal cities, north and south, east and west. Its presence is earnestly invited and cordially welcomed. Its meetings are public and are always well attended, by persons of both sexes. And there the public listens to the discussion of interesting questions in all the departments of natural science, by the ablest and most celebrated men; and if the object of its founders had been to construct and set in motion machinery for the widest diffusion of these sciences, they could not have done more to effect that purpose.[62]

Diffusion, however, was not the only goal of the founders of the AAAS, and a more cautious Joseph Henry reminded his colleagues, "The Association is now attracting much attention and is becoming powerful for good and evil."[63] James Dwight Dana worried that the prestige of office might attract the wrong sort of leadership.[64] Others worried about publicity seekers. Such skeptics were readily persuaded to centralize control of the Association in their own hand in order, they believed, to guarantee its integrity and guide its course.

Bache's 1851 address as retiring president made him the central figure in efforts to direct the Association. Once actively an officer in the AAAS, Bache vigorously assumed responsibility by urging Lewis C. Beck to produce the Charleston proceedings in a scholarly form and to do so rapidly. Then, realizing the need for better coordination within the Association, he encouraged the establishment of permanent officers to whom the details of administration might be assigned. Finally, with the acumen of an experienced administrator, he himself worked to build the standing committee into a controlling agent capable of establishing professional standards within the organization. His own papers were expositions designed to demonstrate the importance of the Coast Survey practically and scientifically. In short, the AAAS provided a podium for promoting his survey and other projects. He arranged to meet those few men conversant with geophysics less formally for discussion.

Opposing Bache in the consolidation of power for both private and professional reasons was William Barton Rogers. He had worked to maintain the Association of American Geologists and Naturalists and encouraged its transformation into the AAAS. Recognizing the distinction between researchers devoted to regular and scientific investigation and men interested simply in hearing the findings of others, he did support his brother Henry's proposal to form two "classes" of membership in 1849.[65] Associate members were to attend without direct participation, while regular members would present papers, engage in discussion, and share the prestige of holding office. This resolution, which would have left power broadly distributed among researchers while distinguishing them from interested observers, was defeated. But by 1854 Rogers realized that the new Association was being manipulated by certain men holding office. Not privy to their discussions, he questioned their individual motivations and their assumption that they alone were capable of directing the AAAS. Constitutional debates and other issues became clouded by personality. Unwilling to acknowledge the exclusive rights of any subgroup of the Association leaders, Rogers fought to keep the constitution democratic so that in principle, as well as in fact, the Association could be protected from oligarchical control. Ensuing debates forced his ambitious peers to specify their goals and demonstrate their procedure of evaluation, although it did not eliminate their power. Rogers's integrity and his standing as a geologist meant his opposition could not be ignored; as the debates became heated, he, too, attracted a group of followers.

Despite their polarity with the AAAS, Bache and Rogers were remarkably similar. Both regretted the specialization of science even as they recognized its inevitability. They advocated government sponsorship of research, worked for better scientific education, sought a specific code of scientific ethics, and recognized a distinction between scientists and amateurs. The manner in which to establish supervision and control became the battleground, and personal philosophy colored the debates. Bache had little patience with well-meaning amateurs and preferred to direct them from a position of authority. The nature of his reports and general comments indicates that he did not find the AAAS meetings conducive to intensive debate. In contrast, William B. Rogers wanted to establish a good reputation for the Association but never denigrated the importance of field observers and indeed maintained their right to present findings to the organization.

Irresolution

The debate in which the two stood as spokesmen for a diverse group of supporters concentrated on the size and composition of the standing committee and the independence of the section meeting. The original constitution of 1848 stated that, in addition to the officers for the current and preceding year, the standing committee should include six members elected "by ballot." By 1850 the standing committee typically nominated its six additional members. As the committee became increasingly powerful and its core membership became repetitious, opposition arose from Rogers and others who resisted the autocratic overtones as well as the use of power by the group.

In particular the autonomy and authority of the special sections seemed under attack. The constitution gave the standing committee power to organize sections by subdividing proposed reports into appropriate scientific groupings; the increasing number of papers could not all be presented in one general session during a single week's meeting. The section chairmen became members of the standing committee, and each section organized its own daily program. When the standing committee in 1851 delayed in forming the sections, Ormsby Mitchell and Henry D. Rogers suggested that the "states' rights" of the sections had been violated.[66] Agassiz, speaking for the committee, responded that the delay was needed because only a limited number of papers were initially submitted and that the immature organization was not yet capable of handling its business. A qualified vote of approval for the standing committee ended the debate, but the Association also recommended a closer look at its constitution. At the Cleveland meeting in 1853 a committee was appointed to redraft the constitution and incorporate resolutions relating to the function of the Association that had been passed in previous years.[67]

At the 1854 meeting the constitutional debate resulted in permanent, outspoken divisions among the attending scientists. When the proposed amendments aroused angry discussion, the question was postponed and the committee directed to print and distribute its recommendations before the Providence meeting. There the committee on the constitution met twice and changed the original draft by adding specific powers for the standing committee.[68] When the new draft of the constitution was presented and recommended for adoption, pandemonium occurred. As the *New York Times* reported, "it was as if a shell had suddenly dropped among combustibles with the fuse burning."[69] The new proposal gave the committee extended power—quite the opposite result anticipated by the dissidents who had recommended the revisions; the standing committee was given authority to "assign papers, arrange the business, suggest places and times of meetings, examine or exclude papers, appoint the local committee, nominate persons for membership, and decide on publication." In effect, the standing committee made all major decisions.

Rogers, although ill, attended most sessions and did manage to keep the "obnoxious" constitution from passing that year. In 1856 the constitutional question was again postponed until late in the meeting.[70] When finally brought forward, the majority report of the committee remained in support of the Providence draft. This draft changed the nomination procedure for the standing committee from "open" nomination to nomination by the outgoing standing committee, making that group, in effect, self-perpetuating. Rogers managed to eliminate that change, and the rest of the constitution was voted into effect.[71] Despite Rogers's sense of triumph, the victory was incomplete, for the standing committee had the rest of its extensive authority explicitly granted.

The authority of the standing committee was intensified by the preplanning of the Bache group. Agassiz became president at the Albany meeting in 1851, and, like Bache, he assumed a dominant role in guiding AAAS affairs during the week-long session. Prior to the meeting, the two determined nominees for their at-large members and decided to promote Benjamin Peirce and then James Dwight Dana for the presidency.[72] Not only did they successfully nominate compatible friends for office, but they also excluded the Rogers brothers from competitive positions.[73] Their manipulation of nominations was probably unnecessary. As Chester Dewey reminded Bache, "scientific men would naturally control the association; they had in the past and they would in the future." He thus felt it was unnecessary and demeaning to distinguish levels of membership and recalled "meetings of the association when it was necessary to make use of means to get funds from those who were not scientific men."[74] Neither of the leading contingents in the AAAS was yet prepared to limit membership exclusively to scientists.

Throughout the turbulent meetings of the decade, Alexander Bache and William Rogers held in common a desire to sustain the organization. Dissatisfactions multiplied among westerners who resented so many trips east for AAAS meetings, among geologists who felt their section had become a subordinate one as the physical scientists took increasing control of what had been their organization, and even among public observers who could not understand the squabbling of the scientists and were offended when their good-willed hospitality aroused complaints. More serious, some of the younger members were critical of the large meetings. After 1853, for example, Oliver Wolcott Gibbs and Benjamin

Gould were vocally skeptical about the value of the annual meetings, and Bache argued vigorously that they must be supportive and direct the group rather than desert it. Even when discouraged himself in 1858, he wrote to his protégé, John F. Frazer, "When we give up the A.S.S. [*sic*] let us do it *bodily* so that the Philistines may enter at once into possession. But do not let us get into a minority by staying away, one & another, & thus until routed."[75] Bache's reasons for preserving an organization that frustrated him were undoubtedly mixed. The meetings did provide an opportunity for men of science to gather for discussion; they had encouraged national science and stimulated interest; and they had instituted certain reviewing procedures that ensured competency in published materials. They also provided a unique platform from which Bache could display the results of Coast Survey research and ask for scientific approval.

The Association had not, however, realized the expectations of most prominent scientists. The men who held major office formulated no new philosophy or program for the Association, and, in fact, their proposals for structural or procedural changes were often simply responses to challenges from the membership. Name-calling and charges of "old fogeyism" directed against persons who questioned their activities substituted for debates on the fundamental questions regarding the criteria for judging research, at least in the public forum. Rather than presenting new research findings or even doing critical reviews in their field, the well-established scientists often lapsed into presentations of material that was reworked or else discussed general topics in science.

Eventually, but not inevitably, they became "old fogeys" themselves. When their power and autonomy were challenged, they reacted with righteous indignation and allowed their proprietary sense of responsibility for the Association to become a justification for maintaining control. The democratic profile of the AAAS was artificial; membership was open but the leadership became largely a self-perpetuating or "closed" elite by the end of the decade. As such it was unable to incorporate the expectations and goals of many in the Association. The leadership did not follow its own injunction to present only matters pertaining directly to science. Geologist Josiah Dwight Whitney expressed his dismay over the religious sentiments that slipped into addresses by Agassiz and Peirce.[76] Others returning from Germany with advanced scientific degrees attended Association meetings intermittently, unhappy with the popular social atmosphere. In 1860 the dissident "young men" nearly fostered a revolt to defeat the vice-presidential nomination and the decision to hold a western meeting at Nashville.[77]

Conclusions

Name-calling on all sides clouds the essential issues which the AAAS membership and leadership debated during these formative years. The personal rhetoric suggests that the participants themselves were unable to clarify specific problems. American science was coming of age. Practitioners' self-consciousness about their unsettled international reputation perhaps inhibited willingness to criticize established scientists. Disciplines were loosely categorized. While scientists limited their own research areas, they resisted the implications of specialization even as they recognized its inevitability. In addition, they were unable to establish criteria by which to judge both a scientist and his research. Peer recognition was implicit and operative as suggested by the leadership roster but without explicit procedures peer approval might be arbitrarily used to defend old friends. This was suggested by the frequently negative assumptions about amateurs, the exclusion of Rogers from the AAAS presidency, and the expansion of power by the self-perpetuative standing committee. Such manipulation of office seriously undermined the credibility of the leadership when they discussed standards and argued for promotion based on merit.

It is possible to view the leaders of the AAAS in the 1850s as pioneers in developing professional standards among scientists in the United States. This argument is sustained by the self-perceptions of many of those leaders and by the development of very specific professional procedures by the end of the century. The failure to implement these ends more completely prior to the Civil War is often attributed to the pressure of public demands and to amateur interference. However, another factor is important: the limits of the leaders themselves. They never committed themselves to a policy of open review, and they appeared to apply nonuniformly even the vague standards available. While the leaders criticized the popularization and the socializing that occurred at meetings including the office seekers and the publicity hounds, they continued to seek office, to present public addresses, and to enjoy local hospitality. Most importantly, they did little to promote new areas of scientific research but instead limited their promotion to agencies already in existence; their activities thus correlated highly with self-interest. Perhaps they sought to do too much—to represent all sciences, to advance research and gain support for science, and even to professionalize their fields—too soon.

The aspirations shared by most of the leaders were noble enough, and the control exercised by the standing committee was abstractly aimed toward promoting research. The leadership was realistic about the structure of American society, and they recognized the benefits to be gained by popularizing science in open evening meetings and by influencing powerful social and political leaders. But their abstract principles and actual practice were not always complimentary because professionalism decreed disassociation of practicing scientists into a creative, self-critical group separate from the mass of curious practitioners. Historians must look with a skeptical eye at the disclaimers as well as the articulated goals of the scientists. The failure to realize professional goals was in part due to a lingering affection for an older pattern of social relationships and to the personal ambition of the scientists themselves. At the same time, it is clear that the AAAS by 1860 superceded local academies as a point of identification for practicing scientists.

The AAAS provides an opportunity to examine collectively a group of scientists who recognized the value of power even as they valued the goals of science. They were not inept, nor were they simply self-serving, but their goals were shaped, not only by the limits of the larger society, but also by their personal limits of vision. The AAAS was firmly grounded in the past even as it formulated a functional and central scientific organization for American science.

APPENDIX I: MEETING DATES, PLACES, AND PRESIDENTS OF THE AMERICAN ASSOCIATION FOR THE ADVANCEMENT OF SCIENCE

This table gives the opening data of each meeting, the city in which the meeting was held, and the presiding officer. Permanent officers were treasurer Alfred Elwyn (1849-1860) and secretaries Spencer F. Baird (1851-1853) and Joseph Lovering (1854-1860). The vice-presidency was intiated in 1857 and held successively by Alexis Caswell, John E. Holbrook, Edward Hitchcock, and Benajmin A. Gould.

Date	Location	President
20 September 1848	Philadelphia	William Redfield
14 August 1849	Cambridge	Joseph Henry
12 March 1850	Charleston	Alexander D. Bache
19 August 1850	New Haven	Alexander D. Bache
4 May 1851	Cincinnati	Alexander D. Bache
19 August 1851	Albany	Louis Agassiz
28 July 1853	Cleveland	Benjamin Peirce
26 April 1854	Washington, D.C.	James D. Dana
15 August 1855	Providence	John Torrey
20 August 1856	Albany	James Hall
12 August 1857	Montreal	Alexis Caswell*
28 April 1858	Baltimore	Alexis Caswell*
3 August 1859	Springfield	Stephen Alexander
1 August 1860	Newport	Isaac Lea
15 August 1866	Buffalo	F. A. P. Barnard

*Alexis Caswell presided in 1857 because Jacob W. Bailey died prior to the meeting; he presided in 1858 when Jeffries Wyman declined to hold office.

APPENDIX II: SELECTED LEADERSHIP
OF THE AMERICAN ASSOCIATION FOR THE
ADVANCEMENT OF SCIENCE

The following leaders were selected on the basis of their active participation in the AAAS. Each individual held at least two offices (not including appointment to a local committee) and presented two or more papers before the Association.

Louis Agassiz	Asa Gray	Matthew F. Maury
Stephen Alexander	Arnold H. Guyot	Ormsby Mitchell
Alexander Dallas Bache	Samuel S. Haldeman	John P. Norton
John Bachman	James Hall	Denison Olmsted
Spencer F. Baird	Joseph Henry	Benjamin Peirce
F. A. P. Barnard	Edward Hitchcock	William Redfield
Waldo I. Burnett	Eben Horsford	Henry Darwin Rogers
William Chauvenet	Franklin Hough	William Barton Rogers
George W. Coakley	Joseph S. Hubbard	Samuel St. John
James H. Coffin	Edward B. Hunt	Benjamin Silliman, Jr.
John H. D. Coffin	Charles Jackson	J. Lawrence Smith
James Dwight Dana	Walter R. Johnson	Even S. Snell
Charles Davis	Jared Kirtland	George Swallow
John W. Foster	John LeConte	John Torrey
Lewis R. Gibbes	John L. LeConte	Sears C. Walker
Robert W. Gibbes	Joseph LeConte	Charles Wilkes
John H. Gibbon	William Logan	Daniel Wilson
O. Wolcott Gibbs	Elias Loomis	Joseph Winlock
William M. Gillispie	Joseph Lovering	Jeffries Wyman
Benjamin A. Gould, Jr.	Patrick H. Lynch	

NOTES

1. The development of the AAAS is the theme of my *The Formation of a National Scientific Community: The American Association for the Advancement of Science, 1848-1860,* to be published by the University of Illinois Press. This present study will not attempt to detail the internal operation of the Association nor to suggest the variety of issues the organization confronted during its early years. It will concentrate on the ways in which the AAAS reflected and shaped the professional pattern of midcentury science.

2. See Nathan Reingold's observation on model transfer in "American Indifference to Basic Research: A Reappraisal," George Daniels, ed., *Nineteenth-Century American Science: A Reappraisal* (Evanston: Northwestern University Press, 1972), pp. 58-59.

3. Raymond P. Stearns, *Science in the British Colonies of America* (Urbana: University of Illinois Press, 1970); Brooke Hindle, *The Pursuit of Science in Revolutionary America, 1735-1789* (Chapel Hill: University of North Carolina Press, 1956). Both suggest the limits of science as well as the difficulty in establishing even informal communication networks in the colonies.

4. The quantity and quality of effort in local societies varied considerably. The fundamental survey of their efforts remains Max Meisel, *A Bibliography of American Natural History: The Pioneer Century, 1796-1865,* 3 vols. (New York, 1924-1929; reprint ed., New York: Hafner, 1967).

5. Arnold W. Thackray, "Reflections on the Decline of Science in America and on Some of Its Causes," *Science* 173 (1971): 27-31.

6. The earliest recorded discussion is Benjamin Silliman, Sr., to Henry Darwin Rogers, 22 December 1834, Rogers MSS, Massachusetts Institute of Technology Archives, Cambridge, Mass. (hereafter cited as MITA). By 1838 Edward Hitchcock and the Rogers brothers were seriously planning an organization; see Emma Rogers, ed., *Life and Letters of William Barton Rogers* (Cambridge, Mass., 1896), 1:154-56.

7. This was Warren's interpretation of its failure. Edward Warren, ed., *The Life of John Collins Warren, M.D., compiled chiefly from his Autobiography and Journals,* 2 vols. (Boston, 1860). Edward Herrick, who had watched early efforts to organize, knew the defeat of Warren's proposal meant "the whole matter would sleep for some time to come" (Herrick to Elias Loomis, 14 June 1839, Yale University, New Haven, Conn.).

8. Sally Kohlstedt, "A Step Toward Scientific Self-Identity in the United States: The Failure of the National Institute, 1844," *Isis* 62 (Fall 1971): 339-62.

9. "Address of the President," *Proceedings of the American Association for the Advancement of Science* 6 (1852):xlvi (hereafter cited as *Proceedings of the AAAS*).

10. The founders seemed to have followed the recommendation of an anonymous commentator on "Scientific Associations" in the *New York Review* 8 (April 1839): 401-17, who suggested that a national organization should at first include only those topics of science to which American men of science had made important contributions, pointing specifically to geology, zoology, and meteorology.

11. Charles Lyell, *Travels in North America: With Geological Observations on the United States, Canada and Nova Scotia* (London, 1845), 2:261-62; Edward Lurie, *Louis Agassiz: A Life in Science* (Chicago: University of Chicago Press, 1960), pp. 131-32. Lack of self-confidence and a preoccupation with gaining approval was consistently noted by visiting foreigners. See Edward Pessen, *Jacksonian America: Society, Personality and Politics* (Homewood, Ill.: Dorsey Press, 1969), pp. 15-16.

12. This was especially true for geologists distant from the centers of activity. See William Barton Rogers to Jacob W. Bailey, 22 October 1843, Rogers MSS, MITA.

13. The Rogers brothers and Edward Hitchcock took this goal seriously. Henry Rogers to William Rogers, 26 September 1838, in Rogers, *Life and Letters,* 1:155-56; James B. Rogers to William Rogers, 1 March 1839, Rogers MSS; Edward Hitchcock to William Redfield, 8 January 1839, Redfield MSS, Yale University. Hitchcock in retrospect suggested the entire group wanted "gradually and quietly to expand so as to embrace all the sciences, and so become an American Association for the advancement of science, and so our proceedings were modeled after the various European associations of this kind." Edward Hitchcock, *Reminiscences of Amherst College . . . also of other and wider life experiences* (Northampton, Mass., 1863), p. 369.

14. L. Pearce Williams, "The Royal Society and the Founding of the British Association for the Advancement of Science," *Notes and Records of the Royal Society of London* 16 (November 1961): 221-33. A similar suggestion is in D. S. L. Cardwell, *The Organization of Science in England: A Retrospect* (London: Heinemann Educational Books, 1957), pp. 46-59.

15. Joseph Ben-David, *The Scientist's Role in Society: A Comparative Study* (Englewood Cliffs, N.J.: Prentice-Hall, 1971).

16. Walter Cannon, "History in Depth: The Early Victorian Period," *Journal of the History of Science* 3 (1964): 20-38.

17. This was a major theme in Vernon Harcourt's address, "Objects and Plans of the British Association for the Advancement of Science," as reprinted in Howard M. Jones and I. Bernard Cohen, eds., *Science Before Darwin: A Nineteenth-Century Anthology* (London: André Deutsch, 1963).

18. Joseph Henry to A. D. Bache, 9 August 1838, Henry MSS, Smithsonian Institution Archives, Washington, D.C. (hereafter cited as SIA).

19. *Proceedings of the AAAS,* 6: xlv-xlvi.

20. Henry Darwin Rogers, "Circular," 10 May 1848, copy in AAAS Library, Washington, D.C.

21. One chapter of my book-length study of the AAAS explains my method of data gathering and analyzes membership during these thirteen years.

22. Charles U. Shepard to Benjamin Silliman, Sr., 25 March 1850, Shepard MSS, Yale University.

23. Lillian B. Miller, *The Lazzaroni: Science and Scientists in Mid-Nineteenth Century America* (Washington, D.C.: Smithsonian Institution Press, 1972) presents brief biographies of these individuals. Older assumptions about the group are challenged in Mark Beach, "Was There a Scientific Lazzaroni?" Daniels, *Nineteenth-Century American Science,* pp. 115-32.

24. Office holding is an indicator of peer recognition. Only four men held office five or

more times without presenting at least two papers; these were Alexis Caswell, permanent treasurer Alfred Elwyn, Samuel George Morton, and the elder Silliman.

25. These college professors taught science (25), medicine (4), and liberal arts (1); one was a college president.

26. Three were at the privately endowed Smithsonian Institution, three at the Coast Survey, two on the Nautical Almanac staff, three in state or local government, and one at the United States Mint.

27. Clark Elliott, "The American Scientist, 1800-1863: His Origins, Career, and Interests" (Ph.D. diss., Case Western Reserve University, 1970). The more productive scientists in his analysis are similarly employed in colleges and government.

28. Ben-David, *Scientist's Role.* The book is useful because it stresses the importance of institutions created by scientists and considers the nature of cultural transfer.

29. Perhaps because the community leaders who enjoyed avocational science were respected by their communities, their interests caused little comment. The persistence of the newspapers in calling the scientists "savants" suggests that the image of a broadly interested intellectual rather than a specialist still dominated the public mind.

30. See especially Edward Pessen, "The Egalitarian Myth and American Social Reality: Wealth, Mobility and Equality in the 'Era of the Common Man,'" *American Historical Review* 76 (October 1971): 989-1034; Frederic Cople Jaher, "Nineteenth-Century Elites in Boston and New York," *Journal of Social History* 6 (Fall 1972): 32-77; Douglas T. Miller, *Jacksonian Aristocracy: Class and Democracy in New York, 1830-1860* (New York: Oxford University Press, 1967). While all these studies concentrate primarily on the social structure of the Northeast, they also suggest the effectiveness of upper-class leaders.

31. Robert Wiebe, *The Search for Order, 1877-1920* (New York: Hill & Wang, 1967). Wiebe argues throughout his study that Americans shifted their interests and alliances to the national level and that local leaders who successfully achieved national recognition gained tremendously in power and authority.

32. Smithsonian Institution, *Annual Report* (Washington, D.C., 1859), p. 109. Founded in 1834, the informal club was disbanded by 1840. See Joseph Henry to John Torrey, 20 December 1834, Torrey MSS, New York Botanical Gardens, New York, N.Y.; Alexander Dallas Bache to Joseph Henry, 13 February 1840, copy in Henry MSS, SIA.

33. B. A. Gould, *An American University* (New York, 1856); Suzanne Keller, "Elites," in *International Encyclopedia of the Social Sciences,* ed. David Sills (New York, 1968), p. 27. Keller points out, "The general functions of elites appear to be similar everywhere: to symbolize the moral unity of a collectivity by emphasizing common purposes and interests; to coordinate and harmonize diversified activities, combat factionalism, and resolve group conflicts; and to protect the collectivity from external danger."

34. John L. LeConte to S. S. Haldeman, 5 November 1849, Haldeman MSS, Academy of Natural Sciences of Philadelphia, Philadelphia, Pa.

35. Bache to Elias Loomis, 7 March 1844, Loomis MSS, Yale University.

36. "The Century's Great Men in Science," Smithsonian Institution, *Report . . . for 1900* (Washington, D.C., 1901), p. 694.

37. This was especially true at midcentury when the two organized the Coast Survey and the Smithsonian Institution. See Henry to Bache, 6 September 1846, Henry MSS, SIA.

38. Henry Rogers wrote the AAAS constitution, William distributed circulars, and James took basic charge of local arrangements for the 1848 meeting in Philadelphia.

39. Rogers to Redfield, 24 August 1848, Redfield MSS, Yale University.

40. James Dwight Dana to Bache, 6 September 1851, Rhees MSS, Henry L. Huntington Library, San Marino, Calif. (hereafter cited as HHL).

41. *Proceedings of the AAAS,* 6:xli-lx.

42. Gould to Bache, 14 August 1856, Bache MSS, SIA. Gould regularly complained about public demands and resented the "interest" expressed by local citizens at the AAAS meetings. His antagonism toward public curiosity at the Dudley Observatory led to a confrontation and his dismissal.

43. A general deference of amateurs and listeners is clear in the public press accounts of discussion at early meetings, as well as in responses to the questionnaire sent out by Spencer F. Baird as permanent secretary in 1851 ("Scientific Addresses," Baird MSS, SIA). The Reverend Dr. Potter in Albany in 1851 suggested "the people and the cultivators of science

had in common a desire simply to see the new results of science which could lead to a juster and more extended appreciation of the great aims and objects of these devoted laborers" (*Albany Evening Journal,* 26 August 1851).

44. Spencer F. Baird to George Marsh, 5 June 1857, Baird Personal MSS, SIA.

45. Phebe M. Kendall, *Maria Mitchell: Life, Letters and Journals* (Boston, 1896), p. 22.

46. Silliman to Bache, 9 August 1850, Rhees MSS, HHL.

47. Edward W. Emerson, *The Early Years of the Saturday Club, 1855-1870* (Boston: Houghton Mifflin, 1917).

48. *The Century, 1847-1946* (New York: Century Club, 1947), pp. 3-24.

49. There could be little illusion of actual assistance from these persons. James B. Rogers wrote to his brother Henry of his work with the first local committee, "None of the Committee here but Morton, P.A. Brown and myself have shown any strong interest in the matter, but the others are some absent and business men only; so that perhaps none should be expected" (9 September 1848, Rogers MSS, MITA).

50. Gould to Bache, 14 August 1856, Bache MSS, SIA.

51. George Englemann to Asa Gray, 29 July 1851, Historic Letter File, Gray Herbarium, Harvard University, Cambridge, Mass.

52. A. Hunter Dupree, *Science in the Federal Government: A History of Policies and Activities to 1940* (Cambridge, Mass.: Harvard University Press, Belknap Press, 1957), pp. 91-115, documents the rapidity of these developments.

53. Henry to Gray, 21 February, 1849, Historic Letter File, Gray Herbarium.

54. Thirty percent of all the committees appointed by the standing committee were to recommend a particular project to the federal government or to a state legislature.

55. Gould to Benjamin Silliman, Jr., 21 September 1860, Gould MSS, Yale University.

56. The controversy involving John Warner of Pennsylvania and Charles Winslow of New York stemmed from their failure to have papers published by the AAAS, and included charges of plagiarism against Benjamin Peirce. Peirce denounced using the public press to arbitrate questions of science, and even John Warner's friends urged him to keep the matter within the scientific community. See J. Peter Lesley to Warner, 26 June 1858, and other detailed materials in the Warren MSS, American Philosophical Society, Philadelphia, Pa. (hereafter cited as APS).

57. Undoubtedly Spencer F. Baird was shocked by a letter from reporter Augustus Maverick asking for "good scientific gossip" or anything "rare and racy" to make up for the loss of such news because of the canceled Cleveland meeting of the AAAS. 9 September 1852, Baird Official MSS, SIA. For the historian, however, the interest in debates and in personality make the public press an irreplaceable source of information that was not published in any formal account of the AAAS meetings.

58. Louis Agassiz to Henry, 19 April 1851, Henry MSS, SIA.

59. John P. Norton to unknown, 9 December 1851, Norton MSS, Yale University.

60. See John D. Holmfeld, "From Amateurs to Professionals in American Science: The Controversy over the Proceedings of an 1853 Scientific Meeting," *Proceedings of the American Philosophical Society* 114 (February 1970): 22-36.

61. Henry to Bache, 13 September 1851, Henry MSS, SIA.

62. *North American Review* 72 (January 1851): 94.

63. Henry to Bache, 13 September 1851, Henry MSS, SIA.

64. James Dwight Dana to Bache, 6 September 1851, Rhees MSS, HHL.

65. *Proceedings of the AAAS* 2 (1849):179.

66. *Albany Evening Journal,* 23 August 1851.

67. *Proceedings of the AAAS* 8 (1854):xi. The committee was A. D. Bache, J. Lawrence Smith, John LeConte, Wolcott Gibbs, B. A. Gould, W. B. Rogers, J. D. Dana, Joseph Leidy, S. S. Haldeman, and A. A. Gould.

68. *New York Times,* 24 August 1855.

69. Ibid.; *Providence Journal,* 21 August 1855.

70. *Albany Atlas and Argus,* 21 August 1856.

71. W. B. Rogers to H. D. Rogers, 1 September 1856, typescript copy, Rogers MSS, MITA.

72. Agassiz to Bache, 2 August 1851, Rhees MSS, HHL.

73. They opposed the nomination of Rogers in 1851 and again in 1860. See Agassiz to

Bache, 2 August, 1851, Rhees MSS, HHL; Peirce to Bache [1860], Peirce MSS, Houghton Library, Harvard University.

74. *Springfield* [Mass.] *Daily Republican,* 10 August 1859.

75. Bache to John F. Frazer, 22 March 1858, Frazer MSS, APS.

76. Edwin T. Brewster, *Life and Letters of Josiah Dwight Whitney* (Boston: Houghton Mifflin, 1909), p. 168. None of the religious comments, doubtless extemporaneous, were published in the *Proceedings.*

77. Gould to Silliman, Jr., 21 September 1860, Gould MSS, Yale University; Bache to Peirce, n.d., Peirce MSS, Houghton Library.

The Early Development
of Scientific Societies
in Canada

PETER J. BOWLER

A considerable amount of material has been published on the origins of Canadian scientific and learned societies, largely in the form of anniversary volumes issued by the societies themselves. As yet, however, little effort has been devoted to the correlation of this material and to the construction of an overall view of the development of Canadian scientific organizations. This paper cannot give a complete history, but by examining a few of the more important early societies it will attempt to deal with some of the general issues facing the historian who seeks to understand this neglected aspect of Canadian history.[1]

The time scale of the paper extends further into the nineteenth century than does that of the others in this volume. This is a result of the comparatively late development of Canadian science, and of the fact that the particular issue to which I have addressed myself inevitably required a study extending at least into the 1880s. I shall concentrate almost exclusively on the development of societies in English-speaking Canada; lack of familiarity prevents me from dealing with the French-speaking community, despite the potential interest of a comparison between the two groups.[2]

As might be expected, learned societies originated in nineteenth-century Canada in the form of local organizations established to satisfy the demands of the intellectuals and scientific cultivators living in or around the small number of reasonably sized towns. But shortly after the midpoint of the century, at least one society—the (Royal) Canadian Institute—had come into being with the aim of uniting Canadian scientists, both amateur and professional, into a truly national organization. It was never very successful in this objective, however, and tended to become another local society confined to the Toronto area. Not until the 1880s did a national society arise, a fact that leaves the historian with the problem of isolating the factors that may have interfered with efforts to achieve national unity in this area. A further problem resulted from the very nature of the first truly Canadian organization, the Royal Society of Canada. The Royal Society was organized specifically for the widely recognized scientist or intellectual, deliberately excluding the amateurs who made up the bulk of the local societies. It thus differed not only from the earlier Canadian societies but also from the popular British and American Associations for the Advancement of

---

[1] Notes to this chapter begin on page 337.

Science, which might have formed the most obvious model upon which to base the structure of the first national Canadian society. This paper will suggest a number of possible reasons for the comparatively late appearance of the Royal Society of Canada, and will also attempt to account for the abrupt change in the nature of Canadian scientific organizations represented by the creation of this Society.

There are, of course, a number of very obvious reasons why Canadian scientists did not achieve any degree of professional unity until long after their colleagues in the United States. Transport developed very slowly at first; the two cities of Toronto and Montreal were not linked by railway until late in the 1850s. Even when satisfactory transportation became available, the total number of professional scientists in Canada remained very small for a country with such a large area. The Geological Survey of Canada employed only a handful of workers and was for some time the only significant scientific enterprise sponsored by the government. The universities were few in number and again employed only a handful of scientists as teachers. But these factors do not, in themselves, provide a complete explanation for the late formation of the Royal Society of Canada. Suitable transportation between the major cities was available for two decades before the Society was formed, and, although the number of scientists began to increase after 1850, there is nothing to suggest that the early 1880s marked a crucial turning point in the growth of Canada's scientific population. (Even in 1882 it was difficult to find forty professional scientists to fill the appropriate sections of the Royal Society.) To understand why Canadian scientists failed to achieve professional unity, one must look not to these factors but to the different motivations that were evident in the formation of scientific and learned societies and that influenced their subsequent interactions.

The early Canadian societies, like their American counterparts, served a function as "information systems" at a purely local level. Yet the development of national societies in the two countries seems to have involved a number of different motivations that can be broadly grouped into two categories. The formation of national societies in the United States has generally been regarded as a result of the operation of "professional" motivations. However difficult it may be to define a "professional" scientist, it does seem that there was a growing sense of identity among those who felt themselves to be committed to science as a means of obtaining their living. This, along with the need for regular contact with other researchers, for respectable journals, and for a means of influencing the government encouraged the organization of national societies and led to the exclusion of amateurs or cultivators from positions of influence within them.[3] It has been suggested that, given a large enough scientific community, this combination of factors can lead to the formation of a national society when adequate transportation facilities are available—as in the case of the American Association for the Advancement of Science.[4] But the professional influences are not the sole determinants; there is, in addition, a purely nationalistic motive based on the desire to illustrate a new nation's prestige by exhibiting the quality of its scientists and intellectuals in the form of an élite group or academy. In America this was evident in the creation of the National Academy, yet it represented merely one additional factor leading to the foundation of a second national body after professional motivations had already laid the basis for creation of the AAAS.

In Canada, on the contrary, it is possible to show that the nationalistic motive was the chief factor involved in the formation of the first national learned society. Professional motivations were not strong enough to unite the widely scattered Canadian scientists; indeed, they tended in precisely the opposite direction, since a number of the more important figures sought some form of professional identity within the AAAS. The Royal Society of Canada succeeded because it was founded by a political figure for a purely nationalistic reason—to demonstrate that the country possessed a body of scientists and intellectuals that could compare favorably with that of other nations. In a sense, Canadian scientists united behind the Royal Society because they recognized a nationalistic purpose diametrically opposed to their professional inclination to become absorbed into the body of American science.

Early Canadian Societies

Perhaps the two most important societies formed in Canada in the early decades of the nineteenth century were the Literary and Historical Society of Quebec and the Natural History Society of Montreal. The Quebec Society was created by the Governor General, the Earl of Dalhousie, in 1824 to promote the collection and publication of documents relating to Canadian history.[5] It did, in fact, perform this function,[6] but the early *Transactions* of the Society also contained a large proportion of papers on scientific topics, chiefly in the field of geology. It would seem that the Society actively encouraged scientific studies in addition to its original objectives.[7]

Dalhousie also played a role in the early development of the Natural History Society of Montreal, becoming a patron of the Society shortly after its formation by a group of amateur scientists in 1827. This Society was incorporated in 1833[8] and began to print a small number of papers in its *Annual Report;* in 1857 it took over the publication of the *Canadian Naturalist* from Elkanah Billings, the paleontologist of the Geological Survey.[9]

Within the purely local context in which they were conceived, both organizations were quite successful. Dalhousie had initially intended the Quebec Society to be limited to 24 prominent local personalities,[10] but this number was soon exceeded, and by 1831 there were already 126 members.[11] In Montreal there was some doubt at first as to whether the Natural History Society could be held together,[12] but the membership soon began to increase rapidly.[13] In 1847 there was a record number of new members, and the Society was still expanding by 1860.[14] Unlike its counterpart in Quebec, the Montreal Society enjoyed the support of a number of professional scientists who contributed to its publications and eventually came to play an important role in the direction of the Society. In the 1850s, the most prominent of these professionals was John (later Sir John) William Dawson, who initiated the teaching of science at McGill University in 1854.[15]

With its alternative interest in historical matters, there was little chance of the Quebec Society expanding into a wider forum for Canadian scientists. But the Montreal group, once it acquired a core of professionals, had the potential to play a much more important role in the country's scientific life. With the active participation of Dawson, the Society succeeded in persuading the American Association for the Advancement of Science to meet in Montreal in 1857, and the adoption of the *Canadian Naturalist* gave it control of a leading organ for the publication of Canadian scientific material. Yet no effort seems to have been made to create a national organization based in Montreal or to encourage scientists from elsewhere in Canada to attend even the Society's Annual General Meeting on a regular basis. The lists of corresponding members from this period included names from Toronto, Kingston, Quebec, and other Canadian localities, as well as a number of foreign scientists.[16] When Elkanah Billings moved from Ottawa to Montreal in 1856, he had to apply to have his status changed from that of a corresponding member to an ordinary member.[17] These facts suggest that other Canadians did not attend meetings in Montreal, nor is there any evidence to indicate that they were actively encouraged to do so.

It may legitimately be asked why the Montreal Society was sufficently outward looking to invite the AAAS to the city in 1857 yet had no vision of itself as the nucleus of a Canada-wide organization. It would seem that, having been founded as a purely local organization, the Natural History Society never managed to break out of this mold. Indeed, there is evidence that by the late 1850s it was having difficulty in retaining support even within its home city. The state of the Society in 1857 has been described as that of "a paralysed, helpless and almost hopeless organization, struggling hard for its very existence."[18] It was noted above that the membership was still increasing at the time, but reference to the Minute books shows that only a handful of members actually attended the meetings.[19] In addition, serious financial problems arose in 1859 to complicate the Society's future.[20]

The decision to invite the AAAS seems to have come directly from Dawson and some of his colleagues who undoubtedly saw this as an opportunity to achieve closer relations with the much larger body of American scientists. They were able to get local support for this move because of the publicity the city would enjoy as a result of the temporary influx of Americans. But Dawson and his friends do not seem to have regarded the Natural History Society itself as anything more than a means of encouraging this type of local support for science. Since the group was still composed largely of amateurs, the small core of professionals can hardly have envisioned scientists from elsewhere in Canada traveling to Montreal to attend their somewhat limited monthly meetings. A complete revision of the Society's role would have been needed to turn it into a nationwide organization, and there was apparently no sense of unity with the other Canadian scientists to encourage such a radical step. The Society retained its local, amateur status, and the move to invite the AAAS should not be taken as evidence of a general desire to expand.

The Royal Canadian Institute

Considering the pattern of Canadian development, it is not surprising that the Toronto area should have lagged behind Montreal and Quebec in the establishment of learned societies. A Mechanics' Institute was founded as early as 1830 and enjoyed varying success throughout the century, but it did not cater to the professional scientists of the area. A Literary and Philosophical Society existed for a brief period in the early 1830s, followed a decade later by the Toronto Athenaeum, a group that finally merged with the Canadian Institute in 1855. The Canadian Institute itself (which became the Royal Canadian Institute in 1914) originated in 1849 with the formation of a small organization for engineers and surveyors.[21] After some dispute it broadened its scope and in 1851 obtained a charter as a "society for the general advancement of the Physical Sciences, the Arts and Manufactures."[22] The membership increased rapidly, so that in 1852 the publication of a *Canadian Journal* was begun, followed in later years by the *Proceedings* and *Transactions* of the Institute.

The men who reorganized the Canadian Institute in 1851 intended it to become a truly national society. As Sir Sandford Fleming later wrote of his co-founders, "They were not satisfied that it should be a local society merely, with its membership confined to the citizens of Toronto."[23] But this emphasis on expansion appears to have been promoted more by nationalism than by any desire to encourage professional unity among Canadian scientists and engineers. There *was* a professional element present, best represented by Fleming himself.[24] Indeed, Fleming's later work on railroads illustrates the practical outcome of the sort of patriotic utilitarianism that was the driving force behind the first expansion of the Institute and that most clearly distinguishes it from the earlier Quebec and Montreal societies. But many of those involved in the reorganization were not scientists or engineers but politicians. Indeed, the Institute's own historian has admitted that during its early years it was dominated by politically oriented "High Tory" elements.[25] Thomas Ridout, one of the founders, had close links with government, links that were exploited in the move to obtain the first charter.[26] As amateur scientists, these men believed that the encouragement of science and technology was essential for national unity and development,[27] but they were not themselves actively engaged in scientific studies. More scientists and engineers joined the Institute after its reorganization—a number of professors from the University of Toronto joined en masse in 1852[28]—but this period seems to mark a decline in the expansionary outlook that had been produced by the earlier spirit of nationalism.

By the late 1850s the Canadian Institute had lost its political affiliations and had become purely a scientific society. Professors from the science departments of the University of Toronto gradually began to take over more of the important offices, and by 1859 it was emphasized that the Institute should be regarded as a "strictly scientific society."[29] A corresponding decline in the membership's political influence is also evident: in 1860 it was found necessary to petition the Legislative Assembly and Council for the renewal of a small grant that had been cut off as a result of the Institute being classed as one of the local mechanics' institutes.[30]

No attempts were made during this time to establish the Institute as a Canada-wide organization. The first president was William (later Sir William) E. Logan, who, as director of the Geological Survey, was perhaps the most respected scientist in Canada. But Logan did not make his home in Toronto, so he seldom attended any meetings and resigned from the presidency in 1853. Subsequent presidents were all Toronto men, and the active membership continued to be drawn almost exclusively from the Toronto area.[31] Some attempt was made to keep up the facade of a nationwide expansion, the most notable effort in this direction being a request in 1859 that the Institute's name be changed to the "Royal Society of Canada." But the Governor General turned down this request, remarking that he did not think the new name suitable for "an Institution having its headquarters permanently established in Upper Canada."[32] (There had certainly been no effort made to hold meetings outside Toronto). The essentially local character of the Institute had become apparent, and there were no further attempts, even at the symbolic level, to create the impression that the group represented the whole of Canadian science. Only in its publications did the Institute fulfill its original function of publishing papers by a wide range of Canadian authors.[33]

A number of factors helped to bring about this modification in the intended nature of the Canadian Institute. With respect to the original hopes of its founders, the Institute was created a few years before the most opportune moment for establishing a national body. Communications across Canada, even between Montreal and Toronto, were still comparatively restricted during the early 1850s. Dawson has given us an eloquent description of the difficulties encountered in traveling between Montreal and Toronto in 1854,[34] and such conditions can hardly have encouraged scientists from elsewhere in Canada to travel to the new Institute's meetings, however energetically they might have been exhorted to do so. By the time a rail link was established later in the decade, the Institute's character had already changed; the earlier utilitarian nationalism had been diluted by the influx of academic scientists into key positions. The new leaders appear to have regarded the society's main purpose as the creation of local support for science in the Toronto area, rather than the foundation of a national organization of scientists. In effect, the Canadian Institute became a Toronto equivalent of the Natural History Society of Montreal. Neither society boasted a sufficiently large core of professionals to make its meetings attractive to scientists from elsewhere in the country, and neither group felt it worthwhile to create a professional union artificially. The limited membership, coupled with the almost inevitable corollary of a lack of any sense of belonging to a Canadian scientific community, restricted both groups to essentially local operations. The Canadian Institute's emphasis on sheer nationalism—which was to be the leading factor in the successful founding of the Royal Society of Canada—had come too soon, and professional ties were not strong enough to act as an alternative unifying force.

The inability of the local Canadian societies to attract a wider membership may be contrasted with (and even partially explained by) the willingness with which a number of Canadian workers sought contact with the much larger body of American scientists. The American Association for the Advancement of Science in particular attracted the attention of a significant number of Canadians. W. E. Logan joined the AAAS at its first meeting in 1848, as did Thomas Sterry Hunt, who was later to serve as Logan's chemist.[35] J. W. Dawson joined in 1856 to present the invitation to meet in Montreal one year later, and by the time that meeting had closed there were at least 135 Canadian members, including the majority of the professional scientists in the country.[36] Of course, a large proportion of these joined only for the Montreal meeting and then allowed their membership to lapse, but it is significant that the AAAS could attract Canadian scientists from a much wider area than could any purely Canadian organization.

Canadian scientists and cultivators *were* prepared to travel to a meeting that provided the opportunity for significant professional contact, and they apparently felt that the AAAS, unlike the National History Society of Montreal or the Canadian Institute, met this need. It is also significant that a number of the more eminent scientists did, in fact, retain their membership in the AAAS. Sterry Hunt (who was educated at Yale and always retained his American citizenship) delivered papers at every AAAS meeting from 1856 to 1880 and was president in 1870. Logan and Dawson both kept up their membership and attended an occasional meeting, while Daniel Wilson of Toronto was president of the anthropological section in 1876 and 1877. L. W. Bailey of the University of New Brunswick read a geological paper at the 1880 meeting. It seems clear that these scientists felt that the AAAS offered them a greater degree of professional contact than was obtainable within the more restricted Canadian scientific community. Furthermore, to the extent that the Canadians looked to the AAAS, their search for professional contacts acted in opposition to the nationalist sentiments that had motivated the formation of the early Canadian Institute. Under these circumstances, there was no chance of professionalism and nationalism acting together within the Canadian scientific community; nationalism alone was the only factor that might stimulate interest in the formation of a truly Canadian society.

The two decades between 1860 and 1880 saw no further attempt to create a national organization for science. A number of new local societies were founded: The Nova Scotia Institute of Natural Science and the Natural History Society of

New Brunswick in 1862, the Ottawa Literary and Scientific Society in 1869, and the Historical and Scientific Society of Manitoba in 1879. The Canadian Institute continued to act as a Toronto society for the popularization of science, although on occasion it also assumed the role of a more general cultural organization. A sudden boost in the Institute's fortunes caused by the move to a new building in 1879[37] appears to have had no connection with the establishment of the Royal Society of Canada a few years later. In the twentieth century the Institute has played an important role in organizing cooperation between government, science, and industry, but its membership has remained largely confined to the Toronto area, where its lectures still serve the cause of the popularization of science.

The Royal Society of Canada

In 1881 the Governor General, the Marquis of Lorne (later Duke of Argyll), organized a meeting to draw up a provisional constitution for a society that would unify the country's scientific and humanistic communities. The first full meeting of the resulting organization, the Royal Society of Canada, took place in the following year.[38] Its aim was to draw together scientists and scholars who were scattered across the country by means of an annual meeting to be held at Ottawa, or occasionally in other cities. At Lorne's insistence, the Society contained sections devoted not only to the sciences but also to French and English literature. In 1883 a grant was obtained from the government to finance the publication of a series of *Transactions,* although the members hoped to remain as independent of the government as possible so they could provide impartial advice on scientific and other matters.

From the beginning it was decided that the Society should be largely a professional body, composed of "residents of the Dominion who have published original works or memoirs of merit, or who have rendered eminent services to literature or to science."[39] Amateurs were thus excluded, apart from the talented few who might equal the achievements of the professionals. This characteristic is somewhat surprising in view of the scientists' awareness of the success of the popularly oriented British and American Associations and the background of the local Canadian organizations. Indeed, there was a strong feeling that the Royal Society would fail through lack of support if the amateurs were not allowed to join. Dawson recorded the presence of such a feeling,[40] yet he himself supported the original policy and argued against the claim that there were not enough eminent Canadian scientists to form a successful organization.[41] All of the principal scientists rallied around the new society and seemed prepared to take the risk that by excluding amateurs they would doom it to an early death. This enthusiasm for an elitist policy suggests that the scientists themselves were interested more in an organization encouraging national excellence than in one that merely drew together all who were in some way interested in science. This preference seems to have arisen from the nationalist element contained within the original proposals, an element that had the power to influence the ideas of scientists who had hitherto felt no need to unite for scientific purposes and who saw amateur science as something that had only been able to flourish at a local level.

Lorne's early statements concerning the Royal Society indicate that he had far more in mind than the mere provision of a stimulus to general scientific and intellectual advancement. Not that he was unaware of this aspect of his idea—indeed, the prospect of encouraging younger scientists by giving them a goal to aim at was partly responsible for his belief that the Royal Society should be confined to men of merit. But this encouragement was specifically directed toward a nationalistic end; Lorne saw the creation of an elite group as a means of focusing the attention of Canadian scientists upon their national identity by showing them that as a whole they could at least begin to compare themselves with the scientists of Europe and America in terms of intellectual attainment. He wrote:

America already bids fair to rival France and Germany in the number of her experts. Canada may certainly have her share in producing those men whose achievements in science have more than equalled in fame the triumphs of the statesmen. These last labour only for one country, while the benefits of the discoveries of science are shared by the world. But widely different as are the qualities which develop patriotism and promote science, yet I would call to the aid of our young organization the love of country, and ask Canadians to support and gradually to make as perfect as possible this their national society.[42]

It may be noted that the United States had founded its National Academy of Sciences during the 1860s, partly as a means of identifying its outstanding scientists. In effect, Lorne felt that an institution paralleling the National Academy, rather than the American Association, would be more likely to succeed in pulling the scattered Canadian scientists together by generating a sense of national unity and purpose. The enthusiasm of amateurs could still be catered to at the local level, although the Royal Society hoped to play a unifying role even here by inviting delegates from the local organizations to its annual meetings. Canadian science, however, would only achieve an identity by showing that it could equal, or at least approximate, the scientific communities of the great nations; for this reason Lorne wanted the actual membership of the Society to be limited to men of some eminence. The same arguments applied to the broader cultural fields the Society encompassed, and indeed the very breadth of these activities illustrates the Society's origins in cultural nationalism rather than scientific professionalism.

The principal Canadian scientists all reacted favorably to Lorne's proposal and seem to have regarded the political benefits of the new organization as being at least as important as the scientific ones. In his address delivered as the Society's first president in 1882, Dawson noted that the creation of a truly national journal would help both the scientists and the country. All were aware, he said, of the "injury which Canadian science and the reputation of Canada" had suffered because of the limitations of the journals published by the local societies.[43] Against those who thought the country was as yet too young to support the Society, Dawson argued that it was vital even at this early stage of development to plan for the future in a manner that would ensure Canada's independence.[44] By following a similar line of thought, he was led to accept the argument that the Society should be composed only of eminent figures, in order to create a center to which Canada and the world could look for evidence of the country's intellectual standing.[45]

In the following year Dawson repeated some of these points and appealed also to the patriotic feeling "which becomes all Canadians in witnessing any effort, however feeble, to sustain and exalt the greatness of our country."[46] Similarly, Thomas Sterry Hunt (although he was still an American citizen) emphasized the national purpose of the Royal Society by comparing it to America's National Academy of Sciences when he gave his opening speech as president of one of the Society's sections.[47]

As it was first constituted, the Royal Society of Canada included almost all of the professional scientists in the country.[48] This fact, along with the admission of the Society's own historian that "some of these were men of mediocrity,"[49] illustrates how small was the country's scientific community even at this late date. Despite their limited numbers, the scientists did hope to gain some professional advantages from the new organization. Dawson's plea for a more reputable journal was based on professional as well as national interest, and the hope was also expressed that the Society would be able to offer advice on scientific matters to the government.[50] It did, in fact, act in this advisory capacity, and was even able to initiate scientific projects that the government later adopted;[51] in this way the members gained some measure of influence on government policies.

However, the Society could not satisfy all of the professional requirements of the Canadian scientists. Contacts were still maintained with outside bodies; indeed, the AAAS met for the second time in Montreal in 1882, followed by the British Association two years later. Canadian scientists probably saw the Royal Society as a means of maintaining professional contacts in addition to those which some of them had already established with the American community, but the Society could not completely replace these wider connections. A spirit of nationalism was clearly the major factor behind Lorne's original proposals and was probably the more significant element governing the organization's early coherence.

Conclusion

The existence of the Royal Society of Canada was made possible only by the increasing size of the country's scientific population and by a revolution in transportation that had, in fact, begun several decades earlier. The growing importance of science in higher education and in government services had made possible the creation of an organization whose members were chosen on the grounds of national or even international merit rather than interest alone. But it was also clear that the Royal Society did not arise out of a recognition by the scientists themselves of the need for professional unity within the country. The first move was made from outside the scientific community, and, although the scientists saw some professional advantages in the new organization, their response was guided to a large extent by a recognition of its value as a means of asserting Canada's political independence. The absence of this nationalistic feeling in the Natural History Society of Montreal and the Canadian Institute (after its first few years) in large part explains the fact that neither of these organizations advanced beyond a purely local status. Thus, to understand the early development of the Canadian societies, it must be recognized that the needs of a scientific community are quite different from those of a political one. A number of Canadian scientists naturally turned to the larger scientific body of the United States in search of professional contacts, and at the scientific level such contacts were, and still are, quite satisfactory. Only when the political motivation of nationalism was introduced did a viable Canadian scientific society emerge. Scientists who were concerned about the status and independence of the country supported the Royal Society despite the fact that the professional advantages of this move were only a marginal improvement over those already enjoyed as a result of membership in the American Association. At a purely professional level, Canadian scientists might never have united, but the creation of the Royal Society made evident to them the existence of a national requirement that contact with the American organization could not satisfy.

This study has indicated the existence of a number of problems in the development of Canadian scientific societies and has suggested that these issues might be resolved in terms of differing requirements for scientific and political unity. The conclusions advanced above can be supported or attacked only in terms of the attitudes of the scientists toward the various Canadian and American societies as revealed by their own writings. There are biographical studies of some of the more important figures, but these are rarely capable of giving the modern historian an insight into a specialized question of this nature. Manuscripts of a number of prominent scientists have been preserved, but an extensive examination will be required to produce information on a given scientist's relationship to the larger scientific community and to the various societies.[52] It is difficult to locate material (if, indeed, any has survived) that can be attributed to lesser known scientists, and little effort has been devoted to the scientific interests of political and other figures who played an important role in the formation of these organizations. The present paper is no more than an outline of the issues that can be recognized in one area of the history of Canadian science. To complete the study of this and a host of related topics will require a large-scale effort devoted to what has hitherto been one of the most neglected aspects of Canadian history.

NOTES

1. My work in this field was undertaken while studying and teaching at the Institute for the History and Philosophy of Science and Technology, University of Toronto, between 1969 and 1972, and owes a great deal to the encouragement of Professor J. Bruce Sinclair.

2. Of the French-speaking intellectual societies, mention should be made of the Institut Canadien of Quebec, formed in 1846, and the similar Institut in Ottawa, formed in 1852. The first scientific journal published in French was the *Naturaliste Canadien* founded in 1868. The Université Laval of Quebec maintained a high standard of science education in the midcentury.

3. For an examination of these tendencies, see Sally Kohlstedt's paper in this present volume, and her "A Step toward Scientific Self-Identity in the United States: The Failure of the National Institute, 1844," *Isis* 62 (1970): 339-62.

4. Ralph S. Bates, *Scientific Societies in the United States,* 3rd ed. (Cambridge, Mass.: MIT Press, 1965), chap. 2.

5. For a history of the Society and some of the documents relating to its foundation, see *The Centenary Volume of the Literary and Historical Society of Quebec* (Quebec: Literary and Historical Society, 1924), pp. 1-104.

6. Literary and Historical Society of Quebec, *Historical Documents,* 9 series (1838-1924).

7. For a list of the Society's early publications, see the *Centenary Volume,* pp. 104-105. The Society owned a mineralogical cabinet, which is cataloged at the conclusion of the *Transactions of the Literary and Historical Society of Quebec* 1 (1829). According to a Captain Bonnycastle, the Society was determined to "advance the march of geological science in Canada," see "Desultory Observations on a Few of the Rocks and Minerals of Upper Canada," *Transactions,* pp. 62-70. That the Society actually organized an expedition for geological exploration seems implied by H. W. Bayfield, "Outlines of the Geology of Lake Superior," *Transactions,* pp. 1-43.

8. The act of incorporation is reprinted in the *Constitution and By-Laws of the Natural History Society of Montreal, with the Ammending Act, 20th Vict., Ch. 118* (Montreal, 1859), pp. 3-9. For a brief history of the Society, see the *Twenty-Eighth Annual Report of the Natural History Society of Montreal* (Montreal, 1856).

9. The full title of the Journal was the *Canadian Naturalist and Geologist,* changed in 1864 to *Canadian Naturalist and Quarterly Journal of Science.*

10. Earl of Dalhousie to the Honorable Wm. Smith, 7 May 1823, *Centenary Volume,* p. 14.

11. The list in the Act of Incorporation is reproduced in ibid., pp. 18−19.

12. The report of the governing committee, 26 May 1828, Natural History Society of Montreal, Minute Books 1:65, Blacker-Wood Library of Zoology and Ornithology, McGill University, Montreal.

13. From twenty-six members at its foundation in 1827 to about one hundred at incorporation in 1833.

14. The statement concerning the 1847 membership is based on the *Twenty-Eighth Annual Report,* p. 5. In 1859 the Natural History Society had a total of 192 life and ordinary members (see the list in the *Constitution*). This rose to 287 in 1862, but fell back to 264 in 1865 (see the relevant *Annual Reports*).

15. For an outline of Dawson's career, see T. H. Clark, "Sir John William Dawson, 1820-1899," in G. F. G. Stanley, ed., *Pioneers of Canadian Science: A Symposium Presented to the Royal Society of Canada* (Toronto: Royal Society, 1966), pp. 101-13. A more recent biography is Charles F. O'Brien. "Sir William Dawson: A Life in Science and Religion," *Memoirs of the American Philosophical Association* 84 (1971). See also J. W. Dawson, *Fifty Years Work in Canada: Scientific and Educational* (London and Edinburgh: Ballantyne & Harrison, 1901).

16. *Constitution and By-Laws* (1859), pp. 25-28; also the *Annual Reports.*

17. Minute Books, vol. 4, 29 September 1856.

18. Bernard J. Harrington, *Life of Sir William E. Logan* (Montreal, 1883), p. 324. Logan, the first director of the Geological Survey, had little to do with the Montreal

Society, possibly because he was out of the city on exploratory trips during much of the year.

19. The attendance was rarely more than fifteen, sometimes as low as six.

20. The *Report of the Council of the Natural History Society of Montreal* (Montreal, 1859), p. 4, laments that the government would not give what was apparently badly needed financial help.

21. W. Stewart Wallace, "A Sketch of the History of the Royal Canadian Institute," *The Royal Canadian Institute Centennial Volume* (Toronto: Royal Canadian Institute, 1949), pp. 123-70; Sir Sandford Fleming, "The Early Days of the Canadian Institute," *Transactions of the Canadian Institute* 6 (1899): 1-24 (semicentennial memorial volume). For a full list of the Institute's publications, see John Patterson, ed., *Canadian Institute: General Index to Publications, 1852-1912* (Toronto: Royal Canadian Institute, 1914).

22. *The Royal Canadian Institute Centennial Volume*, p. 131.

23. Fleming, "The Early Days of the Canadian Institute," p. 2.

24. Lawrence J. Burpee, *Sandford Fleming: Empire Builder* (Oxford: Oxford University Press, 1915). Fleming is perhaps best known for his suggestion of standard time zones.

25. Wallace, "A Sketch of the Early History of the Canadian Institute," p. 125.

26. Ibid., p. 130.

27. These ideas are clearly stated in the Institute's first chapter, reprinted in *The Royal Canadian Institute Centennial Volume*, pp. 130–35.

28. Canadian Institute Minute Books 1:72, 10 April 1852. These books are still in the possession of the Royal Canadian Institute.

29. Ibid., p. 376, 9 April 1859.

30. Printed texts of the petitions may be found in ibid., pp. 526-29.

31. Brief biographies of the officers of the Institute are printed in *The Royal Canadian Institute Centennial Volume*, pp. 117-232.

32. Report of the Meeting with the Governor General, Minute Books 1:380, 3 December 1859. The remark is also quoted by Wallace, "A Sketch of the History of the Royal Canadian Institute," p. 144.

33. Even here, a number of papers by important scientists living outside Toronto (e.g., Logan and Dawson) were merely reprints; see the *General Index* cited in note 21, above.

34. Dawson, *Fifty Years Work in Canada*, p. 102. It is significant that Dawson had to pass through the United States to make the journey.

35. Information on the dates on which Canadians joined the American Association is derived from the lists of members printed each year in the Association's annual *Reports.*

36. In addition to Logan, Sterry Hunt, and Dawson, this list included E. Billings and A. Murray (Geological Survey); G. T. Kingston (director of the Magnetic Observatory, Toronto); H. Croft, W. Hinks, E. J. Chapman, D. Wilson (University of Toronto); J. Robb and W. B. Jack (University of New Brunswick); J. Williamson (Queen's University, Kingston) and E. J. Horan (Université Laval, Quebec). It may be significant that Sandford Fleming, who shared the patriotic ideals of the early Canadian Institute, never joined the AAAS, although other prominent Canadian engineers such as T. C. Keefer did.

37. Wallace, "A Sketch of the History of the Royal Canadian Institute," pp. 150-58. For a contemporary account see the Toronto *Globe*, 9 May 1879. The Minute Book for this period reveals occasional attendances at meetings as high as fifty, where between twenty and thirty had been the normal figure.

38. On the history of the Society, see *The Royal Society of Canada, Fifty Years Retrospect, Anniversary Volume, 1882-1932* (Toronto: Ryerson Press, 1932), especially the introduction by Lawrence J. Burpee. In the Society's original state there were four sections, each with twenty members; the number of sections was increased to five in 1918.

39. Taken from the Society's provisional constitution; see *Proceedings and Transactions of the Royal Society of Canada* 1 (1882-1883): ii.

40. Dawson, *Fifty Years Work in Canada*, p. 179.

41. See Dawson's presidential address of 1882, *Proceedings and Transactions* 1:vi-xi.

42. The Marquis of Lorne, Address to the Royal Society in 1882, *Proceedings and Transactions*, p. vi.

43. Dawson, *Proceedings and Transactions*, p. ix.

44. Ibid., p. vi.

45. Ibid., p. x.

46. Dawson, Presidential Address of 1883 in ibid., pp. lii-lvii.

47. Thomas Sterry Hunt, "The Relations of the Natural Sciences," *Proceedings and Transactions,* sec. III, pp. 1-9.

48. In addition to Dawson and Sterry Hunt, the Society included A. R. C. Selwyn (Logan's successor as head of the Geological Survey), George M. Dawson (J. W. Dawson's son, another prominent member of the Geological Survey), Alexander Murray (who was now head of the Newfoundland Survey), Charles H. Carpmael (of the Meteorological Service), William Saunders (of the Dominion Experimental Farms), Sandford Fleming, Sir William Osler, and almost all of the science professors from the various universities.

49. Burpee, *Royal Society of Canada,* p. 2.

50. A. Todd, "On the Relations of the Royal Society to the State," *Proceedings and Transactions* 1:xlv-xlix. Note, however, that Todd was the parliamentary librarian, not a scientist.

51. Some of these projects are noted by Burpee, *Royal Society of Canada,* p. 5.

52. The present author is familiar with some of the papers of Sir William E. Logan, which do not, however, aid the present study. As an illustration of the problems encountered in this field, it may be mentioned that new material on J. W. Dawson is being turned up almost continuously by the McGill University Archives.

Commentary:
An Historian of Education
Looks at the Newagen Study

RICHARD J. STORR

While I think it would be unfortunate to keep the history of science and the history of education entirely apart from each other, I do hesitate, as a historian of education, to comment upon the particular contributions the papers and discussions at Newagen make to the history of science. Rather, let me speak to a general question that comes to my mind as I think about the conference and about my own field. Indeed, in any field of history, interpretation of the particulars of evidence is both inescapable and necessary. Hence the critical question in regard to any mass of evidence is: What ideas or criteria do we adopt, whether unconsciously or explicitly, to capture the significance of the facts or perhaps even to confer significance upon them?

Obviously, the question raises large philosophical problems, but allow me to put a specific case. There is in the historical study of American education a tradition that resembles the once dominant Whig interpretation of the British past. According to the tradition, the history of education in the United States takes its significance primarily from the emergence of the public school system. Thus the Massachusetts school law of 1647 appears as an anticipation of Horace Mann's work nearly two centuries later. The proposition is that the public school system is a prime embodiment of the democratic ideal: the building of the system is explained as a heroic and ultimately successful struggle—an insistent word in the writing—against the enemies of progress. But, about fifteen years ago, some of us began to argue the case for a more thorough examination of education outside of the school—in the family, the church, and so on. Such study indicates that the identification of the best in education with the public school is itself a product of history and not simply a timeless principle by which progress can be measured absolutely. Now a second generation of revisionists is arguing that the public school system actually fostered bureaucracy and elitism. Still in the name of democracy, the old interpretation has been turned upside down and some fascinating ideas are falling out. Although I do think that both the old and the new interpretations sweep us too hurriedly past important elements of an immensely complicated situation, it would be a digression here to explore the matter in detail. Suffice it to say that the debate renders a historian of education extremely uneasy about what may be only simplistic rather than truly self-evident.

The historian of education wonders if the historical interpretation of science has been influenced by a similar whiggery. The question does not apply where scholarship is descriptive rather than normative; and Newagen was important partly because it did provide an occasion for the publication and collation of much new factual material. Neither does the question apply to efforts, such as were made at the conference, to clarify either the terms used in the past or the taxonomies of the persons and organizations belonging to it. Nor, in the third place, does the question of whiggery apply necessarily to each and every attempt to establish how science in the past contributed or failed to contribute to the development of modern science. One may say: Here stands modern science, for better or worse; let us seek out its roots. That is straightforward enough. Such an approach offers what may be called a relative standard for deciding which institutions were "significant," which were "primitive," or whatever. By that standard, it may not be entirely illegitimate to say that an early institution was a "success," meaning not only that it fulfilled its own stated purposes, but also that its work anticipated the triumph of later institutions. In my field, one is inclined to pass that kind of judgment on a few graduate programs introduced before the Johns Hopkins opened. But the question of whiggery does apply when one drops the quotation marks around "significant" or the other operative words of judgment. Is one then beginning, however unwittingly, to use the achievement of today as an absolute standard of what is better or even best? I seem to recall an idea hovering over the Newagen discussion that any final judgment upon the period before 1860 should be made to hang less upon a perhaps unfavorable balance of immediate successes and failures than upon the bearing that events in that period had upon the later development of American science—that is, that a second or even third conference is needed to put the results of the first in perspective. It simply was not clear to me whether the standard of judgment is to be relative or absolute.

I hope that the use of even the relative standard does not shut off inquiry into whether the years before 1860 were characterized by a distinctive pattern of intellectual and institutional activity and therefore possibly contained the seeds of an order different from that which was actually established after 1860. There is heuristic value in the assumption, which some revisionists declare as a certainty, that ours is not necessarily the best of all possible worlds. In that light, what seems an insignificant lost cause according to a whig interpretation may be perceived as having contained a significant promise of a better world. My argument here is not that we should decide immediately and in a politicized atmosphere whether or not modern science is the best possible, but, quite to the contrary, that it is worth asking, before passing judgment, whether one can detect points in the development of science where a fundamental choice of courses was possible. Can one identify this or that academy, for example, as a signboard pointing toward an alternative way of organizing science—a way that might have had its own kind of brilliance? Of course, some historians are suspicious of contrafactual propositions, yet such a viewpoint does put what actually happened into a cross light that, although admittedly artificial, does help us to see things in relief.

A word about the prospects of research in the history of education and the history of science: both appear to have growing tissue along their outer edges. The history of education has been broadened out by defining education to include all sorts of activities that have a bearing upon the rearing of children or upon growing up in America insofar as that experience has some educative effect—and that is not to speak of adult education. On the side of science, I noticed in the conference that the history of academies takes us across a wide landscape: to the difference between the craft and the scientific approaches to technological development; to the meaning of utility as in the phrase "useful knowledge"; to the possibility of a linkage between the "histories"—civil, natural, and medical; to the impact of apprenticeship; to the historical sociology of the professions; and of course to the whole question of the diffusion of knowledge. The latter topics in particular suggest that the history of American education and the history of American science are spreading outward to meet each other; and I have no doubt that an examination of "research" at a later conference will show the same thing. Perhaps it is obvious, but it seems to be worth explicit notice, that the two fields can (and I think should) be seen as parts of the study of American life, itself considered as an inductive and potentially coherent kind of inquiry. I do not mean that we should collect bare facts about education and science and expect a map of American life to stand revealed like a picture on a jigsaw puzzle; by now such positivism must be dead. However, each of us can usefully concentrate upon education or science most of the time and still look up periodically to assess what is being done in the other field. The process requires analysis as well as fact-finding all along the way and synthesis from time to time, but not, I think, an initial commitment either to a whiggish assumption that American life has been almost inevitably progressive or to the opposite. My point is, of course, that the joint possibilities of the historical study of education and of science should be made the object of full-scale, conscious exploitation. I see the Newagen conference as a step in that direction.

What is at issue is the kind of questions that we put to our material. With regard to education, one may ask not only what shaped particular institutions and American education in general but also what is to be inferred about American society and culture from the fact that Americans created the modes of education they did. For example, what does the massive role assigned to formal schooling, especially schooling under public control and with the apparatus of certification, say about shifting American attitudes toward the responsibilities of the family and the state? Similarly, in regard to the scientific academies, what can we learn from their history about American attitudes toward organization? I was struck by the fact that so many small groups of people, sometimes in fledgling communities, were not content to meet as private clubs but sought to organize formally and took sweeping names: the *American* Philosophical Society; the *United States* Military Philosophical Society; the *Western* Academy; and the *American* Academy of Arts and Sciences. There appears to have been a kind of formalism combined with a sense of grandeur at work in the minds of the academicians. They had the model of the European academies in mind, and the publication of proceedings created a functional need for some degree of organization. A desire to prove that the United States was not culturally inferior to Europe may well have had its effect; the great convention of 1787 may have been an inspiration as an example of constitution framing; civic pride was strong; and perhaps the young nation was given to self-importance.

We may be inclined to be a little condescending toward the pretentiousness in American hopes before 1860 and to dismiss it as an ironic fact that the life of the academies was so precarious only a few years before massive institutions destined to enjoy spectacular success began to emerge. But does the evidence hint at something else: was there a peculiar quality in American life that created a hunger for great institutions—a hunger not unlike that in the stomachs of the real *lazzaroni* as they begged for food? No doubt a direct relation existed in the late nineteenth century between, on the one hand, the rise of big education, big science, and big business and, on the other, the emergence of the country economically from what is today called a condition of underdevelopment. Certainly Johns Hopkins University, the University of Chicago, and other universities rested materially upon accumulations of surplus capital, but is not the psychology of Americans in the earlier part of the century also to be considered? Americans had become accustomed to making great plans for education and science before 1860, and the habit may help to account for the fact that an appreciable segment of the national wealth was presently thought of as indeed a surplus. A kind of upward suction was at work in the minds of Americans as they contemplated the void between what the country was culturally and what they believed it should be. Is the existence of that suction part of the reason why large resources were put at the disposal of academics by the turn of the century and why science was organized as it was when its situation ceased to be precarious? Talk about the American Dream has become hackneyed, but the early history of the academies suggests that a revolution of rising expectations (admittedly another cliché) did begin shortly after the War of Independence ended. Remember how emphatically Dr. Rush declared that the Revolution was not over!

Also, it is worth asking what the history of the academies before 1860 may indicate about the meaning of knowledge to Americans. Obviously, the New World borrowed heavily from the European traditions of learning and science, but was there a characteristically American spin to the idea of knowledge? Do I detect in the papers and discussion of the conference a suggestion that an American style was taking shape and that it was related to a particular conception of knowledge as a public utility? Of course, the idea that knowledge is power was not new, nor was its application to national improvement. Yet one senses that Americans were not simply importing intellectual capital as they worked their way toward strategies for the generation of knowledge and its transmission through an "information system." Again, did the quality of American patriotism, both local and national, affect what knowledge meant? There was John Adams, concerned that his countrymen should be educated to the fullest of their abilities and virtues. I was fascinated by references to the effort within mechanics institutes and societies of arts to remove such boundaries around knowledge as were represented by trade secrets and the Masonic tradition: what exactly can we say about the possibility that there was something in the American situation or in American aspirations that especially favored the democratization of knowledge?

The question applies in regard both to the classes of persons to whom knowledge was made available and to the varieties of information that were allowed the dignity of being considered knowledge. I was reminded of the efforts made before 1860 to broaden the curriculum and audience of the colleges and, at the same time and perhaps by one and the same device, to raise the ceiling of the curriculum to what we now think of as graduate education. The instruments appropriate to the diffusion and advancement of knowledge were not so clearly distinguished from each other as they are now. Mastery of a field was admired, but it was only then being demonstrated—especially to Americans who studied abroad—just how laborious and specialized the roads to mastery might be. But professionalization was beginning, as Nathan Reingold indicated; hence the question is whether the further development of professional science did not, in effect, keep open that gap between experts and even educated laymen, not to speak of intelligent mechanics, which at least some of the early academies were designed to close. It has become a matter of everyday practice to apply the results of scientific investigation instantly and universally in American life, and in that sense science has been democratized; but is it nonsense to suggest that understanding of how scientists really think has yet to become the common possession of Americans? If we wish science truly to be a part of our popular culture, must we not be grateful to those early academicians for taking the first steps toward exploring what attainment of that goal entails?

Early
American Learned Societies
as Informants on Our Past:
Some Conclusions and Suggestions
for Further Research

BARBARA GUTMANN ROSENKRANTZ

American learned and scientific societies of the late colonial and early national period are a source of information about the intellectual commitments and social values of settlers in the New World. Because physical separation from the established institutions of the Old World marked the initial phase of the transfer of a culture, the nature and function of colonial societies followed the formal structure that transplanted Englishmen deemed essential. The shape of early American institutions was largely derived from received tradition, yet, it was strangely incongruent in the provincial setting. The gathering of like-minded men in pursuit of learning presumed a supporting environment. In England numbers alone assured a modicum of success, as did sponsorship by persons of wealth and standing. The impulse to establish learned societies in America attests to the vigor of that tradition and even more to the confidence that a learned tradition granted men far from its source.

The transfer of organizational forms is, however, only a part of the story. English institutional experience is inadequate to account for the generative and staying power of American learned societies. Even when faced with the immediate task of survival, the colonials upheld a mission to establish social order in the wilderness that came from a religious faith linking knowledge of nature with adherence to God's will. Sermons to congregations, proposals to convert the Indians, and letters of information to the Royal Society of London all give evidence that law was sought for and observed in natural phenomena. And when this faith in God's ordered universe came to be articulated in more secular terms at the end of the eighteenth century, the sustaining rhetoric continued to reflect the special obligation of American colonists. In collecting and classifying the flora and fauna of the North American continent, exploring and mapping the terrain, describing and measuring the climate and its effect on human health, Americans had reason to subscribe to societies that gave them status abroad and endowed their pursuits with significance beyond personal gratification. Yet the impulse to establish social order was hardly limited to those few learned men who particularly supported the cause of useful knowledge; in the midst of conflict with England, colonists voicing their different political persuasions called to the attention of the world the philosophic and practical importance of their stance. When the tenuous hold of early settlement was succeeded by assurance of permanence and later independence from England, the leaders of learned societies also argued that New World science had a special opportunity to transform enlightenment into power.

Earlier chapters in this volume suggest that certain assumptions about both the *social function* and the *special character of knowledge* were common to the founders of early American learned societies. Although function and character are surely interlocking conditions, it is useful to acknowledge the circumstances that determined their relationship.

Evidence confirming nature's order may indeed be compelling in a society threatened by discontinuities with its own past and seeking to affirm social stability. In an eloquent assessment of the colonists' efforts to mediate their displacement, Bernard Bailyn has shown that seventeenth- and eighteenth-century settlers experienced potent physical and social threats to accustomed discipline that "radically transformed" traditional practices and processes. By the end of the colonial period, Bailyn observes, "education had been dislodged from its ancient position in the social order, wrenched loose from the automatic and instinctive working of society, and cast as a matter for deliberation into the forefront of consciousness."[1] Bailyn proposes that the function of education in the New World was to identify a normative social structure and simultaneously to provide the means of socialization. Where once the family had been the bulwark of the social continuity and a complement to the traditional order, now schooling played an essential instrumental role. Similarly, in the colonial setting the learned society, although more fragile than its English counterpart, defined a sequence of recognizable social roles in the absence of traditional institutional trappings.

Reingold distinguishes three groups in what he sees as an emerging community of scientific men: the "cultivators" and the "practitioners" of learning were preeminent, although not sharply separated from each other in this early period, while the "researchers" subsequently grew in number with the expansion of scientific occupations and disciplines. Fron Reingold's perspective, the dominant status of the cultivator in the late eighteenth century, as compared with the very limited role of the practitioner group, was largely the result of the immature state of scientific knowledge in the colonies. The need to find patrons to support scientific endeavors in the absence of universities and established centers of learning encouraged the broadest definition of learning, a definition that was reflected in the equal participation of the gentleman cultivator and the expanding practitioner class in founding scientific societies throughout the first half of the nineteenth century. But if one interprets this development of learned societies as part of the hazardous undertaking to establish a stable nation in the absence of accustomed structural underpinnings, efforts to create institutions for the promotion and diffusion of knowledge have a different significance.

[1] Notes to this chapter begin on page 353.

At a time when deference was in bad repute, and yet was still looked to as the surest safeguard against social disorder, learned societies provided a place where social distinctions could reign beyond dispute. Linking social order to the order that bred harmony in nature, membership in a learned society may have protected personal status for the ubiquitous collector of mineralogical specimens. Collegiality was a pleasure justified by scientific pursuits, but we do not know whether at the time this congenial company was viewed unambiguously as a "natural aristocracy" stimulating stability. Looking at this question from a somewhat different point of view, Dupree shows that learned societies provided the "information networks" that created internal cohesion and compensated for the absence of a national center of prestige through the "symbolically national" character of societies established at Philadelphia and Boston. Yet, if uneasiness stimulated organization, not enough has been said about the way in which these learned societies accommodated the tension of these years when many men were suspicious of privilege because organized knowledge was tied to institutions embodying special status. Most of the papers in this volume describe success; only Hindle recounts instances where failure frustrated seemingly practical objectives. We need further research on the public reception of learned societies: who was excluded from membership and how desired participants were recruited. And we need to know what measures were taken to assure success and how the founders characterized their opponents when challenged.

Turning to the question of the character of knowledge as evidenced in the early learned societies, Greene's essay sets out the boundary of useful knowledge by examining the scope of subjects regarded as legitimate concerns. "Improvements" anticipated in Franklin's circular letter of 1743 calling for the formation of the American Philosophical Society ranged from new uses of mathematics to information on animal breeding and brewing of vegetable juices; systematic knowledge included "all philosophical experiments that let light into the nature of things, tend to increase the power of man over nature, and multiply the conveniences or pleasures of life."[2] The parameters of learning included all civil and natural knowledge which "would enrich and aggrandize these confederated States," suggesting that the agenda of scientific societies matched the tasks of the new Republic. For the American Academy of Arts and Sciences, "knowledge of various kinds, and greatly useful to mankind, has taken the place of dry and uninteresting speculations of schoolmen; and bold and erroneous hypothesis has been obliged to give way to demonstrative experiment."[3]

The challenge of these proclamations suggests a departure from past practice, yet we know this same language was used at the founding of the Royal Society of London a century before. Surely some Americans found these words a comforting assurance that "philosophical experiment" would have a home in the New World. For those who believed, with Benjamin Rush, that the Revolution was only one step in the improvement of everything from manners to fecundity and longevity, the notion of useful knowledge was also aggrandized. There were important differences, however, among the leaders of learned societies about the worthiness of some scientific pursuits. Josiah Quincy, an active member of the Massachusetts Historical Society, the Society for the Study of Natural Philosophy, and the American Academy of Arts and Sciences, vented his scorn of the American Philosophical Society in public and private. The source of his animus was complex, but other cultivated Bostonians agreed that the members of the Philadelphia Society "were not famous for A PARTICULAR AND ACCURATE KNOWLEDGE OF ANYTHING, but were distinguished only by a *general acquaintance* with philosophy."[4] The partisan overtones of doubts about the validity and significance of certain investigations does not alter the shared high regard for accurate natural knowledge as the embodiment of lawful order. When the notion of useful knowledge was transplanted to the New World, it frequently took on an added dimension of practical discipline that was consciously articulated by farsighted men.

A decade before the founding of the American Philosophical Society, William Smith, provost of the College and Academy of Philadelphia, described the concerns which had led to the establishment of the College. The trustees of the original Academy, where learning had been limited to English, Latin, and mathematics, decided to enlarge the scope of instruction. "They were very sensible that the knowledge of words, without making them subservient to the knowledge of things, could never be considered as the business of education. To lay a foundation in the languages was very necessary as a first step, but without the superstructure of the sciences would be of little use for the conduct of life."[5] It was precisely this conception of the value of scientific knowledge for the conduct of life that inspired Americans to reflect on the special relevance of Baconian utilitarianism to their situation. Americans recognized the dangers as well as the opportunities of the physical and social environment they occupied, but with all the benefits of useful knowledge potentially accessible through "demonstrative experiment," one senses the urgency to make good the promise.

Urgency and promise were insufficient catalysts to assure universal success. Hindle indicates some of the ways that New York City differed from Philadelphia and Boston, but how local sponsorship translated aspiration into effective organization is an elusive question.[6] And the uneven course of efforts to establish societies for practical arts in New York State suggests that example and exhortation from abroad could not compensate for the absence of a cohesive local leadership. Despite the relatively modest aims of colonials urged on by the London Society for the Encouragement of Arts, Manufactures, and Commerce, most attempts to establish daughter societies foundered. The "premium societies" had a more heterogeneous membership than the societies for promoting knowledge in Philadelphia and Boston, although their commitment to encourage agricultural and manufactured products might have fused differences of status. Agricultural improvement was an interest shared by the learned societies and the societies of arts. Significantly, most of the recommendations made in the *Transactions* and *Memoirs* of the general scientific societies did not find their way into the almanacs widely circulated in the communities where "premium societies" were fostered. Social and geographic distance were obstacles to this exchange, but equally forbidding was the fact that published advice, for instance directions for large scale rotation of crops, was impractical for all but the wealthiest landowner.[7]

There is a clear need for interdisciplinary studies of the growth of technology, the economy, and the social structure of regions where societies thrived and perished. The taxonomy of organizations that John Greene identified as clearly discernible by the turn of the century reflects a useful genealogy of men and ideas: societies for the promotion of knowledge, for the practical arts, and for emerging professional groups laid special claim to subject matter and method.[8] The success of these claims depended on the organization of men and knowledge. Social and cognitive distinctions foreclosed the future of societies of arts composed basically of amateurs, while in urban centers the growth of knowledge and technique gave impetus to a new conception of discipline.

Sinclair's chapter on the Franklin Institute analyzes a crucial aspect of the conception of discipline as it was established in the early decades of the nineteenth century. While historians may argue about the ideological and operational distinctions between science and technology, Sinclair shows that the rhetoric of the American past links mechanic arts with scientific knowledge. The participants in this relationship were responsive to both the social value of this connection and its practical benefits. Sinclair makes the point that the union of mechanic arts and science was accomplished by identifying the principles of science with its methods so that the validation of general laws took place on the engineer's drawing board rather than in the philosopher's study. This shift of workplace was expected to bring tangible rewards and also permit the informed artisan a stake in the progress of science. Just as the definition of useful knowledge had acquired a moral dimension, so too the union of theory and practice should demonstrate the democratizing potential of science. In antebellum America, where licensing of physicians had been revoked because it smacked of special privilege, the notion that scientific knowledge gave the intelligent mechanic status as well as skill had political force.

Several chapters in this volume illustrate the contradictory manner in which scientific knowledge and its use were diffused through early nineteenth-century societies and institutions. Although the ambiguity of egalitarianism in science was as threatening in some quarters as Jeffersonian science had been, a visitor to the United States, Alexis de Tocqueville, saw the emerging ethos in terms of common premises. However inspiring in retrospect, the choice he set before his audience had the unintentional possibility of satire.

We must first understand what is wanted of society and its government. Do you wish to give certain elevation to the human mind, and teach it to regard the things of this world with generous feelings, to inspire men with a scorn of mere temporal advantages, to form and nourish strong convictions, and keep alive the spirit of honorable devotedness? Is it your object to refine the habits, embellish the manners, and cultivate the arts, to promote the love of poetry, beauty, and glory? Would you constitute a people fitted to act powerfully upon all other nations, and prepared for those high enterprises which, whatever be their results, will leave a name forever famous in history? If you believe such to be the principal object of society, avoid the government of the democracy, for it would not lead you with certainty to the goal.

But if you hold it expedient to divert the moral and intellectual activity of man to the production of comfort, and the promotion of general well-being; if a clear understanding be more profitable to man than genius; if your object be not to stimulate the virtues of heroism, but the habits of peace; if you had rather witness vices than crimes, and are content to meet with fewer noble deeds, provided offences be diminished in the same proportion; if, instead of living in the midst of a brilliant society, you are contented to have prosperity around you; if, in short, you are of opinion that the principal object of a government is not to confer the greatest possible power and glory upon the body of the nation, but to insure the greatest enjoyment, and to avoid the most misery, to each of the individuals who compose it,—if such be your desire, then equalize the conditions of men, and establish democratic institutions.[9]

The image of the common man disciplined by work and intelligence may well have been most lifelike when viewed by a visitor. In the United States the 1830s and 1840s were troubled times, when economic disorder threatened opportunity and Irish immigrants and cholera were unwelcome intruders from abroad. It was also a time when a multitude of new learned societies continued to be formed: societies for medical observation, for the study of natural history, for assembling the statistics of populations, and for the support of phrenology to name but a few. The picture of science was as fragmented and multifaceted as the surrounding culture.

The chapters by Cassedy on medicine, by Rossiter on agriculture, and by Shapiro on the Western Academy of Sciences have some common themes that suggest both why it is so difficult to view science as a common enterprise, and how the organization of that enterprise came to assume a distinctive shape in the early nineteenth century. First, a new conception of scientific knowledge developed that called for systematic exploration of the relationship between subject matter and method. This self-conscious attention to method promised rich rewards but also demanded that traditional classifications of knowledge and techniques of study be broken apart and reassembled. Second, the impetus toward specialization threatened the amateur whose intellectual and pecuniary resources had in the past promoted local stability. Contradictory social processes moved toward exclusion of enthusiasm as the basis for participation, yet the profession of competence could hardly be tested by rigorous criteria. Nevertheless, the identifying characteristics of scientific men became more explicit; schooling and experience, evidence of accomplishment, and recognition by peers all assumed a more specific structure and legitimized expertise. At the same time formation and re-formation of local societies and the publication of journals that ended abruptly after a few issues, sometimes reappearing half a decade later, suggest the uneven course of events. It was difficult to find the proper environment in which to locate a cabinet of fossils and just as difficult to locate authority in proper hands. The immediate consequence of this search for legitimacy was centrifugal, frequently casting out accustomed standards and symbols of the culture previously associated with learned and scientific societies.

The ambiguity that had once enhanced membership in such societies by enabling common purpose to impose order on heterogeneous substance and talents now was at best irrelevant. Daniel Drake's encompassing stricture for "accurate observation, judicious arrangement, and logical induction" invited the cooperation of all who called themselves naturalists. Shapiro reminds us that by the 1840s the method of classifying natural phenomena had altered; discipline required distinctions accessible only to the specialist. In Cincinnati the Western Academy ceased to be a viable organization, and scientific men established their authenticity by disassociating themselves from its ranks. Eminence derived from the unique investigation was taken as an indication of provincial isolation rather than local vigor. Cassedy shows that physicians needed to establish their scientific credentials independent of interest in and financial support of learned societies; status could not be shared among professionals without evidence that upheld the claim. And Rossiter's paper describes how the heterodox membership of societies for agricultural improvement scattered. Lacking a single discipline around which to recruit and train experts, agriculture spawned a range of specialties whose allegiance was tied to local situations rather than to scientific skills. Competence was affirmed in the narrow terms of practice, and elevation to professional status was not achieved by unifying theory or method. Eventually, authority in agriculture was organized on a substantially different basis, through the development of government responsibility—another indication of the complex relationship between the growth of knowledge and the institutions that articulate its social functions.

From our perspective it is plausible that learned societies of the late colonial period validated natural knowledge as the agent of social improvement. Dedication to the promotion of knowledge acquired special meaning when firmly attached to the proposition that nature's laws were knowable, while at the same time it gave certain guidance to men's affairs. However, the normative implications of natural knowledge were accepted outside the confines of the learned societies as well as within them. While the learned societies pressed their claim to recognition because of contributions they projected, their importance was in part derived from the membership of men whose status was well established in other spheres. Distinction between the learned and vernacular cultures hardly required proof, and the rhetoric of useful knowledge was too widely shared to suggest usurpation by an elite class or an educated minority.

To discriminate between the functions of different societies for the promotion of knowledge and the arts, it is necessary to set them firmly in the social environment. Success or failure was determined by the matrix of roles that participants brought with them rather than by activities generated within the learned group. Visitors to America remarked on the native propensity for "joining," but mapping the interlocking membership of learned societies shows that some Americans saw utility in making visible the congruence of learning and social values. If the membership of the American Academy of Arts and Sciences was indistinguishable from the membership of the Massachusetts Historical Society, this confirmed an underlying principle of social order without imputing a lesser commitment to either organization.

During the third and fourth decades of the nineteenth century, new societies and institutions reflected in part the growth and spread of population. Distinctions between various branches of knowledge also prompted the formation of new organizations. But the composition of membership had altered as well, indicating a shift in the personal commitment of participants. In the late eighteenth century, public role and interest determined representation, but now occupation tended to be the deciding factor. Achievement was, as always, the measure that promoted access to the company of learned men, but achievement was defined by activity circumscribed by new criteria. While standards were a matter of acknowledged concern, the tension between tradition and new expectations was evident in learned societies as well as in other institutions.

Uneasiness about the growing heterogeneity of the nation coupled with dedication to perfectionist reform was a common characteristic.[10] In the 1840s societies for sanitary reform and temperance unions found that science provided principles to illuminate the causes of deviance and the possibility of cure. But if science was a suggestive reference point for reforming associations, the growth of scientific knowledge set somewhat different conditions for learned societies. The science endorsed by the practitioners who began to dominate the membership lists had the dual function of attracting broad support and diminishing the influence of the marginally qualified.

Since relatively few men could demonstrate professional qualifications, scientific societies faced tasks that strained their resources. Stability simulatneously required an inviting agenda and restricted access to leadership. Kohlstedt notes that, when the American Association for the Advancement of Science welcomed "practicing scientists, interested practitioners, and onlookers," its purpose was to compliment rather than compete with existing societies. Her informative analysis of the social and educational background of members accents the need for a systematic study of the public image of science if the components of organization are to be better understood. Internal antagonisms focused attention at one level where individual roles can be most readily discerned. An examination of the complex environment in which the search for stability evoked contrasting perceptions of external and internal threats to order could account for the accommodations spelled out in the formation of new groups. The difficulty of identifying disciplinary strategies or professional standards prompted important alliances, and the differential durability of these relations can be plotted as an indication of stress points.

The papers in this volume center attention on the life course of specific societies. Within these learned associations the intellectual and social commitments of individuals were played out under constraints that functioned as a screen filtering knowledge of nature and social experience in an effort to resolve contradictory information. The view from within inevitably emphasizes internal coherence, yet the promotion of learning took place in an atmosphere where shared conceptions of nature's order did not obviate sensitivity to the precarious character of social order. The transformation of useful knowledge into learned discipline and scientific practice was influenced by traditions, values, and techniques. Connections between learned men and the larger society changed during the years covered in these papers. The emergence of distinctive classifications of knowledge and the increase in the number of men identified as specialists altered the shape and function of learned societies. By the time of the Civil War connections between science and social order were more distended than before and certainly less accessible to facile generalization. The social space occupied by scientific societies was more clearly defined, implying functions that were at once constricted and aggrandized. And scientific men found that they could project a model for the social accountability of scientific societies that set their affairs somewhat apart from others.

NOTES

1. Bernard Bailyn, *Education in the Forming of American Society* (Chapel Hill: University of North Carolina Press, 1960), p. 21. See also Arnold Thackray, "Natural Knowledge in Cultural Context: The Manchester Model," *American Historical Review* 79 (June 1974): 678.

2. Benjamin Franklin, *The Writings of Benjamin Franklin,* ed. A. H. Smyth, 10 vols. (New York: Macmillan Co., 1905-1907), 2:230.

3. Quoted by John Greene in this volume from *Memoirs of the American Academy of Arts and Sciences* 1 (1875).

4. Josiah Quincy to John Vaughan, American Philosophical Society Archives, Philadelphia, Pa., quoted in Linda K. Kerber, *Federalists in Dissent: Imagery and Ideology in Jeffersonian America* (Ithaca, N.Y.: Cornell University Press, 1970), p. 74.

5. *Account of the College, Academy and Charitable School of Philadelphia in Pennsylvania,* ed. Thomas R. Adams (1759; reprint ed., University of Pennsylvania Library, Thomas R. Adams, 1951), pp. 16-17.

6. French encouragement for L'Académie des Etats-Unis de l'Amérique failed in Richmond and Baltimore as well as in New York and Philadelphia. See Ralph S. Bates, *Scientific Societies in the United States,* 3rd ed. (Cambridge, Mass.: MIT Press, 1965), pp. 11-14.

7. John T. Kelly, "Essays on Early American Almanacs: Popularization of Agricultural Improvement" (Ph.D. diss., Harvard University, in progress).

8. See introduction to this volume, pp. xv-xxv.

9. Alexis de Tocqueville, *American Institutions,* ed. Francis Bowen (Boston: Sever, Francis & Co., 1870), pp. 322-23. This is the same text as *De la démocratie en Amérique,* 1 (1835).

10. For a selection of essays on this subject see David B. Davis, ed., *Ante-Bellum Reform* (New York: Harper & Row, 1967).

Notes on Contributors

PETER J. BOWLER received his Ph.D. from the University of Toronto in 1971 and has published a number of articles on various aspects of the history of biology. He has taught history of science at the University of Toronto and the Science University of Malaysia and is currently teaching at the University of Winnipeg.

SANBORN C. BROWN is Professor of Physics Emeritus at the Massachusetts Institute of Technology. He is the author of *Count Rumford, Physicist Extraordinary; Collected Works of Count Rumford; Scientific Manpower: Dilemma for Graduate Education;* and *Physics 50 Years Later.*

JAMES H. CASSEDY, Historian at the National Library of Medicine, received his Ph.D. in American Civilization from Brown University. As a sequel to his latest book, *Demography in Early America,* he is now preparing a study of nineteenth-century American medical demography.

I. BERNARD COHEN, Professor of the History of Science at Harvard since 1958, is a specialist in the history of scientific ideas. His dominant concern has been the growth of physical thought in the seventeenth and eighteenth centuries and the rise of science in the United States. He is the author of *Introduction to Newton's 'Principia', Benjamin Franklin: His Contribution to the American Tradition,* and other volumes on the development of scientific thought and on science in America.

A. HUNTER DUPREE is George L. Littlefield Professor of American History at Brown University. He is the author of *Science in the Federal Government* and *Asa Gray* and the editor of *Science and the Emergence of Modern America.*

JOSEPH EWAN, Ida A. Richardson Professor of Botany, Tulane University, has combined an interest in field biology and the history of natural history. He has published *Rocky Mountain Naturalists, William Bartram Drawings,* and, with Nesta Ewan, *John Banister and his Natural History of Virginia, 1678-1692.* He edited a *Short History of Botany in the United States* and, most recently, provided the commentary for a reprint edition of Mark Catesby's *Natural History.*

GEORGE F. FRICK is Associate Professor of History at the University of Delaware, co-author of *Mark Catesby: The Colonial Audubon,* and author of the introduction to a reprint of Catesby's *Natural History.*

PATSY A. GERSTNER is Curator of the Howard Dittrick Museum of Historical Medicine and Lecturer on the History of Geology at Case Western Reserve University. Her special interest is British and American eighteenth- and nineteenth-century geology and paleontology. Recent publications include "Vertebrate Paleontology: An Early Nineteenth Century Transatlantic Science," *Journal of the History of Biology* 3 (1970) and "The Reaction to James Hutton's Use of Heat as a Geologic Agent," *British Journal for the History of Science* 5 (1971).

JOHN C. GREENE is Professor of History at the University of Connecticut. His interests include early American science, the history of evolutionary biology, and the historical relations of science and religion. He is the author of *The Death of Adam: Evolution and Its Impact on Western Thought, Darwin and the Modern World View,* and various articles on early American science.

BROOKE HINDLE is Director of the National Museum of History and Technology of the Smithsonian Institution. His publications include the *Pursuit of Science in Revolutionary America, David Rittenhouse,* and *Technology in Early America.*

JAMES M. HOBBINS is Staff Historian of the Joseph Henry Papers at the Smithsonian Institution. A graduate of Cornell and Temple universities, he is currently pursuing his Ph.D. in American history at the University of Maryland. His studies have focused on aspects of nineteenth-century American cultural life.

SALLY GREGORY KOHLSTEDT is Assistant Professor of History at Syracuse University. Her research has emphasized the development of scientific institutions in the United States and the establishment of professionalism in the nineteenth century, as reflected in her forthcoming volume on the American Association for the Advancement of Science.

MARCUS A. McCORISON is Director and Librarian of the American Antiquarian Society. His principal field of interest is the history of American book trades. His most recent book is an edition of Isaiah Thomas's *History of Printing in America.*

ALEXANDRA OLESON is Assistant Executive Officer of the American Academy of Arts and Sciences. She holds degrees from Barnard, the University of California at Berkeley, and Harvard, and is Editor of the *Bulletin of the American Academy.*

NATHAN REINGOLD is Editor of the Papers of Joseph Henry at the Smithsonian Institution. He prepared *Science in Nineteenth Century America: A Documentary History.* The social and institutional settings for science and technology in the last two centuries are his principal areas of concern.

BARBARA GUTMANN ROSENKRANTZ is Professor of the History of Science in the Faculty of Arts and Sciences and the School of Public Health at Harvard University. Her publications include *Public Health and the State: Changing Views in Massachusetts 1842-1936* and, with William A. Koelsch, *American Habitat: An Historical Perspective.*

MARGARET W. ROSSITER is Acting Assistant Professor of History at the University of California, Berkeley. She earned a Ph.D. from Yale University in 1971 and has been a National Science Foundation Postdoctoral Fellow at Brown University and a Fellow at the Charles Warren Center for Studies in American History at Harvard University.

HENRY D. SHAPIRO is Associate Professor of History at the University of Cincinnati. He holds degrees from Columbia, Cornell, and Rutgers universities. His principal interests are in American intellectual and cultural history and in the history of American science before 1870. He has edited *Physician to the West: Selected Writings of Daniel Drake on Science and Society,* with Zane L. Miller, and a collection of autobiographical statements by American scientists contained in the Smithsonian Circulars of 1852 and 1874.

BRUCE SINCLAIR, Associate Professor in the Department of History and Director of the Institute for the History and Philosophy of Science and Technology at the University of Toronto, is the author of *Philadelphia's Philosopher Mechanics: A History of the Franklin Institute, 1824-1865,* and edited, with Norman R. Ball and James O. Peterson, *Let Us be Honest and Modest: A Documentary History of Canadian Technology.* His major research interests are in the history of North American technology.

RICHARD J. STORR is Professor of History at York University. His special interest is the history of education in the United States, and he is the author of *The Beginnings of Graduate Education in America; Harper's University: The Beginnings;* and *The Beginning of the Future: An Historical Approach to Graduate Education in the Arts and Sciences.*

WALTER MUIR WHITEHILL, Director and Librarian Emeritus of the Boston Athenaeum, is the author of *Spanish Romanesque Architecture of the Eleventh Century* and *Boston: A Topographical History.* He has written histories of such learned institutions as the Peabody Museum of Salem, the Boston Public Library, Dumbarton Oaks, and the Boston Museum of Fine Arts.

JOHN VOSS is the Executive Officer of the American Academy of Arts and Sciences and co-editor, with Paul Ward, of *Confrontation and Learned Societies.*

Index

Abert, Johann Joseph, 186
Academic institutions: foreign, 38; and
learned societies, 16, 17, 28–29, 115, 152,
191, 252, 285, 330, 332; and professionalism, 36, 46–47, 300
Academy of Natural Sciences of Philadel-
phia, xvi, xvii, 18, 174–89, 270, 272, 300;
collections, 4, 175–76, 177, 178–80,
188–89; finances, 15, 177, 182; founding,
6, 25, 174–76; library, 177, 181, 188;
members, 2, 8, 25, 176–77; publications,
178, 181–82
"Account of the American Philosophical
Society," 5
Adams, Charles Francis, 152, 156, 166, 168
Adams, Henry, 161
Adams, John, 9, 287, 344; and American
Academy of Arts and Sciences, xxiv,
151–55, 157, 161, 166, 172
Adams, John Quincy, 156, 160, 166, 169
Adams, Samuel, 157, 160, 166
Adams, Thomas Boylston, 156, 165
Adrain, Robert, 5, 17
Agassiz, Alexander, 161
Agassiz, Louis, 12, 14, 16, 23, 141, 161,
213, 215; and American Association for
the Advancement of Science, 302, 311,
313, 319; and National Academy of Sci-
ences, xxiv–xxv, 227
Agricultural, Horticultural and Botanical
Society, 213
Agricultural societies, xvi, 3–4, 30, 89, 95,
96, 121, 279–96; aims, 85–86; county,
xix, 97–99, 289–90; experiments, 87; and
innovation, xviii–xix, 102, 118–19, 166–
67, 280–81, 345–49; lobbying, 292–93;
membership, 282, 284, 286; and professionalization, 279; publications, 13–14,
120–21, 286, 290–91, 297; and science,
279–80; specialization, 280, 351; and
states, 281
Albany Academy, 127, 133
Albany Institute, 40, 42, 130–42, 286;
formation, 98
Albany Institute of History and Art, 143
Albany Lyceum of Natural History, 98,
117, 126–30, 286
Albany Medical College, 140, 141
Albert (prince consort), 110
Alexander, James, 76

Alexander, Stephen, 136
Allston, Washington, 161, 167
Amateurism, 38–39, 182–83, 301, 314. *See
also* Cultivators
American Academy of Arts and Sciences, 9,
30, 31, 92, 151, 162, 189, 300; and agriculture, 283; aims, 9–10, 153, 265, 347;
founding, xxi, 9, 84, 152; and Harvard,
10, 11, 14; and other learned societies,
165, 166, 168, 171, 251, 256; and medicine, 266, 267, 271; members, vii–viii,
11–12, 13, 156–62, 303–9, 352; and
natural history, 25; publications, 11, 12,
15, 24, 30, 153, 161–62
American Academy of Fine Arts, 100, 101,
102, 104, 105
American Academy of Science, 264
American Academy of the Arts, 104
American Antiquarian Society, 252–59;
publications, 258–59
American Association for the Advancement
of Science, 31, 54, 299, 326, 327, 352;
aims, xxiii, 205; founding, ix, xviii, 34–
41, 238, 273–74, 303–5; meetings, 39,
41, 205, 215, 242, 318, 329; membership,
xxii, 321; publications, 5, 313; research,
306–8
American Association of Geologists, 141
American Board of Agriculture, 96
American Chemical Society, ix
American Council of Learned Societies, ix, x
American Ethnological Society, 18–19
American Historical Association, ix
American Institute of Homeopathy, 269
American Institute of the City of New
York, 105–10, 112, 137
American Institution for the Insane, 269
American Journal of Science, 5, 14, 18
American Library Association, 258
American Lyceum, 104
American Medical Association, 189, 268,
269
*American Monthly Magazine and Critical
Review,* 18, 101
American Philosophical Society, 9, 24, 28,
30, 93, 121, 208, 224, 251, 264, 300,
301, 347; and Academy of Natural Sci-
ences, 174, 179, 180, 183, 186; and agri-
culture, 283, 285; aims, xvi, xvii, 3–4,
347; finance, 5; formation, 2, 25, 70, 74,

Library of Congress Cataloging in Publication Data
Main entry under title:
The Pursuit of knowledge in the early American Republic.

Papers from a five-day workshop held by the American Academy of Arts and Sciences, in Cape Newagen, Me., June 1973.

Includes bibliographical references and index.

1. United States—Learned institutions and societies—History—Congresses. I. Oleson, Alexandra, 1939–   II. Brown, Sanborn Conner, 1913–   III. American Academy of Arts and Sciences.
AS25.P87   061'.3   75-36941
ISBN 0-8018-1679-3

Publisher's Note

This book has been reprinted by a new process that greatly reduces production costs and enables the publisher to keep available titles that would otherwise be prohibitively expensive to reprint. One of the characteristics of this process is uniform specifications that require books to be printed and bound in 32-page signatures. Consequently, some books reprinted by this process will contain more blank pages than is customary with conventional methods of bookmaking.